MW01014615

A History of
Western Thought

A History of Western Thought is a comprehensive introduction to the history of Western philosophy from the pre-Socratics to the twentieth century.

Along with in-depth discussion of all the major philosophical movements, Skirbekk and Gilje also look at the historical factors that have influenced Western philosophy, including the natural sciences, social sciences, and humanities, as well as political ideologies such as liberalism, socialism, and fascism.

A History of Western Thought is an ideal introduction to philosophy and the sociological and scientific structures that have shaped modern philosophy.

Areas covered include:

*   Plato
*   Aristotle
*   the Middle Ages
*   the Renaissance and *realpolitik*
*   doubt and belief
*   Locke
*   the Enlightenment
*   utilitarianism and liberalism
*   Kant
*   Hegel
*   Marx
*   Kierkegaard
*   Darwin
*   Nietzsche and pragmatism
*   socialism and fascism
*   Freud and psychoanalysis
*   the rise of the social sciences
*   a glance at contemporary philosophy
*   modernity and crisis.

Gunnar Skirbekk and **Nils Gilje** are professors of philosophy at the University of Bergen, Norway.

A History of Western Thought

From ancient Greece to the
twentieth century

Gunnar Skirbekk and Nils Gilje

London and New York

First published 1972 as *Filosofihistorie* by Scandinavian University Press
second edition 1976, third edition 1980, fourth edition 1987,
fifth edition 1992, sixth edition 1996,
seventh edition 2000 © Scandinavian University Press

English translation first published 2001
by Routledge
11 New Fetter Lane, London, EC4P 4EE

Simultaneously published in the USA and Canada
by Routledge
29 West 35th Street, New York, NY 10001

Routledge is an imprint of the Taylor & Francis Group

© 2001 Gunnar Skirbekk and Nils Gilje
translation © 2001 Routledge

Translated into English by Ronald Worley

Typeset in Perpetua and Grotesque by The Running Head Limited, Cambridge
Printed and bound in Great Britain by TJ International Ltd, Padstow, Cornwall

All rights reserved. No part of this book may be reprinted or
reproduced or utilized in any form or by any electronic,
mechanical, or other means, now known or hereafter
invented, including photocopying and recording, or in any
information storage or retrieval system, without permission in
writing from the publishers.

British Library Cataloguing in Publication Data
A catalogue record for this book is available from the British Library

Library of Congress Cataloging in Publication Data
Skirbekk, Gunnar.
   [Filosofihistorie. English]
   History of Western thought : from ancient Greece to the twentieth century / Gunnar
   Skirbekk & Nils Gilje.
      p.   cm.
   Includes bibliographical references and index.
   1. Philosophy–History.   I. Gilje, Nils, 1947–   II. Title.
B72.S5613   2000
190—dc21   00–059189

ISBN 0–415–22072–6 (hbk)
ISBN 0–415–22073–4 (pbk)

Contents

Acknowledgements

This edition of *A History of Western Thought* is a revised version of the seventh edition (2000) of *Filosofihistorie*.

We would like to express our gratitude to those who have offered us constructive criticism. Special thanks go to Hermund Slaattelid, who wrote the section on Stoicism and certain paragraphs in the discussion of Kierkegaard. We also thank Halfdan Wiik, who wrote a draft of the sections on anarchism and syndicalism, and Joe Garver and David Williams at The Running Head, for their efficient and sympathetic cooperation. Finally, we thank the Scandinavian University Press and Routledge for very good working relationships.

N.G. and G.S.

Translator's foreword

A translation project of this magnitude entails a great many challenges, most of which are connected with trying to convey accurately not only the basic meaning of the text in a different language, but also the nuances that form an integral part of any language.

There are two main difficulties that I would like to outline. Firstly, the Norwegian word *mennesket* is a neuter noun generally translated as 'human being' or 'person'. It may also be translated as 'man'. I have generally used the former alternatives where the original text allowed, but in certain instances, after consulting with the authors, I have retained 'man'.

British philosophy, among other academic disciplines, is often criticized for using 'man' as a generic reference to both men and women. In Chapter 1 and the discussion of Greek philosophy, however, it seems that to avoid using 'man' in order to conform to political correctness is to perform a historical disservice to early thinkers who were often thinking specifically of the male gender. My use of 'man' in this context (as in 'man-in-community') is intentionally ambiguous. In one sense, it may be understood, as referring to both men and women generically – human beings who are part of a community – but it may also be understood, as the majority of early Greek thinkers intended, as a specific reference to *men* in a community.

The second point is one that is well-known in translation from Germanic languages to English. The meaning of the Norwegian noun *vitskap*, 'science', is the same as that of the German noun *Wissenschaft*. 'Science', in this sense, is defined more broadly than it is in English, where it is generally understood to refer to natural science. *Vitskap* includes natural science but also extends to what is otherwise known as the humanities, or human sciences (such as hermeneutics). The intended meaning is generally clear from the context, but at times I have also used 'science' to cover the broader definition that is readily understood in the original language.

I would like to thank Professors Nils Gilje and Gunnar Skirbekk for the good collaboration that we have had during this project. I would also like to thank Judith Larsen for her helpful comments on the manuscript.

Special thanks go to Vivian, Kai, and Aila, who gave me the time and freedom to work on this project. This is for them.

Introduction

Why study philosophy? To put the answer briefly: we study philosophy because it is part of the intellectual baggage that we carry with us — whether we know it or not — so we may as well become acquainted with it!

We can illustrate this with the following dilemma: some people believe that they should not take human life. At the same time they believe that they should defend their country. What should they do in the case of war? If they join the armed forces, they will come into conflict with the precept that they should not kill other people. But if they refuse to join the armed forces, they will come into conflict with the precept that they should defend their country. Is there a solution to this dilemma? Is, for example, one precept more fundamental than the other — and, if so, why? Such people must also question to what extent military action in a given situation will save lives; they must test their precepts thoroughly. The deeper one goes into these questions, the more one works philosophically.

Philosophical presuppositions in the form of such questions and answers are found in daily life whether we recognize them or not. To comprehend them and work with them involves both something that is *personal* — we try to improve ourselves — and something *universal* — we seek true insight as far as possible. If we work in this way, we are working philosophically; and then, we can learn a lesson from what others have thought and said. This is why we should 'study philosophy'.

We could also ask: what can philosophy teach us? Does not science today teach us all that we *can know*? And in so far as science cannot give the reasons for norms and values, we can solve these normative problems by appealing to the laws. For example, our society has outlawed racial discrimination — therefore, what is left for philosophy to do?

But if we lived in a society where, on the contrary, racial discrimination was legal, would we then be bound to respect such discrimination? If we were unwilling to do so, we could appeal to international resolutions on human rights that forbid racial discrimination. But how can we convince those who reject human rights resolutions? Then we might go even further in the search for justification and appeal to religious convictions or to certain fundamental principles of justice that we consider to be self-evident. But how can we persuade people who have different religious convictions or who consider other principles to be self-evident?

A possible solution could be sought by starting with the following reflection: The difference between *knowing* and *believing that we know* is a distinction between having sufficient *reasons* for claiming something to be true and right, and *not* having such reasons. The question of to what extent we can know that certain norms are universally binding then becomes a question of whether or not we have sufficient reasons for the assertion of their universality. But such reasons are not personal: if a reason is valid, it is valid for everyone, and it is equally valid regardless of who states it. A reason that gives us the right to claim knowledge is thus a reason that stands firm in the face of critical testing and counter-arguments. Only claims that can withstand free and open testing from people that hold different views can be said to be valid. This gives us a hint concerning *one* view as to what a reasonable claim might be; and this is a view that can include philosophical (ethical) questions.

Now it is usual to distinguish between what *is* and what *ought to be*, and to say that science describes and explains what is, but that it cannot explain why something ought to be. This distinction might sound reasonable: science, for example, can describe how we learn, but not why we ought to learn. That is to say, science can give us an answer to the question of why we should learn something if we want to achieve a particular goal; for example, having the best possible chance of passing an examination. And we can explain why we ought to take the examination *if* we want a particular job. But these 'ought' questions involve relative goals that are a means in relation to other goals; and the question of why we ought to prefer the ultimate goal in such a means-end sequence cannot be answered by science.

But science can still make a great impact on our attitudes and our actions by clarifying what the situation actually is: i.e., the motives that drive us, the consequences of our actions, and the possible alternatives. Moreover, science can clarify what people, as shown by their words and actions, believe to be right and good, and, hence, show how norms function in society. But it does not follow from all of these facts about norms that certain norms are universally binding.

Thus, when social anthropologists, for example, describe the norms of a society, they mean that these norms are 'binding' in *this* society. But that is not to say that these norms are binding for us, who live in a different society; nor does it mean that these norms, which are believed to be binding by those who live in that society, really are justifiable (say, ritual human sacrifice to the rain god). For example, we may *understand* the norms of a society that practises the exposure of physically and mentally unfit babies without *accepting* them as valid. Acknowledging that certain norms function as though they are binding is not the same as accepting them as being universally valid.

We are not going any further into these problems here – that would be to write the textbook in the introduction. We only wish to hint here how normative problems in our daily lives can lead us into various disciplines and into philosophy – in order to suggest the point of doing philosophy.

As to the relationship between science and philosophy, we would like to add one brief comment about this complicated topic: scientific results are codetermined by the conceptual and methodological presuppositions that the scientific project in question is based on. We can see this point in practice when an issue, such as building a hydroelectric plant, can be analysed from both an economic and ecological perspective; from both a technological and a sociological perspective – or from the perspectives of different groups. Inasmuch as these different perspectives highlight different aspects of the issue under investigation, one perspective alone does not tell the whole truth about this issue. To understand 'what the issue really is', whether building a hydroelectric plant or centralizing a school system, we must become familiar with the different perspectives on the issue. If we call this analysis of different perspectives a philosophical reflection, we can say that such philosophical reflection is appropriate when confronting the problems posed by various disciplines – it helps us maintain some overview in a civilization in danger of being atomized by specialization.

When we, in this introduction, have tried to indicate how philosophical problems arise, we have been guided by our own understanding of what characterizes the central philosophical problems. Others would have emphasized other topics and ways of thinking. This is an important point, because what we have now indicated forms the pattern for this book: an introduction to the history of European philosophy with an emphasis on the problem of natural rights, and on the expansion of science and scientific rationality. There are many threads in this tapestry, but these two are by far the longest and most important.

In comparison to other presentations of the history of philosophy, we have tried to avoid some well-known pitfalls. A history of philosophy will always bear the mark of the authors' academic perspectives, background knowledge, fields of research, and cultural orientation. As a result, every historical presentation represents *one perspective* of prior thought. Inevitably, one will emphasize what one believes to be relevant and important in the historical diversity. No one is able to read Machiavelli, Marx, and Heidegger through neutral glasses. It is an illusion for authors to think that they can write a history of philosophy, or any other historical presentation, from an eternal perspective or from God's point of view. This is the lot of all historians of philosophy, whether they like it or not. Historians are not Munchausens who can lift themselves out of their own academic and cultural setting.

The philosophers of the past have also claimed to have spoken the truth. They challenge our age as much as they did their own. That is why we can only take Plato and Aristotle seriously by trying to take a stand on what they have said. That presupposes that we are able to establish a dialogue that makes it possible for us to test our viewpoints against theirs. This is why a philosophizing history of philosophy is something different from a second-hand reconstruction of the ideas of the past.

We also try to understand past philosophers on the basis of their own presuppositions, while at the same time trying to establish a dialogue with them. We want to listen, but also to answer the voice that speaks.

There are certain areas, however, where *A History of Western Thought* distinguishes itself from existing surveys of the history of philosophy. It is generally accepted that the scientific revolution at the beginning of the modern age challenged the current world-view and generated new epistemological and ethical questions. That is why we find treatments of Copernicus, Kepler, and Newton in all surveys of the history of philosophy. We share this opinion. But we also believe that the rise of the humanities and the revolution within the social sciences raises similar questions. This book goes one step further than the traditional textbooks that generally limit themselves to discussing the influence of the classical natural sciences on our world-view and on our view of man. The sciences that are associated with the names of Darwin, Freud, Durkheim, and Weber represent important philosophical challenges.

Consequently, in this book the reader will find a fairly extensive treatment of the humanities, the social sciences, and psychoanalysis.

Before reading this book, whether you decide to start at the beginning or at the end, it is helpful to keep in mind that you can read a philosophical text in different ways:

1   First, try to understand *what is being said*. Here it is important to emphasize primary sources. But to grasp the philosophical problems, it may often be helpful to read textbook commentaries. In this approach it is important to view any text from the primary sources as a part of the textual corpus to which it belongs; and to view the text in a broader perspective taken from the history of ideas.

2   But the text also derives from *a society* that it is conditioned by and which it, perhaps, conditions. It is therefore helpful to view the text in a historical context. This can also include sociological and psychological analyses; for example, studies of how family background, social status, or political interests may have subconsciously influenced authors and their contemporaries.

3   But the main purpose of a philosophical text is to express something that in one way or another is *true*. This philosophical core can only be grasped in these texts by asking to what extent things really *are* what they are said to be. This requires some sort of dialogue with the text, where it is the best arguments that count, as you put your opinions to the test against the viewpoints and arguments found in the text. Philosophers are not satisfied with trying to find out what Hegel said, or by trying to find out how Hegel's ideas were conditioned by the society of his time; they want to know whether and to what extent his ideas are valid.

The primary task of philosophy is to question; this is something we must do for ourselves, but others may help us along the way. There is no 'final' answer that can be found by looking at the back – or even at the front – of a book. But, as Lao Tzu once said, 'The journey of a thousand miles begins with the first step.'

1 Pre-Socratic philosophy, with a glance at ancient Indian and Chinese thought

THE GREEK CITY-STATE: MAN-IN-COMMUNITY

Philosophy, in the broadest sense of the term, can be found in all civilizations. However, there were some civilizations, such as those of ancient India, China, and Greece, in which philosophy was cultivated more systematically. In these civilizations philosophical thought was put into written form. This gives us, who are living today, better access to those thoughts. The written form also allowed philosophers to record and communicate their thoughts in a different manner than in those civilizations that were based only on the spoken word. That which is written endures. It is possible to return to certain formulations in order to ask questions and to elucidate what was really meant. Analysis and criticism become possible in a radically new way.

A concise history of philosophy must always make certain selections. In this history of philosophy we are going to start with the first Greek philosophers and follow European philosophy up to the present day. On the whole, our selection will include European, upper-class men from the most central regions – there are few women, few from the lower class, and few from the cultural periphery. Such is history, in its standard version. Our task will be to understand what the philosophers said and to find out whether the insight that they have passed on to us is still valid. Our starting point will be Greece, in the sixth century BC.

Before starting on our study of early Greek philosophy, it might be helpful to take a look at the society in which this philosophy emerged. It will be sufficient for us to highlight some central features: the Greek city-state (Greek: *polis*) was in many ways very different from the states of our time. It was, among other things, a *small* society, both in population and geographical area. The city of Athens, for example, had a population of approximately 300,000 in the 400s BC. We can assume that of this number roughly 100,000 were slaves. If we further deduct women and children, we are left with approximately 40,000 free Athenian men.[1] They alone had political rights.

The Greek city-states were often separated geographically by mountains and sea. The city-state consisted of the town itself together with the surrounding area. Agriculture was an important activity along with crafts and trade. It was usually no more than a day's journey from the surrounding areas into the town. The Greek city-state was a close-knit community, a fact that influenced both the political institutions and political theory. For a while, Athens was a direct democracy in which all free Athenian men could participate. The political ideals were characterized by the same intimacy: harmony among equals in the political sphere, the rule of law, and freedom, where freedom meant living in unity under a common law. Lack of freedom was living in a state of lawlessness or under the rule of a tyrant. Problems were supposed to be solved by open, rational debate in a harmonious and free society, governed by laws.

The ideas of harmony and order, both in nature and in society, can generally be said to be fundamental in Greek philosophy, from the first philosophers in the fifth century BC until the time of Aristotle. The political theories of Plato and Aristotle can further be said to have 'man-in-community' as a fundamental concept, and not the individual in isolation nor the elevation of universal law or the state above the individual. For example, human beings were not seen as having 'innate rights'; rights were connected to the function or role that the individual had in society. Moral virtue (Greek: *arete*) was not primarily understood as living up to certain universal moral rules, but rather as fulfilling one's purpose as a human being; that is, finding one's place in society. Plato and Aristotle worked within the framework of the Greek city-state: the system of slavery, for example, was as natural to them as the system of employees and employers is to us.

The geographical conditions contributed to the fact that the Greek city-states were often politically independent, although economically dependent on a certain amount of cooperation to secure the necessary supplies that they could not provide for themselves. After a period of immigration, around the ninth century BC, there was an expansion of the city-states. The areas surrounding each city itself were often barren, and the population grew at a faster rate than the city-state could support. From the eighth century, Greek emigrants started colonizing neighbouring territories (such as southern Italy). Increased trade led to the standardization of weights and measures, and coins began to be minted. Social differences emerged. Instead of straightforward barter of, say, goat skins for grain, goat skins began to be traded for coins, of which the farmers did not always know the correct value. And if one lacked items to exchange, one could borrow coins to buy grain: there were loans and interest on loans, and even new loans to pay off the original loan. Some people became wealthy while many others fell heavily into debt. In the seventh century BC these social tensions led to unrest. As a result, people demanded economic justice. Often a strongman (Greek: *tyrannos*) seized power in order to solve the economic crises. But these absolute rulers often became 'tyrants' in our understanding of the word – they ruled to suit themselves. This created political discontent. By the sixth century BC, the inhabitants began to demand law and equality. The democracy in Athens (400s BC) developed partly as a result of this discontent.

THALES

Life. *Our knowledge of the earliest Greek philosophers and their teaching is scanty. We have little information that is certain and their writings have for the most part been lost. Our presentation is therefore based on conjectures and on an attempt at reconstruction. We do know that Thales lived in the Greek colony of Miletus in the fifth century BC, probably between*

624 and 546. This is partly based on a statement by Herodotus that Thales correctly pre-
dicted a solar eclipse that is believed to have occurred in 585. Other anecdotes tell us that
Thales travelled to Egypt, as was not unusual among the Greeks. It has also been claimed
that Thales measured the height of a pyramid by measuring its shadow at a time of day when
his shadow was the same length as himself.

The claim that Thales predicted a solar eclipse indicates that he understood astronomy.
Such knowledge may have come from the Babylonians. Thales was also said to have had a
knowledge of geometry, the branch of mathematics cultivated by the Greeks. The universal
assumptions in mathematics provided the Greeks with a concept of theory and theoretical
testing: mathematical statements claim to be true in a very different way than statements
about particular events. This opens the door for argumentation and deductive reasoning, with-
out perceptible evidence. It is further claimed that Thales took part in the political life of
Miletus; that his knowledge of geometry and astronomy contributed to an improvement in
navigational equipment; that he was the first to tell the time accurately with a sundial; and,
finally, that he became wealthy by speculating in olive oil because he foresaw a drought.

There is not much to be said about his writings because we lack first-hand knowledge
of them. We must, therefore, investigate what other writers have said about him. In his
Metaphysics, Aristotle writes that Thales originated the type of philosophy that seeks the
origin from which everything emerges and to which everything returns. Aristotle also says that
Thales believed this origin, or source, to be water. *But we do not know exactly what Thales*
meant by this, if indeed he said such a thing. It is with this reservation that we will attempt
to reconstruct 'Thales' philosophy'.

Greek philosophy can be traced back to Thales who lived in the Ionic colony of
Miletus, around the time of Solon. Plato and Aristotle lived in Athens during the
fourth century BC; that is, after the Athenian democracy had succumbed in the war
with Sparta. We shall offer one interpretation of the main features of Greek philosophy up to the Sophists, with emphasis on the issue of change and unity in diversity.

It is said that Thales claimed that 'everything is water'. And here, it is said,
is the beginning of philosophy. To the general reader, with little knowledge of
philosophy, one could hardly have a less promising starting point: 'This is nonsense,
if anything is!' But let us give Thales the benefit of the doubt: it is unreasonable to
attribute to a person the claim that *everything is water*, in a literal sense: that, for
example, this book and this wall are water in the same sense as the water in the
tap. What can Thales have meant?

Before we begin our interpretation of Thales, let us recall a few things that are
always useful to keep in mind when reading philosophy: philosophical answers can
often appear to be either trivial or absurd. If, in an introduction to philosophy,
we study the different answers – for instance, those of 20 to 30 intellectual systems, one after the other – philosophy may appear to be both odd and remote. To
understand an answer, we must, of course, know which question it refers to. And
we have to know what reasons or arguments there are, if any, to support the answer.
As an illustration we could make the following distinctions: when we are studying
physics it is not necessary to clarify constantly what kinds of questions and arguments there are to support the answers. Studying physics is largely a matter of
becoming familiar with the questions and arguments that form the foundation for
the discipline. As students become familiar with the questions and arguments, they

can learn the answers to the questions. These are the answers that are presented in the textbooks. Philosophy, however, is not like this. Here there are various kinds of questions and arguments. That is why we must, in each case, try to grasp which questions a particular philosopher is asking and which arguments he or she is using to support this or that answer. Only then can we begin to understand the answers.

However, in physics we also know how the results or answers can be applied. They equip us to control certain aspects of nature (as, for example, by building bridges). But what can a philosophical answer be used for? We can, of course, use a political theory as a model for reforming society. But it is seldom as simple to say how we can 'use' a philosophical answer. Generally speaking, the point of philosophical answers is not that they can be 'used' but that they enable us to understand something better. We can, in any case, talk about different answers having different implications. It can make a difference which answers we provide to philosophical questions. A political theory, for instance, will have different implications depending on whether we view the individual or the society as being of primary importance. It is therefore important to be aware of what implications a philosophical answer may have.

Hence, there are four points of which we should be aware:

1   the question
2   argument(s)
3   the answer
4   implication(s).

The least important of these is the answer, at least in the sense that an answer only becomes meaningful in light of the other factors.

In this sense it is hardly very enlightening to hear that Thales contended that 'everything is water'. Taken literally, this contention is absurd. However, we can try to guess what the claim means by reconstructing questions, arguments, and implications. We can imagine that Thales was asking what remains *constant* during *change* and what is the source of the *unity* in *diversity*. It seems reasonable to believe that Thales assumed that changes occur, and that there is *one* unchangeable element in all change that therefore is the 'building block' of the universe. This 'unchangeable element' is generally called *urstoff*,[2] i.e., the 'primitive stuff' from which the world is made (Greek: *arche*, also 'principle').

Thales, like everyone else, had seen many things come into existence and perish in water: water evaporates into air, and water turns to ice; fish come into existence and later perish in water, just as other substances (salt, honey) dissolve in water. We see, moreover, that water is necessary for life. Such simple observations may have led Thales to assert that *water* is the fundamental element, the unchanging element in all change and transformation.

Questions and observations such as these make it seem reasonable to believe (in modern terms) that Thales conceived of two states of water: water in its usual fluid state and water in a transformed state, i.e., in gaseous form and in solid form, as in ice, steam, fish, earth, trees – and everything else that is not water in its usual state. Hence, water exists partly as an undifferentiated *urstoff* (plain water) and partly as differentiated objects (everything else).

Thus, the composition of the universe and the transformation of things can be explained as an eternal cycle – from water to other objects and from other objects to water. This is *one* interpretation of Thales. Other interpretations are possible.

water in its differentiated state
water in its undifferentiated state

By this we do not mean to say that Thales actually *started* with a clearly formulated question, and *then* looked for arguments, and *then* found an answer. It is not for us to decide what came first chronologically. We are only trying to reconstruct a possible coherence in Thales' philosophy. But if we keep to this interpretation, we can say the following:

1   Thales asks what is the fundamental building block in the universe. Substance (the underlying)[3] represents the unchangeable element in change and the unity in diversity. The problem of substance subsequently became one of the main issues in Greek philosophy.
2   Thales gives an indirect answer to the question of how change takes place: the *urstoff* (water) changes from one state to another. The problem of change also became a basic question in Greek philosophy.

Thales' questions and arguments are as scientific as they are philosophical. He is therefore as much a scientist as a philosopher. What do we mean by 'science' as opposed to 'philosophy'? Philosophy can broadly be distinguished from four other activities: creative writing, the experimental sciences, the formal sciences, and theology. Regardless of how closely a philosopher may be related to any of these areas, we can say that philosophy singles itself out in the following ways: philosophy, as opposed to creative writing, is supposed to make assertions that can be said to be true or false (in one sense or another). Philosophy does not depend on experience in the same way as do the experimental sciences (such as physics and psychology). In contrast to the formal sciences (such as logic and mathematics), philosophy must reflect upon its own presuppositions (principles) and attempt to discuss and legitimize them. Philosophy, in contrast to theology, does not have a fixed set of presuppositions (such as dogmas based on revelation) that for religious reasons one cannot abandon, even though philosophy always has some kind of presuppositions.

To the extent that Thales bases his arguments on *experience* it may be reasonable to call him a scientist. But given that he seems to ask questions that involve nature *as a whole*, there may be grounds for calling him a philosopher. Greeks at that time hardly distinguished between philosophy and science. This distinction stems from modern times, not Thales' era. As late as the end of the 1600s, we find Newton describing physics as natural philosophy (*philosophia naturalis*). But whether we characterize Thales as a scientist or as a philosopher, it is evident that there is a disparity between his answer and his arguments. In a sense, the answer is 'too large' for the arguments. Thales asserts more than he has a right to, given the arguments we have mentioned. This disparity between arguments and assertion seems to be typical of the first Greek natural philosophers.

Even if we were to choose a reasonable interpretation, it seems clear that the basically correct observations that Thales presumably made did not lead him to the answer. But the importance of Thales' natural philosophy is still overwhelming. If everything is water in various forms, then everything that happens, all change, must be capable of explanation through the laws that apply to water. And water is by no means mystical. It is tangible and familiar, something we see, feel, use. We have full access to water and to its patterns of behaviour. We are dealing with observable phenomena. In hindsight, we can say that this philosophy paved the way for scientific investigation: investigators could posit hypotheses about how water will behave, and then see whether they hold. In other words, in hindsight *we* can say that there was a basis for experimental scientific research.

This means that *everything*, absolutely everything in the universe, is comprehensible to human thought. This is what is revolutionary. Everything is comprehensible, just as comprehensible as water. The universe is, to its furthest corner, penetrable to human thought. Put in negative terms, nothing is mystical nor incomprehensible. There is no room for incomprehensible gods or demons. This is the starting signal for man's intellectual conquest of the universe.

This is why we call Thales the first philosopher or scientist. With him thought moves from *mythos* to *logos*, from mythical to logical thinking. He breaks with the mythological tradition and with the short-sighted connection to immediate sensory impressions. This is, of course, a simplification. The transition from *mythos* to *logos* is not an irreversible event that happened at a particular point in history, i.e., with the first Greek philosophers. The mythical and the logical are continually interwoven both in history and in each individual's life, and the transition from *mythos* to *logos* is in many ways a constantly recurrent task for every epoch and every person. Furthermore, many people claim that myth is not merely a so-called primitive form of thinking that must be overcome, but, correctly understood, represents a genuine form of understanding.

When we say that Thales was the first scientist, and that science was founded by the Greeks, it does not mean that Thales or the other Greek sages had a greater number of isolated facts at their disposal than learned men in Babylonia or Egypt. The point is that the Greeks managed to develop a concept of rational proof, and a concept of theory as the medium of proof: theory claims to obtain universal truth, and this truth stands firm against counter-arguments in a public test. The insight that they were searching for was not only a collection of isolated fragments of knowledge, such fragments often being found within a mythical framework. The Greeks were looking for comprehensive and systematic theories that were supported by universal proof, as in the Pythagorean theorem.

We will not discuss Thales in any more detail. Perhaps he was not really free of mythical thinking. He may have considered water to be living, filled with gods. Furthermore, Thales did not (as far as we know) distinguish between force and matter. Nature (Greek: *physis*) *is* self-moving and living. Nor did he, as far as we know, distinguish between soul and matter. For Thales, nature was probably a fairly comprehensive concept, perhaps corresponding to our concept of 'being'. Hence we may briefly summarize the main points of Thales' thinking in this way:

Premise: change exists.
1   Question: what is the unchangeable element in all change?
2   Arguments: observations of water.
3   Answer: water is the unchangeable element in all change.
4   Implication: everything is comprehensible.

We mentioned that the answer – 'water is the unchangeable element in all change' – does not follow logically from the question and the arguments. And at this point a critique developed among Thales' contemporaries in Miletus.

ANAXIMANDER AND ANAXIMENES

Life. *Anaximander and Anaximenes were both from Miletus. Anaximander lived from approximately 610 to 546 BC and was a younger contemporary of Thales. Anaximenes probably lived from about 585 to 525. There is only one extant fragment attributed to Anaximander besides commentaries by others such as Aristotle, who lived approximately two centuries later. Only three short fragments of Anaximenes' work have survived, one of which is probably not genuine.*

Anaximander and Anaximenes both seem to have started with the same premise and asked the same question as Thales. Anaximander, however, did not find any compelling reason to claim that water is the unchangeable element (*urstoff*). If water is transformed to earth and earth to water, and water to air, and air to water, etc., that means that *everything* is transformed into *everything*, and it becomes logically arbitrary to claim that water or earth or air or anything else is the *urstoff*. Perhaps it was objections of this kind that Anaximander raised against Thales' answer.

Anaximander, for his part, chooses to claim that *urstoff* is *apeiron*, the indeterminate, the boundless in space and time. In this sense he avoids the abovementioned objections. But from *our* perspective it seems that Anaximander has 'lost' something: *apeiron* is not observable as water is. Anaximander explains sensory phenomena, objects and their change, by something that is not sensory. From the standpoint of the experimental sciences this is a loss. But this objection can be said to be an anachronism since Anaximander was hardly trying to develop an empirical science as we would understand it. For Anaximander it may have been more important to find a theoretical argument against Thales. In this sense, Anaximander takes Thales' universal, theoretical claims at his word and *designates* him 'the first philosopher' precisely by showing that it is possible to argue against him.

The third natural philosopher from Miletus, Anaximenes, focused on another weak point in Thales' answer. How does the *transformation* of water in its undifferentiated state to water in its differentiated states take place? As far as we know, Thales does not answer this question. Anaximenes asserts that *air*, which he considers to be *urstoff*, is condensed into water by cooling, and transformed by further cooling to ice and earth. (The jump from ice to other solid objects is an example of the generalizations that are so typical of the early Greek philosophers.) Air is diluted when heated and becomes fire. We then have some sort of physical theory of transitions. The 'aggregate states' of air are determined by temperature and degree of density. We note that Anaximenes has thereby referred to all four substances which were later to be called the four elements: earth, air, fire, and water.

Thales, Anaximander, and Anaximenes are called the Milesian natural philo-sophers. They comprise *the first generation* of Greek philosophers. We will see that succeeding philosophers followed up their thoughts in a logical way.

HERACLITUS, PARMENIDES, AND ZENO

HERACLITUS

Life. Heraclitus was from Ephesus, not far from Miletus. He lived around 500 BC, about 80 years after Thales. Several anecdotes about Heraclitus that are probably without any his-torical basis have come down to us. We can, in any case, form a picture of Heraclitus from the fragments that are extant: he appears to have been a reclusive, bitterly sarcastic philo-sopher who was seldom understood by his contemporaries, and who held an equally low opinion of the mental ability of his compatriots. Hence, Heraclitus is said to have claimed that most people's opinions and positions were like 'toys for children' (fragment 58; D:70⁴). And those that do not understand, according to fragment 2 (D:34), are like the deaf, 'absent while present'. He seems, in addition, to be referring to the judgement of the 'masses' with his claim that 'asses prefer garbage to gold' (fragment 71; D:9). The fact that Heraclitus was appar-ently poorly understood was not necessarily due only to the faulty judgement of the masses. As a philosopher, Heraclitus was given the epithet 'the obscure', and he often expressed him-self in obscure but suggestive metaphors. He had a tendency to express himself in a way that is often near to the mythical, in contrast to the Milesian natural philosophers, who expressly tried to distance themselves from the mythical. Heraclitus does not have the scientific em-phasis that we find with the Milesians. Nor does he use logical, well-defined concepts, as did Parmenides and the philosophers from Elea. Heraclitus employs intuition and vision — his speech is like the voice of an oracle. He is probably referring to himself when he says (fragment 33; D:93): 'The lord whose oracle is in Delphi neither declares nor conceals, but gives a sign.' Heraclitus is said to have kept his writings in the temple of Artemis in Ephesus. In any case, 126 fragments have been preserved from his writings, in addition to thirteen that are probably not authentic.

Other philosophers are mentioned in Heraclitus' writings. Philosophers were no longer solely occupied by phenomena; they were also taking a stand in relation to what other philo-sophers had said about philosophical topics. A philosophical tradition had been established with internal debates and commentaries.

Heraclitus and Parmenides belonged to the second generation of Greek philo-sophers. The first philosopher, Thales, 'opened his eyes' and saw nature (*physis*). Heraclitus and Parmenides were surrounded not only by physis, but also by the theories of the first generation of philosophers. The internal dialogue concerning the unchangeable element in all change began with Thales and Anaximander. Heraclitus and Parmenides, however, started a debate about basic presuppositions.

We said that the first natural philosophers assumed that change takes place. For them, this was a premise, a presupposition. Starting with this presupposition, they asked what was the unchangeable element throughout all change. The second gen-eration seemed to question this premise: does change exist? They make the pre-supposition of the first generation the object of their reflection. To this question, Heraclitus and Parmenides apparently give two diametrically opposed answers:

Heraclitus says that *everything is in a constant state of change or flux*; Parmenides says that *nothing is in a state of change!* Once more, these answers seem at first to be meaningless, but this was not precisely what they said.

To claim that *everything*, absolutely everything, is in a constant state of flux is a logically impossible claim, given the fact that we have to be able to point to objects and recognize objects (which at the very least last a certain length of time) if language is to be possible at all. And without language we cannot make the claim that 'everything is in a state of flux'. However, Heraclitus does not really say that everything is in a state of flux. He says that:

1   everything is in a state of flux,[5] but
2   change occurs according to an unchangeable law (*logos*),[6] and
3   this law involves an interaction between opposites,[7]
4   but in such a way that this interaction between opposites, seen as a whole, creates harmony.[8]

By using an example of our own, we can interpret Heraclitus as follows: everything is in a constant state of flux according to the law of opposition between different forces. For instance, a house is a thing, a thing that is in a state of flux. But the constructive forces will temporarily, over a period of many years, prevail over the destructive forces. The house will stand as long as this situation persists. But the balance of strength between the forces is constantly changing. One day the destructive forces will prevail. The house will fall apart: gravity and decay will conquer the opposite forces. In other words, Heraclitus is not denying that things can last a very long time. But the basic principle that lies behind and supports all transient objects is interaction between forces, and the balance between these forces changes according to laws, *logos*. The underlying substance is not *urstoff*, but *logos*. *Logos* is the hidden unity in diversity.

Even though we have *more* fragments of Heraclitus than of the Milesians, he is still relatively difficult to interpret since he speaks in poetic images. Heraclitus speaks, for example, of fire (Greek: *pyr*). Does he mean that fire is *urstoff*, in the same sense as the Milesian school? Or is he using the word *fire* as a metaphor for change, the consuming fire? Both interpretations are possible.

In one place, Heraclitus says (fragment 40; D:90): 'All things are an equal exchange for fire, and fire for all things, as goods for gold and gold for goods.' If we interpret fire as a primitive substance, then it is possible to suspect a connection between the philosophy of nature and economics: the notion of *urstoff* as the common element through which all things change is connected with the notion of money, gold, as the common point of change for all commodities, the point where the different commodities blend together because they are subject to a common standard.

Heraclitus has been interpreted as defending war, since he says (fragment 83; D:53): 'War is the father of all and king of all.' A more careful reading will here point to Heraclitus' general thesis about the tension between alternating forces: war or conflict (Greek: *polemos*, hence 'polemics'), refers to this cosmological tension; it is this tension that is everything's 'father', that is to say, the basic principle of everything.

Heraclitus talks about the world perishing and reappearing at regular intervals because of a world-encompassing fire. This cycle of ever new fires and new worlds recurs later in the works of the Stoics.

PARMENIDES

Life. *Parmenides was a contemporary of Heraclitus and was philosophically active around 500 BC. He lived in the Greek colony of Elea in southern Italy. Parmenides was reputedly a highly respected man in his native city, involved in public and political matters, including legislation. Parmenides wrote a philosophical poem that we have almost in its entirety. We also have second-hand information such as Plato's dialogue 'Parmenides'.*

An apparent opposite of Heraclitus, Parmenides does not say without reservation that 'nothing is in a state of change'. Parmenides claims that change is logically impossible. We can perhaps reconstruct his argument as follows:

A   (i)   What is, is.
           What is not, is not.
   (ii) What is, can be thought.
           What is not, cannot be thought.

B   The idea of change implies that something *comes into being*, and that something *ceases to be*; i.e., an apple goes from being green to being red. The colour green *disappears*, becoming '*non-existent*'. This shows that *change presupposes non-being*, that which cannot be thought. We are therefore unable to grasp the change by thought. Therefore, change is *logically impossible.*

Now of course Parmenides knew as well as we do that our senses perceive all sorts of change. He therefore posited a dilemma: reason says that change is logically impossible, while our senses tell us that it exists. What should we do? Parmenides, the typical Greek, reasonably tells us that we must believe in reason: reason is correct; our senses deceive us.

The objection that this was madness was made already during his lifetime. An opponent of Parmenides' teaching is said to have stood up and walked back and forth while this claim was being made. But again, let us look at the implications. This is possibly the first time that human beings relied so completely on the logical train of thought that not even the evidence of their senses could shake them. Parmenides is, in this sense, the first rationalist.[9] The fact that he was motivated to follow through with his rational argumentation meant he was one of the first to make a substantial contribution to the development of logical reasoning.

Parmenides thus establishes an irreconcilable division between reason and the senses. We can set it up, schematically, as follows:

$$\frac{\text{reason}}{\text{senses}} = \frac{\text{being}}{\text{nonbeing}} = \frac{\text{rest}}{\text{change}} = \frac{\text{unity}}{\text{plurality}}$$

In other words, reason recognizes that reality is at rest and is a unity. The senses only show us an unreality that is in a state of change and is a plurality. This division, or *dualism*,[10] recurs among several Greek philosophers, such as Plato. But in contrast to the other dualists, Parmenides seems to ignore the senses and sensible objects to such a degree that it seems that everything appearing to the senses is presumed to be devoid of reality. Sensible objects *are not!* If this interpretation of Parmenides is correct, we can almost say that he is a representative of *monism*: what is, is of one kind, not of many, and this reality can be grasped only through reason.

ZENO

Zeno from Elea, was a student of Parmenides who attempted to defend Parmenides' teaching that change is logically impossible, by showing that the opposite teachings, which claim that change is possible, result in logical paradoxes. Zeno attempted to show such a paradox with the story of Achilles and the tortoise:

Achilles and the tortoise are running a race. They start at the same time (time t_0), but the tortoise starts slightly ahead in space. Let us say that Achilles runs 50 times faster than the tortoise. By the time Achilles, at time t_1, reaches the spatial point at which the tortoise started (at t_0), the tortoise will have gone further, 1/50 of the distance Achilles completed between time t_1 and t_0. And by the time Achilles, at time t_2, reaches the point where the tortoise was at time t_1, the tortoise will have crawled even further, 1/50 of the distance Achilles ran between t_2 and t_1. And so on. The lead that the tortoise had rapidly decreases, but the tortoise will always have gone on a little further each time Achilles reaches the point where the tortoise was at the previous point of time; therefore, Achilles will never catch or overtake it.[11]

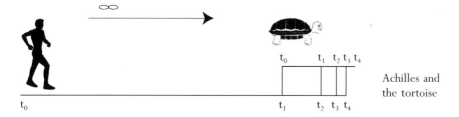

Achilles and the tortoise

It is said that Parmenides had contact with the Pythagoreans, who held a philosophical position similar to Parmenidean rationalism.

THE MEDIATORS: EMPEDOCLES AND ANAXAGORAS

EMPEDOCLES

Life. Empedocles probably lived from c. 492 to 432 BC. He is believed to have lived in the city of Acragas, Sicily, and is said to have taken part in the struggle for a democratic government in his native city. Judging by the manner in which he is mentioned, he was as much a prophet as a natural philosopher.

We have approximately 150 fragments of Empedocles' writings, as well as information from other sources.

What problems did those who came after Heraclitus and Parmenides inherit? This third generation of Greek philosophers had to cope with a parental generation (Heraclitus and Parmenides) who seemed to claim both that everything is in a state of flux and that change is impossible. It is a reasonable reaction to say that both were mistaken; the truth lies somewhere in between: some things are in a state of flux while other things are in a state of rest. And this was how Empedocles and Anaxagoras, the philosophers belonging to this younger generation, responded. In other words, they conceived their task as that of mediating between Heraclitus and Parmenides; and that is why they are called the mediating philosophers.

Empedocles conceived of four elements (or unchangeable primitive substances), fire, air, water, and earth, as well as with two forces, the dividing force (strife) and the unifying force (love). Empedocles differed from the Milesians on two points:

1 There are four unchangeable, primitive elements (not one, cf. Thales or Democritus).
2 The forces exist in addition to the primitive substance (change and force are not intrinsic to the primitive substance; cf. Aristotle).

The four elements are quantitatively and qualitatively unchangeable. There will never be any more or less of them (quantitatively unchangeable). The four elements always retain their own characteristics (qualitatively unchangeable). However, it is possible for *various quantities* of the four elements to join together (aided by the unifying force) to create different objects. Objects such as houses, trees, etc. are created when different quantities of these elements join into a suitable 'clump'. Objects dissolve when the elements are pulled away from each other by the dividing force.

Freely interpreting Empedocles, we can perhaps put it this way: imagine a kitchen with four different ingredients in four drawers – flour, salt, sugar, and oatmeal – the quantities being always constant and the ingredients' properties never changing, even if they are mixed. Various 'cakes' are created when we combine different quantities of the four ingredients. The cakes may later dissolve back into their individual ingredients. That is our interpretation so far.

Therefore, Empedocles managed to create a model that included both change and the unchangeable: change is represented by the 'cakes' that come into being and perish. The unchangeable is represented by the quantities and properties of the four elements.

ANAXAGORAS

Life. *Anaxagoras is said to have lived from around 498 to 428 BC. He spent the early part of his life in the city of Clazomenae, but as an adult he travelled to Athens where he held a central position in public life. He was, for instance, associated with Pericles. But Anaxagoras had to leave Athens when his unorthodox views came into conflict with traditional beliefs. Among other things, he had claimed that the sun was not a god but a large glowing body. We have 22 fragments of Anaxagoras' writings.*

Anaxagoras thought along similar lines to Empedocles. However, he proposed the elements to be 'innumerable': why only four? How can we trace all the different properties that are found back to just four primitive substances? Given that there are 'innumerable' properties, the elements must also be 'innumerable'. To pursue our metaphor of the kitchen, we could say that Anaxagoras basically expanded the number of 'drawers' to include innumerable ingredients. But he explained change, in principle, in the same way as Empedocles.

Anaxagoras, however, conceived of only one force: 'mind' (Greek: *nous*). He seemed to think that this mind or force has set the changes in motion *towards a goal* (Greek: *telos*). Nature is thus teleological, purposeful.

These two mediating philosophers, Empedocles and Anaxagoras, are interesting because they show how natural philosophy was developing toward Democritus and his teachings of atomism.

DEMOCRITUS

Life. Democritus probably lived from 460 to 370 BC and was therefore an older contemporary of Plato (427–347). Democritus came from the city of Abdera in Thrace. He is believed to have travelled to Athens and to have taken several longer journeys to the Orient and to Egypt. Perhaps these journeys were devoted to study and research. Democritus seems to have been a man of extensive knowledge. He was well educated and worked in most of the branches of science in his time. The titles of particular fragments are enough to show the extent of Democritus' interests: 'On Well-Being', 'On Life after Death', 'On the World Order and Rules of Thought', 'On Rhythm and Harmony', 'On Poetry', 'On Agriculture', 'On Mathematics', 'On Correct Language and Obscure Words', 'On Harmonious and Disharmonious Letters', etc. Although we have between 200 and 300 fragments from Democritus, this is only a relatively small portion of his extensive writings. Our interpretations will therefore be reconstructions, even though we also have second-hand information on Democritus.

Democritus' atomism is a stroke of genius precisely because of its simplicity. Only one type of *urstoff* exists: small, indivisible particles. They move about in a void, and their motions are exclusively mechanically determined. We can, in other words, say that Democritus traces nature, in all its richness and complexity, back to a gigantic 'game of billiards' in which an infinite number of very small material particles circulate in a void, and where all the displacements are determined by the collisions that occur. For Democritus, the void, non-being, is a precondition for being: namely, the motion of the atoms. This is a clear break with Parmenides and his disciples in Elea.

question		answer
(what)	1	small, indivisible particles (atoms)
	2	the void
(how)	3	mechanical determinism

These atoms are thought to be physically indivisible (Greek: *atomos*). Their properties are exclusively *quantitative*, i.e., properties that we can describe with physical concepts, such as extension, form, and weight, and not qualities such as colour, taste, odour, and pain. The atoms are so small that they cannot be perceived. We are therefore talking about explaining sensible objects (a house, rocks, fish, etc.) in terms of something that we in principle cannot perceive but can only understand intellectually. All atoms are of the same kind of material. But they differ from one another in form and dimension. However, *each particular* atom's form and dimension is constant. Because different atoms have different forms, there are some that can easily join together while others cannot easily do so. Objects are created when the atoms are 'lumped together' because the mechanical collisions sometimes lead the atoms to cluster and because atoms that collide may join together. Objects dissolve when the atoms that composed them move away from one another. None of the atomic motions are determined by divine or human reason; they all occur mechanically, as in the motion of billiard balls. This is our interpretation so far.

Here we see how the internal development of the Greek natural philosophy led to a first-class explanatory model of substance and change. This model strikingly resembles modern chemical theory.

But since the Greeks did not perform *experiments* to confirm theories such as this – to expect experimentation by them is almost anachronistic – atomism was viewed as a theory of nature along with the other possible theories. It is therefore not surprising that many preferred Aristotle's natural philosophy to Democritus'. After all, Aristotle spoke of things that we can observe – earth, water, air, and fire – while Democritus talked about things that no one can sense. But even though Aristotle had greater influence up to the time of the Renaissance, it was Democritus' theory, through Epicurus and Lucretius, that came to play an important part in the establishment of classical physics during the Renaissance.

An elegant model such as this must, however, pay for its simplicity and economy of principles. There are many common phenomena that are difficult to explain with such a model. What about the qualitative properties that we indubitably experience, such as the colour and smell of flowers, or indignation and sympathy for our fellow man? How can we experience such things if everything that *is*, is quantitative? With the help of a theory of sense perception, Democritus tries to explain how the world appears to be more 'colourful' than the properties of the atoms will allow. He probably thought that all objects send out a kind of mediator atom. When these come into contact with the atoms in the sensory organs, peculiar effects emerge that we perceive as properties belonging to the objects. They *seem* to have colour, taste, and smell but do not possess these properties in themselves; they are added by us. The objects themselves only have properties such as extension, form, and density, and not colour, smell, or warmth. This distinction between properties that objects possess inherently and properties that we attribute to them by our senses came to play an important part in the philosophy of the modern age.[12] But one could ask how we can perceive properties that the objects, i.e., the atoms, do not really possess, while *we*, at the same time, are also atoms and nothing else. Is it not just as much a leap from quantitative to qualitative properties, a leap that we cannot account for if we adhere to a consistent atomic theory that only the atom's quantitative properties exist?

If we disregard this objection, we can see that atomism is also fascinating as a theory of cognition: it only includes atoms – the atoms in the objects that are perceived, mediator atoms that somehow break away from the object and flow out, and atoms in the sensory organs that receive these mediators. Sensory errors, for example, can be explained by disorder in the atoms in the sensory organs, or by the mediator atoms colliding with each other and delivering wrong messages to the sensory atoms. But we are still left with some major theoretical problems.

How can we *know* that the sense impression that we receive really is an accurate representation of the objects around us? This model does not allow us to look at the mediator atoms on the one hand, and at the object on the other, to find out whether the mediator atoms are representing the object as it really is. Neither can we be sure, concerning our own sensations, that the mediator atoms are reaching our sensory organs in proper order; nor can we, by our own sensations, distinguish the message in the mediator atoms from the message of the atoms found in our sensory apparatus. Put briefly, from our own sensations, we do not seem to be able to *know* anything more than that we are experiencing a particular sense impression.

That is to say, this is how it would be if our knowledge of the things around us was based *solely* on sensation. But the atoms are too small to be perceived. We recognize them with our reason. This epistemological theory of our sensory perception of external objects seems to presuppose that the theory itself originates in reason, not through our senses.

We have now followed some important threads in the first Greek philosophy, through three to four generations, from approximately 600 to 450 BC. (Democritus lived, however, until 370.)

First generation   THALES
(ANAXIMANDER – ANAXIMENES)

Second generation   HERACLITUS   PARMENIDES

Third generation   EMPEDOCLES
ANAXAGORAS
DEMOCRITUS

THE PYTHAGOREANS

There is yet another important school of thought in early Greek philosophy, the Pythagoreans. They lived in the Greek colonies in southern Italy from about 540 BC onwards. In a way we can say that the Pythagoreans asked the familiar questions about substance, the fundamental element in nature, and change. But the Pythagorean answers differed from those of the Milesians, the mediating philosophers, and Democritus. The basic idea for the Pythagoreans was not the material elements, but structures and forms, or *mathematical relationships*. The Pythagoreans held that nature can be 'unlocked' by mathematics:

1   The study of harmonics showed a correspondence between mathematics and something as immaterial as music.
2   The Pythagorean theorem showed that mathematics was also applicable to material things.
3   The supposed circular movements of celestial bodies imply that these bodies, too, are subject to mathematics.

The Pythagoreans believed, therefore, that mathematical structures underlie all things (are substance). There were other arguments as well: things perish, but mathematical concepts do not. Mathematics, therefore, is that which is *unchangeable* in nature. And mathematical knowledge is *certain* knowledge, since the subject matter does not change. Mathematical knowledge, moreover, is certain because mathematical theorems are *logically proven*. The Pythagoreans were thus rationalists in a double sense:

1   They advanced rational arguments in the form of mathematical proofs.
2   They believed that reality is found in the mathematical forms 'underlying' all sensory phenomena, and hence that we obtain knowledge of reality by reason (Latin: *ratio*), and not by our senses.

In this sense the Pythagoreans seemed to believe that they had discovered the key to the enigma of the universe. However, although the Pythagoreans can rightly be called rationalists, they conceived of mathematics as something that, through reason, *points beyond reason* toward something mystical. They were rationalist mystics like the Neoplatonists, such as Plotinus. In the Pythagoreans, we thus find religious mysticism and mathematically based rationalism occurring hand in hand.

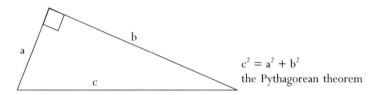

$$c^2 = a^2 + b^2$$
the Pythagorean theorem

Like Parmenides, the Pythagoreans ended up with a dualistic view of the world:

$$\frac{\text{mathematics}}{\text{sensation}} = \frac{\text{certain knowledge}}{\text{uncertain knowledge}} = \frac{\text{reality (the subsistent)}}{\text{the unreal}} = \frac{\text{the eternal}}{\text{the changeable}}$$

The Pythagoreans were to become a source of inspiration for Plato; and later, during the Renaissance, along with Democritus, they played an important part in inspiring the experimental natural sciences. The decisive point was the idea that reality is that which can be conceived in a mathematical language. Reality is not the qualitative multifarious things that we experience through our senses; it is what is measurable and can be expressed in numbers and mathematical formulae. This view may be seen as an idealization since it emphasizes the measurable mathematical aspects of the world, not the world as experienced by human beings. However, it was this 'idealized' view of mathematical concepts and models that paved the way for scientific and technological development in the Renaissance, by establishing classical mechanics and astronomy (cf. Ch. 7).

Politically, the Pythagoreans seem to have supported a hierarchic division of society. Here we can make a general point. Philosophers who excel in disciplines, the acquisition of which requires long years of training and special intellectual or moral faculties, often say that society should be ordered hierarchically: those with insight are to govern and to receive government's honours and privileges. With the

Pythagoreans, we also have an ethics requiring an ascetic way of life. This ethics is associated with a distinction between body and soul, and a belief in the transmigration of souls.

A GLANCE AT ANCIENT INDIAN AND CHINESE THOUGHT

THE BACKGROUND OF INDIAN PHILOSOPHY

Although there was sporadic contact between India and Europe in antiquity – it is sufficient to mention Alexander the Great's invasion of India in 327 BC – we know very little about the intellectual influence of the East on the West, and vice versa. We know that the Greeks received important stimulation from the East, but it is difficult to document a specific Indian source. Indian teaching, as communicated by the Persians, may have influenced the Orphic and Pythagorean schools in Greece; but this is still an open question in the history of philosophy. However, the philosophical and religious traditions in Europe and India do seem to have developed relatively independently of each other from the close of antiquity until well into the 1700s. It was not until the Romantic period that Indian thought was first transmitted to a larger European audience. Our picture of Indian philosophy is still marked by the Romantic enthusiasm for India, especially its expression by the German philosophers Arthur Schopenhauer (1788–1860) and Friedrich Nietzsche (1844–1900).

One may ask whether it is legitimate to talk about an Indian and Chinese *philosophy* at all. The word 'philosophy' comes from Greek and denotes an intellectual activity that has its origin in ancient Greece. Was there anything in India or China that corresponded to classical Greek philosophy? Do we, for example, have reason to talk about a transition from *mythos* to *logos* in the history of Indian thought? It is difficult to give an unambiguous answer. Perhaps this way of presenting the problem is unduly Eurocentric; one could object that Indian thought must be treated on its own premises, not on the criteria set by Greek philosophy.

It is reasonable to assume that in both Indian and Chinese thought there are questions that deserve our attention. We also find an 'internal logic' and discussion in these traditions that are in many ways reminiscent of the history of Greek philosophy. However, we should add that Indian philosophy exhibits many characteristics that we do not find in Western philosophy in the same form. Apparently, Indian philosophy does not distinguish between philosophy and religion as clearly as we are used to. The distinction between *mythos* and *logos*, and that between words and deeds are also made in a different way in India than in Europe. The seminal Hindu text, the *Bhagavad-Gita*, illustrates this difference and can be a useful corrective of too strict a line of demarcation between philosophy and religion in practice: 'There must be a difference between theory (*samkhya*) and practice (*yoga*), / So say the simple-minded, not the wise. / Apply thyself to only one, wholeheartedly, / And win the fruit of both.'[13]

To understand the role of philosophy in Indian culture, we must become acquainted with its historical and religious presuppositions. It will be possible to provide only an elementary introduction in this book. Those wanting a better understanding of Indian philosophy should consult more specialized commentaries.

Between the fourteenth and the twelfth centuries BC, the old civilization in the Indus valley, in what is now Pakistan, was attacked by ethnic groups that presumably came from the region between the Carpathian and Ural mountain ranges. These groups called themselves *Arya* ('noble'), and this is why one speaks of an 'Aryan' invasion of India. It was once widely believed that the Aryan peoples were culturally superior to the 'native' Dravidians. This belief proved to be questionable when, in the 1920s, the Indus civilization was discovered; this was an advanced urban culture along the Indus river dating from the time before the invasion of the Aryans.

India's culture and society is still marked by the original conflict between the Aryans and Dravidians in spite of many centuries of assimilation. This is due not least to the caste system's being probably introduced by the Aryan conquerors. There are many indications that there was originally a distinction between the lighter-skinned 'Aryans' and the darker-skinned 'natives'. Society was later divided into four castes: the three Aryan castes of Brahmans or Vedic priests, warriors and nobles, and artisans and agriculturists, and the lower caste. Significant integration of the different ethnic groups took place over the course of time. New castes were introduced, and non-Aryans were admitted to the upper castes. These processes have continued up to the present day.

Religion united the immigrants. This is embodied in the oldest Sanskrit texts called the Veda of *c.* 1200–800 BC. The Veda may be said to convey the old Aryan world-view. The gods are often associated with the forces of nature, as in Greek, Norse, and Slavonic mythology. This world-view is characterized by an eternal battle between the cosmos and chaos. In this battle, the victory of the gods is not guaranteed once and for all. They need support from man in the battle against chaos. Sacrifices and correctly performed rituals help maintain the cosmic order. It is difficult to call the Veda philosophy. It portrays a mythical world. If we seek a transition from *mythos* to *logos* in Indian spiritual life, it would be found in the *Upanishads*, a more recent and far more comprehensive group of texts of *c.* 800–300 BC. The *Upanishads* critically reflect on the Vedic world-view. They may express a protest against certain aspects of Aryan culture. Newer research seems to have found influences from non-Aryan sources. This is a complicated question that must be left to the historians of religion. It is certain, however, that the *Upanishads* proclaim a new religious and metaphysical doctrine. While the Veda largely consist of hymns, the *Upanishads* consist of *arguments*.

THE *UPANISHADS*

The term *Upanishad* refers to the teaching relationship between the wise man and his student. A philosophical text that provides the content that is communicated in this situation is called an *Upanishad*. Consequently, it can be said that the *Upanishads* resemble Plato's dialogues.

One of the central themes in the *Upanishads* is the idea of an eternal 'round dance' of birth and death. This is the so-called doctrine of reincarnation. The eternal cycle of birth and death is called *samsara*. It is the individual person's innermost 'self' (*atman*) that is reborn in this way. There is lengthy discussion in Indian philosophy of how the *atman* is to be understood. Some of the *Upanishads* seem to assume that the self is a permanent substance (cf. pre-Socratic philosophy) that can be distin-guished from the conscious 'I' or 'ego'. This is a controversial point; but, as we will see, Buddha's criticism of the *Upanishads* is based on this presupposition. Another central assumption of the *Upanishads* is that the *atman* is identical with *Brahman*. It is difficult to find an adequate translation of *Brahman*. Perhaps the expression can be translated as 'the absolute, the all-encompassing, or the divine'. That the *atman* is *Brahman* can therefore mean that the self is identical with the absolute or the divine. We can also recognize such views in the tradition of Western mysticism that individuals or their souls can be one with God (*unio mystica*). Within both Indian philosophy and Western mysticism, as represented in the late Middle Ages by Johannes Eckhart, better known as Meister Eckhart, this unity presupposes an ascetic lifestyle. The *Upanishad* philosophers turn their backs on the world, aiming for an ascetic *flight from it*. The truth is not 'out there', either in texts or in nature. It is inside you. You must learn to 'find yourself'. One can learn *about* mysticism, but that is not the same as having mystical insight. This insight can only be achieved first hand and through personal effort. In India this mystical wisdom is reserved for the priesthood, the Brahmans proper.

The thesis about the *atman* and *Brahman* can be interpreted such that the self *becomes* identical with the absolute. It is under this condition that the individual can be reborn. In Indian philosophy, the 'round dance' of life and death is something that one is to be released from. All Indian philosophy seeks redemption (*moksha*) from the eternal cycle of birth and death. This concept of redemption occupies a superior position not only in the *Upanishads*, but also in Buddhist philosophy. We will therefore take a closer look at why Indian philosophy emphasizes liberation from the cycle to the extent that it does. It undoubtedly has a connection with that philosophy's view of action; more specifically, the doctrine of *karma*. It is our actions that determine whether we are reborn as a Brahman or a lizard – two of millions of more or less dismal possibilities!

Karma is considered a key concept in Indian philosophy. *Karma* means action. All Indian philosophy revolves around the problem of action. The so-called *karma* way of thinking opens up both moral and metaphysical dimensions of philosophy – dimensions that are usually kept separate in modern Western philosophy. This is because *karma* is closely related to the belief in reincarnation, rebirth, and the idea of *moral causality*. By moral causality we mean that the cosmos is permeated by justice: we live in a world where everyone has received what he or she deserves, but where it is possible to rise to a better state in the next life. Put another way: things go well for the good and bad for the bad. All suffering and imperfection in the world is a result of each individual's actions. But what is good and bad will be determined to a large extent by a person's actual caste position. The *Upanishads*, therefore, can be said to legitimize the caste system: people 'deserve' their present caste because each person's caste status is a consequence of that person's previous actions.

The concept of *karma* is not unknown in Western thought. It finds its expres-sion in proverbs such as: 'Everyone is the maker of his future' or 'They have made their bed, and now they have to lie in it'. But, in Western thought, moral causality is not connected to reincarnation. This is a specifically Indian phenomenon.

In Indian philosophy, therefore, moral actions are tied in with the cycle of life-death-life-death. Many Western interpretations of the doctrine of reincarnation – especially within New Age thinking – present it as a positive message about many lives for a person or eternal life. Correspondingly, Nietzsche's theory of the 'eternal recurrence' of all things is thought of as a positive alternative to Christianity's conception of life (cf. Ch. 21, *Übermensch*, will to power, and eternal recurrence). Perhaps we picture rebirth as good news, in that we may replay the game of life again and again, we have the opportunity to live an infinite number of lives, and the sting of death is gone. Such ideas clash with the Indian way of thinking. In Indian philosophy, actions and passions are the main problems. The doctrine of rein-carnation says that our form of existence in the next life will be a reflection of our acts and passions in this life. The analogy of the caterpillar that eats and digests everything in its path is a good illustration: those who have the lusts of a cater-pillar will become a caterpillar in the next life. The caterpillar symbolizes our insa-tiable greed to consume forever without interruption – a typically Western desire! It is essential to escape from such actions and desires.

How can we be liberated from desire and gain control over *karma*? In a short text from the *Bhagavad-Gita*, one of the most important sources of Indian philo-sophy, fire is the central symbol: our desires must be consumed in the fire of know-ledge. This can happen through asceticism and yoga. Those who manage to liberate themselves from *karma* achieve final salvation (*moksha*). But this goal is unachiev-able for most of us. We cannot break out of the cycle of life and death and risk being reborn in millions of different shapes. Even though we cannot all be saints, there is still good reason to try to do our best in this life: those who both do and desire what is good will, according to the philosophy of *karma*, become better creatures in the next life, or will rise in caste. Therefore, the doctrine of *karma*, the idea of reincarnation, and the caste system form a coherent unit in much of Indian philosophy. Within this framework, morality and the social system mutu-ally support each other.

BUDDHIST PHILOSOPHY

Buddhism, a new religion and philosophy, began to take shape in India around the same time as pre-Socratic philosophy appeared in Greece. In this context, 'Buddhist philosophy' refers to beliefs and philosophical positions that can be traced back to the Indian founder of this religion, Siddhartha Gautama (*c.* 563–*c.* 483 BC). We cannot discuss here the other forms of Buddhism that later developed in other cultures, as in Tibet and East Asia.

Siddhartha Gautama left his home and his wife, as did many other holy men in India, to wander as an ascetic wise man. After many years of strict self-mortification, he still found himself in ignorance (*avidya*) about the fundamental questions of human life. He then decided to abandon his self-mortification and return to an ordinary form of contemplative living. After a while, Gautama came forward with a new teaching. He had finally found the right way. He had become 'the Buddha' ('the enlightened one').

In the fifth century BC, the spiritual life of India was still marked by the Vedic tradition, while *the Upanishads* had gained an important place in Indian thought. The

Buddha's new doctrine was sharply opposed to the old Vedic literature and to all forms of ritual and ceremony, while it can also be said to be a critical modification of parts of the *Upanishads*. Paradoxically, the Buddha assumes a fairly unsympathetic attitude towards speculative and religious thought. Modern commentators have therefore, with a certain danger of anachronism, characterized the Buddha as an 'empiricist' and 'sceptic'. Nor do the texts that can probably be attributed to the Buddha prepare the way for the worship that he later became the object of. It has therefore been correct in a certain sense to characterize Buddhism as an 'atheistic' religion, i.e., one without a systematized theology or doctrine about God.

Along with many of the *Upanishads*, the new teaching aims at the individual's liberation or salvation. The Buddha describes this goal as *nirvana* – a term that in many ways corresponds to the term *moksha* in other traditions. Those who want to experience nirvana must learn to free themselves from everything that binds them to this world, including philosophical and religious doctrines. In a brilliant analogy, that of the raft, the Buddha illustrates what he means: a man must cross a danger-ous river. He gathers branches and twigs and ties them together to build a solid raft that will carry him to the other side. When he has safely crossed the river, he says to himself: this raft was really good and useful. I will take it with me, carry-ing it on my head. Thus the man travels on, carrying a raft that he no longer needs. The moral of the story is that the new doctrine resembles the raft. Its purpose is to cross the river, to reach *nirvana*, not to be carried forever. Similar illustrations of the purpose of philosophy have appeared at different times during the history of philosophy: philosophy is an important *tool*, not merely something that is 'nice to have'.

The Buddha's doctrine is both difficult and profound. Here we can only outline some of the main points of his 'fourfold noble truth':

The Noble Truth of suffering (*Dukkha*) is this: Birth is suffering; aging is suffer-ing; sickness is suffering; death is suffering; sorrow and lamentation, pain, grief and despair are suffering; association with the unpleasant is suffering; dissociation from the pleasant is suffering; not to get what one wants is suffering – in brief, the five aggregates of attachment are suffering.

The Noble Truth of the origin of suffering is this: It is this thirst (craving) which produces re-existence and re-becoming, bound up with passionate greed. It finds fresh delight now here and now there, namely, thirst for sense-pleasures; thirst for existence and becoming; and thirst for non-existence (self-annihilation).

The Noble Truth of the Cessation of suffering is this: It is the complete cessa-tion of that very thirst, giving it up, renouncing it, emancipating oneself from it, detaching oneself from it.

The Noble Truth of the Path leading to the Cessation of suffering is this: It is simply the Noble Eightfold Path, namely right view; right thought; right speech; right action; right livelihood; right effort; right mindfulness; right concentration.[14]

The doctrine of the fourfold noble truth was given a pessimistic interpretation by Arthur Schopenhauer. He was the first Western philosopher systematically to occupy himself with Eastern wisdom. Schopenhauer, like the Buddha, took the mis-ery of life and the emptiness of existence as his starting point: everything is per-meated by a foolish, blind, and insatiable need to live. That is why our existence is full of anxiety and pain. Dissatisfaction and pain are the basic experiences; desire is only an illusion that arises when the eternal thirst for life is momentarily quenched. The release from the misery of life can only be attained by denying the will to live. Their solutions go in the same direction: Buddha wants to quench the craving or desire, Schopenhauer wants to quench the *will to live* so that there is no longer any motive for action. Schopenhauer terms as *nirvana* that condition of final redemption, of peace of mind, where all desire is silenced. It may be that Schopenhauer's presentation of the doctrine of the fourfold noble truth is excessively pessimistic; perhaps this interpretation obscures more than it clarifies.

Friedrich Nietzsche, Schopenhauer's student, gave Buddhism a European face. Buddhism's ideal, according to Nietzsche, was to separate man from 'good' and 'evil'. This was the main contribution of Buddhism to the struggle against suffering. In Nietzsche's philosophy, Buddhism became an ally in the struggle with Platonic metaphysics and Christianity: 'the Buddha against the Crucified'.[15] To what extent Schopenhauer and Nietzsche's understanding of the Buddha is adequate is still a disputed question.

Another controversial question in Buddhism is the doctrine of the self. A basic idea of the Buddha is that the world must be thought of in procedural terms, not as things or substances. Therefore, we cannot talk about a permanent self or 'I'; the self cannot be a psychic substance, underlying the individual. What we experience is only a stream of fleeting and perishable states of consciousness that at each moment comprises our personality.

Modern commentators have seen, at this point, similarities between the Buddha and empiricist philosophers such as David Hume (1711–1776). Hume made a similar criticism of the idea of a mental substance (cf. Ch. 12) but had no knowledge of the Buddha. At the end of the nineteenth century, Nietzsche became the spokesman for a similar critique of thinking in terms of substance. This was, surprisingly, a meeting place for premodern and postmodern philosophy.

THE *BHAGAVAD-GITA*

The *Bhagavad-Gita* ('Song of the Lord') is a part of the epic poem the *Mahabharata*. It is viewed today as a seminal text of Hinduism, the dominant religion of modern India. Of unknown authorship, the *Bhagavad-Gita* was probably composed around 200 BC. The text is in the form of a dialogue between Arjuna and his charioteer, Krishna.[16] During the dialogue, Krishna reveals himself to be Vishnu, the Lord of the Universe, God himself.

The *Bhagavad-Gita* presents many problems of interpretation for a Western reader. It examines central questions in the Hindu understanding of morality and reality in fewer than 100 pages. The basic idea appears to be that proper insight provides the basis for action outside the bounds of desire and disgust. Desire and disgust are the real enemies of man. Arjuna is not striving to win power and prestige, but to maintain a just cosmic order. It is up to the individual to assist in this: 'Better one's own duty [*dharma*] [to perform], though void of merit, than to do another's well: better to die within [the sphere of] one's own duty: perilous is the duty of other men.'[17] This quotation does not express any kind of universalist ethic of duty. The caste system is an insoluble part of the cosmic order. Consequently, the individual's duty is conditioned by the caste he belongs to.

The central message in the *Bhagavad-Gita* is a Hindu interpretation of *liberation*. It is emphasized repeatedly that liberation presupposes control over one's actions: 'When all a man's enterprises have neither motive nor desire – his works are burnt up in wisdom's fire – then wise men call him learned'.[18] But liberation is at the same time connected with nonviolence (*ahimsa*). Mahatma Gandhi (1869–1948), in his interpretation of the *Bhagavad-Gita*, strongly emphasized that it is precisely the violent actions that must be consumed in the fire of knowledge. Gandhi interprets the *Bhagavad-Gita* as a timeless text offering a guide to life that still applies to us today.

CONFUCIUS

Greek philosophy was a product of the city-state (*polis*). All its practitioners, without exception, participated in the city-state, which was an autonomous political unit. A place was reserved within its walls for philosophical discussions and other major intellectual activities. The city-state also created a public space for political interaction and discussion, and hence made possible the new form of political praxis that came into play among the free and equal citizens. This provided a foundation for the development of permanent academic institutions such as Plato's Academy and Aristotle's Lyceum – both of which enjoyed significant academic freedom and self-government. Neither India nor China had a similar development. The Chinese city was not a *polis* in the ancient Greek sense. It was not an autonomous entity that could enter into pacts with other states.

The Chinese city was part of a centrally governed administration. Chinese civilization was generally oriented towards the norms of human behaviour, it was a tradition-oriented *culture of scriptures*, but not a culture of *public discourse*. There was little interest in speculative, systematic philosophy, as in Greece, or liberation and salvation, as in India. Chinese civilization had a more practical and pragmatic orientation.

The Chinese philosophers were often drawn from a 'poor nobility' obliged to seek employment in the administrative corps that had developed at the large imperial courts. Many of China's great thinkers came from this class. They were almost without exception learned civil servants, mandarins, who had been certified (and at times even educated) by a bureaucratic system – not so unlike philosophy professors of our time! It was from this social milieu that King Chi came, better known in the West by the name of Confucius (King Fuzi, 'Master King').

Confucius (551–479 BC) lived around the same time as the Buddha, Thales, and Pythagoras. There are no extant texts by Confucius; but central aspects of his thought were written down in *The Analects*, a collection of brief notes from conversations (questions and answers) between Confucius and his students. The dialogues are devoted to social-ethical questions, focusing on proper behaviour. In this work, we get a picture of Confucius as a thinker who was strongly tied to tradition: by a careful study of tradition, individuals can gain an understanding of what their duties are. Tradition also becomes a norm in the efforts to reform the chaotic social conditions in the present. It was, therefore, natural that the study of classical texts had a central place in Confucius' teaching. The dominant attitude is that of *adapting to the world*, not escaping from the world as in Indian philosophy.

Confucius has little interest in natural philosophy and the philosophy of religion. He focuses on the individual, as did Socrates. This attitude is concisely expressed in the following fragment: 'When the stables were burnt down, on returning from court, he said, "Was anyone hurt?" He did not ask about the horses.'[19] The criteria for right behaviour is summarized in the concept of *humanity*. Confucius discusses humanity in words that are reminiscent of the message of the Sermon on the Mount: 'Tzu-kung asked saying, "Is there any single saying that one can act upon all day and every day?" The Master said, "Perhaps the saying about consideration: 'Never do to others what you would not like them to do to you'"' (Book XV, fragment 23, p. 198). This idea of loving one's neighbour is, in Confucianism, often called 'the measure principle': what we expect of others should be the touchstone for our behaviour towards others.

Confucius' teachings about humanity and compassion should not be interpreted in a strictly universalist direction. He defends a straightforward ranking of society. The individual's duty is therefore tied to his social position. The good life was, according to Confucius, realized in 'the five human relations': ruler to state official, father to son, husband to wife, the old to the young, and friend to friend. Each had its own duties. The ruler's relationship to his subjects is well expressed in the following sentence: 'The essence of the gentleman is that of wind; the essence of small people is that of grass. And when a wind passes over the grass, it cannot choose but bend' (Book XII, fragment 19, p. 168). This sentence, too, can be understood as an application of the measure principle. It would perhaps, in this context, mean that individuals, who were themselves subjects, should ask: how would I, as ruler, like my subjects to behave? If the answer is that they should submit, that means that the measure principle is compatible with traditional superiority and subordination.

Confucius did not develop a systematic philosophy. First and foremost, he gave helpful advice on human relations and developed a distinctive teaching of wisdom. During his lifetime he attracted a large group of students. This pragmatically oriented 'Confucianism' has played an important part in Chinese culture and society up to our time. Presenting practical philosophy in the form of sentences, aphorisms, and short essays has not been unusual even in modern China (cf. *Mao's Red Book, Quotations by Chairman Mao Tse-Tung*).

Confucian ethics was further developed by Mencius or Meng Zi (*c.* 371–289 BC). He believed, along with Confucius, that man is innately good and that this goodness can be further developed through education. Like many other Chinese philosophers from this period, Mencius spent his life at royal courts where he guided princes in the two cardinal virtues, humanity (*jen*) and righteousness (*yi*).

TAOIST PHILOSOPHY

While Confucianism developed a philosophy that is realistically and politically anchored, Taoism (or Daoism) is characterized by mysticism and holistic thought. Lao Tzu is often credited as being the greatest representative of the Taoist tendencies in China's cultural life, although we may mention Chuang Tzu (born 369 BC) as another very influential Taoist thinker. We hardly know anything about Lao Tzu's life, except that he is thought to have been an older contemporary of Confucius.

It is believed that he sought a life of obscurity and avoided fame. Lao Tzu's name is inseparably tied to the famous *Tao-te-ching* ('Classic of the Way and Its Virtue'), but it is doubtful that he wrote it himself. It was probably written down by his students.

The *Tao-te-ching* is held to be the classic text in Taoist philosophy. The text is not easily accessible and poses great problems of interpretation. Lao Tzu, like Heraclitus, is often viewed as the 'puzzling' and 'unfathomable'. The *Tao-te-ching* can perhaps best be characterized as a contribution to Chinese natural philosophy or philosophy of being. As such, it distinguishes itself in a definite way from the practically oriented philosophy of Confucianism.

The fundamental idea for Lao Tzu is 'the *tao*'. This is said to be 'indeterminate', 'infinite', 'unchangeable', 'unlimited in time and space', and 'chaos as well as form'. Name-tags such as these can only suggest what it is about. Language, strictly speaking, is not adequate because the *tao* cannot be conceptually defined. Lao Tzu's reflections on the *tao*, however, seem to have many similarities with the type of questions and answers that we are acquainted with from Greek natural philosophy. Anaximander believed that the *urstoff* was *apeiron*, the indeterminate and unlimited. There is undoubtedly a certain family resemblance between the *tao* and *apeiron*. Like Anaximander, Lao Tzu claims that the *tao* is prior to heaven and earth; the *tao* is the point of origin and return for all being. He uses an illustration to show that the *tao* can be viewed as the 'mother of the world', the starting point for the entire diversity of existence. Possibly, we may conceive of the *tao* as the Being of being, the indeterminate primitive power that is the basis for everything that is. In another connection, however, Lao Tzu says that 'being comes from non-being'. Here he may mean that the *tao*, the primitive power or 'being', must be described as 'non-being' to avoid making the *tao* into an object or something existent. Such interpretations are, of course, fraught with a great amount of uncertainty. But if they are reasonable, we can say that Lao Tzu is approaching the problem of substance in the same way as the pre-Socratic natural philosophers.

Lao Tzu's view of cosmic justice has clear parallels with early Greek philosophy. He seems to believe that there is a basic principle of justice in our existence: when something is pushed too far, a reaction occurs: 'It is towards misfortune that the blessings turn, and the blessings rest on the misfortunes.' When something is pushed to its extreme, it turns into its opposite. Too much happiness turns to unhappiness. Extreme unhappiness will turn towards happiness. Therefore, there seems to be a power that intervenes when something moves beyond its natural limits, when *hubris* occurs, and restores the order that should or will be. Heraclitus had a similar conception. In fragment 44 (D:94), he says: 'The sun will not transgress his measures. If he does, the Furies, ministers of Justice, will find him out.' As a result, both Lao Tzu and Heraclitus seem to presuppose a cosmic principle of justice that secures an ordered existence.

It is not difficult to understand that the 'obscure' Lao Tzu was on a collision course with the pragmatic socio-ethical maxims of Confucianism. He also turned explicitly against the Confucian educational tradition, and is said to have claimed that it was better that people had little knowledge than great knowledge; too much education would only serve to corrupt their souls.

QUESTIONS

What characterizes the thought of the Greek philosophers before the Sophists?

What types of questions and arguments can we assume to be presupposed in Thales' thesis that water is the principle of all things?

What implications (consequences) does this theory have? By what justification can we claim that philosophy begins with Thales?

'Heraclitus claims that everything is in a state of change, while Parmenides claims the opposite.' Discuss and take a critical stand on this statement.

Describe Democritus' theory of atomism. Discuss the relation between this theory and Pythagoras' conception of reality.

SUGGESTIONS FOR FURTHER READING

PRIMARY LITERATURE

The Art and Thought of Heraclitus: An Edition of the Fragments with Translation and Commentary, edited by Charles H. Kahn, Cambridge, 1989.
The Presocratic Philosophers, edited by G. S. Kirk and J. E. Raven, Cambridge, 1964.
Hindu Scriptures, translated by R. C. Zaehner, London, 1968.
Analects of Confucius, Beijing, 1994.

SECONDARY LITERATURE

Barnes, Jonathan, *The Presocratic Philosophers*, revised edition, London, 1982.
Heidegger, Martin, *Early Greek Thinking*, translated by David Farrell Krell and Frank A. Capuzzi, New York, 1975.

NOTES

1 There were three groups in Athens: slaves, Athenians, and foreigners living in Athens. Athenian citizenship was hereditary, and foreigners that moved to Athens did not automatically become Athenian citizens even if they (or their parents) had been born in Athens. Athenian women, like the slaves and immigrants, were excluded from politics.
2 Translator's note: the noun *urstoff* in Norwegian is identical in meaning to its German cognate and is usually translated as 'primordial stuff' or 'primitive stuff'. I have chosen to use *urstoff* throughout the text because it concisely summarizes the concept that is being discussed.
3 Substance (Latin: *substantia*): the underlying (Greek: *hypo-keimenon*).
4 Translated into English by Charles H. Kahn in *The Art and Thought of Heraclitus: An Edition of the Fragments with Translation and Commentary*, Cambridge, 1989. [Translator's note: Kahn numbers the fragments differently from the standard numeration found in the Diels-Kranz German translation. I have followed Kahn's numeration of the fragments but for ease of reference have included Diels-Kranz's numeration in parenthesis, e.g. (D:x).]
5 Cf. fragment 51 (D:91): 'One cannot step twice into the same river, nor can one grasp any mortal substance in a stable condition, but it scatters and again gathers; it forms and dissolves, and approaches and departs.'
6 Cf. fragment 37 (D:30): 'The ordering, the same for all, no god nor man has made, but it ever was and is and will be: fire everlasting, kindled in measures and in measures going out.'

7 Cf. fragment 75 (D:8): 'The counter-thrust brings together, and from tones at variance comes perfect attunement, and all things come to pass through conflict.'; and fragment 78 (D:51): 'They do not comprehend how a thing agrees at variance with itself; it is an attunement turning back on itself, like that of the bow and the lyre.'

8 There is thus something 'dialectical' in Heraclitus' thought that is reminiscent of Hegel and Marx: history is driven forward by an interplay of opposites.

9 Rationalist: a person who relies on rational arguments, on reason (Latin: *ratio*).

10 Dualism: a position based on *two* principles – as opposed to monism: a position based on *one* principle.

11 This paradox is typical of Greek thought: the notion of instantaneous velocity (the notion of motion at a mathematical instant) is seen as impossible. Consequently, there are certain questions which cannot be discussed.

12 Cf. the theory of primary and secondary qualities that we find in Locke and Berkeley.

13 *Bhagavad-Gita*, Book V, §4, translated by R. C. Zaehner, in *Hindu Scriptures*, London, 1968, p. 271.

14 W. Rahula, *What the Buddha Taught*, New York, 1974, p. 93.

15 F. Nietzsche, *Werke*, Vol. IV, Berlin, 1972, p. 362.

16 Arjuna is the main character of the *Bhagavad-Gita*.

17 *Bhagavad-Gita*, Book III, §35, p. 265.

18 Ibid., Book IV, §19, p. 268.

19 The quotations here, and in what follows, are paraphrased from *The Analects of Confucius*, Book X, fragment 12, translated and annotated by Arthur Waley, London, 1964.

2 The Sophists and Socrates

THE SOPHISTS

The first question asked by the Greek philosophers concerned *physis* and nature, or the cosmos. We call the first period in Greek philosophy, from about 600 to 450 BC, 'the cosmological period'. But a change took place around 450 BC – at the same time that democracy began in Athens. This change was partially caused by the internal dynamics of early Greek philosophy and partially by political conditions.

We can start with the internal development. If we imagine that we lived during that time as philosophy students, then we would be in this situation: behind us were 150 years of philosophical tradition. Within this philosophical tradition there are many different philosophical positions; some of which contradict each other but all of which are allegedly true. Something must be wrong! At best, one of these systems of thought should be correct. This is a reasonable reaction. It was also the reaction that came.

It is understandable that people gradually became sceptical: here is one philosopher claiming that water is the *urstoff*; one that it is *apeiron*, the undetermined; one that it is air; one that it is fire; and another that it is the atom. One philosopher proposes four *urstoffs* and another an infinite number. One of these answers, at most, is correct. But then what has gone wrong with the others? Attention turns from nature to human thought itself. What is the condition for certain knowledge?

We have a change from pretentious and often ill-founded cosmological speculation to a sceptical critique of knowledge and theory of knowledge; from 'ontology' ('theory of being'; Greek: *onto*, 'being', *logos*, 'theory') to 'epistemology' ('theory of knowledge'; Greek: *episteme*, 'knowledge'). Man does not simply observe objects, and then make assertions. Man's own nature becomes problematic. Thought is thrown back on itself. Man begins to 're-flect'.[1]

Around 450 BC, man himself becomes the centre of interest, as we move into the 'anthropocentric period' (Greek: *anthropos*, 'man'). Along with this epistemological reaction, we also have another turning towards man that allows us to refer to an anthropocentric period: ethical-political[2] questions are now raised in earnest. Man has now become a problem for himself, not only as a being who thinks, but also as one who acts.

This shift towards ethical-political questions is connected to the political changes in Greek society: colonization had put the Greeks in contact with peoples who had alien customs and conventions. Now many peoples have experienced similar things without starting an ethical-political discussion.[3] That the Greeks started asking such questions shows how unusual they were. They managed to do something unique: to ask whether it was *they*, and not the others, who were at fault; and to discuss this question in a clear and objective manner.

Even though the confrontation with other peoples was caused by political circumstances, the ability to debate rationally was a legacy from the 150-year-old philosophical tradition. The Greeks had now, in 450 BC, learned to discuss difficult questions in a clear and orderly manner. Just as the first Greek philosophers had asked about the one unchangeable element in all change, about unity in diversity, Greeks were now asking whether one universally valid morality and political ideal could be found amid all the diversity of different customs and conventions. Formally, the question is the same. But the answers to the question varied. Some believed that there was *one* universally valid morality and political ideal given by God or nature. Others believed morality to be a creation of either society or a single individual, and that there was no universally valid morality or political ideal. It became common, especially towards the end of the anthropocentric period (*c.* 400 BC), to claim that morality is only relative, in the sense that there is no court of appeal for such questions other than the personal opinion of each individual: morality varies, just like taste and pleasure. Those who advocated such viewpoints were often disliked, since the rulers believed that such viewpoints could undermine society. The Sophists (Greek: *sophistes*, 'wise men') led this debate. We will take a closer look at what function the Sophists had.

The Athenian direct democracy functioned more like a close-knit community than a modern corporation in which the connection between members is partial and external. The Athenian democracy was not only a new creation; it was also proof that a limited kind of direct democracy is possible under certain conditions. For instance, it requires a high level of general education. If everyone is to participate in the management of society, then the general educational system must be good. The Sophists directed this 'enlightenment of the people'. They taught those subjects that were necessary for participation in political life: the arts of argumentation and rhetoric, civics, knowledge of human nature, etc. But the natural philosophy was not a prerequisite for participation in politics. The Sophists were at the same time teachers, journalists, and intellectuals: they imparted knowledge and culture to people; above all, to those who were politically active and able to pay their instructors.[4] To the extent that the Sophists themselves took part in enquiry, it was the epistemological and ethical-political problems that they investigated. The Sophists were not a homogeneous group. But we can still say that many of the later Sophists showed a tendency towards scepticism on epistemological questions ('we can't know anything for certain') and towards relativism in ethical-political questions ('there is no universally valid morality or ethics').[5]

Many Sophists claimed that what was called right and just was merely an expression of what an arbitrary tradition or an arbitrary ruler has forced people to accept. There is nothing that *is* right. What we call right is what serves the powerful. Might makes right. Or we could say that right is merely what a majority of the weak have managed to get recognized. And some Sophists said that what we call good morality is nothing more than a concealed expression of what people like. And since different people like different things, morality may be defined in different ways. In a universally valid sense, true morality does not exist. There are only different egoistic sympathies and antipathies.

Because of such relativism, the Sophists gradually started to forfeit public approval. They were paid to teach people to argue and persuade. Since different clients had different interests in many matters, the Sophists, like trial lawyers, had to argue for or against different causes. The client's goal was to win the case, not to get the right answer. The skills that the Sophists taught had to be adapted to this purpose. Consequently, the Sophists often taught debating tricks and deceptions rather than the art of rational argumentation. Therefore, they were in danger of degenerating into hair-splitting quibblers, that is to say, 'sophists' in our sense of the word.

GORGIAS

Life. *Originally from Sicily, Gorgias (c. 483–374 BC), came to Athens during the Peloponnesian war (427). He became known as an orator. A few fragments of his writings survive, and another source is Plato's dialogue* Gorgias. *In addition, the later sceptic Sextus Empiricus tells us about Gorgias' treatise* On That Which is Not, or Nature.

Gorgias originally was to have studied cosmology but is said to have become a philosophical sceptic as a result of his encounter with Eleatic philosophy. In his treatise *On That Which is Not, or Nature*, he denies that knowledge is possible, in view of the paradoxes surrounding movement and change (cf. Achilles and the tortoise). If being is simply that which does not participate in non-being, if all change and movement participate in non-being, and if all phenomena participate in change and movement, then we cannot say that any phenomenon is being, in this terminology. Gorgias is supposed to have gone so far as to say that

1   nothing exists, and
2   if anything did exist, it could not be known, and
3   even if knowledge is possible, it cannot be shared with others.

It has been disputed whether Gorgias really meant this or if these theses merely served as a starting point for exercises to show how rhetoric can persuade people to accept the most absurd claims. But perhaps Gorgias, out of the Eleatic conception of being, non-being, change, and our ability to recognize the changeable, really did conclude that philosophy itself was hopelessly self-contradictory. According to this interpretation, the three extreme formulations form part of a train of thought that ends with the demonstration that philosophy is meaningless. Gorgias may then have gone over to the practice of rhetoric purely as a method of persuasion, because he no longer believed in the possibility of true knowledge. In this view, rational discussion and rational conviction no longer exist, leaving only the art of persuasion.

For Gorgias, rhetoric is to be cultivated as a method of persuasion rather than a medium for argumentation and rational conviction. For him, the foremost point of persuasion is to make listeners change their views and attitudes. To put it briefly, we can say that he is not trying to get the listeners to admit anything, and possibly change their view after attaining true knowledge. Gorgias is not interested in distinguishing true from false, valid from invalid, but rather in influencing an audience. Rhetoric has become primarily a means of manipulation, and not a discourse whose participants are mutually open to be convinced by the best argument.

THRASYMACHUS

Life. *Thrasymachus (born c. 470 BC) was a contemporary of Socrates. We have a few fragments of his writing. In addition, he appears in Plato's dialogue* The Republic.

Thrasymachus is known for his view on rights and justice: right is what serves the strongest. Right is might. The concepts of rights and justice that contradict this are merely expressions of foolish naivety. Thrasymachus is therefore a crass opponent of a universal order of rights, and he interprets existing right as an expression of the interests of the strongest, expressing these views in the first part of *The Republic.*

PROTAGORAS

Life. *Protagoras (c. 481–411 BC) was from Abdera in Thracia. He taught in several Greek cities, particularly in Sicily and mainland Italy, and was a famous teacher. In Athens he was in contact with, among others, Pericles and Euripides. Plato devoted to him his dialogue* Protagoras. *Protagoras left various writings, such as 'About the Gods' and 'Truth or Crushing Arguments'.*

Protagoras' statement that 'man is the measure of all things' can be interpreted as an epistemological thesis: things do not reveal themselves to people the way that the things are in themselves; but it is always only certain aspects or properties of the things that at any one time present themselves to man. For example, a hammer in the hand of a carpenter is a tool to drive a nail. The hammer is handy or awkward, light or heavy. To a physicist, the hammer lying on an observation table is a physical object that is neither handy nor awkward, but which has a certain molecular structure, and certain physical properties, such as weight, elasticity, etc. For the merchant, the hammer on the counter is a product with a particular price and profit, which is easy or difficult to sell or store. This is our interpretation so far.

If we have interpreted Protagoras correctly, his thesis entails that man is the measure of things insofar as things always appear to people in a way that is determined by the circumstances or the duties within which a person is situated at any given time. This view implies a kind of epistemological *perspectivism*: our knowledge is always conditioned by our perspective at any one time and by the perspective on which our knowledge is based. This kind of perspectivism implies an epistemological *pluralism*: there is a plurality of ways of viewing things. This perspectivism also represents a *relativism*: our knowledge of things is determined by our activities or situations – knowledge is relative to our situation.

Does this mean that we cannot distinguish between the true and the false? Not according to our presentation of this thesis: two carpenters will usually be able to find out which hammer is best suited to a particular task, given that they have fairly similar hands, arm strength, etc. And usually two scientists will easily be able to agree on an object's specific weight, elasticity, etc. In other words, this type of perspectivism (pluralism, relativism) that is connected to various situations and professions does not imply that the distinction between true and false is erased. As carpenters, we can speak both truthfully and falsely about the hammer; the same will apply to scientists, merchants, etc. When we, in a particular situation, discuss the object, such as the hammer, as it appears in this situation, we are speaking truthfully as long as what we say is that the object is the way it appears to be in this situation. It is the object itself, for example, the hammer, that we are talking about, not an imaginary object.

But if the object reveals itself only from certain perspectives, how can we know that it is the *same* object, the hammer, that we are talking about when we move from perspective to perspective? One could answer by showing that the various perspectives actually merge: a carpenter is not only a carpenter, he is also involved in family roles, as a father, son, or brother, as well as commercial relationships, such as those with the supplier of his building materials or his customers. Overlaps and fluid transitions exist between perspectives; and that is why we can recognize the same object, such as the hammer, in different contexts.

How can we say all of this? Is the statement we have just made about perspectivism itself a truth that is dependent on a certain perspective? If we answer yes, then we are making what we have said relative. We are approaching scepticism. If we answer no, then we are limiting perspectivism to our knowledge of things: when it comes to theoretical reflection, we are not positing perspectivism.

We have now given a free interpretation of Protagoras. But one fragment by Protagoras indicates that he wished to expand perspectivism beyond the knowledge of things to include the theoretical discussion: 'There are two opposite arguments on every subject.' Is this Protagoras' way of stating as a fact that people do not agree without wanting to decide whether people are speaking the truth or not? Or is Protagoras saying that it is possible in all matters to formulate two equally true, contradictory statements – true in the same sense, and referring to the same issue? The first position is not a problem philosophically; it is just a matter of making a slightly dogmatic claim about an actual state of affairs: 'people contradict one another'. But the second position is philosophically problematic. What does it mean to say that, in a certain case, there are two contradictory claims that are both true in the same sense? And does this thesis apply to itself? If so, then it is possible to formulate a contradiction of this thesis that is also true. But then what is this thesis actually asserting? Sceptical self-dissolution is close at hand.

Protagoras also says: 'With regard to the gods, I cannot feel sure either that they are or that they are not, nor what they are like in figure; for there are many things that hinder sure knowledge, the obscurity of the subject and the shortness of human life.' This fragment also states that there is a limit to human knowledge. We cannot know whether the gods exist or what they are like. But this fragment does not bring human cognitive ability into question in such a way that the fragment itself, that is, the doubt expressed in the fragment, is brought into question.

We have interpreted the statement that man is the measure of all things as a thesis that things always appear in a way that is, at any one time, determined by the situation in which human beings find themselves. But we are constantly moving in and out of these situations. However, were perspective to be determined by social status or an economically determined class, so that the transition between the different basic perspectives was as difficult as the transition from one class to another, then the result would be a sociological thesis about the fundamental difficulties of communication within society. And if people from different groups or classes cannot understand one another, then open communication in the political arena will not be possible. If, in addition, there are fundamental conflicts of interest between social groups, politics will be characterized both by conflict and by a lack of mutual understanding. Politics as rational discussion and governance will then only occur when the socially determined conflicts of interest and conflicts of understanding are removed, along with the social classes.

We see again how we can find our way to different theories from Protagoras' statement. We are not evaluating here whether it is reasonable to ascribe these interpretations to Protagoras. We are only trying to find possible interpretations that represent interesting epistemological or political viewpoints.

If, for example, we were to change our previous interpretation – the sociological one based on class differences – by replacing class with nation, people, or era we would then have a theory about every nation (every people, every era) understanding things in their way. Communication between nations and peoples, or between those alive now and past times then becomes a problem.

If we had said that the basic perspectives were based on age, gender, or race, then we would end up with theories about generational differences, about a lack of understanding between the sexes, or about failure of communication between different races, between the young and the old, men and women, black and white. 'Oh, East is East, and West is West, and never the twain shall meet' (Kipling).[6]

It is noteworthy that, so far, we have been talking about groups of people rather than individuals. We have talked about distinctive ways in which things appear for different occupational groups, different social classes, different nations, different age groups, different sexes, and different races. We can also take Protagoras' thesis about man as the measure of all things to mean that it is individual persons who, on the basis of their own experiences and their own situations, 'stamp' things in their own images, so to speak. The individual person is the measure of all things.

We can note that the world is not the same for those who are happy and those who are unhappy; for those who are paranoid and those who are ecstatic. We know that, as a psychological thesis, this is correct to a certain degree. But if this thesis is made more radical, so that we claim that all knowledge is perspectivized, as determined by the individual's distinctive presuppositions, then we again face a paradox when this claim is used against itself: is this claim, too, merely an expression of the way in which the problem appears to a certain person?

Thus far, we have treated the thesis about man as the measure of all things as an epistemological thesis; as a question about how things appear to human beings. But we could also interpret this as a thesis concerning the normative: man is the measure of all things insofar as the value or importance of the phenomena is relative to man, in one sense or another. We could say, for instance, that things are in themselves neither good nor evil, but only good or evil in relation to a human being or a group of human beings.

Protagoras' argument that we cannot know anything about the gods is twofold: divinity is beyond perception, and human life is short. The first argument does not say that the divine does not exist, but that man cannot perceive it – this implies that perception is a, or the, fundamental basis of human experience. Platonists, for example, would argue against such a view. The second argument, that human life is short, seems to imply that *if* life were longer, we would be able to comprehend more of the divine – in that case, this argument admits both that divinity exists, and that knowledge of that divinity, in one way or another, increases with a longer life.

The thesis that an opinion always has a counter-opinion can, in this context, be interpreted not least as an indirect criticism of unquestioning acceptance of existing norms: regarding the norms that already exist, whether they be ethical or political, there are alternative norms that can be equally well supported. But this argument can also be used to serve tradition: the traditional norms are as good as any others. If the agnostic thesis can be interpreted as an argument against grounding basic ethical-political norms on a divine authority, then this thesis about counter-opinions can perhaps be interpreted as an argument against the attempt immediately to ground ethical-political norms on the prevailing tradition.

One interpretation of the thesis about man as the measure of all things implies that it is society which is the final court of appeal for normative questions. The point of this thesis is that values and norms are valid for the society in which these values and norms are embedded, but not in other societies. It is both relativist and absolutist in the sense that one set of norms and values is said to be valid in the society in which these norms and values are entrenched, but in other societies other norms and values are valid. When we play chess, we have to play by the rules of chess. But when we play rummy we follow different rules, those of rummy. The fact that certain rules are valid in Athens is not in conflict with the fact that different, perhaps conflicting, rules are valid in Persia.

Here we have a confrontation between two basic views of law. The first claims that valid law is the law which actually exists at any given time, or the 'positive' law. The second view claims that valid law is different from law existing; valid law appeals to a 'naturally given' idea of law. In later debates we speak of the conflict between legal positivism and natural rights philosophy. We will see that Socrates and Plato, from a particular conception of natural law, argue against precisely the positivist tendencies found in the Sophists. The question is whether human beings, in one way or another, have access to universal norms, to the knowledge of something that is universally right and true, beyond tradition and that which has been handed down.

The Sophists raised a great many issues connected with ethics, the social sciences, and epistemology – issues that we have since lived with, such as the complex problems of relativism and absolutism, right and might, egoism and altruism, individual and society, and reason and feelings, to list some key terms. We will see that Socrates and Plato took part in this debate surrounding the Sophists. Plato's theory of ideas can be viewed as an attempt to fashion a positive answer to the question of whether one universal ethical-political order exists: the theory of ideas is in this sense a counter-argument to the ethical-political scepticism of the Sophists.

Ages	Periods/persons	Themes	Philosophical styles
600 BC	The cosmological period (Thales to the mediating philosophers)	'External' (nature)	Assertive
450 BC	The anthropocentric period (the Sophists)	Internal (knowledge, ethics)	Sceptical
400 BC	The systematic period (Plato and Aristotle)	External-and-internal	More balanced

Thales	(624–546)	
Anaximander	(610–546)	
Anaximenes	(585–525)	
Pythagoras	(c. 580–500)	
Heraclitus	(c. 500)	
Parmenides	(c. 500)	
Empedocles	(492–432)	
Anaxagoras	(498–428)	
Democritus	(460–370)	
Gorgias	(483–374)	
Thrasymachus	(470–410?)	
Protagoras	(481–411)	
Socrates	(470–399)	
Plato	(427–347)	
Aristotle	(384–322)	

SOCRATES

Life. *Socrates was born around 470 BC and died in 399. His life as an active philosopher coincided with what we have called the anthropocentric period (450–400). He lived, that is, at the same time as the Sophists. Socrates was the first Athenian philosopher and he lived his entire life there. He did not come from the aristocracy; his father was a stonemason and his mother was a midwife. He had a wife (Xantippe) and three children. Socrates, through Plato's dialogues, is among those who have most strongly influenced and inspired the Western spirit. What seems to distinguish Socrates as a human being is his ethical strength, his just and undemanding life, his quick wit, and his outspokenness and good humour. In spite of this, the citizens of Athens were made uncomfortable by his questions when he accosted them on the streets and in the market. The powers that be decided that Socrates, like the Sophists, was corrupting the youth and was a danger to society. He was condemned to drink poison. Socrates did not write anything himself. Our knowledge of his 'doctrine' (if he had one) derives from what others have written about him; primarily the Platonic dialogues. It is therefore difficult to be certain what Socrates really stood for, and how he and Plato distinguished themselves from each other. With this reservation, we will attempt to provide an interpretation of Socrates' philosophy in relation to Plato's.*

Like the Sophists, Socrates was not primarily interested in the philosophy of nature but in epistemology – conceptual clarification (definitions) by the aid of dialogues – and in ethical-political questions. In the latter, Socrates took it to be his mission to refute the scepticism of the Sophists: there are some values and norms that are universally good and right! We can perhaps outline the basic principles of Socrates' ethics as follows: virtue and knowledge form a unity. The person who truly knows what is right will also do what is right. This person will also be happy.

The Greek word for 'virtue' is *arete*, which does not primarily mean virtue in a narrow, moralizing sense; that is, the avoidance of certain actions. Instead *arete* means achieving one's true potential as a human being in society. Virtue is therefore positive, not negative. The essential meaning of *arete*, like the English word *virtue*, is connected with the idea of excellence, whether it be moral excellence or that excellence which is achieved by fulfilling the function or role assigned to one in the best possible way. The person who possesses *arete* performs his or her function in the proper way. Teachers possess *arete* when they teach their classes properly. Blacksmiths possess *arete* when they make good tools. People are virtuous when they achieve all that they can, according to their abilities; i.e., when they realize the true potential of what it means to be a human being.

For Socrates, virtue is in a way equivalent to knowledge (Greek: *episteme*). But his understanding of knowledge is rather complicated. It includes knowledge about ourselves and the situations we find ourselves in. It is, however, characteristic of Socrates that he does not seek this knowledge by collecting experiences, but mainly by *conceptual analysis* and by clarifying the vague concepts that we already have about human beings and society, concepts such as justice, courage, virtue, and the good life. But this is not enough. Virtue is to live the way we *should*. This involves goals or values that we cannot have knowledge of by means of the experimental sciences or the formal sciences. In other words, we must also have insight into the good (Greek: *to agathon*), insight into norms and values, or normative insight. But even this does not seem to be enough. Knowledge must be 'one' with the person; it must be the insight that the person truly represents, not what the person *says* he or she represents.[7]

We therefore have three types of knowledge:

1   factual knowledge about what *is*
2   normative insight into what *should* be, and
3   insight into what the person truly 'stands for'.

This rough, threefold division demands a certain qualification: since Socrates viewed knowledge as knowledge of the self through conceptual clarification – knowledge of oneself as a human being and as a member of society, gained by allowing what one already knows to be clarified and put in its proper place – this self-knowledge will in a way incorporate all three of the forms of knowledge that have been listed. But if we hold to this rough scheme, we can say that Socrates' answer to the Sophists can be found in point 2: there is a universal good! And we can gain insight into it. The insight that we achieve, by conceptual analysis through dialogue, of concepts such as justice, courage, virtue, truth, reality, etc., is, according to Socrates, something firm and unchangeable. With the help of such conceptual analyses, we can arrive at the truth about what the situation is and what we are to do. This applies both to knowledge of actual states of affairs and insight into goals and values, insight into what the good and right are and into what *should* be done.

Now it is unclear whether Socrates believed that we, by the aid of reason alone, by clarifying concepts, can gain full insight into what the good (virtue) is. He sometimes referred to an inner voice that spoke to him. He called this inner voice his *daimon*. This is the Greek name for an impersonal divine power that intervenes in nature and human life. Here it seems that Socrates ultimately tried to ground ethics not only in reason, but also in a divine vision of which man can partake by intuitive insight. Socrates probably never went further than to say that he followed his conscience. Why the voice of his conscience gave him access to a universal morality remains an intriguing question.

But if Socrates perhaps did not reach a conclusive philosophical answer, he still contributed to the search for this answer insofar as he gave morality a certain epistemological foundation: in order to do good, we must know what the good is. According to Socrates, the good is a universal concept. Doing good requires that we know what these ethical universal concepts represent. Conceptual analysis of universal concepts, such as the good, happiness, virtue, etc., is therefore important for ethical behaviour. A particular action is then evaluated by comparing it with these universal ethical concepts. The universal aspect of these concepts is meant to secure both a true knowledge, that is, knowledge of something *universal* and not only of something special and contingent, and an objective morality valid for all people.

Socrates questioned people and tried to get them to think about their own situations and to reflect on the fundamental viewpoints that guided their actions and words. We can say that Socrates tried to 'awaken' them. This is connected with point 3: like a psychiatrist, Socrates did not want people merely to repeat what they heard without having digested it. The purpose of the colloquies, directed by Socrates' provocative 'midwifery', was to bring out what we could call personal knowledge from those he questioned. We will see that the existentialists of later times (such as Kierkegaard) were trying to do something similar.[8]

It is decisive for Socrates that the individual, by means of conversation, will personally realize the nature of the subject. By personally recognizing the truth of a viewpoint, the person acquires that viewpoint as his or her own. Here we encounter a main point in Socrates' criticism of the Sophists. We should not enter into a discussion with our minds made up and use the debate to try to win over the other persons. In a discussion, everyone should try to learn more about the subject itself. Each person's viewpoint should conform to what that person at any time recognizes to be true. Hence, Socrates distinguishes between bad and good convictions, between being persuaded to believe something without understanding the reasons, and becoming convinced that something is true and right since one has understood the reasons that support this conclusion. We could say this is a distinction between *persuading by rhetoric* and *convincing by reason*.

On the one side we have belief without insight, or poorly established opinions (Greek: *doxa*) that a person tries to persuade others to accept. The means here are the art of persuasion: rhetoric in a negative sense. We try to find the best technique to persuade the opponent. The truth of the matter is not really under discussion. Propaganda is a clear example: we gain power by persuading others to acquire certain opinions. On the other side we have an open debate in which increased insight (Greek: *episteme*) is the goal. Here the relationship is built in a dialogue where all participants mutually cooperate to make the subject as clear as possible. The intent is to have the best possible presentation and elucidation of the subject. We thus have communication between persons who recognize each other as equals in the common search for truer insight. Here we do not have a situation in which the strong or deceitful try to persuade the weak or simple-minded; rather, there is a mutual attempt to convince one another on the premise that the goal is to attain better insight for both sides. Such a dialogue promotes mutual growth.[9]

Was Socrates himself never anything more than a man of dialogue, a *convincer*? Some would answer that Socrates also used rhetoric – he, too, tried to 'persuade' by skill with words and argument.

But if the situation is not one in which the participants are reasonable and equal – in which the debaters are intellectually limited by their education – or if prestige and material profit are at stake, a free discussion can be very difficult. And without a doubt, argument is often like this. In such cases, the problem is how to *establish* the conditions for a free and reasonable discussion. Provocation, inappropriate shock, and rhetorical persuasion can play a part. Just as psychotherapists may use psychoactive drugs or other external means when communication has broken down or is not fully established in order to induce voluntary communication, we can here, in the dialogue, imagine that 'persuasion' is being used to bring about a situation characterized by rational 'conviction'. We must therefore distinguish between using persuasion and other manipulative means to achieve a free and rational situation and using these techniques to oppress and control others. If communication also failed in ancient Athens, and if Socrates used persuasion to establish the conditions for proper communication, then it is understandable that he met powerful opposition.[10] Those who interpret Socrates' discourse as inappropriate verbiage or unnecessary rhetoric, may therefore realize that he often found a situation to be too vague for free and reasonable debate. As a result, by using a conversational form and rhetorical means, he tried to lay the groundwork for a common frame of reference, in which the free, dialectical thought process could eventually be developed between the participants. The fact that Plato wrote dialogues with descriptions of scenes and did not go straight to the point, as in a dissertation, points in this direction. In order for two or more people to communicate properly about a subject they must establish a common frame of reference that allows them to grasp the details as clearly as possible. In an ordinary prose text it may not be certain that the reader grasps the author's frame of reference. The dialogue form can perhaps more easily create common ground for the reader and the author. This means that dialogue is preferable to exposition and monologue. As we know, Socrates did not write anything himself, but often engaged in colloquy. Plato is said to have believed that writing expository prose is a dubious undertaking.

We have now come full circle back to the first thesis of our scheme; that is, that virtue is in a way knowledge and can in a certain sense be learned. This also explains the second thesis: knowledge of the right leads necessarily to right actions.[11] This thesis becomes understandable when we are talking about knowledge that we 'vouch for'. If you have insight into the right, you will also be just. It is then unthinkable, by definition, that an individual can apprehend the good without at the same time acting on it. If you first have personally acquired insight into the good, along with correct knowledge of the situation and correct insight into the good, then it is logical that you will do right. Or better: that you do right is the proof that the knowledge truly is personally acquired. The third thesis can, however, still be a source of amazement: right action leads necessarily to happiness. Socrates, a just man who performed right actions, was sentenced to death. Can that be happiness? It is therefore clear that Socrates' use of the word *happiness* (Greek: *eudaimonia*) means something besides desire. Physical suffering and death cannot prevent happiness for Socrates. To be happy seems, for Socrates, to be closely related to being at peace with oneself, and having a good conscience and self-respect. Happiness is thus related to human integrity and identity. The person that excels as a human being, and is as such a *whole* human being, is happy. Happiness, integrity, and virtue are therefore related, just as happiness and virtue are connected with insight into the right and right actions. Whatever else may happen to us is irrelevant to the question of to what extent we are happy. Here we meet features of Socrates' ethics that remind us of Stoicism.

Plato's dialogues present Socrates as a wondering philosopher: in his colloquies he attempts to develop our ability to ask questions. We should realize that we are fallible and that there are many things that we do not understand. In this sense we should recognize that we are ignorant. In a later system such an insight is called *docta ignorantia*, the learned ignorance (cf. Augustine and Nicolas Cusanus). In this sense, when we 'know that we know nothing', we may become receptive to propositions from others possibly concerning new and better answers. Thus, through his philosophical dialogues, Socrates is not only a pioneer in the search for universally valid answers, but also a pioneer in the conception of philosophy as an open and self-critical dialogue that acknowledges our fallible nature.

QUESTIONS

The Sophists introduced a new epoch in Greek philosophy. Describe the philosophical problems that arose during this epoch and how these problems were dealt with by one or more of the Sophists.

It is often claimed that the Sophists were relativists in both epistemological and ethical-political questions. What do we mean by this?

Protagoras said: 'Man is the measure of all things.' Give some interpretations of this statement.

By what method did Socrates seek to arrive at the right insight? How did he view the relationship between right insight, right action, and happiness? In what ways can one criticize this point of view, and how can Plato's theory of ideas be seen as a follow-up of the fundamental Socratic tenet that there is a universal and binding morality?

SUGGESTIONS FOR FURTHER READING

PRIMARY LITERATURE

Gorgias, translated by B. Jowett, Oxford, 1892.
The Symposium, translated by B. Jowett, Oxford, 1892.

SECONDARY LITERATURE

Jaeger, W., *Paideia. The Ideals of Greek Culture*, New York, 1965.
Kerferd, G. B., *The Sophistic Movement*, London, 1981.
Zauker, Paul, *The Mask of Socrates: The Image of the Intellectual in Antiquity*, translated by Alan Shapiro, Berkeley, 1995.

NOTES

1 Later, there was a similar shift among the British empiricists in the 1600s and beyond; from a stubborn systematization (Descartes, Spinoza) to a sceptical critique of knowledge (Locke, Hume).
2 We write 'ethical-political' as a compound word in order to emphasize that the ethical and the political as a rule are connected in the city-state. Cf. the opposition between Aristotle and Machiavelli (Ch. 8).
3 Explorers and adventurers from around the world have encountered new and remarkable cultures, apparently without their confidence in their own customs and conventions being shaken, thus causing them to start asking basic ethical-political questions.
4 The Sophists took fees for teaching; it was therefore the wealthy who initially benefited from their training.
5 The debate about morality that was started by the Sophists pointed towards many of the problems that we have later struggled with. For example, the problem of *proving* morality and legal principles: if we want to prove a moral norm *deductively*, we must have an even higher moral norm to start the proof with. Then we can prove the norm, but only by using a higher norm that is itself unproved. And if we want to prove *this* higher norm, then we end up with the same problem again, and so on. It is like trying to jump on one's own shadow.

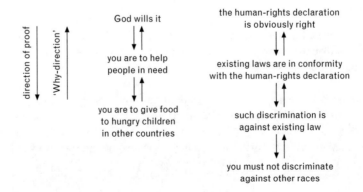

In other words, it is always possible to ask *why?* This logical point applies to *all* deductive lines of argument, not just for deductive lines of argument that apply to norms. Morality and legal principles, moreover, cannot be confirmed by *sensation* or *observation* in the way that descriptive and explanatory statements can: the statement 'John has red hair' can be confirmed or refuted by looking at John. But the statement 'John should go on an errand' cannot be confirmed or refuted by *looking* at something. In other words, the approach used by both the formal sciences (deduction) and the experimental sciences (sensation/observation) is insufficient. There are other ways of arguing ethical-political matters. But the negative result so far makes it understandable that many of the Sophists gradually began to claim that morality and legal principles are valid only relative to various personal or social factors.

6 But, we have to ask, is a theory about every group and every race understanding the world from their own particular perspectives, itself determined by the perspective of one particular nation or one particular race? How can we test the validity of such a theory about nations and races having their own particular ways of perceiving the world? How do we know? Which arguments are we building our case on? And, to begin with, what do we mean by concepts such as nation or race in this connection?

7 We find a similar distinction in psychoanalysis. As a rule, patients are helped very little by repeating what the psychiatrist says about them if it is something that they have not really experienced.

8 Cf. Ch. 19. This point about the 'personal knowledge that a person stands for', is important for pedagogics. Teachers have to take into account *what* is to be learned. And when it comes to literature or philosophy, the purpose of these disciplines is not merely to learn something *about* them, but, among other things, to penetrate into the life and world-views that the various works represent. Two extreme views of pedagogics are therefore unfortunate when it comes to such disciplines:

  1   The authoritarian method, where the student is like a lump of clay which the teacher moulds. The more the teacher presses, the better the moulding! This hardly gives knowledge that the student can embody, nor does it provide a reflective focus.

  2   The liberal method, where the student is like a plant – let us water and nourish it but not interfere with its growth. But people, on their own, are not capable of getting a 2,000-year-old cultural tradition to 'grow' within themselves.

  3   We are left with the Socratic pedagogics; that is, dialogue and co-philosophizing in which the student and teacher are both learning, by 'discussing their way' into a deeper insight into a subject. By allowing the discussion to start from the student's vantage point, one may at best attain a reflective insight which the student can embody. This insight is not 'beaten in' or programmed. Nor will the insight emerge by itself in isolation. Insight is gained through a dialogue about the matter.

9 The distinction between persuading and convincing provides us with a meaningful distinction between genuine and counterfeit authority. A person having genuine authority has the best insight and is able to convince in a free, mutual process of reflection. We are presupposing that all of the participants are, among other things, equally capable of expressing themselves and of participating in the dialogue. On the other hand, the person who can persuade others only by rhetoric or other external means has counterfeit authority.

10 Through discussion, Socrates 'deconstructs' the view of reality held by his respondents, by pointing out contradictions and vague ideas. He shows that the social and moral concepts of his respondents are untenable or insufficient. This is how he is able to create a need for theoretical investigation. But some reacted with disdain for the entire enterprise: not only were the revelations painful for some, but the rulers thought that the disintegration of prevailing opinions was dangerous to the state: even if people's opinions may have lacked any kind of foundation in reality, they were still appropriate for society, functionally speaking – in modern terms, we might say that a half-truth, a slogan, may serve society.

11 Socrates is a psychological *rationalist*; that is, he believes that reason has precedence over the will/feelings insofar as it is reason that first recognizes the good, and it is the will/feelings that are used to reach what reason is pointing to. In opposition we have *voluntarism* which gives the will/feelings precedence over reason – we first *will* something (what we call the good), and then reason finds the *means* for reaching this (and a justification, or rationalization, for willing it).

3 Plato – the theory of ideas and the ideal state

Life. *Plato was born in Athens around 427 BC and died there in 347 BC. An aristocrat by birth, he was related, on his mother's side, to Solon, the lawmaker. Following family tradition, Plato originally planned to enter politics. But things turned out differently. The Athenian democracy had lost the war against Sparta and 'the Thirty Tyrants' had taken over. They were in turn replaced by a new representative government – the same government that sentenced Socrates to death in 399 BC. This presumably sickened Plato of Athenian politics and its abuses. Instead he became interested in the reconstruction of politics. Plato carried on Socrates' attempt to refute theoretically the Sophists' relativism, which Plato viewed as part of the political decline. Setting out to establish the principles on which a healthy political system could be built, he expounded the ideal state. Plato thus turned from the politics of the day to a reflection on what politics is and should be.*

Plato tried three times to turn his political ideas into reality. These attempts were made after he met the tyrant Dionysius I of Syracuse in Sicily, and later under his son, Dionysius II. Each of these attempts was a fiasco; once it was only by the skin of his teeth that Plato made it home to Athens in one piece. Later, he travelled to southern Italy where he encountered the Pythagoreans, who seem to have made an impact on him. Some of the major points shared by Plato and the Pythagoreans are as follows:

1. *a view of mathematics as the essence of all things*
2. *a dualistic view of the universe – that which truly is (the ideas) and the visible world of shadows*
3. *the transmigration and immortality of the soul*
4. *an interest in theoretical science*
5. *religious mysticism and ascetic morality.*

Around 388 BC Plato founded a school in Athens, the Academy. The school was given this name because it was situated in a grove that was named after the demigod Academus. The Academy in Athens offered not only philosophy, but also geometry, astronomy, geography, zoology, and botany. In addition, political education was central. There were also daily gymnastic exercises. The teaching was based on lectures and discussions. The Academy existed for more than 900 years, until AD 529, when it was closed by Justinian. Although only fragments are extant from the pre-Socratic philosophers, we have approximately 30 shorter or longer dialogues by Plato, along with some letters. There are, in addition, secondary sources about Plato, especially Aristotle's commentary. The difficulty in finding out what Plato thought is not due to a lack of extant works, but rather to the way the dialogues are written. Plato himself hardly ever appears in the dialogues, and they do not posit conclusive theses and viewpoints. There is, in addition, the possibility that Plato's views changed during the course of his authorship. We divide Plato's works into three periods:

1 *the early, 'Socratic' dialogues*
2 *the dialogues from his maturity, including* The Republic
3 *the later dialogues, including* The Laws.

Plato comments on the difficulties of communicating what he has to say as follows: 'for it [philosophy] does not admit of exposition like other branches of knowledge; but after much converse about the matter itself and a life lived together, suddenly a light, as it were, is kindled in one soul by a flame'.[1] He does not believe that ordinary readers can easily grasp what he has in his heart. The road to philosophical insight is long and painstaking. It takes time and requires work. It requires fellowship and discussion with others who are seeking the truth. But not even then will we automatically arrive at the truth, as we acquire knowledge in an educational course. Truth comes, when it comes, like a sudden gleam of light in the soul. If we take Plato's words seriously, it will affect the way we approach the problems, and for the expectations that we have for progress in insight and wisdom. The pedagogical simplifications that will be presented in the following pages are therefore extremely un-Platonic! But such simplifications should provide a certain amount of help, enough to allow one to start on the path to wisdom. According to Plato, this road requires patience and hard work, and it never ends; it is our own life. The truth that we find cannot be shared with those who do not walk with us. Truth is not accessible unless one walks the road.

KNOWLEDGE AND BEING

IDEAS AND KNOWLEDGE

Socrates believed that we could achieve objective knowledge by scrutinizing and clarifying the concepts that we have of humanity and society, concepts such as virtue, justice, knowledge, and the good. For example, by conceptual analysis we can find out what justice and the good really *are*. If we are to be able to determine whether an action is good or not, we have to compare it with a pattern or a norm; that is, the good. Insofar as the action resembles this pattern, it is good. By defining universal concepts such as the good and justice, we grasp something that is universal and unchangeable. But what is this *something* that we are grasping? Does it have an objective existence? Can we refer to it as an independent object in our surroundings? Or is it an object of thought that does not exist outside us? These are the kinds of questions that arise about the Socratic conceptual analysis and the claim that universal ethical norms do exist.

Perhaps Socrates was somewhat uncertain how to explain, philosophically, that universal ethical-political norms exist; but with his theory of *the good* as an *idea* (Greek: *eidos*, 'idea'), Plato meant to resolve this issue: the theory of ideas can be seen as a fundamental defence of an objective ethics. Plato supplements Socrates' criticism of the Sophists' relativism.

There is, however, some doubt whether Plato himself really subscribed to 'Plato's theory of ideas'. He actually presents some powerful arguments *against* this theory. Perhaps he was more of a Neoplatonist, like Augustine, than a Platonist. Here it is important to remember that Plato's authorship went through a development which has been interpreted as follows: in his first phase, Plato stands close to Socrates (the Socratic dialogues) – he works with conceptual analysis and conceptual insight; in his middle phase, Plato tries to show that ideas have an independent existence – the theory of ideas (as in the dialogue *The Republic*); and, finally, driven by an internal dynamic in the resolution of the concepts and the universal, Plato expounds a dialectical epistemology (as in the dialogue *Parmenides*).

In *Parmenides*, Plato discusses the criticism of the prevailing version of the theory of ideas, which was based on the question of the definition of the ideas and on the question of how things participate in the ideas. Concerning the former question, the young (!) Socrates is asked whether there are ideas for the One and for the many (and for other mathematical concepts). His answer to this is an unqualified yes. And for the beautiful, the good, and corresponding concepts? Here, too, the answer is an unqualified yes. But for human beings, for fire and water? Yes; but here Socrates is more uncertain. What, then, of hair and mud; do they also have their own ideas? There cannot be ideas for these, according to Socrates. In other words, there is some uncertainty as to what does and what does not have ideas – the criteria seem to be lacking – while at the same time, it seems that valuable phenomena have ideas, not unworthy things. This viewpoint is seen by Parmenides as evidence that the young Socrates is being influenced by public opinion, and is still not capable of independent thought.[2]

In *Parmenides*, Plato continues the dialogue in a dialectical testing of the concept of the one, in relation to the other, in relation to itself, and in relation to the many, based on alternative hypotheses (that the One is, or that the One is not). How to interpret this part of the dialogue is one of the basic questions in Platonic research. It has been argued[3] that Plato, in this portion of the dialogue, is revealing the most important part of his philosophy: a dialectical process of thinking that leads to the boundaries of thought, where the primordial origin of all things tacitly appears, beyond what we can discuss and express; then it turns, and like the light from the primordial origin, wanders 'down', down through the theory of principles and the theory of science, where the ideas appear in their interconnections on different levels, until the light is lost in diversity and sensory chaos. This means that Plato is a Neoplatonist mystic, working with dialectical reason in accordance with the Neoplatonist interpretation (see Plotinus). According to this view, the traditional interpretation of the theory of ideas appears like a tortoise's perspective on truth: the light and primordial origin are seen 'from below', from things and from the sensory world, by abstraction 'upward'. The light from above, which could reconcile the counter-arguments already mentioned, is then not acknowledged. First by breaking away from analytic reason, we can acquire the eagle's perspective, where we, *from* the primordial origin, see 'down', through the world of ideas towards the sensory world – where the world of ideas is seen not as a set of induced, hypostasized universal concepts, but as the light from above that passes from the primordial origin to the sensory world. The idealistic two-part division found in the prevailing interpretation of the theory of ideas is here transcended in favour of a dynamic theory of emanation, of the sort that we find in Neoplatonic philosophy and theology.

However, the theory of ideas can be interpreted in line with the ontological doctrines of the cosmological period, leading to the question, 'What exists?' Some answer that certain substances exist. Others, like Pythagoras, say that structure or form exists. Plato says in this interpretation that the ideas are the primary reality (substance). In order to make the first steps into the theory of ideas plausible, we can take our own everyday reality as our starting point. If we are digging a ditch with a shovel and someone asks us *what* we are working with, we can answer, for instance: 'a ditch', or 'with a shovel and dirt'. But if someone in a mathematics class asks what we are working with, it immediately becomes more difficult to answer. We could answer 'with pen and paper', or 'with chalk and a blackboard'. But these are not good answers, since we could give the same answers to the question about what we are working with in an English or art class. And we are not working with 'the same thing' when we are working with mathematics and when we are working with grammar. They are not the same subjects. But what is the subject of mathematics? We could answer: it is a system of concepts. This puts us on the road to the theory of ideas: a theory that says that besides the things we can perceive with our senses (chalk, ink, paper, blackboard, etc.) there are things that we understand but cannot perceive with our senses; that is, concepts, such as the circle, the triangle, etc.

But is it so certain that these mathematical ideas exist? Isn't it only the chalk on the blackboard that exists, and not these ideas? Then do mathematical ideas disappear when we wipe the blackboard during our break? That seems unreasonable. Or does mathematics only exist 'inside' us? But then how can 30 students in a mathematics class all learn the same thing, for example, the Pythagorean theorem, while some students think slowly and others quickly? Mathematics cannot simply be within us. Mathematics must be something that we can all direct our attention towards, that we can think *about*. The truths of mathematics are universally valid; that is, they are valid for everyone. They are therefore not connected to the subject.

Such simple questions and arguments leave us with something that corresponds largely with Plato's theory of ideas: the ideas, such as the circle and the triangle, are not grasped with our senses; they are intelligible through our reason. The particular circles and triangles that we perceive with our senses are like perishable representations of the corresponding ideas. The ideas are universal and unchangeable, in contrast to the changeable representations. And the ideas are not something within our thoughts. They exist objectively; they are universally valid. We have again used the scheme with questioning and argument in order to understand the answer. And one of the implications is this: if the universe is 'divided into two', that is, if there are two forms of existence – the things that we perceive with our senses and the ideas – then we have already prepared the ground for a universally valid ethics. We have then, in a way, explained how it is possible to say that the good exists as something objective – that is, in the form of an idea.

IDEAS AND THE GOOD

In the previous passage we have asked an ontological question – what exists? – by looking especially at mathematics. But we can also make Plato's theory of ideas understandable with the help of other starting points. If we ask 'what is a good action?', it is not difficult to give an example; say, saving a person who is about to drown in an icy lake. What is good about the action? That you run out on to the ice? That you put a ladder down on the ice? That you draw in the ladder? We cannot *point at* or see the good. It is not anything we can perceive with our senses. Yet we are still certain that the action is good. Why? Because, according to Plato, we already have an idea about good actions that enables us to understand this action as good.

We may ask: what is a concept? This is, as we will see, a controversial philosophical question (cf. Ch. 6, the dispute about 'Universals' in the Middle Ages). We can simplify it in this way: when we talk about John's horse, we are talking about a particular horse that we can point to, a perceptible phenomenon in space and time. If, on the other hand, we are talking about the horse generically, then we can say that we are talking about the concept of horse. Different languages have different words for this concept: *Pferd*, *hest*, *cheval*, *hestur*, etc. Plato maintains that concepts – e.g., the concept of horse, or what we mean or are referring to when we use the words *Pferd*, *hest*, etc. – have an independent existence in relation to the particular objects that are subsumed under them. The particular objects here are specimens of the species, horse. Concepts that are understood in this way Plato calls ideas. If we are talking about horses named Black Beauty and Secretariat, then it is clear what we are talking about. It is Black Beauty and Secretariat. It is something that we can point to and touch. But the concept of horse is not anything that we can find in a stable or pasture; we cannot point to, look at, or touch it. If we are operating with a theory of meaning that says that linguistic expressions have meaning only when they refer to something that exists,[4] then it follows that the word *horse* must refer to something. Since we cannot perceive this 'something' with our senses, it must be an imperceptible something; that is, the idea of horse. Then the idea of horse must be something that exists, even if we cannot perceive it in space and time.

Arguments like these serve to make the theory of ideas plausible. Such arguments suggest the construction of a world divided into two parts; that which *is*, is in two fundamentally different ways, either as ideas or as things we can perceive with our senses:

$$\frac{\text{ideas}}{\text{perceptible things}}$$

This dualism largely corresponds to the division found in Parmenides and the Pythagoreans. For us, it is an important point that this ontological division helps explain how universal ethical-political norms are possible: the good – the ethical-political norms – exists in the form of ideas. If we maintain the usual interpretation of the ideas, we can say that the ideas do not exist in time and space, that they do not come into being, and that they do not perish. They are unchangeable. Black

Beauty is born, grows up, and dies. But the idea of horse remains the same. This means also that the good, as an idea, remains unchangeably the same, whether people follow it or not; whether people know about it or not. In other words, Plato believes that he hereby has shown that morality and politics have a firm foundation that is totally independent of the diversity of human opinions and customs. The theory of ideas can thus be said to secure an absolute and universally valid foundation for ethical-political norms and values. We will see later that there have been other theoretical attempts, such as that by Kant, to explain how absolute and universally valid norms can be possible. This question generally is one of the perennial problems of philosophy.[5]

From the perspective of the theory of ideas we get the following two-part division:

$$\frac{\text{idea}}{\text{perceptible things}} = \frac{\text{unchangeable (the ethical-political Good)}}{\text{changeable (the diversity of customs and opinions)}}$$

EROS AND EDUCATION

Plato does not mean that the world of ideas and the world of perception are *equal*. He believes that the ideas are more *valuable*: the ideas are *ideal*. This viewpoint has been important for the spiritual inspiration that Plato's philosophy has given; for example, for the poets in the Romantic period.[6] Since the ideas are ideal, we should strive for them. Plato believes that a longing for these ideals is implanted in us. This is the Platonic *Eros*: the longing for an ever-increasing vision of the beautiful, the good, and the true.

Hence there is not, for human beings, an immovable, insurmountable barrier between the world of perception and the world of ideas. People live in a dynamic tension between these two worlds: in the world of sense perception, they recognize that certain actions are better than others. This glimmer of the idea of the good in the world of perception enables us to attain a temporary and imperfect insight into the idea of the good. When we seek a clearer vision of the idea of the good, we also become more able to distinguish between good and evil in the world of perception. And when we try to better understand what we encounter of good and evil in the world of perception, we are better able to envision the idea of the good. In this way we have a *process of cognition* with an ongoing interchange (dialectic) between envisioning the ideas (theory) and experiencing the sensory world (practice). This is how we improve our insight, both into the idea of the good and into what is good in this life.

Philosophy becomes in this way both universal — as it relates to the eternal ideas — and concrete — as it relates to our life situation. Philosophy is at the same time knowledge and education. This educational process is an unceasing journey, up towards the ideas (the light) and down towards the perceptible things (world of shadows). Hence, we cannot unreservedly claim that Plato is searching for truth for truth's sake, as is often claimed. Truth is partially attained by moving between insight into the ideas and insight into the life situation here and now; one who has achieved sufficient insight into the ideas will turn back in order to enlighten the world with this insight. Philosophers are not supposed to contemplate passively the ideas, like hermits in a cell; they are also to guide society by virtue of this insight.

SOME OBJECTIONS TO THE THEORY OF IDEAS

The ideas exist independently of time and space. They cannot be described with space-time predicates, just as the concept of *seven* cannot be described with colour predicates. On the other hand, the perceptible things in space and time participate in one way or another in the ideas. It is through perceptible circles, in space, that we are reminded of the idea of circle. But if we understand the ideas as something radically different from the things that we perceive with our senses, so that the ideas cannot at all be described with predicates that apply to space, time, and change, then it becomes difficult to explain how the changeable objects of perception, in space and time, can participate in the ideas. This leads us to a basic problem with the theory of ideas. Here we are not going to pursue the criticism of the theory of ideas. As we have already mentioned, Plato was himself the first critic. We will only point out two objections:

1   Terms such as 'justice' and 'evil' refer to ideas. But the ideas are also ideals. We are then faced with this paradox: 'evil' is an example of such a term; hence, the term 'evil' should refer to an idea of evil. On the other side, evil is not an ideal and therefore an idea of evil cannot exist.
2   The ideas are unchangeable and the sensory things are changeable. The theory of ideas views sensory things as copies of the ideas. But how can the changeable sensory things be copies of the unchangeable ideas? Don't we end up with a logical problem? If these two factors, the ideas and the sensory world, are defined as complete opposites, is it not unthinkable that they can have anything to do with each other?

IDEAS AND TOTALITY

What we have mentioned about the dynamic educational interaction between insight into the ideas and insight into the life situation here and now shows that it is doubtful to claim that Plato is making an absolute logical distinction between the world of ideas and the world of sensation. Furthermore, he does not claim that the various ideas are isolated from one another, like the stars in the sky. The ideas are connected to form a *whole*. For instance, in *The Republic* Plato discussed the question of what is a just action. The dialogue brings out different opinions and different actions that are all called just. When all of these different phenomena and images can be called just, then, according to Plato, it must be because they all participate in an idea that is the idea of justice. It is this idea that makes it possible to discuss these different examples as just. But this also means, according to Plato, that we cannot understand the idea of justice in isolation. The idea of justice points beyond itself; on the one hand, to the virtues of wisdom, courage, and moderation, since justice is the right harmony among these; and, on the other hand, to the idea of the good.

This is how the ideas are woven together. We can therefore not have true knowledge about one idea. Insight into the ideas is insight into connections, into totalities. If we take this to an extreme, we can say that true knowledge is knowledge about 'everything'. But such an insight into the whole, into the ideas in all of their inner relationships, can hardly ever be achieved by man. We can only reach incomplete totalities or, more correctly, incomplete and provisional totalities, since insight into the ideas is achieved by a continual oscillation, partly up and down between phenomena and ideas, and partly in continual transcendence of certain ideas towards others – so that the totality is never reached. On the basis of this interpretation, we can say that the idea of the good (the idea of the One) does not stand for one idea among others, but that the idea of the good represents the very interrelationship between the ideas. This relationship among the ideas is the very foundation of reality, the basic pattern that supports the particular phenomena that our senses reveal to us. This continually transcending holism, or dialectic, can be said to be the core of Plato's philosophy.[7]

THE ANALOGIES

In *The Republic*, Plato presents three analogies to clarify the theory of ideas: the 'analogy of the sun', the 'analogy of the divided line', and the 'analogy of the prisoners in the cave'. In brief, the analogy of the sun indicates that the sun can be compared with the idea of the good: the sun is to the sensory world what the idea of the good is to the world that is accessible only to thought. The sun, like the idea of the good, is sovereign in its world. Just as the sun gives light, so the idea of the good gives truth. And just as the eye sees in the daylight, reason understands in the light of the truth. Reason is the ability that connects us with the idea of the good, just as the eye is the sensory organ that connects us with the sun. But the eye, or the ability to see, is not identical with the sun, just as reason is not identical with the idea of the good. The sun is what makes all things, itself included, visible to us. In the same way, the idea of the good makes all the other ideas, including itself, comprehensible to our reason. Moreover, the idea of the good is the condition not only for the comprehensibility but also for the existence of the other ideas, – just as the sun is not only the condition for our ability to see things, but is also the condition for their existence.

The analogy of the divided line (see diagram) indicates that our ability to know is realized on different levels. First we have the division between knowledge of sensory things (BC) and knowledge of that which only thought can acknowledge (AC). But within knowledge of the sensory, we have a distinction between conjecture (BD – knowledge of the shadows, of the images or copies) and conviction (DC – knowledge of the things that generate these images or copies). Correspondingly, we have, within the knowledge that does not apply to the sensory, a distinction between careful reasoning (CE – knowledge of given presuppositions) and insight (EA – knowledge of prototypes, when the mind, unsupported by images, thinks purely by ideas). In short, we have a distinction, in the spheres of knowledge of the perceptible, between conjecture (BD) and conviction (DC), corresponding to a distinction, in the spheres of knowledge of the world of ideas, between careful reasoning (CE) and insight (EA).

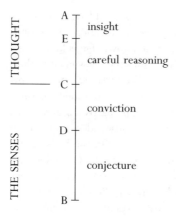

The analogy of the prisoners in the cave also serves to illustrate the relationship between the knowledge we have of the perceptible world and the insight we obtain of the ideas. Inside a cave prisoners have been bound in such a way that they can look only toward the wall at the rear of the cave; behind them is a fire, and between the fire and the prisoners various objects are carried from one side to the other so as to throw moving shadows on the cave wall in front of the prisoners. These moving shadows are conceived as reality by the prisoners. If one of the prisoners got free and was able to see the objects that threw these shadows, he would realize that what he had taken to be reality were merely images of the real objects. Furthermore, if this prisoner emerged into the daylight and glimpsed the sun, he would be overwhelmed, and if he returned to the cave and told what he had seen he would hardly be taken seriously by the other prisoners looking at the moving shadows on the wall. This analogy illustrates the main points of the theory of ideas.

Seen in conjunction with the analogy of the divided line, the analogy of the prisoners in the cave can be said to illustrate how we can ascend in the hierarchy of knowledge, from conjecture to insight – from the world of shadows to the light of day – and finally view the sun itself. Plato's theory of ideas is thus not only ontology, a theory of being, but also epistemology, a theory of knowledge: the perceptible things and most of the opinions we have are changeable and imperfect. This knowledge is not perfect knowledge. We can only have objective knowledge, *episteme*, of the ideas, which are themselves unchangeable and perfect. But by reflecting on our sense experiences and our linguistically formulated representations, we can reach down towards this objective knowledge, since the ideas are in some way what lies 'under' our representations and the perceptible things. For instance, the idea of just actions 'lies under' the various good actions and the various conceptions we have of just actions. This is how we can recognize the idea of the circle behind the various imperfect circles that we perceive in nature; and we can recognize the idea of a just action behind our various linguistically formulated conceptions of just actions. Conceptual analysis of our daily language is therefore more than merely linguistic analysis: conceptual analysis of our common daily language leads us towards insight into the ideas. Furthermore, correlation between the conceptions and the sensory things, which is a condition for knowledge of the perceptible world, is possible because the conceptions and the perceptible things have a common origin in the ideas. Hence, the ideas make even our imperfect knowledge of the perceptible phenomena possible.

THE THEORY OF IDEAS AND THE ROLE OF MAN

We can also illustrate Plato's theory of knowledge by looking at the position that human beings have in relation to the world of ideas and the world of sensation. We can put it this way. Plato introduces the philosophical question of how the individual soul can come into contact with the ideas. This question is raised when Plato (metaphorically?) speaks of human beings having both a pre-existence and a post-existence. The soul, the real person, existed before birth and will live on after death, when the physical body dies. A human being is a creature between the world of ideas and the world of sense perception: the soul belongs to the world of ideas and the physical body belongs to the world of sense perception. Human beings, with a soul and physical body, are thus at home in both spheres. But the real part of a person is, according to Plato, the soul. What we call life is the period of the soul's existence when it is incarnated in the physical body. In a sense, the soul 'dives down' to the world of sense perception, the so-called birth. There it takes on a physical body, but after a while again returns to the world of ideas by liberating itself from the body, the so-called death. The time that the soul is 'under water' is the so-called life. Plato's theory of knowledge can be said to build on this view of human beings: during its pre-existence, when the soul lived in the world of ideas, it was able to view the ideas directly. However, when the soul takes on a physical body (at birth) it forgets everything that it previously knew. But during the course of life the soul is reminded of what it knew before. The sight of imperfect circles in nature can awaken the earlier insight into the idea of the circle. All learning, from birth to death, is therefore a process of recognition. When we *see* the imperfect and perishable circles in the world of perception, we are reminded of the idea of the circle. Learning is rediscovery. We recognize the ideas 'behind' perceptible things.

But this recognition is often difficult. Not all souls are capable of remembering the ideas behind the changeable, perceptible things. Many exist in an epistemological darkness. They live with unsupported opinions and superficial sense experiences (*doxa*) without breaking through to true insight (*episteme*). It is only a minority who in this earthly life manage to envision the ideas behind the perceptible phenomena. Hence, Plato is a pessimist, believing that it requires good abilities and hard training to achieve clear insight into the ideas: the truth is only accessible to a chosen few.

PLATO'S *THE REPUBLIC* AND THE GOOD

EDUCATION AND SOCIAL STRATIFICATION

Socrates said that virtue, in a certain sense, is knowledge, and that virtue can in some way be learned. By talking with people and getting them to think, we can induce them to become virtuous; they will then pursue the right course of action, and it follows from this that they will be happy. Plato supplements this thesis by saying that right knowledge is knowledge of the idea of the good. But Plato has less faith than Socrates that people will be able to achieve the knowledge that is virtue. We can see this as a consequence of the theory of ideas: the ideas are difficult to comprehend. To attain knowledge of the ideas requires good intellectual abilities along with discipline and training. Most people will therefore not be able to achieve adequate insight into the ideas. As a result, most people will not, by their own accord, be able to be virtuous and live a good and happy life. Consequently, the few who do have insight into the ideas, and thus are virtuous by definition, must lead the others on the right path.

This scepticism about people's ability to recognize what is right can also be seen in Plato's reaction to his experience of the dissolution of Athenian democracy: the crumbling of the feeling of fellowship, the Sophists' critique of the traditions, and the execution of Socrates by the democrats. Plato becomes an anti-democrat: people cannot lead themselves. They are not virtuous and competent enough. The 'experts' must take over and secure unity and loyalty. Hence, Plato places himself in opposition to the belief in the people's competence that was one of the corner-stones of Athenian democracy.

In outline, Plato believed that in a healthy city-state power should be placed in the hands of those who are competent – not in the hands of the people, and not in the hands of an incompetent and iniquitous absolute ruler. This could be accomplished by having a universal educational system in which everyone had the same oppor-tunities and all could take their places in the city-state according to their abilities.

A large portion of *The Republic* is devoted to Plato's explanation of his ideal edu-cational system. The main points are as follows. Education is under the jurisdiction of the state, and all children are treated equally, regardless of descent and gender. All students receive the same education from the ages of ten to twenty, the import-ant subjects being gymnastics,[8] music, and religion. For the youths, the goals are a strong and well-coordinated body, an appreciation of beauty, and cultivation of obedience, self-sacrifice, and loyalty. The best students are selected at the age of twenty. They study other subjects (especially mathematics) until the age of thirty. Another selection then takes place, and the best students study philosophy for five years, until the age of thirty-five. Then they go out into the world to learn to man-age the affairs of practical life for fifteen years. When they reach the age of fifty – after forty years of complete education, training, and experience – this carefully chosen elite become leaders in the state. They now have acquired insight into the idea of the good, factual knowledge, and practical experience. They are therefore, according to Plato, absolutely competent and virtuous. And these, the competent, are now invested with authority to govern the other members of society.

Those who are left after the first selection become artisans, labourers, and merchants. Those who are selected at the next level become administrators and soldiers. The educational system thus produces three social classes. First, there are the rulers who have competence along with authority, then those who are involved with administration and military defence, and finally those who produce the prod-ucts that are needed in society: (1) rulers, (2) administrators/soldiers, (3) pro-ducers. The presupposition here is that people are different. The educational system's function is carefully to separate the different types of people and place them where they belong in society. Plato speaks metaphorically about some people being made of gold, others of silver, and others of iron and copper.

Plato also compares the three classes with three functions in society and with three virtues:

Class/profession	Function	Virtue
the rulers (philosophers)	to govern	wisdom
the administrators (the guards)	to administer	courage
the producers (the labourers)	to produce	temperance

Plato does not believe that all people are equally good. Not everyone is meant for political leadership. He believes that state education and rearing will ensure that each man and woman will end up in the right place in society, and thus perform the function in society that they are best equipped for. Those who have a gift for wisdom will govern. Those who are courageous will defend the state. And those who are temperate will produce food and other objects that are needed in society. When each person is doing what he or she is best equipped to do, and when all social functions are thereby performed in the best way (according to Plato), society will be just: the virtue justice is found when there is harmony among the three virtues that have been mentioned. Justice is a virtue that is connected with the community; it is the harmony among the three other virtues:

1 wisdom
2 courage ⎫ justice
3 temperance⎭

It is worth noting that this ideal society is not only thought of from the perspective of theoretical and moral demands. A just society is also a society with reciprocal satisfaction of needs: the wise think, the courageous defend, and the temperate produce. Since different persons have different abilities (virtues) and therefore have different functions in society, they complement one another so that everyone participates in supplying the natural needs, i.e., needs that Plato believed to be natural in the city-state. Here we can see the seeds of a theory of the division of labour and of class division. Plato not only includes the division of labour and trade into his theory as something given to society by nature or by a higher power, but also attempts to justify the division of labour and the division into classes on the basis of effectivity and on the basis of ability. We can put it this way: Plato grounds the division of labour in effectivity: it would be inefficient if each person were personally to obtain everything that he or she needed, like food, shoes, clothes, housing, etc. Specialization allows for better results for all parties. By sticking to one occupation – as a shoemaker, mason, sculptor, administrator, etc. – a person can go further and achieve a higher standard than he or she would be able to do if attempting to work in many different occupations. Specialization allows perfection. In principle, it would have been like this also if all people had had the same abilities. But given that people have different abilities and talents, it becomes even more important for the workforce to be specialized so that each person can do the work for which he or she is best suited. The occupational specialization is connected with trade. Shoes are traded from the shoemaker to the farmer; food from the farmer to the shoemaker. The individual occupational groups are dependent upon one another. As already mentioned, Plato specifies three main occupational groups – producers, administrators, and rulers – each group containing several sub-groups which perform different tasks. This division of labour into different occu-pations, which mutually presuppose one another, produces greater effectivity. On this basis we must say that all the necessary tasks within society are equally import-ant. But Plato also believed that some tasks and occupations are qualitatively higher than others. Thinking holds a higher place than administration, which in turn holds a higher place than production. These qualitatively different tasks are grounded in the abilities of each person, which in a corresponding way are qualitatively differ-ent. In the good society, each person does what he or she is most capable of, and that means that there is a concurrence between high-ranking tasks and high-ranking abilities, and between mediocre tasks and mediocre abilities. The differ-ences in one's place in society are then grounded in innate differences. For Plato, social differences are grounded both ethically and according to ability. The har-monious interplay between the classes and their professional functions is what characterizes the just state. The cardinal political virtue, justice, is therefore pre-supposed by the division of labour and the social stratification.

POWER AND COMPETENCE

One would think that Plato had now achieved his model: an ideal society where power and competence coincide. This society is like a pyramid that 'hangs by a thread', the thread being the invisible bond that exists between the rulers and the idea of the good. And this bond is indestructible since insight into the idea of the good is firmly anchored in the rulers.[9] Even if Plato, in this sense, theoretically solved the problem that he introduced about the relationship between power and competence, he still doubted whether this educational system and system for raising children were sufficiently secured against factions and egoistic discord. Alongside incompetence, this was precisely what Plato believed to be the danger in store for the degenerate democracy in Athens in his time. Plato's cure is the abo-lition of private property and family life for the two higher classes; that is, for those who have political power. His way of thinking is as follows: riches and family life are the origin of the self-interest that can clash with the common interest. Family life 'privatizes' its members. Riches are the origin of envy and conflict. Both weaken the sense of community in society.[10]

Plato preferred to view economics as a political problem: an uneven distribu-tion of goods, a great division between those who have much and those who have little, threatens the stability of society. Furthermore, politicians with economic interests may act in a way that is contrary to the common interest. Plato believed that the city-state ought to be supported by various means; for example: com-petent rulers (education), loyalty to the community (no private property or family for the rulers), self-sufficiency (balance between population and territory), and a defence force.[11]

For Plato, as for most Greeks, *polis* and *oikos* are basic concepts: the city-state and the household. The basis for the good life in the community is a lasting and harmonious maintenance of the common household within the cycle of life and its natural limits. Taking care of the household in a sensible way is thus important.[12] Moreover, the city-state is to have a population that neither rises nor falls; in *The Laws* he mentions 5,040 inhabitants (households), and a territory large enough for them to be able to support themselves, neither more nor less. In this respect, Plato is thinking politically and ecologically – if we may use such modern terms. Political direction is to rule production, not vice versa;[13] and changes or growth that may lead the population beyond its sustainable level cannot be tolerated. Now, of course, there is to be biological growth, in the form of an increase in crops, and human growth, in the form of a better realization of the good life. Plato's entire political philosophy, after all, aims to achieve human growth for each person – in the way that he interprets it – that is to say, the good life in stable and harmonious fellowship in a city-state organized in occupational and social classes.[14]

Egoism is therefore more than a *moral* error, according to Plato. It is a fundamental misunderstanding of what it means to be a human being. Egoists have not understood that self-interest and common interest are the same; that society is not something external to a self-sufficient individual, but that a person is always part of the community. An egoist is like a lunatic who believes that he can place his feet in a bucket and grow like a tree (our analogy). He has completely misunderstood the meaning of human existence. Put in another way, the contrast between egoism and altruism presupposes a distinction between the individual and society, and this is the very distinction that Plato denies: to view the individual and society as two self-sufficient elements is an aberration; human beings and society are inextricably interwoven. The supposed distinction between the individual's desires and his duty to society is therefore a misunderstanding, according to Plato. What a person desires is the same as what the good society demands: that is, the realization of the person's best abilities and the satisfaction of the person's real needs, in harmony with the division of labour, according to a just division of occupations. Those who complain that there is too little freedom in the ideal state have misunderstood what is their own good; namely, that freedom is freedom to realize one's own life, and that one can only realize one's life in society. Those who complain that Plato's system infringes basic human rights have not understood that rights are not something that people have, like teeth or hair, independently of society. Rights are something that are connected with the roles and functions that people have in society.

But isn't there still something uncomfortably authoritarian in Plato's thought? Perhaps there is, in a certain sense, if we take Plato literally, and make him into our contemporary. Authoritarianism appears, among other things, in his dictation of the educational system needed to make competent citizens. He makes no allowance for discussion of the presuppositions in his theory of the state. Its principles are presupposed, without giving the inhabitants the opportunity to discuss them rationally. Free and critical reflection is thus prevented. In Plato's defence, we could say that he probably never intended to found such an ideal state, not even in Syracuse – it was only an ideal, a utopia. Moreover, it is doubtful that Plato was as unwilling to discuss his own philosophy as we have suggested here.

On the contrary, the Platonic dialogues bear witness to his ability and willingness to reflect on his own thinking. Hence, Plato is not as much of an authoritarian as we have implied.

It is difficult to place Plato in relation to the political ideologies of our day,[15] or to discuss him in connection with communism or fascism. It should be unnecessary to say that it is far-fetched to say that his ideal state is socialistic, in most reasonable interpretations of the word. It is tempting to call Plato a conservative, in the sense of being a 'supporter of the established order'. But this is merely a formal definition, because what Plato wants to conserve is the Greek city-state, not, for example, the interests of the nobility or of capitalism. But even in relation to the Greek city-state, it is difficult to call Plato a conservative, one who wants to preserve. For he is not an uncritical admirer of tradition. He is critical of it and asks what is worth preserving and what *can* be preserved. In that sense, he is a radical; that is, 'one who wants to change the established order on the basis of rational criticism'. But, again, this is merely a formal definition. What this kind of radicalism means in each case will depend on what the established order is and what the criteria for rationality are.

It would perhaps be correct to call Plato a radical of the Political Right (*rechtsradikal*): one who places reason above tradition (radical), but who believes that most of tradition passes the test, and thus that tradition is reasonable ('right-wing'). But this label can also be confusing. The expression *rechtsradikal* was used for certain tendencies in Germany during the inter-war period; but tradition and reason were not equivalent in Hitler's Berlin and Plato's Athens.

In his works *The Laws* and *The Statesman* Plato makes more allowances for the difficulties of *realizing* the ideals. He advocates the 'next best state'. He allows everyone to have property and the right to a family life. He also allows society to be governed by laws. He says, furthermore, that the best solution, i.e., the best government, is a combination of monarchy (competence) and democracy (public control). These modifications lead toward Aristotle, who emphasized the possible, what could be realized, and not just the ideal, as Plato does in *The Republic*.

MAN AND WOMAN

Plato's view of women's place in the ideal state helps clarify his view of the relationship between the biological and the cultural, and between the private (*oikos*) and the public (*polis*). Plato advocates a far-reaching *equality* between women and men. This is noteworthy when one takes into account the low place that women had in the Greek society of his time. Plato took this view because he saw the biological differences between men and women as *irrelevant* to the question of which tasks in society each person is capable of performing: that women bear children does not justify a gender-based division of labour in which women do housework and men alone perform public duties.[16] It is on this basis that Plato has been viewed as an early defender of women's rights. Going against the customs of his day, he argues for equal educational opportunities for boys and girls, equality in assignment to the occupation one is equipped for, equal opportunities for social intercourse, equal legal and political rights for all. This must not, however, be interpreted to mean that Plato is advocating general, individual rights in the same sense as in the modern age (from Locke to Mill, cf. Chs 11 and 14). For Plato, these rights are connected to the person's place in society.

For Plato, human beings are primarily spiritual beings, but also intellectual and political beings. The biological holds a less central place in his view of humanity. Therefore, he does not support a biologically based division of labour and hierarchy. This explains his radical point of view. Why shouldn't women as well as men be able to perform public duties? However, this picture of Plato as a theoretician of equal rights should be moderated. Elsewhere Plato expresses the disparaging view of women that was typical of his age.[17]

Considering this disparity in Plato's discussion of the two sexes, it has been argued that Plato actually feared women and their sphere; that is, childbirth and the supervision of new generations. Here, in the sphere of reproduction and socialization, nature and the private life reign. This sphere is beyond the reach of rational control. That is why it must be placed under control, public life becoming all-encompassing and private life actually being abolished. There is to be no private property, no monogamous relationships, and no ties between biological parents and their children. Everything is to be public and in common. As for the view that Plato was a kind of feminist, it is true that Plato gives men and women equal status in society, but this is precisely because he is attempting to eradicate women's traditional sphere. In reality, Plato oppresses women because he fears them, as if they were an uncontrollable force, and their power to form children and young people within the private sphere. We are not going to decide which interpretations of Plato's view of the problems of gender are best. It is at least certain that Plato places the public life over the private, just as he places the intellect and education over biological nature.

THE ETHICAL RESPONSIBILITY OF THE ARTS

Plato's dialogues have made him a classic in literature. He is not only a philosopher, but also a poet; he was a writer of genius. Plato has been, ever since, an inspiration to many artists and poets (above all in the Romantic period). He has been considered not only a philosopher of the pure forms, a mathematical philosopher, and a philosopher of the spiritual forces in view of his religious attitude towards life, but also a philosopher of the Muses and the arts.[18] Nonetheless, Plato was very sceptical of art and artists in his political philosophy. He supported a strict censorship of the arts in the ideal state and the expulsion of artists who would not or could not adapt. How does all of this fit together? What is behind this ambiguous role that the arts seem to have for Plato? The reasons are numerous. But with the reservation that there are problems of interpretation here, as elsewhere, we can make the following analysis.

In the first place it is worth noting that Plato did not make a clear distinction between the true, the good, and the beautiful – or between science, morality, and art – as has been common in modern times since the Enlightenment. In modern times we find, for example, the slogan *l'art pour l'art*, art for art's sake, since art is seen as something distinct from and independent of moral and political concerns. From a modern perspective it makes sense to say that art should only be evaluated on artistic criteria, and not on whether it is good or true, useful or destructive. A work of art can be great art even though it promotes neither morality nor truth! But such a strict distinction between the true, the good, and the beautiful was unreasonable for Plato. On the contrary, his point was that the ideas are connected: as ideas, the good and the beautiful are interwoven. The beautiful points to the good, and the good points to the beautiful. Art cannot be divorced from morality. Ethics and aesthetics[19] cannot be separated. On the one hand, this means that artists are seen as being important to society. But, on the other hand, it means that Plato cannot permit himself to remain morally neutral towards (the) art(s).

There is also another point connected with the theory of ideas that affects Plato's view of the arts. According to the theory of ideas, the ideas represent the true reality. Things in the world of sense perception are, in a way, reflections of the ideas. This means that when a painter paints, say, a deer, he or she is in a sense making a copy of a copy. First, we have the idea of deer, then we have the many deer in the world of sense perception, and finally we have the painting of one of these perceptible deer. Art is thus second rate, or even third rate; it copies the copies! In this sense, art cannot be rated very highly, considered from the perspective of truth. The idea of copying, imitation, is fundamental to Plato's view of the arts. Perceptible things are copies of the ideas, and works of art are copies of the perceptible things. But the ideas are also ideals of the perceptible things and subsequently of the works of art that copy perceptible things. Artists *should* therefore attempt to copy the ideas. This demand is unavoidable, given Plato's philosophy. The theory of art as imitation (Greek: *mimesis*) is thus connected with a demand for truth; first that concerning sensible reality and then that concerning ideal reality, which for Plato is the real reality. But human beings are, during their life-long educational process, constantly oscillating between experience in the world of sense perception and insight into the ideas. This also applies to artists. This is why, for Plato, it is possible to imagine that an artist can be inspired more directly by the ideas, and not only by the perceptible things. The artist then becomes a kind of medium for the ideas. But this, too, is ambiguous, according to Plato, since artists do not have the intellectual guidance of philosophers; therefore, inspired artists cannot give an appropriate account of what is happening to them. They may spoil or garble it. This is why philosophers have to supervise, even when artists exhibit an inspiration drawn almost directly from the ideas.

In *The Republic*, Plato gives careful directions on how the different artists are to work. Poets, for example – with all of their charm, but with their distant relationship to the binding truth – must be controlled by those with insight: 'We must remain firm in our conviction that hymns to the gods and praises of famous men are the only poetry which ought to be admitted into our state.'[20] But this 'quality control' does not apply only to the arts that pertain to words. It applies just as much to music and song, the forms of art that (according to Plato) go straight to the soul. Thus, Plato rejects both the kind of music that feeds the fire of uncontrollable passion and the kind that lulls to a sleepy intoxication. Music, like any other art, is to be a part of the cultivation of the soul and the strengthening of the moral character. Like poetry, it is to promote insight into the ideas, including that of justice, and not to vulgarize or confuse our thoughts and emotions.

Plato is a philosopher who especially emphasizes union; dialectical integration rather than division and distinction. Unity and cohesion take precedence over that which divides. He is thus a 'holist'. And since he does not distinguish between different spheres and tasks, he is not able to accommodate the freedom that these different spheres can offer.

QUESTIONS

Discuss Plato's theory of ideas. Explain the difference between insight into the ideas and knowledge of perceptible phenomena.

'Plato's theory of ideas gives a universally valid foundation for ethical-political norms and values.' Discuss what could be the basis for this claim.

Discuss the connection between Plato's theory of ideas and his doctrine of the state.

SUGGESTIONS FOR FURTHER READING

PRIMARY LITERATURE

Ion, translated by Benjamin Jowett, Oxford, 1892.
Crito, translated by Benjamin Jowett, Oxford, 1892.
Phaedo, translated by Benjamin Jowett, Oxford, 1892.
The Republic, translated by Benjamin Jowett, Oxford, 1892.

SECONDARY LITERATURE

Barker, E., *Greek Political Theory*, London, 1970.
Kraut, Richard (ed.), *The Cambridge Companion to Plato*, Cambridge, 1992.
Taylor, A. E., *Plato, the Man and his Work*, 5th edition, London, 1948.

NOTES

1 *The Seventh Letter*, 341, from a translation by J. Harward, Cambridge, 1952.
2 The next problem is the so-called problem of participation. If ideas and things are thought of in spatial categories, so that each thing participating in the idea takes part in a *portion* of the idea, or so that the idea 'gives' a part of itself to each thing, then we end up with absurd consequences: in the first case, the thing does not participate in the idea, but only in a portion of the idea; in the second case, the idea's identity seems to be lost in a multitude of sub-ideas that each participate in different things. Does Plato then reject the theory of ideas for good after he has worked through such counter-arguments?
3 For example, by the Norwegian Plato scholar, Egil A. Wyller (1925–). See also Wyller, *Platon's Parmenides: in seinem Zusammenhang mit Symposon und Politeia: Interpretation zur Platonischen Henologie*, Oslo, 1960.
4 This is of course a highly debatable thesis. What do significant words like 'or' and 'maybe' refer to?
5 Plato's view of morality as anchored in the 'world of ideas' corresponds to a certain extent with prevailing viewpoints. If you ask people who do not study philosophy why we should not take another life, many would probably answer that we should not take another life 'because it *just is* wrong', 'there *are* certain moral norms'. For example, if we ask about the conviction of Nazi war criminals in Nüremberg, many will probably say that the verdict was just, because there *are* certain moral norms that apply in all places at all times. Few will accept that the accused should not have been convicted because ethical and political principles are relative in relation to changing customs and conventions, and to different laws in different societies. If those who accept the verdict in Nüremberg as objectively right choose their words more carefully, there are surely many who would formulate something that resembles a Platonic standpoint: norms *exist*, independently of space and time. Ethical-political norms exist in addition to perceptible things.

6 Cf. 'Napoleon' by the Norwegian poet Henrik Wergeland, in *Henrik Wergeland: Poems*, translated by Jethro Bithell, Oslo, 1960, p. 8.

We are the germs in the slime left by spirits;
Souls unfold like the butterfly
Out of the chrysalis, heightening
Power of spirits:
Higher and higher, through spirals,
Rises the army of spirits
Up to God.

7 It follows from this that Plato is *against* the investigation of phenomena based on fixed, academic divisions (such as the divisions between psychology, sociology, politics, economics, ethics, etc.): true insight is ultimately 'interdisciplinary'.

8 From *gymnos* – 'naked'; cf. *gymnasium*. Moreover, the educational content is not specified by Plato. His plan is not to be understood as a public educational system in the modern sense of the term.

9 Since Plato is presupposing universally valid and unchangeable norms for human behaviour (the ideas), we can say that the conception of the natural rights (cf. Ch. 5) has roots in his thought. At the same time, it is important to remember that Plato mainly seems to have in mind the Greek city-state, and not an international community. Corresponding comments can be made in connection with Aristotle.

10 Cf. E. Barker, *Greek Political Theory*, London, 1970, pp. 239 ff. It is claimed that Plato introduces 'communism'. This is an unfortunate choice of words. True, we can talk about communism in Plato in the sense that property, to a certain degree, is to be *common* – Latin *communis* – from which the word *communism* is derived. It is in this sense that we can talk about communism, for example, in early Christianity. Today, the word *communism* is usually associated with Marxism, and Marxist communism says that political power emerges from economic control over the means of production; while Plato, in his theory of the ideal state, describes a society where the rulers do not have any possessions. That is, there is communal ownership among Plato's upper classes, but this communal ownership seems to apply more to the consumption (goods and family members) than to the production side of things (land, tools, ships, etc.).

11 In *The Laws* Plato moderates some of the viewpoints of *The Republic*. He went back on his claim that private property and family life should be abolished for the two upper classes: with the nature of people being what it is, it would be nearly impossible to require communal ownership or the rotation of sexual partners under state management, especially with the resulting dissolution of the relationship between parent and child – even though Plato still believed this to be the best solution.

12 *Oiko-logi*, Greek: *oikos*, 'household' and *logos*, 'sense, reason'. The word *ecology* is a recent construction from the nineteenth century.

13 The idea of exponential growth would be an absurdity for Plato, a presumption (*hubris*) that leads to imbalance (*chaos*).

14 When Plato's city-state is occasionally called communistic, the term can be the source of confusion. His state has also been called 'fascist': the state stands above the individual. But this characterization is also warped. In recent times we have indeed seen a contrast between individualism and collectivism, the former claiming that the individual is everything and the state is nothing, and the latter that the state is everything and the individual nothing. But in the Greek city-state we generally do not have either the 'individual' or a 'state' that is *distinct* from the individual. With Plato there is a moral community where the good citizen assumes that people are performing their rightful functions in society. The distinction collectivism/individualism (and liberalism/fascism) is thus inadequate to describe Plato's city-state.

15 But isn't Plato anti-democratic? He hands all power to the experts and lets the people be governed from above. This is correct. But we need to add that the 'experts' in Plato's ideal state are of a different kind from those that *we* have in our society. Our experts are experts by virtue of their actual knowledge of a *particular* section of reality, on the basis of certain conceptual and methodological presuppositions. Our experts are not experts on 'the good'. They are not experts on what *ought* to be, on which *goals* we should have for society and for human life. They can only tell us that *if* we want to achieve this or that goal, then we need to do this or that. The experts cannot tell us, any more than any one else, what goal we should have. That is why we can justify *democracy* over expertise in our society: the experts, as experts, have no competence to say how things *should* be. Therefore, people, lay people, are fully within their rights to participate in politics, to take part in deciding what kind of society we are to have. But it is not possible to justify democracy this way in the ideal society that Plato was conceiving because here the 'experts' are also experts in *goals and values*. They have, after all, the best insight into the idea of the good. And having the best insight into the idea of the good also makes them the most virtuous. *If* the kind of experts that Plato is talking about did exist, and if it is not possible for *everyone* to be such an expert, then, theoretically, it is not easy to defend democracy as an ideal form of government. The

objection that Plato is anti-democratic thus becomes a problem. However, we can object that Plato's distinction between the experts and the people – between those who have complete competence, both in how things are and how they should be, and those without competence – is nothing more than a postulate. The *real* problems arise from the fact that no one is all-knowing and no one is completely ignorant, about either facts, values, or perspectives. The problem of the relationship between a government of the people and a government where power is held by those who are competent is therefore much more complex. But, some will claim, Plato can at least be said to make demands that are beyond reach. He demands things of people that hardly anyone is able, or willing, to do. But *what* is it that the people *really* want? What people *say* they want is not always what they really want. But how does Plato know what people 'really want'? And doesn't he claim that people 'really want' something that they in all actuality will not be able to attain; for example, to live for society, to be partially without family and without private property. Plato would probably answer that his educational system ensures that every person will come to his or her right place in society; i.e., that each person *ought to* do that which he or she has the ability to do, that which he or she is *best equipped* to do. The tasks in the ideal society are thus not beyond anyone's ability. On the contrary, each person is allowed to live in accordance with his or her best ability. What we really want is to be able to realize precisely the abilities we have, in the *best* way. What is best is determined by the idea of the good. There is no other basis for determining what we *ought to* do than the idea of the good. It is *the idea of the good* – which is one and unchangeable – that determines what is good, *not* the arbitrary and changing opinions of people who have not envisioned the idea of the good. Thus, what a person really wants is what he or she is capable of, what he or she ought to do. There is, in theory, no contradiction between self-interest and common interest.

16 We are indebted here to Seyla Benhabib and Linda Nicholson, 'Politische Philosophie und die Frauenfrage', in *Handbuch der politischen Philosophie*, I. Fetscher and H. Münkler, Münich, 1987.

17 Cf. *Timaios* 42 a, where men are said to be the superior sex, or *The Republic* 395, 548 b, and *The Laws* 781 a–b, where he warns against women as a source of socially harmful vices.

18 'Muses'; refers to the nine Greek goddesses, 'Muses' who represent the arts and sciences: Clio (history), Euterpe (lyric poetry), Thalia (comedy), Melpomene (tragedy), Terpsichore (dance), Erato (love poetry), Polyhymnia (sacred song), Urania (astronomy), and Calliope (epic poetry).

19 *Aesthetic*, from the Greek: *aisthétikos*; from *aistanesthai*, 'to sense' (perceive).

20 *The Republic* 607 a.

4 | Aristotle – natural order and man as a 'political animal'

Life. *Aristotle was born in 384 BC in the Ionic city of Stageira on the coast of Macedonia. His father was a physician at the Macedonian court. It is possible that his father's profession played a part in awakening Aristotle's interest in biology. In any case, Aristotle's thought is in many ways influenced by biology, just as Plato's thought is influenced by mathematics.*

At the age of 17 or 18, Aristotle came to Athens and became a student at the Academy. He remained there for about 20 years, until Plato died in 347. The contact with Plato had a great impact on Aristotle as a philosopher, even though he eventually moved away from Plato's philosophy and developed a philosophy that, on many points, can be said to stand in opposition to Plato's teachings. This applies to the theory of ideas, but also to Plato's political theory: while Plato, in a sense, looks up towards the ideas, Aristotle looks out towards the many particular phenomena. While Plato attempts to develop a theory of an eternal and perfect ideal state, Aristotle, starting with an investigation of existing forms of state, attempts to find the best among the states that can be realized. But these differences between Plato and Aristotle should not be emphasized so strongly that we overlook the similarities that exist between them. After Plato died, Aristotle travelled on various study tours. He especially studied aquatic wildlife. As a descriptive biologist, he learned to observe and classify (but not to experiment – experimentation began in earnest during the Renaissance).

For some years, Aristotle was tutor to the young crown prince of Macedonia, the future Alexander the Great. But it is doubtful that they had any impact on each other. Aristotle was primarily concerned with the city-state, not with the idea of an extensive empire that included both Greeks and Persians.

After Alexander came to power, Aristotle moved to Athens and started his own school, the Lyceum (335 BC).[1] The school lasted for over 860 years, longer than almost all of the present European universities. Aristotle established a library at the Lyceum and there founded the first museum of natural history. And at the Lyceum, he organized research of various kinds, often as a group effort; for instance, with the help of younger assistants, he collected systematic descriptions of 158 different forms of city-state government in Greece. From this mammoth work we have only one portion about the history of Athenian constitutional development. The courses offered at the Lyceum included philosophy, history, civics, natural science (biology), rhetoric, literature, and the art of poetry. Most of the extant writings attributed to Aristotle are probably notes from his academic lectures. When Alexander died in 323, the Athenians turned against Aristotle because of his Macedonian past, and he left Athens. He died the following year at the age of 62 (in 322).

We have many of Aristotle's works, but many others have been lost. His writings were to a great extent edited by his students. Towards the end of the Middle Ages, Aristotle's works were arranged in order and systematized as required reading material in the various educational centres around Europe. But the authentic Aristotle was a searching philosopher, not a man with a closed and complete system of thought, that offered all the answers.

IDEA OR SUBSTANCE

PLATO AND ARISTOTLE

Aristotle and Plato both believe that human beings are enabled to live a worthy life only in a community; and, by community, they both mean the Greek city-state. But the general opposition between the idealistic rationalist, Plato, and the critical, *common-sense* philosopher, Aristotle, also becomes evident in their views of society: Plato criticizes the actual conditions by an appeal to the demands of reason; he sees politics as a task: that of bringing the actual conditions closer in line with the ideal. Aristotle, on the other hand, starts with the existing forms of the state; and reason, for Aristotle, is a means of classifying and evaluating that which actually exists. This means that Plato looks beyond the existing order towards something qualitatively new. Aristotle is searching for the best of what already exists. What he says is more realistic, in the sense that it fits in better with the political conditions of the city-states during his time.

This characterization of Plato and Aristotle is, of course, a simplification. But it can still serve to point out certain differences that apply to both their purely philosophical and their political theories. However, calling attention to their differences should not hide the fact that the two have much in common. And the connective thread in the development from Plato to Aristotle is related to the fact that Aristotle *argues* against Plato — that is, Aristotle marshals arguments against Plato; he does not just present a new outlook. We can say that Aristotle represents a kind of rational continuation of Plato, without taking a stand as to which of them was the better thinker. For example, Aristotle criticizes, as does Plato, the so-called Platonic theory of ideas.

SUBSTANCE AND PROPERTIES

While Plato, in the prevailing textbook interpretation, says that the ideas are what *really* exist, Aristotle claims that what exists independently are particular things, or 'substances', to use Aristotelian terminology. The Eiffel Tower, the neighbour's horse, and this pencil are examples of particular things, of substances in the Aristotelian sense: they exist independently. The height of the Eiffel Tower, the golden colour of the neighbour's horse, and the hexagonal cross-section of the pencil, on the other hand, are properties that do not exist independently of the tower, the pencil, and the horse. Substances have properties, and properties exist as properties of the substance; but, beyond this, properties do not have any independent existence. We can look at various yellow objects and talk about the property 'yellow', and speak correspondingly of other objects and properties. But this does not make the property yellow an independently existing idea, according to Aristotle.

The property yellow exists only in, and because there are, yellow things.[2] Correspondingly, we can look at Black Beauty, Secretariat, Trigger, and other horses and talk about them, as horses. We are then disregarding the individual and accidental properties of each of the particular horses and focusing on what is characteristic of all of them, as horses. Whether they are golden or brown is thus not essential, nor whether they are thin or round, good-natured or stubborn. These are non-essential properties when we consider what the essence of a horse is. But there are other properties that a horse cannot be without if it is to remain a horse; for example, being a mammal, and having hooves. Such properties can then be called essential properties: they express what characterizes that kind of substance. From this distinction between *essential* and *non-essential properties*, we can formulate a *concept of species*; for example, the species *horse*, which consists of the essential properties of a horse.

Aristotle is thus claiming that substances are what actually exist, but that properties and species possess a relative existence insofar as they exist in or with the substances (particular things):

$$\frac{\text{the brown door}}{\text{brown}} = \frac{\text{particular thing (substance)}}{\text{property and species}} = \frac{\text{independent existence}}{\text{relative existence}}$$

Therefore, Aristotle brings the ideas down to the level of things: properties and species exist, but only *in* particular things.[3]

In outline, we can interpret the relationship here between Plato and Aristotle as follows. Both Plato and Aristotle believe that conceptual words (names of properties, like 'red', 'circular', etc., and names of species, like 'horse', 'human being', etc.) refer to something that exists. But Plato believes that these 'somethings' are ideas that exist 'behind' the sensible phenomena: we say, rightly, that this is a chair and that it is blue; but, to see this, we must already possess the idea of chair and the idea of blue. It is the ideas that enable us to see the phenomena for what they are; for example, as a chair, as blue. Aristotle believes that these 'somethings' are the forms that exist in the sensible phenomena. But this should not be understood too literally. According to Aristotle, with the aid of reason we can perceive the universal, or the forms. By disregarding what is unique in Black Beauty, I am able to envision the universal form of horse. I can see Black Beauty, but the form of horse that indeed exists 'in' Black Beauty can only be explicitly known by abstraction from the sensible and the specific.

For Plato, sense experience is an imperfect form of knowledge. True knowledge is insight into the ideas. And this insight into the ideas involves looking into a world of ideas 'behind' the world of sensation. For Aristotle, sense experience, the empirical, has a more positive status. According to Aristotle, ultimately only particular things (substances) do exist. But we can, with the aid of reason, distinguish the universal forms *in* these things. By a process of abstraction we recognize the universal forms in things. In other words, sense experience and reason have a more equivalent status for Aristotle than for Plato.[4] We will come back to this opposition between Platonism and Aristotelianism in connection with the controversy over universals (Ch. 6).

ONTOLOGY AND EPISTEMOLOGY

SOME BASIC CONCEPTS

Philosophical theories about the fundamental forms of existence, like the theory of ideas and the theory of substance and of properties, are called *ontology* ('theory of being'). Philosophical theories about the fundamental forms of knowledge are called *epistemology* ('theory of knowledge'). For Aristotle, the first step in the path to knowledge is that we experience particular things with our senses; the next step is an abstraction from the accidental to the essential and universal. The essential and universal is then captured in a definition; for example, that of horse as a species. Once we have a definition of the essential properties of a species, we have know-ledge on a higher level, since the themes of our knowledge are unchangeable and essential. Hence, Aristotle views the acquisition of knowledge as a process that moves from sense experience to insight into essence; as a process of abstraction in the direction of a definition about something that is essential and universal. Although Aristotle claims that it is the particular things, substances, that have independent existence (as is claimed in his ontology), he believes that the knowledge we should seek is knowledge of essential and universal properties (as is claimed in his epistemology). After we have moved from insight into the particular to insight into the universal and essential, we can use this insight to make logically valid infer-ences that allow us to reach other true propositions: if we know that a horse is a mammal, and that Black Beauty is a horse, we can deduce that Black Beauty is a mammal. Aristotle is known for formulating the so-called syllogism about valid and invalid implications of this kind.[5]

In addition to knowledge in the form of perception of particular things and of insight into substance-related essences, Aristotle invokes practical wisdom. He also refers to insight into unproved, but incontrovertible, basic principles. We will return to these forms of knowledge later (Knowledge and praxis), but first we are going to take a closer look at the insight into essence that Aristotle is seeking. Insight into essence is not just insight into the definition of a species. To understand a phe-nomenon, we have to know the *causes* that make it what it is. But Aristotle's under-standing of *cause* (Latin: *causa*) tends to be more comprehensive than the usual understanding of the word. The fundamental properties of all things and the fundamental causes that make them what they are, are treated in the Aristotelian ontology, the key words of which are as follows:

1   substance
2   form/matter
3   four 'causes'
4   actuality/potentiality; change
5   theology.

THE FOUR CAUSES

Each particular thing (substance) consists of *form* and *matter*. A lump of clay has a certain form, and the clay itself is the matter. A potter can transform this lump of clay into a jar, so that this lump of clay (with form and matter) becomes a *new* particular thing, now having a more refined form. What makes the clay a jar, is a certain form that is combined with a particular material, the clay. The form tells us what kind of thing the jar is. The material is what the jar is made of. But a jar is not something that makes itself. A potter makes the jar. When she begins, she has certain ideas of what the jar should look like in order for it to fulfil its purpose, i.e., preventing water from running out. By working with a suitable raw material, she makes the jar. With this simple example we can illustrate *Aristotle's teaching of the four causes*. The clay jar is codetermined by four 'causes', or principles.

1   The representation of the finished jar is the purpose that the entire creative process is directed towards: *the final cause (causa finalis)*. This is the teleological principle, which says that a process of change is guided by its purpose (Greek: *telos*).

2   The potter's preparation of the raw material is the moving force, or the source of motion, in the process: *the efficient cause (causa efficiens)*. This is the principle of causality, which says that a process is determined by external mechanical forces.

3   What the jar is made of is the matter: *the material cause or principle (causa materialis)*. The material principle consists of that from which things are made. This principle corresponds to matter (mentioned above).

4   And finally we have the (different) forms that the lump of clay/jar has at any time. This is *the formal cause or principle (causa formalis)*. The formal principle consists of the properties that things acquire. This principle corresponds to form (mentioned above).

These four 'causes' (principles) have, in different ways, become a part of the philosophical debate and are continually the basis of discussion. The doctrine of the formal principle (cause) is part of the debate surrounding the Platonic ideas, of the controversy over universals in the Middle Ages, and of today's debate about nominalism and realism.

In addition, the discussion has been vigorous when it comes to the relationship between the efficient cause and the final cause. During the Renaissance, many rejected the teleological principle (*causa finalis*), and in modern times we have a continuing debate about the relationship between explanations based on purpose and causal explanations in the social sciences and the humanities.

The concept of matter presents many problems. We can talk about matter as *material*, such as clay, rock, or wood. The same material, such as a piece of wood, can serve for different things, the leg of a chair or an axe handle. The same material can have different forms, depending on what the carpenter has planned. But we can also imagine two chair legs being identical to a tee. They have the same form. The forms, or properties, are universal. In the mass production of needles, all the products look the same. They all have the same properties – shape, size, colour, etc. But they are different units – they are not all the same needle – because each has its own matter. That which makes them into many particular things, and not one thing, is that they possess their own matter and that they therefore can be found in different spatial locations, for example, side by side; but that several needles never occupy the same space. Matter, in this sense, is what individuates, that is, what makes a thing into a *particular* thing. In this sense, matter (*materia secunda*) is seen as the principle of individuation. But what is matter before it is formed? Can we even talk or think about that which is without form? This sense of matter (*materia prima*) is a problematic concept. In addition, matter, in the Aristotelian tradition, is usually associated with *the feminine*, and the form or the formative, with *the masculine*.

We have illustrated here the four principles (or causes) with an example from the world of craftsmen or artisans. This is in keeping with Aristotle's thought. His reflections are often based on the creative processes found in the various crafts. But, at the same time, he also uses biology as a reference point. The four causes apply, in principle, to all things. When it comes to organisms that form themselves anew throughout their lives – like roses and cats – we can say that the final cause and the efficient cause lie, in a sense, within these things themselves. They possess the purpose, and moving force, within themselves, and not because of an external agent such as a potter. Here we have a distinction between *nature* and the *work of human beings* (culture). Natural things possess all four principles *in themselves*, as opposed to the things that are made by human beings. But not all things in nature are organisms or man-made objects. Non-living, natural things, like rocks and water, are not determined by growth, nor by human goals or formative intervention. Here it becomes more problematic to talk about a final cause.

CHANGE AND COSMOLOGY

Aristotle's theory of 'natural' and 'forced' motion illustrates the notion of a final cause in connection with inorganic nature – non living things that are not man made. It is worth noting that Aristotle defines four types of change:

1   *substantial change*, where a substance (thing) comes into being and perishes, as when a horse is born and dies
2   *qualitative change*, where a substance (thing) changes properties, as when a leaf changes from being green to being gold
3   *quantitative change*, where a substance (thing) receives more (or less) of a property, as when a cat becomes plump and heavy, or thin and light
4   *spatial change*, where a substance (thing) changes its spatial location, as when a stone falls to the ground or an arrow is shot towards a target.

The theory of 'natural' and 'forced' motion belongs to the last type of change. The starting point is that all things are composed of the four elements – fire, air, water, and earth – where the first two elements reach upwards (fire more strongly than air), and where the last two reach downwards (earth more strongly than water). Different things are composed of various amounts of these four elements. Things that have mostly earth in them will, therefore, naturally reach downwards. Those that have mostly water in them will naturally cover these 'earth-rich' things. Those that have mostly fire will seek greater heights, while those that have mostly air will place themselves under those containing mostly fire. This means that the action *fall*, for instance, is explained by this Aristotelian doctrine of particular things 'seeking their natural place' in accordance with their composition by the four elements. This is how the falling motion is explained by the *final cause*. To use all of the four types of causes, we can say that a thing's natural place is the final cause, that its weight is the efficient cause, that the path leading to the natural place is the formal cause, and that the material composing the thing is the material cause. When we shoot an arrow in a horizontal direction, it first moves in a horizontal direction and then gradually declines and falls at an angle towards the ground. The arrow will not fall straight down when it is released from the bowstring. The arrow is put into motion, forcing it to fly in a different direction than its 'natural' movement would have taken it, namely, a fall straight to the ground. The arrow is thus 'forced' in a direction that it would otherwise not have gone. This is Aristotle's doctrine of forced motion. In the Renaissance such phenomena began to be explained in a different way. The concepts of natural and forced motion were criticized and rejected, along with the notion of final causes in nature (cf. Galileo).

In astronomy, Aristotle distinguishes between the universe's lower and upper spheres. The theory of natural and forced motion applies to the part of the universe that is closest to the Earth ('sublunary', under the moon). The stars and planets, on the other hand, belong in the upper sphere, where their orbits describe perfect circles at a constant speed. Here there are three basic astronomical assumptions:

1   The universe is divided into two spheres, one lower and one upper, each with its own laws of motion.
2   The orbits in the upper sphere are circular.
3   The celestial bodies move in these orbits at a constant speed.

The universe is, moreover, conceived as finite.

All these assumptions are included in the so-called Ptolemaic world-view (cf. Ch. 5, Astronomy) that dominated astronomy until the conflicts that ushered in the new age gained a foothold. The new theory of mechanics (Galileo and Newton) rejected the Aristotelian understanding of motion on the surface of the Earth, and the new theory of astronomy (Copernicus, Kepler, and Newton) rejected the Aristotelian understanding of nature in celestial space: according to this new understanding, the entire universe is subject to the same laws, and celestial bodies move in elliptic orbits, at varying speeds (in a boundless universe).

ACTUALITY-POTENTIALITY AND HIERARCHIC-ORGANIC WORLD-VIEW

The Aristotelian distinction between form and matter is closely related to the distinction between *actuality and potentiality*: the seed of a pine is *here and now* (actually) only a seed, but it carries within itself *natural capacities* (potentialities) to become a tree. In the tree's growth, the *capacities* that the seed carries within itself are *realized*. The potentiality is thus actualized. Aristotle generalizes this biological aspect to apply to *all* things: all particular things are a tension-filled mixture of potentiality and actuality, and all things seek to actualize their potentialities. Aristotle thus gives a biological explanation for change, not a mechanical explanation, as the Milesian philosophers and the atomists did: change, for Aristotle, is the actualization of potentialities. This is how Aristotle avoids the problematic concept of non-being, in connection with the concept of change. Change is not an oscillation between being and non-being. Creation is not an emergence of something from nothing, *ex nihilo*. Change based on biological development and creative craftsmanship involves a realization of existing capacities. The possible *is*, qua potentiality.

From this theory about the interplay between actuality and potentiality, we can say that *the real* for Aristotle, as for Plato, is not identical with that which is actually given. The real is for Aristotle that which strives for *actualization*. The exception is pure actuality, which is real without potentiality and hence without the urge towards actualization. Reality has a dynamic dimension of depth. Exploring reality cannot be limited to registering and synthesizing actually given facts. Exploring reality should also include seeking the underlying, dynamic process of actualization. And philosophy, from this point of view, is to criticize the actually given, from an insight into how the real, really is. Aristotle, in this way, ends up with a hierarchic universe:

pure actuality
human beings
animals
plants
inorganic things (rocks, earth)
pure potentiality (pure matter).

At the bottom of the scale are lifeless things (rocks, earth, etc.). Then come plants, which, according to Aristotle, have a higher form of existence: they have a reproductive and vegetative soul (Greek: *psyche*, 'soul, life principle'). They reproduce and take in nourishment. Then come the various animals, which, along with the ability to reproduce and take in nourishment, also have a sensitive soul – they feel – and a motory soul – they move (run, swim, fly). Finally, we have human beings, who, along with the vegetative, reproductive, sensitive, and 'motory' soul, also have the ability to reason. Reason (in a broad sense) is the unique 'soul' of human beings. Man is the rational animal.[6] Reason is the *form of human beings*, the form that transforms the animal forms – the ability to reproduce, to take in nourishment, to sense, to move – so that the animal forms become the material for the human being's specific form, reason (Greek: *nous*). Even though a human being is also an animal (possesses all of the abilities that animals possess), the animal properties are, as it were, transilluminated and enobled by reason.[7]

Human beings are the highest creatures with material existence. At the top of this hierarchic universe, Aristotle imagines a first principle, God, who is pure actuality, that is to say, without potentiality, and consequently without change. God rests in himself. Aristotle's metaphysics thus culminates in a *theology*, a teaching about the highest being. This is not a personal God: Aristotle thinks of the highest being as *the unmoved mover*, who is at rest. This highest principle is pure act, having no potentiality. But for this reason it is the final end (Greek: *telos*) for everything else. The unmoved mover is what all things move towards (each in its own way and within its limits). The lowest level in the hierarchic universe is pure matter (potentiality); the concept of pure matter represents a 'border' concept that we, strictly speaking, cannot imagine, since it does not possess actuality (actual properties).

In Aristotle's hierarchic universe, each particular thing has an inclination to realize its potentialities in the best way. There is, in all things, an 'upward' yearning. Each thing's purpose (*telos*) is the realization of its capabilities. The actualization of the thing's potentiality is, in this sense, teleological. This yearning and this actualization through change are located in each thing. But each *species* has its given place in the universe (cf. Darwin, Ch. 20). This world-view exerted great influence by, among other things, being adopted by several Christian philosophers, such as Thomas Aquinas, in the thirteenth century.

ARISTOTLE AND ECOLOGY

It is typical of Aristotle that his starting point is often *living* nature, and not, as for Democritus, inorganic nature. We can talk here about a choice between two models of explanation: one that takes its concepts from the field of biology and one that takes its concepts from the study of inorganic things. Democritus tries to explain everything by mechanical, inorganic concepts and laws – the billiard-ball model – but finds it difficult to explain biological and social phenomena. Aristotle, we could say, attempts to explain everything with biological, organic categories – the organic model. Aristotle, then, maintains that all things, including rocks and air, have their 'natural place', and that a thing seeks its natural purpose.[8] We could also say that Aristotle uses the concept of action as his starting point, as opposed to Democritus, who starts with the concept of event. An event is an occurrence in nature that we investigate through observation, and where the establishment of causal laws often is the goal of the investigation. An action is a social phenomenon that presupposes a person who acts intentionally – that is, a person who in one sense or another is conscious of what he or she is doing. Aristotle's theory of causes is especially applicable to goal-oriented action. Purely natural events do not fit in quite as well with the Aristotelian theory of causes. On the other hand, philosophers like Democritus who start with events have difficulty in accounting properly for social phenomena, i.e., phenomena that are connected with action, intention, subject, and intersubjectivity.[9] For Aristotle, natural philosophy[10] is, in a way, a description of nature as we experience it. Aristotle conceives of basic elements like earth, water, air, and fire, and notions such as up and down, etc.; that is, general concepts for the experience of nature.[11] Or perhaps we should say that the natural philosophy is, for Aristotle, defined by ecology, not physics. For him, there are various species and principles of life, each with natural functions and limitations that no creature can violate without harm. An ecological crisis that leads to the extinction of higher forms of life does not violate the fundamental order of things according to the mechanistic world-view of Democritus: a universe of material particles, possessing only quantitative properties, and moving mechanically in a void. Such a world is fundamentally unaffected by an ecological crisis. The categories that Democritus uses to understand the universe are ecologically neutral, and hence, from a practical perspective, inadequate.

Nor can we grasp the ecological dimension simply by supplementing a mechanical atomism with subjective categories such as human values and experience of quality,[12] because an ecological crisis in an ecosystem involves destructive changes on the Earth even if the human race did not exist. In medicine, the distinction between sickness and health is one that, in a sense, is grounded in the living body, whereas physics alone cannot distinguish between health and sickness. What is needed is a natural philosophy that comprehends the ecological. But since human beings participate in the ecological balance, this philosophy of nature must accommodate both man and nature.

Among early Greek philosophers we find a view of nature as a whole, *physis*, in which human beings are seen as a part of a natural framework. The teaching about the interaction found in nature as a whole by the Greek natural philosophers, is in this sense an ecological philosophy. *Physis* is a functional totality in which each thing functions according to its purpose. To go beyond one's natural function is *hubris* (presumption), and that can lead to disorder (*chaos*). The harmonious realization of each thing's natural attributes, within its natural place, is right, in nature as well as in society. The positive interaction between the different forms of life and the environment, within nature's finite borders, composes the *cosmos*, the universe as a finite and harmonious whole.

We might recall that today pollution affects water, air, and earth, and our energy comes ultimately from sunlight. Fire, air, water, and earth were the basic elements for Aristotle and the other Greek natural philosophers.

For Aristotle, each thing has its natural place. Pollution is 'misplacement': things are placed in contexts where they do not belong and, in that sense, where they should not be. In Democritus' atomic universe there is no pollution in this sense.

In contrast to Democritus, Aristotle uses concepts in pairs, such as up/down, dry/wet, and warm/cold: the differences between desert, tundra, and rainforest are important ecologically. But, in the mechanistic world-view, these differences are not recorded as essentially different conditions. The same applies to the differences between the living and the non-living, and between the different principles of life among living creatures: for plants, the ability to take in nourishment and to reproduce; for animals, the additional ability to move and feel; and for human beings, the ability to reason. Ecology, then, seems to point beyond a mechanistic-atomistic view of nature, as in Galileo and Newton, to the natural philosophy of Aristotle and other Greek philosophers.

KNOWLEDGE AND PRAXIS

FORMS OF KNOWLEDGE

While the dialectician, Plato, sees a connection between the various forms of knowledge and their problems, so that he does not really make a sharp distinction between the theory of ideas and the doctrine of the state, ethics, aesthetics, etc., the analyst, Aristotle, seeks to distinguish among the various disciplines. He distinguishes between the theoretical, the practical, and the poetic disciplines (corresponding, respectively, to *theoria*, *praxis*, and *poiesis*) that are related to knowledge (*episteme*), practical wisdom (*phronesis*), and art or technical skill (*techne*). The goal of the theoretical disciplines is to determine the truth. Aristotle takes three theoretical disciplines into account, namely, the philosophy of nature, mathematics, and metaphysics. Natural philosophy seeks to determine the perceptible and changeable things. Mathematics seeks to determine the unchangeable, quantifiable properties.

Metaphysics seeks to determine the unchangeable forms in so far as they exist independently. He is, in this sense, talking in terms of an increasing level of abstraction, from natural philosophy, through mathematics, and on to metaphysics. The goal of the practical disciplines is to lead to wise actions through acquired, ethical competence. Such ethical competence (*phronesis*) can only be gained by personal experience in the company of mature people who are experienced in various social situations, who know how to recognize these various situations and how to respond to them. This is a different kind of experience from sense experience. It is an experience that everyone must undergo in order to gain the competence to evaluate social events. To a great extent, therefore, we can talk about 'tacit knowledge', in the sense that such knowledge cannot be communicated by propositions alone, but only when the persons concerned themselves participate in and experience what is at stake. It is interesting that Aristotle classifies ethics and politics as 'practical' disciplines. When it comes to politics, it means that he distances himself from the view that politics is only a struggle for power, as in the notion of *Realpolitik* beginning with Machiavelli. For Aristotle, politics has to do with open, enlightened interaction in which people mutually mould and cultivate each other, and seek to achieve fair and good solutions to their problems.

Aristotle emphasizes the importance of the acquisition of ethical competence. We will later see that there are those who limit ethics to the question of the justification of universal, ethical principles (as in Kant's categorical imperative), and those who view ethics as a question of the maximization of utility (like utilitarians such as Bentham). By the concept of *praxis*, Aristotle shows that he also recognizes the need to acquire the capability to make fair, ethical judgements, and that includes cultivating the individual in the company of others, and goes beyond what we can learn in the form of theoretical justification or criticism of norms.

The goal of the poetic disciplines is to produce something. They are creative (*poetic*). This production can take place through artistic creation; that is why poetry and rhetoric are included here. But this can also take place by technical production, and here Aristotle is thinking about different kinds of crafts.

Finally, it is worth noting that Aristotle, the father of logic, classifies logic as a tool (Greek: *organon*) that is part of all disciplines without being itself a discipline alongside of the others. We can put it this way: Aristotle turns language into an object of research, and finds what he sees as the inner structure of language: the logically correct deductions (proofs). Since language is a part of all academic disciplines, an investigation of logically correct deductions will be an investigation of something that is common to all disciplines.

Within the theoretical disciplines, Aristotle has a special interest in knowledge that is absolutely certain in the sense that what is claimed by these propositions necessarily has to be true. Aristotle seeks this kind of knowledge in what he conceives to be essential properties in the different substances, as in his ontology. It is therefore important to be able to express this kind of certain knowledge (of general properties of the substances), and it is also important to be able to *move on* to *other* equally certain statements, by the use of valid arguments. Logic as a *theory of argumentation*, or a *theory of proof*, plays exactly this role in Aristotle: by logically valid inferences we can move from one set of true and certain statements to other equally true and certain statements. Logic secures this transition. Aristotle analysed logically valid inferences, or *syllogisms*, involving two premises and one conclusion, where the conclusion follows with logical necessity from the premises. Here is one example:

Premise 1: All human beings are mortal.
Premise 2: Socrates is a human being.
Conclusion: Socrates is mortal.

There are three terms in a syllogism ('human being', 'mortal', and 'Socrates'), two terms in each premise, and two in the conclusion. The term that is common to the two premises (the 'middle term') does not appear in the conclusion. There are also words like 'all', 'some', or 'no(n)'. In this way, we have various forms of syllogisms, some being valid and others invalid. First, two valid inferences:

Premise 1: All M are P.
Premise 2: All S are M.
Conclusion: All S are P.

Premise 1: No M is P.
Premise 2: All S are M.
Conclusion: No S is P.

We realize that these two inferences (traditionally called Barbara and Celarent) can be presented as relationships between sets:

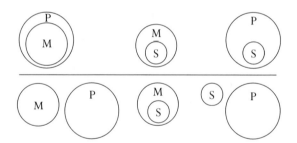

An example of an invalid inference is the following:

Premise 1: Some M are P.
Premise 2: Some S are M.
Conclusion: Some S are P.

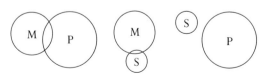

We may have a valid inference and a false conclusion. Take the following example in which one of the premises is false, the inference (Celarent) is valid, and the conclusion is false:

Premise 1: No bird has feathers.
Premise 2: All crows are birds.
Conclusion: No crow has feathers.

Only when both premises are true can we be sure that a valid inference gives a true conclusion – the point being that we have to distinguish between the question of whether an *inference* is *valid* and the question of whether the *premises* are *true*. (It does not help to be logical if we have not checked that all premises are tenable!)

Aristotle believes that all logically correct deductions presuppose undemonstrable principles; for example, the principle of contradiction: the same thing cannot be an attribute and not be an attribute of the same subject at the same time and in the same way. This, according to Aristotle, is a first principle that cannot be proven, but that is indispensable for any rational use of language.

ANTHROPOLOGY AND SOCIOLOGY

An infant, like a seed, has inherent capabilities that can be realized. But human beings do not 'grow', like plants. They live, as creatures of reason. They can themselves fall short of realizing their best capabilities, while the seed can not. This is why human beings have developed the practical disciplines, ethics and politics, to help them manage their lives, in the attempt to realize the best human capabilities.

Generally, according to Aristotle, the best human capabilities are connected with the unique human 'soul', reason: a rational life is the universal goal for all human beings. But *our* goal is to realize *our* best capabilities in the society that we live in; that is, to find *our* style (*ethos*), to find *our* place in community, the place where we best can realize our personal capabilities. This is virtue (*arete*).

Because we do not know *everything*, like the gods, and are not ignorant, like plants and animals, we *can* make mistakes: 'I may have had the capability within me to make something of myself, but I failed.' This is a recurrent theme of the tragedy that belongs to human life, but not to the life of the gods or the animals.

Aristotle proposes that people need to experience progressive stages of socialization in order to be able to fulfil their best capabilities: a person must develop through the family, the village, and finally the city-state, in order to be a fully developed human being. Only then can people realize their potential. People's nature – what capabilities (potentialities) they have – first appears (is actualized) by means of these three social groups:

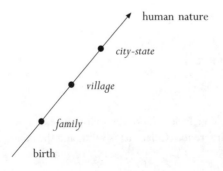

A growing number of needs, from elementary needs (family) to complex needs (city-state), are met, and we end up with increasing levels of realization of human nature. In other words, the human nature does not reveal itself in the primitive and brutish life. This nature first appears when the human being has become civilized. It is worth noting that, for Aristotle, the human being is primarily male. As we will see, women, according to Aristotle, are primarily connected to the family and the local environment. That is where they can best realize their capabilities. Aristotle distinguishes, moreover, between men who are free and autonomous persons – man in the best sense – and men who have a slave mentality by nature: slaves in the city-state were usually employed in physical labour, and such a life was, for Aristotle, less valuable than the life of the free Greek men. Aristotle also thought that those enslaved were slaves by nature. For Aristotle, there is a correlation between the slave's work in bondage and his personal attributes. From both perspectives, the slave is *below* the free Greek man. In this way, Aristotle places both slaves and women below free Greek men: both belong at home in the household (*oikos*), not in the public life of the market place (*agora*); and women and slaves are by nature, according to their attributes, on a lower level than the free men who appear in the public places of the city-state. When we say that man realizes his nature in the city-state, we must then keep in mind that, for Aristotle, this does not apply to women and slaves.

The community, society, is thus nothing external to the human being. The community is a necessary condition for human beings to be able to realize their best capabilities. In other words, man-in-community is the basic concept, not the individual in isolation from society, nor society (the state) in isolation from the individual. The city-state is self-sufficient, not the individual. Man reaches self-realization as an actor in civic life, as a social being. Aristotle thus conceives of man as a 'political animal' (Greek: *zoon politikon*). But at the same time, he believes that Plato goes too far in emphasizing that a human being is a part of the community. 'The nature of the state,' says Aristotle, is 'to be a group, a group of people.'[13] That is, in theory, and in political practice, we must not standardize; we must not enforce a greater unity than what is natural. We have said that the uniquely human principle of life is reason, in a broad sense. Human beings must live in community principally so that they can realize their ability to reason. Satisfactory fulfilment of reason presupposes the good city-state. *Logos* and *polis* are interconnected. Human nature is *not* shown by those who live irrationally without reason and logic, or by those who do not make use of the unique human 'soul' in company with others, but only by those who live in a rational, social community.

Some have claimed that Aristotle is unclear when it comes to the question of whether the good life is a life in theoretical activity or a life in rational, political community. But when it comes to the relationship between the rational, political community and necessary, productive labour, it is clear that Aristotle believes that the former is good for human beings, is a goal in itself, but that physical labour, along with accompanying recreation, does not represent the good life, and has no value in itself. Therefore those who carry out such work, whether they are slaves or not, cannot realize human life at its best. The class differences in Aristotle's age take shape here as a distinction between those who do manual labour and those who pursue intellectual and political activity. Aristotle believes that this moulding process, 'humanization', takes place primarily in intellectual and political activity, not in physical labour.[14]

The differences in the views of man and society between Aristotle and Plato become clear in their view of women. While Plato distinguishes sharply between the private sphere and the public sphere, and inclines to do away with the private sphere by turning the state into a large family having common property and common children, Aristotle believes that family and state fulfil different functions. The family provides a framework for meeting primary needs, like nourishment, reproduction, and raising children. The state makes it possible for male citizens to realize themselves politically and intellectually. There are positive transitions from the private to the public. In addition to the socialization that takes place within the family in the private sphere, we are further moulded in the village, and finally by life in the city-state, in the public sphere. There is therefore no opposition between the private and the public, but, instead, there is an inner connection. The family, then, should not be abolished. On the contrary, the family is a fundamental institution for socialization and communication. Correspondingly, Aristotle cannot accept the sharp distinction that Plato makes between the biological and the cultural. For Aristotle, human beings are spiritual beings that *at the same time* have all the animal's principles of life.

Aristotle is thus closer to the prevalent opinions of his day than Plato. Aristotle shares the traditional view that men are superior to women, and even uses biological arguments to support it. Thus, Aristotle believes that it is the man's sperm that provides the child's form, while the woman only contributes the matter. This unique use of the Aristotelian concepts of form and matter was possible because it was then not known that genetic properties are derived from both the sperm and the egg. For a long time it was believed that the man's sperm embodied microscopic human beings. (There were, however, rival theories about reproduction in antiquity, and Plato for a time held the view that women and men both contribute equally.)[15] Aristotle also believes that women have a lower body temperature than men in line with the prevailing conception that warm creatures are superior to cold creatures. Thus, the woman is inferior to the man.

THE GOOD LIFE

When it comes to his view of ethics, Aristotle distinguishes himself from Plato on several points. We have seen that Aristotle criticizes Plato's theory that the ideas have an independent existence in relation to things. This criticism also applies to the idea of the good. The good, that is the goal for human life, is, for Aristotle, not something independent of man. The good is found *in* the way that human beings live. For Aristotle, the good is happiness or bliss (Greek: *eudaimonia*), a state which precisely requires that people realize their best capabilities in community, through the three stages of socialization, so that each person finds his or her place in society, i.e., becomes virtuous. Aristotle thinks that a life of theoretical activity is especially suitable for bringing happiness, especially for those who possess good theoretical capabilities. But different persons have different capabilities and potentials. Therefore, the good life does not have to be the same for everyone. Aristotle thinks, moreover, that we cannot be happy if we are afflicted with severe physical suffering (pain). Here he parts company with Plato (Socrates), who appears to think that both pleasure and pain are irrelevant to happiness.

The existentialists often hold a *heroic* view of life: 'Either–or', 'Be what you have to be wholly and completely, not a little bit here and a little bit there' (Henrik Ibsen, *Brand*, Act I). That is: concentrate on one capability, and realize it to its fullest – even though this may be at the expense of other capabilities. For Aristotle, the Greek, the good life is harmonious. Every capability, intellectual, athletic, political, personal, and artistic, is to be nurtured and realized in a well-balanced manner, according to each person's predisposition. Aristotle also applauds moderation, that is, the harmonious realization of all good capabilities. Thus, courage is a virtue, because courage is the golden mean between cowardice and recklessness.[16]

Friendship (Greek: *philia*), says Aristotle, is one of the virtues that we can least do without. Friendship involves mutual, not hidden, goodwill. Thus, friendship is a mutual attitude between persons. We can, for example, 'love money', but money does not love us. We can also be in love with a person without knowing that person and without that person realizing it. Friendship, on the other hand, requires mutual knowledge and mutual recognition. Friendship requires time to develop, time for companionship. Companionship is both a goal and a prerequisite for friendship. Friendship is a goal in itself. It becomes perverted if it is used as a means for something else. To develop a friendship – to become virtuous in such a relationship – is something more than merely justifying the norms that can be used to evaluate actions. The main task is that of developing our capabilities, of acquiring the attitude that is a prerequisite for choosing correctly between alternative actions. It means that we must gain moral sense. Theoretical knowledge of norms and values is not the same as this practical wisdom (Greek: *phronesis*). Practical wisdom is derived from an ethical competence that is acquired through personal experience under the guidance of experienced people. It provides the discernment necessary for reasonable evaluation of the different (often ambiguous) situations in which we find ourselves. What is reasonable in each case can only be learned by this form of thoughtful practice. The so-called golden mean points back to such an acquirement of moral competence that can distinguish between what is reasonable and what is unreasonable in concrete situations.

THE JUST SOCIETY

Aristotle, like Plato, is preoccupied with the concept of *justice*. Aristotle distinguishes between justice based on existing right and justice based on principles of equality. Justice based on *existing right* includes both the explicit and implicit notions of justice found in a society. This covers both the existing laws and legal tradition *and* the traditions of what is legally acceptable. Justice on *principles of equality* is based on the conviction that each case of a certain kind is to be treated in the same way. This has to do with a requirement of consistency: if we do not treat similar cases alike, we are inconsistent, and, consequently, both irrational and unjust. This implies a 'natural rights' element in the principle of justice: it is seen as something universally valid, beyond what might be the existing legal practice (cf. Ch. 5, Stoicism).

Aristotle distinguishes between two kinds of justice on the basis of equality: what we can call justice as equality in trade and justice as equality in distribution. Equality in trade exists on the economic level through the market. A fair trade is a trade whereby one receives just as much as one gives. (Cf. the idea of an equal, and thus fair, trading value in the market, Ch. 13, Economic liberalism.) On the legal level, we should restore the balance after one person has inflicted harm or injury on another person. Fair restitution is what makes amends for the harm done. Fair punishment is to inflict equivalent damage/loss in quantity, but not in kind. Aristotle does not support the principle of 'an eye for an eye, a tooth for a tooth'.

An ordered society not only allows economic growth and legal control, but also establishes arrangements for distributing rights and duties, prosperity and burdens. What is to be distributed? And to whom? What is to be distributed may be taxes and fees, material benefits and legitimate power, the right to vote, or military duties. The salient point here is what is meant by stating that these things are to be distributed fairly by being distributed equally: equally, with regard to what? 'To all according to effort', or 'to all according to need'? Or equally regarding power, or riches, or virtue? Or an equal part to each person ('one man, one vote')? Aristotle advocates both egalitarian rules for distribution (equal parts to each person) and hierarchic rules for distribution (equal with regard to special functions and roles).

Aristotle distinguishes between practical and poetic disciplines, and includes ethics (moral theory) and politics (theory of the state) among the practical disciplines. We can say that for him, *praxis* is behaviour that is a goal in itself, and *poiesis* is behaviour whose goal is something different from the behaviour itself (preferably something new that is created by the behaviour).[17] In other words, children at play realize (approximately) the concept of *praxis*, and the electoral candidate who drinks a cup of coffee at the retirement home to win votes represents (approximately) the concept of *poiesis*. If we make friends to achieve benefits, we pervert something that should be a goal in itself, namely, friendship, by using it to achieve something else. Much of what we do represents *praxis* and *poiesis* in varying degrees and proportions.

When Aristotle primarily characterizes politics and ethics as *praxis*, and not as *poiesis*, this means that politics and ethics, for Aristotle, are actually types of behaviour that are in themselves an end: the end of rational social interaction, where people, in community, discuss problems. Society should be no larger, geographically or in population, than where people can know one another and can discuss their common problems. And society should not be so complex that one does not know *what* one is doing when one does it; that is, that actions do not get lost in a complicated and opaque society where so many different actions overlap that people lose the ability to see the consequences of their actions. But at the same time it is clear that even in the city-state of Aristotle's day, it was difficult for politics to be *pure praxis*. When the citizens of the city-state tried to solve the problems they discussed, they had to approve of actions where things and people, in various degrees, were used as means to achieve something different; that is, *poiesis* actions. For example, a decision could have been taken to use labourers to carry amphoras of wine aboard a galley, which was then rowed by slaves to the coast of the Black Sea, where the wine was traded for grain.[18]

From his experience in the city-state, Aristotle could view politics and ethics largely as rational, free interaction, as *praxis*; and rhetoric and poetry as *poiesis* undertaken to influence people (and to create something new). Aristotle's doctrine of the state, or politics, does not include political manipulation or empirical sociology. For Aristotle, politics, as a discipline, is primarily a normative and classificatory political science organized as follows:

1 collecting and classifying information about various city-states
2 pointing out the rules and ways of life that lead to the best life for citizens.

Aristotle supervised the collection of descriptions of 158 Greek city-states, and this material was classified according to the following scheme:

law	monarchy	aristocracy	limited democracy
lawlessness	tyranny	oligarchy	extreme democracy[19]
	one	few	many

Aristotle discussed which forms of the state are best, and emphasized, among other things, political stability: the opinions of the people must be heard; if not, the state will be unstable. And the state must be governed by law; if not, it will be unsafe for its citizens, corrupt, and subject to the arbitrary whims of those who rule. Thus, we must have a society governed by laws where people are permitted to express their views. In opposition to Plato, Aristotle believes, moreover, that public opinion can express cogent, considered insights. For Plato, 'the experts' had *all* the insight that was worth having. Public opinion was simply inferior. Aristotle thinks that a government by a 'good tyrant' never represents a genuine alternative to a society governed by laws. To be subordinate to another human being is to be not free but enslaved. Another person decides which 'style' (*ethos*) we should have. But to live virtuously and with dignity is to personally realize our own life, not to be 'trained' by others, like an animal. If we live under a common law, we can – within the limits of the law – safely realize our capabilities in society. A government by law, for Aristotle, is a condition in which people are able to realize their capabilities in the best way. Aristotle thus supports the view that public opinion is to be heard, and that the state should be governed by laws. On both points, he distinguishes his conceptions from Plato's ideal state in *The Republic*. But even for Aristotle the law is not universal: it is the established customs and the rules that apply to free, Greek men. Slaves and barbarians are not included, as the law does not apply universally.[20]

As we have mentioned, Aristotle discusses among other things the question of equality: equality with regard to *number* leads to democracy, government by the people. Equality with regard to *property* leads to plutocracy, government by the rich. Here Aristotle sees conflicting demands of power. What, then, are fair demands? How can they be balanced against each other? Property provides responsibility, according to Aristotle, and that is good for the state. And property indicates (more often than not) the presence of valuable capabilities. Ideally, it should be wisdom and virtue that count most, but they are difficult to measure. Riches, on the other hand, can be measured. But public opinion, the number of people in a group, must also count. Good insights may be found in the masses, and the government may become unstable if the masses are excluded. Aristotle says that everything should count for something. Property, education, birth, contacts – and number – everything is to count 'a little' in the distribution of power.

After extensive discussion, Aristotle comes to the conclusion that a limited democracy is the best state that we may hope for. This state is governed by law and it is a 'mixed government': the democratic principle of quantity (number) and the aristocratic principle of quality. Politics is based on laws so that everyone can be free, and so that many citizens can have a say in what goes on – many, but not all. Again, Aristotle avoids the extreme. 'The middle class' is to have the most power. It is neither rich nor poor. It has enough members that the state will have a broad base in the people, and few enough to ensure a basic transparency within the city-state. This form of government provides the best balance between public opinion and intelligent administration. For Aristotle, it is important that this is the most *feasible* form of government. He has little good to say about Plato's impracticable ideal state.[21]

ART – IMITATION AND CATHARSIS

With his four causes (or principles) Aristotle is able to make a distinction between things of nature and things of culture. The things (substances) that possess all four causes within themselves, including the moving (efficient) cause and the final cause, are things of nature. A standard example is the seed that under normal developmental conditions will grow into the plant that it is supposed to be, without interference by human beings, who provide neither efficient cause nor purpose to the process. On the other hand, the things that require interference by a human being to go through a change, both in terms of the efficient cause and of the final cause, are things of culture. The standard example here is the lump of clay that is transformed into a vase.

Things of culture are related to the creative actions of a human being. Such actions may be of two kinds. We may talk about obtaining something that nature does not provide, but that is useful for human well-being, as in tool production. Or we can talk about imitating nature, creating a copy of something that is found naturally, like a picture of a thoroughbred horse; that is, a work of art that gives us joy, without being useful. Both of these kinds of actions are included in the Greek word for art, *techne*. But it is the latter that corresponds to what we today understand by art. Art in the latter sense is, for Aristotle, characterized by two things. It pertains to copying, or *imitation*. And it pertains to that which gives joy in itself, independently of its usefulness. What is useful is good for something else, and this 'something else' is a good in itself. Art, however, represents something that is good precisely in itself. For Aristotle, the essence of art is that of a copy that gives joy in itself.

The basic idea of art as copying (or imitation) is an inheritance from Plato. But since Aristotle reinterprets the theory of ideas, he also views art as imitation (and cognition) differently from Plato. For Aristotle the 'forms' are *in* particular things. The perceptible things, then, have a higher status (in relation to forms) than for Plato. Art as the copying of perceptible things is therefore of more worth for Aristotle than for Plato. At the same time, Aristotle has a more democratic view of the insight that is needed to guide society and to live a virtuous life. Consequently, Aristotle has a more positive (cognitive and political) evaluation of the various forms of art.

Aristotle is more analytically discerning than Plato. Aristotle distinguishes, for example, between *theoria* (metaphysics, mathematics, philosophy of nature), *praxis* (ethics, politics), and *poiesis* (actions whose purpose is apart from the action itself [cf. *techne*]). The different activities are to a greater extent distinguished from each other. This allows more 'self-determination' (on its own premises) for each activity. For example, the aesthetic can, to a greater extent than in Plato, be evaluated primarily as aesthetics. The view of art as copying is connected with the notion that human beings by nature have a desire to learn and experience joy in learning and perception. Aesthetics comes from the Greek word *aisthanesthai*, which means to perceive. The imitations of the real teach us to perceive things in a special way. We see, for example, new sides of something; or we experience, in a new way, something we have previously seen; or we recognize something that we have already seen or experienced. The aesthetic perception is pleasurable both for 'the producer' (the artist) and for 'the consumer' (the person who experiences the work of art), in the sense that this experience is a good in itself (and not only useful for something else). But artists do not only need to imitate something that actually exists. They can also imitate what should be, and what should not be. A poet can, for example, present good and evil persons, heroes and criminals. Consequently, there is also in Aristotle a transition from aesthetics to ethics. For Aristotle, the function of art is also a moral one: it can purify, or cleanse. Most deeply, its function is *catharsis*, refining purification and cleansing.

The idea of art as catharsis is connected with inherent notions of harmony in Greek culture: the universe, the *cosmos* (the root of our word *cosmetics*), is in its essence harmonious and therefore beautiful. The ugly and the evil are disharmonic, out-of-balance. Therefore, sickness is understood as an imbalance among the different body fluids. If we have too much blood (*sanguis*), we become sanguine. If we have too much phlegm (*phlegma*), we become phlegmatic. If we have too much bile (*chole*), we become choleric. If we have too much black bile (*melaina chole*), we become melancholy. Bloodletting is therefore an appropriate therapy. An attempt to disrupt nature's harmony and balance represents an arrogance (*hubris*) that the gods will punish. The good society is one that is in harmony with itself; i.e., it is self-supporting and self-governing. In short, it keeps within the limits set by nature. The good life is a harmonious realization of the capabilities that we possess. Then we are virtuous. We should realize our potential in a well-balanced way. It is precisely because of this that we must avoid extremes, like cultivating certain sides of ourselves at the expense of others, or in such a way that we go beyond our natural capabilities and potential, or abuse the resources that have been given by nature. The ecological implications here are fairly clear. The notion of exponential growth could serve as a prime example of destructive insanity.

In accordance with these points of view, Aristotle ascribes to art the function of re-creating spiritual balance. By experiencing works of art, as in music and drama, we can restore harmony and peace, eventually ennobling our mind. Here there are two interpretations:

1   Art is *catharsis* in the sense that we can 'let off steam'.[21] By experiencing a drama, with heroes, villains, and grand feelings, we can find a release for suppressed passions and uncontrollable feelings, so that we can recover our harmony and resume living by the ideal of *the 'golden mean'*. This is the therapeutic interpretation, in line with the medical therapy based on the theory of fluids: those who have excessively grand and intense feelings can find

release for them through art and can thus experience a kind of spiritual blood-letting. And those whose feelings are too fragile can be filled with a moderate dose of emotion.

2   Art is *catharsis* in the sense that we, as human beings, are purified and educated through our encounter with art. The point is then not that we rid ourselves of certain emotions (as in spiritual bloodletting), but that we, through our experiences, *ennoble* our mind. We aspire to personal growth beyond the ordinary.

For Aristotle, art is a good (or purpose) in itself for the person who is experiencing the work of art. The creative process may also, for the artist, be a good in itself; but at the same time, the point of the creative process is to achieve a product, the work of art. Hence, the creative process is predetermined by a purpose that lies apart from the process itself. In this connection, it is natural to mention Aristotle's treatment of rhetoric as a means to gain a hearing. Here, as in art in general, Aristotle has a more positive attitude than Plato. According to Aristotle, rhetoric has a place in public debate.[23]

QUESTIONS

Explain Plato's view of the ideas and Aristotle's view of the substances and discuss the relationship between these two viewpoints. Discuss their similarities and differences.

Explain Aristotle's view of what exists and what knowledge is, and compare Plato's view in this respect.

In Aristotle's philosophy we encounter the concepts of form and matter, potentiality and actuality. Explain what he means by these concepts and explain what role they play in his philosophy. Give examples.

Compare Aristotle's view of nature and that of Democritus. In what sense can it be said that Aristotle has an ecological view of nature?

Discuss the relationship between Aristotle's ontology and his ethics.

Describe Plato's and Aristotle's views of women, and explain how each of these views is connected to basic concepts in their respective philosophies.

SUGGESTIONS FOR FURTHER READING

PRIMARY LITERATURE

The Nichomachean Ethics
Posterior Analytics
Metaphysics
Rhetoric
De Anima

These texts are found in *The Complete Works of Aristotle*, revised Oxford translation (2 vols), edited by Jonathan Barnes, Princeton, NJ, 1984.

SECONDARY LITERATURE

Barker, E., *The Political Thought of Plato and Aristotle*, London, 1906.
Jaeger, W., *Aristotle. Fundamentals of the History of His Development*, London, 1967.
Lear, J., *Aristotle: The Desire to Understand*, Cambridge, 1988.

NOTES

1 Cf. *lycée*, French secondary school.
2 For example, Aristotle uses arguments of the following kind: if the idea of *the green* is what all green things have in common, we have two alternatives. First, we can say that the idea of the green is *itself green*, but then the idea of the green is, at the same time, an element proper to itself. And we can then ask whether there is not a *third something* that is common to the green idea of the green and the particular green things (and then we can again ask the same question about this third something; this is called the 'argument about the third man'). Second, we can say that the idea of the green is *not* green, but then it becomes difficult to make sense of the claim that the idea of the green is what all green things have in common.
3 The Aristotelian distinctions often seem, to begin with, simple and easily understandable. But when we look closer at them, they soon become complex. For instance, we may ask: *what* remains in the independently existing particular object when all the properties having a relative existence are removed?
4 For Aristotle, knowledge *starts* with sense experience. But by reflecting on sense experiences, such as the sense experiences of different horses, human beings can recognize the form of *horse* that is *in* these particular horses. And by further reflection on the forms, philosophical knowledge becomes possible. We can say that Aristotle views the different theoretical sciences as different *grades of abstraction* from everyday experience: in *the world of life* we have immediate sense experience of material things. *Physics* represents an abstraction from the distinct and accidental properties of particular material things: not this rock, here and now, but the rock as a physical object, with a certain weight and a certain motion, is the object of physics. *Mathematics* represents a further abstraction: this time from the thing's material properties, so that the thing appears only as geometric forms or numerical values (numbers). Finally, by means of further abstraction, we come to *metaphysics*, in which we are concerned with the completely universal principles and properties. Aristotle can thus be said to move from sense experience and *upwards*, by means of abstraction. Plato, on the other hand, starts, in a certain sense, 'up', and moves 'down' towards the world of sense: the dialectical insight into the ideas is what is certain (when this insight first is attained). We move 'down', through mathematics, physics, and the humanities, towards more and more changeable objects which then give more and more transient and uncertain insight. (Thus, for Plato, no one begins in the world of ideas. We all have to wander 'up' and 'down' in a lifelong attempt to attain the best possible insight into the ideas.)
5 This Aristotelian theory of knowledge that emphasizes inductive inferences leading towards definition of essence, and deductive inferences from this definition, was greatly criticized during the expansion of the new experimental sciences in the 1500s and 1600s (cf. Ch. 7).
6 We may compare the Aristotelian tripartite division of plants, animals, and human beings, based on the life principles of taking in nourishment and reproduction, sense perception and effort, and reason, with Plato's tripartite division of the producers, the 'controllers', and the thinkers.
7 From this we can go on to talk about *overdescribing* and *underdescribing* a phenomenon. To attribute human properties to animals is to overdescribe animals. That is what we do in adventures and fables, as when the fox and the bear talk to each other. Speech is an ability that is connected with the rational principle of life that human beings possess, but not animals. A description of such talking animals is then not true. But if we do not attribute to human beings anything more than animal properties, we underdescribe human beings. To describe them this way is to a certain extent true – because human beings also possess all of the animal principles of life – but it is, in a qualitative sense, insufficient. Animism – the attribution of spiritual properties to rocks and trees – is a type of overdescription that is not very common in our society. However, to view human beings exclusively as representing principles of life that are below the human principle of life ('naturalistic reduction') is a type of underdescription that is not quite so unusual for us ('human beings are after all nothing more than physiological organisms'). But what is the correct description of human beings? That remains a difficult and controversial question.
8 From *our* conceptual terms, this description applies well to plants and animals, but not quite as

well to lifeless things. Thus, Aristotle and Democritus represent two alternative *monistic* natural philosophies.

9 The theoreticians first appearing during the Renaissance who interpreted events as seen from the natural sciences could hardly explain the social sides of reality. And since the social sciences seriously began to take shape in the last century, we have lived continually with this tension between *action* and *event* in connection with the basic problems investigated by the social sciences.

10 This natural philosophy was called 'physics', that is, a doctrine about *physis* ('nature'). Because the Aristotelian writings that discuss the first philosophy were placed *after* the philosophy of nature ('physics'), the first philosophy was called *metaphysics* (*meta ta physica* 'after physics').

11 We could say that Aristotle's natural philosophy springs from his interest in understanding the nature that human beings experience, unlike modern scientists, who are interested in *controlling* nature – in the latter case, the experimental hypothetical-deductive method and abstract mathematical concepts are the correct ones (cf. Ch. 7, The dispute over method).

12 Not only does the mechanistic view of nature have a tendency to misplace the qualitative 'leftovers', like sensory properties and values, for human beings, but this mechanistic perspective on nature also goes hand in hand with an emphasis on the human ability to control phenomena in nature. Descartes' distinction between the thinking thing (*res cogitans*) and the extended thing (*res extensa*) parallels a view of society that divides all being into two: the profit-calculating leadership and the raw materials. Whether the raw materials are animals, rocks, or human bodies, they are all objects for the calculating subject, who by virtue of intelligence can exploit and control the objects.

13 *Politics*, 1261a 10ff.

14 This view is in conflict with, among other things, the opinions of Hegel and Marx, who both claimed that *labour* represents formation, 'humanization', in history: 'the master' is necessary, but only as a catalyst; it is not the master, but 'the servant' who, through labour, gains knowledge and insight, and who, through labour, creates history, and moulds human beings. But the positions are, of course, not easy to compare on this point, since Aristotle lived at the beginning of a historical development that Hegel and Marx had behind them and that they could reflect on. We will later see how Hegel and Marx take over the idea that human beings first become themselves through a social development; but Hegel and Marx see this as a *historical* development, that is, a development that takes place over many generations, and not only as a development for each individual person.

15 See Anne Dickason, 'Anatomy and Destiny: The Role of Biology in Plato's Views of Women', in Carol C. Gould and Marx W. Wartofsky (eds), *Women and Philosophy*, New York, 1976, pp. 45–53.

16 This is a typically Greek idea. Even the idealist Plato emphasizes that education is to begin with *gymnastics* and *music*, and end with *practical duties*: all abilities are to be harmoniously developed.

17 *Poiesis* also means *creating something new*. Poetry, then, is *poiesis*, not *praxis*.

18 The view of politics, in light of the distinction between *praxis* and *poiesis*, has varied along with the changing forms of society. Perhaps we can make a rough sketch of it in this way: along with the transition from the city-state to the great Hellenistic empire, a certain depoliticization and political indifference developed due to the lack of political rights in a despotic, mammoth state. But the introduction of the absolute monarchy after the Renaissance, when national kings restructured the feudal aristocracies, led to the view of politics as *Realpolitik*, as manipulation (Machiavelli); i.e., as *poiesis* in Aristotelian terminology. Later, society became more and more complex, in step with industrialization: the discovery of gold in America could create unemployment in London. Society was no longer immediately transparent to its members. Specialists who could explain the implications of people's actions were needed: as a result, empirical sociology developed (Comte). But gradually, as bureaucratization and manipulation increased (M. Weber), there has been a reaction, where, among other things, we seek to find a more important place for *praxis*, for rational interaction that is meaningful in itself. Aristotle's distinction between *praxis* and *poiesis* has thus again become current within a society completely different from the Greek city-state.

19 Democracy: government by the people; plutocracy: government by the economically powerful; oligarchy: government by a small group of all-powerful persons; monarchy: government by a single ruler.

20 In that respect, Aristotle is not advocating natural rights. On the other hand, he advocates certain norms for interpersonal relations that are objectively seen to be the best. Thus, he thinks that *justice*, which for him is characterized by law and by equal treatment, is a valid basic principle. If we emphasize that Aristotle recognizes universally valid ethical-political principles, we can say that natural rights theory does have its roots in Aristotle (just as in Plato).

21 It is worth noting that Aristotle takes for granted that *few* are rich and that *many* are poor. That it is theoretically possible to have many who are rich and few who are poor is uninteresting to one who is starting with the realities of Aristotle's day. Aristotle considers a large gap between the rich and the poor as *politically* dangerous (it makes for unstable conditions), as well as *morally* deplorable. Like Plato, Aristotle believes that the main purpose of the state is *ethical*: the good life.

22 From the Greek *katharizo*, 'I cleanse'.

23 Cf. rhetoric's place within the university tradition (Ch. 6).

5 The late classical period

SECURING THE INDIVIDUAL'S HAPPINESS

FROM GREEK CITY-STATE TO HELLENISTIC EMPIRE

Plato spoke for the view that society may be an object of rational study, and may be influenced by intelligent leadership. And Aristotle spoke for the view that society is defined by the relationship among free, morally equal members of society, that it must be governed by law, and that the government must be based on free discussion, not on power alone. As an ideal these viewpoints were to live on, even after the Greek city-states were assimilated into the Hellenistic empire, although after this assimilation it became even more difficult to realize these ideals. Aristotle and Plato understood that the type of politics they espoused presupposed a relatively small society. Aristotle thought that the city-state, the *polis*, had to have a reasonable size: not so small that it is dependent on others, and not so large that its inhabitants do not know one another and that discussion becomes difficult in large assemblies. As we know, Plato claimed (in *The Laws*) that the city-state should have 5,040 citizens (households). Plato and Aristotle both thought that this city-state should be an independent unit. But the individual Greek city-states were dependent on each other and on the world around them. And towards the end of the fourth century BC we have the formation of a new state: the Hellenistic empire. This transition from city-state to empire entailed changes on both the institutional and the intellectual levels.

During the entire Hellenistic-Roman period, from *c.* 300 BC to *c.* AD 400, states were large, both geographically and in population, and included peoples diverse culturally, religiously, and linguistically. The local community, where all could participate, was weakened, even if the cities, both in Hellenistic and Roman times, did have a certain amount of internal self-rule and could from time to time assert themselves politically. The result was large states with power concentrated in certain central agencies, whether the state was a monarchy or a republic. As a means of holding together a national mosaic of different ethnic groups without natural solidarity, the king was sometimes depicted as divine, a policy that strengthened the state's central authority. The dissolution of the relatively autonomous small states and the tendency to concentrate power involved an increasing political powerlessness among the people. In addition to all of the relatively powerless, *free* men, we have the even more powerless *women* and *slaves*.

NEW CONSTELLATIONS: INDIVIDUAL AND UNIVERSAL LAW

Much of what was written during the Hellenistic-Roman period has been lost. The presentation in this chapter is a hypothetical reconstruction. With this reservation, we can probably say that this political powerlessness of the people in early Hellenism, was reflected on the intellectual level as a general tendency to refrain from philosophical speculation about society – there is so little that we can do! – and to concentrate on one thing: how can a person secure his or her own happiness? For example, regardless of how Epicureanism and Stoicism differed, and how great the variations were in these two schools, we can, to simplify, say that both of these philosophies, which were in many ways dominant during the Hellenistic-Roman period, focused on this one question of how to guarantee the individual's happiness. The answers differed, but the basic question was in essence the same.

As a general hypothesis, we can say that there was a universal change from concern with man-in-community to concern with the isolated, private individual. To put it briefly, in the Greek city-states, people were generally seen as an organic part of society. Each person was supposed to find his place and to realize himself in participation in various public activities. Each person's nature and worth were thus linked to the community. When the city-states declined and the Hellenistic-Roman period began, we encounter at the same time

1   the idea of a universal law valid for all human beings and embodied in each individual
2   the idea of a private individual with a basic value in himself, independent of his particular upbringing and social status.

This is, of course, a simplification. Already in certain pre-Socratic philosophers we find a tendency to view the individual as being self-sufficient, while at the same time we find traces of the view that there are universal norms and principles that apply to everyone. It can still be interesting to entertain this hypothesis that the concept and the reality of *the particular individual* arise around roughly the same time as the concept and the reality of *the universal state*. The classical Greek notion of 'man-in-community', which was linked to the city-state, lost ground. On the one side, we have the particular individual, and on the other side, an empire – on the one hand, the virtue and happiness of the individual; on the other, the concept of universal law, valid for everyone everywhere. It is as if there were a dichotomy between the particular and the universal:

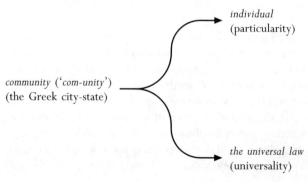

individual
(particularity)

community ('*com-unity*')
(the Greek city-state)

the universal law
(universality)

For most Greeks, the law applied only to people in a local community. But as a dialectic counterpart to the view of the human being as an individual, we now have the view of the law as a universal law applicable to all persons regardless of nationality and social standing. This is one of the roots of the concept of natural rights: there is a *universal*, *normative law* above all existing laws that applies to everyone. It follows that all people are, in principle, subject to the same law, and that existing law in a society is subject to appeal to this universal, natural law.

We will come back to the concept of the individual in our discussion of liberalism in the eighteenth century. It will now suffice to indicate that such a change from man-in-community to the individual and to universal law coincided with a loss of political involvement, and a development of the ideal of a unique personhood and a private happiness, under a common law. The Greek unity of ethics and politics was blown apart, and the emphasis moved to the ethical in a private sense, while the political moved to the background. Only the Roman Stoics valued politics. But the word *politics* then took on a different meaning from that of Plato and Aristotle: it came to mean primarily the general, legal principles of ruling an empire, not the rational discussion regulating public activity in the local community of a *polis*.

EPICUREANISM – SECURING THE INDIVIDUAL'S WELL-BEING

The term *Epicureanism* is derived from Epicurus (341–271 BC). In his school, The Garden, known for its friendly and cultivated atmosphere, women and slaves were also welcome, an unusual practice in antiquity.

Epicureanism answered the question of how to secure each person's happiness as follows: enjoy life, but with consideration. That is to say, the good life is a life of well-being and an absence of pain and suffering. To achieve the maximum well-being and the minimum suffering during our life, we must *calculate*. For example, should I seek brief, intense pleasure now, taking a chance on suffering later, or should I delay pleasure now, in the hope of attaining long-lasting well-being later? We ought to weigh gain and loss for the alternative options. In other words, this is the province of the cultivated, self-conscious hedonist! Seek pleasure, but let it be calculated pleasure. To put it bluntly, don't get involved in politics or other matters that entail worry and risk. Instead, live in a protected circle where you can enjoy your cheese and wine in peace and quiet. The Epicureans, then, were not sensualists who blindly plunged into an immoral life of overindulgence. On the contrary, Epicurus recommended caution and deliberation in life, because it is only pleasure that we are in *control of* that *guarantees* happiness. We can summarize the Epicurean philosophy of life in two points.

1   The only good that exists is pleasure.
2   To secure maximum pleasure, we must enjoy only the pleasures that we can control.

A doctrine that takes pleasure (Greek: *hedoné*) as the highest (only) good is called 'hedonism'; i.e., the philosophy of pleasure. We might say that Epicureanism is hedonism informed by precaution and deliberation. In the first place, the Epicureans did not view pleasure as momentary sensual lust; Epicureanism emphasized more refined and secure forms of well-being, like friendship and literary pursuits. If we want to secure our private happiness, we should pursue these more certain and refined pleasures.

At the same time, Epicureanism deprecated political activity, which can cause much worry and little certain pleasure. It did not view the state or society as something that has value in itself.[1] Only pleasure – and pleasure is necessarily the individual's pleasure – has value in itself. The state and society are only good when they promote the individual's pleasure and prevent the individual's pain. Laws and conventions only have value as a means of promoting individual interests.[2] What keeps people from breaking the law is the fear of punishment; that is, fear of pain. Everything is based on individual pleasure. Good morality or a good system of law is what maximizes individual pleasure. There is no foundation for right and morality beyond this. (But *who* determines that the pleasure of ten other people outweighs *my* displeasure? And how can I *compare* different kinds of pleasure?[3])

The natural philosophy that we find in Epicureanism – and that largely seems to correspond to Democritus' materialistic theory of atoms – supported, in a way, this philosophy of life: since everything is material, including the soul and the distant, indifferent gods, we should not allow ourselves to be frightened by religious strictures.

Unlike Epicurus' teaching, a radical hedonism which says that physical pleasure/enjoyment is the *only* thing that counts in life may appeal to persons having relatively good access to all goods and services, and who can count on a surplus of pleasure and enjoyment in relation to need and suffering. But for the great majority of people in antiquity, such a theory could easily have had fatal consequences: if most people tried to 'calculate' the relationship between suffering and pleasure, the average answer might turn out to be negative. The sum of suffering would easily exceed the sum of pleasure. According to radical hedonism, such a life would not be worthwhile. It was therefore not merely eccentricity when the hedonistic philosopher Hegesias in the third century BC recommended suicide. For people condemned to suffering by a grim fate, pure hedonism could become advocacy of suicide.

STOICISM – SECURING THE INDIVIDUAL'S HAPPINESS

MAIN POINTS OF STOICISM

The Stoics were generally more doubtful than the Epicureans of our ability to control the external good. The Stoics therefore recommended that each person become independent of external factors. If we want to secure our happiness, we must learn to be as independent of these uncontrollable external things as possible, and learn to live in our inner selves, which we can control. The Stoics claimed that happiness is really not dependent on any external good. They took the same position as Socrates and Plato: the only condition for a person's happiness is that he or she lead a virtuous life, and virtue is based on knowledge. The Stoics maintained this position with complete consistency. To live virtuously is the only good for a human being. Not to live virtuously is the only evil. Everything else is, in the final analysis, irrelevant or without importance when it comes to the question of living happily.

Life, health, prosperity – or death, sickness, pain, and poverty – cannot affect the happiness of the wise and virtuous person. The differences that we find in people's external circumstances do not indicate whether they are happy or unhappy. Whether we meet adversity in life or are externally successful and gain honour and recognition does not matter; nor whether we are rich or poor, masters or slaves. The decisive distinction is that between the wise and virtuous, and those who are not so. The former are happy. The latter are not. Knowledge, virtue, and happiness are linked to the inner life and are independent of all external circumstances.

What insight and virtue is it that can render a person indifferent to all decrees of fate? The Stoics said that virtue is living in accordance with reason, with *logos*. *Logos* is the leading principle in the cosmos, as Heraclitus said. They also called this principle God, the divine fire, or fate. People can open themselves to *logos* so that their souls become harmonious and ordered in accordance with the cosmos. In a way, the soul then reflects the order and harmony that rule in the cosmos. The most important insight is probably the realization that everything is ordered wisely and that it is neither possible nor desirable to interfere in events. Everything is guided by *logos*, or God. Man's task is to learn to accept joyfully everything that happens. 'Whatever happens to you, you should bear it as if you wanted it to happen to you. Because you ought to desire it if you knew that everything happens according to God's will.' This was written by Seneca, a Roman Stoic.[4] The Stoics thus preached an ascetic morality with respect to the external world and education for inner strength of character. A person is to show a Stoic serenity, that is to say, passionlessness (apathy), in the face of the decrees of fate.

To this Stoic position on how we can secure our happiness, it is possible to object that it may be just as difficult to master 'the inner' sphere as it is to master many external circumstances. This objection is certainly weighty. But, at the same time, we should remember that the ability to control nature (illnesses, crop failure, etc.) was relatively small during the Hellenistic-Roman period. If, for us, it seems to be easier to remove an appendix than to control our anger, the situation was reversed in antiquity. It was therefore not completely unrealistic for the Stoics to recommend that people control what could be controlled, namely, their own minds. Corresponding to the change from man-in-community to the private individual, the *mind* was understood to be something inward, divorced from both nature and the social world. This was, in a sense, un-Greek: ethics was now divorced from politics. Each person was to cultivate the self, independently of society and environment. We find the idea of a private morality, divorced from society. Perhaps epicureanism never found very many adherents. Stoicism, on the other hand, had a large following and influence, not least in Roman times. And both the ethical and the legal ideas in Stoicism had an impact on medieval philosophy. But Stoicism was not a homogeneous movement. A fundamental development took place within it, from Greek to Roman Stoics.

THE CYNICS

The Cynics were one of the so-called Socratic schools in antiquity. The name points to a certain connection between Socrates (and the Sophists) and philosophical tendencies in the Hellenistic-Roman time.

The Cynics may be said to represent people with few goods. Instead of inciting such people to futile rebellion, the Cynics encouraged them to learn to be satisfied without the goods that they could not have anyway. The Cynics withdrew from society and lived in a simple and partly primitive manner – something they thought was a natural way of life for man (in direct opposition to the Aristotelian understanding of human nature). Hence the Cynic Diogenes from Sinope (*c.* 404– 324 BC), who lived in a barrel, praised the natural and despised the artificial. If cultivated hedonism is purely escapism,[5] and individual hedonists (Hegesias) preached a self-effacing ideology, the Cynics taught the underprivileged to be satisfied with what they had, even if they had hardly anything.

GRECO-HELLENISTIC STOICISM

With the Greco-Hellenistic Stoics – Zenon (*c.* 326–264 BC), Cleanthes (331–233 BC), and Chrysippos (*c.* 278–204 BC) – we find a kind of 'middle-class' emphasis: duty and character formation are emphasized, and not just ascetic withdrawal from the world. In addition, the Stoics began to formulate a natural law that applies to all people. Stoicism changed further after it increasingly became an ideology for the upper levels of society: the Stoic emphasis on duty and character formation and belief in universal laws appealed to the Roman upper class, who eventually turned Stoicism into a kind of state ideology. At the same time, the world-renouncing features of lower-class Cynicism were suppressed in favour of a state-supporting morality based on duty and the cultivation of a strong and responsible character. Only a vestige remained of the original withdrawal from the world: a distinction between the internal and private, and the external and public. Stoics write down their innermost thoughts in private (Marcus Aurelius the philosopher), while at the same time publicly performing their duties to society (Marcus Aurelius the emperor).

ROMAN STOICISM

With the Roman Stoics – Cicero (106–43 BC), Seneca (4 BC–AD 65), Epictetus (*c.* AD 50–138), and Marcus Aurelius (AD 121–180) – the earlier ascetic and individualistic withdrawal from the world shifted to a tension between withdrawal and political duty. In the Roman Stoics we can trace the change in Greek political concepts that we previously postulated; roughly, it meant that a person was no longer considered an organic part of a group, but an individual under a universal legal code and system of government. All individuals were, in principle, equal before the law, and their rights were determined not by their function, but by the universal law that is applicable everywhere at all times. Here we meet the idea of *natural law* in its fully developed form.

Just as a person's world is part of the cosmos, so that person's reason is part of the universal reason. Correspondingly, human laws are aspects of the eternal law that apply to the whole cosmos. That is why we, in principle, can distinguish between the laws of society that are in accordance with the eternal law, and those that are not. We can thus distinguish between laws that are valid by virtue of their conformity to the eternal law, and those that claim to be valid only because they exist, without being valid according to the universal, natural law. Human reason, which in its various forms has its basis in a common world reason, is a given, something that exists. This is an essential point in natural law theory: the legal-political laws are grounded in a universal law of nature. The foundation for the laws is not something created by individuals or by groups, as by powerful persons deciding what is law and what is right ('might is right'). The valid laws exist. And because they exist, we can discover them, explicate them, and make known what we have discovered. But we cannot invent laws. The foundation for law is thus raised above humanity's arbitrary wishes. It is also raised above the diversity of actually existing, and partly conflicting, legal codes. The foundation for law is then not relative. And because all individuals share in the universal reason and the common law, all people are fundamentally similar. The natural law applies to all people everywhere. The basic features of the Stoic view of right were largely adopted by Roman statesmen and legal scholars, including the eclectic Cicero, whose works were often read in later centuries. The Stoics distanced themselves from the claim of certain Sophists that a universally valid right or morality does not exist, and that laws are only relative. In the same way, they opposed the Epicureanean view that laws are only valid as long as they promote people's individual desires. In rejecting relativism and holding that a universally valid right exists, the Stoics agreed with Plato and Aristotle. But on the source of the law, and how legal principles can be justified, the Stoic interpretation differed from Aristotle's. According to Aristotle, the basic legal principles are connected to human society, primarily the city-state. Here these basic principles are potentially present and, to some degree, in actuality. By collecting information about the legal codes of various city-states and systematizing this information, we can find out the best rules for society. In this way we find out what legal norms exist in a good society. By comparison with these norms we can identify what is bad in the existing code, and we can formulate new laws. For example, according to Aristotle, the wealth of the state should be distributed more harmoniously: large disparities between people cause tension in society. A degree of equality of citizens is necessary if a society is to be healthy. Therefore, it is an important goal of the legal code to create a reasonably balanced distribution of wealth. This means that Aristotle advocates a *certain* equalization of social differences, although he by no means supports complete equality. He accepts, among other things, slavery and class divisions, and he criticizes the democrats for a too simplistic view of equality. The starting point for the Stoic view of law is not, as in Aristotle, the city-state and man-in-community, but the universal reason, which is present in each individual: in each person there is a spark of the 'divine fire', another word for reason. For the Stoics, this is a person's true nature, common human nature. The Stoics derived natural law from this universal reason. This common nature, universal reason, is the source of law, to use an expression from Cicero.

A human being is not primarily a social being, as in Aristotle, but an individual possessing a spark of the universal *logos*. This allows human beings to found society, to formulate a legal code, and to promulgate laws. Those who are best able to make just laws are the wisest persons. In them reason is present in its purest form. 'In the soul of the wise is found the perfect law,' says Cicero.[6] In Cicero we see how the Stoic view of natural law, which claimed that there is an unchangeable, universal legal code above all given and changeable legal systems, can also be used to justify existing laws. Hence he claims that the old Roman 'rights of the fathers' largely expressed this universal law. Existing law and existing inequalities are thus justified by natural law, according to Cicero. This points to something principally ambiguous in natural law theory: it can be used to justify existing law, just as it can be used to criticize existing law. It can function both as a conservative and a transforming force in society. (Cf. the Church-state relationship, Ch. 6.)

But does not Stoic natural law claim a fundamental *equality* among all human beings? How can one, then, at the same time accept existing differences? The answer is partly found in a certain ambiguity in the Stoic view of equality: everyone participates in the common *logos*, and all people are, in this sense, equal; but at the same time, it is basically irrelevant to a good and happy life whether one is rich or poor, king or slave. The main goal, therefore, is not to intervene in the world in order to change it. The main goal is that we meet all of the decrees of fate with a perfect serenity. In other words, it is not clear that the fundamental equality is influenced by the actual social differences; it is not clear that the fundamental equality requires actualization of equality in the material and political areas. For Cicero, the statesman, the answer may also be found in *realpolitik* conditions: regardless of the fundamental equality of human beings, existing societies function only through the differences. Differences are inevitable. Thus, Cicero does not see the need for the legal code to secure a reasonable distribution of property. It is a basic principle, according to Cicero, that we should not hurt others, as by stealing property, and that we should keep our promises. Thus, he strongly emphasizes that property ownership is to be respected and that contracts are to be honoured.

Through Cicero's writings, especially *On the Laws*, *On Duties*, and *On the State*, Stoic thinking had a great influence on Roman legal thought. 'True law is right reason in agreement with nature; it is of universal application, unchanging and everlasting; it summons to duty by its commands, and averts from wrongdoing by its prohibitions. . . . We cannot be freed from its obligations by senate or people. . . . There will not be different laws at Rome and Athens, or different laws now and in the future, but one eternal and unchangeable law will be valid for all nations and all times. . . . Whoever is disobedient is fleeing from himself and denying his human nature, and by reason of this very fact he will suffer the worst penalties, even if he escapes what is commonly considered punishment.'[7]

The idea of innate, inviolable individual rights and the idea of an eternal and universal law are connected. Such thoughts fit in well with the Roman Empire, with its different peoples: ideas such as these provided the basis for a certain amount of tolerance – at least as an ideal, if not always as a reality.

In a way, the Roman Stoics had a universal sense of collective responsibility that the Greeks largely lacked. The Stoics advocated a cosmopolitan solidarity and humanity. They had a religious conviction that all people participated in a cosmological and moral whole. But the ideal of such a cosmopolitan brotherhood can also be interpreted as an attempt, in theory, to overcome the lack of intimacy in the Roman Empire: there was a great distance from Bethlehem to Rome, and there was a great distance from the individual to the emperor. To overcome this distance, the Stoics postulated a harmony between the individual and the universe. They spoke of the fire that is both in God and in man, and that thus vouches for the brotherhood of man.

The Stoics also spoke of a fire that at regular intervals destroys everything, as at Armageddon, after which the world begins anew, but the new world repeats what happened in the previous world. This new world continues until a new fire devours it; the process then repeats itself, with new worlds and new fires. The Stoics thus had a *circular* view of world history. The world does not move forward, linearly – or upwards or downwards – but *circularly*. Everything repeats itself like the four seasons. These cosmological ideas about fire probably functioned as a justification for the Stoic philosophy of life. If everything repeats itself, it is not possible to better the world. We can only endure the best we can. One person is an emperor, another is a slave. There is nothing we can do about it. We can only play the role we have been given with as much dignity as possible. Such a cyclic philosophy of history can thus be fatalistic and antirevolutionary. But this is not strictly necessary. What if this cyclic process includes the idea that we, at a certain point, revolt or carry out social reforms? In some of the Roman Stoics there is at least the trace of a wish for social reform. In opposition to the Cynics – who thought simply that people were equal but that nothing could be done about it – these Stoics thought that everyone was, in principle, equal before the law, but not in reality: equality does not exist at present, but it is an end. Human legislation and humane politics are means to realize the ideal, if only that could, to some degree, be done.

There is also a seed of social criticism in that the natural law and the laws in the Roman state were not obviously identical. And this dichotomy between the literally universal (the laws of the empire) and the ideally universal (natural law) became a theoretical basis for the distinction between the emperor and the pope, as we will see later. Jurisprudence, as a discipline in its own right, can be said to have been founded by Roman lawyers, whose thinking was generally close to Stoicism.

All the movements that we have mentioned are sometimes called the Socratic schools, since they, each in its own way, carried on Socrates' legacy. They shared the Socratic opinion that virtue is happiness, and that virtue can, in a certain sense, be learned. If we keep to the interpretation that we have indicated above, and say that these movements attempted to answer the question of how a person's happiness can be secured, we can probably conclude that none of these philosophies of life had a satisfactory answer. Some of their answers presupposed material wealth – and relatively few were wealthy in antiquity. And all of the answers reflected the common view that people could not always escape unhappiness: even the most convinced Stoic did not always manage to feel happy when struck down by a painful and deadly illness. In that sense, none of these doctrines of the philosophies of life could guarantee a person's happiness. This was the conclusion that gained support towards the end of antiquity: the doctrines of the philosophies of life, created by man for man, could not fulfil what they had promised. How, then, to secure happiness? The answer was close at hand: by supernatural means, by religion. Towards the end of antiquity there was an increasing religious longing.

NEOPLATONISM

Neoplatonism sought to meet the religious longing that emerged in Hellenistic times. The Neoplatonist doctrine places the individual in a larger cosmological picture, and portrays evil as a privation, as non-being, the body (matter) being seen as non-being and the soul as being. The goal is to liberate the soul from its mortal frame (the body), so that the personal soul can experience the all-encompassing union with the world-soul. Plotinus (205–270 AD), who lived in Alexandria, Egypt, developed an interpretation of Platonism that deviates from the dualistic theory of ideas, and that instead conceives the universe as a hierarchic interplay of light and darkness. The core of the universe is said to be the inexpressible 'One', which we, through our reason, can approach, but not describe: it is the final basis (*Urgrund*) of the universe. It radiates Being to all that is, like a source of light that illuminates the surroundings in such a way that the light rays diminish as they radiate from the source of light until they are extinguished in the dark. This doctrine of radiation, or emanation, implies that the spiritual *Urgrund* is Being in the highest potency and the centre of power that upholds all things, while matter is conceived as non-being. Hence there is a hierarchy from the immaterial and inexpressible *Urgrund* (the One) down to the increasingly material and perishable phenomena. Through their spiritual nature, human beings can seek to approach this *Urgrund*. But as a bodily being man partakes of the non-being of matter. Therefore there is a tension between soul and body. But human beings can seek to approach the *Urgrund*. The goal is a union of the soul with the forces of light coming from the One (the *Urgrund*). This union cannot be expressed propositionally. Hence it is an inexpressible union, *unio mystica*.

Neoplatonism focuses on supernatural forces. But still it is a *doctrine*, not *life* – even though Neoplatonism was experienced by some as a concrete reality. But only with Christianity, with its message of a living, personal God and a redeeming paradise, did the religious longing find a satisfying answer for a larger group of people. In the fourth century, Christianity became the official religion of the Roman Empire. Antiquity ebbed away and the Christian Middle Ages stood at the door.

SCEPTICISM

The Sceptics of antiquity, such as Pyrrho (*c.* 360–270 BC), Carneades (*c.* 213–128 BC), and Sextus Empiricus (*c.* 200 AD), were primarily concerned with epistemological questions; generally, they tended to adopt a cautious or negative view of epistemological questions of truth and rightness. They thus belong to the epistemological tradition of the Greek Sophists – just as the Epicureans and Stoics adopted and developed further the tradition of moral philosophy of Socrates.

However, in an epistemological sense, scepticism is an ambiguous concept.[8] It can, for example, be helpful to distinguish between the type of sceptic who directly or indirectly claims that we cannot know anything (cf. our interpretation of Gorgias) and the type who does not claim that we cannot know anything, but who keeps searching without taking a stand (Greek: *sceptikos* 'enquirer'). We will outline a few modern interpretations of important sceptical arguments, stemming from Hellenistic Scepticism.

THE SENSES DO NOT GIVE US CERTAIN KNOWLEDGE

The sense impressions that a person receives from objects in the world are dependent not only on the objects, but also on the relationship of the object to the person having the sense experience (such as distance), on the conditions of the sense organs, and on the general condition of the person having the sense experience (whether the person is awake or asleep, sober or drunk, etc.).[9]

We recognize these problems since our senses sometimes 'deceive us', as in varying emotional states, varying visual angles and distances, and various forms of intermediate conditions, like water, fog, steam, etc. All of these influence our sense impressions. Moreover, there are various differences in perception between individuals; what is sweet or cold for one individual may not be so to another.

The ancient Sceptics emphasized that we can never extricate ourselves from these difficulties: they apply, in principle, to all of our experiences of external objects. There is no neutral access to the objects that could allow us to extricate ourselves from these difficulties and perceive the objects as they really are. Or, to put it in a different way, there is no authority to guarantee that a sense impression faithfully reflects reality, that it really corresponds to the object in question.

That most people usually agree that they have similar sense impressions of given things does not solve these epistemological problems, according to the Sceptics: we have no guarantee that everyone is not in error. Moreover, it is often difficult to know whether people mean the same thing when they say that they are perceiving the same object.

To recommend an impartial attitude in observation is all well and good. But that does not get us any further either, because it does not touch on the basic difficulties, even if such an impartial attitude may be helpful in practice. The basic epistemological difficulty, according to this sceptical argument, is that a sense impression is always the result of several factors that in various ways influence the result, and not only of one pure and uninfluenced signal from the object. In other words, human beings are incapable of recognizing an object's true nature. We have no method of acquiring knowledge that can extricate us from this dilemma. The distinction between true and false sense impressions is thus problematic; that is, the senses do not lead us to true and certain knowledge.

It is worth noting that the Sceptics, with this argument, do not seem to have meant that we, in our daily lives, should ignore what our senses tell us. To survive, we must, in practice, take notice of our sense impressions. What the Sceptics think we should reject is the belief that our senses give us certain knowledge of the world. The observations that salt always tastes salty (for most people) and that fire always burns (for almost everyone) lead us to a subjective certainty, but this does not give us the right to claim anything about an object's true nature.

INDUCTION IS NOT A VALID INFERENCE

Induction is inference from a statement about a property in a *finite* number of cases of a certain kind that this property applies to *all* cases of this kind: 'All mules observed up to now, 45,987 cases, have been grey-brown; therefore, all mules are grey-brown.' But this is not a compelling inference, because there is no guarantee that a mule of a different colour will not turn up. Induction thus may lead to claims that are stronger than warranted. Induction is therefore not a valid inference.

DEDUCTIONS DO NOT LEAD TO NEW KNOWLEDGE

Deduction is inference from a set of given statements (premises), with the aid of definite rules, to a specific statement. And this statement is true if the given statements are true and if the rules of deduction are valid. If we know that all human beings can speak and that Socrates is a human being, we can conclude that Socrates can speak. But this does not lead us to new knowledge. The deduction does not say anything new in relation to what is already implied in the premises. Deductions are, in this sense, sterile or tautological. Or, to put it in another way, to the extent that we can support the claim that all human beings can speak, we must begin by confirming that all human beings, including Socrates, actually can speak. If we can support such a general statement ('all human beings can speak'), we have already included Socrates. Therefore, there is nothing new in the derived claim ('Socrates can speak').

DEDUCTIONS DO NOT PROVE THEIR OWN PRESUPPOSITIONS

All deductions take their own premises (and rules of deduction) for granted. It is always the derived statement which is proven, never the premises. Certainly, such a premise can in principle be proven as a deduction in a new syllogism. But then there are new premises that are part of this deduction, premises that are themselves unproven in this deduction.

This means that we here have a 'trilemma': either we carry on in an infinite process of supporting premises ('regression *ad infinitum*'), or we move in logical circles ('vicious circles'), or we break off the proof at a logically arbitrary place ('decisionism'). Other alternatives do not exist for deductive conclusions. Therefore, in the final instance, no basic principle can be proven deductively.[10]

CONFLICTING OPINIONS HAVE EQUALLY GOOD REASONS

Moreover, like Protagoras, the Sceptics in antiquity thought that our opinions of a more comprehensive nature, such as those about political and social issues, are characterized by conflicting viewpoints of which the arguments for and against are equally good. One opinion is just as well founded as another. Opinions are partly expressions of varying habits and customs (traditions), not of true insight.

In conclusion, we can say that the Sceptics' criticism was directed against the validity of sense experience, induction, and deduction, meaning that we cannot have certain knowledge of external things or of universal principles (universal claims or presuppositions). The Sceptics differed in how far they took such criticism. Pyrrho, who is generally considered the founder of the Sceptics, thought that the objections to the possibility of knowledge were so far-reaching that the only defensible position was to refrain from taking one. Others, like Carneades, placed greater emphasis on clarifying different degrees of insight.

The Sceptics' extreme claim that knowledge is impossible undermined itself. Such a position is self-evidently inconsistent. Radical scepticism is therefore paradoxical, and thus untenable. An important point in the interpretation of the Sceptics is therefore the question of what they really did claim: how comprehensive and absolute was their doubt, and in what sense did it take the form of an unproven statement that claims to be true?

Perhaps we can interpret the view of the Sceptics to mean that they, for practical reasons, lived in accordance with their sense impressions and current opinion, but without taking a stand as to the possible truth of these opinions and impressions, almost like students who learn their lessons without asking whether what is written there is true or not. Hence, the Sceptics' view is that we are correct in refraining from taking a stand on whether or not various statements are true. Sceptical persons neither accept nor reject a standpoint as true or false. They are content to observe, without passing judgement.

When other philosophers asserted something, the Sceptics did not deny this in the sense that they asserted something else. They were satisfied with showing that it is problematic to claim true and certain knowledge of this matter. They attempted to show that it is problematic to assert anything at all about the matter – without themselves taking a stand on it. The question remains of where the Sceptics could have got this insight that it is correct to refrain from taking a position. Is this a true and valid insight?

Regardless of how the Sceptics can best be related to this question, they seem to have thought that they had something important to say about human life. For example, if religious beliefs lead to anxiety and uneasiness, the Sceptics counsel that we cannot know anything for certain about such things, and thus we should not worry about them. A sceptical attitude should therefore give a person peace of mind. Just as the Stoics found a road to happiness and peace of mind through liberation from external needs, and the Epicureans sought the same thing through joy in calculated pleasure, so the Sceptics sought liberation from faith, from metaphysical and religious convictions: since we basically do not know anything, and everything is therefore equally valid, nothing should disturb our peace of mind.

As Pyrrho took a more radically sceptical position – we cannot know anything – Carneades developed scepticism as a doctrine of degrees of knowledge, or as a doctrine about what is probable, a 'probabilism' with a certain empiricist twist. Although Carneades thinks that we lack criteria for determining the truth of a proposition, he thinks that we can still evaluate the probability of the propositional content of a statement. For example, when we have many different, but mutually harmonious sense impressions supporting our view of a phenomenon, we have a better reason for accepting this view than if the sense impressions conflicted. The more sense impressions we have that correspond harmoniously with each other, the more probable our total picture is. Correspondingly, the harmony between the impressions of several observers will also make a picture more probable than if different observers had conflicting impressions.

With an increasing number of impressions that harmonize with one another, those of one observer as well as those among different observers, the composite image will appear more probable – even if we cannot believe that this view gives a true picture of the world. In practice, this is still sufficient, as when a judge assesses how several testimonies harmonize with one another and thus provide a sufficient basis for rendering a verdict: even if we do not find the truth, we can assess the support for a verdict.

From this moderate scepticism, which emphasizes the probable, it is not far to a policy of systematic collection of new information and systematic analysis of the harmony and dissonance within the collected material. From here, the step to empirical research is not far. But Carneades does not seem to have gone further than to recommend the testing of given information. A wish or need for systematic collection of new information does not seem to have occurred to him. Still, in Carneades, we find an emphasis on how important it is constantly to test statements for probability, according to experience and consistency. Here, we have the means for better practical knowledge, even if the real essence of things is not known to us.

We mentioned that the scepticism of antiquity had its roots in the Sophists. Afterwards, scepticism emerged in different settings, as in the theologian and philosopher Augustine at the beginning of the Middle Ages, in the rationalist Descartes, and in the empiricists Locke and Hume at the beginning of the new age.

THE SCIENCES AND OTHER DISCIPLINES IN ANTIQUITY

We have mentioned that the boundary between philosophy and science was not fixed in antiquity. Until now, we have mostly emphasized philosophical contributions. In this section, however, we will emphasize the establishment and development of some central branches of science during this period. For practical reasons, we can only provide brief glimpses of these sciences.

HISTORIOGRAPHY

In the speculative cosmological tradition, with its tendency to seek the unchangeable, we find the historians, Herodotus and Thucydides, who placed a greater emphasis on *experience* than on cosmological speculation, and who made the *changeable* an object of research.

Herodotus (484–425 BC) and Thucydides (460–400 BC) deal with events which are defined with regard to time and place, in opposition to mythological events that usually are without temporal or geographical placement ('once upon a time . . .'). Herodotus and Thucydides searched for relatively demonstrable causes for the transitory events in the past, such as psychological factors and power struggles between states. To be sure, the divine does come into the picture in Herodotus, especially in the form of fate, as the unpredictable that we must take into account when it comes to historical events.

In all of this, Herodotus and Thucydides were part of the shift towards the scientific way of thinking. In opposition to most of the Greek philosophers of nature, they viewed the transitory and changeable as a valuable research field, and were therefore central in strengthening the empirical, scientific ideal. They emphasized observation and description of existing, changeable reality, in opposition to rational, but often untenable speculations on the unchangeable element behind all change.

MEDICINE

In view of the speculations of the pre-Socratic philosophers of nature, we can say that Hippocrates (*c.* 460–375 BC) advocated an empirical-scientific ideal within medicine corresponding to what Herodotus and Thucydides had championed in historical writing: emphasis on observation and practical experience, not speculation.

Hence, Hippocrates is part of a factual, experientially based trend in antiquity. Today Hippocrates is probably best known for his formulation of the medical code of ethics that bears his name, the Hippocratic oath:

> I swear by Apollo the physician, and Æsculapius, and Health and All-heal, and all the gods and goddesses, that, according to my ability and judgment, I will keep this Oath and this stipulation – to reckon him who taught me this Art equally dear to me as my parents, to share my substance with him, and relieve his necessities if required; to look upon his offspring in the same footing as my own brothers, and to teach them this art, if they shall wish to learn it, without fee or stipulation; and that by precept, lecture, and every other mode of instruction, I will impart a knowledge of the Art to my own sons, and to those of my teachers, and to disciples bound by a stipulation and oath according to the law of medicine, but to none others.
>
> I will follow that system of regimen which, according to my ability and judgment, I consider for the benefit of my patients, and abstain from whatever is deleterious and mischievous. I will give no deadly medicine to any one if asked, nor suggest any such counsel; and in like manner I will not give to a woman a pessary to produce abortion. With purity and with holiness I will pass my life and practise my Art. I will not cut persons labouring under the stone, but will leave this to be done by men who are practitioners of this work. Into whatever houses I enter, I will go into them for the benefit of the sick, and will abstain from every voluntary act of mischief and corruption; and, further from the seduction of females or males, of freemen and slaves.
>
> Whatever, in connection with my professional practice or not, in connection with it, I see or hear, in the lives of men, which ought not to be spoken of abroad, I will not divulge, as reckoning that all such should be kept secret. While I continue to keep this Oath unviolated, may it be granted to me to enjoy life and the practice of the art, respected by all men, in all times! But should I trespass and violate this Oath, may the reverse be my lot.[11]

This version of the code of medical ethics has become a classic text. It displays a reflective, moral view of the relationship between doctor and patient and between doctor and society. Moreover, it displays the caution in medical practice that Hippocrates stood for: the doctor should not at once grasp the knife, and operate. For Hippocrates, a doctor should primarily be a physician who prescribes medication rather than intervenes drastically. Behind this lies the view that a doctor should work *with* nature, not *against* it. The goal is to restore nature's balance and harmony by stimulating nature's own processes. If this seems far too passive for us today, it may be helpful to clarify two points. First, surgical procedures were more dangerous in antiquity than they are today, owing to factors such as antisepsis and technical equipment. Secondly, Hippocrates had a view of nature similar to that of Aristotle. Everything seeks its place, and human beings, with both a mind and a body, seek health; that is to say, they seek regulation of natural functions and abilities, and harmonious balance. In this process the doctor can act as a counsellor who advises on diet or lifestyle, as well as a physician, since it is the 'whole' person that is to be made well.

Greek surgeons practised dissection and even human vivisection (on prisoners condemned to death), and thereby improved their anatomical and physiological knowledge: they were enabled to describe the inner organs in more detail, and to uncover the functional relationship between organs; for example, that linking the eye, the optic nerve, and the central nervous system. Such knowledge is necessary if we are not only to describe the progression of various illnesses and experiment with medicines in relation to the observation of external symptoms, but also to explain why things happen.

Galen (*c.* AD 130–200) was a follower of Hippocrates, and an Aristotelian. He too emphasized that natural things seek harmony, and that the doctor is to assist cautiously in this process. Galen opposed the theory that material atoms are the basic elements of nature. Such a view misrepresents the processes of life, according to Galen. Therefore, he rejected the concept of medical therapy based on the theories of nature proposed by Democritus and Epicurus. Galen eventually achieved considerable fame and remained an authority on medicine until the end of the Renaissance.

In accordance with the views of his day that the physical state of the body is governed by a balanced relationship among the various bodily fluids, he attempted to account theoretically for the various temperaments in terms of an imbalance in this relationship: the sanguine person has too much blood (Latin: *sanguis*), the phlegmatic has too much phlegm (Greek: *phlegma*), the choleric has too much yellow bile (Greek: *chole*), and the melancholy has too much black bile (Greek: *melaina chole*). Here we meet the classical Greek ideas of balance and harmony.

JURISPRUDENCE

From the Sophists and Socrates through Plato and Aristotle, and throughout the entire Stoic school, judicial reflections are central. This applies to basic, theoretical questions about the law's source and justification: is there a universally valid and binding basis for law, or is law ultimately only an expression of power and tradition? We have followed this debate from Thrasymachus and Socrates, and on to the Stoic version of natural law theory. We will later follow the discussion further, through Christian theology in the Middle Ages and on to the modern ways of treating the question.

To the further theoretical reflections on law belongs a compilation of utility calculations, as in Epicureanism; this method discusses the effects of legal decisions. This is a problem later to be studied in the utilitarian tradition by thinkers like Bentham and Mill, who gradually attempted to gain social insight in order to determine whether laws function as they were intended. In the theoretical reflections on law in antiquity there were, moreover, various discussions of what kinds of conditions lead to social decline, generally in the form of theories inspired by biology of the rise, development, maturation, degeneration, and dissolution of states. For example, we find such theories of the decline and fall of states in Aristotle and Plato. These authors offer various observations of developments in certain societies, and classic discussions about what legal and other steps should be taken to influence the process.

It is worth keeping in mind how engaged the Greeks were in the political and legal realm. It is also worth keeping in mind that many of the leading Roman Stoics were statesmen with first-hand knowledge of the legal system; Marcus Aurelius was an emperor, Seneca a senator, and Cicero a statesman at many levels. Roman law later became the basis of European law. Roman law became so well-developed not only because of its theoretical legacy, but also because the Romans sought to create a common legal system for an empire with many different ethnic and cultural groups. To create a common legal system for such a diverse society (without espousing cultural conformity), one must raise the level of abstraction and formulate general rules that can be a common denominator for everyone.

Hence we can say that jurisprudence developed into a professional, normative hermeneutics (Greek: *hermeneuein*: 'interpret'); that is to say, that a professional corps was trained to rule on particular cases in light of universal, normative laws and rules. Education then became concerned not only with knowledge of the written laws (and how a good society is built up), but also with the practical judgement needed to recognize a new case as a case of a particular type (that is subject to a particular law). This is the kind of practical wisdom that Aristotle refers to in his discussion of ethics and politics; that is, a competence to interpret law in the light of inherited and politically approved judicial views.

MATHEMATICS

From Pythagoras to Plato we have seen how central mathematical ways of thinking have been in philosophy. Reflections on the Platonic ideas and their existence can rightly be seen as reflections on the basic problems of mathematics. This debate continued from these Greek philosophers to the controversy over universals in the Middle Ages, and on to our time. The problems of objective knowledge, valid deduction, and proof are also basic problems in mathematics.

The Greek mathematicians, such as Pythagoras, promoted precisely the formal and operational side of mathematics by developing a concept of proof for their statements, namely, a mathematical proof consisting of logically correct deductions from self-evident axioms. An axiomatic-deductive system consists of axioms, deductive rules (inference rules), and proven statements (theorems) that are obtained by means of these axioms and rules.

Euclid, who lived around 300 BC in Alexandria, wrote a textbook in mathematics on this theoretical basis that remained fundamental for the subject until recent times. Newton used it in his physics, as Descartes and other philosophers had used this system of reasoning as a model of rigorous thought.

PHYSICS AND CHEMISTRY

We have seen how the early natural philosophers developed concepts that led to a mechanistic theory of atoms (Democritus, Epicurus), a theory that later was to have a great influence on the establishment of the experimental and mathematically formulated natural sciences in the Renaissance. But in antiquity this theory seemed too speculative to most people. It spoke of things that we, after all, could not perceive. It was therefore the Aristotelian view of nature that gained acceptance; the chief virtue of this view of nature lay in its descriptive perspective of nature as we experience it, and in its ecological perspective of the interplay between species and environment, in a non-evolutionary context.

The Greeks had thus developed the basis for many of the concepts that were to be decisive in the establishment of modern, empirical natural science. Now, in retrospect, we can say that what they lacked was the experimental method. But this is not completely correct. For example, Archimedes (287–212 BC) did perform scientific experiments. He was born in the Greek city of Syracuse in Sicily, but studied in Alexandria. He is especially known for his principle of the buoyancy of fluids. It is interesting that Archimedes at the same time worked as a technical inventor, or engineer. Such a close relationship between intellectual and practical work was unusual in antiquity, when physical labour, which was largely based on slavery, was disparaged. Archimedes was also a great mathematician and perhaps went even further in that field than as a physicist. Perhaps he was an even more important mathematician than Euclid, upon whose works Archimedes actually based his own. When the Roman army captured Syracuse in 212 BC, Archimedes was deep in thought about some geometric figures that he had drawn in the sand. Approached by some Roman soldiers, he rebuffed them in irritation, saying, 'Don't step on my figures!' They responded by killing him.

ASTRONOMY

The study of astronomy was pursued from the very beginning of the Greek philosophy of nature. We have mentioned that Thales predicted a solar eclipse. And we have mentioned the part that the Pythagoreans attributed to the harmony between the celestial bodies. In Aristotle we find a fully developed world-view in which the heavens arch over everything with their spheres and unique laws. The 'heavenly' is above the 'earthly', not only spatially, but also qualitatively. Here we have a mixture of observation and speculation. But there was also a strong element of practical interest in astronomy among seafarers who navigated by the stars and planets; among those concerned with time-measurement and the calendar, and among astrologers.

Ptolemy, who lived in Alexandria approximately 100 years after Christ, systematized and perfected the wealth of astronomical knowledge available at that time, on the basis of an Aristotelian view of the Earth, stars, and planets; that is to say, he developed a *geocentric* world-view. This model of the universe, with the Earth as the centre and a qualitative hierarchy from the terrestrial to the celestial was dominant until the coming of Copernicus and Kepler after the Middle Ages.

But again it is worth noting that the heliocentric model had already been proposed in antiquity. Aristarchus, who lived around 270 BC, posited that the Earth is a sphere that moves in a circle around the sun. This theory suffered the same fate as Democritus' theory of atoms: in its own day it was thought to be too speculative. It seemed to contradict the immediate experience that we have of the stars and planets moving around us and of an immovable Earth. There were also theoretical reasons for not accepting the heliocentric model: Aristotelianism held a strong position at that time and taught that it was meaningless to claim that the Earth was in motion, since everything's natural motion takes place in relation to the Earth. Therefore, when Copernicus began the battle against the geocentric world-view it was necessary to question Aristotelianism at the same time. Finally, medieval Christian theology became involved in the controversy, since the Church believed that the geocentric view was biblical. Hence, the controversy about astronomy in the Renaissance became especially bitter because it threatened established religious convictions.

PHILOLOGY

From their intense discussion of earlier writings, the Greeks developed great competence in the interpretation of texts, or hermeneutics. Thus, Aristotle often used references to earlier philosophers in his own interpretations. Gradually, with the passage of time, the need arose to edit, classify, and explicate the classic texts. This took place in Alexandria, where an extensive library was founded. Texts such as Aristotle's writings were edited, and philological exegesis was developed. Alexandria became a centre of education.

The Jewish philosopher Philo, who lived in Alexandria from about 25 BC to AD 45, is one of these exegetists who sought to mediate between various traditions and languages, not the least between Greek philosophy and the Hebrew Old Testament. We will see later (Ch. 6) how Christian theology arose out of a need to mediate between Greek philosophy and the Christian interpretation of the Bible: exegesis was further developed in Jewish and Christian commentaries on the Bible, and the Islamic commentaries on the Koran. It is worth noting that it was no longer only the Greek language that prevailed, but also Latin, Hebrew, and eventually, Arabic. From antiquity and into the Middle Ages, these were the languages for education. When the universities were established in the Middle Ages, it was Latin in the West, Arabic in the south (all the way to Spain), and Greek in the East. As part of the philological activities in antiquity, we can also mention the developments in the field of grammar. In addition, work was done in rhetoric, especially by Aristotle.

FEMALE SCIENTISTS IN ANTIQUITY

In antiquity women were excluded from philosophical and scientific activity, with few exceptions, such as the Epicurean school. At the centre of learning in Alexandria, however, was the famous female scientist, Hypatia (*c.* AD 370–415). She was a Platonic philosopher competent in mathematics and astronomy. Known for her knowledge and other intellectual abilities, she was murdered on her way to the library during a period of rioting. This marked a turning point for Alexandria as a centre of learning, and thus for all intellectual life in antiquity. The old institutions were in the process of decay and migration of scholars began. Antiquity, the old times, was in transition to what we later have learned to call the Middle Ages; that is, the period between the old and new eras.

QUESTIONS

Explain the basic moral concepts of Epicureanism and Stoicism. Compare these two moral philosophies and point out similarities and differences.

Which were the questions discussed by the Sceptics? Can we doubt everything?

Explain the main ideas of Neoplatonism (Plotinus).

SUGGESTIONS FOR FURTHER READING

PRIMARY LITERATURE

Marcus Aurelius, *Meditations*, Ware, 1997.
Marcus Tullius Cicero, *Selected Letters*, Oxford, 1925.

SECONDARY LITERATURE

Barker, E., *Social and Political Thought: From Alexander to Constantine*, Oxford, 1956.
Brehier, Émile, *The Philosophy of Plotinus*, Chicago, 1978.
Gerson, Lloyd P. (ed.), *The Cambridge Companion to Plotinus*, Cambridge, 1996.
Næss, Arne, *Scepticism*, Oslo, 1969.

NOTES

1 Value in itself: 'autotelic'; Greek: *auto*, 'self'; *telos*, 'goal'.
2 Laws and conventions have 'heterotelic' value; that is to say, they have value, *telos*, by being a means *for something else* that is a goal in itself.
3 At the end of the 1700s, the utilitarian Jeremy Bentham proposed a method to *evaluate various kinds* of pleasures. We will come back to its problems in our discussion of Bentham in Chapter 14.
4 *Quaestiones naturales III*, praefatio.
5 Escapism: *flight*.
6 *De legibus*, II, 5.
7 Cicero, *De re publica*, translated by C. W. Keyes (Loeb Classical Library, Cambridge, MA, 1928), Bk. III, xxii.
8 Cf. Arne Næss (*Scepticism*, Oslo, 1969, pp. 2–7), who from the discussions within ancient scepticism calls the sceptics who state and defend a sceptical position, 'academics', and the sceptics who do not make such claims but who continue their philosophical enquiries, 'sceptics'. Næss' discussion of Pyrrho (based on Sextus Empiricus) is a treatment of scepticism in the latter sense.
9 We find corresponding arguments in Democritus (and Protagoras): a human being's sense experience of external objects occurs by means of a transmission of mediator atoms from the object to the human sensory organ. But since all of our cognition of external things depends only on sense impressions which arise in our sensory organs, we have no guarantee that sense impressions give a correct report about the external objects. The sense impression in the sensory organ is, of course, dependent on *both* the impression from the objects *and* the condition of the sensory organ.
10 But is this not a remarkable statement? Cf. reflexive (self-referential) argumentation (Chs 15, Transcendental knowledge and 27, Hannah Arendt).
11 The Hippocratic oath, published by the American Medical Association.

6 The Middle Ages

CHRISTIANITY AND PHILOSOPHY

The Roman Empire was divided in the fourth century AD, and just before the year 400 Christianity became its dominant religion. During the fifth century the invasion of the Germanic tribes gained momentum and the Western Roman Empire fell. Antiquity drew to a close and the Middle Ages began.[1] We will first look at certain changes that took place once Christianity had become the dominant religion in the Roman Empire. Afterwards we will look at some changes that occurred during the transition from the Roman Empire to medieval society. We have said that social conditions in the Hellenistic-Roman period probably led to a certain political resignation and lack of interest in theoretical philosophy. Philosophy especially focused on personal ethical problems. But during late antiquity, this philosophy of life was felt to be insufficient, and many people began to seek a *religious* answer. Neoplatonism and, to some extent, late Stoicism expressed this reawakened religious longing. And Christianity found good soil for its growth.

Christianity appealed to *everyone*. It proclaimed *hope* for everyone. In spite of political powerlessness and material suffering, in spite of evil and weakness of character, there is hope for everyone. Our lives are part of a dramatic historical process at the end of which we can expect just compensation for the suffering and injustice of this life. Above all, there is a Heavenly Father who can extend mercy and salvation to sinners and the pious alike.

For the first Christians, the encounter with Hellenistic intellectuals would have been in the following terms. The intellectuals were educated in Greek and Hellenistic philosophy and lived in a different conceptual world from that of the Bible. How should Christians respond to these intellectuals? Should they attempt to 'translate' the Bible into the language of the intellectuals in order to convert them to Christianity? Or should they condemn all philosophy as a heathen folly and speak the language of the Bible to the intellectuals as well?

Here, therefore, there were two different strategies. Anachronistically, we could call the first strategy 'catholic' (faith and tradition). This strategy accepted that the philosophical tradition was also created by God. Christians should therefore respond positively to this tradition and not be afraid to express Christian beliefs with the help of philosophy. We could call the second strategy 'Protestant' (faith alone): it maintained that in the Bible, and only in the Bible, could Christian truth be found, and this truth must not be contaminated by heathen traditions, such as that of Greek philosophy. The first strategy turned out to be the more effective, and the result was a Christian *theology* which attempted to make the biblical message understandable with the aid of Greek and Hellenistic philosophy. Christian theology thus starts as apologetics; that is, as a defence of Christianity against the objections of contemporary non-Christian intellectuals. At first we have, above all, a synthesis between Christianity and Neoplatonism, although late Stoicism also played a part. This theological synthesis was dominant from about 300 to 1200 AD, covering most of the Middle Ages. In the thirteenth century, Aristotle was rediscovered by the Western Christian world, and we have a synthesis between Christianity and Aristotelianism. This theological synthesis later became the dominant philosophy of the Roman Catholic Church.

In the Middle Ages, philosophy and theology were the two main branches of learning that claimed to lead to true insight. Natural science in our understanding of the word hardly existed in European culture until the late Middle Ages. It is therefore natural that the relationship between faith and reason was central during this period. The two disciplines, philosophy and theology, had to find their place in relation to one another: which questions belong to philosophy and which to theology? The close relationship between philosophy and theology in the Middle Ages is often presented as if theology, in a sense, held philosophy in its clammy grip; that is, philosophy was the 'victim'. But we can just as well turn this around and say that it was Greek and Hellenistic philosophy that damaged theology (Christianity): theological doctrines (dogmatics), such as those of the Trinity and the superiority of the soul to the body, were formulated in a language that suited Hellenistic (Neoplatonic) philosophers. But theology remained trapped in this philosophical terminology, even after people stopped thinking in Neoplatonic terms. It was therefore theology that 'suffered' as a result of this coexistence between theology and philosophy.

It is not our place to determine who 'subdued' whom. Instead, it may be appropriate to warn against moralizing over the historical decrees of fate, since we then may easily overlook the historical 'necessity' in the events. We can instead ask this question: what did Christianity bring, in the way of new opinions, into the philosophical and intellectual environment? Simply stated, the new concepts were as follows:

1   an anthropocentric view of man
2   a linear view of history
3   a conception of God as a person and a creator.

The Greek philosophers largely viewed man as a creature among others in the cosmos; a high-ranking creature indeed, but still, without a unique position. There are rocks and earth, plants and animals, human beings and gods – all within the same finite universe. It is different in Christianity: God is a person who exists beyond this world, and the world – with rocks, plants, animals, and man – was created by God so that man could be saved. The universe is secondary in relation to man and God. Everything in creation is centred on mankind's struggle for salvation on the Earth.

The notions of salvation and sin gained ground at the expense of traditional Greek views of morality, such as virtue and the realization of the good life. And salvation is for each person. Human beings have an infinitely higher value than anything else in creation, and all human beings have, in principle, the same high value. This means, at the same time, that the Stoic ideas of natural law and universal brotherhood and equality coincided with Christian concepts: a universally valid law exists, namely, God's word, and all human beings are equal because they were all created by God in God's image.

Both cosmologically and axiologically, man is at the centre. At the same time, history, not nature, is essential. And history is not circular, as in Stoicism, but linear. History moves *forward*: creation, the fall of man, the birth of Christ, his life and resurrection, the struggle between sin and salvation, all anticipating the Day of Judgement.

POPE AND KING: TWO RULERS IN ONE STATE

The Middle Ages, which lasted from around AD 400 to 1500, was not characterized by a homogeneous and static social system. The geographic differences could also be great. In outline, we can still say that the main system of governance in Middle Ages was a *feudal* system in various forms. By this, we mean a society in which the relationship between the king (or emperor) and the nobility takes the form of a mutual contract whereby the king grants to the noblemen (his vassals) fiefdoms, and the noblemen in return pledge military support and taxes to the king. There was also a contract between the vassals and the peasants, whereby the vassal was to protect the people of his fief and the people, in return, were to give a portion of their harvest to the vassal.

This feudal system could create both strong and weak kingdoms. But by around the year 1000, the tendency was on the whole towards a strengthening of the power of the state, although the balance of power between the king and his vassals could shift. But by the end of the Middle Ages, it was the king who, for the most part, was dominant: we end up with centralized states, in which, by the seventeenth century, all legal power was concentrated in the king, who had become an absolute monarch.

After Christianity became the dominant religion, definite political changes occurred that had a fundamental impact on the political life and thought of the Middle Ages. Two authorities became entwined, the secular and the ecclesiastical. These authorities developed and the relationship between them changed from the fourth century until the end of the Middle Ages. In what follows we will not discuss the various phases of this historical development, but only certain theoretical points in connection with a historical comparison of the two rival authorities.

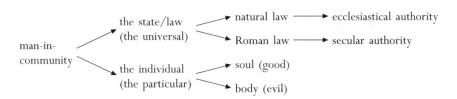

We have said that a kind of dichotomy arose between the individual (the particular) and the state/law (the universal) during the transition from the Greek city-states to the Hellenistic-Roman Empire; and that a dichotomy developed within the universal between natural law and the existing laws of the empire. The latter dichotomy can be interpreted as an attempt to justify existing laws. It is a common view that in order to justify a moral norm (N_2), we should have a more fundamental norm (N_1) that can serve as the premise for a logical deduction leading to the first norm (N_2):

N_1  natural law

N_2 Roman law

To justify existing laws which claim to be universally valid (N_2), we can thus appeal to an absolute law (N_1) that lies behind these existing laws, and of which they are an expression. In this way, natural law could justify the existing Roman laws. But this justification is a two-edged sword, since natural law can also be used to impugn the existing laws. People claiming to be the rightful interpreters of natural law may condemn existing law as a violation of natural law. In other words, the important question is, *who* are the legitimate interpreters of natural law?[2]

As long as the Roman emperors held all the power, including that of interpreting natural law, everything was under control. A momentous change occurred when these rulers accepted the Christian Church as the interpreter of the law. Instead of maintaining his personal divinity, and, consequently, his right to interpret the law, the emperor could entrust this interpretation to another authority, the pope and the Church. As long as the Church is in harmony with the state, the situation will remain satisfactory, from the state's perspective. But precisely because the Church, as a relatively independent institution, was authorized to adjudicate on basic ethical and religious questions, a situation was created of potential conflict between the ecclesiastical and the secular powers.

Thus, the view of the Church as servile to the state must be modified. Since the Church was the authorized interpreter of ethics and religion, the people had a certain forum for a legitimate criticism of the secular rulers. This was probably important for the idea of freedom in Europe.

It is true that the Church more often than not preached obedience to the secular rulers. It is, after all, written: 'Let every soul be subject unto the higher powers. For there is no power but of God: the powers that be are ordained of God. Whosoever therefore resisteth the power, resisteth the ordinance of God: and they that resist shall receive to themselves damnation' (Romans 13: 1–2). This exhortation to obey the rulers of the day can be seen as the solution to a strategic (and theological) dilemma for the early Christians. Should they shun questions about society and put all of their trust in the life to come? If so, Christianity could easily have developed anarchistic characteristics, leading to conflict with the rulers. Or should Christians support a compromise in which the Church is autonomous in spiritual matters and subservient in secular matters? We find the latter strategy in Gelasius' teaching about the two powers (authorities), which was a basis for the coexistence between the state and the Church in the Middle Ages.

But this ecclesiastical appeal for obedience to the secular rulers was ambiguous since the Church could withdraw the appeal if it found that the secular authorities did not meet ethical and religious standards. The point is that the Church, as a relatively independent authority, occasionally had the political power needed for such sanctions. In theory, state and Church were to cooperate. But since these were relatively independent authorities who had the same subjects, the people's loyalties were often divided at times when it was difficult to give both the pope and the emperor their due. And, practically speaking, it was impossible to distinguish sharply between the secular and ecclesiastical powers: those who were to have only spiritual power had to have a certain economic basis for their mission. They had to have a certain amount of secular power. And those who were to hold the secular power had to possess a certain spiritual authority.

Christianity became the dominant religion in a society governed by two authorities, the state (*regnum*) and the Church (*sacerdotium*). Every member of society was subject to both of these authorities and had a double loyalty. But the relationship between the two authorities was filled with conflict. Pope Gelasius I (the end of the fifth century) defended his position against the Byzantine Empire, and thereby he was defending, in reality, the Church in declaring that the two powers (*potestates*) were *both* of God and were therefore both equally legitimate. The two authorities were also said to have different tasks: the Church had spiritual tasks, the state worldly tasks. And the two authorities were mutually to assist each other. For 800–900 years, this doctrine was accepted by representatives of both the Church and the state. But this agreement soon proved to be more theoretical than real. The doctrine of the two 'swords' was subject to different interpretations. We can hardly blame Gelasius that the doctrine proved to be vague and ambiguous. This ambiguity was rooted in the actual situation, which no doctrine could change, even if the purpose of the doctrine was to make coexistence possible and to legitimize coexistence by answering the question of where the boundary between spiritual and worldly power should be.

To administer the sacraments and to proclaim the Gospel are spiritual tasks. But these spiritual acts presuppose a certain right to control properties, such as monasteries and churches. That is to say, the spiritual power must necessarily possess a certain amount of secular power. On the other hand, to be involved in secular politics is to act on the basis of certain values. And if the spiritual power includes authority over morality and values, it becomes impossible to engage in secular politics without intervention in the spiritual field.

AUGUSTINE – FAITH AND REASON

Life. *Augustine was born in Tagaste in North Africa in* AD *354. His mother was a Christian, but his father was not. As a young man, Augustine lived a riotous life in Carthage. He first joined one of the popular religious movements of his day,* Manichaeanism, *which taught the strict dualism of good and evil in the universe, and which claimed that man has two souls, one light and good and one dark and evil. A person's actions result from the conflict between these two souls. Augustine recognized himself in this doctrine: it explained the evil in the world.*

But Augustine's communion with Manichaeanism did not last. Its teachings did not lead to the moral life that he sought. He was also dissatisfied intellectually. He was now drawn to scepticism, but neither was it acceptable to Augustine. He then turned to Neoplatonism (Plotinus). Here Augustine thought that he had found a satisfactory answer to the question of evil. The Neoplatonic view of the spiritual as the real met with his approval. He found intellectual peace in Plato and Plotinus.

But Augustine's own experiences conflicted with the Neoplatonic confidence in reason: right insight leads to right actions. Augustine had in fact realized that he was unable to live in the way that he knew to be right. At the same time, he thought that the Christians lived a more moral life than he, even though they, theoretically, were weaker. Augustine began to feel that Christianity offered a superior doctrine of salvation, although he theoretically disliked Christianity. At this point Augustine went to Milan as a teacher of rhetoric, where he was attracted by Ambrose's sermons. And around the age of thirty Augustine converted to Christianity. He returned to North Africa, where he became a bishop. The remainder of his life was devoted to ecclesiastical and spiritual service. Augustine died in 430, around the same time that the Vandals overran the Western Roman Empire.

Augustine wrote a number of books, all in Latin. We will mention only four of the best known. In Contra academicos *('Against the Academics') Augustine dealt with his past as a Sceptic by attempting to refute scepticism. In* De libero arbitrio *('On the Freedom of the Will') he discussed the problem of evil and of free will. In* Confessiones *('Confessions') Augustine portrayed the struggles in his own soul. This book illustrates the development from early Greek antiquity to Christian late antiquity: we do not meet a sober, rational Greek citizen, but rather an idiosyncratic person torn by an inner struggle between soul and body, in which the emotions emerge as a stronger force than reason. In* De civitate Dei *('The City of God') Augustine worked out his theory of history and hence the doctrine of the two 'cities', the earthly city and the city of God.*

PHILOSOPHY AND THEOLOGY

Augustine lived after Christianity had become the dominant religion, after the division of the Roman Empire, and immediately before the invasion of the Germanic tribes destroyed the Western Roman Empire. While the Roman Empire faced destruction, the ecclesiastical institutions were developed. These institutions eventually assumed the task of perpetuating the cultural legacy of the Latin and Greek worlds. In addition, the Church, along with Byzantine and the Teutonic principalities, was assigned certain political responsibilities as the power of the emperor diminished. Thus, Christian theologians also became political ideologists.

Augustine emerges as one of the first great theologians to mediate between antiquity and the Christian era which followed: he created a synthesis of Christianity and Neoplatonism. In Augustine we thus find the new Christian concepts that we have already mentioned: man in the centre, history as a linear development, and a personal God who has created the universe out of nothing. In Augustine these concepts merge with the philosophy of antiquity: not only is everything centred on man insofar as God has created everything *for* man and insofar as man, created in God's image and destined for salvation, is the paragon of creation. But as a result of his refutation of scepticism, Augustine claims that the most *reliable knowledge* is that of the *inner* being of man. Introspection (of our inner life) leads to more certain insight than sense experience. Man's inner being takes epistemological precedence. The argument is that the subject and the object 'coincide' through introspection, while sense experience is always uncertain because the subject and the object are different. And the inner being is, for Augustine, more of a battleground of various feelings and various impulses of the will than a region of calm rationality. The inner being is a playground for irrational impulses, for sin, guilt, and the longing for salvation. But Augustine does not believe, like the Stoics, that we, by our own strength, can govern this inner life: we need grace and 'superhuman' assistance. Indeed, Augustine holds that we have free will, but at the same time he emphasizes that we are completely subject to God's predestined plan of salvation.

Furthermore, Augustine largely shares the Neoplatonist view of the relationship between soul and body: the soul represents the divine in man. The body is the root of the sinful. We must, as much as possible, free ourselves from the body and concentrate on the soul, on the inner being, so that we can approach the spiritual source of existence in the universe, God. But, for the Christian Augustine, the idea of original sin comes in addition: the soul too is (directly) affected by sin.

Just as Augustine interpreted the struggle between God and the Devil as a struggle within each person, he found the same struggle on the historical level in the opposition between the city of God (*civitas Dei*) and the earthly city (*civitas terrena*). Just as *each* individual life is a struggle between salvation and sin, so history is a struggle between a good state and an evil state.

Augustine's doctrine of the city of God and the earthly city was not clearly defined as a political theory, primarily because Augustine was thinking theologically, not politically. He was comparatively little concerned with how particular political systems are to be actualized. With this reservation we can still say that Augustine's presentation of this struggle between the two 'states' was probably influenced by his own political situation: the Christians were accused of causing the fall of the empire, and Augustine had to counter such accusations. And *one* interpretation is that Augustine probably thought that the Church in a way represents the divine 'state' and the empire, the earthly 'state', although he left this unclarified. But Augustine did not view the earthly state as something that is accidental and unnecessary. On the contrary, because of each person's corrupt nature (the Fall), a strong earthly state is necessary to control human evil. The earthly state is therefore a necessary evil, as long as the historical conflict between good and evil continues – that is to say, during the time between the Fall and Judgement Day.

This view of the earthly state is distinguished from the Aristotelian and Thomist views of the relationship between man and society, the view of man as naturally a social being. We also see that Augustine's view of the state is distinguished from the Platonic view of the state as an ethical educator for the perfect life. Plato seeks the ideal, while Augustine has enough problems keeping evil under control.

For Augustine, there is no sharp distinction between politics and morality/religion, between the prince (the politician) and the priest: politics has a directly moral function. It is an authoritarian means of controlling moral evil. That is to say, this is a simplification of Augustine's view of the state and politics *after* the Fall. *Before* sin came into the world, human beings were equal; and Augustine assumes that human beings were then, by nature, social beings. But sin made an organized state system necessary, with the use of force and a clear division of authority between the rulers and the subjects – both as punishment and as a security measure. Even without sin, however, it would still be necessary to have a certain amount of order in society, and thus a certain form of government, but coercion would be unnecessary. In a sinful state, the rulers are appointed by God to keep order; therefore, they do not derive their authority from the people. The rulers of such a state are God's men, and citizens have a duty to obey these rulers as they do to obey God.

But how can an evil state correct the evil in man? This is where the good state comes in:[3] the Church as an organization is necessary for the salvation of the soul, both by the moral and religious education of the soul and by keeping a watchful eye on the earthly state and its corrective measures. All of this became a central dogma in later times: the Church as an organization is necessary for salvation. And the empire was now a Christian state, in the sense that all of its members were subject to both the emperor and the pope.

We have previously seen that epistemological questions were important for the Sophists and Socrates, and for Plato and Aristotle. In late antiquity, epistemology had an especially central role for the Sceptics. With the rise of Christianity, the realm of epistemological questions broadened: in addition to the earlier questions about what we can know, we have questions about what we can believe in a religious sense; that is, about the relationship between religious faith and secular wisdom, between Christian revelation and Greek thought. As we mentioned earlier in this chapter, this is the starting point for Christian theology: some Christians looked at biblical faith and Greek thought as essentially different. Christians should therefore not attempt to justify or to understand the Christian faith with the aid of philosophy and reason. Tertullian (*c.* AD 160–222) is a representative of this deprecatory attitude towards philosophy. The formulation *credo quia absurdum* ('I believe because it is absurd') was an expression of his viewpoint. That is to say, faith is independent of reason. If reason were to claim that faith is meaningless, that claim would therefore be irrelevant to faith. This represents an extreme position on the relationship between religious (Christian) faith and worldly wisdom.

Another position was one that promoted a certain common sphere of faith and reason. The usual statement of this position among the early theologians was the view that faith has the 'right of way' in an epistemological sense: if a conflict should arise between faith and thought, faith is right. This is the basic position for most Christian theologians, from Augustine to Thomas Aquinas. But within the latter position there could still be different emphases. One view is that faith has preeminence in the sense that it is by virtue of faith that thought is possible: *credo ut intelligam* ('I believe in order to understand'). This means that without revelation and faith, people would be blind to essential aspects of life. Augustine shares this viewpoint. Another view is that faith does have pre-eminence, but only in regard to the latest Christian revelations taken on faith:[4] to a great extent, both faith and reason are independent and hold an equal position. They have unique aspects and aspects in common, but there is a harmony of faith and reason in their common area.

REFUTATION OF SCEPTICISM

The Sceptics had asserted that certain knowledge is not accessible to us (cf. Ch. 5). Augustine thought that he could refute this claim, precisely by showing that certain knowledge is possible. Here, we will point out four areas where Augustine believed that certain knowledge could be found:

1   Even when our senses deceive us and we say that everything we experience is doubtful, we still cannot doubt our own doubt, and, thus, our own existence. Since I doubt, then I, as a doubter, must necessarily exist. Hence we have a truth which is irrefutable, which rises above all possible doubt: that a person who doubts, exists. Thus it is shown that there is certain knowledge in this area. Certain knowledge has been shown to be possible, and scepticism is thus refuted. We are here disregarding the notion that there may be more moderate forms of scepticism that are not refuted by this. Augustine's way of thinking is reminiscent of Descartes' well-known formulation about 1200 years later: *cogito, ergo sum* ('I think, therefore I am') (cf. Ch. 9). That the subject's immediate certainty about the self is seen as a basis for certain knowledge is a 'modern' feature of Augustine's thought.

2   When we extend doubt as far as possible, we are left not only with the insight 'I exist', but also with the insights that 'I want', 'I think', 'I feel', and 'I know'. Shortly, we are left with several indubitable cognitions about ourselves as cognizant beings: when the cognizant self claims to be conscious of its own mental state, this is certain insight. When I want, when I love, when I doubt, and when I know about all of this (that I exist, that I love, that I doubt), I can, with complete certainty, claim that I have certain knowledge. Thus, Augustine thought that scepticism can be refuted by insight into our internal states. Introspection, in opposition to sense experience of external things and events, leads us to certain knowledge.

    Here we may object that the Sceptics probably would not have denied that instantaneous statements of our current mental states can represent reasonably certain knowledge – as long as we are not making any mistake when we use language to express what we thus experience. The question is whether such momentary statements can be known to be true after the passage of time, and the experienced state has passed. Augustine seemed to think that statements about our own inner state represent certain knowledge, even when time has passed and the experienced state is passed. This means that we can have certain knowledge about ourselves beyond the momentary knowledge. But in such cases we have to trust our memory, which is fallible; and we have to trust linguistic expressions that, in principle, always can seduce us. However, Augustine was convinced that he could show that introspection does give us certain knowledge even beyond the momentary experiences, or at least that introspection gives us a more certain insight into our inner life than the senses give us about external events.

3   A third area where Augustine thought that he could find certain knowledge and refute scepticism is mathematics. For example, we recognize that the statement $3 + 3 = 6$ is certain knowledge. Mathematics represents truths that cannot be doubted. In mathematics, we have truths that are necessary and unchangeable, as opposed to what we recognize through our deceptive senses.

4   Finally, Augustine claimed that certain logical principles cannot be doubted. The Sceptics also used these principles to make their points. The Sceptics presupposed, for example, that knowledge cannot, at the same time and in the same sense, be both certain and uncertain. This meant that the Sceptics presupposed the so-called principle of contradiction (cf. Aristotle, Ch. 4,

Knowledge and praxis). To what extent a Sceptic had to presuppose the truth of such principles or whether it is possible to base thought on such principles as hypotheses is not for us to decide here. Augustine did, at least, use this argument against the Sceptics of his day to show that, even in this area, there is certain knowledge.

By such arguments, Augustine attempted not only to refute scepticism by showing that certain knowledge is possible with regard to self-reflection and introspection, mathematics, and logical principles, but also to emphasize the epistemological pre-eminence of the inner life and the logical forms above the senses and the external world. And this led to a basic feature in Augustine's philosophy, its close relationship with Neoplatonic thought (Ch. 5): the individual soul and its spiritual life are higher and nobler than the external sensible things, and higher still are the pure forms of mathematics and logic which we 'behold' with our thoughts. In other words, that which we have the most certain knowledge of – our inner life and the pure forms – is also that which is most essential and most real in the universe. This is how epistemology and ontology (the doctrine of knowledge and the doctrine of being) harmonize with one another. Furthermore, for Augustine, as a Christian, the arguments for certain knowledge of our inner lives and of the pure forms simultaneously represent a worldly support of faith in an eternal truth that is the highest being, namely, God. Hence we have a Christian version of Neoplatonism. This is the core of Augustine's philosophy.

AUGUSTINE AS A CHRISTIAN NEOPLATONIST

For the Neoplatonist Plotinus, the universe is an expression of a timeless creation, or emanation of existence, from the ineffable One, so that the universe can be arranged in various grades of existence and rank depending on the distance from the One. This emanation is eventually lost in non-being, which is matter.

Augustine made a synthesis between Neoplatonism and Christian faith. The One is reinterpreted as the Christian God. Revelation, through the life of Christ and the Bible, represents a historical proclamation, for man, of God's essence and God's plan. Through the revelation of Christ, and their belief in that revelation, Christians gain a certain access to what, for Plotinus, was the ineffable One. Faith provides the light that makes it possible for the Christian to glimpse the source of the light. Thus, at the highest point, faith takes an epistemological precedence over secular wisdom, while at the same time enlightening secular wisdom (*credo ut intelligam*, 'I believe in order to understand').

The Neoplatonists thought of the relationship between the One and the world as somewhat static and impersonal. Here, the eternal laws that rule are impersonal. The wise person's insight into the One, by *unio mystica*, can be realized at all times by those who have the strength to lift themselves so high. This highest insight is thus not conditioned by history. For Augustine, as a Christian, revelation is rooted in history by Christ's birth and teachings. Man's community with God in faith is thus historically conditioned. The same applies to God's creation of the universe; creation has its first origin and creation will come to an end. The existence of the universe is fundamentally historically changeable and precarious. Furthermore, the Christian God is not an impersonal principle, but a living personal God, whom human beings can love and fear, to whom they can pray, and to whom they will personally answer. The laws of the universe are not impersonal; they are an expression of a personal will, which creates and rules over everything. Thus, not only do change and historicity figure as basic features of the universe, but also man's inner spiritual life comes to the fore, and in such a way that the source of the universe is essentially understood as a will – the will that man can only partially recognize through the revelation of God's word, i.e., through Christ and the Bible. Here we meet, moreover, a Judeo-Christian conception of creation, as God is said to have created the universe out of nothing (*creatio ex nihilo*). This is a radical view of the old question of change.

The universe is not conceived, as for the Neoplatonists, as an eternal emanation from the One, so that the universe is really the One, and so that this emanation loses itself in matter as non-being. God, according to Augustine, is the independent, spiritual force that has created the universe, both the spiritual and the material, and created it out of nothing. This means that all things are not on the same level, that the Creator and the created are separate from each other. Pantheism is thus excluded.

Because God and the world are separated in this way, Augustine cannot entertain the idea of a mystical union with God; that is, that a human being, in an ecstatic state, can achieve union with the One. God, in his independent majesty, can never become one with the world. A human being's fellowship with God in faith is a relationship between two persons; it does not mean that the human soul enters the world spirit. On the other hand, Augustine shares the view that it is through our inner life that we come into contact with God. As spiritual beings created in God's image, we can by faith have fellowship with God, internally. God's presence in our inner life is something that believers have knowledge of through introspection, according to Augustine, even if God is and remains unattainable by our mundane reason. The principle of 'creation out of nothing' also means that the body, the material, is not merely an emanation whose existence is lost in non-being. For Augustine, the physical and sensible things are a created reality. Evil is thus not to be found simply in our attraction to the material. For Augustine, moral evil is primarily a misuse of the will, not a lack of being. However, Augustine attempts to understand metaphysical evil as a privation of existence, in line with Neoplatonic thought.

The changes in the basic Neoplatonic concepts that Augustine thus makes entail a change in the way these concepts are used and a change in intellectual atmosphere. Concepts such as creation, person, will, love, sin, and salvation emerge as fundamental metaphysical concepts. What is cosmologically important is not nature, nor the pure ideas, but, rather, the relationship between God and man, a relationship that is of a personal kind. With Christianity man thus moves into the centre of the universe. Not only is man a noble creature, but also the universe was largely created for man and for man's devotion of his life to the Creator's purpose and laws. This applies, in principle, to all human beings, in that all are created in God's image. And this devotion to God is a varying relationship in which will and faith, passion and sin, and love, punishment, and salvation all have a part.[5]

The relationship between human beings, both in reality and in the ideal, is, for Augustine, characterized by the same concepts. Feelings and will, sin and punishment are central. In this connection, the relationship between man and woman is one of tension in an interesting way: in Augustine's basic Neoplatonic view, the spiritual is above the physical. Spiritual love between man and woman is therefore noble. But physical love between man and woman is something lower.

KNOWLEDGE AND WILL

The will plays an important role in Augustine's philosophy. It is viewed as a decisive factor in our spiritual life. Reason and knowledge, of course, play a part, as in making choices, but the will still takes precedence over reason. Augustine's emphasis on the will, and on feelings, means that he holds what we could call an existentialist conception of faith, in opposition to an intellectualist view of faith: believing is not just accepting something as true; it is passionately and intensely asserting that something is true. (Cf. Søren Kierkegaard's 'Subjectivity is truth', Ch. 19.)

At the same time, Augustine's emphasis on the will entailed his opposition to the common Greek conception of the will as a force engaged to reach what reason has recognized as being good. The Greeks had, in general, an intellectualist view of man (reason takes precedence over the will), while Augustine had a voluntaristic view of man (the will takes precedence over reason). In accordance with this voluntaristic viewpoint, and in harmony with common Christian thought, Augustine also claims that feelings play a decisive role. He thinks that feelings in fact play a larger role in human life than many intellectuals think, and, moreover, that many feelings are ethically valuable. From this background, he attacks the Stoics' dispassionate attitude, claiming that a good person (a good Christian) *should* feel love and compassion, shame and regret. The good person is, above all, filled with love, for God and for other people – not only friendly goodwill, but burning and sincere love. Augustine's view of the will and the question of what an ethically correct choice is, is also connected with his philosophical-theological view of man's free will, original sin, and the problem of evil.

From the start, Augustine thought that he could attribute absolute free will to man: our actions depend greatly on our own will. We can desire to seek God and follow his word, or we can wilfully not follow him; that is to say, we can choose sin. It is only through free choice that we can have sin. Evil thus stems from man's free will, to man's wilful misuse of the will. In addition to this, Augustine thought that certain forms of evil are expressions of absolute absence of 'Being' and, hence, of 'the good' – in a Neoplatonic sense. In other words, human beings are free, and only by freely choosing what is evil can they sin. But why do human beings freely choose to sin? And why did God create human beings capable of sin by an act of their will?

Later in life, however, Augustine presented an almost diametrically opposed doctrine: the freedom of the will is attributed only to the first man, Adam. Adam could freely choose between sinning and not sinning. But since he chose to sin, human nature became deeply corrupt, including all of humanity. All other human beings cannot avoid sinning. Choice and freedom no longer seem to be present. Since all human beings have to sin, and actually do sin, Augustine also thought that all deserve eternal damnation. But God still allows, by his grace, a certain minority to escape damnation. Since everyone is sinful, the selection of those to be saved is not due to their own merit or virtue. Since we all, in essence, are equally sinful, this selection is arbitrary. The great majority will be damned, and an arbitrarily chosen minority will be eternally blessed. Furthermore, Augustine held that this entire process was planned by God in advance. This is the core of Augustine's doctrine of predestination. Everything that happens has been predetermined by God.

On the one hand, God has foreknown everything. On the other hand, human beings act freely. Is this not a contradiction? God foreknows human actions, but they remain free, says Augustine. And he suggests that there are two kinds of time perspectives. We live in 'temporal' time. God, on the other hand, transcends this conception of time, since he has created time along with the universe. From this perspective, God does not foreknow a human action in the sense that he, at a previous point in time within a temporal frame of reference, perceives what a coming action will be. God foreknows a human action in the sense that he is *beyond* temporal time, and thus exists simultaneously with time. Thus, God's prescience does not predetermine a human action – just as we, when we remember an action from the past, cannot be said to determine this action. God foreknows everything by seeing everything that happens, since he himself is beyond all time, but he thus determines just as little as do we when we remember a past action.

These are difficult concepts. Some will think that they contradict what Augustine says elsewhere about free will. It should be mentioned that Augustine put forward these ideas during a theological debate with the Manichaeans. Perhaps in the heat of this debate Augustine went further than he normally would have done. But these conceptions can generally be seen in connection with Augustine's own experience of man's hopeless battle against sin, with God's mercy as the only hope.

Seen from a Christian perspective, the idea of predestination must still appear to be problematic.[6] If it is decided in advance who will be saved and who will be damned, why did God reveal his word in the Incarnation of the historical Christ? Who, then, did Christ come to save? Is not, then, the Incarnation and all of Christ's works and suffering – that is, the core itself of Christianity – basically superfluous? Or does all of this show precisely that mundane wisdom cannot grasp the Christian truths of faith? Or perhaps the moral is that if we, by our reason, could understand God's works, revelation and Christianity would be unnecessary for us.

Augustine's view of the relationship between the Christian truths taken on faith and mundane knowledge is that certain revealed truths can be grasped by reason, while others surpass our understanding; at the same time, no truths taken on faith can ultimately conflict with reason when reason is correctly understood. Among the revealed truths that Augustine thought we could understand were those of God's existence and the immortality of the human soul.

THE PROBLEM OF UNIVERSALS, AND THE SCHOLASTICS

The designation 'the problem of universals' refers to the medieval debate on whether or not universal concepts, universals, exist and, if they do exist, what form of existence they have. But this discussion is not unique to the Middle Ages. The basic issues in the problem of universals may be found in the debate between Platonism and Aristotelianism, and the conflict is just as current today as it was then.

The following two terms were generally used in this controversy: 1) *universalia* (singular: *universale*) denoted universal concepts, that is to say, properties like brown, circular, etc., and species like human being, horse, etc.; 2) *particularia* (singular: *particulare*) denoted particular objects, that is to say, this brown door, this round lamp, etc. Plato's ideas are closely related to *universalia*. (But Plato's ideas are not only universal concepts but also ideals.) Moreover, in Plato's philosophy, *particularia* are the perishable objects in the world of sense experience. In Aristotle, on the other hand, *particularia* correspond to substances, the independently existing particular objects, and *universalia* correspond to the universal forms of the substances.

The different viewpoints in the problem of universals are determined by which answer we give to the question of to what extent *universalia* exist: those who claim that *universalia* are *real* are called '*realists*' (or 'conceptual realists'). Those who claim that *universalia* do not really exist, but are only *names* (Latin: *nomina*), are called 'nominalists'. These are the two extreme positions. But there are many variations of these viewpoints, and there are mediating positions.

PLATONIC REALISM

Plato claimed that the ideas (*universalia*) possess the highest and most real form of existence, and that they thus exist independently both of our comprehension and of whether there are perceptible phenomena that reflect the ideas. This view is *extreme realism* (Platonic realism): the universal of 'justice' exists, according to this extreme realism, independently of whether we comprehend what justice is, and independently of whether just societies exist. In other words, *universalia* possess a completely independent existence: if a nuclear catastrophe wiped out all people and all things, *universalia* would continue to exist. In the Middle Ages, this extreme realism was often characterized by the expression *universalia ante res*; that is, *universalia* exist prior to the objects. The phrase 'prior to' (*ante*) shows that *universalia* exist independently of the objects, since things, including human beings, are created by God out of his thoughts (*universalia*).

ARISTOTELIAN REALISM

Aristotle claimed that *the forms* (*universalia*) exist *in* particular things (*particularia*). Through *particularia*, we can, with the aid of thought, recognize *universalia*, but universalia do not exist independently of the things: according to Aristotle, there is not a universal 'justice' that exists independently of whether a just person or a just society can be found. Justice does not possess an independent existence, but exists only *in* just societies and just individuals. This position is also a form of realism, since *universalia* are said to exist, to be real. But here, *universalia* are not said to possess a higher form of existence than *particularia*; moreover, the existence of *universalia* is not said to be totally independent of *particularia*. In the Middle Ages this position was usually characterized by the expression *universalia in rebus*, *universalia* in the objects. The universal (the form) of 'circle' existed before human beings, and will exist after they are gone; but the existence of the universal of 'circle' is dependent on round objects.

Now, other thinkers claimed that *universalia* (such as justice) existed neither in the objects nor independently of the objects, but that *universalia* are only names used for practical reasons to refer to objects that resemble one another. Instead of listing the proper names of all horses, we talk about 'horse'; that is, we use a common name, a universal. This *nominalism* was generally characterized by the expression *universalia post res*; that is, *universalia* exist after the objects. That is to say, we first learn about particular objects, and then we ascribe common names (*universalia*) when it is practical to do so. The nominalists could say that the concepts exist *in* individual consciousness, but not as anything independent of individual consciousness.

There are various mediating positions between the viewpoints that we have mentioned. In the Middle Ages, for example, some claimed that *universalia* are *ante res* ('prior to the objects'), as seen *from the perspective of God*, who has created the objects after his own thoughts. But *universalia* are *in rebus* ('in the object'), as seen *from the objects* as they actually are; at the same time, *universalia* are *post res* ('posterior to the object'), as seen *from human cognition*, which is here understood as a process starting in the sense experience of particular objects. Thomas Aquinas may be said to have held such a viewpoint, which is thus a kind of harmonizing synthesis of various views.

We have mentioned here different answers to the basic question in the controversy about universals. Earlier, we sketched some of the arguments, in Plato and Aristotle, and we have mentioned how the different answers have different implications: realism, for instance, makes it possible to claim that there is an objective morality which is accessible to reason. In the Middle Ages, moreover, many philosophers thought that realism harmonized best with Christian theology. At times, the nominalists were considered heretics.

We will see that the views of the relationship between faith and reason, which are generally different in Catholicism and Protestantism, are connected with the position taken in the controversy about universals. In early medieval philosophy, realism predominated. In Thomas Aquinas, in the high Middle Ages (1250), we meet a moderate realism: *universalia* exist in God's thoughts (*ante res*), in the particular objects (*in rebus*), and as abstractions in human thought (*post res*). But in the late Middle Ages, nominalism gained ground, as, for example, with William of Ockham and, later, Martin Luther.

Medieval philosophy, often called 'scholasticism' – i.e. the philosophy learned at school – is generally divided into three periods:

1   Early scholasticism is usually placed in the period from Augustine, around AD 400 until around 1200. This period is, in many ways, characterized by the thought of Augustine and the Neoplatonism by which he was influenced. Prominent in that period are the Irish monk John Scotus Erigena (ninth century); Anselm of Canterbury (1033–1109), known for his so-called ontological argument for God's existence (see this chapter, God and the world); and the sceptical and open-minded Frenchman Peter Abelard (twelfth century), who especially contributed to shaping the typical scholastic method of discussing philosophical questions.

2   The period of high scholasticism lasted from around 1200 until the early fourteenth century. This is the epoch of the grand systems and syntheses, with men like Albertus Magnus (Albert the Great; d. 1280), his student Thomas Aquinas, and Aquinas' primary philosophical opponent, John Duns Scotus (d. 1308).

3   Late scholasticism lasted from the early fourteenth century until the Renaissance. The major philosopher of late scholasticism is the Englishman William of Ockham, who declared that faith and reason are essentially different, who defended nominalism and the turn towards the empirical, and who thus heralded the advent of the philosophy of the new age.

Theologically, the problem of universals was a debate about the relationship between faith and reason. As in the tradition from Tertullian to Luther, the Christian nominalists emphasized the uniqueness of faith and revelation, which reason could not comprehend. According to the nominalists, if reason could comprehend what revelation teaches us through God's word and faith, the whole point of the Incarnation would be weakened. The Christian realists viewed this differently. Thus, Christians influenced by Neoplatonism who proposed, with the aid of reason, to approach God (the primordial source) could do so only if the concepts of our mind correspond to something real. This presupposes an ontology (theory of being) and an epistemology (theory of knowledge) of the kind that was developed in the so-called realist position in the problem of universals.

The doctrine of original sin (that man, as a species, inherits a sinful nature), the mystery of the Eucharist (that the bread and wine become Christ's body and blood), the doctrine of the Trinity (that God is simultaneously one person and three persons: the Father, the Son, and the Holy Spirit), and the doctrine of the Atonement of our sins (that Christ can expiate mankind's guilt and thus make salvation available to everyone) were all viewed, by many Christians as truths of the faith which could be most easily understood from the viewpoint of conceptual realism.

THOMAS AQUINAS – HARMONY AND SYNTHESIS

Life. *Thomas Aquinas was born in 1225 near the city of Aquino, not far from Naples. He studied at the Benedictine Abbey of Monte Cassino, and then at the University of Naples, before joining the newly formed Dominican order in spite of opposition from his family. At the age of about 20 he went to study in Paris where he met Albertus Magnus, studied under him later in Cologne, before returning to Paris. Aquinas' life was filled with work and travel to centres of learning, resulting in a prodigious collection of writings, although he was barely 50 years old when he died (1274). He was canonized in 1323, only 49 years after his death. In 1879 his philosophy was adopted by the Roman Catholic Church.*

Aquinas' best-known works are probably Summa theologiae *('Handbook of Theology'), and* Summa de veritate catholicae fidei contra gentiles *('On the Truth of the Catholic Faith Against Non-Christians'). The former was intended to be used in schools; the latter to assist Christian missionaries. In addition to these comprehensive, but rapidly completed theses, he wrote a series of texts with a philosophical and theological content: commentaries on the Bible,* De regimine principum *('On Kingship'), and* Quaestiones disputatae *('Disputation Questions', discussing evil, truth, the soul, and other subjects).*

LAW AND JUSTICE

Most of Aristotle's works were long unknown in Western Christendom. Aristotle was rediscovered around 1200 AD. At first the Church was hostile: Aristotle was a pagan. In 1210, Aristotelianism was forbidden at the University of Paris. But it soon proved that Aristotle could not be banned, and Thomas Aquinas created a theological synthesis of Christianity and Aristotelianism. This synthesis would prove to be so vital that the Roman Catholic Church finally adopted Thomism as its favourite philosophy.

Most of the Aristotelian concepts recur in Aquinas, but they are reinterpreted in a Christian framework. Aquinas 'Christianized' Aristotle. Aristotle's first cause is exchanged with the Christian God. But Aquinas also distinguished himself from Aristotle when it came to consideration of *law*. Aquinas did not live in the city-state, but in feudal society. Since we have already discussed Aristotle, we will begin by pointing out certain unique features of Aquinas in connection with the relationship between faith and reason, and in connection with law.

The Thomist synthesis of Christianity and Aristotelianism is characterized by *harmonization*: harmonization of God and the world, and harmonization of faith and reason. In the problem of universals, Aquinas accepted a moderate (Aristotelian) conceptual realism: concepts exist, but only *in* objects. Our knowledge begins with sense impressions, but we recognize the universal principles in objects (*universalia*) by abstraction. This has theological implications for Aquinas: with our natural reason we can recognize many of the universe's principles, including evidence that the universe was created by a Higher Being (Aquinas' proofs of God's existence). In other words, reason and revelation (faith) merge.

sense impressions/reason

There are Christian truths that can never be apprehended by reason (C–D, such as God's essence). But reason can lead us towards God. And for certain truths (B–C) we can possess both insight apprehended by reason and insight apprehended by faith (according to Aquinas, this includes insight into God's existence).

As for Aristotle, the universe is, for Aquinas, ordered hierarchically, but with the difference that Aristotle's first cause is exchanged for a personal God.

God
angels
man
animals
plants
rocks, earth

Like Aristotle, Aquinas considered man a social creature. That human beings live in society is a condition of their ability to actualize themselves. Politics is therefore a natural activity that allows the realization of human attributes. This means that political science is largely independent of revelation: even heathens can live a good life to a great extent. Here again we have a harmonization of Greek and Christian thought: it is true that human beings can lead a virtuous and happy life without revelation. And it is the statesman's task to prepare the way for this realization, whether that statesman (the prince) is a Christian or not. But beyond virtue and happiness stands the final goal: salvation. And that is the priest's task to encourage. Thus, the statesman's task naturally merges with the priest's task, since a civilized life (virtue and happiness) is the basis for salvation. The political-ethical stage possesses a certain amount of independence of the religious stage, while, at the same time, the political-ethical stage is the first step in the direction of the religious stage.

Aristotle viewed the city-state as the final stage of human self-realization. For Aquinas, who lived in a Christian feudal society, the final goal is eternal salvation in the next life, and the highest social environment is the law-regulated, Christian society. For Aristotle, virtue is self-realization in a local, exclusive society through active participation in civic life. For Aquinas, virtue is self-realization through a moral way of life within a stable, all-encompassing social hierarchy governed by law, but in which only a few actively participate in political activity – a minority govern and the majority are governed.

Law, for Aquinas, is a *decree of reason* made by a ruler for the common good of those subject to the law, and for whom the law is promulgated. Thus, the law is normative. Aquinas discusses different laws that are related: the eternal law is a decree of reason expressing God's provision for the entire creation. Since everything is subject to God's provision, everything is subject to the eternal law. But rational creatures are subject to the eternal law in a more definite way than other creatures. Rational creatures are themselves a part of God's provision; they provide for themselves and for others. They participate in the eternal reason since they themselves can naturally perform right actions and seek right goals. This actualization of the eternal law in rational creatures is the natural law. This is how rational creatures can use their reason, or *lumen naturale* ('natural light'), to distinguish good from evil. In other words, we recognize the natural law through rational reflection. This is an ability belonging to all rational beings, pagans as well as Christians. Aquinas thus thinks that we can recognize good and evil independently of revelation. He thinks that these laws are something that is evident, something that exists objectively and that is universally valid. The natural law is one and the same for all people. Hence, Aquinas gives a theological version of natural law theory.

The advantage that Christians have over non-Christians is knowledge of the divine law through revelation. But the divine law applies basically to salvation. When it comes to what must be done to live a good life, non-Christians can also have sufficient knowledge through rational acknowledgement of the natural law. Again, we see the harmonization: a relative independence of the political-ethical life, while at the same time, everything is ultimately subject to the divine order.

Theologians who consider will to be God's essence understand good as that which God at any time wills. Thus, if we do not know God's will, we cannot know what good is. And if God had so wished, he could have ordained different criteria of the good. Christians, who know God's will, are thus in a unique position with respect to insight into the good. And recognizing the good is not so much a question of rational reflection as of correct faith; that is to say, it is a consequence of revelation and grace. For Aquinas, God is, above all, rational, willing what is rational and what is good. God cannot desire evil. He desires what is good because it is good; the good is not good because God wills it. (An extension of this problem is the question of God's omnipotence and of the wholly good and omnipotent God's relationship to evil.)

Human law is, for Aquinas, the laws in force in a society. He distinguishes between practical and theoretical reason. Both forms of reason are based on unproven principles, as in Aristotle's principle of contradiction. But while theoretical reason conforms to things in nature to attain knowledge, practical reason concerns rules and norms for human behaviour. While, for theoretical reason, it is the object that gives us knowledge, practical reason prescribes what our behaviour ought to be. Since the conditions of our active life are not universal and necessary, but individual and arbitrary, the ability to make practical judgements should be a part of practical reason. Nothing else is needed, according to Aquinas. The method, in other words, must be appropriate to the matter at hand. Hence we have different methods for different conditions. And not all methods need be equally strict. Thus, Aquinas advocates a flexible conception of adequate criteria in ethical and political questions.

For Aquinas, therefore, reason mediates between the universal laws and human behaviour (cf. the Stoics). By virtue of our reason we voluntarily follow the law. Therefore, only rational beings are subject to the law and, strictly, only those rational beings that can actualize reason. The exercise of power and punishment by the rulers is necessary when someone violates the law. Offenders must be forced back into law-abiding behaviour so that they do not harm themselves or others. Avoiding harm is a fundamental goal of the law. But beyond this is the positive realization of the good life. Here, the guide is virtue, not only the law. In addition to the cardinal virtues of wisdom, courage, temperance, and justice, Aquinas cites the Christian virtues of faith, hope, and charity. As we have already mentioned, salvation is the ultimate virtue for Aquinas, an extension of the legal-moral dimension.

In his view of the relationship between state and Church, Aquinas was a moderate papal supporter: he thought that the Church was above the state, and that the pope could excommunicate a tyrannical king. But at the same time, Aquinas accepted the Gelasian doctrine of the two powers, and he did not think that the Church's moral superiority should develop into legal superiority. As an Aristotelian, he thought, moreover, that society was naturally given; no ecclesiastical leadership is needed in matters of state. But at the same time, there is no absolute distinction between society (reason) and Christianity (faith) – the spiritual and worldly tasks merge to a certain degree.

ONTOLOGY

Aquinas sought a synthesis of faith and reason in the form of a harmonization of Christian revelation and Greek philosophy, especially Aristotelianism. But this synthesis also included influence from Neoplatonism, transmitted through Augustine. And the legacy from Aristotle reached Aquinas through Arab philosophers such as Averroës (see this chapter, Arabic philosophy and science).

ESSE *AND* ENS

Thomist philosophy can be characterized as a philosophy of *Being*, a philosophy about existence – not only of persons, but of substance in general. The concept 'to be' (Latin: *esse*) holds a fundamental position for Aquinas.[7] Thomism is essentially an 'ontology', a theory of being. This fundamental concept in Thomist philosophy, *esse*, is not directly identical with God. Ultimately, what we can comprehend with our mind is this fundamental *esse*. Beyond that which *is*, we can imagine nothing. What, then, is entailed by this *esse*, this Being? First, we can say that every particular thing that *is*, is an existent thing, a being (*ens*), such as this book, this tree, this chair, this person, etc. *Esse*, or Being, is not, on the other hand, one of these particular things. *Esse* represents '*is-ness*', which is common to all beings. *Esse*, we could say, is what makes a being into a being. It is the Being of beings. Being is thus itself 'no-thing', not a being among other beings, but that which is particular for all beings to the extent that they exist. Being (*esse*) is thus more fundamental than any particular being (*ens*).

We can, however, through thought, comprehend Being in and by the particular existing phenomena, according to Aquinas. But to penetrate beyond Being again with our thought, in order to know God, or the meaning of Being, is not possible. Through thought we can arrive at Being as something without boundaries and without blemish, as something infinite and perfect, but we cannot, through thought, comprehend what this means. Being thus marks the limit of human cognition. Everything which can be thought, including thought itself, is determined by Being. Thus, Being represents philosophy's great mystery; that something *is*, is the very mystery of Being.

If we then turn our attention to the various existing things and phenomena, we can first mention that Aquinas distinguishes between the fact that a thing is and what a thing is, between existence (*existentia*) and essence (*essentia*). What can be determined of a thing, what can be limited and conceptually understood, and thus defined, is the thing's essence – its 'whatness'. But the fact that it is, its existence, can be comprehended only directly and intuitively; it cannot be explained and further defined.

THE CATEGORIES

Among the many definitions that can be formulated about various things, about their manner of being (as that certain things are round, others flat, others smooth, etc.), some definitions apply to all things and phenomena, to all beings. Such universal definitions are called categories. We have the categories of, for instance, quality, quantity, relation, action, and passion, as well as time, space, and order (for external things).[8]

ACTUS AND POTENTIA

Among these basic characteristics common to all beings are *actus* and *potentia* – a conceptual pair reminiscent of Aristotle's actuality and potentiality. For Aquinas, as for Aristotle, this conceptual pair indicates a dimension of depth in the universe: in each creature there is a dynamic interplay between what appears to be real (actual) and what is latent (actualizable). Change occurs when latent possibilities are actualized. In living beings, like plants, animals, and human beings, the urge for change may be internally motivated, whereas in inorganic beings, like stone, soil, and water, change is caused by external conditions. The notion of change is thus tied to the doctrine of *actus* and *potentia*, as in Aristotle. And for Aquinas, as for Aristotle, the universe is hierarchically ordered according to the various levels of *actus* and *potentia*. From God as *actus purus*, all potentialities are actualized downwards to *materia prima*, which represents the concept of pure potentiality without actualization (see this chapter, God and the world).[9]

CAUSES

The doctrine of act and potency, and thus of change, is also connected with the doctrine of the four causes or principles (again, as in Aristotle): *matter*, or what something is made of; *form*, or what matter is characterized by; the *efficient cause*, which forms matter by external influence (causally); the *end*, which gives a direction or purpose to the process.

FORM AND MATTER

When the particular being (*ens*) thus stands in the tension between potentiality and actuality, where change can mediate and where the four 'causes' form the basis, we also have the distinction between form and matter (for example, shape and material). As in Aristotle, this provides a basis for a hierarchic order of all beings (see this chapter, Law and justice) — according to what form they actualize: inorganic things, plants, animals, human beings, and angels — from the lower towards the higher, from pure potentiality to pure actuality, from pure matter without form to pure form without matter. Pure actuality (*actus purus*) has actualized all of the potentiality it possesses, and can therefore not be changed. Thus, pure actuality is eternally the same. This points, for Aquinas, in the direction of God. This indicates to him that it is rational to believe that God exists; but it does not give us insight into what God is in his essence.

These are notions that resemble Aristotle's. But they also have clear parallels with Neoplatonism and its hierarchic world-view in which the primordial source is the fountain of Being, which then emanates and gradually moves towards darkness and non-being. But while Aristotle and Aquinas, in a sense, start at the bottom, and move upwards step by step, the Neoplatonists may be said to start with the primordial source (God, the ideas) and move downwards from there. The former attempt to illuminate the highest principles from the perceptible phenomena. The latter attempt to illuminate the perceptible phenomena from the highest ground.

This difference shows precisely the basic difference between these two types of philosophy, the Neoplatonic and the Aristotelian. This difference is reflected in the different view of *universalia*: radical conceptual realism (Platonism) conceives that thought can quickly penetrate into the essence of the universe through comprehension of the universal characteristics of all beings, while moderate conceptual realism (Aristotelianism) is more careful to move from the forms in the particular phenomena towards the more universal characteristics.

SOUL AND BODY

In the hierarchic world-view, the lowest beings are inorganic things (rocks, earth, air, etc.). They are without inherent activity and organic unity. They are thus passive, and are only changed by external pressure (an efficient cause). The plants are above the inorganic things because plants have their own inherent activity and organic structure. They can change through their own driving force (final cause). Next come the animals, who have a greater degree of inherent activity and a higher degree of organic structure than the plants. As a result, the higher animals can actively pursue a goal (as when the fox hunts the rabbit). In man, personal activity is the freest and organic structure the most advanced. Human beings can, freely and independently, both set goals and actively achieve those goals.

Human beings are, for Aquinas, the highest material beings. A human being is body and soul at the same time. This is in contrast to the Neoplatonic view of the body as a non-real covering for the soul, which is regarded as the genuine human being. This also means that bodily love, with reproduction as its goal, within marriage, has a positive status for Aquinas, in opposition to the Augustinian view. This positive view of the material body also contrasts with the radical distinction between body and soul that we find in Descartes.

Thomism, too, claims that the soul is one and indivisible, and that it does not vanish when the body dies. The soul is immortal. Ultimately, the human soul holds an independent position relative to the body. For Aquinas, the human soul has two main functions, namely, cognition and will. The will is understood as an activating force that follows cognition. Cognition comprehends what is good as a goal, and the will then initiates action to achieve the goal. Cognition is therefore the primary component, and the will is better understood as an impulse that is dependent on what is set before it as a goal. Therefore, Thomism represents a form of intellectualism in its view of human beings and their behaviour: reason takes precedence over the will. The opposite position, voluntarism, claims that the will takes precedence over reason (cf. this chapter, Knowledge and will).

EPISTEMOLOGY

Aquinas incorporated the theory of knowledge in his general philosophy. This was, in many ways, usual before the later rationalists (such as Descartes) and empiricists (such as Locke) placed epistemology in the centre. The Thomist view of knowledge can be characterized as realistic in the sense that it assumes that we can gain knowledge about the world. His view is thus opposed to epistemological scepticism. Aquinas further maintains that we gain knowledge by sense experience and by reflection on what we have experienced. This is in opposition to the Platonic view that emphasizes an independent path to insight into the ideas, and in opposition to the Kantian view that emphasizes that the knowing subject fundamentally shapes the sense impressions from the external world. In other words, Aquinas holds that knowledge begins with sense experience. Nothing is in the intellect without first being in the senses. Sense experience applies to particular, concrete phenomena. By sense experience, we receive direct impressions of these perceptible phenomena. We do not create these objects. From the sense impressions of the perceptible phenomena we can then, with our intellect, recognize common traits in the various phenomena and formulate concepts.

Here we again encounter the basic problems of the controversy about universals, in which Aquinas took a moderately realistic position. It is, however, worth

noting that his position can be interpreted and stretched in the direction of
nominalism: if we say not only that cognition starts with the sense experience of
particular things, but that particular things (*particularia*), for Aquinas, are the most
important ontologically, and that concepts (*universalia*) are merely human abstractions of particular things, we end in nominalism. This was exactly the interpretation that arose after Thomism and high scholasticism, as in William of Ockham.
But the reasonable interpretation of Aquinas is that of a moderate realism: although
cognition begins with the sense experience of particular things, this does not mean
that direct sense experience has a higher status than the intellect's recognition of
concepts. All cognition starts with the sense experience of particular things, but
the universal concepts that we derive from this do not then need to be understood
as pure abstractions created by human beings. Regardless of whether the concepts
are known from the background of sense experience, they can be said to have an
independent ontological status. Aquinas claims that they *exist* in the objects, and that
we, by thought, recognize only the concepts which are manifested in the objects.
That which is recognized afterwards, in time (*post rem*), is not inferior in ontological rank or epistemological status. *Universalia* exist independently in the objects,
and by recognizing *universalia*, we gain insight into the basic features of reality.

For Aquinas, both particular objects (*particularia*) and the forms or concepts they
include (*universalia*) are created by God. In the same way that sense experience and
thought are both God-given cognitive abilities in man, both things and concepts
have a common origin in God. Moderate realism, which involves a certain equal-
izing coordination of *particularia* and *universalia*, thus has a foundation in Christian
teleology; namely, in the idea of God as a creator by means of *particularia* as well
as of *universalia*. Furthermore, this means that God, in a way, has secured the correspondence between our cognition and the external world. Our sensory abilities
were created so that we can recognize the sensible creation around us. And our
cognitive abilities were created so that we can recognize the universal forms
around us. God, as Creator, is here a kind of guarantor that reliable knowledge is
possible. God is then understood as a rational and good God, not as an 'evil spirit'
that will either deceive us or act irrationally. (Cf. Descartes, on God as guarantor,
Ch. 9, Descartes – methodical doubt . . .)

Aquinas' view of the sciences may be clarified on the basis of what we have now
mentioned: all human knowledge builds on the sense experience of particular
things. But particular things have two aspects that we can distinguish by thought,
namely, form and matter. Matter is a condition for motion and change. It is, moreover, matter that individuates particular things, that is, makes it possible for two
things to have the same form without being identical, since each thing's matter
occupies a space that another thing's matter cannot occupy at the same time. When
we recognize something about an object, it is the form that we recognize. The form
is what makes the thing recognizable. The form is the thing's structure and appearance; the form makes it possible to characterize the thing by what it is – round or
oval, green or yellow, etc.

Knowledge of external, material things is gained, according to Aquinas, when
we ignore something in order to focus on something else. Knowledge necessitates
that we abstract from something. Through various degrees of such abstraction, the
various sciences arise, such as natural philosophy, mathematics, and metaphysics.

In *natural philosophy* we study material things, like trees, horses, and tables. But our subject of study is what makes them into a tree, horse, or table, that is, their form or essence, and not what makes them into this particular tree, this particular table, or this particular horse. In other words, we look beyond that which individuates; that is to say, we abstract from the matter to the extent that the matter individuates. But we do not abstract from the matter to the extent that the matter makes the object perceptible, because it is of perceptible things that natural philosophy seeks to know the nature. In natural philosophy, then, we abstract from the matter as an individuating principle, but not as that which makes sense experience possible. We seek a thing's essence to the extent that it is perceptible, but not as a particular, distinct thing.

In *mathematics* we abstract from the matter both as an individuating factor and as that which makes sense experience possible. A mathematician studies a thing's measurable properties and structures. Both the individuating aspects of this horse and the fact that it is a perceptible object are here abstracted. They are uninteresting to mathematicians, who are interested only in the purely quantitative sets and relations.

In *metaphysics*, we encounter the third and most extreme degree of abstraction. Here, too, we start with the simple, perceptible things. But we abstract not only from the individuating and the perceptible aspects but also from the quantitative attributes. In metaphysics, it is only the thing's *esse*, its being, that is interesting – *that* it *is*, and furthermore, the basic forms connected with *esse*, namely, the categories.

This is how the three types of theoretical science arose, according to Aquinas – as exemplified by natural philosophy, mathematics, and metaphysics. The objects of these sciences appear by abstracting from the perceptible, particular things. The theoretical sciences do not have their own objects, as in the form of independent, existing essences or ideas. The objects of the theoretical sciences exist in the material objects. Aquinas' epistemology and his doctrine of the sciences are thus connected with his experientially oriented perspective and also with his moderate conceptual realism.

ANTHROPOLOGY AND MORAL PHILOSOPHY

Aquinas' anthropology and moral philosophy, like his ontology and epistemology, have distinct Aristotelian features. In opposition to the Neoplatonic tradition (for example, Augustine) Aquinas thinks that the worldly and social life, like the body and its functions, are something natural and basically positive. Theologically, this means that these things are also viewed as having been created by God. Just as Aquinas thinks that man can, naturally, recognize important aspects of creation, apart from Christian revelation and faith, he also thinks that man, apart from Christianity, can live a good social life and can, to a great extent, gain knowledge of the ethical norms of life. Being created by God, we have an ability to know, apart from Christ's words and revelation. We have our *lumen naturale*, or natural light. Moreover, we can live a rational and social life apart from Christ's words and independently of Christian discipline. Thus, Aquinas did not share Augustine's voluntaristic and pessimistic view of man.

Since Aquinas largely bases his thought on Aristotle, important aspects of the Thomist doctrine of human nature become purely philosophical theory, without Christian or biblical elements. This distinction between mundane wisdom and Christian faith is not a handicap for Aquinas, but, on the contrary, forms a major point in his view of the relationship between philosophy and Christianity, and between secular knowledge and Christian faith. A major point in Aquinas' moral philosophy is that human beings have capabilities (potentialities) which they can in various ways realize (actualize). Good actions are those which, to the greatest degree, realize the specifically human capabilities that best fulfil human nature.

In his view of the essence of human nature, Aquinas also follows the Aristotelian view: man is both a rational and a spiritual being. Good actions, therefore, especially realize these rational and spiritual capabilities. But Aquinas, like Aristotle, does not reject the notion that man is a mundane creature, or that different people have varying capabilities. As a result, there are several ways of life available to us; for example, the contemplative life and the active life. But regardless of what we choose on the basis of our abilities and position, Aquinas recommends, like Aristotle, that we proceed with moderation. The extreme is not natural, and is not based on the good.

Aquinas' moral philosophy builds on the notion that actions have a purpose. We aspire to some kind of goal. This goal is primarily to actualize our uniquely human capabilities. Our task is to realize our own variation of these capabilities in the situation in which we find ourselves. As an aid in this goal-oriented way of life, we can rely on our reason. The goal is mainly to become rational, but at the same time, the means of its realization is by reason. This realization occurs when we are educated in practical wisdom, and advised by mature persons about what is required and which actions are appropriate in various situations. That man is capable of goal-oriented actions is taken for granted by Aquinas: reason takes precedence over the will. We do what reason recognizes as good. We aspire to the goals that reason points out.

Aquinas assumes *universal* moral norms or laws. There are unchangeable and universally binding moral principles. That people may understand these laws and principles differently does not prove that they are relative, but only that our ability to comprehend them is fallible. Aquinas is thus a representative of the natural rights tradition. Philosophically, this is a consequence of his Aristotelian perspective. Theologically, this is a consequence of his view of God: God, who has created us, desires the good. The good is not relative to God's will, but God wills the good. In opposition to this, we have Luther's voluntaristic view of God. Yet Aquinas does not think that mundane reason and ability to lead a secular life are sufficient for us. The highest goal of man is salvation, and what is needed for salvation goes beyond what is needed for a socially and morally acceptable life. This is because revelation and faith are needed for salvation. Faith is needed to enlighten the goal of salvation for us, and faith and training are needed to help us achieve this highest goal.[10]

Here we see the transition in the Thomistic anthropology and morality from what we could call the Aristotelian-Christian to the specifically Christian. By this we mean that Aquinas finds that Aristotelianism is largely in harmony with Christianity, but, at the same time, he emphasizes that the Christian's ultimate end goes beyond Aristotelianism. This means that morality is not independent of religion. Even non-Christians can, according to Aquinas, find the correct moral norms and live a truly moral life. This is because they are created by God, with reason and with the capability of living a rational and social life. But they cannot achieve salvation, because salvation presupposes the Christian revelation.

Aquinas' positive view of the secular in relation to ethics is also reflected in his conception of the state and of society: man is a social being. He sees the state and society, along with structures like family, occupation, and estate, as natural aspects of being human. Aquinas does not view the state as a necessary instrument of discipline as Augustine does. The secular state and its institutions are, in and of themselves, good and rational. But the state should not become a goal in itself. And the secular state and its institutions can, of course, fall into decline and be corrupted in various ways.

GOD AND THE WORLD

Most scholastics thought that rational arguments for God's existence could be made. These arguments are often called 'proofs of God's existence'. Here the word *proof* can be misleading. These are not proofs in a deductive sense (cf. Ch. 7, The dispute over method). Besides, deductive proofs cannot prove their own premises, such attempts leading either to an infinite regression, to a vicious circle, or to an arbitrary break in the deductive chain. Nor are they proofs in the sense of empirical confirmation, as in the experimental sciences. The proofs under discussion are philosophical. They purport to prove that sense experience points beyond itself, towards something that we can call God.

It should also be noted that we are speaking about justifying our faith in God's *existence* – that God is – not of knowing how God is. When it comes to the question of God's essence or properties, Aquinas holds that we can answer this question only through revelation and faith, not mundane reason. Finally, it is worth noting that these arguments for God's existence are not decisive for the believing Christian. Revelation and faith are the appropriate means for a relationship with God. But these arguments are useful, especially against unbelievers.

When we talk about such proofs of God's existence as a form of rational argumentation, it is obvious that what counts as sufficient and persuasive reasons will vary with the various basic philosophical views. Neoplatonists, Thomists, sceptics, and followers of Luther have different fundamental views, and therefore react differently to the question of what are sufficient reasons in this connection. We can put this in more detail: Neoplatonists do not really use such proofs of God's existence, since they start, as it were, with the primordial source, with God, and descend to the world. For the Neoplatonists, it is rather the existence of the world that requires proof! The nominalists (followers of Luther) do not really require proofs of God's existence either, since they think that reason cannot rise above perceptible particular things; beyond this, there are only faith and revelation, and therefore no rational arguments for God's existence. Only the Aristotelians, in a broad sense, recognize proofs of God's existence since they ascribe to reason a field of operation beyond perceptible particular things (conceptual realism), and since they start at the bottom with perceptible particular things, and then ascend (moderate conceptual realism).

In the following discussion, we will first consider the so-called ontological argument for God's existence stated by Anselm. Afterwards, we will look at the 'five ways' – five proofs of God's existence stated by Aquinas.

ANSELM'S ONTOLOGICAL ARGUMENT FOR GOD'S EXISTENCE

Anselm's argument for God's existence goes roughly like this: our idea of God is an idea about perfection (the Highest Being). We cannot imagine a greater perfection. Independent existence is more perfect than relative existence (as in fiction). Thus, God, as the greatest perfection, must exist independently. The gist of this argument is that the idea of perfection is itself perfect, and that perfection must exist since perfection without existence is less perfect than perfection with existence. (Cf. Descartes' argument for God's existence, Ch. 9, Descartes – methodical doubt . . .)

This so-called ontological proof of God's existence was criticized already during Anselm's life (1033–1109). (It was later attacked by, among others, Kant, who, on the basis of his philosophy, criticized all attempts to prove or disprove God's existence, Ch. 15, Transcendental philosophy – theory of knowledge.) The criticism, in part, is that we cannot derive God's existence from the concept of God. Here there might possibly be some nominalist overtones. The critics argued, for instance, that the concept of perfection does not need to be perfect, just as the concept of brown does not itself need to be brown. To those who objected that we cannot derive the existence of something from its idea, Anselm could respond with conceptually realistic arguments about the existence of immaterial phenomena. If we have a clear idea of the Pythagorean theorem, we know, according to conceptual realism, that this theorem exists. And God is immaterial. It is therefore irrelevant to introduce arguments based on ideas of material phenomena, but it is relevant to introduce arguments about ideas of immaterial phenomena, like mathematical concepts. Thus, arguments for and against must be evaluated in light of the different basic philosophical positions. This shows, at the same time, how philosophical education is required in theological discussions, even in those instances where we reject philosophy's ability to answer religious questions.

AQUINAS' COSMOLOGICAL ARGUMENT FOR GOD'S EXISTENCE

Aquinas' so-called cosmological argument goes roughly as follows: the universe contains change. Seeds become trees, children grow up, and so on. But each such change in a phenomenon points to something besides this particular change, to something that is the origin of the change. Each phenomenon in change thus points to another phenomenon that originated the change. The point is that a change cannot simultaneously be its own cause. Another phenomenon is necessary in order to cause change. In this way, we can move from that which is changing, to something that is the cause of this change, and, again, from this cause to its cause, and so on. Thus, we will be able to go further and further backwards. A concrete example is the retracing process that starts temporally with children and moves back to parents. But we cannot imagine that this retracing from the moved to the mover can go on infinitely. There must be a first stage. Anything else is unthinkable. There must therefore be a first cause that is itself not caused, but that is the origin of all change and all motion. This first cause is the prime mover, and this we call God, according to Aquinas. It is worth noting that he does not say that the first cause is God, but that this is what 'we call God'. This line of argument is thus meant to show that it is reasonable to claim that God exists, but the argument is not meant to show what God is, beyond that of being the first cause.

Several objections to this argument for God's existence have been presented: a challenge has been raised to the premise that everything that changes must necessarily receive an impulse to change from something else. Cannot things change on their own? This leads us into a discussion of what a thing is and how it relates to forces of change. Aquinas' view is based on the doctrine of *actus* and *potentia* and the four causes. Another objection is that it is not rationally compelling to claim that there must be a first cause because we cannot imagine an infinite regression. Cannot the universe be infinite in the sense that it does not have a starting point? Finally, it has been claimed that it is not the existence of the Christian God that is made probable, but, at best, the existence of a first cause that does not need to be a person, much less the Christian God. We need other reasons to be able to claim that the first cause is identical with the God of Christianity. Aquinas' own formulations show that he was aware of this difficulty, and therefore did not intend to stretch this argument too far.

AQUINAS' CAUSAL ARGUMENT FOR GOD'S EXISTENCE

The causal argument corresponds to the cosmological, but builds especially on the connection between cause and effect: every effect of a cause points back to the cause, which again points back to a prior cause, and so on. While the first cosmological argument for God's existence builds on the doctrine of act and potency and on the so-called causes by conceiving of change in a broader sense, this causal argument for God's existence builds on the special direct relationship between cause and effect.

AQUINAS' ARGUMENT FOR GOD'S EXISTENCE BASED ON NECESSITY

The argument for God's existence based on necessity is roughly as follows: everything on the Earth is basically contingent in the sense that its existence is not necessary. It could have been different from what it is. Other things and phenomena could have existed instead of those which do exist. This applies to things, events, and persons. It is not necessary that you or I exist. Or that New York and London exist. But it is unthinkable that everything is contingent. Thus, there must be something which is necessary. And this 'we call God', according to Aquinas.

AQUINAS' ARGUMENT FOR GOD'S EXISTENCE BASED ON THE IDEA OF A HIGHEST DEGREE OF PERFECTION AND OF BEING

Aquinas' fourth argument for God's existence is roughly as follows: we see that all that exists is more or less perfect and has more or less of Being. Therefore, we can imagine a gradation of being and of perfection. This hierarchic order points beyond the earthly towards something that is perfect and that is absolute Being – and this is what 'we call God', according to Aquinas. This line of argumentation builds on Aquinas' hierarchic world-view that we mentioned earlier.

AQUINAS' TELEOLOGICAL ARGUMENT FOR GOD'S EXISTENCE

Aquinas' so-called teleological (or physio-teleological) argument for God's existence is roughly as follows: we experience order in nature (*physis*) and hence we trace a purpose (*telos*) behind it. The universe appears to us to be well-ordered and well-structured. This order in the world and its many subtle connections point to a fundamentally rational and good design, and this, again, indicates a rational spirit that has created this design and that actualizes it in the universe – and this 'designing' spirit, according to Aquinas, is what 'we call God'.

This line of argument is based on the doctrine of the final cause, or purpose. The notion of a final cause became a matter of discussion for adherents of the mechanistic world-view, which rejects such teleological causes (Cf. Ch. 7).

THE PROBLEM OF EVIL

If God is the cause of everything, is he also the cause of evil? We will, in closing, briefly mention some of Aquinas' arguments on the problem of evil.

Some of what we call evil is necessarily a consequence of the fact that we live in a finite universe. Thus, things must be limited in space and time. Things do not last for ever, but are perishable – man included. These limitations, and the evil they entail, are therefore necessary, even in the most perfect universe. They can therefore not be ascribed to God's will.[11]

Much of what we believe to be evil only appears so to us from our finite position. Seen from a larger perspective, this apparent evil would vanish. Still, some evil is real and is caused by God. This is the evil that results when God punishes us for our sins. However, neither is this evil primarily caused by God, but, on the contrary, by human sin. Man's sin, the real evil, does not come from God, but from man's free actions. It is true that God has given man free will, to live uprightly or to sin. But the actual misuse of free will, the evil action, is not caused by God. This evil is evil precisely in the sense of non-being, as a privation of the good and of God. And this non-being *is* not and therefore has no cause, not even God.

MARSILIUS OF PADUA AND WILLIAM OF OCKHAM – FROM SYNTHESIS TO SCEPTICISM

The Thomist synthesis, with its harmonization of faith and reason, and Church and state, stands as the apex of thought in the High Middle Ages (thirteenth century). This was a relatively stable society with cultural and religious unity, in spite of regional divisions – a *universitas hominum*, a human community, in spite of the feudal hierarchy. A common Christian culture, with man in the centre, existed, but it is worth noting that man was thought of as a part of society and as a creature whose *raison d'être* was God. In the High Middle Ages the pope and the Church reached the peak of their power. The struggle between the pope and the emperor had been won by the pope.

Under Popes Innocent III, Gregory IX, and Innocent IV (1198–1254), the Church reached the peak of its secular power. The popes had come off well in the conflict with the emperors Otto IV and Frederick II; they had secured extensive authority, including supervision of appointments and agreements, a voice in questions of war and peace, supervision of the care of widows and orphans, direction of the persecution of heretics and the right to confiscate their property, and the right to intervene in revolts against the Church and the social order. But this *universitas hominum* with ecclesiastical supremacy was not to last for ever. Around the year 1300, we find that French clerics were behaving like Frenchmen, not like the pope's servants. Loyalty to one's country had become stronger than faithfulness to the pope. The national state (in this case, France) had become a political entity that was stronger than universal Christian brotherhood, even among the clergy.

The growth of the well-organized national state led to a tension-filled cooperation between the king and the aristocracy, a tension reflected, ideologically, in the conflict between absolutism and constitutionalism. Hence, the question of the relationship between rulers and subjects came under greater scrutiny: if the king has absolute power, his subjects must show absolute obedience. Is it then *never right* to rebel against an unjust and tyrannical ruler? Similarly, the question arose of the legitimization of absolutist and constitutional power: does the king have absolute power by God's grace? Do the national assemblies have a legitimate claim to power by virtue of their representative nature? These are in a sense traditional problems, but they now became, to a greater extent, a subject of debate. In the fourteenth century, the ideological conflict centred on the question of the relationship between the king and his subjects, and that between the pope and all other Christians. Should the king (or the pope) have absolute power, or should power also reside in the traditional, representative assemblies and be subject to ancient laws and customs?

Marsilius of Padua (1275/80–1342), author of *Defensor pacis* (1324), was an Aristotelian opponent of the pope. But in addition, Marsilius held views that foreshadow the Reformation and Protestantism. Like Thomas Aquinas, Marsilius claimed that society is self-sufficient; that is to say, it needs no theological or metaphysical justification. For Aquinas, faith and reason were in harmony, as were the sacred and the secular; therefore, this self-sufficient society remained grounded in God. However, Marsilius claimed that society is *independent* of the Church.

Marsilius' radical dichotomy between politics and religion, state and Church, was connected with his nominalistic view of faith and reason. He rejected the Thomist harmony of Christian and rationalist (secular) truths, and claimed that there is a radical distinction between truths of faith and truths of reason: reason (like society) is self-sufficient in its area. And faith builds on revelation (such as that of the Bible) and is applicable to the hereafter, not to politics. Marsilius did not reject religion (Christianity). Atheism is basically a French invention of the eighteenth century! But he 'interiorized' religion to the extent that it largely became something overrational and consigned to the hereafter, something private and nonpolitical. Religion thus became a 'private' question, and the Church, in his theory, almost a voluntary, nonpolitical organization.[12]

All social activities, according to Marsilius, should be under the control of the state. And he viewed clerics as a social group. They should not have any other rights or privileges than those allowed by the state. There should not be any special,

Church law (canonical law); and priests, like the pope, should be appointed and dismissed by society. In the religious sphere, there are no religious truths of reason so difficult to understand that they must be interpreted by certain highly qualified persons. Faith and reason are separate. And the Bible is thus the only source of religious insight. Hence there is no reason to give more credence to the words of the pope than to those of other Christians. Consequently, there should be Church councils to decide questions of faith, according to Marsilius.

There is, then, both secularization and Protestantism in Marsilius' thought: *secularization*, because the natural – the biological functions, and the useful functions in society – are emphasized at the expense of the religious and ethical goals; and *Protestantism*, because Marsilius determines that religion is private, making a sharp distinction between faith and reason. At the same time, Marsilius, as a voluntarist, placed greater emphasis on the will than on rationality. But, like the first reformers, Marsilius still conceived of *one* universal Christian faith.

William of Ockham (1285–1349), a Franciscan, was a politically conservative defender of medieval constitutionalism against the pope's 'absolute monarchy'. Philosophically, he was a nominalist and voluntarist, and from the perspective of the history of ideas, a predecessor of Martin Luther and Protestantism.

Aquinas was a conceptual realist. Concepts and principles *exist* in the universe. By reflecting on these concepts and principles, we can gain real insight into problems such as the origin of the universe (God as Creator). Ockham was a *conceptual nominalist*: the only things that exist outside our consciousness (extramentally) are perceptible things (physical *particularia*). The concepts exist only in our mind as particular phenomena (mental *particularia*). We can reason about the perceptible and mental *particularia*. There is therefore no basis for theological speculation on the *universalia*. Theology and our relationship to God are primarily based on the Bible and our faith in what is written there. Nominalism thus leads to a certain distinction between reason and faith. Metaphysics and speculative theology are, in a sense, excluded. This means that intellectual activity is directed away from philosophy and towards the experimental sciences. We will later return to this shift towards experimental science.

Since revelation (the Bible) is the only source of Christian truth, it is difficult to justify an ecclesiastical hierarchy with the pope as the absolute ruler: the ability to read the Scriptures and the Christian faith are generally distributed more democratically than is theological education. Ockham therefore opposed the thesis that the pope should have the final say in religious questions. He proposed the establishment of assemblies (councils) to limit and censure the power of the pope. But he also realized that councils are fallible. Still, Ockham did not become a sceptic – a common development in the sixteenth and seventeenth centuries in France. He thought that enlightened criticism from representative councils would lead to truth. And he did not seem to doubt that truth is *one*.

MARTIN LUTHER – VOLUNTARISM AND NOMINALISM: FAITH ALONE

In the sixteenth century, the Roman Catholic Church was officially split. Even if the reformers, to start with, wanted only to reform the Church, their theological originality and political connections led to a revolution that turned the Church's view of tradition and of faith and salvation upside down. Theologically, Martin Luther (1483–1546) became the advocate of the Bible and the individual's faith against tradition and the pope. Therefore, the individual stood more isolated in relation to God, without the mediation of tradition and the Church. At the same time, the Reform movements adopted a critical position on the traditional view of salvation. The radical, Puritan sects rejected ecclesiastical-sacramental salvation as magic and superstition. As a result, the Reformation participated in the historical process that excluded magic from the world (cf. Max Weber on 'demystification of the world', Ch. 24).

On theological questions, Luther followed, in a different manner, the modern way (*via moderna*); that is to say, William of Ockham's nominalism. In practice, this meant a certain critical attitude towards medieval philosophy's view of a reasonable and well-ordered cosmos. In Luther's thought it is also difficult to find traces of the Aristotelian anthropology that we find in the Thomist tradition. Luther's pessimistic anthropology looks back to Augustine and forward to Hobbes, Nietzsche, and Freud. In line with Ockham, Luther gives faith primacy over reason. All that man needs to know about questions of faith is found in the Scriptures. Christians need neither the Fathers of the Church, the Church councils, nor the pope to tell them what to believe. Luther also mistrusts allegorical or philosophical interpretation of the Bible. Hence, he is blind to his own presuppositions in biblical interpretation (cf. his view of 'Scripture as the only authority'). The only thing we really need to know is that God reveals himself to man, who is the passive recipient of God's *grace*. Faith gives us immediate or direct contact with God. For Luther, faith alone (*sola fide*) is the only means of justification for man: 'Remember what has been said, namely, that faith alone, without works, justifies, frees, and saves.'[13] On the other hand, Luther claims that reason guided by faith may be the handmaid of theology. But when reason sets itself up as the judge of articles of faith, independently of faith, it is the work of the Devil. Such arrogance is unforgivable and must be purged by forcing reason to accept as truth that which, from a philosophical perspective, appears false and absurd. Consequently, reason cannot be the basis of a code of ethics. Thus, Lutheran fideism can easily become irrationalism.

Luther's theology also has an interesting voluntaristic trait ('voluntarism', from the Latin *voluntas*, 'will'). When God draws the line between good and evil, right and wrong, he does it as an act of sovereign will. The right and good are not right and good because God is bound by a moral standard, but because God *wills* them to be so. He could, in principle, have drawn this dividing line differently (God's omnipotence). He is God, according to Luther, and we can therefore not apply a rule or measure to his will, which is the rule for all things: 'For it is not because he is or was obliged so to will that what he wills is right, but on the contrary, because he himself so wills, therefore what happens must be right.'[14] We cannot place rules and norms above God's will. If we do so, we are placing another creator above the Creator (cf. Hugo Grotius' criticism of this voluntarism, Ch. 8).

Luther's thought thus seems to blend with Ockham's nominalism and ethical-theological voluntarism: from a nominalistic perspective, Luther could confute the view that there are ethical principles that God, too, must submit to. Voluntarism also anchors Christian ethics in God's decisionist will.[15] Thus, God is understood as an unbound and absolute majesty. In a political context, we meet this argument in Thomas Hobbes' legitimization of the absolute monarchy. In a sense we can say that both the world and moral standards are contingent for Luther – they could, in principle, have been different than they are.

Luther's political thought revolves around the relationship between spiritual and secular power. Formally, Luther here argued for what became a modern distinction between Church and state; in practice, the Church suffered a certain loss of authority in relation to the state. For Luther, we here have two regimes founded by God, but with different functions. The secular regime is instituted to maintain right and order in society. This regime uses the sword ('The sword of the state is to be red and bloody'). The spiritual regime uses the word and appeals to the conscience of both subjects and rulers.

The doctrine of the secular regime is connected with Luther's pessimistic anthropology: a human being is actually a fierce animal that must be restrained with chains and ropes.[16] A society without the secular regime will therefore be chaotic and a war of man against man (cf. Thomas Hobbes, Ch. 8). Because we are sinful and evil, God keeps us in check with the law and by the sword, so that it will not be easy for us to enact evil. For Luther, human beings are not the social and political animals they were for Aristotle and Thomas Aquinas. The medieval harmony and synthesis have definitely fallen apart.

Luther's doctrine of the two regimes implies an important distinction between the inner and the outer person. The secular regime is limited to external actions. It regulates life, property, and earthly things, but it cannot legislate the inner person. Here, God rules alone. Thus, the inner person does not belong under the secular sphere of power. Consequently, Luther says that heresy cannot be stopped with the sword. The word of God must be the weapon: 'Heresy is a spiritual matter which you cannot hack to pieces with iron, consume with fire, or drown in water. God's word alone avails here'.[17] In principle, this allows an important distinction in the philosophy of law between internal attitudes and external actions. Here we also see the outline of a distinction between morality and legality. The secular regime can punish only external actions, not internal thought. It was a long time before this idea had practical consequences.

Since the secular regime is founded by God, insurrection against the state is simultaneously insurrection against God. The insurgent becomes an enemy of God. When the state wields the sword, it is thus a 'service to God', according to Luther. Thus, in the conflict between the peasants and the princes (the Peasants' War of 1524–5 in Germany), Luther vehemently attacked the peasants: 'You have to answer people like that with a fist, until the blood drips off their noses.'[18] Since Luther thought that the state is an authority founded by God, he could acknowledge the legitimacy of the leaders of the secular regime as God's 'executioners and hangmen'.[19] In the light of Luther's times and the political-theological tradition, such a justification is understandable. In the light of recent German history, on the other hand, this principle of unquestioning obedience to rulers has turned out to be a questionable legacy.

Luther's harshness is also evident in his anti-Semitic works (for example, 'On the Jews and Their Lies' [1543]). Here he claims, among other things, that it is the Christian's duty to burn synagogues, destroy Jewish homes, and subject Jewish youths to forced labour. In view of the anti-Semitism and Nazism of the twentieth century, such texts have unpleasant associations, not least because they could so easily be used in Nazi propaganda. But it is still unreasonable to trace a direct descent from Luther to Hitler. On the other hand, it seems clear that not all of Luther's thought is useful today – either theologically or politically.

THE UNIVERSITY TRADITION

The oldest European universities can trace their origins back to the Middle Ages. It is often difficult to say precisely when a university was founded, because the sources are limited and because the very concept of university was unclear in the Middle Ages. For example, it was claimed that the University of Paris was a continuation of Plato's Academy, which, via Rome, was transferred to Paris. Historically, of course, this is not very probable, but there is still a grain of truth in it: the European universities which emerged at the end of the twelfth century had certain roots in the educational system of antiquity. The universities adopted the Greco-Roman idea of *the seven liberal arts* which it behooves a free man to learn. These can be divided into two groups: the first group, *trivium*, or the threefold way, comprised grammar, rhetoric, and logic. Here we find the disciplines which in antiquity were thought to be necessary for the orator and statesman. The second group, *quadrivium*, or the fourfold way, comprised geometry, arithmetic, astronomy, and music. These were disciplines which both Plato and the Pythagoreans had given the central place in their educational systems. We can say, in many ways, that the liberal arts, or *artes liberales*, of antiquity especially the *trivium* disciplines, formed the basis of the medieval university tradition.

This continuity between antiquity and the Middle Ages has not always been so obvious. Historians in the eighteenth and nineteenth century often thought that the culture of antiquity disappeared in the early Middle Ages and did not reappear until the Renaissance. Today the picture is more complicated. We know that the Middle Ages had three intellectual cultures which were relatively independent of each other, but which all, in their own way, assimilated the legacy of antiquity; namely, Byzantium, the Latin monasteries, and the Arabic cultural centres. Throughout the Middle Ages, in the east, there was a Greek-speaking centre of learning in Byzantium. (Constantinople did not fall to the Turks until 1453.) In Western Europe part of the wisdom of antiquity 'hibernated' in the monasteries. In a sense, only Christianity and the Church survived the fall of the Roman Empire. The art of reading and writing was preserved only within the ecclesiastical institutions. From the sixth century, the monasteries were the primary sources in the West of literary study and education for men and women. In a divided Europe with different languages and different peoples, the Church was the only unified and centralized institution capable of preserving a common European culture.

This monastic culture was a Latin-speaking one. The Greek language fell rapidly into disuse. Thus, the key to Greek science and its methodical perspectives was lost. Arabic culture, on the other hand, preserved the learning of antiquity. The most important works were translated into Arabic at an early stage. Latin-speaking Europe became reacquainted with scientific literature on a large scale through its contact with the Islamic culture in the tenth century, especially in Córdoba.

In Western Europe, then, a portion of the learning of antiquity was preserved in the monasteries. Remains of Greek and Roman rhetoric and logic thus lived on as the framework of a new content. The monk, the priest, and the missionary studied rhetoric with the Bible as a textbook, the liberal arts remaining the intellectual basis. Nor were the 'dark' centuries devoid of enlightened scholars such as Gregory of Tours (*c.* 538–594), the Venerable Bede (*c.* 673–735), and Isidore of Seville (*c.* 560–636). In the liberal arts, the focus was primarily on the first group (*trivium* – 'trivial literature'). The disciplines of the second group, the so-called *quadrivium*, were not central in the early Middle Ages. Nor was much of the scientific study of antiquity considered relevant by the monks. It was only when scholarship in Europe became socially integrated with the development of state and urban culture that the learning of antiquity could again be relevant. We see traces of this in the Carolingian Renaissance (*c.* 800): Charlemagne's powerful empire lacked an efficient administrative structure. This created the need for a new educational system. As a result, monastic and cathedral schools were established, out of which the first universities developed.

In many ways, the university was socially and intellectually a new creation at the end of the twelfth century. In this system, the word *universitas* refers to a students' or teachers' guild. The modern use of the term *universitas* first became prevalent in the fifteenth century. The first universities had one important feature in common – they were all located in a city, small or big. The rural monastic schools could not keep pace with the 'educational explosion'. No medieval universities developed in the countryside. Only cities had the capacity to accommodate the growing student populations.

Already in the first universities we find an attempt at specialization. In Salerno and Montpellier, students specialized in medicine. Bologna became an early centre for law. North of the Alps, the cathedral school in Chartres became a centre for the study of *artes liberales*. At the end of the twelfth century, Paris emerged as an important centre for theological studies. Oxford University became recognized for scientific research at an early stage. These institutions of learning quickly gained international status. They accepted students from all over Europe to be educated as physicians, lawyers, and theologians. In a certain sense, it was the benefits to society that formed the basis for the success of the universities. A *studium generale* specializing in, for example, law, met a social need. There was an urgent need for qualified lawyers in both the state and the Church.

Specialization also led to many students having to supplement their education at another university. If one studied in Paris in preparation to become a bishop, then, in addition to theology, one also needed legal and canonical knowledge. For this, one had to travel to Bologna. The itinerant students, or 'vagrants', were an important feature in medieval society. They had a hard life of journeys on foot, which lasted months or even years.

The university quickly gained a central position in the city landscape. Around the year 1200, Paris is thought to have had a population of about 50,000. Of this number, ten per cent were students. Such a large group was both a source of social irritation and an important source of income for landlords and merchants. The relationship between the students and the rest of the population was therefore not always without friction. Violence was not uncommon. A decisive turning point, after many years of student rebellions and boycotts, was marked by the papal bull *Parens scientiarum* of 1231 – the 'Magna Carta' of the University of Paris. This stated that the university had the right to create its own statutes, rules, syllabi, and standard degrees. At the same time, diplomas from different universities were conceived as equivalent, or at least 'convertible'. The university was finally recognized as a corporation, an institution with a certain autonomy: it had the right to decide educational content and form without external interference. Thus, the university gradually gained freedom to teach, independently of Church and state. It had its own privileges and autonomy. An important development in the university institution had taken place.

Already by the thirteenth century, the university was divided into four faculties: theology, law, medicine, and *artes* (at which were taught the seven liberal arts). The first three comprised the 'higher' faculties. The faculty of arts was a preparatory and general education faculty. All students were required to start at the faculty of arts. They had to remain at this faculty for several years in order to be able to study at one of the other faculties. Such a long period of preparation may seem excessive. But we must remember that medieval students began to study at the age of fourteen or fifteen, so they probably needed some general education!

The division into faculties already shows that it was difficult to find a place for mathematics and the scientific disciplines within the medieval university. It seems to have been primarily the *quadrivium* disciplines that were difficult to place. Few courses of study of the thirteenth century offered disciplines such as mathematics, geometry, and astronomy. But here we should note that several universities in the thirteenth century had scholars who studied the sciences without having teaching duties. At Oxford and Paris, Robert Grosseteste (1175–1253) and Roger Bacon (1215–1294) made great progress in optics. In the fourteenth century, mathematics, for example, gained a central position at Merton College, Oxford. A similar renaissance of mathematics took place in Paris in the middle of the fourteenth century under the leadership of Nicholas Oresme (*c.* 1320–1382).

An important feature of the medieval university was the formal disputation. Here one sharpened one's logical tools and learned to appreciate good arguments. Such discussion and debates were often inspired by Peter Abelard's (1079–1142) logical argumentation form, *Sic et Non*. Besides the lectures (*lectio*), the disputations (*disputatio*) were an important element in the medieval educational system and pedagogics (even in our day, the doctoral candidate must undergo a long and hard disputation). The disputation exercises could be quite inventive: 'Should a monster born with two heads be baptized as one or two persons?'

Studies at a medieval university were primarily a question of textual study. The study of medicine was, for example, primarily a textual study of Greek, Latin, and Arabic authorities. We have a course description from Bologna for the four-year programme in medicine. There were four lectures each day. The first year was devoted to the Arab philosopher Avicenna (Ibn-Sinâ) and his textbook of medicine. The second and third years were devoted to Galen, Hippocrates, and Averroës (Ibn-Rushd). The fourth year was mainly used for reviewing the syllabus. Human autopsies were first performed in Bologna around 1300. In 1396, the king of France gave the university in Montpellier permission to dissect corpses. In Montpellier, students studying medicine also had to go to a hospital to observe and practise surgery. Personal observation is important, it was said, because surgery is primarily about being daring. Once, when the *magister* was trepanning (operating on the skull), a student fainted when he saw the pulsation of the brain. The comment of the *magister* may be of interest for new students of medicine: 'My advice, therefore, is that no one should perform an operation before he himself has seen the operation being performed.'

The medieval university was not without student democracy. In many places, the students had more power and influence than in our days. In Bologna, for example, there were student guilds that elected and dismissed chancellors and professors. The students could fine the lecturer if he started his lecture too late, if he did not stick to the course of study, or if he skipped difficult passages in the text. If the students boycotted a lecturer, he became unemployed. The strong position of the students at this university was due to the fact that they came from rich families and paid the lecturers' salaries. The city of Bologna first started to pay salaries to lecturers around 1350.

The university tradition of the Middle Ages was a tradition formed by men. We know little about women's contribution to the intellectual life of medieval society, although they held a central position in the monasteries and hospitals. Recent research has shown that during the Middle Ages several women were prominent in philosophy and theology. Here we often talk about a 'hidden female tradition'. Perhaps the best-known of them was Hildegard of Bingen (1098–1179), who founded a cloister near Bingen, Germany. She wrote several books, including *Scivias* ('*Know the Ways of the Lord*'). She initiated the feminization of the concept of God. Similarly, Julian of Norwich (b. *c.* 1340) spoke of God as 'our Mother'.

Much of the intellectual conflict in the medieval university concerned nominalism and realism. During the fourteenth century, nominalism gained a strong position within the university, and various attempts to stop its advance failed. Nominalism became 'the modern way' in philosophy. Traditional realism became 'the old way'. The modern way pointed towards Luther, theologically, and towards British empiricism, philosophically.

ARABIC PHILOSOPHY AND SCIENCE

Most of the philosophical and scientific legacy of the Greeks was lost in the West in the period between the fall of the Roman Empire and the great cultural renaissance in the twelfth and thirteenth centuries. In the Dark Ages, however, Greek philosophy and science were preserved in the Arabic-Islamic cultural sphere. It is at the same time important to emphasize that the Arabs were not passive recipients of Greek culture and science. It is more correct to say that they actively acquired the legacy from Hellenism and carried it on in a creative way. This acquisition was the source of a new scientific tradition that was to dominate intellectual activity until the scientific revolution in the sixteenth and seventeenth centuries.

Even though Arab dynasties had come to power in areas previously under Roman control, there was no interruption of the intellectual life in Egypt or Syria, Iraq or Iran. In Syria, Iran, and other places, there was a living Hellenistic tradition of philosophy and science. Here, the works of Aristotle and other Greek philosophers were translated into Syriac at an early stage. The great breakthrough in the cultural transmission, however, took place with the Abbasid caliphs in Baghdad. The reign of Harun al-Rashid (786–809) marked the start of the first comprehensive Hellenistic renaissance in the Arabic world. It started as a great translation project. Much of the work was initially completed by Christians with Syriac as their cultural language. Al-Rashid actively supported scholars who studied Greek and who translated Greek philosophical and scientific works. He also sent envoys to the west to purchase Greek manuscripts.

An important part of the translation work consisted of expanding the Arabic vocabulary and in developing philosophical and scientific concepts corresponding to the Greek concepts. Hunayn ibn Ishaq (808–873) played an important role in this process. Significant portions of Greek culture were assimilated in this enriched language – with the exception of rhetoric, poetry, drama, and history, which held little interest for the Arabs. Their interest focused on philosophy (Aristotle, Plato, and Neoplatonism), medicine, optics, mathematics, astronomy, and occult disciplines like alchemy and magic. By the end of the ninth century, Baghdad was established as an Arabic centre of learning. It was not only Hellenistic culture that the Arabs acquired. In the east, there was significant contact with Iran, India, and China. As early as the ninth century, the mathematician Al-Khwarizmî (c. 800–847) used Indian ciphers – so-called Arabic numerals – in arithmetic calculations.

The great task of translation and cultural mediation gave rise to new libraries, which were usually associated with mosques and *madrasah* (Islamic schools). In the tenth and eleventh centuries, there were already hundreds of libraries throughout the Arabic world, with large collections of books. At its peak, the library in Baghdad is said to have housed almost 100,000 manuscripts. In comparison, the Sorbonne (Paris) had 2,000 manuscripts in the fourteenth century, approximately the same as the Vatican library in Rome during the same period. It can also be mentioned that the Arabs learned from the Chinese how to make paper in the eighth century. In the tenth century the use of paper was so extensive that the use of papyrus for writing died out. Paper production first began in Europe around 1150, and then, typically enough, it was the Arabs in Spain who were the pioneers.

The Arabs' most important contributions to the development of science were made in the fields of medicine, astronomy, and optics. The Arab physician and philosopher Abu Bakr al-Razi, usually called Rhazes (865–925), is thought to have been the first to study children's diseases like measles and chickenpox. Rhazes wrote several textbooks which were widely circulated, not only among the Arabs, but also in the West. His works were translated into Latin in the seventeenth century.

Ibn-Sinâ, or Avicenna (980–1037), carried on Rhazes' work. As a physician, Avicenna was greatly influenced by Galen (cf. Ch. 5, The sciences . . .). His major work, *The Canon of Medicine*, was a broadly constructed synthesis of the best of Greek and Arabic medicine. It was used as a basic textbook in medical education at European universities in the sixteenth century.[20] Avicenna was also an important philosopher. Like many Christian theologians, he attempted to formulate the truths of Islam in concepts of Aristotelian logic and later Greek metaphysics (Neoplatonism). For Avicenna, God was the first cause, or the Creator. The created world should be understood as a series of emanations from God: the emanation of the divine light created the human soul, and human life should be a journey back to the light, God. The decisive point in Avicenna's philosophy was his view of matter. In keeping with Plato and Aristotle, he seemed to reject the idea that

God created matter *ex nihilo*: the emanations from the divine light filled the matter, but did not create the matter. This was the starting point of a bitter conflict within early Islamic philosophy. Avicenna's Neoplatonism was, in several works, attacked by Al-Ghazali (1058–1111), one of the great Islamic mystics and theologians. His main point was that the God of the philosophers is not the God of the Koran. When philosophy comes into conflict with the Koran, philosophy must yield. As we know, similar conflicts were occurring in the Christian world around the same time.

The challenge from Al-Ghazali was met by Ibn-Rushd, or Averroës (1126–1198). In the West, he is often considered the most influential Arab thinker. Averroës was born in Córdoba and received a thorough education in the scientific disciplines of the day. For a time, he was a judge in Seville and Córdoba and ended his career as the personal physician of the caliph in Marrakesh. In Europe, Averroës was especially known for his comprehensive analyses of Plato and Aristotle. He exercised considerable influence on Thomas Aquinas, and Averroism marked scholasticism until the seventeenth century. In the conflict with Al-Ghazali, Averroës claimed that there could not be any contradiction between philosophical conclusions and the Koran: 'Since this religion is true and encourages a study that leads to knowledge of the truth, we, the Muslim community, know that research with the aid of argumentation does not lead to conclusions that oppose that which the Scriptures have given us. For truth does not contradict truth, but harmonizes with it and witnesses to it.'[21]

How, then, do we explain apparent contradictions? Here, Averroës introduced a principle of interpretation which has also played an important part in Western philosophy: he explained that not everything in the Koran should be taken literally. When a literal interpretation of the verses of the Koran seems to conflict with reason, the verses must be interpreted metaphorically or allegorically. From this brief presentation of the conflict between Al-Ghazali and Averroës, it should be apparent that fundamentalism has a long history. It is an old and well-known challenge within both Islamic and Christian philosophy.

Outstanding contributions were made in several areas by Arab scientists; among them, Ibn al-Haitham, or Alhazen (965–1039), holds a unique position. His work in optics was in many ways a breakthrough for this discipline. Ibn al-Haitham also made great advances in the study of lenses, and of spherical and parabolic mirrors. Moreover, he was an eminent representative of an experimental approach to optical phenomena and made a careful analysis of how the eye works. Today, Ibn al-Haitham is viewed as the greatest Arab physicist. He considerably influenced many Western scientists, including Roger Bacon, Johannes Kepler, and Isaac Newton.

The Arabs were also advanced in the field of astronomy. In particular, they worked on the development of mathematical models to solve the problems surrounding the discrepancy between theory and observation. At the Meragha observatory in Iran, Ibn al-Shâtir (d. 1375) had corrected and further developed the Ptolemaic system so that it largely became mathematically equivalent to the later Copernican system.[22] Until Copernicus, the Arab astronomical models were far more advanced than those of the West.

In almost all areas of astronomy, mathematics, medicine, and optics, Arab scientists were among the most advanced in the Middle Ages. For more than six centuries, the Arabs were technically and scientifically ahead of the West. But why did not Arabic science give rise to *modern* science? Why did the scientific revolution occur in Europe in the sixteenth and seventeenth centuries, and not in the Arabic-Islamic world? And perhaps even more puzzling: why did Arabic science *decline* after the fourteenth century? Why did Arabic philosophy and science stagnate? It is not possible to give a comprehensive answer to these questions here. We will merely indicate a possible answer.

The Arab philosophers and scientists with whom we have become acquainted were all Muslims. They based their work on Greek philosophy and science, but without 'Islamicizing' the problems and the results. This was at first tolerated, but they were subjected to increasing criticism by religious leaders. In the twelfth and thirteenth centuries, the religious pressure increased. The so-called foreign sciences could count on support only if they could be justified religiously or had a religious function: astronomy, geometry, and arithmetic were important because Muslims had to know the correct times to pray and the direction of Mecca. But from a religious perspective, many disciplines were criticized for being useless or for undermining the Koranic world-view. The increasing Islamization of the Greek sciences seems to have led to a restriction of research fields. This Islamization was perhaps one of the most important causes of the stagnation and decline in the fifteenth century.

Furthermore, a serious problem was the lack of an *institutional* foundation for the sciences in Arabic culture. The Arabs' main educational institution was the *madrasah*. These colleges, which started to flourish in the eleventh century, were Islam's primary cultural institution. They were primarily dedicated to the religious or Islamic sciences. All areas of education focused on the study of the Koran, the lives of the Prophet and his followers, and Muslim law (*sharia*). Philosophy and the natural sciences were not part of the course of study, but major texts were copied in the schools and added to the libraries. Many philosophers and scientists worked as teachers in the *madrasah*, but they did not lecture in Greek philosophy and science. Engagement in 'the foreign sciences' became therefore a matter of private activity or was connected with the mosques (astronomy) and the royal courts (medicine). Independent Arabic science was never institutionalized and sanctioned by the religious and political elite in the Arabic-Islamic world. Nor did medieval Islam recognize guilds and corporations. Therefore, it became difficult to legitimize and to develop professional groups of students and teachers. As a result, it was almost impossible to establish autonomous academic institutions with internal self-government – as was characteristic of late medieval European universities. Perhaps the most important cause of the stagnation in the fourteenth century is that the Arab world never developed independent universities that were tolerated or supported by either secular or religious officials.

QUESTIONS

Explain the main points in Augustine's view of God, the human being, and the world. Describe also his doctrine of the two states and of history.

Discuss Augustine's view of the relationship between knowledge and religious faith.

Show how Aquinas tried to harmonize philosophy and Christianity. Refer to his view of natural cognition.

Explain Aquinas' view of laws and their foundation.

Explain the different positions of 'the problem of universals'. Explain especially Aquinas' and Luther's positions.

Discuss Luther's nominalism and voluntarism (if you like: compare with Aquinas).

SUGGESTIONS FOR FURTHER READING

PRIMARY LITERATURE

St Augustine, *The City of God*, translated by Marcus Dods, New York, 1994.
St Augustine, *Against the Academicians*, translated by Peter King, Indianapolis, IN, 1995.
St Augustine, *Confessions*, translated by Henry Chadwick, Oxford, 1991.
St Augustine, *On Being and Essence,* Thomas Aquinas, Toronto, 1949.
Thomas Aquinas, *On the Truth of the Catholic Faith*, 5 vols, New York, 1955–57.
Martin Luther, *Works: American Edition* (55 vols), edited by Jaroslav Pelikan and Helmut T. Lehmann, St Louis/Philadelphia, 1955–.

SECONDARY LITERATURE

Gilson, E., *History of Christian Philosophy in the Middle Ages*, London, 1980.
Huff, Toky E., *The Rise of Early Modern Science. Islam, China and the West*, New York, 1993.
Thompson, W. and D. J. Cargill, 'Martin Luther and the "Two Kingdoms"', in D. Thomson (ed.), *Political Ideas*, Harmondsworth, 1969.
Tranøy, K. E., 'Thomas Aquinas', in *A Critical History of Western Philosophy*, New York, 1965.

NOTES

1 The name 'Middle Ages', *medium aevum*, was given retrospectively by those who regarded the period *between* antiquity ('the old times') and the Renaissance ('rebirth' of the culture of antiquity) as the Dark Ages.
2 The term 'natural law', of course, is used here in the philosophical sense, not the scientific.
3 We are here interpreting the ecclesiastical state as being identical with the good (God's) state.
4 For example, the divinity of Christ, and his birth into history, death, and resurrection.
5 Cf. the Bible's claim that the greatest virtues are 'faith, hope, and charity' (where hope is also hope for salvation).
6 Cf. corresponding problems in Calvin.
7 Cf. the word *interest*, derived from *inter-esse*; literally: 'between being'.
8 Here Aquinas is again indebted (as he so often is) to Aristotle. See also the discussion of Kant's categories (cf. Ch. 15, note 4).
9 According to Aquinas, each creature has the potentiality to become a *special* being, such as a human being (and not a dog) or a horse (and not a cat). When a creature has actualized its potentiality (*potentia*), it is *in actu*. If a creature by the actualization of its potentiality becomes what it is 'meant to be', as when a calf becomes a cow, this possibility may be called its *positive* possibility. But a calf may also

become veal, and that may be called its *negative* possibility. When a creature's positive possibilities are not actualized, something is *lacking* (for this creature). Thus, for a blind person, the ability to see is lacking. This lack is different from a lack that is due to a creature's generic lack of a certain potentiality, as horses cannot fly like birds.

10 Note the difference between Aquinas' view of good actions (attaching importance to good actions when it comes to man's hope of salvation) and Luther's view (emphasizing God's grace alone).

11 Cf. Leibniz' so-called *theodicée* (argument that this is the best of all possible worlds), Ch. 10.

12 This is Marsilius' view. But, as we know, the Church at that time was not a voluntary, nonpolitical organization. In the countries of the Reformation, the princes largely filled the political vacuum that appeared when Rome had to withdraw. And the rule was that the citizens should have the faith of the prince (*cuius regio, eius religio*). One's choice of religion was not more 'private'.

13 Martin Luther, *The Freedom of a Christian* (1520), translated by W. A. Lambert, revised by Harold J. Grimm, in *Luther's Works: Career of the Reformer: I*, vol. 31, edited by Jaroslav Pelikan and Helmut T. Lehmann, Philadelphia, 1957, p. 348.

14 Martin Luther, *The Bondage of the Will*, translated by Philip S. Watson in collaboration with Benjamin Drewery, in *Luther's Works*, vol. 33, p. 181.

15 Decisionism: determination by a free *resolution*, a decision, not by a universal standard.

16 Martin Luther, *Temporal Authority: To What Extent it Should be Obeyed*, translated by J. J. Schindel and revised by Walther I. Brandt, in *Luther's Works*, vol. 45, p. 91.

17 Ibid., p. 114.

18 Martin Luther, 'An Open Letter on the Harsh Book Against the Peasants', in *Luther's Works*, vol. 46, p. 65. Luther's style in this work is worth scrutiny: 'The peasants would not listen; they would not let anyone tell them anything, so their ears must now be unbuttoned with musket balls till their heads jump off their shoulders. . . . He who will not hear God's word when it is spoken with kindness, must listen to the headsman, when he comes with his axe' (pp. 65–6). 'Let no one have mercy on the obstinate, hardened, blinded peasants who refuse to listen to reason; but let everyone, as he is able, strike, hew, stab, and slay, as though among mad dogs' (p. 73).

19 Martin Luther, *Temporal Authority*, in *Luther's Works,* vol. 45, p. 113.

20 Nancy Siraisi, *Avicenna in Renaissance Italy: 'The Canon' and Medical Teaching in Italian Universities after 1500*, Princeton, NJ, 1987.

21 G. F. Hourani, *Averroës on the Harmony of Religion and Philosophy*, London, 1961, p. 50.

22 Victor Roberts, 'The Planetary Theory of Ibn al-Shâtir', *Isis*, 57 (1966), pp. 365–78.

7 | The rise of the natural sciences

THE DISPUTE OVER METHOD

The rebirth of the culture of antiquity, the Renaissance, has definite significance for the foundation of the experimental sciences. When the Eastern Roman Empire fell in 1453, a number of men of learning fled to the West. Their arrival led to a rediscovery of ancient Greek philosophy, especially Plato – just as the Arabs a few centuries before had made possible a renewed knowledge of Aristotle. This injection of Greek theories, in the fifteenth century, helped to create the conditions that made possible the founding of experimental science. On the one hand, we had *adequate concepts and theories* – from Greek philosophy – and *logical method* – from training in scholastic philosophy in the Middle Ages – and, on the other hand, we had a newly awakened *interest in the exploitation and control of nature* – a secularization of interests typical of the Renaissance.

We have mentioned earlier that the transition in the late Middle Ages from conceptual realism to nominalism was, in a way, a shift of interest towards concrete things, and that this may have played a part in promoting the rise of the experimental sciences. But the *speculative* Greek theories were also important; for example, Democritus' mechanistic theory of atoms and – above all – the conceptual-realistic, Neoplatonic philosophy of mathematics, which, among other things, exercised a great influence on the early Renaissance thinker Nicholas of Cusa (1401–1464), and later on Copernicus and Kepler. But whatever the role of these various factors, this combination of theory and practical interest in utilizing things, was unique to the Renaissance. It was the first time in history that such a combination had appeared. In most cultures, there was interest in utilizing things, but adequate theories and social conditions were lacking. The result was magic and medicine men, not science and technology. The ancient Greeks were in many ways unique. To put it briefly, they had the theories, but not the interest in exploiting nature. For Greek philosophers, theories had a value in themselves.

What we have just said is of course a great simplification. The rise of the natural sciences in the Renaissance was the result of a long process, in which we had a development of scientific concepts within medieval philosophy and a development of technology within crafts and agriculture.[1] With this reservation we can say that the natural sciences did not arise by theory alone, nor by practical interest alone. Both factors had to exist simultaneously. And this was what happened in the Renaissance.

By the end of the seventeenth century, classical mechanics, the foundation of the experimental, mathematical sciences, was established. There were now three intellectual activities which dealt with truth: theology, philosophy, and natural science – in comparison with only theology and philosophy in the Middle Ages. It was therefore important for philosophy to find its place in relation to science. Much of philosophy in the newer age – as for the rationalists Descartes and Leibniz, the empiricists Locke and Hume, and the transcendental philosopher Kant – was an attempt to find the boundary between philosophy and natural science. Still, it is not correct to say that philosophy forsook theology for natural science. Christian theology was long the unmistakable background for most philosophers, including Descartes, Locke, and Berkeley.

The establishment of experimental science was not easy. In the Middle Ages, the scholastics had debated well. Intellectually, the High Middle Ages was a rationalistic period. But the arguments mainly concerned other arguments, not nature. Learned men knew how to marshal effective arguments against their opponents. But now the task was to understand and master nature. How does one do this? How does one set about it?

For us, the answer is simple. It can be found in any science textbook that we use in secondary school. But, at that time, the answer was anything but simple. And it took at least two centuries before the right questions to ask, the appropriate concepts and methods to use, were found. This period, which can be characterized by the expression 'the dispute over method' (fifteenth and sixteenth centuries), was in many ways a time of intellectual confusion. This was the age of alchemy, the age of Faust. There was a burning interest in mastering nature, in making gold out of lead, in finding the elixir of eternal youth. But no one knew how to do these things.

The Renaissance was not simply the period when the light returned – in contrast to the Middle Ages as the 'Dark Ages'. Instead, it was generally a time when the light was almost extinguished! In many ways, Renaissance philosophy was more intellectually confused than medieval philosophy.[2] Nor should we make the mistake of simply reversing the generally positive view of the Renaissance. The intellectual confusion in the Renaissance was a consequence of the attempt at radical innovation and of the fact that it took the innovators some time to find their way.

During the course of the seventeenth century, the experimental sciences began to take shape. The intellectual confusion in the Renaissance represented a transitional phase that was necessary in order that intellectual life could make a new start.

The new infusion of Greek philosophy was especially rich in elements of Democritus' thought – nature is composed of small material particles that circulate in a void – and of the teachings of Plato and the Pythagoreans – mathematics is the key to natural processes. A science developed that used the mathematical language (formulae, models, and inferences) and quantitative concepts (mass, force, acceleration, etc.) familiar to us from classical mechanics. And this was a science neither purely deductive nor purely inductive, but hypothetico-deductive.

In order to comprehend this change, we should keep in mind some elementary points in general methodology. In mathematics and logic we start with certain premises (axioms), and with the aid of certain rules of deduction we arrive at proven statements (theorems). We call this form of reasoning the *deductive* method (cf.

Euclid). In contrast to deduction is *induction*: this is a form of reasoning based on the application of a statement true in a *finite* number of cases of a certain kind to *all* cases of this kind.

For example, for eight years we have been observing the ducks at Smith Mountain Lake, and all that we have seen have been grey. We conclude that 'all ducks are grey'. We have thus made too strong a claim because we have not observed *all* ducks. It is quite possible that there are ducks at Smith Mountain Lake that we have not seen, nor have we seen all ducks in all other places, nor, of course, all of the ducks which existed before we were born, nor all the ducks which will live in the future. The relationship between what we have observed and what we have concluded is like the relationship between a finite number and infinity. Now, of course, we can *test* this conclusion reached by induction, 'all ducks are grey', by making new observations and by collecting information from others who have been looking for ducks in other places and at other times. If someone has seen a duck which is not grey, our conclusion will be *refuted*. But regardless of how many new observations we make of grey ducks, the relationship between the number of such observations and the number of *possible* observations will be like the relationship between a finite number and infinity. Conclusions reached by induction can thus be refuted, but *never completely confirmed.*[3]

In the dispute over method in the Renaissance, it became strategically necessary to free enquiry from the deductive scientific ideal that had virtually dominated scholastic philosophy in the Middle Ages (but not Greek philosophy). Purely logical deduction just does not lead to (logically) *new* knowledge. The conclusion we arrive at is already implicit in the premises. Deductive answers are certain but sterile for those seeking *new* knowledge. And in the Renaissance, it was precisely new knowledge that was sought. The disadvantage of deduction is not that it might be incorrect, but that it is sterile.

Thus, one of the ideologues in this epistemological conflict, Francis Bacon (1561–1626), attacked deduction as a scientific ideal. But it still seems clear that deduction played an important part in the new science. What was decisively new lay in a dynamic combination of hypotheses, deductive inference, and observation. This new combination is known as the *hypothetico-deductive* method.

When we inductively generalize from the statement, 'the 7,645 ducks that I have observed at Smith Mountain Lake, are grey', to the statement, 'all ducks are grey', we are not introducing new concepts. We are always talking about grey ducks. In addition we are guilty of a conclusion that is not logically valid. Bacon's defence of the inductive method thus entails a logical problem. But if we propose the hypothesis that the balls rolling on this table follow the formula $F = ma$ (force is equal to mass times acceleration), we are *jumping* from concepts on the level of observation – balls, table, etc. – to concepts expressed in the formula on the level of abstraction – force, mass, acceleration. We can never *see* 'force', 'mass', or 'acceleration'. These are concepts constructed in connection with an hypothesis, and they are all formulated in the language of mathematics. In other words, we do not conceive of a formula of the type $F = ma$ in an inductive manner. To formulate a hypothesis, often in mathematical language, is something other than induction. We *invent* the formula. *How* we arrive at the formula is, for that matter, irrelevant. It may as well be something that jumps out of our coffee cup.

Whether a hypothesis is tenable or not is decided by testing. From the hypothesis, we deduce certain statements about things that must occur if the hypothesis is true. And we then try to determine whether they do occur. Deduction is thus part of testing a hypothesis.[4] That is why we call it the hypothetico-deductive method.

deduction:

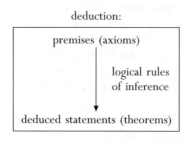

induction:

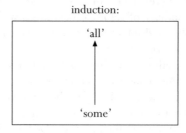

hypothetico-deductive method:

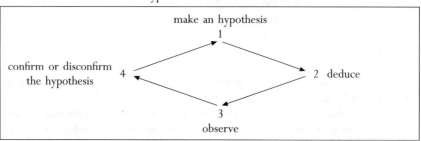

If an hypothesis is tested adequately, and if the testing does not disconfirm the hypothesis, it will become a theory – which may lead to new knowledge. This knowledge is still not absolutely certain. It is always possible that future observations will disconfirm the theory. Thus, in practice, hypothetico-deductive research implies a continuing alternation between the proposal of hypotheses, and deductions with observation and testing. In practice, the research process becomes an unending spiral.

Since testing often requires the construction of special conditions – completely round balls, perfectly smooth tables, no disturbing wind, etc. – we need controlled experiments. The testing must be done systematically and with special focus on features that may weaken the hypothesis, in order to test it adequately.

With the hypothetico-deductive method we can predict and thus perhaps control the processes of nature. Here we have a fusion of theory and practical application. That is to say, knowledge based on the hypothetico-deductive method can give us both insight into and control over natural phenomena. Knowledge is power (Francis Bacon).

Here we have mentioned three methods – deduction, induction, and the hypothetico-deductive method – and we have mentioned that it was usual, at the time when the natural sciences were founded, to emphasize the conflict between induction and deduction, since the new sciences were not yet conceived of as hypothetico-deductive. This was how the methodological problem was perceived from the perspective of natural science. However, during the Reformation a renewed importance was attached to textual analysis and hence to another kind of method. The Protestants wanted to return to the Bible. But how is the Bible to be understood? Many centuries had passed since it had been written; how could people during the Reformation fully understand a text shaped by ancient Judaic tradition? None of the three methods we have mentioned can help. The explication of texts from an alien culture is not a problem of control in a technological sense, but of penetrating the horizon of understanding from which the author in question wrote. The interpretive method, hermeneutics, thus gained a new interest during the Reformation, although hermeneutics is basically as old as philosophy itself.

Just as some philosophers were fascinated by the *concepts* used in classical mechanics, some also were fascinated by the *method*. But these philosophers had different opinions about what this method was. Thus, some philosophers thought that the new and essential could be found in the empirical and sceptical attitude. We see this especially in the British empiricists (Locke, Berkeley, and Hume), who emphasized a criticism of knowledge based on experience. Other philosophers thought that deduction and mathematics were essential. We see this especially in the classical rationalists (Descartes, Spinoza, and Leibniz), who emphasized deductive systems. We will return to these two main branches of philosophy in the seventeenth and eighteenth centuries, and follow them up to Kant's transcendental philosophy.

Francis Bacon, the defender of the inductive method, wrote both about the new science (*Novum Organum* ['*The New Tool*']) that would give us power over nature, and the new society (*Nova Atlantis* ['*The New Atlantis*']) that, by virtue of the new science, would be an earthly paradise. He expressed the dream of technological control of nature. Technological rationality is the discipline that should lead us into this new society. In other words, the methodological and the political problems are placed in close connection with one another, and it is only science that will be the means of mastering nature in order to create the good society. Today, it is clear that Bacon's claim was largely correct. Hypothetico-deductive science has made it possible to improve our living conditions, and this science has played a part in the formative process by which man became autonomous.[5]

Bacon distinguishes himself both from Aristotle – who thought that the good society primarily needs good praxis – and from the Middle Ages – where paradise was in the hereafter, and where this world was viewed as something practically unchangeable. Bacon writes about a political *utopia* that, in contrast to the static ideal state in Plato, is permeated by a progressive historical development. It is a secular development. It is society that must be changed, and the goal is *in* this world, not the hereafter. In other words, the modern faith in progress has begun to take shape. The divine history of salvation is no longer the core of history; instead, man's ability to utilize and control nature is the core. History moves forward, but directed by man.

Bacon is a forerunner of the Enlightenment, in the sense that he wants to help his fellow man progress towards truer insights and sounder attitudes. He thus tries to show how thoughts and attitudes can easily be distorted and limited. He discusses four types of prejudices:

1   The idols of the tribe (*idola tribus*) are misconceptions stemming from human nature, such as wishful thinking, thinking that abstractions are real things, and accepting immediate experience without delving more deeply into things.
2   The idols of the cave (*idola specus*) are misconceptions stemming from each person's unique disposition, education, and background. We all interpret events from our own perspective!
3   The idols of the market place (*idola fori*) are distortions of language. We use expressions like 'fate' and 'first mover' as if they were unambiguous with clear referents.
4   The idols of the theatre (*idola theatri*) are misconceptions stemming from the philosophical tradition.

Here there is an entire programme for enlightenment and the struggle against ignorance and prejudices.

As usual, Bacon's thought foreshadows the Enlightenment in the eighteenth century.

ASTRONOMY – COPERNICUS AND KEPLER

THE SCIENCES AND THE CONCEPT OF EXPERIENCE

The scientific upheaval that perhaps most affected the ordinary person's self-image was the shift in astronomy from a geocentric to a heliocentric world-view. Astronomers also use the hypothetico-deductive method and concepts of material bodies and of motion. However, their immediate experiential basis is systematic observation, rather than experimentation. It may therefore be helpful to point out three different conceptions of experience.

1   When we talk about *life experience*, we mean neither systematic observation nor experimentation, but the formation and education of a person by personal experience. In psychology, we use this conception of experience when we talk about the socialization of children. Here we are talking about developing concepts and building competence. When children, for example, learn to pretend, they have developed the capability to distinguish reality from appearance, and to use this distinction in social situations. This kind of life experience involves something that cannot be communicated to other people unless they

have had similar experiences themselves. Hence, there is an element here of 'tacit knowledge' which cannot be communicated by words alone. We generally have such life experiences in the company of others, who often help us attain such understanding. This type of personal experience is thus accessible to others.

2   In science we have experience in the form of *systematic observation*. We observe and record certain types of events, according to particular concepts. On the basis of conceptions of political science, we observe, for example, the Greek city-state and record the result in a form which is understandable to others who are interested in the same topic (cf. Aristotle). Or we observe the varying anatomical features of reptiles and birds on the Galápagos Islands (cf. Darwin). Or we observe the planets by measuring their positions and movements (cf. Tycho Brahe). We not only 'see', but we also perceive by means of certain concepts; we are not trying to see everything, but only certain features within the chosen field of study. The result is then recorded so that it will be useful to others, and can be assimilated by others. Thus, this kind of experience can be controlled interpersonally. By measuring and using mathematical concepts in describing observations, we make it easy for others to understand precisely what we are saying. On the basis of these experiences, we can formulate hypotheses that may be strengthened or weakened by new observations; we can, in other words, conduct research by means of the hypothetico-deductive method.

3   However, in certain instances we can *influence the conditions* of the experiences we are seeking. For example, we are not content with random observations of falling objects; we design tests in which the appropriate objects are made to fall from a suitable height. We are thus able to have continually new experiences at times that suit us and as many times as we need. In this way, we can determine the factors we want to keep constant and those we want to vary. Thus, we can systematically vary the weight and volume of the falling objects, or we can vary the distance of the fall for the same object. To put it briefly, we can *experiment* as scientists do today, in fields ranging from physics to psychology. In astronomy we can alter our observational situation by varying our equipment, for example; but we cannot experiment with the research objects, such as the sun, the Earth, and other celestial bodies. However, we can construct thought experiments and make theoretical and technical models of the movements of the stars and planets.

All science makes use of experience in the sense of systematic observation (no. 2 above), but only some sciences involve experimentation with the research objects (no. 3). We can also say that all scientific activity requires interaction (among researchers) as in the type of learning that we called socialization or the formation of human beings (no. 1): learning a science is not only acquiring knowledge of certain facts, but is also concerned with how these facts have been discovered, and that entails an introduction to certain modes of thought and action. The dispute over the world-view in sixteenth-century astronomy can be clarified on the basis of these points. The actual events are well known. We shall here focus on some points of philosophical interest.

COPERNICUS AND THE HELIOCENTRIC SYSTEM

Nicolaus Copernicus (1473–1543) developed an astronomical model with the sun as the centre of the planetary system, a heliocentric system, which conflicted with the prevailing geocentric system that went back to Ptolemy and had the sanction of the Church. The heliocentric system was a highly rational construction with fairly weak observational support. The Copernican model was apparently simpler and easier to use than the Ptolemaic. But the heliocentric principle was not new. The Greek astronomer Aristarchus had long before proposed a heliocentric model. Nevertheless, with his theory, Copernicus was challenging the Church and the Aristotelian tradition, beginning a conflict that was to continue throughout the Reformation and the Renaissance. Copernicus did not seek this conflict. He published *On the Revolutions of the Heavenly Spheres* ('*De revolutionibus orbium coelestium*'), under pressure, at the end of his life. But Copernicus' theory soon began to have a great effect on the intellectual climate of his day. The heliocentric system was revolutionary, and not only for the Church and for the Aristotelian-Ptolemaic tradition. It also revolutionized the immediate life experience. Copernicus invited his readers to imagine themselves outside the centre, and to observe the universe from a completely different perspective. His theory required the ability to see the world and mankind from a completely new perspective: man, as subject, had to view the universe, and himself, from a completely different point of view. This reflexive distancing and reversal of perspective has been called *the Copernican revolution*. Kant used this revolution to interpret human cognition in a new way. For others, this was seen as a realistic critique of an overly optimistic faith in human reason and man's unique standing in the universe. Previously, man had viewed the world from a personal perspective; now he had to give up this false self-exaltation and view himself as mere dust in the universe! Later, with Darwin's theory of evolution and Freud's theory of the unconscious, the vain faith in human reason was finally reduced to its true worth! These theories became a standard source of criticism of the traditional confidence in human reason and human superiority in the universe. But this criticism presupposes, of course, that the critics have good reasons for their pessimism in regard to man – and if they have such insight, things are still not so bad.

The heliocentric theory, which was based on systematic observations and mathematical models, thus represented a challenge to the time-honored life experience. This brought man to a crisis of self-perception. We cannot trust the immediate testimony of our eyes that the Earth is at rest and that the sun moves across the firmament. With reference to our discussion of the different types of experience, we can say that new theories based on scientific experience (type 2) transformed man's life experience (type 1). In other words, man's view of himself became scientific.

But this change in man's view of himself was ambiguous. It not only represented a kind of cosmic degradation of man, but it also gave man a new, positive self-consciousness: the new world-view undermined the belief that the celestial spheres were unique and qualitatively superior to that part of the universe inhabited by man. Moreover, there was the potential of a new, positive self-image due to the progress that man had made in exploring the universe; here were the roots of the secular and scientifically based faith in progress that arose at the time of the Enlightenment. This was, perhaps, a presumptuous but definitely not a negative self-image.

KEPLER AND THE ORBITS OF THE PLANETS

Like many other pioneers in later times, Johannes Kepler (1571–1630) lived in the tension between the old and the new.[6] He rejected the idea that the celestial spheres are qualitatively different from the Earth, and he sought mechanistic explanations of the planets' orbits. But for Kepler, the mathematical laws of the planets' motion were embedded in a profound metaphysical dimension. This mixture of mathematics and metaphysics points to a relationship with older thought, going all the way back to the Pythagoreans. Kepler was convinced that God was a mathematician and that mathematical forms prevail in the perishable world of the senses. At the same time, the interest in mechanistic explanations for everything in the universe, high and low, helped lay the foundation of the new natural sciences.

Kepler adapted the Copernican model: the orbits of the planets are not circular with the bodies moving at a constant velocity, but *elliptic*, with the sun as one focal point. A celestial body moves at varying velocities depending on its distance from the sun. He made this adaptation with the aid of observations by the Danish astronomer Tycho Brahe (1546–1601). Hence, Kepler was able to formulate the laws of planetary motion. In this way he was able greatly to simplify the Copernican model. This accentuated the question of which model best corresponded with reality. Is the heliocentric theory not only 'more economical' (simpler), but also *true*? Consequently, the conflict with the Church intensified. When Newton's theory of the force of gravitation was later able to explain why the planets move in elliptic orbits at varying velocities, the argument for the heliocentric system was correspondingly strengthened: the Copernican-Keplerian theory gained strong support from another central theory in science.

Towards the end of his life, Kepler became the chief astrologer for the great general Wallenstein and cast horoscopes for him. He also had to engage in a bitter struggle to save his mother from charges of witchcraft.

KEPLER'S LAWS OF PLANETARY MOTION

1 The planets move in elliptic orbits, one focus of each ellipse being occupied by the sun.
2 The radius vector connecting the sun and the planet sweeps out equal areas in equal times.
3 The squares of the periods of revolution of any two planets are in the same ratio as the cubes of their mean distances from the sun. (The mean distance is half the length of the major axis of the ellipse.)

PHYSICS – GALILEO AND NEWTON

It is natural to view Galileo Galilei (1564–1642) and Isaac Newton (1642–1727) as representatives of the mathematical-experimental natural sciences. In their work, the new physics began to take shape, in conflict with the Aristotelian tradition. We have already mentioned the concepts of material particles, mechanistic causal explanations, and the hypothetico-deductive method, all of which entered into this new experimental, mathematically formulated natural science.

Life. *Galileo Galilei was born in Pisa in 1564. He died in 1642, the same year that Newton was born. Galileo studied medicine, natural science, and mathematics. He had also strong interests in the humanities and was well acquainted with Greek and Latin literature. By 1589 — at the age of 25 — he had become a professor of mathematics at Pisa, without having taken a single university degree. Two years later he was appointed to a prestigious professorship in Padova. Simultaneously he cultivated his humanistic interests. For example, he lectured on the location of hell in Dante's* Divine Comedy *and wrote several essays on literary topics. He was also a master of the dialogue in the Platonic pattern. Among his main writings we may mention* Messenger from the Stars *(1610),* Dialogue about the Two Major World Systems *(1632), and* Dialogue about Two New Sciences *(1638).*

NEW DISCOVERIES

In 1609 Galileo heard reports of a new invention in the Netherlands. A lens grinder had assembled lenses and constructed the first telescope. Prompted by this report, Galileo made his own telescope. Although not its inventor, he was the first to employ the telescope and the knowledge he gained thereby in the dispute over the geocentric and the heliocentric theories. It is not sufficient to make contingent observations and discoveries; we must also understand what these discoveries mean and find their *theoretical* implications. This was Galileo's strength.

With his new telescope Galileo made several interesting discoveries: on the moon he observed mountains and valleys. Consequently, the moon was not a perfect sphere, as was believed earlier. Physically, the moon apparently resembled the Earth. Galileo also discovered that the planet Venus had phases similar to those of the moon, and he saw no fewer than four moons orbiting Jupiter. He also detected dark spots (sunspots) and 'torches' on the surface of the sun. All these observations could be interpreted as arguments *against* Aristotle/Ptolemy and *in favour of* Copernicus/Galileo. The Aristotelian-Ptolemaic tradition in astronomy had assumed that everything in the firmament, the so-called *supralunary* world ('the world above the moon'), was perfect. Galileo's observations showed that neither the moon nor the sun had a perfect surface, or the shape of a perfect sphere. Accordingly, Ptolemy was wrong! The fact that Venus had phases suggested that the planet revolved around the sun, and not around the Earth, as the geocentric theory claimed. In the geocentric system the Earth has a unique position. The Earth was held to be the only celestial body with a satellite, namely, the moon. Since we know that the moon revolves around the Earth, we have reason to believe that the other celestial bodies do the same. Thus, the discovery of Jupiter's moons weakened the geocentric argument. In the same way, Galileo established a chain of circumstantial evidence that little by little demolished the geocentric theory. He published the most important discoveries in the short paper *Messenger from the Stars* (1610).

It is often said that Galileo had the best observations and the best arguments on his side and that the opponents represented only an irrational reaction to the new astronomy. This interpretation of the controversy is untenable and anachronistic. In the early seventeenth century the good arguments were fairly equally distributed. The major traditional astronomer of the day, Tycho Brahe, had advocated a compromise between the geocentric and the heliocentric systems, and no astronomer made better observations of the positions and movements of the stars and planets than Brahe. His system probably gave better predictions than that of Copernicus.

However, the greatest problem for Copernican astronomy was the fact that its basic hypotheses seemed to correspond so poorly with our daily experience. We cannot perceive that the Earth is moving; the heliocentric hypothesis is not immediately supported by our sense experience. If the Earth not only rotates on its own axis from the west to the east at great speed, but also revolves around the sun in a huge orbit, we ought to notice this movement in our daily life. But in fact we do not notice anything of it! If the Copernican hypothesis were correct, we should, for instance, expect movable objects on the surface of the Earth to be thrown off, like water from a revolving grindstone. And we should expect the wind always to blow toward the west, and the clouds always to move westwards. Luckily, this is not so. The Copernican theory seemed to mean that cannon balls could be shot further westwards than eastwards. Of course, this is not so. If the Earth rotates, why does a stone dropped from the top of a high tower fall straight down? Why does its path not slope behind (given that we define the direction of the Earth's movement as forward)? Not until Newton was there an adequate explanation of these phenomena.

Early in the seventeenth century these examples furnished counter-arguments to the heliocentric theory. Such examples apparently refute the Copernican hypothesis. Consequently, adherence to Aristotle and the geocentric position was not completely irrational. Galileo himself must have been in doubt. He was more than fifty years old when he defended the heliocentric system publicly. Nor was his grasp of the heliocentric position perfect. Like Copernicus, he held that the planets revolve in perfect circles around the sun. The circle hypothesis is a traditional view. The proponents of the geocentric astronomy had also held that the planets' orbits are circular. Although Galileo knew the work of Kepler, he was not able to accept the idea that the orbit of a planet is an ellipse with the sun as one of the foci. Nor could Descartes. This is an important point to keep in mind when we examine the proceedings of the Inquisition against Galileo.

'THE GALILEO AFFAIR'

In 1615 Galileo went to Rome to show his telescope to the pope. At this time Galileo had supporters among both the Jesuits and the Augustinians. Nor was the pope directly opposed to his work. But, for the Church, there was a major scriptural objection: according to the best opinion, the Bible endorsed the geocentric system. This was certainly an *interpretation* of the Bible, but it had solid textual support, and it had been approved by the Fathers of the Church. For instance, the miracle in the book of Joshua (10:12–13), when God stopped the movement of the sun, was often referred to:

> Then spake Joshua to the Lord in the day when the Lord delivered up the Amorites before the children of Israel, and he said in the sight of Israel, Sun, stand thou still upon Gibeon; and thou, Moon, in the valley of Ajalon. And the sun stood still, and the moon stayed, until the people had avenged themselves upon their enemies. . . .

> So the sun stood still in the midst of heaven, and hasted not to go down about a whole day.[7]

How should the Copernican theory explain such texts?

All parties in this controversy assumed the Bible to be infallible, but that its interpreters could be mistaken. The Church accepted also that many statements in the Bible could not be interpreted literally. Thus, the Fathers of the Church had developed allegoric and moral interpretations of problematic passages. This was a conception of interpretation which Galileo also could accept, namely, 'that the Holy Scripture can never lie or err, and that its declarations are absolutely and inviolably true. I should have added only that, though the Scripture cannot err, nevertheless some of its interpreters and expositors can sometimes err in various ways. One of these would be very serious and very frequent, namely to want to limit oneself always to the literal meaning of the words.'[8] According to Galileo, we should above all avoid a literal interpretation of the cosmological and astronomical statements in the Bible.

Galileo knew that the literal message of the Bible is geocentric. This he explained by the so-called accommodation theory: the language and the formulations of the Bible are accommodated to the needs of simple and ignorant people. To avoid confusion, it is based on the geocentric world-view. In principle the Bible can also be reconciled with the Copernican view. But the Bible is no textbook in astronomy. As Galileo emphasized, it does not even mention the names of all the planets. The task of the Bible, Galileo says, is to tell us how to reach paradise, not how the celestial bodies move. Even if the theory of accommodation is today accepted by most Christians, it was at the time of Galileo a controversial position, not least because it was developed by John Calvin and had support in the Protestant world.

This controversy was also related to the question of what should be accommodated to whom (and how). Thereby arose complicated questions on the natural sciences and the interpretation of the Bible. Galileo took as his point of departure the idea that scientific knowledge can never conflict with a correct interpretation of the Bible. God reveals himself both in the Bible and in the book of nature; he is the author of both. And he cannot contradict himself. It is therefore always possible to harmonize the truths of the Bible and those of nature, according to Galileo. This view was also accepted by enlightened members of the Church. More problematic were Galileo's ideas on how this accommodation and harmonization should be achieved. According to Galileo, scientific theories should be our tool in interpreting the Scriptures.[9] The interpretation of the Bible is thus to be accommodated to the natural sciences. And scientists are therefore in a better position to understand the Bible than theologians. This view could certainly not be accepted by the Catholic Church. That would have been a renunciation of its authority in religious questions. Luther and Protestantism had shown where that might lead.

It is easy to see why Galileo's position was unacceptable to the Church. Firstly, it was an implicit attack on the authority of theologians to interpret the Scriptures. Secondly, Galileo questioned the competence of theologians to resolve conflicts between science and religion. Thirdly, Galileo represented the hermeneutic position that the scientist can determine the correct interpretation of the biblical view of the cosmos. Many people regarded this as a dangerously individualistic tendency

— a slippery slope toward Protestantism: the interpretation of the Bible should not be left to each individual — least of all to scientists!

The visit to Rome in 1615 was planned by Galileo as a scientific crusade. He wanted to demonstrate his new discoveries and strike a blow for the Copernican view, but he also wanted to be exonerated from the accusations of heresy. For Galileo personally, the process was successful. The accusations were withdrawn by the Inquisition. However, the pope referred the controversial questions on astronomy and theology to a special commission of theologians. This is where the problems began. On 24 February 1616 the commission unanimously found the Copernican system to be philosophically and scientifically untenable, and heretical. Simultaneously, the Inquisition forbade propagation of the Copernican view. This was a great defeat for Galileo.

At the end of the 1620s the theological and political situation was somewhat changed. The new pope, Urban VIII, was enlightened and liberal, and Galileo thought that the time was ripe for a new offensive. But how could he outflank the ban on arguing in favour of the Copernican view? He decided to write a book in the form of a Platonic dialogue, but without a dogmatic conclusion, so that he could not be held responsible for the opinions expressed in the dialogue. This book was entitled *Dialogue about the Two Major World Systems*. It was presented to the pope in 1630 and was allowed to be printed in 1632.

It is in the form of a dialogue among three persons: Simplicio is an Aristotelian who defends the Ptolemaic-geocentric world-view, Salvatio a spokesman for the Copernican system, and Sagredo a student seeking enlightenment. The dialogue indirectly defended Copernicanism. It created a great stir and provoked a forceful theological reaction. In the spring of 1633 Galileo was summoned to appear before the Inquisition in Rome. Under threat of torture he had to abjure the view that the Earth moves, and he was sentenced to life imprisonment (later commuted to house arrest). *Dialogue about the Two Major World Systems* was put on the Index of Prohibited Books — where it remained until 1835. The sentence against Galileo was to prove a great disaster for the Catholic Church, since it showed the Church in a bad light, and the advancement of science in the Catholic world was retarded.

At the end of his life Galileo was allowed to live in his own villa near Florence. He was now blind and deaf, but he dictated to his closest friends his last book, *Dialogues on Two New Sciences*, which was printed in the Netherlands in 1638.

DECONSTRUCTION OF THE COSMOS AND MATHEMATIZATION OF NATURE

Galileo played an important role in the history of science. Among other achievements, he discovered the laws of falling bodies and constant accelerated motion. He was also said to have 'discovered' the new experimental method. Moreover, he holds an important position in the history of philosophy as a renewer of Platonism.[10]

Today this picture of Galileo has been somewhat modified. His status as an important experimenter has been questioned. It has even been claimed that he cheated in his observations, and that he often had to fall back on rhetoric and dubious arguments. In his writings he presented a series of 'thought experiments', but that does not mean that he carried them out (or that they could be carried out). It should, however, be emphasized that Galileo actually did carry out experiments and that he made important discoveries of a practical nature. But both as a philosopher and as a physicist, he was more of a rationalist than an empiricist. He fully realized that Aristotelian physics is closer to the experience of daily life than the new physics. But, like Plato, he placed reason and mathematics above our sense experience.

Galileo's most important *philosophical* contribution was the 'deconstruction' of the Aristotelian cosmos and the dissolution of the old teleological view of nature. The Aristotelian universe was replaced by a geometric or Euclidean universe. That meant that a hierarchic and limited cosmos was replaced by an open and endless universe. The old distinction between 'the world under the moon' and 'the world above the moon' had broken down. For Galileo all phenomena are on the same ontological level: the same laws of nature are valid throughout the universe. Astronomy and physics are based on the same principles. With Galileo a whole world-view collapsed. A new approach to nature was under way. The natural attitude of our everyday life was replaced by a methodological approach that can hardly be called 'natural' at all. In what follows we shall take a look at how Galileo revolutionized our world-view. Aristotelian physics was in many ways an advanced nonmathematical interpretation of nature. Its initial observations are simple and convincing: it seems 'natural' to us that heavy objects fall 'downwards'. We would be as surprised as Aristotle if a heavy object, such as a big stone, were suddenly to rise from the ground. This would be seen as 'unnatural'. If we strike a match, we expect the flame to turn 'upwards', not 'downwards'. Aristotelian physics explains such phenomena. Crucial in this connection is the idea that all things have their natural place. Each thing has, in accordance with its nature, a definite place in the cosmos. There is a place for everything and everything has its natural place. When everything is in its place, nature appears to be a harmonious cosmos. In our empirical world we certainly perceive that objects move and change their places. Such movements and changes are either the expression of a cosmic disorder, a *forced* movement, as when we throw a stone into the air – or a *natural* movement, as when the stone returns to its natural place. Natural movement has a definite and natural end. This is, however, only true for the 'world under the moon'. The 'world above the moon' is characterized by eternal and circular motion, as in the planets revolving around the Earth.

With the new physics, the Aristotelian notion of movement broke down completely. In a vacuum, there are no 'natural places', and a body will never 'know' where to move. Nor, strictly speaking, can we place concrete, observable objects in a geometric space, which can accommodate only idealized phenomena. Only geometric bodies can be located in a geometric space.

For Galileo it was no longer possible to conceive of all things as seeking their natural places, the heavy ones at the bottom and the light ones on top. It no longer made sense to think of natural motion that ceases by itself. According to the principle of inertia, all objects remain in their state of rest or constant, linear motion as long as no external forces intervene. At this point, Aristotle would certainly have objected that nobody has ever seen constant, linear motion. And Galileo would have agreed: such a motion is possible only under idealized conditions. This is where mathematics enters the picture: objects in linear motion in a vacuum are not observable physical objects, but geometric solids moving in a geometric space. This form of idealization also deliberately ignores such factors as friction, resistance, and the non-Euclidean character of all physical phenomena.

For Galileo the struggle for the new physics also became a struggle for a new *ontology*. Prior to all empirical and experimental enquiry of nature, he points to a basic philosophical problem: what is the role of mathematics in the questions we raise with respect to nature? Galileo answers that all questions must be raised in a mathematical language, because the book of nature is 'written' in this language: 'Philosophy is written in the great book that lies before our eyes – I mean: the universe. But we can only read it when we have learned that language and are well acquainted with the signs by which it is written. It is written in the language of mathematics, and its letters are triangles, circles, and other geometric figures. Without these means it is impossible for a human being to understand as much as a single word.'[11] In this way Galileo advocated a *mathematical ontology*. The innermost essence of reality is mathematical. The unchangeable in all change are mathematical forms.

Galileo's view of nature and of mathematics places him in the tradition from the Pythagoreans and Plato: the essence of nature is ultimately numbers. Our senses do not give us immediate access to this dimension of reality. The mathematical science of nature does not investigate the experienced and qualitative nature of Aristotle, since its objects lie 'below' the perceptible nature. It belongs to an idealized 'world of ideas'. This is what makes Galileo a Platonist. In the *Dialogue about the Two Major World Systems*, it is the Aristotelian Simplicio who doubts the role of mathematics in the study of nature. For Simplicio, the natural processes are 'for the most part such or such': they are always qualitative and individualized; no phenomena are absolutely identical. In experienced nature there are no circles, triangles, or straight lines. There is nothing that corresponds to geometric or mathematical concepts. The processes of nature are therefore not quantifiable. Physics is not 'applied' geometry.

The Aristotelian approach is not unreasonable. In a certain sense we cannot quantify quality. Galileo's natural science has therefore no room for sense qualities such as colour, smell, and taste. They do not belong to the 'objective' nature and are not part of the essence of reality. Sense qualities are 'subjective' and occur in the experiencing subject. This theory of the subjectivity of the sense qualities, which originated with Democritus, was later accepted by Descartes and the British empiricists. For Galileo, the theory of the subjectivity of the sense qualities means that sense experience cannot be the most important source of knowledge. At least, sense experience has to be guided by mathematical reason. Here, too, there are parallels with the Pythagoreans and Plato: mathematical reason is the only tool by which we can grasp the essence of nature. Hence, Galileo is more of a rationalist than an empiricist. At the same time, this rationalism is combined with an *experimental examination* of nature. In practice, this means that Galileo tries to find mathematical solutions to concrete physical problems – questions connected to the movement of falling objects, of projectiles, and of pendulums.

Galileo understood mathematical truths to be strictly self-justifying. This knowledge could not have been otherwise. In mathematics, Galileo says, we have the same absolute certainty that only nature itself can have. Here we lift ourselves to a divine level where human knowledge and God's knowledge unite: 'As to the few mathematical truths that are understood by the human intellect, I believe that our knowledge can be equal in certainty to the divine knowledge'.[12] In the field of mathematics there is thus no room for compromise or negotiation. Who dares to correct God?

Galileo thought that insight into mathematical relations was an innate knowledge. This is also the Platonist and rationalist opinion. Plato had argued in a similar way in his dialogue *Menon*. For both Plato and Galileo, mathematical knowledge is something we all possess, but for most of us it is 'deep down'. However, what has been forgotten can still be remembered (cf. *anamnesis*, 'remembrance', in Plato). The process of remembering can be compared with that of relearning a forgotten language; in this case, an alphabet of circles, triangles, etc. It is typically through a *dialogue* that we manage to remember that which is forgotten. This strategy, too, Galileo shares with Plato.

Hence, geometry is to play a crucial role in the founding of the new natural sciences. In the language of geometry the phenomena can be described in a measurable way. Therefore, the geometric language also facilitates technical solutions: for instance, building blocks with right angles, plane surfaces, and uniform dimensions do make it easier to build houses and walls than natural stones with various shapes and dimensions. Similarly, we can use geometric concepts to describe mechanical systems of wheels, circular motions, and transitions between linear and circular motions. Such devices should make it possible to exploit the natural energy of wind and water. The speculative Pythagorean-Platonist theory, according to which mathematics – here geometry – underlies all phenomena, could thus be a fruitful idea both for the new experimental sciences and for the development of technology. With the development of experimental procedures, technology was drawn into scientific work. The Pythagorean-Platonist view, apparently remote from life, was thereby given a practical application, by pioneers such as Galileo Galilei. In addition, geometry influenced not only the world-view, the concepts and methods of science, and the practical development of technology, but also the art of the day, as in the use of perspective in painting and the use of geometric forms for aesthetic reasons in architecture.

NEWTON: THE TRIUMPH OF PHYSICS

Sir Isaac Newton, the son of a yeoman, became a professor of mathematics at Cambridge University and president of the Royal Society. He was a pioneer in physical science as well as a giant in Western intellectual history in general. His major work *Philosophiae naturalis principia mathematica* was published in 1687. As is well known, he worked out the three laws of motion and the law of gravitation, the theory of the infinitesimal calculus (at the same time as, but independently of, Leibniz), and the theory of the composition of light. His physical theories reinforced earlier theories, both in astronomy (Kepler's laws of planetary motion) and in mechanics (Galileo's laws of falling bodies). In Newton's physics, we find hypothetico-deductive research, which in essential points is experimental, and we find conceptions of material particles, the vacuum, and mechanical forces acting at a distance, expressed in a mathematical language. The idea of acting at a distance broke with the accustomed way of thinking of, among others, Galileo and Descartes (whom Newton had carefully studied in his earlier years).

Newton emphasizes the role of mathematics, especially geometry, in the new physical science. On the basis of measurements geometry allows us to treat numbers and figures, such as lines and circles, in a precise way. Hence it is the task of physics to investigate the forces of nature by using the concept of motion clarified in this way, and to explain the other natural phenomena on the basis of these forces. Newton's famous laws of motion and gravitation are as follows:

Newton's first law: a body at rest remains at rest and a body in motion remains in uniform motion in a straight line unless acted upon by an external force.

Newton's second law: the acceleration of a body is directly proportional to the applied force and is in the direction of the straight line in which the force acts.

Newton's third law: for every force there is an equal and opposite force or reaction.

Newton's law of gravitation: two bodies mutually attract each other with a force that is proportional to the product of their masses and inversely proportional to the square of the distance between them.

Newton was also interested in theology, writing extensively on that subject, and alchemy. He sought to achieve transformations of one substance into another. His efforts in chemistry were less successful than his work in physics and mathematics.

With Newton, physics became an example of the triumph of science over tradition and prejudices, and Newton became a major predecessor of the Enlightenment. Just as the emerging natural science had previously inspired the philosophers, partly in the formation of the mechanistic world-view, partly for rationalistic as well as empiricist positions, so Newton gave new impulses to philosophy. We especially see his influence in Kant, who sought to establish the epistemological basis for the new physics. According to Kant, not only are space and time grounded in unalterable features of our experience, but since the category of cause is necessarily present in our cognition, the new science has also given us a defence against the sceptical objection that we cannot be sure that the principles governing what happens today will also shape what happens tomorrow, an objection that seems to destroy the foundation of the experimental method, which presupposes a certain constancy in the universe.

As the primary founder of the new physics, Newton remained a symbol of human achievement: science became connected with the idea of progress. Francis Bacon's conception of knowledge as power, and as a source of prosperity and progress, became widely accepted and implemented in the time that followed. Science, not theology, emerged as the rightful authority in questions of truth and became man's means of controlling the processes of nature. Philosophy and religion had to find their place in relation to the new sciences. This is the social and intellectual significance of the emergence of the mathematical and experimental natural sciences.

THE BIOLOGICAL SCIENCES

We have seen how the new astronomy and the new physics emerged from inner conflicts with earlier academic traditions and in conflict with established notions and interests in philosophy and theology. These are conflicts which took place simultaneously on the theoretical and the institutional levels. However, in the university tradition from the late Middle Ages, it was theology, law, and medicine that comprised higher education, and led to academic professions. There were also internal developments and internal conflicts within these disciplines during the transition to the newer age. In theology, there were the Reformation movements, with roots going back to nominalist conceptions (directly to Luther and indirectly to Ockham). In jurisprudence, there were debates about more secularized policies for legal institutions, and various versions of contract theory and natural law theory, debates which continued from Althusius and Grotius, Hobbes and Locke, to the Enlightenment and the declarations of human rights (in North America and France). In medicine, among other things, there was the transition to a modern, scientific perspective, exemplified by Harvey's theory of the circulation of blood in the first half of the seventeenth century. We will glance at the development within the biological disciplines, using medicine as our starting point.

But first it may be appropriate to note that all of the three higher university disciplines at that time – theology, law, and medicine – were normative, hermeneutic disciplines: theology interpreted the Holy Scriptures, jurisprudence interpreted law and legal affairs, and medicine interpreted disease. For theology, the normative was found in revelation; for jurisprudence, the normative was found in natural law and in statute law; and for medicine, the normative was found in the idea of promoting health and longevity.

Inspired by the mechanistic world-view, medicine, too, searched for mechanistic explanations. A conflict developed between the traditional Aristotelian view of biological phenomena and the new Galilean-Newtonian ideal of science.

Paracelsus (1493–1541) – also known as Theophrastus Bombastus von Hohenheim – was a Swiss physician and scientist. He was still essentially within the Aristotelian tradition, which was also connected with Hippocrates and Galen: sickness was an imbalance of the basic elements in the body. For Paracelsus, these basic elements were salt, sulphur, and mercury; here, he was linked with the alchemist tradition of his day. For us today, it is easy to point out his uncritical speculations. Yet, the alchemists, with their development of laboratory techniques, still played a part in laying the foundation for the emergence of chemistry. Hence, Paracelsus the physician, also sought special ingredients in herbs in order to cure certain diseases. In this search we find traces of a fruitful scientific method, even if the notions he had about which ingredients led to which effects were often rather fantastic. Paracelsus can be said to typify the Hippocratic medical tradition in the sense that he emphasized medical practice and experience, in contrast with tendencies towards more interpretive medicine (in which physicians place more emphasis on interpreting diseases than on curing them, let alone explaining them). The medical profession, however, had vague boundaries. Thus, operations were, to a large extent, performed by 'barbers', not by physicians.

The transformation of medicine into a science took place under the influence of the new physics, and eventually, under the influence of the new chemistry, and this process gained momentum in the nineteenth century. But this process required renewed knowledge of anatomy and physiology. This meant that the ban on human dissection had to be broken so that physicians could profit from the legacy of antiquity. Leonardo da Vinci (1452–1519) was a pioneer in anatomical research through dissection, although here we must also mention Andreas Vesalius (1514–1564).

William Harvey (1578–1657) was an English anatomist whose investigations led to the revolutionary concept of the circulation of blood. Harvey viewed the cardiovascular system as a closed system, in which the heart functions as a pump. This brilliant mechanical-causal explanation was far better than the older theory that the blood disappeared and was created again. Hence, medicine gradually took shape as a scientific discipline, in accordance with the development of anatomy on the one hand, and physics and chemistry on the other.

The conflict between the Aristotelian and Galilean-Newtonian perspectives was expressed in the opposition between vitalism and the mechanistic view of the biological sciences: can all aspects of organic (living) nature be grasped with the same mechanistic and materialistic concepts that we find in the new physical sciences, or do the biological disciplines require unique concepts to comprehend the processes of life? Those who claim the latter are usually called 'vitalists', and those who deny it are often called 'reductionists'. The last-named attempt to explain the processes of life in the same way as the phenomena of inorganic nature; hence, they 'reduce' biology to physics (cf. the problem of reduction in Hobbes, Ch. 8). Thus, Aristotelians are vitalists, while adherents of the Galilean-Newtonian view of science are reductionists in biology.

In medical practice a doctor must, at the same time, both scientifically examine the patient and consider the patient's self-image and social situation. We may, for instance, reject the view that a mechanistic perspective is sufficient for all medical problems, but still retain the mechanistic perspective for *scientific explanations* of biological phenomena. We might reason as follows: indeed, we do have a completely unique experience of our own body, as a living body. Those who view their own sexuality exclusively in biochemical terms are insane. Here there is a recognition of psychosomatic processes. But the question remains: which observations or scientific explanations should thereby be different in the biological disciplines?

This conflict has now lost some of its intensity, but in debates about man's nature in relation to evolution or so-called holistic medicine, similar problems may emerge. The same is true, to a certain extent, in the debate about ecology.

MAN AS *SUB-JECTUM*

Today it is common, in referring to the Renaissance, to talk about a revolution in fundamental perspectives, about a *paradigm shift*.[13] We shall illustrate this point by referring to three different sciences: astronomy, mechanics, and optics.

PARADIGM SHIFT IN ASTRONOMY

Let us start with a reminder: the prevailing view in astronomy until the Renaissance was based on the notion that the Earth is the centre of the universe. The sun, the stars, and the planets revolve around the Earth. This view was connected with theological and philosophical views of the Earth, man's home, as the centre of creation. This is the geocentric world-view. Against this view it was claimed, with increasing intensity, that it is not the Earth that is the centre, but the sun: the Earth, like the stars and the planets, revolves around the sun. This is the heliocentric world-view. The change from the geocentric to the heliocentric world-view took place in connection with a precise formulation of the planets' orbits. Yet the geocentric world-view had not been disproved by new observations. The geocentric world-view could also account for the new observations; but in order to cover all of the observations, the theory became more and more complicated. The scientists' opinions were divided. Not all scientists thought that the heliocentric world-view was correct. Who was right then? We might say: both theories and neither. From the kinematic point of view, whether we look at the Earth or the sun, or any other point in the universe as 'the preferred point' is a question of our choice of the frame of reference. All data can, from this perspective, be accounted for regardless of which frame of reference we choose.[14]

This conflict between the geocentric and the heliocentric world-views illustrates how different theories can account for the same data. This is what is called a diversity of theories, in the sense of a diversity of explanation. The point is of epistemological interest since it means that if one theory has been developed to explain a given problem, the possibility is not excluded that other theories can also be found. There are, in other words, good reasons to be tolerant of competing scientific explanations. There may be, on the level of theory, different views, and the idea of *one* true synthesis of all scientific insight, *the* scientific world-view, thus becomes problematic.

What, then, took place during the transition from the geocentric to the heliocentric world-view? In modern terms, we could say that there was a 'shift in paradigm', a change of perspective and premises, which cannot be explained as a falsification of the superseded theory. Such a shift occurs when a circle of scientists who have developed a new basic theory have displaced the scientific school that previously dominated the field. In such instances, there will be great communication problems between the competing schools since the opposition is so fundamental.

During the Renaissance, the controversy over the geocentric and the heliocentric world-views had a deep impact on the view of man. After having lived in the centre of a finite universe, man found himself located on a small planet among other planets in an infinite universe. The world became less 'homelike'. The French philosopher and physicist Blaise Pascal succinctly expressed this scientific *and* existential experience: 'The eternal silence of these infinite spaces frightens me' (cf. also Ch. 9).[15]

PARADIGM SHIFT IN MECHANICS

There was also a paradigm shift in mechanics, but here it was largely a transition from a theory unable to account for the observed data to a theory that could account for the available data: the transition from an Aristotelian to a Galilean-Newtonian mechanics. Aristotle attempted to explain the motions of inorganic objects – like rocks, wagons, and arrows – from the doctrine that all things seek their natural place: heavy things (rocks) fall down because their natural place is close to the surface of the Earth. Light things (smoke) rise because their natural place is high. The motions of inorganic objects are thus, in a certain sense, explained by their goal:

they seek their natural place. It is obvious that inorganic things do not possess any notion of a goal, and it is equally obvious that they do not do anything themselves in order to reach their goal. But in Aristotle's hierarchic view of the universe, different things naturally belong at different levels.

Hence, in a way, Aristotle found it easy to explain the motion of falling. It is given in his premise that heavy things fall. The problem for Aristotelian physics, in connection with falling, is that of velocity. Aristotle thought that heavy objects fall faster than light objects. According to the new mechanics, all freely falling objects attain the same velocity. This opposition is sometimes presented as though Aristotelian physicists neglected observation. If they had only looked, they would have corrected their views! The matter is more complex. Aristotle had a different conception of space than that of the new mechanics. For Aristotle, space is always filled. He rejected the idea of an empty, frictionless space. Space is to be understood as an element analogous to air and water. Hence, the medium in which the object falls always offers resistance. Therefore, if we drop a lead ball and a goose feather in an air-filled space, the lead ball will of course fall fastest.

Newtonian mechanics is based on completely different premises: space is empty, that is, free of resistance. Objects remain in their condition of motion in regard to velocity and direction until they collide, thereby changing their velocity and direction. This basic view does not harmonize with our everyday experience of objects, but represents a bold conceptual model. Only in special attempts, where, for instance, the resistance in the material or in the air is eliminated, can we empirically test this theory. Therefore, a connection between such abstract models and systematic experiments may be established.

From Aristotle's perspective it became difficult to explain how an arrow could continue in its path in an almost horizontal direction. Why did not the arrow seek its natural place at once? In Aristotle's thought, the horizontal movement must be explained. The vertical movement, the fall, is given in the premises. In Newtonian mechanics, the arrow's horizontal movement is explicable: that an object remains in its condition, with regard to velocity and direction, is precisely the basic presupposition. But why does the arrow then fall towards the ground? Here, the fall itself must be explained. Gravity is the cause: objects attract one another. The reduction in velocity must also be explained: friction explains this. In other words, without denying the more certain empirical foundation for the new mechanics than the Aristotelian, we may point out how these two theories illustrate an interesting point about the diversity of theories: what could be seen as roughly the same state of affairs — here, motion — is explicable by different theories in which the premises in the first theory are what should be explained in the second, and vice versa.

Which paradigm shift occurred in the transition from the Aristotelian to the Galilean-Newtonian mechanics? This was, among other things, a transition to a more systematic, experimental natural science in which mathematics in some way or another plays a part in theories and observations. It was a transition to purely mechanical causes, since all teleological viewpoints have been excluded. This last point is not the least important for our understanding of man as well as nature. The conflict between mechanistic causal explanations and teleological explanations continues in our age, as in the discussion of the unique aspects of the social sciences.

PARADIGM SHIFT IN OPTICS

We may say that the paradigm shift in the Renaissance meant that things became *objects*, and that human beings became *subjects*. In order to clarify what this means, we will take a brief look at *optics*. Earlier, optics had been viewed as the science of vision. Therefore, human beings, as seeing and cognizant beings, were studied in optics. In the Renaissance, optics became the science of light rays, refraction, and lenses – without reference to the eye that sees. The eye now became an object that we look *at*. The eye that perceives the eye was no longer a subject of optics. The seeing eye and the cognizant human being became the province of philosophical epistemology.

The objects of science thus became pure objects, objects that have quantitatively measurable properties, and that are purged of all subjectivity. Not only were cognition and thought eliminated, but also colour, smell, taste, etc. – the so-called sensory qualities – which were interpreted as something a human being, the subject, adds to sense impressions of the object.

Here we have a radically new way of perceiving things and human beings. The traditional hierarchy of different forms of being, from inorganic things to plants, animals, and man – each with its unique capabilities – has been reduced to a simple dualism: *objects* with quantitative properties that we discuss and explain, and *subjects* who, by thought and action, investigate the objects. Objects belong to science, while the subject acquires an ambiguous, dual status: we can, on the one hand, investigate the human being, the subject, scientifically. Thus, a human being is a kind of object. On the other hand, the human being remains cognizant of science. There is therefore an epistemological 'remnant' in the subject. But how this should be understood, ontologically and epistemologically, soon became a controversial topic – the result was a dispute over the relationship between body and soul, and over the varying theories of knowledge of the rationalists, the empiricists, and the transcendental philosophers.

Even the terminology represented something new. The word *subject* is derived from *sub-jectum*,[16] 'that which is thrown under', i.e. 'the underlying'. Before the Renaissance, man was not the genuine *sub-ject*. The underlying (cf. *sub-stance*) could just as easily be things. That man becomes a subject, and things in their diversity become objects – that which presents itself to the cognizant subject – was thus something new and revolutionary: a human being was now largely understood as the fundamental (as *subjectum*), and things were, in various ways, understood as objects of knowledge for the cognizant subject (things were thought of as objects). Philosophy in the seventeenth and eighteenth centuries, from Descartes and Locke and on to Kant, reflects how epistemology, based on human beings, had now become the common basis for philosophy. Philosophy in these times is thus rightly called a philosophy of subjectivity. In Descartes' thought, the individual person's doubt and certainty are the starting point; in Locke's thought, it is the individual person's experiences and thought. The common starting point is man as subject.[17]

The occurrence of man as subject and nature as object was thus connected with the shift in paradigms within science. This process of making man a subject and nature (and man) an object implies at the same time a relationship of exploitation, of the subject's power over the object. The causally explanatory sciences give the subject a power over the objects. This power relation takes the form of predictions and technical maxims that can serve as the means to achieve given ends. The scientific-technical development gained momentum. A human being was no longer, ideally, a social being, *zoon politikon*, living in harmony with a household, *oikos*, within a reasonable community, *polis* and *logos*. A human being had become a *subject* who, with technical insight, has assumed overlordship in a universe of *objects*. The Renaissance is not so much a rebirth, as a birth, out of tradition, of something radically new – a turning point in history.

QUESTIONS

Describe the conflict between the geocentric and the heliocentric world-views.

Explain what we mean by the mechanistic world-view. Compare this view with that of Aristotle. Discuss the difference between a teleological and a mechanistic world-view.

Explain also what we mean by the 'mathematization of nature'.

Explain what we mean by 'the dispute over method'.

Describe the various paradigm shifts in the Renaissance.

SUGGESTIONS FOR FURTHER READING

PRIMARY LITERATURE

Newton, I., *Mathematical Principles of Natural Philosophy*, Berkeley, 1971.
Galileo Galilei, *Dialogue concerning the Two Chief World Systems, Ptolemaic and Copernican*, translated by S. Drake, Berkeley, 1967.

SECONDARY LITERATURE

Bernal, J. D., *Science in History*, vols I–IV, London, 1969.
Koyré, Alexandre, *Galileo Studies*, Sussex, 1978.
Kuhn, T. S., *The Structure of Scientific Revolutions*, Chicago (1962), 1970.

NOTES

1 On the relationship between science and practical insight, see J. D. Bernal, *Science in History* (I–II), London, 1969.
2 With Thomas' cool, rational style in mind, we can quote something that a Renaissance natural philosopher, Giordano Bruno (1548–1600), allowed one of the personages in a dialogue to say about matter: '[when] Aristotle – in the *Physics* – wants to enlighten the problem of matter, he uses the female sex as a mirror – a sex, I say, whimsical, frail, changeable, weak, miserable, nasty, base, bad, petty, despicable, unworthy, shameless, depraved, empty, vain, confused, crazy, faithless, lazy, sneaky, dirty, ungrateful, dull, crippled, imperfect, unfinished, cut off, amputated, worn down – rust, vermin, infection, corruption – dead – I say.' This can serve as a reminder of how questionable is the common practice of upgrading the Renaissance at the expense of the Middle Ages. (*Della Causa, Principio e Uno*, translated from the Norwegian by R.W.)

3 Cf. Popper, Ch. 26.

4 See, among others, Karl Popper, *The Logic of Scientific Discovery*. Popper says that theories that *cannot be falsified* are not *scientific* theories (Ch. 26).

5 The process of becoming autonomous does not apply only to the ability to *do* more things (build bridges and space stations); science, not least in the Renaissance and early modern period, was prone to make people autonomous by giving them *liberating insight* into relations which had much to do with a person's self-image and view of the world, without this insight always being of practical use, at least not at that time. An example of such insight is that achieved through the investigation of space.

6 A. Koestler, 'Johannes Kepler', in *The Encyclopedia of Philosophy*, vol. IV, 1972.

7 Galileo to Gastelli (21 December 1613), in Maurice A. Finocchiaro (ed.) *The Galileo Affair: A Documentary History*, London, 1989, p. 49. This book contains all the important documents relating to the proceedings against Galileo.

8 Ibid.

9 Ibid. p. 93.

10 This interpretation of Galileo has been elaborated especially by the French historian of science, Alexandre Koyré, in his book *Galileo Studies*, Hassocks, 1978 (originally Paris, 1939). Our interpretation of Galileo is indebted to Koyré.

11 Galileo, *Il Saggiatore*, 6th question.

12 Galileo, *Dialogo sopra i due massimi sistemi del mondo*, Bari, 1977, p. 144.

13 Today, the theoreticians of science who most strongly stress the fundamental characteristics of such shifts in paradigms within the history of science tend to view the change as something almost irrational, in view of the internal development of science. It thus becomes problematic to talk about scientific progress. Paradigms change. But does science move forward? See Thomas S. Kuhn, *The Structure of Scientific Revolutions*, Chicago, 1962 (1970). Cf. Ch. 26 about Kuhn. See also Paul Hoyningen-Huene, *Reconstructing Scientific Revolutions. Thomas S. Kuhn's Philosophy of Science*, Chicago, 1993. On astronomy in the Renaissance, see A. Koyré, *From the Closed World to the Infinite Universe*, New York, 1958, and S. Toulmin and J. Goodfield, *The Fabric of the Heavens*, London, 1961.

14 Logically, one has a choice. The argument (from perspectivism) above is based on a kinematic point of view.

15 Pascal, *Pensées*, §206.

16 See M. Heidegger, 'Die Zeit des Weltbildes', in *Holzwege*, Frankfurt am Main, 1957.

17 In the history of philosophy it is usual to point at *contrasts*, such as those between Plato and Aristotle, between the Stoics and Epicureans, or between rationalism and empiricism. But these contrasts are only contrasts in view of some common problem. Whether we choose to emphasize the contrasts or the parallels reveals as much about us as about the subject under discussion.

8 | The Renaissance and *realpolitik*[1] – Machiavelli and Hobbes

MACHIAVELLI – POLITICS AS MANIPULATION

Niccolò Machiavelli (1469–1527) lived in Italy at the end of the Renaissance. In his works *Il principe* ('*The Prince*') and *Discorsi sopra la prima deca di Tito Livio* ('*The Discourses*'), Machiavelli discusses why political leaders rise and fall, and the best means to hold on to power. In *The Prince* he advocated absolute monarchy, and in *The Discourses* he advocated a republic. But both works express a *realpolitiker* view of government: the political results are what count.

In the sixteenth and seventeenth centuries there was a tendency for the king to continue to expand his power base until he could rule as an absolute monarch. In this period there was mutual support between the king and the citizenry. It is probably as correct to say that the nation's king promoted the citizenry and free capital as it is to say that free capital, through the citizenry, promoted the nation's king. Be that as it may, with the absolutism of the seventeenth century and with early capitalism and the emerging free citizenry, the feudal society eventually crumbled. But this was a lengthy process, and one that did not proceed at the same rate in all places. The transition from a feudal economy to capitalism was not abrupt, but gradual. We will here be content with emphasizing a few points.

In the Middle Ages, it was largely taken for granted that there was an objective natural law providing the norm for good and right; and this applied also to kings and emperors. There were limits for displays of power. And society was viewed as a large community having mutual duties in order to satisfy human needs. It is true that there were different estates, and it is true that some people were poor and others wealthy. But society was generally viewed as a community based on a mutual contract. And it was society that was sovereign, not the head of state. Man was considered a moral and religious creature. Ultimately, the state's task was moral. And Church and state were to be concerned with their respective areas.

Roughly, we may say that at the same time that the centralized state power was being strengthened in the late Renaissance, human beings were again becoming individualized, just as in the transition from the city-state to the empire: it was not the community but the individual that was the starting point. And the individual was usually understood as being egotistic. To prevent internecine conflict, a strong ruler with unrestricted power was needed. In other words, we have a division between isolated individuals and the state's absolute power. But in the late Renaissance, individualism was often grounded biologically and materialistically (Hobbes), and the state's absolute power lay in the hands of one person who was the monarch of a national state, and not of a cosmopolitan empire.

Machiavelli was Italian. Unlike Spain, France, and England, Italy was divided into many small states that were in constant conflict with one another. Milan, Venice, Naples, Florence, and the Vatican State intrigued against one another and against foreign states. The pope functioned as an Italian local king in this game. And social life was, in many ways, characterized by an unbridled egotism. Creating a stable state became a goal for Machiavelli.

Machiavelli lived during the transition from the Middle Ages to early modern times. His conception of being a citizen was closely related to certain points of view in the Middle Ages: honour and fame were fundamental. His method was consistent with the humanist approach of the day: using historical examples in order to clarify current affairs. And this secularized way of thinking showed a relationship with aspects of the intellectual life in the seventeenth and eighteenth centuries.

Machiavelli's political theory is a doctrine of the mechanics of government. Superficially, it is a diplomatic 'game theory' for absolute princes. This theory was immediately applicable to the political struggle between the small states in Italy; at the same time, Machiavelli's political theory includes features that are typical of the Renaissance, and that distinguish it from the political theories of both ancient Greece and the Middle Ages. A presupposition for Machiavelli is that man is egotistic. There are hardly any limits to man's desire for things and for power. Since resources are scarce, there is conflict. The state is founded on the individual's need for protection against the aggression of others. Without enforcement of the law, there is anarchy. Therefore, a strong ruler is needed to provide security for the people. Machiavelli takes this for granted without entering into a philosophical analysis of man's essence. A ruler must, then, assume that human beings are evil. A ruler must be hard and cynical to secure the state and thus the life and property of the people.

Even though human beings are always egotistic, there are various degrees of corruption. Machiavelli deals with good and bad states, and with good and bad citizens, and he is interested in the precise conditions that make a good society and good citizens possible. Good states are those which maintain a balance among the different egotistic interests, and which are thus *stable*. Bad states are those in which the egotistic interests are in open conflict. And the good citizen is the patriotic and combative subject. In other words, the good state is the stable state. *The end* in politics is not the good life, as in ancient Greece or in the Middle Ages, but simply to gain and retain power, and thereby maintain stability. Everything else is a means — including morality and religion.

Machiavelli distinguishes between those who work to *gain* power and those who *have already gained* power. The difference between *The Prince* and *The Discourses* is, to some degree, an expression of this distinction between the problem of creating a stable state and the problem of retaining power. Machiavelli thought that the ancient Roman republic and Switzerland in his day were examples of stable states and relatively uncorrupted societies. Here, he thought that the people could, to a great extent, govern themselves. No despot was necessary. But in Italy, in his day, the task was to *create* a state. Here, a strong and ruthless prince was necessary. And Machiavelli is probably best known for his theories of how a leader can win power in a corrupt society. Machiavelli's interest in the problems of power is thus neither immoral nor amoral, but is moral in so far as the purpose is to prevent chaos. The goal is the good state or, more correctly, the best possible state – given the nature of man (according to Machiavelli).

Machiavelli thinks that a politician who pursues such a goal virtually creates the state: by making laws and enforcing them, the prince institutes the political order. Again, we see the contrast with the Middle Ages and Greek antiquity. For Machiavelli, existing law and morality are not absolute and universal, but something instituted by a ruler. This is the theory of the foundation by the sovereign prince of the national state. *L'état, c'est moi*; 'I am the state' (Louis XIV).

Because law and morality are founded by the prince, the prince is himself above them. There is no legal or moral standard by which he can be judged. His subjects can only show absolute obedience to their ruler, since it is the ruler who *defines* right and morality. But if one of the subjects manages to seize power, *he* should be obeyed by all, including the deposed ruler.

Machiavelli has been accused of having a double standard: the prince is to impress morality and virtue on the people, but he should himself be concerned only with the acquisition of power. Hence, there is a distinction between public and private morality. The subjects have one morality and the ruler has another. But, in fact, by Machiavelli's presuppositions, there is no double standard. There is only one morality, the prince's will. The prince wants to create a stable state, gain power, and retain it. And it is implicit in Machiavelli's thought that this is the only way to protect the citizens against mutual aggression. Given that human beings are fundamentally egoistic, and given that morality is nothing more than the prince's will, the accusations of a double standard dissolve. On the other hand, the distinction between private morality and public morality may be said to indicate a certain political realism: if we want to understand how politics *actually* functions, we should be aware that politics often uses categories other than those used in private life. What in private life is called 'murder' is, in politics, 'inflicting a great loss upon the enemy'. Politics has its own categories, its own morality – its own '*raison d'état*'. In other words, talking about murder in ordinary warfare is as inappropriate as talking about checkmate in rummy – it is confusing two different games. We may criticize this point of view, but Machiavelli is largely correct in pointing out that this is mainly the way things are.

A conquered people have moral attitudes and opinions *prior to* the prince's attempt to reorganize society. In this sense, morality is without normative import, i.e. for the prince. The prince must, however, consider the existing morality as one of several factors he must take into account. Nor does the morality that the prince eventually impresses on the people have any normative import for him; this, too, is a means in a political strategy. But the prince's own political policy ultimately has a moral core: that of securing stability in society.

We can thus say that Machiavelli subordinates morality to politics in the sense that he views morality, both that which a people has inherited and that which the prince establishes for that people, from a strategic perspective in which the prince's goal is to ensure a stable state. Private morality, in the sense of the citizens' morality, is thus subordinate to public morality, in the sense of the prince's fundamental goal that is identical with the state's fundamental goal. Here it is worth emphasizing that Machiavelli and the medieval theoreticians had different interests. In the Middle Ages, political theory had primarily concentrated on the ideal goals without always attempting to explain how one should realize these goals. Machiavelli, on the other hand, is interested in the means. He is interested in how politics is carried on here and now. Machiavelli provides a journalistic, empirical description of how politics functions in his day. He distinguishes in a certain sense between morality and politics – between the goals worthy of pursuit and the political means which are in and of themselves neither good nor bad but only more or less effective in the work of realizing these goals; and he attempts to describe the political means actually used in politics without considering whether they are good or desirable.

The sharp distinction between ends and means is something relatively new. Most Greek philosophers and Christian theologians had taken it for granted that certain actions (means) were blameworthy, like stealing and murder, regardless of whether they led to desirable ends. From this sharp distinction between ends and means, Machiavelli may claim that *the end justifies the means*: it was right and good for Romulus to kill his brother Remus because this led to a universal good.

It goes without saying that religion has a low position in Machiavelli's thought. All interests and all goals are secularized. The only role left for religion is to create a unity in the group. Machiavelli therefore thinks that it may be good for people to be religious. And the prince may just as well give the impression of being pious if he can achieve something by it.

Machiavelli is mostly interested in the purely political game. He has relatively little understanding of the economic conditions needed for exercising power. Moreover, he had an ahistorical anthropology: human nature is unchangeable. Therefore, we can learn to master the political situations in our day by studying those of previous ages (cf. *The Discourses*). We may therefore, to a great extent, have a timeless political science where the purpose is not to understand the essence of politics, but to learn to gain power. That is to say, Machiavelli's method is 'ahistorical' in *our* terms. But, viewed from his day, Machiavelli was thinking historically: like the humanists, he wrote history based on examples, individual stories used to explain his own times.

Aristotle viewed ethics and politics as a unit, which was *praxis*. Machiavelli *distinguished* between ethics and politics; and, in politics, the end justifies the means. The means are manipulative and amoral, beyond moral evaluation. And they can be empirically investigated. The goal is ultimately to maintain peace and order. Aristotle assumed universal norms and a constitutional form of government. Machiavelli allowed the Prince's will to define law and morality – but the final end is given: political stability. At the same time that politics became manipulation, the need arose for a social science that can give rulers authority over the actions of others. Machiavelli advocated both an empirical investigation of politics and a manipulative politics. In later times, Machiavelli became most famous, and notorious, for the doctrine of politics as manipulation, for the political amorality which many (such as Mussolini) interpreted as justifying unrestrained displays of power.

Machiavelli sought political insight by starting with particular events in the past and present. By studying these particular events he thought that he had gained practical insight that would aid all those who ruled a state or who wanted to seize power. It should be insight of the type 'if – then': *if* we act thus or thus, *then* this or that will occur. He assumed that human nature basically remains unchanged throughout history, or, more precisely, he assumed that history and man are subject to cyclical changes; for example, in the form of the rise, flourishing, and decline of states. Machiavelli thus assumed that we can construct universal generalizations from various isolated cases. If such insight did not always turn out to be accurate after all, it was because an unavoidable uncertainty, *Fortuna*, limits our ability to control events.

A common objection to this approach is that if we start with what is held to be unchangeable human attributes, we encounter great difficulty in grasping what is radically changeable, the creative element in society. As he explained various events in his day by means of psychological concepts, like egotism, supported by simple political concepts and a cyclical view of history, Machiavelli was not well equipped to grasp deeper socio-historical changes.

POLITICS BY CONTRACT AND POLITICS BY NATURAL LAW – ALTHUSIUS AND GROTIUS

From the beginning of the seventeenth century, political theory became more distinct from theology. Thus, the German Johannes Althusius (1557–1638) established a contract theory that built not on religion, but on social groups. Here the notion of a contract is used to explain both social groups and the ruler/subject relationship. The various groups – family, corporation, local community, nation – have different tasks and the groups are constituted by *different contracts*. Sovereignty always resides in the people, that is to say, not in individuals but in organic communities, hierarchically ordered in the society, from the family to the state. The people give power to the king and the civil servants on the condition that they keep their part of the contract. In this way, Althusius was able to explain how the king and the bureaucracy hold certain power while the sovereignty always resides with the people. This is all explained by *consent*, contract, between groups, and not by specifically religious concepts.

When the national states were established, the question arose of the relationship *between* these independent states. There was no longer any institution that could regulate the relationship between them; moreover, the legal conceptions found in the national states were based on the opinion that laws are created by a national king, and that they are therefore applicable *only* to *his* state. The Dutch lawyer Hugo Grotius (or de Groot, 1583–1645) provided a juridical solution to the dilemma by returning to the idea of natural law: there are certain laws that are *superior* to the individual national states, and that regulate the relationship between them. By developing the idea of natural law, he provided the basis for an international law superior to those of particular states. His efforts on this point gained approval and became incorporated in the concept of international law that resulted in the League of Nations, the Nuremberg trials, and the United Nations. Grotius lived during the Thirty Years' War (1618–48). As a result of religious-political conflicts, he was sentenced to imprisonment for life in 1618, but he escaped (concealed in a bookcase) to Louis XIII in France, where, among other activities, he entered the service of Sweden as a diplomat (1634). But when Queen Christina summoned him to Sweden, the harsh climate and his weak health led to his death. (Cf. Descartes' unfortunate demise there five years later.) The Thirty Years' War stimulated the idea of establishing a legal code to which disputing states are subject. This war also led to the idea of a division between political and legal issues, which are public, and religious questions, which are private. Grotius expressed both of these ideas. The idea of natural law, developing from Stoicism through Christian theology, was adapted by Grotius such that this law was divorced from theological and sacramental ties. This was not an expression of an anti-ecclesiastical view, but adaptation of natural law to a new situation in which the political and legal aspects were more separate from the religious. If international law was to apply to everyone, the foundation in natural law had to be independent of Christian theology. Between states, and in states, a more secular basis was therefore sought for political and legal agreement. In this sense, Grotius updated the idea of natural law for a new situation.

Grotius' best-known work is *The Law of War and of Peace* ('*De jure belli ac pacis*'). As the title indicates, Grotius dealt here with the idea of a law that is applicable to all conditions, including war: God has given human beings a natural need for fellowship (*appetitus societatis*), and this can be recognized by all human beings independently of revelation or theology. The need for a peaceful coexistence is fundamental, and in order for this to be realized certain laws must be respected by everyone. For example, promises must be kept and equality practised. This natural law theory entailed a rejection of the voluntaristic view of God as Creator and as the Giver of norms (cf. Luther). Things are not as the voluntarists say, that what God at all times *wills*, is by definition right; on the contrary, God wills right because it is right. Right is therefore lasting and universal, and can be acknowledged by everyone.

Grotius mentions some conditions that must be fulfilled in order for a state to be an equal member of the international community: it is unimportant whether the state is large or small, but the state must be stable and able to honour its treaties. These are criteria that are also used today. Of course, the problem is that there is no institution to enforce this international law. Such an institution existed, to a certain extent, in the Middle Ages, in the Church. But after the Reformation, the Church was divided and largely integrated into the particular states.

HOBBES – THE INDIVIDUAL AND SELF-PRESERVATION

Life. *Thomas Hobbes (1588–1679), an Englishman, lived at the time of the English Civil War. He learned Latin and Greek at the age of six and began at an early age to study at Oxford University. He was associated with Lord Cavendish and often travelled in an official capacity. He thus met several prominent persons of his day (such as Galileo). Hobbes took refuge in Paris during the first part of the English Civil War, but returned to Cromwell's Britain. At 88 years of age he translated Homer into English. His best-known work is the* Leviathan *(*Leviathan, or the Matter, Form, and Power of a Commonwealth Ecclesiastical and Civil*) of 1651. Among his other works are* De cive *('On the Citizen') (1642),* De corpore *('On Body') (1655), and* De homine *('On Human Nature') (1658).*

SOCIETY AS THE MECHANISM OF A CLOCK

Hobbes lived in politically unstable times during the civil war between the royalists and the Parliamentarians. His political writings focus on the need for a strong government that can secure peace and order. Hobbes thus supports an absolute monarchy. But the ideological support that Hobbes gives is ambiguous. Peace and order are essential for Hobbes, but whether or not the government is an hereditary monarchy is of less significance. Hobbes' political theory can be seen as at once strongly individualistic and strongly absolutist. Here, as in many other instances, there is no contradiction. Social atomization and strict political intervention can go hand in hand; when people are not bound to one another by social bonds, it may become necessary to use external force to prevent anarchy.

In Hobbes' case, this association of individualism and absolute government may be interpreted as an expression of the situation at an early and unstable stage in the development of the national state and market economy: the state needed a strong king who could abolish the old privileges of the nobility and secure peace and order, and who could guarantee that customers and rivals keep their trade agreements. In a situation of universal competition of man with man for survival, the only means of securing life and property is a strong government under an absolute monarch.

Hobbes seems to hold some of the same views as Machiavelli: society and politics should be understood rationally and scientifically, and human nature is basically unchangeable and ahistorical. But Hobbes is not content with a merely descriptive method, with generalizations based on the study of particular events, as was Machiavelli. He seeks a more secure method; he attempts to go deeper, to a foundation that offers a profounder explanation of the immediate social phenomena.

Hobbes is one of those philosophers inspired by the new sciences, and his natural philosophy is clearly marked by this influence: ultimately, the universe is composed of material particles that move mechanically. Hobbes' philosophy is thus ultimately a theory of motion. The parallel with mechanics is clear.

But at the same time, Hobbes is a rational metaphysician. He seeks, as did the rationalistic philosophers before him, a fundamental principle to explain the various changing surface events. He seeks an absolute and unchangeable basis. Being a philosopher of the late Renaissance, he seeks this basis in man. Man is the *subjectum*, the basis from which society should be explained.

How does he proceed? He comments on his method in *De cive* ('*On the Citizen*'). Here he uses *a watch* as an analogy. When we want to understand how a watch works we take it apart. We examine the various components and their properties. Then we put the watch back together, and by putting the parts together in such a way that the watch works again, we acknowledge how the parts relate to one another and how the watch functions. We have then understood what a watch is.

His idea was to divide society into its parts in a similar fashion, examine the parts, and then put them together again so that we may see how they relate to one another and how they function. By so doing, we will understand what society is. This cannot happen by actually dividing society, but only by imagining that that is what we are doing. This example illustrates several important points in Hobbes' 'dissolving – composite' method. The method starts by dividing up a phenomenon, and then reassembling it. This is a method of *analysis* and *synthesis*. Society is thus explicable on the basis of its component parts. But this does not mean that Hobbes thinks that society consists of its parts *alone*. The watch does not consist of its parts alone. When the parts are put together, something qualitatively new emerges, whether it be the watch or society. Hence, Hobbes does not reduce the whole to its parts. But he says that the whole can only be understood by its parts and their properties, *as well as* by their functional union. This method thus attempts to explain something given, by referring to its underlying elements. We can say that Hobbes seeks an explanatory principle that lies deeper than the level of observation.

If we return to the example of the watch, we can say further that Hobbes is looking for a functionalist explanation: understanding the watch means understanding how it works. The only properties of the parts that are of interest are those important for its ability to function: that the spring is tight and can drive the watch, that the cog has teeth that can connect with the other teeth and transfer motion. Whether the spring is green or red is irrelevant to the watch as a functioning system. Nor is it profitable to divide its parts any further: we understand what the watch is from the joining of springs, cogs, etc., without needing to know anything about the atomic structure of these parts. It is true that the spring and the cog are what they are, as functioning parts, because of the material particles from which they are built. But we do not need to know anything about this to find out what a watch is. A watchmaker does not need to be a physicist.

A watch is of course made by somebody. And it is used by someone to tell the time or as an accessory or a status symbol. But, according to Hobbes' example, we do not need to know anything about who made the watch or why, or what the watch is used for. To understand the watch is to understand its parts in their functional interconnection. It is to understand how the watch works, how it functions. The watch's workings are determined by the mechanical motion of its parts. To understand the watch is to understand how it runs. In this sense we can say that Hobbes' explanation is *functionalistic*.

We may say that Hobbes' example points to a cybernetic model. It is not merely that all the parts fit into a functionalist whole in which each part mutually presupposes the other parts. It is also that certain parts drive mechanisms and others steer mechanisms. If we think of a grandfather clock with a weight and pendulum, we can say that the weight is the driving force that makes the clock run, while the pendulum is what regulates, or disciplines the driving force so that the clock runs at an even rate. Without the weight, there is no movement. Without the pendulum, there is no ordered movement.[2]

If we now apply this argument to society, we can say that Hobbes rejects attempts to explain social phenomena by means of social phenomena. We must consider the basic elements. He also rejects the notion of explaining society by means of a deity who has a purpose for society (teleology). He seeks the functional connection between the parts, but he does not reduce society to its isolated parts. Nor does he break the parts down any more than is necessary to explain their functional social connection. According to this interpretation, it does not make sense to call Hobbes simply a reductionist.

How does Hobbes arrive at the component parts in society and how does he understand them? He uses a kind of *thought experiment*: let us imagine that the state did not exist; what would human life be like then? Hobbes is thereby trying to find out what it is that makes the state possible, what it is that explains and justifies our existence in a political society, in a state. He therefore asks what life would be like if the state *did not exist*. To understand what it means to live in a state, we must be able to understand what it is to live without it. Hobbes uses his doctrine about *the state of nature* to clarify what it would be like to live without a state. Using concepts like the individual, everyone's fear of everyone else, and the contract entailing the surrender of personal freedom, Hobbes tries to understand phenomena such as the state, authority, and power.

Hobbes argues that human beings without a state would feel unsafe. Without the state, we would be left to fend for ourselves. But since we need material goods to survive and since there is a scarcity of the goods that we must have, at the same time that we all, by nature, try to survive, there is bound to be competition among us for these goods. No one can be safe in this individual struggle for survival because no one is invulnerable, and there is a relative equality in strength and shrewdness among human beings. There will therefore be continual conflict. This is the so-called state of nature with everyone fighting against everyone else. The component parts are thus the particular human beings, or *individuals*. Their basic aim is *self-preservation*. This is the result of the analysis by which Hobbes wishes to explain social phenomena.

It is Hobbes' contention, the example of the watch serving as a model, that social phenomena, such as solidarity, interaction, freedom, etc., can be explained by the individual desire for self-preservation. He does not think that solidarity is nothing more than the desire for self-preservation, but he thinks that a social phenomenon such as solidarity needs an explanation, and that it cannot be explained by itself or by any other social phenomena, but only through the individual desire for self-preservation. According to this explanatory model, everything that we immediately experience, like positive and concrete ties between human beings (for example, love, empathy, and ties to home and community), must be understood in light of the individual's basic desire for self-preservation. Society may be explained by a reconstruction based on underlying elements and driving forces. From this perspective we can say that Hobbes does not deny that social unity and empathy exist, but he does try to determine what these factors actually are. In addition, we see that Hobbes does not need to go further than self-preservation. While it is true that human beings are made up of small material particles in mechanical motion, those particles are not included in the explanation of society any more than the atomic structure is a necessary part of the explanation of the watch. One does not need to have insight into the inner structure of matter in order to understand society.

The example of the watch means that the idea of a state of nature is not thought of as referring to an event in the past.[3] This idea of a state of nature is the result of an analysis, of a thought experiment in which the state is eliminated. The idea of the state of nature is not a historical hypothesis about something that has happened, but a thesis as to what is needed in order to make society possible. We could say that Hobbes attempts to explain social phenomena by means of psychological notions. Some may object that this is turning things upside down; on the contrary, social phenomena should be the basis for explaining psychological phenomena. The question as to what requires explanation and what offers explanation is thus a controversial one. How can we resolve the dispute scientifically? However, for

Hobbes, as the Renaissance philosopher, the *individual* is the basis of explanation; that is, the individual understood on the basis of self-preservation. That is to say, the individual accounts for three sources of conflict: competition, uncertainty, and the aspiration for honour. As a motivation, fear is the most important. Fear is what drives a human being into a politically ordered society. Within such a society, everyone's fight against everyone else is abolished as regards security of life, but financial competition and the aspiration for honour can continue.

How does Hobbes put the parts together again in such a way that an ordered society can arise? He points out that everyone in the state of nature lives in a continual state of fear, ultimately, the fear of sudden death. But as long as everyone is trapped in a state of mutual distrust and conflict over material benefits, there is little that any person can do to change the situation. Spontaneous reason tells the individual what is best to secure life and vitality, and *that* is self-defence; it is to take part in the struggle against others.

However, it would be to everyone's benefit if all were to agree to order society differently, establishing a power that secured life and health for everyone. How does one arrive at this point? This is the salient point of Hobbes' theory. Certainly, the state of nature clearly represents a less satisfactory solution than the ordered national society, viewed from the individual's egotistic interest in securing life and vitality. But reason in its spontaneous form is only an aid in the struggle for existence. It says, correctly, that it is best for the individual to prepare for the prevailing condition of discord. The individual cannot change this. But at the same time, Hobbes counts on an enlightened self-interest of a more reflective and forward-looking kind. This self-interest says that an ordered society is best. The salient point is how the various individuals can reach agreement to follow the reflective, forward-looking reason rather than the spontaneous and short-sighted reason; that is to say, how they can unite to create a common state.[4]

If we take society as a fact and say it is the expression of an agreement between egotistic individuals dictated by everyone's common long-range and enlightened self-interest, we can attempt to understand society as being founded on a *social contract* that is acknowledged by reason. The social contract is that which constitutes society. It explains the social phenomena in politics and social life in general. The state is established by this contract. According to Hobbes, the contract is based on the idea that everyone gives up freedom to a state body. The state is characterized by the fact that all legitimate physical force is gathered in one body. Without physical force the contract could be broken. Physical force is the only thing that can prevent people from breaking the contract agreed upon in order to secure life and health for everyone.

Using the watch as a cybernetic model, we can say that the desire for self-preservation can be compared with the weight (or the spring), the force of nature, and that the ruler can be compared with the pendulum (or the movement), the disciplining, steering factor. Power must be united, be *one*. This is a certainty for Hobbes. Whether this unity is located in a king or in a parliament is of secondary importance. The point is that there is a body with physical power that can exercise the sovereignty of the state. A distribution of power or a decentralized popular government would imply a dissolution of the unity that makes the state possible: power in one body. Hobbes does not perceive the contract that creates the state as a contract between the king and the people. It is a contract between individuals. The person who becomes the head of state is not personally a party to the contract. Therefore, the ruler *cannot* break his part of the agreement, because, as ruler, he is not a party to the contract. The ruler is thus absolutely sovereign. So far, Hobbes lends his full support to absolutism.

It is true that Hobbes thinks that the ruler should not interfere with the individual's right to buy and sell freely or to enter into agreements with others. He further mentions that the ruler cannot command individuals to kill or harm themselves – this would go against the individual's essence: self-preservation. But these are empty words as long as there is no power to prevent the ruler from interfering in these areas. Hobbes further gives the ruler the full right to use censorship. The ruler can rightfully determine which viewpoints are harmful and which may be presented to the people. Up to this point Hobbes seems to support absolutism without reservation. But the support is conditional. If the absolutist king loses control of society, that is to say, that he is no longer able to provide security for individuals, each person must again trust in his or her own power. We return to a state of anarchy, to a universal civil war, and a new contract and a new ruler must emerge. This means that a king who is overthrown does not have any right to regain the crown. For an absolutist king, an ideology that defends the inherited position of the king is preferable. A combination of the right of inheritance and God's grace is the best defence for the absolutist monarch.

But there is nothing in Hobbes' theory that says that there should be only *one* king. Hobbes' point is that one or several persons should enforce law and order. This being the case, Hobbes provides a poor defence of royal absolutism. Furthermore, *the individual* is what is fundamental to Hobbes, not the king. The struggle between egotistic and isolated individuals is the basis for the state and the monarchy. The state and the monarchy are only the means for securing the self-preservation for individuals.

By his model of explanation, there is not much Hobbes can say about class relations. What we have, as a basis for explanation, are egotistic individual, and the state that constitutes society. Classes and groups are to be explained, they are not principles of explanation. A model of explanation that has egotistic-rational agents as a basic presupposition for society transcends the problems of absolutism and points to the future, as a predecessor of the models of explanation in the political and economic theory in the emerging liberalist tradition. Hobbes thus became a spokesman for what is called methodological individualism.

The state, founded on the contract and sustained by physical power, is the basis of all social phenomena. There is thus no real distinction between state and society, between the administrative bodies and the immediate community. The social ties are constituted by enlightened self-interest mediated by the state. Here, Hobbes clearly distinguishes himself from earlier views, such as those of Plato and Aristotle, of human beings as social beings with a natural capacity for fellowship. For Hobbes, everything having to do with society can be traced back to the state and further back to the individual's desire for self preservation. Individuals are basically asocial and society is really secondary to the individual. The state and society are not one with the individual's essence, as they were for Plato and Aristotle, but are something that human beings have created by means of a contract based on concurring self-interest.

THE NATURAL LAW AS A RULE OF REASON

Hobbes talks about *laws of nature* in connection with human behaviour, and concludes that they are norms or general rules arrived at with the aid of reason. The first and basic natural law is that everyone should try to achieve peace if it is possible to be so. And the entire concept of natural rights is found in the following rule: if we cannot achieve peace, we must avail ourselves of all the devices and powers of war. A *right* is a freedom to act or to refrain from acting. A *law* prescribes what one should or should not do.

In the state of nature it is natural rights that rule, and hence the freedom to act in unscrupulous self-defence based on the desire of self-preservation that is recognized by reason. When a state is established, the natural laws come into force; these are rules of reason based on what all individuals understand that they ought to do, out of enlightened and long-term self-interest, in order to preserve life and the social conditions for a secure life. The rules of reason are, for Hobbes, norms of the type *if – then*: if we live in a state of nature, then we must use all possible means of self-defence. If we live in an ordered society, we must uphold peace. In both cases the rules of reason are based on man's basic instinct, self-preservation. Of the two possibilities, the latter is the best alternative.

In the philosophy of classical natural rights, the natural law is something ideal, above man, so to speak: norms that we should try to reach. For Hobbes, the norms in natural rights are dictated by material factors, by instincts and enlightened self-interest. Natural rights and the natural laws are explained by the individual's egotistic nature.

THEORY OF MOTION

We have so far looked at Hobbes' political philosophy without discussing his natural philosophy. We will now give an outline of one interpretation of Hobbes based on his natural philosophy; that is, a radical mechanistic-materialistic interpretation. However, from what Hobbes says about his method and from the direction he takes in his social philosophy, there is little reason to claim that Hobbes simply *reduces* social phenomena to mechanistic-materialistic phenomena; in other words, that he maintains that social phenomena exist only as material particles that circulate mechanically. But such a radically materialistic and reductionist interpretation is not uncommon, and it does give us the opportunity to illustrate some interesting philosophical points.

We can then say that Hobbes' basic concept is ultimately motion, which is used to explain everything else. The concept of motion is understood quantitatively, according to the mechanistic-materialistic world-view: *that* which moves are material particles, which change their spatial location by thrusts. The opposition to Aristotle is clear. For Aristotle, the basic concept of change entails a realization of potentialities, and there is both an efficient and a final cause. For Hobbes, all change is to be explained by physical motion, and there is only one cause, the efficient cause.

Aristotle, we may say, attempts to explain physical motion by means of a qualitative conception of change, whereas Hobbes tries to explain qualitative change with the aid of a conception of quantitative motion. When an apple's colour changes from green to red, Aristotle explains this as a change whereby the apple's potential for the colour red is actualized through the process of becoming ripe. The green apple is the material cause of the red apple, and this change entails both an efficient and a teleological cause, as well as a formal cause. For Hobbes, this change, too, is to be explained by the movements of material particles.

When the laws of particle motion can explain all things, there is no basis for teleological explanations. Everything that happens must be explained by the same mechanical causes that we have in the ideal case of mechanical interaction between completely round balls on a frictionless plane. Everything that happens, happens necessarily. Even human actions are determined. Society can then be interpreted as a diversity of human atoms that whirl around and bump into one another. And we can imagine two forms of society: a society with disorder and hard collisions between human beings, that is, anarchy, and a society in which human atoms move harmoniously because a unifying force coordinates the movements, that is, a society in the true sense of the word.

Political and social relations may thus be traced back to individual psychological relations, and these again to physiological conditions that are in turn traced back to mechanics. This is the analysis; reducing society to basic material elements and their mechanical moves. And once we have determined what the underlying elements and forces are, we can reconstruct society. We have a synthesis, back from mechanics to politics. Everything, absolutely everything, should therefore ultimately be explicable with the aid of mechanics, i.e., from mechanistic-materialistic concepts. In spite of the problems in reducing social and mental phenomena to physical phenomena (reducing actions to events), mechanistic materialism is fascinating also when it is applied to political theory: the attempt is made to explain everything from simple principles. There are no other forces or principles in society than those found in mechanics. Complexity is the only thing that is greater in the particle constellations we call society. Everything that happens can be understood from a simple theory of motion.

LIBERALITY AND LIBERALISM

Hobbes' political theory is not only a very consistent doctrine. This theory is also suitable as a simplified depiction of the situation of the citizenry in early capitalism: a collection of human atoms that struggle daily for survival in a world where there is a scarcity of material goods. The ties that bind these human atoms together are the enlightened self-interests, and they need the state, with an absolutist government, as a means of ensuring that trade agreements are kept. The state exists for the individuals. It has no value in itself. At the same time, this is understood as an eternal truth: this is the essence of man and of the state, through all time.

If by liberalism we mean a political theory that supports tolerance, Hobbes is not a liberal. It is then natural to trace liberalism back, for example, to Locke (Latin: *libertas*, 'freedom'). But if we define liberalism by the basic concepts *individual*, *contract*, and *state*, and not by psychological attitudes or moral values, Hobbes can be viewed as a predecessor of liberalism. This terminology requires that we clearly distinguish *liberalism* (*liberalist*) – basic concepts: individual, contract, state – from *liberality* (*liberal*) – as a positive, moral attitude in favour of tolerance and juridical freedoms. By this terminology, Hobbes can be called a 'liberalist', but not a liberal, while Locke is both a liberalist and a liberal; and socialists can, from this, be liberals, but not liberalists.

With this terminology we can depict some interesting connections between ideologies at different stages of modernity, from early capitalism, with hard struggles for survival and with the need of an absolute king (Hobbes), through a more established capitalism when it is important for the citizenry to point to inviolable rights vis-à-vis the absolute king (Locke), and on to an established private capitalism and *laissez-faire* liberalism (Adam Smith). The basic concepts – individual and state – seem to be largely the same in these different phases of liberalism. But from the early to the fully established capitalism, there is a certain change in the view of human nature – from self-preservation, through inviolable rights, to pleasure and profit (cf. utilitarianism, Ch. 14). We can say that the concept of freedom presupposes that there is some agent or subject that is free. Freedom is not a concept that stands on its own. A philosophy of freedom presupposes necessarily a doctrine of what *is* free, and in what way it is free. For the liberalists this is *the individual*, understood as a self-sufficient, rational-egotistic agent. It is therefore not arbitrary when we define *liberalism* as a form of *individualism*. Liberalism cannot be understood without the social philosophy or ontology that it presupposes – just as little as any other doctrine of freedom can be understood without the accompanying doctrine about *what* it is that is free, and in relation to what.

It should be emphasized, however, that usually the term *liberalism* is used about the political-economic theories that view freedom as a basic value and the individual's enlightened self-interest as the underlying driving force, where the state has the task of securing the field of action for the independent agents. That is to say, the state must guarantee peace and order, and the right to own property, so that rational predictable actions become possible, but there must be clear restrictions on any further intervention by the state.[5] From the common use of the word – according to which individual liberties are crucial and the state should act predictably – it is unnatural to call Hobbes a liberalist.[6]

QUESTIONS

What are the new ideas of man, society, and the state in Machiavelli and Hobbes?

'In Aristotle ethics and politics are connected with each other, while Machiavelli separates ethics from politics.' Discuss this assertion, and clarify Machiavelli's view of politics.

'Plato and Machiavelli have essentially different views on morality and politics.' Discuss this assertion.

Hobbes advocates a mechanistic world-view and uses concepts from classical mechanics to explain social phenomena. Discuss his political theory from this background. Explain especially Hobbes' legitimation of unlimited state power.

SUGGESTIONS FOR FURTHER READING

PRIMARY LITERATURE

Niccolò Machiavelli, *The Prince* and *The Discourses*, translated with an introduction by Max Lerner, The Modern Library, New York, 1950.
Hobbes, Thomas, *De Cive or The Citizen*, New York, 1949.
Hobbes, Thomas, *Leviathan*, Cambridge, 1991.

SECONDARY LITERATURE

Habermas, J., 'The Classical Doctrine of Politics in Relation to Social Philosophy' in *Theory and Practice*, London, 1974, pp. 41–82.
MacPherson, C. B., *The Political Theory of Possessive Individualism. From Hobbes to Locke*, London, 1962.
Skinner, Q., *Machiavelli*, Oxford, 1981.
Watkins, J. W. N., *Hobbes' System of Ideas*, London, 1973.

NOTES

1 *Realpolitik*: German term. Politics based on material ('real') factors, especially as distinguished from ethical objectives. Politics by the use of power, including manipulation – disregarding moral considerations. The aim of *realpolitik* is political strength, as for a state in its foreign policy. The means that are used for this purpose are evaluated only by their expediency for this aim, not by independent ethical standards.

2 Instead of *weight* and *pendulum*, we could say *spring* and *movement*.

3 When we emphasize here that Hobbes' idea of a state of nature is a principle of explanation, not an empirical (historical) thesis, it may be appropriate to remind the reader that Hobbes possibly had a certain basis in experience from his own day to build on: in Hobbes' day, a large part of the population was extremely poor and miserable; mere survival was a struggle for these people, especially during the English Civil War. And in international relations there was always (potential) war among nations.

4 What is problematic is not so much that we can question how such a unity and agreement could actually come about. Here we are discussing the theory about the state of nature as a non-historical model of explanation. The problem is how we can use this model to understand a change *from* anarchy *to* an ordered society, since the forward-thinking reason, which points beyond the state of nature, is in reality powerless as long as people live in a state of nature.

5 Cf. Jürgen Habermas, *The Structural Transformation of the Public Sphere*, Cambridge, MA, 1989.

6 To define *liberalism* and *individualism* as equivalent in meaning is contrary to normal linguistic usage: even if any form of liberalism can be said to be individualism, this does not mean that any form of individualism is liberalism (cf. individualistic features of the *rechtsradikal* cultivation of the superhuman).

9 Doubt and belief – man in the centre

DESCARTES – METHODICAL DOUBT AND CONFIDENCE IN REASON

Life. *The Frenchman René Descartes (1596–1650) studied scholastic philosophy at the Jesuit school at La Flèche, but he soon began to doubt the value of learning: most disciplines were without a firm foundation, according to Descartes. He abandoned his books and began to wander. For a time he fought on the Protestant side in the Thirty Years' War. At his winter quarters in Germany in 1619, he developed the basic ideas of the method he was to use. He was then 23 years old. Ten years later he moved to the Netherlands to live and study in peace. In 1649, he went to stay with Queen Christina in Stockholm. He could not adjust to the harsh climate in Sweden and died in February 1650.*

Descartes wrote both in French and Latin. His central writings include the famous Discours de la méthode *(1637) and the scholarly* Méditations métaphysiques *(1647). The* Discours de la méthode *is one of the first works in French. He also wrote* Principes de la philosophie *and* Règles pour la direction de l'esprit.

COGITO, ERGO SUM

Descartes was simultaneously a spokesman for the new and a representative of the old. He wished to start over and ground philosophy on a new and secure foundation, but at the same time his roots were deep in the scholastic tradition, as shown, among other ways, in his argument for God's existence.

In philosophy there were endless conflicts, observed Descartes. The only certain method is the deductive mathematical method. And Descartes thus made *the deductive system* his scientific ideal. It became the determining factor in his philosophy. If philosophy is to be a deductive system, like Euclid's geometry, we must find *completely certain and true* premises (axioms), because in a deductive system, the conclusions (theorems) are of little value if the premises are uncertain and only half-true. The scientific ideal that Descartes borrowed from mathematics and from deductive elements of the scientific method thus led to the question of how we can find absolutely certain premises for this deductive philosophical system.

This is where Descartes' *methodical doubt* comes in. Methodical doubt is a means of filtering out all the propositions that we *logically can* doubt in order to find the propositions that are logically beyond doubt – and we can use *these* propositions as premises in the deductive system. Thus, the purpose of methodical doubt is to determine not what is *reasonable* or *unreasonable* to doubt, but what is *logically possible* to doubt. Methodical doubt is a method of eliminating all the statements that cannot be premises in a deductive philosophical system. But for Descartes, methodical doubt has definite presuppositions. The individual is the singular thinking subject who asks the questions, not, for example, a community of researchers. Hence it is not surprising that the answer, the certainty which is to end doubt for Descartes, is the certainty of the thinking individual. This result, the firm ending of doubt, is in a way built into the way he raises the question.[1]

Descartes discusses different kinds of knowledge and tests them with methodical doubt.

1   He first discusses the philosophical tradition. Is it, in principle, possible to doubt what the philosophers have said? Yes, says Descartes, because they have been and are in disagreement on many points.

2   But what about our senses? Is it logically possible to doubt them? Yes, says Descartes. And his argument goes like this. It is a fact that we are sometimes subject to illusions and hallucinations. A tower, for example, may appear to be round but later turn out to be square. Hence we have two conflicting sense impressions about the same thing. But, in practice, we place more confidence in the one sense impression than in the other. We maintain, for example, that the tower is actually square because it looks square when we are close to it, although it looked round when we were far away. In practice, moreover, we can ask other people to confirm what we think we have seen. In practice, therefore, we do not, as a rule, find it difficult to find out whether the tower really is round or square. But this example shows that our senses can be mistaken, and that we do not have any other means of verifying one sense impression except by another sense impression. But if one sense impression *can* be mistaken, so could the sense impression that we use for verification. And if we want to verify this 'control sense impression', we must again use a sense impression that also, in principle, may be mistaken. And so on to infinity. Logically, therefore, it is possible to doubt all sense impressions. Thus, our senses cannot provide us with *absolutely certain* premises for a deductive philosophical system.

3   As a special argument, Descartes mentions that he does not have any criterion for determining whether he is awake or dreaming, and that he, therefore, for this reason too, may, in principle, doubt what is apparently a certain sense impression. This dream argument is the same kind as that mentioned above (the sequence involved in verifying sense impressions). In both cases Descartes asks for an absolutely certain criterion, and in both cases he concludes that he cannot find such a criterion: the criterion that we have for determining whether a sense impression is correct is *another* sense impression; but if one sense impression may be wrong, the *criterion*, namely, other sense impressions, *may* also be wrong. The criterion that we have for determining whether we are awake is that we *think* we are awake, but we may also dream that we think we are awake.

4   Finally, Descartes discusses logic. Again, he applies methodical doubt to the *criterion*. We have no other means of verifying a line of argumentation except

by other lines of argumentation. And if the first line of argumentation is, in principle, fallible, it is, in principle, possible that the other lines of argumentation are fallible. In principle, therefore, we *can* doubt logical arguments. Clearly, doubting the validity of lines of argumentation is not quite the same as doubting sense impressions, since it is *by virtue of* such lines of argumentation that Descartes argues that lines of argumentation are, in principle, fallible.

But here we do not need to look any closer at Descartes' argument. It is sufficient for us to state that Descartes is attempting to find out not what is reasonable to doubt, but what, in principle, is logically possible to doubt. And we have seen that Descartes, with this strict requirement, has rejected philosophy, sense perception, and logical reasoning. None of these kinds of insight are so absolutely certain that they can be used as premises in the deductive philosophical system that Descartes wants to create. Here we may add that Descartes proposed the following thought experiment in order to substantiate the doubt of everything that we think we know: imagine that there is a powerful and malicious demon (*un malin génie*) who is deceiving us so that we are mistaken without being aware of it – that is, that there is an 'evil spirit' who unnoticeably feeds us wrong opinions. Then we would not be able to have confidence in what we think we know. The question is: how can we know that this is not the case? How can we know that we are not being deceived by such a demon?

Does anything pass the test? Descartes says that there is: in principle, he cannot doubt that he himself is conscious and that he exists. Even if he doubts everything, he *cannot* doubt *that he doubts*, that is to say, that he exists and is conscious. We therefore have a 'candidate' that passes the test, and that is, in Descartes' formulation, '*I think, therefore I am*' (*cogito, ergo sum*).

The statement *cogito, ergo sum* represents, for the person who makes this statement, an insight that he or she cannot reject. This is a reflective insight that cannot be rejected: he who doubts cannot, as a doubter, doubt (or deny) that he doubts and thus that he exists. This is not a logical inference (from premise to conclusion), but an insight that the doubter cannot reject.[2] Even if the evil spirit should confuse us, we cannot doubt our own doubt. This is a small start for an entire deductive system. But Descartes now establishes a kind of proof of God's existence. He moves from the conception of something perfect to the existence of a perfect being, God.

GOD AND RATIONALISM

Descartes' starting point is that he has a conception of a perfect being. He further assumes that this conception of something perfect is itself perfect, and he assumes that he himself is not perfect, since he is filled with doubt and uncertainty. In addition, he assumes that the effect cannot be greater than the cause. (When something causes something else, there cannot be more in that which is being caused than in that which causes, because if this were not so, something that is caused could have arisen from nothing; but nothing cannot be the cause of anything.) Since he views the conception of perfection as a perfect conception, he thus concludes that the conception of a perfect being cannot be caused by something that is imperfect. Since he himself is imperfect, he cannot be the cause of this conception. The perfect conception of something perfect can be caused only by a perfect being. Therefore, when Descartes has such a perfect conception of a perfect being, this conception must be caused by a perfect being, that is to say, God. Thus, the perfect being exists; God exists.

A perfect God would not deceive man. This gives us confidence in a criterion: everything that is as self-evident as the statement *cogito, ergo sum* represents an insight that is certain. Here we see the starting point of Descartes' rationalistic epistemology: the criterion for valid insight is not empirical support (as in empiricism), but that the ideas appear *clearly and distinctly* to our reason.

Descartes claims that it is just as self-evident to him that there is a thinking being (soul) and an extended being (matter) as that he himself exists and is conscious. Hence, Descartes postulates the doctrine of *res cogitans* (soul) and *res extensa* (matter) as two fundamentally different phenomena and as the only two phenomena that exist (besides God): the soul is only conscious, not extended. Matter is only extended, not conscious. Matter is understood by means of mechanics alone (mechanistic-materialistic world-view), while the soul is free and rational. We shall return to the logical problems that arise with this dualism.

The existence of a God who will not deceive us refutes the notion of an evil demon, given that a perfect God is a mighty God. But given such a God, how can it be that we are so often mistaken? The answer is that we still make mistakes because we do not proceed in a systematic and critical manner to analyse that which presents itself to our thoughts and our senses. We should therefore grasp what is clear and distinct; moreover, we should use our reason critically to distinguish between what is true belief and what is not. All in all, this means that we still can have some confidence in our reasoning and also in our sense impressions. The condition is that we should be critical and methodical in our use of these sources of knowledge. With this background, Descartes now returns to the types of insight that he earlier rejected as being fallible, *in principle*, and says that they are, *in practice*, useful. But this 'rehabilitation' still does not apply to previous philosophy.[3]

Thus, the development of Descartes' argument is that he first asks whether it is logically possible to doubt philosophical theses, sense perception, dreams, and logical reasoning (the methodical doubt), so that he finally arrives at the insight of reflection that, at least, it is impossible to doubt our own doubt (*cogito, ergo sum*). All claims of knowledge that are just as compellingly certain as this must also be accepted as true. Descartes has thus discovered a criterion for truth. He then proceeds with his proof of God's existence on the basis of his conception of perfection; a conception that he himself, as imperfect, cannot have originated. God must be the origin of this conception. God exists, as perfect, and therefore cannot deceive us: that which we, by means of critical evaluation, conceive of as being completely clear and distinct must therefore be something in which we can have confidence. Hence, Descartes rehabilitates our theoretical arguments (that he previously doubted), and he also thinks that we, after appropriate testing by means of reason, should be able to have confidence in the testimony of our senses. In this way Descartes first moves critically down to a sure foundation (*cogito*, God) and then finds a new and critical confidence in our theoretical and perceptible insight.

Descartes' *criterion of truth* is thus *rationalistic*. What reason (*ratio*) arrives at as being clear and distinct, in systematic and deliberate reasoning, can be accepted as true. Sense experiences should be subjected to verification by reason. Sense experiences are inherently less confidence-inspiring than reason.[4]

Most of Descartes' philosophizing is devoted to finding acceptable premises. He never advances to the development of a strictly deductive system. For Descartes' rationalistic successor, Spinoza, it is almost the opposite. He places the main emphasis on the deductive system itself.

We may add that the doubt about the criteria for certain insight was well known in Descartes' time.[5] The conflict between Roman Catholics and Protestants was related, among other things, to the question of the *criterion* of Christian truth. Protestants did not accept ecclesiastical tradition as the criterion. That is to say, Protestants objected to the determination of Christian doctrine by appeal to tradition. Generally, Protestants did not doubt that what Roman Catholics said would be true *if* tradition was accepted as the criterion (or as the court of appeal). Protestants doubted this very criterion! How do we know that tradition is a true criterion for Christian truth? And Protestants set up another criterion: *the Bible alone*, *Sola Scriptura*, while Roman Catholics had the Bible and tradition. But Christians did not agree on how to interpret the Bible. The Protestant view of the Bible was therefore often formulated as follows: *the Bible as the Bible's teachings appear to my conscience*. Each individual's conscience became the criterion. But the Roman Catholics replied that this is more arbitrary than tradition: how do we know that each individual's conscience is a true criterion for Christian truth? Luther and Calvin, as we know, posited partially different teachings. If each individual's conscience is to be a criterion, will not Christian doctrine be dissolved in an infinite number of private opinions, and will not the Church disperse into a multitude of small sects? This conflict between Protestantism and Roman Catholicism led to one of the basic problems in philosophy: the question of justifying the criteria for truth.[6] How do we justify the basic principles? In Descartes' time many French Roman Catholics had become sceptics as a result of this debate: *que sais-je?* 'what do I know?' (Montaigne, 1533–1592.) They found that it was impossible to justify the first principles, the criteria that we use to justify other statements. Therefore, they thought that it was not possible to decide between the conflicting criteria that divided Roman Catholics and Protestants. But this also meant that neither was it possible to argue against the faith that they now had – as a result, these French sceptics remained Roman Catholics.

It is generally thought that Descartes did not have a political theory. However, in *Discours de la méthode* (second part), he says, in connection with architecture, that a city should be planned by one person, from a unified perspective. This will give better results than if the houses are simply built gradually, in the style of different builders and without plan. The view that Descartes expresses here seems, among other things, to be in clear opposition to Burke's conception of the wisdom of tradition that grows through the experience of the generations and the conditions of local life. Burke detested those who, with the stroke of a pen, would raze what already exists, and refashion everything anew according to their own reason. For Descartes' conception of architecture and city planning to be realized it would require that a competent person be found with the power to obtain the land, materials, equipment, and labourers to build the new houses. This seems to entail a type of enlightened absolutism: the concentration of power in the hands of the person with competence, and powerlessness and obedience among the people.

THE MECHANISTIC WORLD-VIEW AND THE RELATIONSHIP BETWEEN SOUL AND BODY

The holders of the mechanistic world-view conceived of the universe as comprised of an infinite number of small, indivisible, material particles, having exclusively quantitative properties, that move about in space, and that collide only in accordance with mechanical laws, and not with intention or purpose. These concepts proved to be fruitful in mechanics, and they fascinated a number of philosophers – such as Hobbes, Descartes, Leibniz, and Spinoza – to such a degree that these philosophers, in different ways, applied the same concepts in philosophy.[7]

But the fact that certain concepts are fruitful when used within one aspect of reality does not mean that these concepts give a true picture of *all* phenomena in the universe. The transference of concepts from classical mechanics, which is a scientific theory, to the mechanistic world-view, which is a philosophical theory, therefore presented some interesting challenges: the philosophical theory was far more ambitious than the scientific one. Thus, the mechanistic world-view, as such a philosophical theory, ran into philosophical difficulties, as we have already seen in Democritus' theory of atoms. If these quantitative concepts are to give a true picture of everything, how can we explain our experience of colour, smell, pain, etc. – that is, qualities – and how can we explain the distinction between material and mental phenomena? For those fascinated by mechanistic and materialistic concepts, the following dilemma thus arises: on the one hand, we experience qualities (sense qualities: smell, colour, taste) and mental phenomena (*I* and *you*, in contrast to *it*). On the other hand, qualities or mental phenomena cannot exist if these mechanistic and materialistic concepts are the only true ones. There are different solutions to this dilemma, all of which depend on our level of belief in the mechanistic world-view.

Hobbes, we may say, was the most orthodox materialist. To some extent, he can be said to have claimed that qualities and mentalistic phenomena are 'basically' materialistic and mechanistic. As a consistent position, this is called materialistic monism.

Descartes tried to have it both ways: nature (*res extensa*) is as the mechanistic and materialistic concepts indicate, but the soul (*res cogitans*) is not. This position is usually called psychophysical dualism. Descartes defined these two areas, *res extensa* and *res cogitans*, as logical opposites, while claiming that they mutually influence each other, and while having a conception of influence that requires an *identity* between cause and effect (cf. his proof of God's existence). Hence, Descartes was caught in a logical dilemma since he postulated an identity between two factors defined as logically different. This is a logical-philosophical problem, a conceptual problem, not a problem that can be solved by empirical research.

Neither of these philosophers doubted what we experience, namely, the correlation between what happens in the body and what happens in the soul. On the contrary, the experienced correlation of body and soul was the starting point. The problem for these philosophers was how this correlation could be *explained* theoretically. In their attempts to explain, they consistently used mechanistic concepts. For instance, we may try to avoid the Cartesian dualist dilemma by denying that there is a real causal connection between the body and the soul: when two clocks show the same time, it is not because they influence one another, but because they have been made and set to show the same time. This is how it is with the body and the soul. When I want to raise my arm and when my arm rises, it is not my will that leads to my arm's rising, but the body and the soul are so in tune that this takes place in parallel. Or we may say that the soul and the body are only two manifestations of the same reality. This position could be called psychophysical parallelism (cf. Spinoza).

materialistic monism – Hobbes
psychophysical dualism – Descartes
psychophysical parallelism – Spinoza

PASCAL – THE REASON OF THE HEART

Blaise Pascal (1623–1662) had already, at the age of 16, written a treatise on geometry that made him famous. But he early devoted himself to Christian faith and theology after a dramatic personal conversion. There is a direct line from Augustine through Pascal and on to the modern Christian existential philosophers. In French cultural life Pascal and Descartes stand at two opposite poles, as representatives of two opposing traditions.

In his *Pensées* Pascal pleads for the reason of the heart while, at the same time, arguing that we can neither prove nor disprove religious beliefs, and that for this reason alone we have everything to win and nothing to lose by faith in God. Existential insight and choice – here, choosing the God of the Bible – are basic themes that Pascal shares with the existential philosophers of our own day.[8]

Pascal can be said to belong to the realm of the rationalists since his existential despair at our cognitive uncertainty represents a kind of inverted rationalism: or, better, Pascal shares the horizons of the rationalists. He has the same cognitive ideals requiring certainty, about the great metaphysical and religious questions. But Pascal does not believe that these rationalistic expectations of answers can be met. He therefore ends in an existential despair that represents a restrained polar opposition to the rationalistic confidence in our cognitive abilities.

VICO – HISTORY AS A MODEL

The new historical consciousness, which had its climax in the nineteenth century, was clearly foreshadowed by the Italian philosopher of history Giambattista Vico (1668–1744). Vico's *magnum opus*, *Principi di una scienza nuova* (1725), is difficult and was little known during his lifetime, but its main idea is easy to grasp: according to Vico, we can have clear and certain knowledge only about what we ourselves have created.[9] Vico was primarily thinking about society and history, but also about all the institutions and ordinances that constitute a society. What man has created is fundamentally distinguished from what is created by God, namely, nature. Since nature is not created by man, but by God, only God can fully and completely understand it. We may describe the processes of nature and elucidate how physical phenomena behave in experimental situations, but we can never gain insight into *why* nature behaves the way it does. Man can only know nature from the outside, from an observer's perspective. We can never understand nature from within as God does. The only things that are completely understandable and intelligible are those that we understand from within, when we recognize that man is the creator.[10] Consequently, for Vico, the distinction between what is constructed and what is given by nature has important epistemological implications.

Firstly, the *Scienza nuova* represents a corrective to Cartesianism. Descartes had claimed that humanistic studies could not provide us with certain knowledge. In addition, the humanities have a low status: what is the point of studying the social conditions of ancient Rome, Descartes asks ironically, when we can never learn any more than Cicero's maid knew? As we see, Vico turns this round: we can have certain knowledge only in sciences where man himself has created the research object. This applies both to geometry (here we 'make' definitions, axioms, and rules of inference) and to historiography. Within natural science we can never achieve the same degree of certainty.

Secondly, Vico anticipates the debate in our day within the philosophy of science about the relationship between the humanities and the natural sciences. The difference between the humanities and natural science, says Vico, concerns not only two different methods, but also different relationships between the subject of cognition and the object of cognition in the two types of disciplines. For Vico, society, culture, and history are products of the human spirit.[11] Therefore, in the 'new science', the researcher seeks to understand society and culture as expressions of human intentions, desires, and motives. In the humanities we are not concerned with the Cartesian distinction between subject and object. Here the object of cognition is itself a subject (human beings and the societies they create). In the humanities the researcher is, in a certain sense, personally a participant in the lives and activities of other human beings. On the other hand, the researcher will always remain an observer of nature. This is the background that requires different methods in the humanities and the natural sciences.

Vico's epistemological reflections also touch on one of the basic questions in historiography: how can we today understand what earlier historical epochs and alien cultures have created? When historians and philosophers express themselves about the past, says Vico, they do so without historical consciousness. They attribute to earlier times an insight that is present only in their own day. But man's mental and intellectual perspectives vary from epoch to epoch. The knowledge that was formulated and applied in one age would hardly be formulated or applied in another. For example, it is an anachronistic mistake, Vico emphasizes, to assume that the natural rights of our day existed in the childhood of humanity. Natural rights thinkers like Hobbes and Grotius forget that it took some 'two thousand years for philosophers to appear in any of them [i.e., developed a modern theory of natural law]'.[12] Above all, we must guard ourselves from the idea that people in the past had developed a language, an art of poetry, and a rationality that correspond to those of our day.

If we want to understand the people of the past, we must work through their language. Philology is therefore important. We must put ourselves in their situation and learn to see things from their perspective. In our time, this is taken for granted, but not in Vico's day. We possess something that Vico struggled to attain, what we now call 'historical consciousness'.

But how can we immerse ourselves in foreign cultures and epochs? Vico is critical of the view of radical Enlightenment thinkers that the Bible is merely a compendium of myths and legends that are, in fact, 'prejudices' and 'forgery' instigated by clerics. Instead, myths are proof that man in earlier times organized his experiences in conceptual schemes that differ from those of later epochs. The ancients saw the world through mythological glasses. Their world can only be reconstructed by using our imagination or empathy. Through imagination, *fantasia*, we can feel our way into other people's situations; through fantasy we can participate in their lives and understand their world from within. *Fantasia* is the ability to imagine different ways of categorizing the world. If we reject myths as 'prejudices', we forfeit the ability to understand how people in earlier ages thought, and how they acted from a mythical understanding of reality and in this way changed themselves and their world. Vico thinks that we can learn to use our fantasy methodically in the study of the past if we can remember what it was like to be a child. We often wonder at a child's strange combination of words and associations, at the 'poetry', the 'irrationality', and the inability to draw logical conclusions. Such must also have been the primitive and prelogical mentality of early human beings, says Vico. Just as the child becomes an adult, a rational and moral individual, early peoples gradually developed the ability to think rationally. Vico sees an analogy between a people's development and an individual's development; phylogenesis (development of the species) resembles ontogenesis (the development of the individual). All peoples have a childhood, youth, adulthood, old age, and death. This process involves a cyclical pattern which repeats itself endlessly.

For Vico, the insight that we gain with the aid of our fantasy is not knowledge based on facts in a normal sense. Neither is it knowledge based on the relationship between concepts. It resembles more the insight we think we have about the character and conduct of a close friend. Vico claims that because we have a common human nature we can understand other human beings from within. We can, in other words, interpret their actions as an expression of intentions, desires, and reasons. We begin to approach such an insight when we try to understand what it meant to live in Plato's Athens or Cicero's Rome. We can gain such an insight, according to Vico, only by the use of empathy or *fantasia*. In this way Vico attempts to identify an insight or knowledge that is neither deductive nor inductive (nor hypothetico-deductive). Hence he wants to provide humanistic studies with a new research programme and new methodical principles.

The *Scienza nuova* is at once a synthesis of philology, sociology, and historiography. Vico emphasizes what we may call epochal understanding. In this perspective, history contains three main epochs: 1) the age of the gods, 2) the age of the heroes, and 3) the age of men. For Vico, this indicates the 'ideal eternal history' that all nations pass through. Of course, he did not think that history takes the same path everywhere. But to some degree, the different nations approach some archetypal pattern in history: a nation arises, matures, and dies. New nations repeat the same cycle. Vico is aware that an 'ideal eternal history' cannot be fully traced back to particular individuals' intentions, and also that a person's actions often have unforeseen consequences. In this connection, Vico talks about divine providence's unsearchable ways in history. However, he distinguishes his view both from the

Stoics' understanding of fate and Spinoza's view of necessity. God, or divine providence, does not interfere directly in history, but, rather, divine providence realizes by means of human actions something that no one had thought of.[13]

In light of the 'ideal type' model, we can move closer to the content of Vico's view of history: early man was filled with horror and fear when confronted with the forces of nature. Intention and purpose was ascribed to nature. All of existence was, in a certain sense, sacred. These people had still not developed the universal concepts and articulate language of later ages. Their world-view was based on an analogical and associative way of thought.[14] They imagined traditions, customs, and institutions to be determined by the gods. The right and truth were mediated by oracles. The first 'natural rights' were understood as being granted by gods. The form of government was theocratic. Thus, this was a way of life in which everything was interconnected and conditioned by man's primitive 'nature' or mentality. This was the *age of the gods* according to Vico's scheme. In this phase, man developed religion, art, and poetry appropriate to his manner of life and emotional stage. In the second phase, *the age of the heroes*, strong fathers became the leaders of families and tribes. Weak individuals sought protection and became slaves. A picture of this epoch is found, according to Vico, in what we call Homer's *Iliad*.[15] The Homeric heroes sing; they do not speak in prose. Metaphors predominate over technical terms. The wisdom of the epoch is 'poetic' — not philosophical and discursive. In this period there is also an internal connection of world-view, poetry, and manner of life.

Social differentiation created an inner dynamic in the age of the heroes. The slaves' lives and what they produce are in the hands of the masters.[16] Gradually, the slaves begin to realize their own strength and require less protection. They become 'humanized', learn to debate, and demand their rights. The challenge from the slaves leads to the masters joining forces to put down the rebellion of the oppressed. This conflict is the source of aristocracy and monarchy. For Vico, Solon (*c.* 630–560 BC) was the first spokesman for a new egalitarianism.

Solon encouraged the oppressed to reflect and to realize that 'they were of like human nature with the nobles and should therefore be made equal with them in civil rights'.[17] Vico thus anticipated Hegel's dialectic of master and slave (cf. Ch. 17). When those who are governed are recognized as the equals of those who govern, says Vico, it is unavoidable that the form of government must change. Thus, the state changes from an aristocracy to a democracy. In this period of transition, language also changes its character. We move into a 'prosaic' age. Human beings learn to use abstractions and universal concepts. Philosophical wisdom replaces poetic wisdom. The 'moderns' distinguish between the sacred and the profane, between the temple and the tavern. In this third historical epoch, which Vico calls *the age of men*, the *individual* appears for the first time, and also *individualism*. Individualism and egotism create tendencies to disintegration and dissolution. The last 'modern' human beings in antiquity are the Cynics, the Epicureans, and the Stoics. The decline ends in barbarism and the Middle Ages begin a new cycle.

According to Vico, all peoples go through such a cyclical pattern (*corsi e ricorsi*). It is unclear whether he interprets this historical process as an 'eternal recurrence of the same', or as a dialectical, spiral pattern. The driving force in the process is man himself; through war and conflict he creates new ways of life and institutions that again reflect his view of existence. Hence, Vico foreshadows Hegel's and Marx's dialectical view of history. It was not far from the truth when an expert on Vico characterized him as an 'imaginative historical materialist' (Isaiah Berlin).

In a certain sense, we may also say that Vico introduced the so-called historicist principle of individuality; that is, every culture and epoch is peculiar and unique (cf. Ch. 16). New ways of life are neither better nor worse than previous ways; they are merely different. In keeping with this principle of individuality, Vico denies that there are absolute aesthetic standards. Each epoch has its own form of expression. What we call Homer's epic is thus the expression of a heroic age and a barbaric ruling class – because only conditions of this kind could have produced the view of life and man that we find in the *Iliad* and the *Odyssey*. Later epochs, Vico emphasizes, could not have created such epics because people in Homer's time literally saw things that we no longer see. In the same way, heroic and democratic personages (such as, respectively, Moses and Socrates) must be viewed as specific and characteristic expressions of the mentalities and ways of thinking of two different epochs. Similarly, Nero's refined cruelties are an example of an age in dissolution and decline. In keeping with this principle of individuality, Vico claims that the dominant form of government is conditioned by the character of natural rights in the period. The conception of natural rights is also anchored in the morality and custom that ultimately reflect the view of reality and way of life prevalent in an epoch. We can thus find a definite *unity* in the institutions of a given society. This unity is an expression of man's resources and ways of thinking. Hence, Vico develops a historicist principle of individuality that we later encounter in Herder and Hegel, and in German scholarship in the humanities (*Geisteswissenschaft*).

QUESTIONS

Explain the role of methodical doubt in Descartes' philosophy.

How did Descartes arrive at '*cogito, ergo sum*'? What role does this statement play in his thinking?

Explain Descartes' proof of God's existence.

Explain Descartes' view of the relation between the soul (*res cogitans*) and the body (*res extensa*). Discuss the problems inherent in this point of view.

Discuss Vico's conception of the humanities.

SUGGESTIONS FOR FURTHER READING

PRIMARY LITERATURE

Descartes, R., *A Discourse on Method* in *The Philosophical Works of Descartes*, Cambridge, 1931.

Descartes, R., *Meditations on the First Philosophy* in *The Philosophical Works of Descartes*, Cambridge, 1931.

Pascal, B., *Pensées and Other Writings*, translated by Honor Levi, Oxford, 1995.

Vico, G., *The New Science of Giambattista Vico*, Ithaca, NY/London, 1968.

SECONDARY LITERATURE

Berlin, I., *Vico and Herder. Two Studies in the History of Ideas*, London, 1976.

Coleman, F., *Neither Angel nor Beast: The Life and Work of Blaise Pascal*, New York, 1986.

Craukroger, S., *Descartes. An Intellectual Biography*, Oxford, 1995.

NOTES

1 That a thinking individual is the epistemological starting point is characteristic of much of philosophy in early modern times, including both the rationalists and the empiricists. The idea that cognition can be intersubjective first moved to the forefront at a later stage, as in the historically oriented Hegel, and in Peirce, who was interested in the community of researchers and the progress of scientific cognition. At the same time, the notion that cognition can be associated with actions, with what we do, came more into focus (from Hegel and Marx, through Peirce to Wittgenstein). In modern times, from Nietzsche to the so-called postmodernists, the criticism has mounted against the belief in reason and progress, whether this belief is thought to be anchored in autonomous subjects or in a free community of researchers.

2 The insight inherent in '*cogito, ergo sum*' is not to be understood as a conclusion from given premises. This '*ergo*' does not point to a logical inference from '*cogito*' (as premise) to '*sum*' (as conclusion). It is an insight that cannot be rejected, an insight that entails that I, as a doubter, simultaneously think ('*cogito*') and am ('*sum*').

3
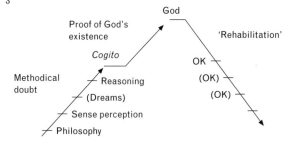

4 See later the conception of experience in the empiricists, such as Hume, who understood experience as perception, which is again interpreted as simple sense impressions. For the empiricists, this is the basis of knowledge. See also Hegel, who viewed experience as life experience.

5 Cf. R. H. Popkin, *The History of Scepticism from Erasmus to Descartes*, Assen, 1960.

6 Cf. Aristotle on proving the first principles, in *Metaphysics* 1005b5–1006a28.

7 There were, however, different views, among adherents of the mechanistic world-view, of how matter, forces, and space were to be understood. For example, Newton thought that the absolute void exists, while Descartes and Hobbes rejected this notion.

8 *Pensées.* Translated by W. F. Trotter, London, 1952.

> 'Man is only a reed, the frailest thing in nature; but he is a thinking reed. It is not required that the whole universe should arm itself to crush him; a breath of wind, a drop of water is sufficient to destroy him. But were the universe to crush him, man would still be nobler than that which slays him. For he knows that he dies and that the universe has the better of him. But the universe knows nothing of this.' (§55)
>
> Let us just as well give up the attempt to seek certainty! Our reason is always fooled by the changing outward skin. There is no secure point for the finite being between the two infinites. (§20)

'The heart has its own reasons which the mind does not understand [*Le cœur a ses raisons, que la raison ne connaît point*]. Faith is a gift of God. Do not think that we believe it to be a gift of the mind! There is a great distance between knowing about God and loving Him. It is the heart that knows God, not the mind.' (§97)

9 Vico's main idea was in a sense already formulated by Hobbes. See 'Six Lessons to the Professors of the Mathematics', in Molesworth, W. (ed.), *English Works*, vol. 7, pp. 183 ff.: 'Of arts, some are demonstrable, others indemonstrable, and demonstrable are those the construction of the subject whereof is in the power of the artist himself, who, in his demonstration, does no more but deduce the consequences of his own operation. The reason whereof is this, that the science of every subject is derived from a precognition of the causes, generation, and construction of the same; and consequently where the causes are known, there is place for demonstration, but not where the causes are to seek for. Geometry therefore is demonstrable, for the lines and figures from which we reason are drawn and described by ourselves; and civil philosophy is demonstrable, because we make the commonwealth ourselves. But because of natural bodies we know not the construction, but seek it from the effects, there lies no demonstration of what the causes be we seek for, but only of what they may be.' For Hobbes, this principle has no consequences for history as a science. Kant also touches on Vico's main point, but Kant does not establish any distinction between the natural sciences and human science. Kant says (in relation to the natural scientist): 'Reason only realizes that which it itself creates out of its own plan' (*Critique of Pure Reason*, B xiii). Not until Herder, Droysen, and Dilthey do we find a thematization of history and the humanities that follows up Vico's attempt to establish a new human science.

10 G. Vico, *The New Science of Giambattista Vico*, revised translation of the third edition by Thomas Goddard Bergin and Max Harold Fisch, Ithaca, NY, 1968, p. 96 (*Principi di una scienza nuova* (1744), *Opere filosofiche*, Florence, 1971, p. 461): 'But in the night of thick darkness enveloping the earliest antiquity, so remote from ourselves, there shines the eternal and never failing light of a truth beyond all question: that the world of civil society has certainly been made by men, and that its principles are therefore to be found within the modifications of our own human mind. Whoever reflects on this cannot but marvel that the philosophers should have bent all their energies to the study of the world of nature, which, since God made it, He alone knows; and that they should have neglected the study of the world of nations, or civil world, which, since men had made it, men could come to know.'

11 Vico's main thesis plays a central part in Wilhelm Dilthey's interpretation of the philosophy of the humanities. See his *Der Aufbau der geschichtlichen Welt in den Geisteswissenschaften*, Frankfurt am Main, 1970, p. 180: 'Only that which the spirit has created, can it understand. . . . Everything that man, through his activity, has put his mark on, forms the object of the humanities.'

12 G. Vico, *Principi di una scienza nuova*, p. 95.

13 As human beings are created by God, they will never be able to understand fully how they fit into God's plan, how he uses human nature to realize his purpose with man. From a slightly different perspective, we could say that the disciplines that see man as, respectively, 'nature' and 'spirit' are radically different (cf. Vico's distinction between natural science and the humanities).

14 According to Vico, we can still find traces of this world-view in our own language: we no longer believe that a river has a mouth yet we still talk about 'the mouth of the river'; for us, the hurricane does not have an eye, but we normally refer to 'the eye of the hurricane'.

15 Vico emphasized, that more than one author composed the *Iliad* and the *Odyssey* (he maintained that six centuries separate the composition of the two works). Nor was the *Iliad* the work of one man, but a product of the people (cf. folk poetry). Vico thus began the controversy on the 'Homeric question'.

16 Cf. G. Vico, *Principi di una scienza nuova*, p. 209.

17 Ibid., p. 133.

10 Rationalism as a system

SPINOZA – GOD IS NATURE

Life. Baruch Spinoza (1632–1677) was born in Amsterdam into a Jewish family who had fled from the Portuguese Inquisition. As a youth, he studied rabbinical philosophy and theology, and was viewed as a promising candidate for the rabbinate. But Spinoza soon showed independent thinking, encouraged by his studies in natural science and Descartes' philosophy. His independent and questioning attitude led him into conflict with the Jewish community. When neither prayers nor threats managed to turn him from his heresy, the 24-year-old Spinoza was expelled from the community under a curse. After this, Spinoza withdrew to live a quiet simple life. He earned his living by grinding lenses for optical instruments. As a result, he was free and independent. He later turned down the offer of a position at a university to devote himself wholly to his philosophical pursuits. In spite of the conflict surrounding his philosophy and accusations of atheism and materialism, no one could criticize Spinoza's way of life. His serene life, distant from worldly passions and ambitions, was that of the exalted philosopher who exhibits a complete harmony between life and doctrine. Spinoza suffered from tuberculosis, and died at the age of 45.

Spinoza wrote in Latin. Most of his writings were published after his death. His Short Treatise on God, Man and his Well-Being *('Tractatus brevis de Deo et homine ejusque felicitate') indicates in its title what were to be major themes in Spinoza's philosophy: God, man, and man's well-being. Among his other writings we may mention* Treatise on the Correction of the Understanding *('Tractatus de intellectus emendatione'), published anonymously in 1670, and* Theological-Political Treatise *('Tractatus theologico-politicus'). His main work is* Ethics Demonstrated According to the Geometrical Order *('Ethica ordine geometrico demonstrata').*

SUBSTANCE AND ATTRIBUTE

Spinoza belongs to the classical rationalistic school along with Descartes and Leibniz. Spinoza is one of the great system builders. As a rationalistic system builder, he is, like Descartes, inspired by Euclidean geometry. Spinoza has the utmost confidence in the ability of human reason to arrive at absolutely certain insight, with axioms and deductive inferences. Of the connecting themes in the history of ideas, we can mention parallels with Stoicism in Spinoza's moral theory, a connection with pantheism in his theory of nature, a connection with liberal Bible criticism in his

religious ideas, and a connection with the new demand for tolerance in his political philosophy.

In his *Treatise on the Correction of the Understanding* Spinoza discusses the basic
ethical question of the supreme good, rejecting, as an inferior good, the things most
people seek, such as honour, riches, and pleasure. For Spinoza, the question of the
supreme good is connected with the question of the supreme form of knowledge,
and in this question he points to four paths of cognition:

1   We gain knowledge by hearsay but without personal experience of the matter.
    This is, for example, how we find out about our own date of birth.
2   We gain knowledge by direct, personal experience.
3   We gain knowledge with the aid of logical inferences since, by means of de-
    ductive methods, we infer true statements from other statements that we
    already know to be true. This path to the acquisition of knowledge is certain,
    but it presupposes that we already have true statements from which we can
    make our inferences.
4   The fourth and final path to the acquisition of knowledge is direct intuition.
    This is the only path that gives us clear and certain knowledge and that leads
    us to the essence of things. Here we see similarities with Descartes' view of
    intuition and evidence.

The first path to the acquisition of knowledge is second-hand and uncertain. The
second path is also, in principle, uncertain, since we may always misunderstand
what we experience (cf. Descartes' arguments on the fallibility of sense experience). The third path presupposes, as we have mentioned, that the starting points
are well-founded. Therefore, if we are to have certain insight, there must be a
fourth path of direct, intuitive insight. And we cannot deny, without ending in
sceptical self-dissolution, that we, in some sense or other, do have certain insight
– for example, we must be able to say that we have certain insight into the fact
that we cannot have certain insight by means of the first three paths to knowledge,
a statement which presupposes that we already possess the fourth type of knowledge. This is how we could argue in support of Spinoza's rationalism.

In his *Theological-Political Treatise* Spinoza discusses historical biblical research
in the conviction that philosophy and theology are, in principle, different things.
Philosophy is a science whose goal is truth, but theology is not a science, and
its goal is the practical conduct required for a pious life. This work caused a great
commotion.

In this treatise he emphasizes the question of tolerance. The different kinds of
government may have good and bad sides, but the decisive point is that there be
freedom of faith, freedom of thought, and freedom of expression. Spinoza seeks to
justify his view of politics by means of his theory of human nature. According to
Spinoza, man's essence is the will to live, to preserve life. But to understand what
this entails we must know more about Spinoza's philosophy.

Spinoza's *magnum opus*, *Ethics Demonstrated According to the Geometrical Order*, is
simultaneously a study of ethics and metaphysics. In structure, the work is modelled on geometric systems. Spinoza starts with eight definitions and seven propositions, from which he deduces several metaphysical-ethical conclusions. Even if we
can question the validity of the inferences in a strictly logical sense, there is no

doubt that the work represents a complete, unified philosophical system. His *Ethics* is apparently a dry and abstract work. But behind the formality, there are stimulating ideas about the human condition, with suggestions on how to escape from the anxiety and passion of a pointless, unenlightened life towards a free, serene life where we may view life and the universe from the eternal perspective, *sub specie aeternitatis*. This means knowing and recognizing the underlying laws of nature, and thus gaining peace of mind and freedom by realizing their necessity. Behind the mathematical form we thus find a vision of man's place in the universe. The first chapter in the *Ethics*, 'Of God', is about the basic structure of the universe. Man has a subordinate position, but by virtue of reason he can recognize the divine and thus arrive at the supreme good. The second chapter, 'Of the Nature and Origin of the Mind', also discusses the more metaphysical doctrine of the universe and man. But in chapter III, 'Of the Origin and Nature of the Affects', and in chapter IV, 'Of Human Bondage or of the Strength of the Affects', the doctrine of affects is central. The great obstacle that hinders us from reaching true happiness and serenity is the passions, the affects. We continually allow ourselves to be influenced by various external forces. The mind loses its equilibrium, and we perform actions that lead to unhappiness. The passions control and reduce us; they turn us into slaves of the desire for wealth, honour, and pleasure. In the fifth chapter, 'Of the Power of the Intellect, or of Human Liberty', redemption is reached in this passion play: the wise person's insight into the necessary essence of the universe and the obliteration of the distinction between the self and the rest of the universe. But Spinoza's passionless study of the passions does not entail a rejection of all affects or feelings. He distinguishes between good and harmful affects. Good feelings are those which increase our activity. Harmful feelings are those which make us passive. When we are active, we are ourselves the author of our actions to a greater degree. We act more from ourselves and are more free, according to Spinoza's definition of freedom.

Activity is not understood as pursuit of business or frenetic action on the external level. What is worth striving for is to free ourselves from arbitrary external influence by allowing our spiritual power, our true essence, to shape our actions and our lives. Our true essence lies in an active, intellectual cognition that contributes to ending our isolation and allowing us to identify ourselves with nature (God). Thus, the fifth and final chapter of *Ethics* is called 'Of the Power of the Intellect, or of Human Liberty'. Through our intellect, through the active intellectual cognition of the connection of everything with God, we ourselves become free because our identity now embraces the All and is no longer a narrow ego frustrated by that which perishes and changes in isolated events. Through this cognition, we arrive at the supreme happiness through the intellectual love of God (*amor intellectualis Dei*). This human love of God is, at the same time, caused by God. The intellectual love of God is therefore not only our love of God, but also a love *from* God. Our love of God is God's own love (Chapter V, proposition 36): 'The intellectual love of the mind towards God is the very love with which He loves Himself . . . the intellectual love of the mind towards God is part of the infinite love with which God loves Himself.'

Spinoza is a rationalist in the sense that he thinks we can gain knowledge about the essence of a thing by means of rational intuition; he is also a deductionist since he, like Descartes, starts with mathematics as an ideal for science. But while

Descartes is mainly concerned with finding absolutely certain axioms so that the deduction itself is in the background, Spinoza starts with the axioms and places the emphasis on the inferences, on the system. Thus, on the first page of the *Ethics* we find the definition of the basic concept *substance*: 'By substance, I understand what is in itself and is conceived through itself, i.e., that whose conception does not require of another thing, from which it must be formed'. What is *substance*? We have previously, for instance, used this Latin-derived word to designate a concept in Aristotle's philosophy. Substance is that which exists independently. For Aristotle, this was particular things like brown doors and round towers, in opposition to properties like brown and round. These properties merely have a relative existence since they are found only as the properties of particular things. One way of approaching Spinoza's conception of substance is to say that it represents a kind of absolutization of the Aristotelian definition: 'Substance is that which exists by itself *alone*, absolutely alone, and that which is understood by itself *alone*, absolutely alone.' To say that substance is that which exists totally independently and which is understood through itself alone, without the participation of anything else, is to suspend the concept of substance as a concept of particular things. A brown door exists only because someone has made it, and the concept of brown door already suggests door frames and actions such as opening and closing. In other words, the door does not exist completely independent of everything else, nor can it be fully understood without our having to understand something or other that is not a door. Therefore, the door is not a substance according to this new absolute definition.

Correspondingly, we can proceed to consider other particular objects, things created by man, organisms, and inorganic things. In any case, particular things must be delimited from other particular things, and this delimitation already implies that particular things cannot be understood completely independently of everything else: the limit itself, and the fact that the limit borders something else, must sooner or later become a part of the definition of the thing. This means that no particular thing that in one way or another is delimited from something else can be conceived of as substance on the basis of this new definition. But on the basis of this definition, what is substance? We must say that substance is *one* and *infinite* since all delimitation is excluded by the definition of substance. Substance is *one* because there cannot be more than one substance in the world; otherwise, the relationship of the first substance to the second substance (other substances) would have to be included in our full understanding of substance – something that contradicts the definition. And substance is *infinite* in the sense that limits in time or in any other way do not apply to it. Nor can anything else be the cause of substance since this other thing would then have to be included if we are to comprehend substance fully; and, according to the definition, substance can only be understood through itself, alone. Spinoza expresses this by saying that substance is *causa sui* ('*cause of itself*').

If there is a God, God cannot be something different from substance since the relationship to this other, to God, must then be included in our comprehension of substance. Thus, substance cannot be distinguished from God. Substance is *God*. Correspondingly, substance cannot be distinguished from nature. Substance is *nature*. Spinoza's doctrine of substance thus represents *monism*: everything is one, and everything is understood on the basis of this one. Since God and nature are both substance, we end up with *pantheism*: God and nature merge. And since substance is not created, and nature is substance, we cannot say that God is the creator of nature. The attacks on Spinoza's philosophy by Jewish and Christian circles is thus understandable.

But what, then, *is* substance? If by this question we are asking for a definition that we can *imagine*, that we can in any way picture, we have asked an inadequate question. We can, for instance, imagine a triangle, a square, etc. because we can form a mental image of it. We may be able to continue in this way for a while: a ten-sided figure, an eleven-sided figure? But sooner or later we will not be able to continue. We cannot imagine, in this sense of the word, a 1,001-sided figure, or the difference between a 1,001-sided figure and a 1,002-sided figure. But we can *think* about this in the sense that we have the concepts of a 1,001-sided figure and of a 1,002-sided figure. In other words, there is much that we can think about, conceive of, but that we cannot imagine, in the sense of a mental image of it.

If substance cannot be imagined in this sense, we cannot ascribe to God such attributes that we can imagine. But can we think about substance, have a concept of substance? Yes, in a sense. Substance appears to us in two ways, either as extension or as thought. Substance has infinitely many ways of manifestation, but these are the two manifestations with which it appears to us. Spinoza talks about two *attributes*: the attribute of thought and the attribute of extension. These are two equally valid forms of appearance for the one, underlying substance.

Particular extended things, like this book, are *modi* (singular: *modus*) under the attribute of extension, just as particular thoughts are *modi* under the attribute of thought. What we are immediately in contact with are the different *modi* of the two attributes of substance. We do not have direct access to substance. We might try to clarify the point by the following example. Imagine looking at something through coloured glasses, say, a green lens and a red lens, so that the object is perceived not directly but respectively as green and as red. And when there is a correlation between the green thing (one *modus*) in the green lens (one attribute) and the red thing (another *modus*) in the red lens (another attribute) – that is, a correspondence between the two *modi*, in the attribute of thought and in the attribute of extension – this is not because there is a causal connection between the lenses (the two attributes), or between the thing seen as green and the thing seen as red (between the two *modi*), but because it is the same thing (substance) that we see through different lenses (attributes). Particular phenomena, including the individual, are thus more or less complex *modi* within the two attributes of substance. Ultimately, everything is, so to speak, connected in substance. Everything (except substance) has a relative or limited existence in relation to substance. Extension and thought are not two independent basic elements, as they are for Descartes (cf. Descartes' *res cogitans* and *res extensa*); the two attributes, extension and thought, represent two aspects of the same substance.

NECESSITY AND FREEDOM

The relationship between substance and attribute is not a causal relationship. It is not that something first takes place in the substance and then causes corresponding events in each of the two attributes. What happens, happens in the substance, but it reveals itself in two aspects, thought and extension. The relationship between substance and attributes has a strictly necessary character, since the attributes represent the two manifestations of substance. However, it is not really correct to talk about a relationship *between* substance and attribute, as if we were talking about two phenomena which stand in relation to each other. The attributes are only the manner of appearance of the substance. Nor, for the same reason, can we talk about *coercion*, if by coercion we mean that *one* phenomenon influences *another* phenomenon against the other phenomenon's will or essence, because, basically, there is only one phenomenon, substance. What takes place in thought and in the extended field cannot be the result of coercion by the substance, since everything that takes place in thought and in the extended field is merely the form of appearance of what takes place in the substance.

This view also embraces political conditions. Human beings appear precisely as *modi* of the two attributes, as an extended body and as a thinking soul. Not only is what takes place in the soul and body always coordinated without there being any form of influence of one on the other, since they are both expressions of the same event in substance, but also what we do and think is necessarily determined by substance, without there being any form of coercion, since we are, fundamentally, aspects of substance. Here we see how the question of freedom is determined by the question of how we understand human nature. Since a human being, for Spinoza, is, fundamentally, one with substance, it is meaningless to say that a human being is *free* of substance or that a human being is *coerced* by substance, if the words *freedom* and *coercion* are used in such a way that they presuppose a relationship between two relatively independent phenomena.

Spinoza accepts the mechanistic perspective in regard to the attribute of extension. What happens in the extended field is causally determined. But human beings are not causally determined by substance. Causal determination is included in the form of appearance which the events in substance have in the extended field.

If everything in the two attributes follows God's infinite nature just as necessarily as it follows from the nature of a triangle that the sum of the angles is always 180 degrees, what is God's, or substance's, infinite nature? Substance is one with the laws of nature. But Spinoza seems to view the laws of nature in the light of geometry rather than physics. Substance, and what takes place within it – that is to say, what truly takes place – is, fundamentally, conceived of in terms of logical and timeless structures. The universe is not a conglomeration of physical and psychical phenomena, divided from one another, and determined by changes and placements in space and time. The universe, substance, is rather a timeless and static whole which, in a way, rests on its own logical structure.

But does Spinoza deny that individuals exist? And does he deny that the individual may more or less be free? Fundamentally, there is only substance. The individual person is a *modus* of the substance. But, relatively, particular people have their own existence and their own freedom to whatever degree they can act on the basis of their own nature. Freedom is thus a task which requires that we know our own nature precisely. To understand our own nature, for Spinoza, is to say that we understand ourselves as aspects of the whole, as *modi* of substance. Put in more common terms: understanding ourselves also entails understanding the relations and connections in which we live. Understanding ourselves is to understand more than ourselves in a narrow sense. It is to understand ourselves as a part of a situation, within a whole. To put this in social terms, we must understand ourselves as being determined by the community, as internally determined in identity, in essence, through socialization and interaction within a given society. The more we manage to liberate ourselves from narrow and petty ties and frustrations, the more we manage to recognize ourselves as being internally determined by a comprehensive social and physical reality, the freer we become. This is so because when we in this sense manage to widen and deepen our self-understanding, whatever happens is conceived as something that belongs to our own being. When our own identity is thus conceived as being more comprehensive, we will face less coercion since there will be fewer events that appear to us as something else. But we gain such an 'all-encompassing' identity only when we solemnly recognize this reality. We must personally recognize the truth of our inner connection to 'all that is'. An identity like this cannot be achieved unless it is recognized as true.

That the truth will make us free is thus an idea that we meet in Spinoza, as we meet it in various formulations in Socrates and Stoicism, in Christian thought, in the philosophy of the Enlightenment, and in Freud and the modern critique of ideology. But what truth is and how it can liberate us is, of course, the salient and controversial point.

For Spinoza, the liberating and redeeming truth is something that arises out of the *(re)cognition* of our connection with the totality, a (re)cognition that, at the same time, entails an expansion of our identity in relation to substance.

For Spinoza, we may say that the point is that we cannot understand anything, not even ourselves, without seeing it in a larger interconnection, from the right perspective. To understand what it means to be human is to understand how we fit into nature. To understand ourselves is always to understand more than just ourselves. We must understand correctly the situation in which we live. Ethics, along with the liberating self-understanding that shapes our identity, thus points towards an understanding of the totality, or of substance. Therefore, *ethics* is necessarily *metaphysics*.

LEIBNIZ – MONADS AND PRE-ESTABLISHED HARMONY

Life. *Gottfried Wilhelm von Leibniz (1646–1716) was German, but as a philosopher in the era of Louis XIV, he wrote his books in French and Latin. Leibniz's entire manner of life contrasted with Spinoza's. Unlike the reclusive Spinoza, Leibniz was quite a public person who developed his talent in the most diverse fields, theoretical as well as practical. He was, for example, interested in mining, political reforms, the treasury, legislation, optics, transportation problems, and the establishment of scientific institutions. Leibniz, moreover, travelled extensively, and he left a collection of more than 15,000 letters. Among other things, he was in contact with various royal courts and with several princes. On the theoretical level, Leibniz dealt with philosophy, theology, law, physics, mathematics, medicine, history, and philology. He is especially known for developing the differential calculus (around the same time as, but independently of, Newton).*

We will mention three of his works. Essays in Theodicy *('Essais de théodicée' [1710]) discusses the question of the relationship between God and evil. Where Leibniz attempts to exculpate God for the evil in the world: this world is the best of all possible worlds.* Monadology *('Monadologie' [1714]) discusses the construction of the universe, in which the ultimate and fundamental elements are 'monads'. Leibniz also wrote a critical analysis of Locke's epistemology*, Nouveaux essais sur l'entendement humain *(1703)*.

PURPOSE AND CAUSE – A NEW SYNTHESIS

Leibniz attempted to reconcile the mechanistic world-view with the idea of a teleological universe. Briefly, this attempt at reconciliation is based on Leibniz's acceptance of mechanistic explanations as a kind of surface explanation while claiming that the universe, on a deeper level, is purposeful and teleological, and that the apparently blind, mechanistic causes ultimately originate in divine purpose. Correspondingly, Leibniz says that the things that on the surface give the impression of being material and passive, are, in essence, forces. We will briefly see how Leibniz meant to build a non-materialistic, teleological 'basement' beneath a mechanistic and materialistic universe.

Particular things can be subdivided until we reach certain indivisible basic physical elements which may be characterized as centres of force. Leibniz calls these *monads*. Monads are thus the basic elements on which the universe is built. These monads have different degrees of consciousness, ranging from the inorganic elements up to the human soul. The monads thus form a hierarchy. At the same time, each monad is unaffected by all the others. Monads are 'without doors and windows', as it were: they do not communicate with one another; they do not influence one another.

That they still move in time, so that there is a correlation between mental and physical events, is because all the monads are somehow 'programmed' equally – they are all put in motion by a common plan, that of God. God is thus a kind of universal engineer who ensures that the monads move in time; for example, he ensures that soul and body are coordinated. All things, all monads, communicate in this sense through God. And it is here that we see the teleological aspect of the universe. Leibniz says that the monads are part of a pre-established harmony.

THE BEST OF ALL POSSIBLE WORLDS

If God is the engineer guiding everything that takes place in the universe, how can evil exist, God being at once good and reasonable? Leibniz distinguishes between two kinds of truth, the necessary truths and the truths that could have been different. The necessary truths (logic) could not be denied by God. As for the truths that could have been different (empirical conditions), God chose, as a good and reasonable being, the best possible combination. Viewed in isolation, it seems to man that certain conditions could have been improved; but if we had been able to see the whole, as God did, we would know that, all in all, the world we live in, that is to say, the combination that God chose, is the best possible combination.

Leibniz can therefore say that everything has its reason: either it is logically necessary or it is justified in being as it is in order for the whole to be the best possible world. Therefore, we live in the best of all possible worlds. In this way, Leibniz's philosophy represents a defence of the world that God chose. God is justified in regard to the evil in the world. In political terms, we could say that this, at the same time, represents a defence of the society that exists. If we live in the best of all imaginable worlds, and if the suffering and need that we find are the least possible that we could suffer, there is little reason to want to change society. This theodicy thus functions as a legitimization of both the prevailing form of society and the existing inequality in living conditions and power.

In a political connection, we may say that Leibniz's philosophy represents a clear *individualism*: each monad is unique and is not influenced by other monads. Yes, there cannot be two identical monads (individuals), because God chose the best possible, and it is not possible to choose rationally between two completely identical phenomena (since the reasons to choose one are just as good as those to choose the other). Since God *has* chosen and since the choice is a rational one, there can be no individuals (things) that are completely alike. An extreme metaphysical individualism follows from this: the universe is composed of an infinite number of individual substances. At the same time, these different individuals stand in a harmonious relationship to one another, without influencing one another directly: they interact, so to speak, indirectly, via the pre-established harmony. From a political perspective, it is possible to interpret this to mean that Leibniz does not think of human beings as master and slave in the feudal sense in which the identity of one person is defined in relation to another, while the one dictates to the other. For Leibniz, interaction between people takes place without apparent force, the individual's spontaneous behaviour being based on internalized norms (a pre-established order). This seems to apply to agents in a market where no one acts on the basis of apparent force, but from the principles of market economy, which everyone has internalized.[1]

QUESTIONS

Describe the basic ideas of Spinoza's ethics.

Explain the basic ideas of Leibniz's view that we live in 'the best of all possible worlds'.

SUGGESTIONS FOR FURTHER READING

PRIMARY LITERATURE

Spinoza, Baruch, *Ethics*, translated by R. H. M. Elwes, London, 1919.
Leibniz, Gottfried, *Monadology*, translated by Robert Latta, Oxford, 1898.
Leibniz, Gottfried, *Théodicée*, translated by E. M. Huggard and edited by Austin Ferrar, London, 1951.

SECONDARY LITERATURE

Hampshire, S., *Spinoza*, Harmondsworth, 1970.
MacDonald Ross, G., *Leibniz*, Oxford, 1984.

NOTE

1 Jon Elster, *Leibniz et la formation de l'esprit capitaliste*, Paris, 1975.

11 Locke – enlightenment and equality

Life. John Locke (1632–1704) was the son of a Puritan, a Parliamentarian lawyer. As a young man, Locke reacted against scholastic philosophy, at the same time taking an interest in natural science, especially medicine and chemistry. He saw it as his vocation to carry out an intellectual 'cleansing', that is to say, a critical testing of our knowledge. Locke says that it was the endless discussions of moral and religious questions that moved him to ask whether many of our concepts are not hopelessly unclear and inadequate. He felt that philosophers should proceed gradually and tentatively like natural scientists. Before we can deal with the big questions we need to examine our tools, that is, our concepts. Locke begins therefore with a critique of knowledge and linguistic analysis. But his interest in the 'tools' did not keep him from being concerned with the matters at hand: he is one of the classical thinkers in pedagogics and in political theory.

His Two Treatises of Civil Government *(1690) has been called the bible of liberalism. The first treatise attacks one of the ideologists of absolutism, Sir Robert Filmer (1588–1653). The second develops Locke's own ideas about the state and natural rights. The work was seen as a defence of the constitutional monarchy of William of Orange, but in France and North America these ideas were to acquire a revolutionary implication. In addition, Locke wrote works such as* A Letter Concerning Toleration *(1689–92), Some* Thoughts Concerning Education *(1693), and* The Reasonableness of Christianity *(1695), along with the epistemological* Essay Concerning Human Understanding *(1689).*

EPISTEMOLOGY AND CRITIQUE OF KNOWLEDGE

CONCEPTUAL CLARIFICATION

John Locke is a transitional figure in the history of ideas. His roots go back to the theory of natural rights as well as to nominalism (Ockham). He was influenced by the rationalist Descartes, but at the same time he opposed Cartesian rationalism with empiricist arguments. He is a forerunner of the Enlightenment but also a pioneer of British empiricism, a philosophical position that eventually led to sharp criticism of important aspects of the philosophy of the Enlightenment (cf. Hume's criticism of the concept of reason).

The rationalists thought that clear concepts give us insight into essential aspects of reality. If we have a clear concept, we also have certain knowledge. They had great confidence in our ability to gain this kind of certain insight (provided that we use reason correctly). It is true that the rationalist Descartes appeals to doubt, but primarily as a means of starting correctly. However, the various rationalists did not agree among themselves about what should be seen as clear and distinct, that is to say, as true. This provided fertile soil for rebuttals of rationalism. The standard argument, from Locke to Kant, is that insight into concepts does not necessarily confer insight into reality: even a clear conception of a perfect cat who can read and write does not mean that such a cat exists! And even if we have a clear conception of a perfect being, God, we cannot be certain that God exists. We cannot make inferences from concept to existence.

Locke supported doubt, not as a temporary position before we finally gain infallible knowledge, but as a permanently doubting and testing attitude. The process of cognition does not lead to absolute certainty but to partial knowledge. Our task is that of improving the knowledge we have, gradually and critically, as we do in the natural sciences. The nascent natural sciences thus led to different attitudes and cognitive ideals for Locke than for the rationalists Descartes, Spinoza, and Leibniz. Here it may be useful to recall that Locke was especially fascinated by medicine, an empirical science in which observation and classification play a key role. Already in antiquity there was a connection between medical science and an experientially oriented, theory-sceptical philosophy (Hippocrates).

Like most philosophers in the seventeenth and eighteenth centuries, both rationalists and empiricists, Locke was interested in epistemology. He was trying to gain insight into what human cognition can achieve, and, crucially, what its limits are. By discovering these limits, we can free ourselves from what we believe incorrectly to be true. But while epistemology for the rationalists, with their critique of knowledge, was a springboard for launching philosophical systems, the therapeutic and knowledge-promoting force of the critique of knowledge was an independent goal for Locke and the empiricists. This is naturally connected with the fact that the empiricists' analysis of cognition entails a more considered view of our cognitive abilities. The insight we gain through concepts alone is limited and fraught with problems; an appropriate acquisition of knowledge takes place in the empirical sciences through testing and gradual improvements.

In his epistemological 'cleansing work', Locke looked beyond philosophical cognition alone. He was seeking not only to know what knowledge is but also to promote its acquisition, to further its growth in the sciences. Philosophy is not a superior master science, but it can serve the sciences, as, for example, by clarifying concepts and exposing pseudo-insight. Conceptual clarification is necessary for several reasons. If we do not use clear concepts, it is impossible for others to know what we mean. If what we say can be interpreted in different ways, and if there are reasons for claiming that the one interpretation is true and the other is false, we cannot take a stand on the original formulation before we have clarified which interpretation we are talking about. Thus, in intellectual discussion and scientific research, precise expression is imperative.

According to Locke, academic language can easily lapse into vague abstractions that apparently express profound wisdom, but that are really only a misuse of language. Language may thus deceive us. This applies both to the speaker and to the listener. Those who express themselves in vague and abstract concepts often do so in good faith. It is therefore often difficult to convince them that they are misusing language. The traditional, philosophical discourse, with terms like 'substance', 'innate ideas', 'infinity', etc., is, for Locke, a typical example of how vagueness can pass for profound wisdom. Eliminating misleading abstractions is thus an important therapeutic activity. The users of language may then be freed from delusions. Here the relationship with the Enlightenment becomes apparent: linguistic clarification liberates us from inherited delusions. It guards us against fanaticism that is based on unclear and distorted ideas. It helps to make reasonable behaviour possible in public discussion and in scientific work.

We may say that being rational entails the will to seek truth, and this again means willingness to test our own viewpoints; that is to say, to test them against the opinion of others in an open and free discussion. The search for truth thus presupposes a certain intellectual freedom and tolerance. We discuss controversial scientific or political issues with others because we do not exclude the possibility that others *may* be right, that we can learn something from them. A discussion thus presupposes a certain undogmatic and open attitude: we maintain what we think to be right on the basis of available arguments, but we immediately change our view according to changes in the arguments – we change our view when the arguments require it, but only then. This indicates a certain connection between epistemology and social philosophy. But what is a convincing argument? Even today, this is a controversial question.[1]

Locke was a torchbearer for the new scientific culture that found expression in the enlightened and progressive citizens of Britain at the end of the seventeenth century: he inaugurated the Enlightenment. We will see later how Locke formed a political philosophy in accordance with these ideas. But first we will take a closer look at Locke's epistemological viewpoint.

THE ORIGIN OF KNOWLEDGE

Locke's critique of knowledge entails a demand for linguistic clarification and experiential justification. This critique of knowledge is connected with Locke's general view of what knowledge is. On the question of what sources of knowledge we possess, Locke says: 'Whence has it [the mind] all the *materials* of reason and knowledge? To this I answer, in one word, from EXPERIENCE. In that all our knowledge is founded; and from that it ultimately derives itself.'[2]

Locke thus says that the *materials* for reasoning and cognition come from experience. Hence, we should infer that that which does not build on this material is not really knowledge. In such instances, we use words without experiential backing, and what we say may not be accepted as knowledge. But what is experience? This word is in itself ambiguous. We speak, for example, about religious experience, about professional experience, and about pure sense experience. Locke distinguishes between experience as external perception (*sensation*) and as internal perception of our own mental operations and conditions (*reflection*). And what we experience in this way are really simple impressions (*ideas*).

Locke generally thinks that these basic experiences are acquired passively. These passively acquired *simple ideas* are then, in different ways, actively processed by the mind. This is how the rich diversity of our *complex ideas* arises. In part, simple ideas which regularly appear together lead to compound representations, as when the regularly appearing simple ideas of the sides of a house lead to the representations of the house itself. And partly, the mind functions more creatively by forming complex ideas, like the ideas of a centaur, of substance, or of private property.

A salient point is the question of to what extent the reasoning and knowledge that build on experience as their material, that is, on simple ideas, represent something different from and greater than these ideas. In other words, we must ask whether knowledge is nothing more than the sum of the ideas of perception on which it is built, or whether there is something more to it.

Here we have a problem of reduction that corresponds to the problem we had in connection with Hobbes: is the watch reducible to its parts? If we answer that knowledge is reducible to its parts, we end up with a radical empiricist position: knowledge is only that which can be fully traced back to experience. Moreover, when experience is interpreted as simple ideas of perception, the thesis says that knowledge is only that which can be completely and wholly analysed in simple (external and internal) ideas of perception. On the other hand, if we answer that the formation of knowledge starts with simple ideas of perception – experience is, in this sense, the material of knowledge – but that knowledge still entails something qualitatively different from the sum of these ideas, we have another thesis. A more precise formulation of this thesis will depend on how the formation of knowledge based on the material of simple ideas is understood.

The first alternative entails some difficult problems; for instance, the problem of self-reference: can this thesis itself be reduced to simple ideas of perception? This radical empiricist interpretation would starkly oppose Locke's epistemology to his political theory, which has clearly rationalistic elements (such as the notion of human rights). There are thus good reasons for choosing the latter alternative for a treatment of Locke's view: knowledge arises from experience, simple ideas of perception and reflection, but the mind uses this material actively in such a way that the knowledge which arises represents something qualitatively different from simple ideas. (Cf. Hobbes: the watch is something qualitatively different from the parts, although it is composed of the parts.) According to this interpretation of Locke's epistemology, the human mind plays an active part in the formation of knowledge. As for the question of the validity of complex ideas, the test is whether the different elements in a complex idea can be traced back to simple ideas of perception. But this test does not mean that complex ideas basically *are* the sum of simple ideas of perception. The test means only that separate, simple experiences, *qua* material for knowledge, represent a necessary, but not sufficient condition for knowledge. If this necessary condition is not fulfilled, we do not have knowledge.

As an example, Locke mentions the notion of *infinity*. Does this notion represent knowledge or pseudo-knowledge? To find out, we must investigate how this notion is formed. We will then see, according to Locke, that we never experience infinity directly. What we experience or, more correctly, perceive, is, for example, that different lengths can always be extended a little further. If we imagine this process as unceasing, with a continual extension of the preceding portion of the line, we reach the concept of an infinite line. A corresponding argument can be made for the concept of time. This shows, according to Locke, that our notion of infinity is largely valid – if we do not ascribe more to the notion than what we can experientially support; that is, that we do not claim that an infinite something *exists*, but only that we can imagine infinity by generalizing from given experiences. Then we may use such a notion of infinity.

That a notion of infinity is *clear* does not guarantee its epistemological acceptability. This is a criticism of Descartes' view that the clarity and distinctness of a notion entails the existence of what the notion designates. Only by establishing empirical evidence can we really talk about what exists. The test of knowledge is based on the empirical justification, not on personal experience. That we personally experience something as being clear is not enough. A test by perception or introspection is required.

Locke's theory of the formation of knowledge is thus that we, at birth, are like a blank slate (*tabula rasa*) – there are no 'innate ideas' – that external objects provide us with simple ideas of perception that are a compound of the true properties of the external things and the sensory qualities that we add to them, and that we, from our mental operations and conditions, have simple ideas of reflection. From this material, the mind forms the various kinds of complex ideas, as previously mentioned. We thus acquire knowledge that builds on simple ideas of perception and simple ideas of reflection, without being reducible to these ideas.

A distinction between primary and secondary qualities was common during Locke's day. In the mechanistic world-view, it was common to say that external objects have only properties like extension, form, solidity – the so-called primary qualities, without which the things cannot be imagined. These primary qualities are in principle copied in our sensory organs in an adequate manner, in the form of corresponding ideas. But, in addition, we experience by means of sensory organs; for example, we perceive taste, smell, colour, and warmth. These are secondary qualities that do not originate directly in corresponding primary qualities in the things. In the things, these primary properties are found in the form of quantitative forces and conditions that, in their influence on our sensory organs, provide us with the sensory, or secondary, qualities. This is the thesis of the *subjectivity of sensory qualities*: sensory qualities are dependent on us, on the subject.

We may ask whether it is meaningful to distinguish between sensory qualities, such as colour, and primary properties, such as extension. Can we imagine extension without colour? If the answer is no, and if we think that colour is a property dependent on the cognizant subject, it is problematic to claim that primary properties (such as extension) are independent of human beings. But if *all* properties, including the so-called primary qualities, are dependent on the cognizant subject, we are left with idealism: we can no longer talk about objectively existing properties in nature; that is, properties in the things that are independent of the subject. These are the kinds of problems that led to a self-critical development within British empiricism, from Berkeley to Hume.[3]

We may also ask how we can know about external things if it is true that sensory impressions on the retina (and in other sensory organs) are the final basis of our knowledge. If we do not see the tree in the forest outside us, but only the 'tree pictures' on the retina, we surely cannot *know* that there is a tree in the forest. The model based on epistemological access in the form of sensory impressions from external things in our sensory organs is thus problematic.

What we have now indicated represents a standard criticism of so-called representative realism, that is to say, of the epistemological theory that external things exist independently of our consciousness (epistemological realism), but that these external things are only accessible to us via images, representations, in our sensory organs. This model of knowledge, which is meant to explain how we recognize the external world, apparently entails our inability to reach out to the external world.

Furthermore, it is even unclear what a simple sensory idea is. When I read this book, is it then the entire book, the entire page, one line, one word, one letter, a part of a letter – or something else – that is the simple sensory idea? Moreover, it is commonly pointed out that Locke uses the word *idea* ambiguously: partly in the sense of 'concept', and partly of 'immediate sense impression'.

In principle, the complex ideas are of two kinds: those which are meant to apply to states of affairs in the world, and those which apply only to the relationships between concepts. For the latter kind of complex ideas, the test of knowledge is a question of consistency, of to what extent the concepts correspond with one another. For the former, there is also a question of the correspondence with simple ideas.

Locke thinks that axioms in ethics and mathematics can be tested.[4] Furthermore, he allows the concept of God and the concept of substance. But he maintains that all concepts which stand for complex ideas need analysis. This applies to words like 'virtue', 'duty', 'force', and 'substance'.

Locke's analysis of the concept of *substance* is especially well known. We often see that certain simple ideas operate together, in definite ways. We often say, therefore, that these ideas belong to one thing and we give them a common name. This is how the properties round, green, sour, hard, etc., appear in connection with what we call an unripe apple. On a day-to-day basis, we view the unripe apple as a thing. Through analysis we see that this complex idea is composed of a set of properties that appear together in a regular way. But when we talk about the unripe apple as if it were something that exists in a way that transcends all the particular perceptible properties, we are talking about something of which we cannot have sense impressions. Such a something that somehow underlies the properties and binds them together is often called substance (the underlying). We may say that Locke's point is not that we should stop talking about substances or things – he himself talks about them – but that we, through analysis, should prove that we then have concepts of a quite different kind than when we talk about simple percept-ible properties. In such an interpretation, Locke's point is not to criticize our use of language, but to make us more aware of what we are really saying when we use such complex concepts.

In this sense, Locke does not assume a radical empiricist position, if we thereby refer to the view that only that is knowledge that can be traced back to simple experiential impressions. He partly assumes a moderate empiricist position (cf. his criticism of the concepts of substance and of infinity), and partly a certain ration-alist position (cf. his view that we can rationally acknowledge the existence of inviolable human rights). Hence, it is not entirely correct to call Locke the father of empiricism if we mean by empiricism radical epistemological empiricism. But Locke at least contributed to the foundation of a tradition that runs from Berkeley and Hume to, among others, the logical positivists – and in Hume and the logical positivists we find fairly radical empiricist viewpoints.

The word *empiricism* is also applied to attitudes and viewpoints that are not char-acterized by a strictly epistemological position, but that instead express a positive

attitude towards the experiential sciences and an attitude of doubt towards speculative systems of a logically unclear and empirically unverifiable nature. Such a
sceptical and open attitude, along with a desire for conceptual clarification and
experiential control, came to mark much of the intellectual life in the eighteenth
century, especially in Britain. And if we call this attitude empiricism, it is clear that
this empiricism was not affected by the arguments that we mentioned previously
in connection with the radical version of the empiricist theory of knowledge. By
this terminology, where empiricism is such an attitude, we may, without reservation, call John Locke an empiricist – although it is doubtful if we may at the same
time call him the father of this empiricism, since a certain empiricist attitude can
also be found in earlier philosophers. We can add that such an empiricist attitude
is today, in many ways, an integrated part of our scientific civilization.[5]

Another distinction that can be made in connection with empiricism is a
distinction between what we could call conceptual-empiricism and verification-
empiricism. Conceptual-empiricism is roughly the epistemological position that
concepts arise from experience, and verification-empiricism is roughly the epistemological position that statements are ultimately confirmed by experience (observation).[6] Both positions can be presented in different ways depending on the various
notions of experience, of a concept, and of verification and falsification of statements. Conceptual-empiricism aims to clarify what makes concepts meaningful.
(A meaningful use of concepts is a necessary, but not sufficient, condition for
statements to be true.) Verification-empiricism aims to clarify how we confirm and
disconfirm statements – how we may know that they are true or false – whether
they are theoretical or observational statements.

POLITICAL THEORY – INDIVIDUALS AND THEIR RIGHTS

Locke, like Hobbes, conceives of the *individual* as a basic element, and he regards
the state as being created by a social contract among individuals, so that the state
of nature is thus abolished. In this sense, the doctrine of the state of nature does
not serve as a doctrine of the genesis of the state, of how the state actually arose,
but as a doctrine that explains what the state is, and thereby also legitimizes the
state. But these concepts have a milder character in Locke's thought: they do not,
as in Hobbes, entail everyone's struggle against everyone else, a crass principle of
self-preservation and absolutism. There are free citizens who, from enlightened
self-interest, live in a society governed by law and by a representative government
in which the individual citizen is guaranteed certain rights, especially the right to
own property.

Locke's state of nature is not an anarchistic state of war, but a form of life where
individuals have unrestricted liberty. Here, human beings are equal, by nature. This
equality is something that we can recognize with our minds. Equality means the
freedom to be our own master, as long as we do not harm anyone else. Furthermore, this equality and freedom mean that we freely rule over our own bodies and
thus whatever we achieve by means of our bodies, that is to say, the result of our
work, or property. When individuals attempt to escape from the state of nature
into a politically ordered society, it is not because of a fear of death, but because
they realize that they are safer in an ordered society than in the state of nature.

Here we may say that Locke, as opposed to Hobbes, distinguished between *society*, which functions spontaneously, in a regulated manner, and which may exist within a state of nature, and the *state*, which represents a political arrangement, and which is a product of a political contract. A politically ordered society, for Locke, is not a despotism. It is a state under majority rule, subject to certain regulations: each individual possesses inviolable rights that no ruler should touch. This is thus a constitutional rule. For Locke, the maximization of individual liberty and a constitutional government grounded in the individual's rights are two sides of the same coin. For Hobbes, the state's purpose is to secure peace, to safeguard the individual's survival. For Locke, the state's purpose, above all, is to safeguard private property. Here, Locke's view is certainly opposed to the common opinion in antiquity and the Middle Ages that the state's task is primarily *ethical*: to make possible the good life, to allow man's ethical-political self-realization in the community. In this traditional view, securing private property is less important than this basic ethical task. Safeguarding property is a goal only to the degree that such safeguards are necessary for people to live worthy lives. The emphasis that Locke places on the notion that the state should primarily protect property is therefore striking, seen from a traditional perspective. It is thus tempting to view the priority that Locke gives to this point as a reflection of the dominant view of his day that protecting private property is paramount.

Locke also had a theory of the relationship between labour and property rights. In the state of nature, before society was established, people could make free use of everything around them. But when the individual works on a natural thing, as by transforming a tree into a boat, the individual puts something of himself or herself into that thing. The individual gains a personal interest in the thing, which has become private property. And when the individuals move from the state of nature to society via a contract, it is implicit that society should safeguard this private property.[7]

Locke is not an advocate of *laissez-faire* liberalism, that is, an economic system in which the state plays a minimal role, and the wealthy have free rein. Like most of his fellow citizens then — Britain at the end of the seventeenth century — Locke supported an economic system in which the state adopts a protectionist role *vis-à-vis* native industry and similar industries in other states. The state should protect private property, maintain order, and pursue a protectionist trade policy in regard to other states, but not supervise or control trade and industry. The economy should be based on private capital. Nor should the state intervene in social problems, as by regulating personal incomes and improving the living conditions of the poor. In this area, Locke followed radical liberalism: the individual's own work is basic; the state should ensure the legal but not the social and economic equality of citizens. As in *laissez-faire* liberalism, Locke seems to think that there is a natural harmony between the egotism of the individual and the common good.[8]

Locke thinks that sovereignty is vested in the citizens in community. But since the citizens have approved the social contract, they must accept the will of the majority. He is thus clearly against absolutism: the aggregate will of all the citizens, not the king by God's grace, is sovereign. But it is difficult to say why the majority should rule, once the social contract is approved. Why should a minority be excluded from the practical use of the sovereignty of which they, in principle, partake? The answer is pragmatic: for society to function, it is necessary for the minority to submit to the majority. But this answer is not satisfactory. Cannot society function when a strong minority rules?

Locke's emphasis on the majority, however, suits the legal equality that the citizenry at that time sought – against the traditional privilege of the nobility. But Locke does not support a majority rule in the sense of a representative government with general voting rights. Locke does not hold that everyone should have the right to vote. He is well satisfied with the political system after 1689, in which the right to vote was limited to the property-owning classes: the middle class and nobility. The liberalist civil democracy was, for Locke, a democracy of the citizens. Thus, what we have said about the majority's will, in Locke's theory, should not be taken literally.

Beyond that, it is worth noting that Locke is concerned with limiting the power of rulers. Executive and legislative power should not reside in the same body. Here, Locke supports the principle of the distribution of powers in government (cf. Montesquieu). The notion of natural rights is, for Locke, based on the idea of the inviolable human rights of all people. This idea has an important role for Locke: these rights should secure the individual and private property against the state's interference. This version of natural rights is important in the political defence of citizens against absolutism.[9]

In the presentation of Locke's political philosophy that we have given here, how-ever, there is a certain conflict between, on the one hand, the thesis that all peo-ple have the same rights, and on the other hand, the defence of a political order in which the power lies in the hands of those who have property. How can this conflict be resolved?

To deal with this issue, we must go back to Locke's theory of the state of nature and the voluntary contract on which society is based. In connection with the state of nature, Locke emphasizes that all people are equal: 'A state also of equality, wherein all the power and jurisdiction is reciprocal, no one having more than another, there being nothing more evident than that creatures of the same species and rank, promiscuously born to all the same advantages of nature, and the use of the same faculties, should also be equal one amongst another, without subordination or sub-jection.'[10] But at the same time he says, with a constant reference to the state of nature: 'Thus, the grass my horse has bit, the turfs my servant has cut, and the ore I have digged in any place, where I have a right to them in common with others, become my property without the assignation or consent of anybody.'[11] Is then the *servant* not an equal individual? On the contrary, in the latter quotation, the servant is placed on the same level as the horse. The work that the servant and the horse per-form becomes 'my property'. This indicates that the servant was not included as a member of the political community in Locke's day: when one talked about people, about the individual, it normally referred to men of the middle class and nobility.[12]

Individuals, for Locke, are adult persons who voluntarily enter into agreements, *contracts*, with one another. Just social arrangements are those which can be recon-structed as a result of such contracts. This is a modern view: individuals, that is to say, adult persons – without feudal ties and hierarchic arrangements – freely deter-mine, from an enlightened self-interest, how society should be organized. Locke also applies this view of contracts in interpersonal relations to marriage: 'Conjugal society is made by a voluntary compact between man and woman, and though it consist chiefly in such a communion and right in one another's bodies as is necessary to its chief end, procreation.'[13] The attempt to analyse so many interpersonal relationships by means of the idea of a voluntary contract may, in hindsight, seem oversimplified, but it is important to realize that in Locke's day concepts such as 'individual' and 'contract' represented new and exciting perspectives on man and interpersonal relations, from politics and economy to marriage. We will follow this line of thought about individual and contract – within political and legal theory, within economic thought, and within theory of the private sphere (the relationship between woman and man, and between child and parent) – up until the rise of the critique of contractarian thought and its faith in individual rationality of choice. Thus, David Hume replaced the contractarian idea with emotions and conventions; Edmund Burke appealed to tradition; and Hegel emphasized the mutual formative processes inherent in socialization, and criticized, for instance, the view of marriage as a contract, as in Kant.

With this set of problems in mind, we will examine three points of Locke's theory about the state of nature:

1   Originally, all human beings had everything in common, but the individual had a duty to take care of himself or herself and therefore to work. However, 'every man has a property in his own person. This nobody has any right to but himself. The labour of his body and the work of his hands, we may say, are properly his. Whatsoever, then he removes out of the state that Nature hath provided and left it in, he hath mixed his labour with it, and joined to it something that is his own, and thereby makes it his property.'[14] The individual's labour confers the right to *own* the product that he or she has made. This means that property eventually becomes *private* property, and that *inheritance* as such does not give the right to property. All this applies to the state of nature. With the transition to the politically ordered society, the right of ownership, as a right of private property, is maintained; at the same time, Locke accepts the principle of property by inheritance – a principle not compatible with his first thesis that private property results from the individual's own labour.

2   The individual has the right to own as much property as he himself can use. He does *not* have the right to squander the things that he owns by virtue of his own labour. Since Locke is speaking here of an economy based upon barter, he thinks that the right of ownership is naturally limited for everyone. The crops that a person has grown, and that he uses personally are his private property. But no one has the right to allow crops to rot.

3   Finally, Locke assumes that there are *enough* resources to satisfy the basic needs of *all* mankind. He justifies this by saying that there is enough land for everyone, and, moreover, that working the land is what essentially adds value to our property. As for the extent of our resources, he says, among other things: 'There is land enough in the world to suffice double the inhabitants'.[15] At that time, the population was around half a billion. Scarcely 200 years later, the population had doubled. Today, the population has grown tenfold.

Now, according to Locke, since each person lives from his or her own labour without squandering, while there are enough resources for everyone, there is a certain harmonious equality among people. This version of the state of nature is thus characterized by a barter economy, with private property being created and limited by individual efforts and by private consumption. But 'the invention of money, and the tacit agreement of men to put a value on it, introduced (by consent) larger possessions and a right to them'.[16] In other words, at a certain point, prior to the political social contract, man entered into a 'tacit and willing agreement'[17] to introduce *money*. And along with money there arose an unfair distribution of land. For with money, with silver and gold, a man may 'rightfully and without injury, possess more than he himself can make use of by receiving gold and silver, which may continue long in a man's possession without decaying for the overplus'.[18] We may store money, unlike crops, without it rotting or rusting. Money is not destroyed, even when it is acquired in enormous amounts. Therefore, there is no longer a natural limitation to what each person may rightfully own. Locke developed these ideas under the presupposition that there are enough resources for everyone, and that private property is the result of the individual's own labour.

Thus, with money, a material inequality develops. Some own much, others little. But this inequality originated in a *voluntary* contract between individuals, by the introduction of money. The large properties have thus arisen rightfully. The poor, therefore, have not reason to complain because all, according to Locke, have entered into the agreement to introduce money. At that point, society, in a political sense, had still not been founded. We were still in a state of nature. There is therefore no reason to blame society, in a political sense, for the material inequality that arose along with the entrance of money.

Political society is considered to have been founded by a new contract, the veritable social contract. But why should such a contract be necessary? Do not things function well as they are, in this revised, monetary state of nature? There are two reasons for leaving this state of nature: everyone is interested in securing life, and those who have property are interested in securing this property. Everyone is therefore interested in such a social contract, even if the premises vary.

The political society that we thus end up with is essentially British society in Locke's day; that is, the time of the Civil War in the mid-seventeenth century. It is a state with the political power in the hands of the property owners and with certain legal rights shared by all citizens. How can Locke's theory, which starts by asserting that everyone is equal, legitimize a society based on economic and political inequality? And how can a political theory propose inviolable rights for everyone while legitimizing economic inequality and voting rights limited to property owners?

We have seen how Locke attributed the economic inequality not to a fault in society, but to a voluntary agreement freely entered into by individuals.

Locke also held that those who have property are those who put into practice reason in society. Since those who vote and exercise political power should be reasonable, this means that voting rights and other political rights should be reserved to the property owners. This means that material inequality, i.e., the inequality in property, is consistent with inequality in reason and political power. The voluntary agreement to introduce money had many consequences! And the underprivileged cannot blame society or the privileged for these inequalities, which, in fact, derive from this voluntary agreement. But even those who do not own anything are potentially reasonable. Even they can improve themselves and achieve rationality. Here we see the seed of the belief in progress that we find in the

Enlightenment: through material and cultural progress, all people may, in principle, eventually become reasoning citizens. The belief in progress could thus make it easier to accept the current inequalities: everyone will do well in the future.

From this interpretation of his political theory, Locke emerges as a defender of the status quo in the Britain of his day: he legitimizes its political and economic inequality by universal and humane principles of the inviolable rights of individuals, in which the mediating element is the notion of the voluntary contract. But the same ideas took on a different and more socially critical implication in other countries, such as France. And through the French philosophers of the Enlightenment and the American Revolution (the founding fathers),[19] Locke's political ideas had a great influence on later developments.

In short, we might say that Locke is a representative ideologist of liberalism in the phase of capitalism when the citizenry did not need an absolute monarch to curb the nobility and unite the national state, but instead wished to eliminate the absolute monarch and directly control the government. Locke's liberalism starts with the idea of a social contract and inviolable individual rights, and the political ideal of placing sovereignty in the hands of the people. Accordingly, the legislative power should be exercised by a national assembly that represents the bourgeoisie and the landowners, and the executive power should reside in a government which respects the inviolable rights of the individual.

QUESTIONS

How does Locke view the relationship between knowledge and sense experience (perception)? How can this view lead to a critique of knowledge?

Explain how the concept of a social contract is fundamental to Locke's political philosophy, and clarify his view of the rights of the individual.

Clarify the basic features of Hobbes' and Locke's political theories and discuss the claim: 'Modern theories of the state of nature and the social contract represent a radical break with basic political concepts of antiquity (as in Plato and Aristotle).'

SUGGESTIONS FOR FURTHER READING

PRIMARY LITERATURE

Two Treatises of Government, critical edition with introduction and notes by Peter Laslett, Cambridge, 1970.

An Essay Concerning Human Understanding, in *The English Philosophers from Bacon to Mill*, New York, 1939.

SECONDARY LITERATURE

Macpherson, C. B., *The Political Theory of Possessive Individualism. Hobbes to Locke*, Oxford, 1964.

Yolton, J. W., *John Locke and the Way of Ideas*, Oxford, 1956.

NOTES

1 See the debate within the philosophy of science that starts with logical positivism, Popper's thesis on falsification, and the ensuing debate surrounding Kuhn, in addition to Apel and Habermas (Chs 26 and 27).
2 Locke, *An Essay Concerning Human Understanding*, Book II, 'Of Ideas', Chapter I, 'Of Ideas in General, and their Original', §2.
3 Cf. the debate in analytic philosophy about 'sense data', as in Alfred Jules Ayer (1910–1989), *The Foundations of Empirical Knowledge*, London, 1940.
4 *An Essay Concerning Human Understanding*, Book IV, Chapter III, §18.
5 Locke is a kind of Thomas Aquinas of his day in the sense that Locke, like Aquinas, tried to grasp conceptually the spirit of his entire age. The ambiguity in Locke's philosophy may thus be related to the ambiguity of his day: not only were there different forms of philosophical thought, but also society was fragmented and in a state of transition. Locke's ambiguous views of the mind and of experience make it possible to read him both 'backwards', that is, from the perspective of Aquinas – the mind forms abstractions on the basis of the material provided by the senses – and 'forwards', that is, in the direction of Kant – the mind actively forms the material of experience.
6 On the latter, cf. logical positivism, Ch. 26.
7 As we will see later, the theories about what value is (Adam Smith and Karl Marx) start with the view that the value of a commodity is the work that is put into it.
8 It is around the mid-nineteenth century that we first have a transition from *laissez-faire* liberalism to social liberalism, since one recognizes that, as a rule, unlimited private initiative, without social and economic equality, does not lead to the best possible result for everyone.
9 If Locke had been a radical empiricist, there would have been a contradiction between an empiricist epistemology and a political theory supporting the notion of natural rights. How can empiricists *know* that the individual possesses inviolable rights? What simple sense impression tells them that we *should* not violate these rights?
10 *Two Treatises of Government*, Part II, §4.
11 Ibid., §28.
12 The concept *individual* in liberalism does not, as a rule, apply to children, women, or servants; instead, it applies to the paterfamilias: it is he, disposing of private capital, who enters into contracts and who, on a rational basis, maximizes profit and pleasure. The attributes that liberalism ascribes to the individual do not apply very well to the maid and stable boy.
13 *Two Treatises of Government*, Part II, §78.
14 Ibid., §27.
15 Ibid., §36.
16 Ibid., §36.
17 Ibid., §50.
18 Ibid., §50.
19 Cf. Thomas Jefferson's (1732–1826) use of the expressions 'the laws of nature' and 'self-evident':

> A DECLARATION BY THE REPRESENTATIVES OF THE UNITED STATES OF AMERICA, IN GENERAL CONGRESS ASSEMBLED*
> July 4, 1776
> When in the course of human events, it becomes necessary for one people to dissolve the political bands which have connected them with another, and to assume among the powers of the earth the separate and equal station to which the laws of nature and of nature's God entitle them, a decent respect to the opinions of mankind requires that they should declare the causes which impel them to the separation.
> We hold these truths to be self-evident, that all men are created equal, that they are endowed by their Creator with certain inalienable rights, that among these are life, liberty, and the pursuit of happiness, that to secure these rights, governments are instituted among men, deriving their just powers from the consent of the governed, that whenever any form of government becomes destructive of these ends, it is the right of the people to alter or to abolish it, and to institute new government, laying its foundation on such principles, and organizing its powers in such form, as to them shall seem most likely to effect their safety and happiness. Prudence, indeed, will dictate that governments long established should not be changed for light and transient causes; and accordingly all experience hath shown, that mankind are more disposed to suffer while evils are sufferable, than to right themselves by abolishing the forms to which they are accustomed.
> *This was Jefferson's original title.

12 Empiricism and critique of knowledge

BERKELEY – A CRITIQUE OF EMPIRICISM FROM WITHIN

Life. George Berkeley (1685–1753) was an Anglo-Irish philosopher who became the Anglican bishop of Cloyne. His best-known works are A Treatise Concerning the Principles of Human Knowledge *(1710) and* Three Dialogues between Hylas and Philonous *(1713).*

'ESSE' IS 'PERCIPI' – IDEALISTIC EMPIRICISM

Berkeley viewed himself as at the same time an advocate *for* common sense *against* metaphysics, and *for* a theistic (Christian) view *against* atheism and materialism. He thought that he could reconcile these viewpoints, that is, common sense and Christian faith, by claiming that matter does not exist, and that God communicates directly with us through our perceptions. Berkeley posited such viewpoints out of a critical development of the seminal epistemological ideas of earlier empiricists like Locke.

Locke had distinguished between secondary and primary qualities. The primary qualities – extension, form, solidity – are comprehended by us as they are in the things themselves. The primary qualities in things are represented by our sense impressions of them. On the other hand, the impressions of colour, smell, taste, etc. that we think originate with the thing, do not express the same properties in the thing. But the thing causes these impressions by influencing our sensory organs.

This is the thesis of the subjectivity of sensory qualities: we comprehend external things by the influence of certain stimuli from these things, qualities such as colour and taste; that is, attributes that cannot be found in the things themselves, but which are produced in us by impressions from the things.

Hence, Locke distinguishes between the world as it appears to us (ideas, sense impressions) and the world as it actually is, independently of our senses, and the nature of which we can only infer. Berkeley rejects this: that which we sense is the actual and only world. There are no imperceptible objects beyond our perceptions (as it were) that cause the world we experience. Berkeley's argument is that it is meaningless to maintain such a distinction: can we imagine extension (a primary quality) without colour (a sensory quality)? No, says Berkeley. The idea of extension, as in a rose, cannot be imagined as divorced from some kind of notion about colour. It is true that we, by means of a thought experiment, can eliminate the rose's red colour. But when we think about the rose's extension, we think of it as being white or grey or visible in some way, that is to say, as being distinguished from its surroundings because of its colour. The rose's extension is imagined in contrast to the surrounding room by virtue of colour contrast. We must at least draw the boundaries of the rose; for example, by drawing a black line against a white background.

But if we cannot distinguish between properties that things have independently of us and properties that depend on us, we must say that all properties are, in reality, subjective: colour, smell, taste, and heat are properties that we can show to be dependent on us, and if all properties are to be of one kind, extension, form, and weight must also be dependent on us.

The thesis about secondary qualities is closely related to the mechanistic world-view. If we hold that the concepts of mechanics reveal things accurately – and this is just the philosophical view that we call the mechanistic world-view – it is tempting to try to explain the remaining properties from the subjective perspective. But the notion of secondary qualities may also arise independently of the mechanistic world-view; for example, some properties may be shown to be dependent on the condition of the observer. They are relative in relation to the observer. Thus, the same water may seem warm when we place a cold hand into it and cold when we place a warm hand into it. Is the water then warm or cold? Or is it both warm and cold? If we answer the latter question affirmatively, we must ascribe conflicting properties to the same thing. Some thinkers have held that the best answer is that the thing in itself is neither warm nor cold, but that these properties are in some way relative to the subject who perceives. Similar arguments about relativity can be made in connection with the perception of colour, smell, and taste. However, the fact that we can show certain properties to be relative does not mean that we *must* claim that these properties do not belong to the thing itself. But the latter claim of the subjectivity of sensory qualities is *one* way of explaining relativity.

But are not the primary properties, and indirectly also the sensory qualities, connected to external things, to material substances? It is precisely this that is metaphysical speculation, according to Berkeley. What do we really *know* about such material substances? If all that we know originates in sense impressions, we cannot know anything at all about material substances. The idea of such material substances is a metaphysical construction. An everyday conception of matter, whereby, for example, we can say that a piece of cheese is material, is something different from the philosophical conception of matter, in which matter is a general name for all material things, a name that is meant to refer to invisible substances. The conception of matter that Berkeley rejects is not the usual, everyday conception, but a philosophical conception of matter. Berkeley thus interprets the common conception of matter as a collection of sense impressions: a piece of cheese is the set of sense impressions that we, under normal conditions, understand as a piece of cheese. The first step in Berkeley's immaterialism is thus a rejection of the idea that matter is something different from properties; the second step is an interpretation of the properties as sense impressions.

But do we not have to imagine the subject along with the sensory organs, on the one hand, and the material things on the other hand, so that the sense impressions from external things are captured by our sensory organs? No, says Berkeley. This entire epistemological model of *representative realism*[1] is based on a postulate of the existence of external material things. This is something that we, strictly speaking, cannot know anything about on the basis of the model itself, since the only thing we really know on the basis of this model is that we have different sense impressions. These sense impressions are the final, and only, basis of knowledge. And from this basis it is impossible to know anything about what caused this basis, namely, the so-called external material things.

But will this not mean that we can no longer distinguish between reality and illusion? No, says Berkeley. The sense impressions that appear regularly, and not by our will, represent reality. Those that appear irregularly, and perhaps by our will, are not to be trusted in that respect. We have regular sense impressions about what we call the *wall*, and we do not have these impressions by our own volition. We know that we will not get anywhere by trying to walk through the wall. This is a reality. However, we can, to a certain extent, summon up the idea of a leprechaun at will. This is not reality. Nor is a nightmare determined by our will: it appears irregularly, especially in relation to experiences we have had of corresponding things in other conditions. There is therefore no basis for saying that what we experience during a nightmare is real.

Therefore, Berkeley thinks that he can maintain the distinction between reality and illusion.[2] What do we mean when we talk about reality? Well, we mean that we have regular sense impressions that do not appear according to our will. This is all that we mean, and can mean, by the word *reality*. To add that such impressions originate from a nonsensible material substance is not to provide a better explanation, but only to create confusion with metaphysical constructions.

To say that something *exists* is the same as saying it is comprehended: *esse* is *percipi*. But does this mean that the wall disappears when I turn away and no longer perceive it? That the wall exists means that the wall is sensed (or comprehended) when we turn towards it, under normal conditions of sight. To exist is thus to be perceivable by a conscious being. That something exists does not, then, mean that it actually is perceived, but that, under normal conditions, it can be perceived. Put negatively: that which cannot be perceived does not exist.

SUBSTANCE OUT, GOD IN!

Berkeley did not think that existence depends on perception. He thought that the principle that *to be* is *to be perceived* implies that there is *someone* who perceives. The concept of perception is necessarily connected with the concept of subject (soul). There must exist someone who perceives. For this subject, it is true that to exist is *to perceive*; *esse* is equal to *perceiving*. This is where the human consciousness, the subject, comes in. But there is also a consciousness that embraces all reality, according to Berkeley, a consciousness that always perceives everything that is perceptible. This is God. God is thus that which sustains all things. Therefore, *esse* is equal to *percipi*: all things exist in so far as they are comprehended by God.

God is the being who secures the regularity, the ordering of experience, that is to say, of reality. The necessary connections in the events originate in God.

Berkeley's proof of God's existence is as follows. There are ideas (that is, sense impressions) that I can produce and dissipate by my own will, and there are ideas that are not subject to my will. The latter must have a cause outside myself. What can cause them? Not matter, because matter does not exist. Not other ideas, because ideas are passive. Hence, it must be another spirit (subject). This spirit must be powerful since it can cause all of this. And it must be good and wise since it can create such a regular order. This spirit is the Christian God.

Since God is not an idea, we cannot perceive God. God, in this sense, is not in the world, that is to say, not an idea among the ideas. But that there is a world, an ordered diversity of ideas, shows that there must be a God. God thus plays approximately the same role for Berkeley that matter does for Locke and thing in itself (*Ding an sich*) for Kant. God is the unperceived cause of all perceptions. God has a double role in regard to sense impressions. He is the cause of our sense impressions, and he himself perceives all sense impressions.

But what have we gained by substituting the notion of God for the philosophical conception of matter? The answer may lie in the notion that matter is dead, while God is creator, sustainer, and giver. To the notion that God is the cause of all sense impressions, we may object that this notion resembles Locke's theory of matter as the cause of all sense impressions. To the idea that God perceives all sense impressions, we may object that no one else can perceive our own sense impressions. There is something striking about the idea that something essentially private can be shared with others.

We have seen how Berkeley, from a critical development of empiricist epistemology, reaches a form of *idealism*, since he traces properties and existence back to the subject, and reaches *theism*, since God is really the One who sustains it all. Whether this is also an expression of *common sense* is, of course, another question. And Berkeley encounters some difficult problems; for example, that of how we perceive and comprehend *the same*, inasmuch as sense impressions are private and there are no external objects. Even if we say that God imbues us all, qualitatively, with the same sense impressions of a wall, there are, still two different sense impressions that you and I, respectively, have of 'the wall'. It is probably acceptable to common sense that two people who drink the same wine or smell the same rose each have their own sense impression, but it is hardly acceptable to claim that two people who see a wall, because they have different sense impressions, do not see the same wall.

Thus, from Berkeley's epistemological position, we end up with a dualism of forms of being: consciousness and impressions, that which comprehends and that which is comprehended. In this way, Berkeley accepts, as does Locke, that there are mental substances. And like Locke, Berkeley bases his system on both human subjects and God. But, in opposition to Locke, Berkeley decisively rejects the idea of an external, material substance. We will see that Hume develops an empiricism in which even the existence of mental substances is rejected. There are only *impressions* that remain.[3]

Berkeley criticizes the use of general concepts, arguing that to imagine something is to have a visual picture of it: we may, in this way, form representations of centaurs and leprechauns; that is, we can use sense impressions to create such imaginary combinations. These are combinations made from simple sense impressions, but in a way that is not credible. According to Berkeley, only those impressions that are simple, or that are combined as they regularly appear, can normally be conceived of as being credible. We can be cognizant of credible combinations by perceiving their stable and regular occurrences. But we *cannot* perceive *man*, *matter*, *life*, etc.; that is to say, we cannot perceive universal ideas.

Thus, Berkeley out of conceptual nominalism, rejects the philosophical conception of matter: matter is considered to be a universal concept, but we cannot form representations of universal concepts. Since only that exists that we can imagine, matter does not exist. We use words like *horse* and *human being* as abbreviations, to make speech easier. But using language in this way must not deceive us into believing that universal concepts such as those of *horse* and *house* exist. In Berkeley's theory of language, words refer to sense impressions. The sense impressions are the word's meaning. The word *apple* refers to the sense impressions that signify apple; that is, the meaning of the word *apple* is the bundle of sensory impressions that we have of the thing. The word *matter* is meaningless since it does not refer to such sense impressions.

HUME – EMPIRICISM AS CRITICISM

Life. David Hume (1711–1776) lived during the Enlightenment as a contemporary of Voltaire and Rousseau. Hume developed his basic philosophical ideas early. His A Treatise of Human Nature *was published when he was 28 years of age. Hume had expected a great stir to follow its publication, but, at first, little interest was shown. However, Hume's philosophy eventually came to awaken the greatest interest, and today he is considered one of the foremost empiricists. Hume's most important philosophical works are* A Treatise of Human Nature *(1739),* Essays Moral and Political *(1741), and* An Enquiry Concerning Human Understanding *(1749). He also wrote a multivolume* History of Great Britain *(1754–62).*

For Thomas Aquinas, natural law theory was anchored in an objective order created by God. For Locke, natural law theory was related to man as the acting subject; the inviolable rights are those of the individual. Throughout the eighteenth century, natural law theory was attacked by the adherents of both Romanticism and empiricism. Adherents of Romanticism attacked the universal aspect of natural law theory, claiming that *all* peoples have unique laws that are determined by the special historical development that they have undergone. Empiricists attacked natural law theory through an epistemological analysis whereby the empiricists concluded that we cannot have the normative insight that natural law theory presupposes.

EMPIRICIST EPISTEMOLOGY – 'IDEAS' AND 'IMPRESSIONS'

The philosophers of the Enlightenment appealed to reason. Reason was the weapon that was to defeat irrational traditions and prejudices. But at the same time, this conception of reason was anything but clear. The Scot David Hume was an empiricist, in an epistemological sense. For him, there were only two kinds of knowledge: that founded on experience, ultimately, sense perception, and that founded on conventionally designed rules about the relationships between concepts, such as we find in mathematics and logic, according to the empiricist interpretation. We cannot have knowledge that goes beyond these two kinds of cognition. We cannot have knowledge about what we cannot experience, such as God or objective norms.

This empiricist epistemology had important implications not only for theology and ethics, but also for the experiential sciences. According to this theory, there is no core within the natural sciences, such as a law of causality, that is above all possible doubt. This was one of the points in Hume's theory to which Kant reacted. We will later see how Kant attempted to refute Hume's position, but here we will sketch the argument on which Hume based his position. First, we will examine Hume's version of empiricism as a theory of knowledge, which is close to what we called radical empiricism in our discussion of John Locke.[4]

On the question of the origin of knowledge, Hume makes a distinction between what he calls 'impressions' and 'ideas'. *Impressions* are strong and vivid perceptions, including immediate sense perceptions, such as sights and sounds. But direct psychological experiences, like hate or joy, are also impressions. Impressions thus embrace both external and internal perceptions. Hume conceives *ideas* as mental images that are based on those immediate sense perceptions, or *impressions*. Ideas are thus based on impressions, and the relationship between *impressions* and *ideas* is such that ideas cannot arise without preceding impressions.[5]

The sense *impressions* that we receive are combined and ordered by us so that they create our various *ideas*. Ideas in this sense can be everything from the idea of a house to the idea of a fundamental law, or the idea of a geometric pattern.[6] All such ideas ultimately arise from internal and external impressions. The boundaries of knowledge are found between the ideas that can be traced back to such impressions and those that cannot. This is the distinction between what does and does not represent knowledge. The question, so to speak, is whether the ideas have their 'pedigree' in order; that is, whether it is possible to trace all the elements of an idea back to internal and external impressions. Where it is not possible to do so, we have inappropriate ideas. Here, epistemology becomes a critique of knowledge since it rejects such ideas as being unacceptable and untenable. Hume is radical in his critique of knowledge: on this basis – as we shall see – he rejects the notion of a material substance (in keeping with Berkeley), as well as the notion of a spiritual substance, including the notion of God (in conflict with Berkeley), and he attacks the concept of causality. It is against this background that Hume attacks metaphysics in his interpretation of natural science and mathematics: for him, mathematical ideas reveal nothing about reality. They only illuminate the relationship between concepts. Thus, they can be said to be 'analytic'. Hence, it is not a question of a possible correspondence with internal or external impressions, but only of logical relations between concepts. (Note that this is a nominalist interpretation of mathematical concepts, in contrast to realistic or Platonic interpretations; cf. Ch. 6, The problem of universals . . .) The ideas of the experiential sciences, on the other hand, can in principle be traced back to such impressions. These ideas may thus be said to be 'synthetic' in the sense that they do reveal something about reality. In these cases, this process of tracing ideas back to impressions will largely be successful, but not always, as we will see when we discuss Hume's attack on the concept of causality in the next paragraph.

It is claimed that metaphysical ideas do reveal aspects of reality, although they cannot be traced back only to internal and external impressions. These ideas are therefore liable to the empiricist critique of knowledge. Hence Hume considers the ideas of a material substance and a spiritual substance to be examples of such metaphysical illusions. Hume follows Berkeley in his attack on the idea of a material substance: our sense impressions derive only from the various sensible properties. We do not sense any material substance that supposedly lies behind these sense impressions. For example, we experience this table, in the sense that we have diverse visual impressions that can be supplemented with other sense impressions if we touch it, strike it, etc. But we do not have sense impressions of 'something' that would be the 'carrier' of these impressions. It is true that all such sense impressions appear in constant groups, in the sense that they appear regularly in definite associations. We call such stable groups of impressions a table, or chair, and so on. This is also sufficient. Nor do we have impressions of any underlying material substance 'behind' these groups of properties, or need to postulate such a substance. Therefore, the idea of a material substance is an untenable metaphysical idea.

Hume has a similar argument against the idea of a spiritual or mental substance: we have access only to internal impressions. These often appear in definite, more stable associations. Hence, we talk about an ego that lies 'behind' impressions and unites them. But really, this ego is also a metaphysical illusion since we cannot have internal impressions of any such substance, behind these impressions of various properties and associations. Nor is it necessary to postulate any such thing. It is enough to keep to these properties in their various associations. The idea of an underlying ego is grounded in an association of properties that consistently appear together. That is all.

THE EMPIRICIST CRITIQUE OF KNOWLEDGE – THE NOTION OF CAUSALITY

In the light of this discussion of Hume's empiricist epistemology we will take a closer look at his attack on the concept of causality. It might be claimed that when we have observed innumerable times how billiard balls affect each other by mechanical forces, we may, from this experience, *know* how the balls will act in the future. We can detect laws of causal connections, as about what happens on a level surface when ball *A*, having this or that velocity and mass, strikes ball *B*, having this or that velocity and mass. The laws of the connection between cause and effect tell us what effect *necessarily* will take place, if some cause occurs. Hume discusses viewpoints like these and asks, on the basis of his *empiricist* theory of knowledge, whether we can really *know* such causal laws. When we talk about *causes*, says Hume, we think:

1   that something follows something else
2   that there is contact between two phenomena
3   that what happens after this contact happens necessarily.

In other words, *the concept of cause*, according to Hume, has the following characteristics:

1   succession
2   contact
3   necessity.

But how do we *know* this? What gives us this idea? According to empiricist epistemology, knowledge is only that which is rooted in experience. A *succession* of events can be *seen*; that is to say, the idea of succession is *knowledge* because this idea is based on experience. *Contact*, as between ball *A* and ball *B*, can also be *seen*. Here too, we have knowledge. Moreover, we can *see* that succession and contact are repeatable, time and time again, when we continually carry out new attempts. In other words, we have knowledge of a *constant repetition*. So far so good. But how do we *know* that what happens, happens by *necessity* (when one ball strikes another ball)? What experience tells us that this is *necessary*? Can we *see* the necessity? How could we see? As a pink gleam? Obviously not. Can we *hear* the necessity? For example, as a low buzzing sound? Of course not. Nor is necessity anything that we can feel or smell, or in any other way have simple sense impressions of. Hence we cannot have knowledge of necessity at all.

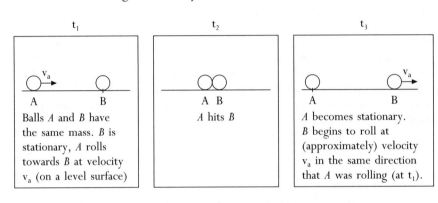

We may object that, although we may not have knowledge from simple sense impressions of the necessity in the relationship between cause and effect, we may still gain knowledge of this necessity through induction: when a ball rolling on a level surface strikes another ball (with the same mass) that is stationary, we have always observed that the moving ball becomes stationary, and that the ball that was stationary begins to move with the same velocity as the first ball. We can repeat this experience and observe this example of a causal connection many times. Therefore, we infer inductively that this will always happen: that it must always be the case. That is to say, this causal connection happens by necessity, and we *know*, therefore, that identical 'collisions' in the future will also have the same effect. Hume's answer is simple: we *know* only what we have experienced. But we have not experienced all cases in the past and present, and we have no experience of the future. Therefore, we cannot say that we *know* that something will happen in the future.

It is important to keep in mind what Hume says and what he does not say. Hume does not claim that there is not a necessary connection between cause and effect, but only that we cannot *know* anything about such a possible necessity. In other words, Hume's thesis is epistemological, not ontological. Moreover, he does not say that we should not expect the balls to act in the same way in the future as they have up to the present. Hume says only that we cannot know this, in his own sense of the word *know*. Hume would, of course, not think it wise for us to jump from the Eiffel Tower in the hope that we will not hurtle to the ground as always previously has happened, but float gently down on the other side of the Seine! ('We do not *know* that we will fall to our death in the *future* just because that has been the case *until now*.') Hume's point is *epistemological*: we must distinguish between different kinds of knowledge.

1 *Direct experience*. We have knowledge of what we experience directly, or have experienced directly. But such a particular experience does not tell us that causal connections *must* come into force. And this kind of experience bears no relation to the *future*.
2 *Induction*. If, on the basis of a finite number of direct experiences, we claim that something must happen in the future, we are saying *more* than we can really *know*.

But this does *not* mean that we are not wise in expecting it to happen.

Hume found it crucial to distinguish sharply between logical and experiential insight. If we say 'A > B and B > C, then A > C', we know with complete certainty that it must be so. It is logically necessary that 'A > C', given the premises and the common rules of inference.[7] Logical insight is thus 100 per cent certain. This is not so with experiential knowledge. It is, in a sense, imaginable that ball *A* striking ball *B* (under the same initial conditions) will occasionally lead to different results – for example, that ball *B* bounces straight up instead of starting to roll across the surface[8] – and it is imaginable that the balls might behave differently in the future than they have up to now. It is also imaginable that new experiences will show that previous observations were erroneous.

Our conclusion is as follows. Logical knowledge is 100 per cent certain, but it does not tell us anything about the world. Experiential knowledge tells us something about the world, but without being 100 per cent certain.

In summary, for Hume, there are *only* these two forms of knowledge:

1 logical knowledge, which is about the relationship between concepts (not about the world)
2 experiential knowledge, which is based on simple sense impressions (internal and external).

And, according to Hume, the concept of causality is composed of the following components:

1 succession ⎫
2 contact   ⎬ repetition
3 necessity ⎭

If this conception of causality is to represent knowledge of the world, *all* of its components must stem from experience. This does not turn out to be the case for point

3 in the diagram, necessity. The idea of necessity cannot stem from simple sense impressions and an inductive inference — for example, that the future will be like the observed past — does not give us knowledge in a genuine sense.

For Hume, therefore, the next question is how we can have a conception of causality that contains a component that does not represent knowledge in an empiricist sense. The answer is finally psychological: when events happen in the same way again and again, we form *expectations* that the same process will happen in the future as well. It is this expectation by us that creates the idea of a necessity in reference to causal connections.[9] We see in this way how Hume's epistemology opposes the idea that the experiential sciences give us a 100 per cent certain insight into the universal laws that must apply in the future as well as in the past: there is, according to Hume, no reason, no rational intuition, that gives us access to necessary and unchangeable principles in nature — just as there is no reason that gives us access to universal moral norms. We may conclude that what we know about causal relationships is based on experience (sense perception). From this source of knowledge, we cannot *know* that causal connections happen with necessity, because we do not perceive the 'necessity'. Nor can we know (that is, know with certainty) whether observed conditions in the past will also apply in the future.

Hume, however, does not leave us with this critical empiricist analysis of the concepts of cause and reason. In keeping with the notion that our expectations lead to our ideas that events happen necessarily, Hume emphasizes what he calls *natural belief*. By virtue of natural belief, we order the world and the events around us in such a way that we can get along quite well in life — even if reason and what we, in a strict sense, can know are not as much help as many earlier philosophers thought. Hume's notion of common practical knowledge, or natural belief, is a basic notion that recurs both in his theory of knowledge and in his moral philosophy and political theory (in terms of common impartial feelings and sympathy). Here it is important to add that Hume, as a philosopher in the eighteenth century, has a positive view of scientific research and progress. Although, in his epistemology, he rejects the notion that absolutely certain results are achievable, he emphasizes the value of a stepwise and self-correcting progression in the experiential sciences.[10]

MORAL PHILOSOPHY – THE DISTINCTION BETWEEN 'IS' AND 'OUGHT'

Since the notion of natural rights rests on the idea of certain universally valid norms or values, Hume, as an empiricist, denies that the notion of natural rights represents knowledge: values and norms are not expressions of knowledge, but of feelings, and feelings can be neither true nor false. We may reconstruct Hume's point as follows: we witness a morally despicable action, such as a murder. We see the murderer lift the knife. We see the knife penetrate the victim. We hear a scream. We experience all of this. We see it or hear it. And when we report this, what we say is true, as long as we do not deliberately lie. We may also, in good faith, say something that is false because our senses have deceived us, or because we have witnessed a fictitious murder, as in a film set, without knowing it. The point here is that we can use the concepts of truth or falsehood. What we are talking about is something that applies, or could apply, to an action of this kind. But, according to

Hume, we cannot in the same way experience the action as being morally repugnant. The aspect of the action that we consider morally repugnant is not a property of the action, along the same lines as the properties we just mentioned. Just as necessity is nothing that we experience when ball A strikes ball B, but, rather, something that is grounded in our expectations, so an action's being morally repugnant is not anything in the event itself, such as the murder, but something within us. The notion of moral repugnance is grounded in our feelings about the case. We feel a moral repugnance. The action as perceived is neither moral nor immoral. Moral repugnance is nothing that we sense. It is connected with our feelings. We experience actions and attitudes as being morally good or bad, and we think that certain things should be done and that other things should not be done. All that has to do with such moral evaluations, norms, and values arises out of our feelings, not out of the actions we experience directly.

To take a less extreme example, if we say 'Paul has blond hair', we can determine whether this statement is true or false by *looking at* Paul's hair. But if we say 'Paul ought do his homework', what should we look at to find out whether the statement is true or false? There is nothing we can *look at* to determine the truth or falsehood of this question. Since empiricism claims that we can know something only via experience, that is, sense experience, we can never confirm or disconfirm the latter statement. (However, a rationalist, like Plato, would claim that by rational intuition we can know whether certain ethical and political statements are true or false.)

Schematically, we can express the opposition as follows. On the one hand, we have *is*-statements, or descriptive statements, such as 'Paul has blond hair'. These statements may be true or false. On the other hand, we have *ought*-statements, or normative statements, such as 'Paul ought to do his homework'. These statements can be neither true nor false because they do not claim something about reality or about concepts. Such statements express feelings. And feelings, in opposition to reason, *motivate* us to action.

The normative – goals, values, norms – can be neither true nor false. The question of whether a statement is true or false is determined by an experientially based use of reason, as in the empirical sciences. But this experientially based use of reason, here called 'reason', cannot evaluate goals, values, or norms. That is to say, 'reason' in this sense can of course evaluate what *means* will best lead to a given goal, and what we ought to do or ought not to do in order to attain the goal. And 'reason' can, in principle, tell us whether a goal is realizable or not.[11] Of course, 'reason' can also, in certain instances, show us that we are pursuing internally conflicting goals. But the experientially based use of reason *cannot* tell us what basic goals and values we ought to pursue, since these normative questions fall outside the boundaries of 'reason', of the experientially based use of reason. These normative questions can be neither true nor false. Norms and values are ultimately grounded in feelings, not in reason. This distinction between the descriptive and the normative, between reason and feelings, is what Hume refers to when, for example, he says, ''Tis not contrary to reason for me to prefer the destruction of the whole world to the scratching of my finger.'[12]

However, Hume does not think that everything is 'subjective and relative' since the basic goals and values are grounded in feelings. Here he distinguishes himself from certain Sophists who also claimed that the normative is grounded in the emotions, but who, from this, drew relativistic and sceptical conclusions: they thought that feelings vary from person to person, and that the normative could therefore not be considered universal. Hume, on the contrary, relies on a certain common basis for the normative, although the normative is grounded in the emotions: we can take an impartial and disinterested position on what is taking place, and when we do so, we will all have the same feelings towards a particular action. And this common feeling of disgust or admiration entails a universal agreement on normative questions. Thus:

1   we take an *impartial* position
2   we will *all* then have the *same* feeling towards the action
3   from this feeling, we will make a *correct* evaluation.[13]

PRACTICAL CONFIDENCE AND CONVENTIONS

Hume thinks that we have emotional reactions not only to actions, but also to the attitudes of the person who is acting. From observing the pattern of the particular actions of a person, we form expectations of how this person will act in new situations. This is how we form moral evaluations of other people,[14] and views of their moral character. Therefore, Hume allows that we can speak morally not only about actions, but also about persons and their character.

Hume describes notions not only of natural sympathy and antipathy, but also of what we could call culturally determined patterns of reaction, those patterns that we, while growing up, learn through the traditions and mores of our culture. Virtues like justice and honesty are thus tied to inherited conventions in society. These are virtues we learn through socialization, and that prompt us to react emotionally. They are not something that we think up and then decide to follow in cooperation with others.[15]

There are pleasant and unpleasant feelings. The pleasant feelings are, for Hume, connected to what is *useful to us*, what stimulates us to act and to survive. Hence, there is a utilitarian component in Hume's moral philosophy (cf. Bentham and Mill): the social order is good and just when it promotes general welfare and secures life and well-being.

Hume emphasizes both the natural emotions and the learned conventions that imbue us with emotional patterns of reaction. Hume, like Edmund Burke, opposes the more rationalistic moral conceptions such as the theory of the social contract (as expounded, for example, by Hobbes and Locke). Conventions, confidence in natural emotions, and learned patterns of reaction are, for Hume, more basic than contracts and agreements. Laws, institutions, and governments are useful for people who live in society. Their legitimacy is grounded in our emotional loyalty, which, again, is an indication that we, through the learned conventions, find them useful.

The distinction between descriptive and normative statements, between 'is' and 'ought', has a practical impact: it means, for instance, that we can never deduce normative statements from descriptive premises alone. The conclusion in the statement, 'The prime minister's plan will increase the gross national product by 0.5 per cent; therefore, his plan ought to be approved', is logically inadequate. We cannot say '*therefore* . . . ought to' without having normative statements in the premises; for example:

a   The prime minister's plan will increase the gross national product by 0.5 per cent.
b   Plans that increase the gross national product ought to be approved.
c   *Therefore*, the prime minister's plan ought to be approved.

Analyses in which we ask about the various ways to *confirm* or *disconfirm* statements are important if we want to take a stand on what is being said. An insight into methods of confirmation and thus into classification of statements is not only of theoretical interest. In the above example, a normative statement is concealed in the premises. Since, today, there are often different groups of experts who have the authority to decide to what extent descriptive statements (such as *a*) are true or false, concealment of the normative statement in the premises (as in *b*) would be the same as undermining the right of the people to make decisions in normative questions. That is to say, the result restricts democracy in favour of the power of the experts. The distinction between 'is' and 'ought', between facts decided by experts, and goals and values that are decided by all of us, is thus an important point in the defence of democracy. And there is, without a doubt, something correct in this distinction: if I have a bottle of liquid, I can ask a scientist to determine whether it contains water, spirits, or acid – and whether I, by drinking the contents, will have my thirst quenched, become drunk, or die. But if I ask whether I *ought to* drink the contents, the scientist *qua* scientist cannot give me an answer, for it depends on what I *want* to achieve, and what I *ought* to want to achieve.

Hume's political theory, like his moral philosophy, appeals to people's basic attitudes and feelings, as he conceives them: all people have an ability to empathize, a sympathy for their fellows, and this empathy is the foundation of an ordered community, of society. Therefore, society is not based on a contract, but on a basic convention – or, more correctly, a convention passed not by resolution, but by the immediate experience of common feelings and interests. Rules and laws – and conventions in a more superficial sense – arise out of this basic feeling of community. Hume emphasizes the importance of stability, order, and authority so strongly that his political theory acquires a conservative tone: a liberal, common-sense British conservatism, with a penchant for liberty and reforms, on the basis of a historically inherited social order that is ultimately based on compassion.

It is significant that Hume gives feelings, habits and conventions the place in ethics and politics that he takes from reason. This was to be one of Kant's complaints in his treatment of Hume's critique of reason. But, at the same time, these were ideas that Romanticism and the conservative attitude towards the Enlightenment took hold of: in politics and ethics, conventions, habits, and feelings are more important than cold reason; feelings and tradition take precedence over reason, as in Edmund Burke. Hume's standpoint, that conventions are good when they provide stability and order, is reminiscent of a conservative version of utilitarianism: conventions are good because they are useful.

In his theory of knowledge, as in his theory of values, Hume appeals to common, practical knowledge, or natural belief; to natural confidence, and common reactions and attitudes. This basis of appeal is not infallible, but it is what we have, and, according to Hume, that is good enough.

EMPIRICISM AND RATIONALISM – LINES OF CONFLICT

Finally, we shall briefly discuss some main points of the two epistemological positions, empiricism and rationalism. The epistemological position of rationalism is roughly characterized by the view that we have *two kinds of knowledge*: in addition to the *experience* of particular phenomena in the world and in our inner being, we can obtain *rational insight* into essential properties in terms of universally valid truths. Rationalism and empiricism conflict especially on this kind of insight. The rationalists[16] claim that by *rational intuition* we gain insight into universally valid truths concerning (for example) God, human nature, and morality. The empiricists[17] deny that there is a rational intuition which gives us such knowledge. They hold the epistemological view that we gain knowledge only by *experience* – which they ultimately view as sense experience. In addition, we gain insight by analyses of concepts and deduction, as in logic and mathematics. But neither of these two kinds of insight teaches us anything about the essential properties.

The rationalists, we may say, think that we can recognize reality by means of concepts alone, while the empiricists trace knowledge of reality back to experience: by clarifying concepts of different kinds, like freedom, interaction, virtue, the good, or God, we gain insight into something real, according to the rationalists. The matter becomes complex since the empiricists and the rationalists understand the various forms of knowledge somewhat differently. Here we will indicate only two different interpretations of the concept of experience: experience can be interpreted as a passive process of perception in which the subject is supplied with simple impressions of external things. The subject then combines these impressions according to whether they have developed together or not, according to likeness and contrast, and so on, so that knowledge of these things can be established (cf. the empiricists). Or experience may be interpreted as something that is already structured by the human constitution (cf. Kant) or by human interests and activities (cf. Marx and Habermas).

The insights of mathematics and logic are also understood differently. For Plato, the conceptual realist, mathematical insight refers to something (to the greatest degree) existing: the mathematical ideas. However, mathematics can also be interpreted as a man-made game in which we have relations between concepts of the posited rules and abstracted premises, but without mathematics being considered to represent something that exists objectively (the nominalistic interpretation).

Here we have indicated some ways that experience and mathematical insight can be construed. This may be sufficient to show that it is not only in their view of rational intuition that empiricists and rationalists differ. Furthermore, there are different consequences of empiricism and rationalism. A rational intuition, for example, permits insight into normative questions. A purely empiricist point of view denies that knowledge exists in normative questions. Thus, everyone – empiricists and rationalists – agrees that we can have knowledge of normative questions in the sense that we can know that this or that person maintains that this or that norm is correct. The disagreement is in the question of whether we can have normative insight in the sense that we can know that this or that norm is correct.

Being an empiricist is not the same as being a scientist who works empirically. An empiricist maintains empiricism as a philosophical (epistemological) viewpoint. An empirical scientist can just as well be a rationalist as an empiricist, according to the way the terms are defined here.

Against the background of the new natural sciences, we have seen how the question of the origin of knowledge arose, and we have mentioned two types of answers – the rationalist and the empiricist – with somewhat different implications. But more needs to be said about the arguments *for and against* these two positions.

Empiricism may be seen as a reaction to rationalism, the argument behind this reaction being that the use of rational intuition has not led to the *same* results for the various rationalists, such as Descartes, Spinoza, and Leibniz. In other words, the empiricists seized on the rationalists' own *disagreement* about what is intuitively rational. And to *what* do we then appeal? A *new* rational intuition? Hence, say the critics of rationalism, it is not possible to gain true insight by rational intuition.

This argument has much in its favour. But the rationalists can reply to the empiricists that the empiricist thesis is itself not meant to be an *analytic* truth that does not reveal anything about reality of the kind expressed in the statement 'a bachelor is an unmarried man'. But is the empiricist thesis, that all knowledge stems from experience, then *itself* a truth of *experience*?[18] On what kind of experience could this thesis possibly be based? It seems clear that the empiricist thesis is not itself a truth of experience, but a thesis *about* all truths of experience and about the distinction between meaningful and meaningless statements. The empiricist thesis therefore cannot belong to either of the two types of insight that empiricism accepts, namely analytic truth and empirical truth. This means that the empiricist thesis indirectly declares itself to be impossible. Put another way: the empiricist thesis can offer true insight only if there is a rational intuition that empiricism is correct, but such an intuition is denied by empiricism. If the empiricists can accuse the rationalists of being dogmatic in defence of a questionable doctrine – 'the rationalists themselves disagree about what is intuitively rational' – the rationalists can accuse the empiricists of undermining themselves – 'the empiricist thesis renders empiricism impossible'.

There are also other forms of opposition between the rationalists and the empiricists. Both movements were seeking *clarity*, but they held different views about what clarity is. The rationalists sought that which is 'clear' in the sense of 'self-evident'. This is where rational intuition comes in: when something appears completely clear, as self-evident for this intuition, what this intuition is telling us is true.

The empiricists sought what is 'clear' in the sense of 'observable', 'empirically testable', and in the sense of 'in keeping with normal linguistic use'.[19] They were sceptical of what is said to be clear in the sense of self-evident. For the empiricists, the task was to elucidate language in order to, among other things, present the concepts in such a way that they can be tested by experience.

The rationalists and the empiricists each contributed in their own way to stimulating the awareness of clarity – an impulse that was influential during the Enlightenment in the eighteenth century.

QUESTIONS

Discuss Berkeley's empiricist idealism (immaterialism).

Explain Hume's epistemological (empiricist) critique of the concept of causality.

Give a summary of the main points of Hume's philosophy. Comment on this statement: 'Hume gives feelings precedence over reason'.

SUGGESTIONS FOR FURTHER READING

PRIMARY LITERATURE

Berkeley, George, *A Treatise Concerning the Principles of Human Knowledge*, edited with an introduction by G. J. Warnuk, London, 1967.
Hume, David, *An Enquiry Concerning Human Understanding*, Oxford, 1963.
Hume, David, *A Treatise of Human Nature*, edited by Ernest C. Mossner, Harmondsworth, 1985.
Hume, David, *Dialogues Concerning Natural Religion*, edited by N. Kemp Smith, Edinburgh, 1947.
Hume, David, *An Enquiry Concerning the Principles of Morals*, edited by L. A. Selby-Bigge, Oxford, 1894.

SECONDARY LITERATURE

Thomson, J. F., 'Berkeley', in *A Critical History of Western Philosophy*, edited by D. J. O'Connor, NewYork/London, 1965.
Kemp Smith, N., *The Philosophy of David Hume*, London, 1941.
Price, H. H., *Hume's Theory of the External World*, Oxford, 1940.
Stewart, J. B., *The Moral and Political Philosophy of David Hume*, New York, 1963.

NOTES

1 *Realism*: external things exist, and they are *presented* to the subject by sense impressions that represent the things.
2 Berkeley's distinction between reality and imagination rests on a distinction between ideas that are clear and distinct and those that are not, and between ideas that are not subject to our will and those that are. Strong and distinct ideas that are lively and well ordered, and that are, moreover not subject to our will, represent reality. To *comprehend*, to perceive – to have ideas – embraces, for Berkeley, both sensing and thinking, and thinking both as *conceptualizing* and as having *'pictorial' notions*. We might object that to sense a mouse is something different from imagining a mouse. And imagining a circle, in the sense that we have a mental image of a circle, is something different from thinking of the concept of circle.
3 The debate concerning immediate impressions and the problem of the external world has continued up to our day; for instance, we find it in G. E. Moore, A. J. Ayer, and others. *One* statement of the problem is as follows. It is usual to claim that empirical statements cannot be absolutely certain (cf., for example, Descartes' doubt). If we are eager to find observation statements that are *absolutely* certain, it is tempting to say that statements limited to our immediate experience fulfil this requirement. When we perceive a red surface, and state our perception of this red surface, the statement is absolutely certain. We have then not said that there is something that *is* red, and that others would also be able to sense. This *immediate sense impression*, without requiring more than that it is perceived here and now by a person, is often called a *sense datum*. But such sense data exist only for the perceiving

subject. With what right can we talk about external objects? The problems of sense data thus lead to the problems of Berkeley's idealistic empiricism: can we have cognition of an external world, and about other subjects? Is it meaningful to talk about anything external, beyond sense data?

4 Ch. 11, Epistemology . . . Bluntly stated, this empiricism claims that *knowledge* is based only on *experience*, that *experience* is to be understood as *sensation* (sense perception), and that *sensation* is to be conceived as ultimately consisting of *simple sense impressions*.

5 We therefore have the following method: 'When we entertain . . . any suspicion that a philosophical term is employed without any meaning . . . we need but enquire, *from what impression is that supposed idea derived?*' An Enquiry Concerning Human Understanding, Section II, 'Of the Origin of Ideas', 17.

6 Hume says that 'different ideas are connected together' by 'the principles of association'. Ibid., 'Of the Association of Ideas', 19.

7 I.e. 'if A is greater than B, and B is greater than C, A is greater than C'.

8 But if we imagine the two balls, A and B, as solid bodies, and thus understand that they occupy a definite space that no other solid bodies can fill (without the balls being deformed), we can probably say that we know that an impact will occur when we slowly push one ball in the direction of the other. At least, we know this in the sense that we know that certain things will *not* happen: for example, the ball that we push forward will not roll right through the ball that is stationary, like a shadow passing through another.

9 Hume says that 'the mind is carried by a *customary transition*, from the appearance of one to the belief of the other'. An Enquiry Concerning Human Understanding, Section VIII, 'Of Liberty and Necessity', 71.

10 Cf. Popper's view that scientific progress is both desirable and possible, namely, as a fallible, but self-correcting process (Ch. 26).

11 Notice that the word *reason* is ambiguous here: Hume attacks the rationalistic understanding of reason, but at the same time, he talks about reason in another sense, similar to an experientially based use of reason.

12 *Treatise of Human Nature*, Book II, Section III, p. 463.

13 The following, supplementary comments may be in order. Hume started with feelings. And *feelings* are, to begin with, neither rational nor irrational. Of course, feelings may also be inappropriate or unreasonable, as when we have misunderstood the situation and reacted emotionally to something that, on closer examination, turns out to have been a misapprehension – for example, we react with rage at a fictitious murder because we do not realize that we have been watching a film being shot, and not a real murder – or when we are mentally ill, and respond with joy and laughter when other people experience great pain. In the first instance, we have misunderstood reality; in the second instance, we are not able to react normally and sanely. In both instances, the feelings are unreasonable or inappropriate.

14 Cf. how Hume, in his epistemology, understands the transition from observation of particular events to expectations of necessary causal connections.

15 Many of Hume's points are pursued in modern 'communitarian' political theory; see, for example, Michael Sandel (ed.), *Liberalism and its Critics*, Oxford, 1984.

16 Latin: *ratio*, 'reason', hence *rationalism*.

17 Greek: *empiri*, 'experience', hence *empiricism*.

18 See Arne Næss, 'Reflections about Total Views', *Philosophy and Phenomenological Research, 25*, pp. 16–29, 1964.

19 Cf. 'normal linguistic use' as a basis for philosophical analysis and critique in modern analytic philosophy (*ordinary language philosophy*).

13 The Enlightenment – reason and progress

MODERNIZATION AND SCIENCE

In the last half of the seventeenth century, Britain strongly influenced the political debate. But after the constitutional monarchy was established, the theoretical debate subsided in Britain. Energy was expended on concrete political activity – domestic activity, for political reforms, and foreign activity to build up the empire. In the first half of the eighteenth century, the smouldering political debate was fanned to a flame in France. Political theory in the eighteenth century was, to a great degree, marked by the French philosophers of the Enlightenment.

Under Louis XIV (1638–1715), the absolute monarchy was firmly established in France: the national assembly was dissolved; the noblemen were, to a great degree, reduced to civil servants and courtiers of the king; and the government became centralized. But Louis XIV finally was overtaken by political difficulties at the end of his reign, and in the wake of this, political debate developed. Political discussion in France was awakened as people reacted against the government's mismanagement. They criticized absolutism for not being sufficiently effective and rational. But these critics did not demand another form of government. They wanted a more enlightened and effective absolute monarchy. At that time, France did not have viable institutions dating from before the absolute monarchy that could 'sustain the criticism'. It was thus difficult to attain moderation and to make the government more effective with the help of relatively representative institutions, like the British parliament. A change had to come in the form of a political upheaval. This upheaval came in 1789 with the French Revolution.

The French did not only lack political institutions. The tradition of political theory had been largely severed. As a result, the French, at the beginning of the eighteenth century, imported British ideas on a grand scale. The ideals were Locke and Newton – the new liberalism and the new science. The French thinkers of the Enlightenment took the British form of government as their model. The French intelligentsia were Anglophiles ('admirers of the English'). Voltaire visited Britain in the 1720s, and Montesquieu came in the 1730s.

The Enlightenment in the eighteenth century was thus connected with social changes and with scientific progress: important scientific societies, like the Royal Society in Britain, were established already by the middle of the seventeenth century. Simultaneously, scientific journals and other publications promoting enlightenment appeared. Large collections of works on all aspects of the knowledge of the day were published (such as the French *Encyclopédie*). There was a corresponding modernization of universities throughout the eighteenth century, especially the German universities at the end of this period.[1] There was a renewal of academic development in the universities, where, among other subjects, the humanistic disciplines were developing most markedly (cf. Ch. 16). By the end of the century, a new intellectual era had emerged. As the twentieth century approached, the scientization of society set in with increasing strength – not only in business and administration, but also in ideas and attitudes. In spite of the many and always changing opposing forces, the programme of the Enlightenment continued to move forward.

The political debate in France during the eighteenth century had its source in the literary salons of the urban middle class. In this elegant setting politics, philosophy, and literature easily mingled. This debate, perhaps, did not lead to much that was new and original. It was largely a matter of old ideas being applied to new contexts. But when old ideas are thus applied, they often acquire a different implication. Here, too, British political thought, which at this time was rather conservative in Britain itself, functioned as a critique of society under the absolute monarchy of France. Thus, the idea of a natural law that was above the king, and that ascribed certain inviolable rights to the individual, served stability and social conservatism in Britain. But in the context of French absolutism, this idea functioned as a critique of the regime. And while it was meaningful to talk about such rights in Britain – because they existed there – the idea of such rights became abstract, speculative, and removed from reality in the French setting. The French imported Locke's concept of human rights without having the practical political experience of the British. The notion of human rights was simultaneously radical, an attack on the absolute monarchy, and speculative, without a concrete political anchoring. The French version of the British ideas was often bitter and critical – not marked by the British mixture of down-to-earth conservatism and common sense reformism.

The bitter tone was also connected to the fact that class differences in France were more irreconcilable than in Britain. The clerics owned one-fifth of the land and had certain privileges. The nobility was also privileged, although they had less political power than they had had previously. At the same time, the bourgeoisie was more influential than in Britain. The powerful French merchants felt that they pulled the weight for the others: the nobility and the priesthood were parasitic and privileged, and the power of the king was ineffective. The leading critics came from this upper bourgeoisie. And the ideological conflict was the notion of human rights and liberalism (Locke) in opposition to the absolute monarchy and the traditional privileges of the nobility. Moreover, natural science (Newton) was opposed to religion and the power of the priests. The philosophers of the Enlightenment opposed *reason to tradition*, and, by means of reason, hoped to achieve happiness and progress in the struggle against privileges and ignorance.

The period of the Enlightenment was thus marked by progressive optimism within the expanding middle class: a newly awakened confidence in reason and in man. There was a secularized Messianism, in which reason supplanted the Gospel. By the aid of reason, man would now uncover the innermost essence of reality and achieve material progress. Man would gradually become autonomous, dispensing with groundless authority and theological tutelage. Thought was liberated because man felt himself to be self-governed and independent of revelation and tradition. Atheism became fashionable.

But it soon turned out to be more difficult to realize the expected progress than the French Enlightenment philosophers of the eighteenth century had thought. It is true that the Enlightenment philosophers seemed to be correct when they claimed that reason (science) might lead to great material progress, but their conception of reason was far too ambiguous; it included logical, empirical, and philosophical knowledge, and both descriptive and normative insight, without considering the political difficulties in realizing this progress.

Fairly simplified, the following were the basic elements of the philosophy of the Enlightenment: man is good by nature. The goal of human life is well-being in this world, not blessedness in the next. This goal can be achieved by man alone through science (knowledge is power). The greatest obstacles in reaching this goal are ignorance, superstition, and intolerance. To overcome these obstacles, we need enlightenment (not revolution). Through more enlightenment, man automatically becomes more moral. Therefore, through enlightenment, the world will move forward.

Furthermore, we can formulate the following points:

1   Reason is possessed by *all* (not just the initiated, that is, the privileged).
2   Natural law secures the individual's rights (against privileges and against tyranny).
3   The moral theory of enlightened self-interest holds that we should seek the best for ourselves.
4   Sociologically, there is a harmony of self-interests: to fight for our own interest is to contribute to *everyone's* well-being.
5   An ideal state secures property rights and individual liberty and is efficient (state-protected private capitalism, nationally; protectionism and colonization, internationally).

The first two points form part of a version of natural rights philosophy (cf. Locke). The last three points are included in liberalism and utilitarianism (cf. Helvétius, Adam Smith, and Jeremy Bentham).

WORLDLY WELL-BEING

These were not ideas that served an absolute king or a nobility. But they were appropriate for the growing middle class who wanted to protect and secure private initiative and private property rights so that trade and industry could expand quickly. We have shown how liberalism may be presented as a social-philosophical *individualism* (cf. Ch. 8, Liberality and liberalism, Ch. 11, Political theory . . .), at the same time hinting at a change in the notion of man as an individual (an idea developing from Hobbes, through Locke to Adam Smith). Liberalism, moreover, may be characterized as rationalism to the extent that the individual is understood as a rational agent.[2] This confidence in the individual's ability to make a reasonable choice of means in order to achieve useful results is found in liberalism and utilitarianism, and in Enlightenment philosophy.

The political liberalism in this period emphasized *pleasure/happiness* and *utility* as basic motives and basic values. Here we have a transition to *utilitarianism* (cf. Bentham, Ch. 14). Utilitarianism involves partly a psychological thesis about what motivates us, and partly an ethical thesis about how we can determine whether an action is ethically good or bad. The ethical thesis emphasizes the consequences of what we do – whether the result of the action gives pleasure and utility for ourselves and/or for as many others as possible – and not the attributes of the agent, such as the agent's state of mind, or motive and attitude. We thus distinguish between a consequentialist ethics (as in Helvétius and Bentham) and an ethics of good will (as in the ethics of duty in Kant).

The utilitarians sought to establish an objective principle for determining when an action is right or wrong. They formulated the principle for their philosophy of pleasure as follows: an action is right to the degree that it contributes to creating the greatest possible happiness for the greatest number of people.

It is common to object to utilitarianism on the grounds that different values (states of happiness) cannot be compared – how can we, for example, objectively compare the happiness we derive from reading a book and that we derive from eating well? But in practice, utilitarianism primarily centred on *negative* values, that is, *preventing* suffering and unhappiness in various forms. It was more concerned with preventing pain than finding pleasure. And one can argue that, in practice, there is general agreement about what should be considered a deprivation (for example, lack of protein and of fresh air), although there is disagreement about what is the best meal and the best sport. What we could call the practical precedence of the 'negative' may thus weaken some of the criticism that is based on the view that values are incommensurable, and hence that no consensus is possible in questions of value. But why am *I* not more important than others? Or, rather, is every individual's happiness and pain *equally* important? Here, it will suffice for us to point out that utilitarianism as a political ideology builds on egalitarianism, a philosophy of equality, which takes it for granted that no individual (*qua* individual) has any unique position above anyone else. The objection is also raised that we cannot always know ahead of time what the final result of an action will be: if utilitarianism is to function as an objective criterion in situations of choice, we need to know which alternative will give the best long-term result before we act. But we do not always know this. Here, we could answer that the agent's well-founded opinion is sufficient. But then we waive the objectivity that utilitarianism desires: the criterion for a good action is no longer the objective result, but the agent's optimal deliberations.

It may be further objected that utilitarianism, as liberalism, focuses too strongly on the individual, and that the importance of the complex social interplay of institutions and traditions is overlooked. To this, it may be said that the model of rational agents is part of the establishment of modern economics (since the time of Adam Smith), and that it comprises a vital tradition in modern sociology. Here we should recall that individual-oriented liberalism and utilitarianism arose *before* the social sciences were fully developed, and these schools were part of the establishment of important traditions within these sciences.

Liberalism emphasizes freedom of expression and freedom of speech. Here, political liberalism and Enlightenment philosophy converge. The defence of such liberal virtues, however, is based not only on the view that tolerance is a value (a 'good'), but also on the view that open and free debate is a prerequisite for our being able to arrive at genuine insight in science as well as in politics. Liberality is a condition of rationality — including our own rationality. This is an important insight for the question of what characterizes a scientific community of researchers. Liberality as a condition of rationality is at the same time important for democracy, both in the public formation of opinion and in enlightened deliberation.

MONTESQUIEU – DISTRIBUTION OF POWER AND ENVIRONMENTAL INFLUENCE

The French lawyer, Charles-Louis de Secondat, later Baron de Montesquieu (1689–1755), was one of the foremost political theoreticians of the 1700s. Montesquieu is especially known for two basic contributions: the theory of the *separation of powers* as a condition of freedom, and the theory of the effect that different *surroundings* have on politics.

In his *On the Spirit of the Laws* ('*De l'esprit des lois*' [1748]) Montesquieu proposed a double thesis concerning law: a natural rights thesis that different laws are formulations of one and the same law, and a sociological thesis that these different formulations of the law are determined by different kinds of surroundings, social and natural. Montesquieu thus avoided both the relativism that often arises when we deny the idea of natural rights, and the sterile dogmatism that appears when we postulate a universal, natural rights law without explaining how this law is connected to concrete conditions. *On the Spirit of the Laws* elaborates this connection between the various surroundings and the corresponding, specific formulations of the law.

The idea of natural rights itself was not new. Nor was the thesis that we recognize this law with the aid of a common reason. What was relatively new was Montesquieu's recommendation that we study the interconnections between the surroundings and the formulations of the laws in an empirical way. However, this notion was not completely new. Both Aristotle and Machiavelli had previously recommended it. Nor was Montesquieu fully empirical in his own treatment of the surroundings. It is largely limited to a fairly correct intuition that, for example, climate, soil, forms of trade, ways of production, and customs have an influence on politics and legislation.

In addition, Montesquieu made a classificatory presentation of three forms of government (republic, monarchy, and despotism) and three corresponding principles (virtue, honour, and fear). The latter tripartite division (which is reminiscent of Aristotle) was probably determined by the political interests of Montesquieu's day: the republic is the idealized picture of ancient Rome. Despotism is the horrifying picture of what France could become. And the monarchy reflects Montesquieu's view of the British government as an ideal for France. Even though Montesquieu did not fully succeed in meeting the requirements that he himself had set for scientific research, he was still an important advocate of freedom and of political realism and a scientific attitude. Montesquieu pleaded for British institutions and thus for freedom. And Montesquieu thought that in Britain there was a division of power between the juridical, the executive, and the legislative institutions. This division gained significance in the history of ideas through the North American and French declarations of political freedom at the end of the 1700s.

The principle of the division of power is an ancient idea. We find it in Plato's *The Laws* and in Aristotle's *Politics*. We find it, to some degree, actualized in the empires of the Middle Ages. And we meet this idea in Locke's thought. But Montesquieu, the jurist, developed the thesis of the division of power and placed an emphasis on having a system of legal control and a reasonable balance between the various branches of government. The division of power is to apply to the relationship between a juridical function, an executive function, and a legislative function.

HELVÉTIUS – THE INDIVIDUAL AND PLEASURE

Claude-Adrien Helvétius (1715–1771) set out to explain man on the basis of natural science. He accepted only scientific explanations, while holding that such explanations fully explain all phenomena, including social and psychological phenomena. Helvétius did not start with self-preservation, like Hobbes. For Helvétius, the driving force is self-interest. Human beings seek pleasure and avoid pain. Pleasure and pain are by definition individual egotistic factors: we may empathize with others, but we cannot feel their pain. Helvétius explained how these driving forces function in simple psychological terms: all behaviour may be reduced to automatic pleasure seeking and avoidance of pain.[3] For Helvétius, human beings act in accordance with a simple principle whereby each choice of action is based on finding the means that give the most individual pleasure. Thus, Helvétius held to a purposive theory of motivation.

Helvétius denied that there is any other kind of knowledge than that based on experience. That is to say, Helvétius was an empiricist. And this implies that Helvétius could not accept that we can have insight into normative questions. The idea of natural rights must thus be rejected. As a compensation for the lack of a normative measuring standard, Helvétius had a theory that human beings *actually* seek pleasure and avoid pain. But he presupposed this to be *good*. To the degree that he was an epistemological empiricist, Helvétius did not have a basis for claiming the latter point. He could then not claim that he *knew* that something is 'good'; that is to say, that he *knew* that something is normatively valid.

As a thinker of the Enlightenment, Helvétius held that people need information only about their self-interest: when people know what leads to pleasure and what leads to pain, they will seek what leads to pleasure. What we call 'good' is nothing more than pleasure. And when *each person* seeks what is good, the result will be good for *everyone*.

This idea of harmony in the relationship between self-interest and common interests was essential for the liberalist utilitarians. On the principle that the goal of society is *the greatest possible happiness for the greatest number of people*, they could promote proposals for political reform in favour both of self-interest and of the common good – since a maximization of individual pleasure would automatically lead to the greatest universal good, according to this idea of harmony in the relationship between self-interest and common interest. Helvétius was, however, not a wholehearted defender of such a liberalist politic. On the principle of the greatest possible happiness for the greatest number of people, he proposed an eight-hour work day, among other things.

We see that Helvétius was a liberalist according to our definition: the basic concept is the *individual*. But for Helvétius, self-preservation was not the most important thing for the individual (as in Hobbes), nor were inviolable rights (as in Locke); the most important was the maximization of pleasure. And Helvétius was a *utilitarian*, a philosopher of utility, in that he considered the question of to what extent an action is right or wrong to be based on the extent to which the action has useful or useless *consequences*, that is, provides pleasure or pain for the involved individuals. We will take a closer look at Helvétius' theory as a psychological variation of economic liberalism, and we may outline his theory as follows:

1   Psychological thesis: everyone actually seeks to maximize his or her pleasure.
2   Ethical thesis: this is good.
3   Sociological thesis: when everyone seeks to maximize his or her pleasure, we have the greatest possible happiness for all.
4   Ethical thesis: this is good.

In this rough formulation, all of the theses are problematic:

1   The first thesis is either empirically false or void of meaning. If the concepts are used in a *normal* way, we may quickly establish that at least some people occasionally do not act to maximize their own pleasure: for example, a Buddhist monk who deliberately burns himself to death. Here, the thesis is empirically false. But if we define the concepts such that 'to act' is identical with 'to seek pleasure', this empirical counter-argument carries no weight. Even a Buddhist monk who burns himself to death during a political demonstration acts from 'pleasure', according to the present definition. But such a definition makes the thesis a tautology (of the type 'A = A'). Here empirical arguments no longer carry any weight, but the price is that the statement is void of meaning. It does not say anything about reality. And now we are using an unusual concept of pleasure.
2   The second thesis is a normative thesis. But normative theses do not have any epistemological value, according to empiricism. To the degree that the liberalists are radical epistemological empiricists, they do not have the right to assert this thesis (as a truth).
3   The third thesis is also empirically false (or void of meaning). The development in Britain at the beginning of the 1800s – with miserable conditions for the working class – was a powerful counter-argument. (And against the background of this experience, liberalism in Britain acquired a tendency to social liberalism.)
4   The fourth thesis may be refuted in the same way as the second.

We will see that we may analyse economic liberalism (*laissez-faire*) along the same lines by replacing 'pleasure' by 'profit'.[4]

The Greeks had a cyclic view of history, while Christianity introduced a linear view of history. During the period from the 1600s to the 1700s, we find a new and secularized version of this view of history as a linear process that moves forward. In the literary salons, interest shifted from poetry to science and technology. As long as the patrons of the Parisian salons viewed literature as essential, it was not reasonable to say that history moved forward. Was Racine more important than Homer? As long as the primary concern was literature, it could just as easily be said that history went backwards as forwards. But as these salons were, above all, interested in such things as how fast the stagecoach could travel between Orléans and Paris, it became reasonable to talk about progress. The stagecoach travelled faster and faster. Thus, history seemed to move forward. This shift in interest was, of course, not accidental. If an industrial society is to function, the intelligentsia must, to a certain degree, be concerned with and appreciative of technological advances. The Enlightenment philosophers expressed this faith in progress: enlightenment will create material progress and well-being.

This faith in progress was a mixture of realism and naivety; realism, because all of this was actually becoming scientifically and technologically possible, and naivety, because (among other things) the political problems were underestimated by the Enlightenment philosophers. In fact, enlightenment has proved insufficient to achieve general welfare. After World War I, if not before, the faith in progress received its death blow. Today, hardly anyone is optimistic about the future in the naive and innocent sense of the Enlightenment in the 1700s.

Towards the end of the 1700s, the new middle class began to establish itself in Western Europe – first in Britain, later in France, and also in Germany. This transition took place on several levels; ideological, political, and economic. After the establishment of capitalism, political liberalism, including freedom of religion and freedom of assembly, eventually followed. There was a tendency to a constitutional system with a government that was controlled by public opinion through regular elections, even though voting rights were limited, and with a political authority that secured life and property without interfering in economic life.

ECONOMIC LIBERALISM

ADAM SMITH

The Scot Adam Smith (1723–1790) is regarded as the founder of classical economics as an independent discipline. His main work was *The Wealth of Nations* (1776). But his book *The Theory of Moral Sentiments* (1759) shows that Smith did not support the theory of man as *only* an economic agent.

Smith claimed that commodities and production are what actually determine the wealth of a nation, and not the amount of gold and silver. He attacked economic protectionism: the government should meddle as little as possible in trade and industry. The economy functions best when its freedom is greatest. When all industrialists and merchants seek to maximize their own profit, the general affluence will also be greatest. When the economy is thus allowed to function without governmental interference, it will follow natural laws, as all seek to maximize their economic advantage. Prices will become natural, that is to say, just. And the result is the greatest possible affluence in the country. Adam Smith was thus a *laissez-faire* liberalist.[5]

Smith viewed self-interest as the motivation of *economic* life, as Bentham viewed the search for pleasure as man's basic motivation.

'The Smithean problem' is that of reconciling economic and moral philosophy. As a moral philosopher, Smith defended the notion that we should act on the basis of sympathy and concern for other people. As an economist, he claimed that the businessman should follow self-interest, he must seek to enrich himself – even at the expense of others. The logic of the market, according to Smith, implies that private vices can be turned into public virtues by means of the market's 'invisible hand'. From a moral perspective this is still problematic: what is good cannot, without question, be promoted by immoral actions. An answer to the Smithean problem requires that we distinguish between the market/economic sphere and the interactions of daily life. However, Smith emphasized that the market must be regulated by law and justice. This means that Smith worked not only with a market economy, but also with a juridical-national framework and a sphere of interpersonal interaction. The Smithean problem was later treated as a question of the relationship between 'system' and 'life world' by Jürgen Habermas (cf. Ch. 27).

Just as Democritus' atomistic ontology is fascinating because it reduces everything to simple terms; so too does this economic atomism (individualism). Complicated social phenomena become simple and lucid. In principle, individuals always seek their own economic advantage; and, in principle, they act strictly rationally to achieve this goal. Therefore, we may predict what the astute person will do in various situations. The human universe becomes, in this model, a kind of economic billiards in which advantage-seeking individuals manoeuvre on the table for profitable contracts. We may thus ignore the 'irrational' features of human beings and of social institutions and power structures – or, more correctly, the attempt was made to explain all economic activity by this model. It was from these concepts that Smith and other liberalist economists created and developed a model for rational action among several individuals – a game theory for economic man, *Homo economicus* – and hence, they were the founders of one of the first social sciences: classical economics. In other words, the basic concepts mentioned in Smith's economics correspond with the basic concepts of classical liberalism. But Smith supplemented the traditional liberalist concepts with a theory of natural price: individuals meet one another at the market for mutual exchange of commodities, and the price of an item is determined by the relationship between supply and demand. This presupposes a free market; that is to say, the state and political institutions do not intervene by regulating the prices. This model of explanation of price regulation presupposes that we are atomized individuals who think about our own gain, and that the various commodities are independent of one another so that each of the agents can prioritize the different goods and thus choose among them. This is the model for pure market exchange where the state and monopolies are completely eliminated.

Of course, Smith knew that factors other than supply and demand influence prices, such as governmental policies and the hereditary privileges of the nobility. But just as Bentham used his calculus of pleasure both to describe and to criticize, Smith used his model as criticism as well as description. Thus, he attacked those factors that interfere with the free market. Smith's political theory was not only pure theory, but also a political programme: the factors that interfere with the free market *should* be eliminated because they obstruct the natural order. Like the classical liberalists in political theory, Smith the economist thought that free individualism would ultimately lead to social harmony, to the greatest possible material prosperity.

Smith had, moreover, *another* theory of price regulation, a theory of fair commodity prices. This second price theory proposes that the value of a commodity is equal to the work that is put into it. If a carpenter takes ten hours to make a chair and a farmer five hours to produce a sack of potatoes, the chair is worth two sacks of potatoes. If the price is decided thus, it will be fair since all receive as much as they give. Trade is fair because all traders receive as much as they give.

But it is still difficult to determine the value of the work that goes into an item. Time cannot be the only determining factor: some workmen are quick, others are lazy; some are trained, others are not. Moreover, this price theory is in some opposition to the price theory of supply and demand: if the price is determined by supply and demand in a free market, the price of one commodity will vary because of the relationship between supply and demand even though the work put into the item remains constant. We can therefore hardly justify a price that is set by supply and demand by claiming that the price is equal to the amount of work that was put into the item.

RICARDO AND MALTHUS

David Ricardo (1772–1823) and Thomas Malthus (1776–1834) reinforced Smith's economic *laissez-faire* liberalism. But while Smith thought that a free and 'natural' capitalism would benefit all classes, Ricardo and Malthus thought that the working classes must necessarily live near the subsistence level. Nevertheless, Ricardo supported a radical *laissez-faire*: with the absence of governmental interference, the best possible harmony of self-interests will automatically appear, even if the workers, unfortunately, must always live in material need.

The line of thinking behind this theory is as follows: Malthus claimed that poverty in the lower classes is unavoidable because the population has a tendency to increase exponentially, while the amount of food tends to increase only along a straight line.

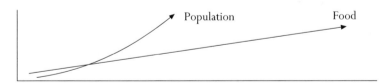

Therefore, the increase in population will always overtake the increase in the amount of food. To put it brutally, a wage increase will not lead to an increased standard of living for the lower classes, but only to more children growing up. The masses must therefore always live at subsistence level, as long as there are no moral or social norms that can reduce the birth rates. This theory seemed to prove that poverty in the lower classes is a natural necessity. It goes against nature for capitalists to give higher wages to the workers or for the state to provide social security. This will only lead to an unnatural increase in the population, that is to say, an increase in the population for which there is no demand (i.e. available work), and this will again lead to more starvation and death. The economy must therefore be allowed to follow its own laws. The state should not carry out social reforms.

The benefits of work may be divided into three: wages for the workers, profit for the capitalists, and rent for the landowners. Therefore, wages should be minimal, that is, just enough for the workers to survive and reproduce the labour force. Another conflict was that between the capitalists (industrialists and merchants) and the landowners. In this conflict, the liberalists claimed that the landowners comprised a *parasitic* group. The landowners rented out the land, but they did not produce anything. Therefore, the capitalists, who are productive, should receive proportionately more and the landowners proportionately less. (Later, Marx made the same attack on the capitalists. For him, the capitalists were the parasites, and the workers were the producers.)

The theory that wages incline towards the subsistence level thus represents a clear breach with the theory that *laissez-faire* liberation leads to improvement for everyone. Hence, the optimistic expectation of progress also has its death blow: it was no longer possible to justify inequality now by holding out expectations of improvement later. But this theory of wages justified the present inequality on a new basis: what we have is after all the best possible arrangement; it is natural and the best we can have; anything else will give worse results. At the same time, the theory of wages meant that we could not think only in terms of individuals: here, there were classes in opposition to one another. Ricardo assumed that on a long-term basis the economy — partially as the result of an increase in population and a finite amount of space for food production — will tend towards stagnation, with low wages and low profit (cf. later theories about built-in crises and zero growth).

Ricardo and Malthus described a private capitalism that fleeced the workers with the claim that such exploitation is natural. This crass *laissez-faire* doctrine was the culmination of liberalism. From the mid-nineteenth century, social liberalism influenced political theories (John Stuart Mill) and led to social reform (factory laws, the right of workers to organize).

ROUSSEAU – REACTION AGAINST THE PHILOSOPHY OF THE ENLIGHTENMENT

Life. Jean-Jacques Rousseau (1712–1778) was born in Geneva into a Calvinistic environment. His mother died early, and when Jean-Jacques was ten years old, his father had to flee from Switzerland. The boy was raised by his relatives and early began the life of a wanderer, mostly in France and in the French-speaking part of Switzerland. Around the age of 30, Rousseau settled temporarily in Paris and met philosophers of the Enlightenment such as Voltaire. He sent the children that he fathered on Thérèse Levasseur to a children's home. In 1750, Rousseau won a prize offered by the Academy of Dijon for an essay on the subject 'Has the progress in the sciences and in the arts contributed to the improvement of morality?' In his answer, he opposed the dominant optimism about progress. Rousseau had just as many difficulties with the Enlightenment philosophers as he had with people in general: he continued his life as a wanderer, both geographically and spiritually. In 1766 he met Hume in London, but soon had a falling out with him as well. Rousseau died in 1778 and his ashes were later placed in the Panthéon in Paris.

His works include Discours sur les sciences et les arts *(1750),* Discours sur l'origine et les fondements de l'inégalité parmi les hommes *(1755),* Du contrat social *(1762),* Émile, ou de l'éducation *(1762), and* Confessions *(1782).*

We have said that French Enlightenment philosophy may be interpreted as an ideological weapon for the emerging French in the 1700s, who struggled against absolutism and against the privileges of the nobility and the clergy, in order to gain power for themselves. In this struggle, the French supporters of the Enlightenment often used notions like the individual, reason, and progress. Theoretically, objections could be raised against these notions, and this theoretical criticism soon emerged: a philosophical analysis of the concept of *reason* (especially Hume, but also Rousseau), a philosophical and sociological criticism of the concept of the *individual* (Rousseau, but also Burke), and a sociological criticism of the *faith in progress* (Rousseau).

Jean-Jacques Rousseau was a very complex person and thinker, and here we can give only *one* interpretation of certain aspects of his authorship.

The cultivation of reason and optimism about the future among the Enlightenment thinkers could, in its extreme forms, be shallow and unclear. It was therefore easy to attack these ideas and transform them to their *negation* in order to vindicate the cultivation of feelings and sceptical pessimism. The Lisbon earthquake in 1755 was enough to shake the optimism of that day: if we live in a perfect world, how can something like this happen? The sceptical Voltaire had an easy target in his novel *Candide*, in which he made a laughing stock of the naive forms of optimism about the future and the self-satisfied belief that we live in the best of all possible worlds.[6]

Rousseau continued this purely negative reaction to Enlightenment philosophy. While the Enlightenment philosophers may have practised a somewhat one-sided cultivation of reason, Rousseau advanced a cultivation of feelings. Where the Enlightenment philosophers paid homage to the individual and to self-interest, Rousseau praised the community and the general will (*la volonté générale*). Where the Enlightenment philosophers praised progress, Rousseau proclaimed a 'return to nature'. This does not mean that Rousseau was in opposition to the Enlightenment on all points. He often fully shared the viewpoints of the Enlightenment philosophers, such as the view that man is basically good. But while the Enlightenment philosophers thought that evil originated in the ignorance and intolerance maintained by tradition and privilege, and that the remedy is therefore enlightenment – when reason and science triumph, the good in man will emerge in step with the progress of civilization – Rousseau thought that evil originated in civilization. This was the sensational part of his prize-winning essay for the Academy of Dijon: civilization has led to an artificial and degenerate life. Here we meet Rousseau's criticism of the faith in progress as a prelude to Romanticism: civilization and the sciences pervert the natural good in man.

Therefore, Rousseau proclaimed that we ought to return *to nature*. With this, Rousseau hardly meant that it is desirable to live primitively. Rousseau strongly emphasized that a human being is a part of the community. His point seems to have been that we ought to return to nature in the sense of 'living a natural and virtuous life in a community'. Rousseau's thesis thus rejected *both* what he saw as over-refined decadence and uncivilized primitivism.

We may interpret Rousseau's attack on the Enlightenment philosophers as a reaction of the lower-middle classes *against* the upper classes:[7] Rousseau opposed the simple virtues and values of ordinary people – like family life, compassion, religious reverence, and faithful labour in crafts and agriculture – to the sophistication and the cold and calculating reason of the great merchants and the scientists. Far from wanting to return to primitive conditions, Rousseau extolled the simple life of the lower-middle classes. He defended the simple moral intuition and unreflective faith of the humble people against the caustic wit of the intellectuals, who apparently did not regard anything as sacred. Rousseau thus represented the irritated and confused lower-middle classes, who were convinced of their own moral superiority, but shocked by the intellectual criticism of the time-honored faith and customs, and who feared that this criticism would threaten their most basic values. And since the lower-middle classes lacked the learning to defend their values rationally, they often countered with a general condemnation of reason and sentimental praise of feelings.

Since the decent lower-middle-class citizen did not personally have any direct use for scientific and economic advances, the changes in society did not always appear to be 'progress'. The lower-middle-class citizen was more often struck by the terrifying aspects of innovation and by what seemed immoral and inhuman. The upper-class citizen praised the individual and advocated freedom of trade and freedom of expression. But these are virtues for the strong. For the weaker members of society, the virtues were rather those of solidarity and community. Rousseau, like the lower-middle classes, also praised family life and general interests. Virtues like solidarity were probably more equally distributed than the ability to make rational and profitable calculations. Therefore, the lower-middle classes (and the workers) often emphasized equality, not individual freedom and personal careers. The lower-middle classes were often more traditional and conforming, while the ruling classes concentrated on rational self-interest and demanded the right to choose for themselves. We will not take this interpretation of Rousseau as one of the lower-middle class too far. But perhaps this interpretation gives us a grasp of some of his basic attitudes.

From Rousseau through Kant there is a tendency for philosophy to be used to defend religion and morality against attempts to attribute all valid insight to the natural sciences. And from Rousseau through Burke and Hegel, there is a tradition that questions the individualistic concept of the individual, and that tries to conceive of the community and the individual as interconnected.

For Rousseau, there was a certain tension in this interrelationship between the individual and the community. Here, we will concentrate on Rousseau's criticism of the individualism that ruled during his day. This individualism, which runs from Hobbes through Locke and on to the French and British liberalists in the 1700s, conceives of the individual as someone who is fully developed – with self-interest, the ability to calculate, desires for pleasure and profit, conceptions of property, language, and the ability to trade. All of this was prior to the development of the state, which was seen as a means of protecting private initiative and private property. The state has no value in itself.

In keeping with the individualistic theories of the state as having been created by a contract, Rousseau also followed a line of argumentation that began with the state of nature, and that ended with a social contract. But, for Rousseau, it was not just a matter of two distinct notions, a state of nature and a society shaped by the state, and of the transformation of the one into the other: the formation of society by a contract. Rousseau's mental experiment reconstructed the gradual development of society and man, the eventual result of which is the politically organized society.

Thus, we can say that Rousseau was still closely related to Plato and Aristotle. Like them, he sought the origin of human abilities such as language, reason, and virtue. And like these Greek philosophers, he pointed to community: human beings develop these abilities through communal life. The fully developed human being and society are thus of the same age. Basically, we cannot imagine the fully developed individual without society. In line with Plato, Rousseau moved one step further. Not only is the fully developed human being connected with the community in an internal way, as a citizen-in-society, but the community has value in itself. The community comprises the concrete ties, the close feelings that bind family and friends together. Rousseau attacked the view that naked, rational self-interest can hold a society together. What binds human beings together in a community are deep-rooted feelings and attitudes, not superficial calculations about profit and pleasure. The community is based on feelings, not on reason. Here, Rousseau articulated an important criticism of liberalist individualism. Rousseau, like the ancient Greeks, saw society as a *small* society, as in the 'city-state' Geneva.

Rousseau was no nationalist, although his ideas were later applied to the national state. For Rousseau, individualism, like nationalism and cosmopolitanism, was basically a distant abstraction. What is real and concrete are the family and the local community where the citizens know one another and are interrelated. Thus, Rousseau represented a conservative reaction to the individualism and the nationalism of which the upper classes were the exponent. As we will later see, both the conservatives and the socialists viewed close communal ties as fundamental – in contrast to the liberalist individualism.

Both individualism and collectivism *distinguish* between two factors, the individual and the state. But Rousseau, like Plato earlier, basically criticized the distinction itself: what is fundamental is man-in-community. We could add that Rousseau was no revolutionary: he supported the right to own property – while criticizing the inequality in property conditions (in his *Discours sur l'inégalité*).

Thus, Rousseau's ideas pointed in different directions. He held that society is necessary and has a moral value. Therefore, Rousseau was not *against* all forms of civilization or *for* a simplistic 'return to nature'. And to the degree that he thought that human beings are actually a part of a community, his use of expressions like 'state of nature' and 'social contract' are somewhat problematic. But he praised the individual's way of life in the 'state of nature', and he condemned the society of his day for having suppressed man's natural virtue, wisdom, and happiness.

Rousseau thus thought that we must avoid both primitivism and decadent civilization, and strive towards a genuine community. But what is a genuine community? The political realities of his day were marked by individualism and nationalism. And when Rousseau's ideas about genuine community were taken over by others, they were transformed to a glorification of both the national (secular) state, the 'Führer' state (Hitler), and the party state (Lenin). If Rousseau had a relatively clear position against the rather mechanistic and atomistic view of society held by the liberalists, it is not clear how his thoughts are related to political conservatism and socialism.

Thus, the basic concept of the general will of the people is marked by an unclear definition. This general will is not the sum of the viewpoints of the political parties or of the representatives in the national assembly. The general will is, in some indefinable way, 'the people's' genuine will. According to Rousseau, the general will comprises society's interests, in opposition to all the special interests.

Furthermore, Rousseau held that the general will 'is always right'. If any persons want something other than the general will, that is to say, what the people 'really' want, such persons do not really know what is in their own best interests or what they really want. Therefore, it is not a matter of compelling everyone to submit to the general will. According to Rousseau, where the general will rules, there is never compulsion. But the salient point is how we are to find out *what* the general will is each time a public question arises. We must also ask, *who* has the authority (and power) to ascertain what the true will of the people is? Moreover, it is of course doubtful whether all individual desires really coincide in *one* general interest. Rousseau did not properly explain how we can ensure, *institutionally*, that the general is given a hearing, so that illegitimate power groups do not decide on what the 'general will' is. Nor did Rousseau explain how we are to secure the interests of the minority.

Although the liberalist tradition often overlooked the organic aspects of society, this tradition did offer a comforting sense of developing the institutional patterns that can secure the political process against flagrant misuse of power. Rousseau's organic view of society largely neglected the institutional problems. From the theory of the general will, both a Hitler and a de Gaulle may claim to be the true spokesman for the people's genuine interests, raised high above the various special interests. Here we end up with both an institutional and a theoretical problem: when it is unclear how the general will is to be expressed institutionally, we run the risk that arbitrary rulers will impose their will as the general will.

In the local community, the home and village, it may be relatively harmless to follow the general will. Here we may have a kind of direct democracy. But it is dangerous to base a modern society on such a general will that is not secured institutionally. Hence, Rousseau's organic theory of society, with its emphasis on the emotional ties between people and its neglect of the institutions, tends to result in an irrational and romantic cultivation of community. Rousseau's lack of an institutional theory meant that the idea of a general will has served both the permanent revolution (as in Robespierre or Mao) – the spontaneous will of the people should lead the government – *and* the stable national state (as in Burke) – the will of the people is created by a continuing tradition.

EDMUND BURKE – THE CONSERVATIVE REACTION

The Irish-born philosopher Edmund Burke (1729–1797) is often called the father of conservatism, as John Locke is considered the father of liberalism. Burke's writings, such as his *Reflections on the Revolution in France* (1790), were a reaction to the outbreak of the French Revolution, and to the cultivation of reason by the

Enlightenment philosophers. The latter placed reason above tradition, and the ahistorical individual above the community. Burke reversed this: tradition is wiser than the theories of intellectuals. The community and history, not the isolated, ahistorical individual, are fundamental. We may therefore summarize Burke's conservatism as a negative reversal of liberalism during the Enlightenment.

Liberalism in the Enlightenment	Burke's conservatism
reason above tradition	tradition above reason
individual (not community and history)	community and history (not the individual)

We may thus talk about a conservative reaction embodied in Burke. And this reaction did not only occur on the theoretical level. Politically, Burke represented a reaction to the radicalism of the French citizenry during the revolution: the king, the nobility, and the clergy were swept out of the political arena. From a French perspective, Burke was thus a defender of the nobility against the citizenry.

Just as we may take liberalism as the ideology of the upper middle class, we may interpret conservatism as the ideology of the nobility. Prominent ideologists within French conservatism at that time, such as the Roman Catholic royalists Joseph de Maistre and Louis Bonald, fit well into such an interpretation. However, it is probably just as correct to view the conservative ideologies towards the end of the 1700s (such as those of Hume and Burke) as the expression of a criticism of liberalism emerging from the citizenry itself. That these conservative ideologies were suitable for the nobility is another matter. If we use the following schema as a basis, liberalism and conservatism emerge as both theoretical and political opposites:

	Liberalism	Conservatism
Social anchoring	upper citizenry	citizenry and nobility
Basic concept	individual (contract, state)	man-in-community
Attributes	ahistorical individualistic-egotistic (maximization of pleasure/profit, individual freedom from coercion)	historic-cultural: having values in common (meaningful life, harmonious realization of abilities in a historic-organic community)

Liberalism and conservatism had in common that they were both anchored in an upper class: conservatism in parts of the middle class and the declining nobility, who under a previous and more feudal economy had been dominant; liberalism throughout a flowering middle class, supported by a private-capitalistic economy.

Like most political labels, the word *conservatism* is used in somewhat different ways. We may, for example, use a *formal* conception of conservatism, defined as 'wanting to preserve that which exists', without any specific definition of what exists, whether it be economy or environment, culture or forms of governance, or whether it be a feudal, capitalistic, or socialistic society. The opposite of *conservative* in this sense is *radical*, in the sense of 'wanting to change what exists'.

This is a definition that disregards the historical aspect, to the extent that we may ask whether Thomas Aquinas, Joseph Stalin, or Ronald Reagan were 'conservative' in the sense that each of them wanted to preserve essential aspects of his own society. In opposition to this formal conception of conservatism, we may consider conservatism to be something that is determined by its content, so that we understand conservatism to mean wanting to preserve something particular (whether in the cultural, social, political, or economic order). It is then natural to talk about a wish to preserve particular values, such as meaningful forms of life in a traditional local community, or ecological diversity. We may use the term *'value conservatism'* to refer to this type of conservatism that is determined by its content.

Like other ideologies, conservatism is at the same time a phenomenon *in* society, determined by social and historical conditions, and a theory that claims to tell the truth *about* society.

If we wish to refine the conception of a conservatism that is determined by its content, it may be useful to start with the earlier phase of conservatism (as in Edmund Burke), when conservatism was clearly opposed to the liberalism of the day (for Burke, its main opposition was to the radical French Enlightenment philosophers). Whereas the liberalists worked with the basic concepts of the individual, reason, and progress, and opposed the autonomous, free, and equal individual to tradition with its inherited attitudes and structures, conservatism centred on the basic notion of man as a being inseparably shaped by what has been handed down, a heritage that may, and should, be improved with care, but that may not be abolished, on pain of disaster. While liberalism can be said to be a social-philosophical individualism that originated in isolated, free individuals, enlightened by self-interest, all seeking their own best interest – so that social life is considered to have arisen as the unintentional harmony of the selfish actions of individuals – this conservatism may be said to have the organism as its model: society is far more complex than the liberalists, with their fascinating, but simplified models, can envisage. For the conservatives, everything is connected, and so tightly interwoven, that no one could survey it all and change it to something better by simple and radical measures, that is, revolutionary changes. Society is a complex organism that grows, not a mechanism that may be changed overnight by simple adjustment. Reforms will often be necessary, and desirable, in order to preserve the valuable aspects of existing structures, but reforms must be carried out carefully, step by step. Each individual and each party must recognize that tradition embodies a wisdom deeper than any one person's finite understanding. And we must recognize that there are no simple, final solutions that give us the right to abolish our heritage and introduce something new and better out of hand. A society is based on the interplay between groups and generations. Social development takes time.

Thus, conservatism, like liberalism, is not only a theory of particular political institutions, like forms of government and of juridical-economical rights and systems. It represents a basic view of what society and man really are, and of what we may know about them. It claims to have the most adequate means to understand society correctly, and thus to act correctly.

In this there is also a claim that conservatism knows better what is valuable than the competing ideologists. But it is not only on questions of value that the different ideologists have different views. It is not simply that what we have called value conservatism places a greater emphasis on meaningful and historically situated life, in a normative sense, than does liberalism — while liberalism, on the other hand, places a greater normative weight on the individual's chance to maximize private benefits according to enlightened self-interest. The differences between these ideologies may be traced back to fundamental differences in the view of what we, as social creatures, *are* and *can know*.

It is not unusual to say that an important difference between liberalism and conservatism lies in their respective views of freedom — put roughly, conservatives view order and authority as being more important than individual freedom, while liberalists view individual freedom as more important, so that order and authority are only justified when they serve this freedom. But our view of what freedom is and of how valuable it is, is linked to our view of what man and society are, views that often remain unexpressed in everyday political discourse and therefore are not discussed with regard to their tenability. When we talk about freedom, we assume that there is *somebody* who is free from something or someone; in other words, we necessarily have certain basic opinions about what man really is and what society really is (hence, the various social-philosophical and epistemological opinions on the relationship among individual, community, and cognition).

To a certain degree, conservatism may agree with socialism in opposition to the more radical conceptions of the individual in classical liberalism. In line with this critical attitude towards liberalist individualism and in line with a more positive view of order and authority, conservatives also have a more positive (or pragmatic) view of the role of the state in society than does classical liberalism (whether it be economic liberalism or cultural liberalism). Conservatism may be distinguished from fascist cultivation of order and authority in that conservatives support a social order that grows organically, and distance themselves from the political view that a new order may be created by compulsion and violence.

To a certain extent, Edmund Burke accepted Hume's criticism of reason and of the idea of natural rights. And he largely accepted Rousseau's criticism of individualism during the Enlightenment. Like Hume, Burke placed feelings, habits, and conventions in opposition to reason. And, like Rousseau, he opposed the community to individualism. But he viewed feelings, habits, conventions, and community in a historical light: history and tradition are sacred and demand respect. Politically, this meant that Burke was against all reform that according to his view, is based on theoretical constructions, and does not grow organically out of the past. Both revolutionary changes and conscious social planning are suspect. Society must grow like a plant. Like gardeners, we are to carry out moderate cultivation (political reform), but we are not to interfere with organic growth by revolution and planning. For Burke, tradition has a value and a wisdom in itself. Thus, Burke also represented a certain formal conservatism: what has been preserved over a certain amount of time has the right to life and ought to be respected. But if this formal conservatism is carried too far, we end up respecting mere opportunism, and defending all kinds of impositions in the name of conservatism, as long as they persistently 'exist'. Even though Burke was clearly antirevolutionary and unambiguously praised historical continuity, there were still *particular* situations that he wanted to preserve. He was hardly an opportunistic formal conservative.

Burke thus argues in favour of a society that is not based on calculated self-interest, but on organic groups, like family and neighbourhood. In these intimate groups, people are bound to one another with concrete, emotional ties without external principles or demands.

This concrete community would vary somewhat from people to people. There is no one set of customs and conventions that is correct in all places. These different forms of life are largely based on *conventions*, not on nature. But *as* conventions, they are unavoidable. That is to say, we *must* have some form of life that is based on conventions. But through drastic changes in the forms of life, some of the social-creative intimacy may be lost. Therefore, we must respect and protect the various organic forms of life that do exist. It was on this basis that Burke defended India's culture and religion against British capitalists. On this point, we see an opposition of political implications between a radical liberalism that holds an abstract conception of the individual in which all individuals are, in principle, identical to the extent that they are said to seek only pleasure and profit, and a value conservatism that favours historical and cultural diversity in the forms of life and the richness and complexity of human behaviour. This value conservatism thus perceives many things that the mechanistic liberalism cannot see with its atomistic 'glasses', such as community, history, and social and human complexity.

Radical liberalism has, in a way, the same advantage as Democritus' atomic theory: by simplification, it expresses a rational model for certain aspects of reality. Thus, this kind of liberalism is fairly appropriate to comprehend market economy. For the value conservatives, the problem is reversed. The theoretical picture is, in a cultural connection, more adequate, but at the same time, all of this organic complexity may be *too* overwhelming. Value conservatism tends to claim that society is so complex that we cannot conceive of it all. This is typical of Burke: society and history are wiser than individuals and their assumed reason.

But this modest view of our ability to comprehend society may turn into a kind of irrationalism: feelings and prejudices are just as reliable as an insufficient reason.[8] And this view may, in turn, lead to political passivity: society is too complex to be understood. Society is so complex that we cannot do anything to change it. This was not Burke's view. Burke wanted *to change in order to preserve*. But this tendency towards political passivity burdens organic value conservatism. In practice, this political passivity could indirectly support the privileged and the free development of capital. In this sense, *laissez-faire* liberalism and value conservatism *may* have the same political consequences.

We have already mentioned that the value conservatives were culturally anchored in a way that the radical liberalists were not (Burke's criticism of the East India Company). In addition, the value conservatives were socially anchored in a way that *laissez-faire*-liberalists were not. The value conservatives often wanted to maintain traditional hierarchic systems, but, at the same time, they had a feudal lord's paternal compassion for the lower orders. Disraeli and Bismarck are examples of such compassion: paternal authority and compassion for the children not yet come of age.

For Burke, this paternal attitude meant that he did not support universal voting rights or the abolition of inherited rights (that is, privileges). He viewed both the individual and the masses with suspicion. On the other hand, he trusted in the wisdom of the people. But, as in the case of Rousseau's general will, it was here a question of how we are to find out what the people really think – since we are not to hold general elections. Here, Burke was more concrete than Rousseau. Burke supported a constitutional monarchy, controlled by a hereditary, wealthy nobility – which Burke thought to be a relatively impartial and socially conservative group – a monarchy with institutions giving expression to the wisdom and feelings of the people.

QUESTIONS

Explain the basic ideas of the Enlightenment. Explain also the ideas behind Rousseau's criticism of the Enlightenment and Burke's conservative criticism of the French Revolution.

Discuss the relation between Adam Smith's economic theory and the basic concepts of utilitarianism (as in Helvétius).

SUGGESTIONS FOR FURTHER READING

PRIMARY LITERATURE

Burke, E., *Reflections on the Revolution in France*, Oxford, 1993.
Malthus, T., *An Essay on Population*, London, 1967.
Montesquieu, *On the Spirit of the Laws*, London, 1975.
Ricardo, D., *The Principles of Political Economy and Taxation*, London, 1969.
Rousseau, J.-J., *The Social Contract* and *Discourses*, London, 1975.
Smith, A., *The Theory of Moral Sentiments*, Oxford, 1976.
Smith, A., *The Wealth of Nations*, London, 1961.
Voltaire, *Candide*, Oxford, 1978.

SECONDARY LITERATURE

Cassirer, E., *The Philosophy of Enlightenment*, Boston, 1955.
Habermas, J., *The Structural Transformation of the Public Sphere*, Cambridge, MA, 1989.
Koselleck, R., *Critique and Crisis: Enlightenment and the Pathogenesis of Modern Society*, Oxford, 1988.

NOTES

1 Thus, Kant was one of the first great philosophers to be a university professor.
2 Although the basic motives of the individual's actions were interpreted differently by the various liberalist theoreticians, they all viewed the individual as an agent who can and ought to choose consistently and rationally between different means of achieving a goal – what we often call purposive rationality (cf. M. Weber, Ch. 24).
3 Thus Helvétius tried to understand human actions in terms of a simple notion of motivation, psychologically conceived. He did not try to reduce everything to pure mechanics. Nor did he envisage an autonomous and discursive rationality of the kind discussed by modern thinkers like Hannah Arendt and Jürgen Habermas (cf. Ch. 27).
4 We do not deny that it is scientifically possible and often fruitful to use the concept of 'economic man' as a hypothesis; that is, to proceed tentatively, in research and economic practice, under the

assumption that human beings, statistically, are motivated by economic gain – but without claiming that this is 'man's (ahistorical) essence'.

5 The expression *laissez-faire* refers to economic liberalism: '*laissez-faire, laissez-passer*', that is, allow the products to be freely created and freely traded ('freely' meaning 'without governmental interference').

6 Voltaire was especially attacking Leibniz.

7 There are parallels between the ideas of the *Sans-culottes* (radical mass movement during the French Revolution) and of Rousseau: these shared ideals included direct democracy, equality in property, a sovereign 'general will', and public education of all members of the state.

8 Many have thought that reason represents something universal and secure, while feelings are unstable and vary from individual to individual; a morality based on feelings is therefore *relative*. Burke viewed this differently: many attitudes and feelings are more stable and universal than many intellectual positions, which may often change just as quickly as the current fashion. Rooted, common 'prejudices' offer a good guarantee of moral stability.

14 Utilitarianism and liberalism

JEREMY BENTHAM AND JAMES MILL – HEDONIC CALCULUS AND LEGAL REFORM

BENTHAM

The British jurist Jeremy Bentham (1748–1832) was one of the so-called philosophical radicals who pressed for legal reforms in British society. Hence, he criticized certain aspects of that society. But the critic must have a normative standard from which to criticize. In line with the utilitarian-empiricist tradition, Bentham accepted neither the idea of natural rights nor that of contract theory. The only justification for authority and for political changes are human needs, namely, *utility* and *pleasure*. Here, Bentham followed Helvétius:

1   Pleasure and pain are the *causes* of human action; therefore, we can influence human behaviour by changing the relationship between pleasure and pain.
2   Pleasure is what *justifies* legislation and political authority.

We have previously mentioned that the first point in this scheme may represent an unacceptable simplification, and that the second point may entail a logical short-circuit insofar as something that is normative, namely, justification, is held to follow from something that is descriptive, namely, the assertion that everyone seeks pleasure.

Bentham followed Helvétius in that he took the utilitarian principle of the greatest possible happiness (utility) for the greatest number of people as the fundamental normative standard. What is new in Bentham's thought is that he, more consistently than the others, used this principle as a guideline for legal reforms, and that he developed a system for calculating what provides the most pleasure.

Bentham's calculation of pleasure and pain considers the various factors that determine which actions and situations, as a whole, provide the most pleasure. This calculation involves the intensity of pleasure or pain, how long the pleasure or pain lasts, how certain it is that pleasure or pain will occur, how long that pleasure or pain will persist, how many persons are involved, and how various experiences of pleasure and pain interfere with one another.

As we previously indicated, it is perhaps more reasonable to talk about a calculation of pain than a calculation of pleasure, since we probably have more in common, in our reactions and attitudes, in the avoidance of certain basic lacks than in ranking different positive activities or benefits. In practice, utilitarianism and liberalism were more an attempt to avoid the negative than to realize the ideal.

Bentham's recommended calculation of pleasure and pain is strikingly reminiscent of a calculation of profit. But while profit is calculated with comparable units, like pounds and pence or marks and pfennigs, it is difficult to see how different experiences of pleasure and pain can be comparable. How can we compare the value of pleasure in the quiet enjoyment of good food and the wild ecstasy after passing an examination? Bentham never managed to solve this problem. His calculation of pleasure is thus problematic. Still, he occasionally expressed himself as if he truly meant that we do act on the basis of such rational calculations.

We note once again that individualism is in a way built into the concept of pleasure itself.[1] Pleasure is individual. The state or the community can have neither pleasure nor pain. In line with this, 'the greatest possible happiness' was also understood as the 'greatest possible happiness for the greatest possible number of particular individuals', since happiness is best understood as pleasure.

It is still worth noting that the concept of utility is not individualistic in the same way as the concept of pleasure. While the concept of pleasure points to individual experiences, the concept of utility points to desirable consequences. The philosophy of utility, utilitarianism, is thus primarily a consequentialist ethics: the criterion for good/desirable actions is to be found in to what degree the consequences are 'useful'. Opposition is here an ethics of good will, in which the criterion lies in the ethical intent of the agent who acts. Utilitarianism has the merit of apparently fitting in well with common situations in our culture: we often choose by evaluating alternatives and consequences, as we take certain preferences for granted. And when the preferences are those that we seek, it is easy to explain the motivation. But utilitarianism may seem to conflict with the concept of justice: if, in a given situation, it leads to the greatest utility (happiness) to convict an innocent person, this would be ethically correct, according to a common interpretation of utilitarianism. But this view conflicts with the basic sense of justice.

For Bentham, the emphasis on the individual is transferred to the field of the philosophy of language. Bentham claimed that it is basically only those words that refer to particular things that have meaning. Words that do not refer to particular things – words like *rights*, *general prosperity*, *property*, etc. – are, ultimately, factitious. He thought that the use of words like *rights* and *principles* tends to conceal reality instead of uncovering it – and social reality, according to Bentham, is ultimately the pleasure and pain of the particular individuals.

It is clear that words like *honour*, *fatherland*, *progress*, etc., are *often* used to mystify and manipulate. Thus, there is something healthy in Bentham's nominalism.[2] But when Bentham seems to think that all such words are mystifying, it is Bentham himself who is in danger of concealing aspects of reality, namely, the social interconnections. To the degree that Bentham rejects all conceptual terms, he makes it difficult to grasp the specifically social aspects of society, like anonymous power structures. The price of Bentham's nominalism may thus be a certain blindness and thereby a certain powerlessness in regard to dominant tendencies that may be irrational and harmful.

As we mentioned, Bentham uses the principle of the greatest possible happiness (pleasure, utility) for the greatest possible number of individuals as a standard for criticizing existing laws. Instead of asking what punishment a criminal 'deserves', Bentham asked, on this principle, what measures might lead to fewer crimes and better human beings in the future. Punishment of one or of a few individuals, which in itself inflicts pain, is only just if the result, as a whole, provides greater pleasure. With this approach, Bentham contributed to humanizing the legal system, just as he contributed to making legal practice more effective and more rational. But even if the practical consequences were good, his theoretical deliberations were somewhat problematic. Bentham often overlooked the historical variety in human values and motivations. Man, for Bentham, is basically ahistorical: man is at all times and in all places seeking the same goals (pleasure) and driven by the same forces (seeking pleasure). Just as Bentham, the nominalist, largely overlooked the social institutions and saw only individuals, so Bentham, the liberalist, had a tendency to overlook history and to reduce human beings to a timeless abstraction. History, for Bentham, is a collection of traditions, habits, and customs that can justify their existence only if they can withstand a critical investigation based on the principle of the greatest possible happiness for the greatest possible number of particular individuals. In this sense, Bentham concurred with the Enlightenment philosophy's criticism of tradition.

Bentham's philosophical radicalism was especially directed against the ineffectiveness and inhumanity of the legal system. He was not as concerned with economic reform. On the contrary, he thought that the right to private property provided security and thus pleasure. In this, we find support of the economic status quo, although here there is also the seed of a demand for a more equitable distribution of property. Like most liberalists, Bentham seemed to presuppose a kind of harmony of various particular interests: when all seek to maximize their pleasure, it is for the best for *all* individuals. But Bentham did *not* think that such harmony appears *automatically*: active legislation, based on the principle of utility, is required, and this legislation should be actively implemented in the sense that its aim is an intended change.

JAMES MILL

Another representative of British philosophical radicalism at the turn of the century was James Mill (1773–1836). He argued for a strong government under the control of a representative, elected assembly founded on general voting rights. He had little sympathy for the rights of the minority, which, for him, was the overprivileged nobility and the priesthood. He therefore supported the majority, as expressed by a representative government, and advocated general education. Everyone should go to school; education should be intellectually and ethically liberating; and the enlightened majority should rule. This is in line with the Enlightenment philosophy of the 1700s.

Like the other philosophical radicals, James Mill contributed to a more effective and democratic legislation and administration in Britain. At the same time, it was clearly the influence of these philosophical radicals that led to the introduction of certain social reforms in the mid-1800s (poverty laws); that is, laws enacted for the benefit of the underprivileged. Thus, the philosophical radicalism of Jeremy

Bentham and James Mill is linked to the social liberalism of John Stuart Mill and Thomas Hill Green.

JOHN STUART MILL – SOCIAL LIBERALISM, AND LIBERALITY AS A CONDITION OF RATIONALITY

Life. John Stuart Mill (1806–1873), the son of James Mill, was raised according to the principles of his father. He studied Greek at the age of three, Latin at the age of eight, and political economy and logic at the age of twelve. Not until after a personal crisis was John Stuart Mill able to liberate himself from his father's (and Bentham's) thinking. He tried to formulate a liberalism that did not have the weaknesses that he felt existed in earlier liberalism. He had a close relationship with Harriet Taylor (1808–1859), whom he married in 1851. John Stuart Mill wrote not only about political theory, but also about logic and epistemology, in such works as On Liberty *(1859),* Utilitarianism *(1863),* The Subjection of Women *(1869), and* Principles of Political Economy *(1848).*

Economic *laissez-faire* liberalism, as exemplified by Ricardo, reached its climax in Britain before 1850. Already by then, outrage was rising over the miserable living conditions of the industrial workers. Social politics had begun, in line with Bentham's social reformism. But this social politics should not be understood merely as a consequence of certain theoretical standpoints, such as Bentham's utilitarianism. At the same time, there was a spontaneous political reaction inspired by the increasing social deprivation of the lower classes. This reaction could partially be explained by fear of political unrest and partially by compassion for the workers.

The workers themselves faced a double struggle: against the conservatives, who were concentrated around the land-owning nobility; and against the liberalists, who were concentrated around industrialists and businessmen. The primary goal of the workers was to ensure basic incomes, reasonable working hours, and lasting contracts of employment. For the workers, the means was solidarity. Solidarity, not individualist freedom, became the cornerstone of the labour movement. When facing opposition from both the conservatives and the liberalists, it might turn out that the workers preferred the conservatives: a patriarchal nobleman who felt some responsibility for 'his' people might be better than a *laissez-faire* liberalist industrialist. In 1867, the Conservative government granted many workers the right to vote.

In this situation, the British liberalists were in a dilemma: either to become socialistic or lose the support of the workers. The liberalists in Britain chose the first course, and British liberalism was eventually transformed into a social liberalism with national obligations, gaining the broad support of the people. The liberalist theory then had to be revised. The theories of Bentham, Smith, and Ricardo of the relationship between the individual and the state, and between freedom and coercion, had to be rewritten. This meant that the basic feature of liberalism, as we have defined this concept here, namely, individualism, was eventually modified by the incorporation of the concept of society and of social scientific thought.

John Stuart Mill was a philosopher who was marked by utilitarianism, liberalism, and empiricism, but who was also critical of the earlier versions of these theories. Thus, he tried to modify classical liberalism with the aid of social science, and in political theory he was a pioneer of the social liberalism that rejects *laissez-faire* and emphasizes active legislation.

Although John Stuart Mill became an adherent of utilitarianism, he found himself critical of Bentham's version of the hedonic calculus, in which utility is explained as pleasure without distinguishing qualitatively between the higher and lower forms. We could say that Bentham tried to explain the qualitative aspects, that is, what is morally and juridically a correct decision or a correct action, with the aid of a quantitative comparison of the various states of pleasure and pain that, in different ways, are supposed to follow from the various alternative actions. John Stuart Mill reinterpreted the concept of utility in such a way that it allowed for *qualitatively* different forms of pleasure and pain. The comparison of the qualitatively different states of utility is then determined by a consensus or by a majority decision by competent persons, that is, people who from personal experience understand the basic alternatives.

Mill thus thought that from the very beginning we must distinguish between qualitatively different levels, that is, between a morally good and a morally bad (or less bad) experience of joy. From the perspective of common linguistic use, this is reasonable. From this perspective we would say that the sadist's delight in harming the victim is evil and that the nurse's joy at the patient's progress is good, even though the sadist's and the nurse's experiences of pleasure are equally intense, equal in duration, etc. But even by using a quantitative calculation of pleasure, this qualitative point could, to some extent, be made when all of the involved parties, over time, are taken into consideration: the greatest possible happiness for the greatest possible number of people, considered in a long-term perspective. We would then probably observe that the sadist's delight leads to more negative results than the nurse's, and that the nurse's action is therefore *best*.

Among the most important values, Mill included personal freedom, self-respect, integrity, and social well-being. Mill defended freedom of speech, freedom of the press, etc., because he viewed these freedoms as desirable qualities. These liberal virtues, however, are also important for rationality and the search for truth: the free debate in the public square – without internal and external obstacles – is a condition for the possibility of our arriving at reasonable viewpoints.[3]

For Mill, however, public opinion was an ambiguous matter. Public opinion, on the one side, may appear coercive and suppressive of viewpoints that are supported by minority groups. On the other hand, Mill assumed that public opinion may be formed and improved by a free discussion between reasonable individuals: this public discussion may lead to the result that prejudices and mistakes can be corrected, as long as the discussion is open and free. The discussion may then serve to enlighten various opinions, even though the discussion does not lead us towards *one* truth. A free discussion may, at least, allow the different perspectives and viewpoints to be expressed more clearly, both for the adherents and for the opponents.

It is only when a viewpoint is publicly expressed, and therefore can be contradicted and defended, that this viewpoint is recognized for what it is. This means that we really do not know what we ourselves think until we have heard the counterarguments. In order for the truth to come out as clearly as possible – in order for all of us to gain the best possible insight into what we really think, by recognizing as clearly and fairly as possible what the opponent thinks – we must have free, public debate. Freedom of speech and freedom of expression are necessary conditions for open discussion.[4] We may say that liberality is a condition for rationality.

As a social philosopher and political reformer, John Stuart Mill is known for his work to help misjudged and oppressed groups, from the workers' fight for parliamentary representation, and the African-American's position in North America, to the discrimination against women on various levels. Concerning the oppression of women in his day, he argued for general voting rights and for the recognition of married women's property rights. This struggle for equality and liberation was a part of the progressive liberalism of which Mill was a champion: all adults are, in principle, equal, both politically and judicially. We all have the right to realize our potential when it does not lead to harm for others. Race, gender, or social background are, in this connection, irrelevant in the sense that we all have the same political and legal rights independently of biological and social conditions. Mill worked closely with Harriet Taylor on these issues.

By thus starting with inviolable individual rights, Mill positioned himself within a modern tradition going back to, among others, Locke. In this respect he distinguished himself from Plato, who thought in terms of man-in-community. But, at the same time, there are certain parallels between Mill and Plato in the view of man, since they both de-emphasized biology in relation to the political. Here, Mill and Plato stand on the same side in opposition to Aristotle. The various views on women found in these thinkers – Plato, Aristotle, and Mill – illustrate the following oppositions and parallels. Aristotle viewed women in light of biology and in light of the social position they held in his day. Plato viewed women as reasonable beings, in principle raised above biology, but anchored in the community of the city-state. Mill viewed women from the perspective of universal, individual rights, relatively independently of their biological-social anchoring.[5] In accordance with his view of universal individual rights, Mill emphasized that women have the right to choose between motherhood and a career. Such a freedom of choice was included in Mill's conception of universal political and economic rights. But for women who choose motherhood, Mill assumed that their practical roles in the family were fixed as understood in his day. He did not envisage a change in the traditional family roles. Such ideas belong to our day.

Although Mill, in his normative thought, emphasized universal principles based on the individual, he was, in his view of society, aware that the social milieu is important in the formation of the individual. In particular, this concept comprises the social-liberal aspect of Mill's thought. Here the parallels can be seen with early British and French socialism, as inspired by thinkers like Owen, Saint-Simon, and Fourier. John Stuart Mill distanced himself from James Mill's belief in a strong majority government: it is not only the strong minority group (an aristocracy) that may tyrannize over a weak majority (the remainder of the people). A majority may also tyrannize over a minority. A representative form of government is not enough to guarantee the liberty of minority groups or of individuals. John Stuart Mill was therefore concerned with the question of how society can ensure decent living conditions for free and responsible persons. He was concerned with how social attitudes, such as intolerance and aggression, may suppress a free personality.[6]

On this point, John Stuart Mill moved beyond classical liberalism: he recognized that anonymous social forces are decisive influences on how people live. We not only have explanations in terms of asocial human atoms and an external state system. Society also is a field of investigation in addition to the individual and the state. However, John Stuart Mill did not think in a systematic sociological manner, for sociology was still in its infancy. He provided a principal defence of personal liberty rather than a structural exposition of the forces in society.

Moreover, his thought still, to some degree, remained within the classical distinction, internal–external, private–social. Thus, he discussed personal liberty as something that belongs within a protected field of privacy, and as something that involves only the individual personally. But John Stuart Mill did not provide a satisfactory criterion for this distinction between the private and the social spheres. Still, the decisive factor is that the naive, *laissez-faire* liberalist view of coercion as external governmental interference is rejected. The social liberalist John Stuart Mill recognized that there are a coercion and a power that are beyond the state and the laws. This meant that the minimum amount of legislation and of governmental interference was not identical with the maximum freedom, as the *laissez-faire* liberalists thought.

John Stuart Mill did not accept the *laissez-faire* liberalists' theses of the natural laws of the market and of self-regulating competition. Thus, he advocated criticism of the economic system. The free market and its laws are not a natural state of affairs that must not be touched. If we think that there is an undesirable socio-economic situation in a country, we may intervene through legal reforms.

The basic ethical intuition expressed by John Stuart Mill was indignation at the unjust and inhumane aspects of the British society of his day. If John Stuart Mill's theory was occasionally problematic, his writings were still driven by a social and moral responsibility. And in his defence of personal liberty and demand for an active legislation to lay the groundwork for this liberty, John Stuart Mill contributed to the formation of basic attitudes within social liberalism, even though the social forces were not recognized in a more satisfactory way in his day. Sociology was still just coming into its own (A. Comte 1798–1857, E. Durkheim 1858–1917, and M. Weber 1864–1920). But the emerging field of empirical social research held a strong appeal for John Stuart Mill.

THOMAS HILL GREEN

The transformation of liberalism into social-liberalism that John Stuart Mill initiated continued throughout the 1800s. The result was liberalism 'with a human face': this meant ethical co-responsibility and the recognition of the individual as a social being, and a public policy governed by social institutions; in short, it meant a recognition that sociological notions are necessary to understand human beings and politics.

Thomas Hill Green (1836–1882) continued the criticism of the simplified psychological and ethical theory that formed the basis of classical liberalism; he pointed out that a person is necessarily linked to the social community. In other words, for Green, the internal criticism of liberalist individualism had shattered the individualist position, leaving a position that, in many ways, may remind us of that of Aristotle. But Green did not live in a Greek city-state. Green distinguished himself from Aristotle both by viewing the community as a Christian community and by viewing politics as a means of arranging the social conditions to make a moral life possible.

Freedom, for Green, was not only negative freedom, freedom from coercion, but a genuine freedom, in the sense that self-realization really is economically and psychologically possible in an ethical community. Laws restricting the actions of certain persons are necessary in order to establish genuine freedom for all. Therefore, social and educational policies become important. Green's goal was a moral life, not 'liberty' and not the maximization of pleasure or profit. Through reform legislation, politics are the means of attaining this goal. Here, liberalism has become humanistic and socially aware. What remained of the liberalist individualism was, among other things, the view of human beings as being morally equal, equal in worth and respect.

If we define 'liberalism' as an individualist ideology, Green was not a 'liberalist', although he was 'liberal', that is, tolerant and humane. Green's liberalism extended to both conservative and social-democratic attitudes. His appreciation of the religious and the ethical aspects of life, and his emphasis on the view that security and stability are necessary to man, reflect conservative ideas. At the same time, there is a theme that develops from Green to the liberal, social-democratic basis of the Fabian Society (established 1884); that is, reform socialism without the theory of class struggle. The British Labour Party was formed within this tradition of social welfare and control of business, although not complete state management, and without the dogma of an unavoidable class struggle that rejects compromise solutions and parliamentary cooperation with conservative parties. In Britain, liberal socialism (Labour) and social liberalism largely converge.

From the early 1860s – after the publication of Darwin's *On the Origin of Species* – parallels were drawn between a free market, in which competition between the agents determines their fate, and biological theories of 'the survival of the fittest'. The thesis of the survival of the fittest may be viewed as a biological and evolutionary reinterpretation of *laissez-faire* liberalism: just as the natural competition for food and mates allows the fittest animals to live and reproduce, so that the most vital genetic traits are preserved, unrestricted economic competition will also result in the best human beings flourishing and bequeathing their superior genetic traits to a future society, while the inferior genetic traits are weeded out. All social aid to the poor and to the 'unfit' is undesirable because it leads to a population with inferior genetic traits. A biological *laissez-faire* liberalism of this kind entails certain theoretical problems. The first problem is that it conceives of society in biological terms and thus overlooks the specifically social aspects. The second problem is that it attempts to deduce a *norm* from a (claimed) *fact*: it attempts to deduce what will lead to the 'best' results, the 'best' individuals – and what therefore 'ought' to dictate our political decisions – from the theory of the preservation of vital genetic traits. We might also formulate the objections as follows. Are those best able to survive in a liberalist market economy the best and most valuable members of society in every way? What about an 'unfit' poet, a misunderstood scientist, or an unselfish and self-sacrificing idealist? That 'the best' is defined as those who best survive in a particular society can easily lead to the view that this society is the 'best' society, since this society allows 'the best' to survive!

JOHN MAYNARD KEYNES

John Maynard Keynes (1883–1946), one of the foremost British economists in the period between World War I and World War II, was prominent both as a practical economist and as an economic theoretician. A basic idea of Keynes was the rejection of *laissez-faire* liberalism:[7] the time has passed when capitalism can be advanced by great individuals. The state must now play an active role in economic life. But Keynes was not a socialist; he did not think that the state ought to take over those activities that had traditionally been in private hands. The state (the government) should perform the new tasks that are not taken care of by the private sector, such as well thought-out control of credit and monetary exchange, the establishment of the extent of saving and investment by society as a whole, and regulation of population numbers. And when unemployment and stagnation threaten, the state should play an active role in managing the economy.

In other words, Keynes was by no means an opponent of capitalism. However, he claimed that liberalism and private capitalism were outdated. And he recommended reforms that he thought would lead to a modern capitalism: a capitalism characterized by strong governmental activity. Keynes was one of the foremost defenders of a state capitalism. Thus, he attacked both *laissez-faire* liberalism (private capitalism) and socialism.

In 1936, after the great Depression, he published *The General Theory of Employment, Interest and Money*. This became a classic for modern capitalist economists. One of Keynes' new features was his emphasis on the problem of full employment, a problem that the liberalist economists had often 'solved' by taking full employment as a given presupposition. According to Keynes, full employment is something that can be only approximately achieved by a well-thought out economic policy. It is not automatically produced by the free reign of market forces, as a natural harmony. In order to achieve an approximately full employment, the state must exert a certain amount of influence on consumption, by means of, among other things, fiscal policy and public investment – but the interference of the state should not become so comprehensive that the right to own private property is endangered. According to Keynes, the right to own private property (capitalism) has the decisive advantage of being based on the decentralization of power and on self-interest. Keynes viewed his reforms as necessary to avoid crises in capitalism. Without government organization, there would be no capitalism.

We may say that Keynes was important in political theory because he represented the view that liberalism and private capitalism should learn from economic crises. He embodied the transition in theory from private capitalism and *laissez-faire* liberalism to a government-organized capitalism, that is, to a capitalism with the social-liberal and social-democratic characteristics later found in social democracy.

QUESTIONS

Describe what is meant by utilitarianism. Explain especially Jeremy Bentham's utilitarianism.

Explain the philosophical views underlying liberalism (from Locke to John Stuart Mill). Explain also John Stuart Mill's views of censorship and of the freedom of expression.

SUGGESTIONS FOR FURTHER READING

PRIMARY LITERATURE

Bentham, J., *An Introduction to the Principles of Morals and Legislation*, London, 1982.
Keynes, John Maynard, *The End of Laissez-Faire*, London, 1927.
Mill, J. S., '*On Liberty*' and '*Considerations on Representative Government*', London, 1976.
Mill, J. S., *Utilitarianism*, London, 1964.
Works of Thomas Hill Green, edited and introduced by Peter Nicholson, London, 1997.

SECONDARY LITERATURE

Berlin, I., *Four Essays on Liberty*, Oxford, 1986.
Cacoullos, Ann R., *Thomas Hill Green: Philosopher of Rights*, New York, 1974.
Duncan, G., *Marx and Mill. Two Views on Social Conflict and Harmony*, Cambridge, 1973.
Ryan, A., *The Philosophy of John Stuart Mill*, London, 1970.

NOTES

1 Cf. the individualism in hedonistic Epicureanism, Ch. 5.
2 On the term *nominalism*, cf. Ch. 6, The problem of universals. On the use of comprehensive concepts, cf. Ch. 26, on Wittgenstein, and Ordinary language philosophy.
3 Thus, we may also say that freedom is 'useful' since it makes it possible for us to recognize what is true.
4 Cf. the view of the discussion, the dialogue, as a path towards the truth (or, at least, better informed opinions) in Plato, the Enlightenment philosophers, and Kant and Habermas.
5 See Susan Moller Okin, 'John Stuart Mill, Liberal Feminist', Chapter 9 in *Women in Western Political Thought*, Princeton, NJ, 1979.
6 It is thus understandable that John Stuart Mill wrote an enthusiastic review of Tocqueville's book *La Démocratie en Amérique*. Tocqueville was especially interested in the oppression of individuals who held deviant opinions. See Ch. 24.
7 John Maynard Keynes, *The End of Laissez-Faire*, London, 1927.

15 Kant – 'the Copernican revolution' in philosophy

Life. Immanuel Kant (1724–1804) spent his entire life in the East Prussian city of Königsberg, now Kaliningrad. His father was a craftsman and a pietist, and Kant was in many ways marked by a pietistic Protestantism. Externally, his life was simple. He started as a tutor and ended as a professor. His lifestyle was punctilious and unvarying to the point of pedantry. His life was devoted to his theoretical pursuits. His three critiques are important: the Critique of Pure Reason *(1781), the* Critique of Practical Reason *(1788), and the* Critique of Judgment *(1790). Of interest for his political theory are* Fundamental Principles of the Metaphysic of Morals *('Grundlegung zur Metaphysik der Sitten' [1785]) and* Perpetual Peace *(1795).*

TRANSCENDENTAL PHILOSOPHY – THEORY OF KNOWLEDGE

In the German-speaking states, the Enlightenment represented, initially, cultural renewal rather than political change. The ideas of the Enlightenment spread among both the upper classes of the state officials and the middle class, and university life was strengthened both academically and structurally.

Kant entered into this process. He was close to the philosophers of the Enlightenment. He sought to establish man's autonomy through an enlightened, universal use of reason. But like Rousseau, he distanced himself from the intellectual atheism of the Enlightenment philosophers. As a philosopher of the 1700s, Kant's work was devoted to an epistemology based on the particular individual. Here, the empiricists, the rationalists, and Kant were on common ground. In many ways, Kant stood within the liberalist tradition; at the same time, he represented a decisive break with the empiricist and utilitarian tendencies that predominate towards the end of the 1700s. The break took place when Kant launched his transcendental philosophy as an attempt to refute both empiricism (Locke, Hume) and rationalism (Descartes).

We will first examine Kant's transcendental philosophy in the context of his theory of knowledge and his moral theory, before we discuss the aspects of Kant's philosophy that apply to his political theory.

Hume criticized the Enlightenment concept of reason by distinguishing sharply between the descriptive and the normative. His position was that the only knowledge we can have about the world and about ourselves, namely, knowledge based on experience, can never be absolutely certain since it is always theoretically possible that new impressions will contradict the experiential impressions on which we have based our views until now: that is, not even the natural sciences are absolutely certain. In other words, apart from insight into the relationship between concepts – which, it is worth noting, does not provide us with insight into reality – no knowledge is absolutely certain. And ethical insight does not exist. The world was apparently more uncertain after Hume. The role that rational intuition and reason had played for both the classical rationalists and for the Enlightenment philosophers was for Hume, to a large degree, taken over by feelings and habits.

For Kant, Hume's sceptical empiricism was a scandal: Hume had undermined both morality and the natural sciences![1] Kant set himself the task of proving that there is something within ethics and within the natural sciences that we can acknowledge with our *reason* as being *strictly necessary and universally valid*. This was Kant's starting point. He wanted to show that reason is given a far too modest role in the empiricist Hume's thought. But at the same time, Kant did not return to classical rationalism (as in Descartes). He tried a third way.

Kant's project was not only an internal philosophical debate with Hume. As a philosopher working during the Enlightenment, Kant was also interested in scientific progress. He seemed to view Newton's physics as a lasting triumph of science. Something indisputably true had been discovered. For example, Newton's physics deals with the concepts of space, time, and causal connection. It was formulated mathematically, and it built methodically on experiment. Kant wanted to bring philosophy into the same secure position as that of the natural sciences; at the same time, he viewed it as his task as a philosopher to show why the foundation for experimental science is unshakable: when we perform experiments, we systematically isolate, combine, and vary some conditions in order to observe and measure the properties of phenomena that depend on these. We measure, for example, the pressure of a gas at a constant temperature by varying the volume, as Robert Boyle did. We then assume that other people can do the same, and that we ourselves can repeat the experiment at any time and in any place. If we do not assume that the universe is uniform, throughout space and time, and that we can repeat an experiment, the experimentation will be without value, and the methodical basis for the new experimental science will be undermined. Of course, new experiments may lead to different results, so that earlier results must be rejected. This is precisely the point with experimental science. In the same way, what we previously held to be constant may prove to be variable factors. Even this is a part of the experimental process in science. But if we doubt, in principle, the basic uniformity of the universe, the point of the experiment disappears – just as the notion of universal natural laws disappears.

Kant rejected this kind of scepticism, and he did so by arguing that the forms of perception, space and time, and some basic notions, such as that of causality, are inherent in the human mind. Kant's reaction to Hume was thus a position not only in an internal philosophical dispute, but also in a dispute concerning our confidence in science.

For Kant, the rejection of Hume's scepticism lay in a shift of the epistemological perspective. Copernicus and Kepler had gained a better grasp of astronomical data by denying the traditional doctrine that the Earth and man are at the immovable centre of the universe in favour of the hypothesis that man and the Earth revolve around the sun. In the same manner, Kant reversed the basic opinion that cognition occurs when the subject is influenced by the object, in the sense that he turned the relationship around and asserted that we must imagine that it is the object that is influenced by the subject; that is, the object, as we know it, is formed by the subject's way of experiencing and thinking. This shift in epistemological presuppositions is called *the Copernican revolution in philosophy*. This is the core of Kant's theory of knowledge.

Kant tried, in a way, to create a synthesis of empiricism and rationalism by attempting to avoid what he saw as empirical scepticism and rationalistic dogmatism. Instead of a rational intuition of supersensory objects – such as God and moral norms – Kant introduced a reflexive insight into the fundamental *conditions* of experience. Insight into such epistemological conditions is called *transcendental* insight. By discussing the central features in Kant's philosophy, we will shed some light on what is meant by this expression.

The starting point is that Hume was wrong. There *is* a necessary and universally valid order in experience. For instance, the principle of causality is universally valid. Therefore, there must be something that structures and orders our experience. But Kant agreed with Hume that immediate experience and induction do not provide insight into something that is necessary and universally valid. Therefore, whatever orders and structures our experience cannot itself proceed from experience. This ordering and structuring faculty must thus be found *within* us.

In other words, Kant presupposed a dualism of subject and object: since the ordering power cannot lie in the object, it must lie in the subject. This is the Copernican revolution in Kant's theory of knowledge: whatever orders and structures our experience, so that it is subject to universally valid principles, stems not from the things that are the objects of cognition, but from ourselves.

Kant simply *took for granted* that there is something in our cognition that is necessary and universally valid. He did not ask *whether* this is so, but *how* this can be so.

But in what sense can such an ordering power lie 'within us'? We may use an illustration: if we always wear glasses with green lenses, everything we see – houses, rocks, trees, etc. – will necessarily appear green. Everything we look at will always have the colour of our lenses. If we know the colour of our lenses, we will know with complete certainty that what we look at will have that colour, even if we do not know what we will be looking at. Thus, using categories of content and form, we may say that the content is determined by the outside, but we always imprint the content with our form (here the colour green). The ordering faculty within us is like the lenses of our glasses, and the various impressions that 'hit' our glasses are the content of experience. What we see is the synthesis, of sense impression and of colour – the content that is formed.

In this sense, Kant agreed with the empiricists that all knowledge *starts* with experience. But at the same time, he claimed that all knowledge is *formed by the subject*. All sense impressions take the form that we impose upon them. They follow the forms of perception, of space and time. However, we do not have genuinely ordered experiences until the sense impressions are conceptually conceived; that is, when our mind makes use of its categories, such as the principle of causality, to order the perceived diversity. Therefore, Kant had a somewhat different conception of experience than the empiricists.

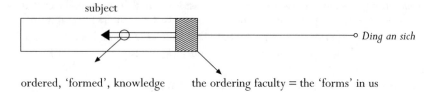

subject

ordered, 'formed', knowledge   the ordering faculty = the 'forms' in us

Kant also presupposed that *all* human beings have the same principal 'forms'. *All* knowledge, for *all* people, *must* therefore be shaped by these forms. In this sense, the forms are *universally valid* and *necessary*.

The 'forms' that Kant sought are not of a psychological nature. It is, for example, a psychological fact that people suffering from paranoia 'see' the world ('form' their knowledge) in a particular way. But the forms that Kant sought are the completely general features of all knowledge, such as *space*, *time*, and *causality*.[2] These are forms that must be *presupposed* in all empirical investigations, and therefore cannot be critically investigated by empirical psychology.

But why create such a complex theory of knowledge? The answer lies in what we have already mentioned: Kant took *for granted* that there is something that is universally valid and necessary in our knowledge, and this theory of knowledge *explains* how this can be possible.[3]

But in what sense is it plausible to claim that space, time, and causality are universally valid and necessary forms? Kant answered that our knowledge of things *must* always be marked by space and time (forms of cognition, or forms of sense experience) and causality (one of the twelve categories).[4] We may try to illustrate Kant's point with the following thought experiment.

A traffic constable enters the police station to report a collision. But to the question of *when* the collision occurred, he answers that it did not take place at any particular time. To the question of *where* it occurred, he answers that it did not take place at any particular place. It just happened. Finally, to the question of what *caused* the collision, the constable answers that nothing caused it. There were no cars that drove too fast or recklessly. The collision just happened, suddenly, without any preceding causes. It is obvious to the police chief that this constable is talking nonsense. To put it another way, we do not need to collect any evidence to show that this report is mistaken. The mistakes that the constable has made are more basic than mere experiential mistakes. He did not report an incorrect time, a wrong street name, or an inaccurate speed and incorrect driving direction. The constable *could* have lied about all of these things, and the police chief *could* have checked the validity of his report by inspection. But the mistakes that the constable made were not experiential (empirical) mistakes, but something more fundamental. A collision that did not take place at any particular time or place, or as the result of some cause, is completely *incomprehensible*. In other words, space, time, and causality are necessary and universally valid forms because our knowledge *must* be marked by time, space, and causality in order to be *comprehensible*; that is, in order to be knowledge. Space, time, and causality are conditions for the possibility of knowledge.

The opposition to Hume is clear.[5] Since we always possess the same forms within us, everything that we may experience must be shaped by these forms. Therefore, we *know* something certain about the *future*: regardless of *what* we experience, the experience will be shaped by time, space, causality, etc. Thus, certain formal structures within our knowledge are *universally valid*. These structures apply to all people, and they apply in the future as well as the present and the past. Therefore, there are certain fundamental features of the natural sciences (or, more generally, the empirical sciences) that are necessary and universally valid.

These forms or structures are not in the object, but are in *all* subjects. To call them subjective is therefore ambiguous. They are *not* subjective in the sense that they are accidental or fallible. On the contrary, they are found in all subjects as the epistemological precondition for the possibility of objective, that is, true, knowledge.

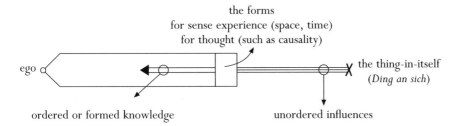

As a precondition of knowledge and experience, the forms are *prior* to experience. Insight into these forms, therefore, does not belong to some empirical science, such as psychology, but to the philosophical reflection upon the epistemological conditions of these empirical sciences.

Up to now, we have tried to make Kant understandable without raising objections to his philosophical thought. We will now mention a common objection: Kant thought that sense impressions stem from an external reality, the thing-in-itself (*Ding an sich*). But at the same time, he said that we can comprehend *only* the sense impressions that *are formed*. The unformed influences and the thing-in-itself are therefore incomprehensible. The concept of thing-in-itself is thus a problematic concept that, on the one hand, is necessary in order to explain the origin of experience, but that, on the other hand, cannot be experienced.

So far, we have discussed Kant's epistemological model. We will take a brief look at the *types of knowledge* that he defines:

1   analytic (*a priori*) – e.g. 'A bachelor is an unmarried man.'
2   synthetic (*a posteriori*) – e.g. 'This house is green.'
3   synthetic (*a priori*) – e.g. 'Every event has some cause.'

The first type of knowledge applies to the relationship between concepts, the second type to the formed sense impressions, and the third type to insight into the *forms*.

Kant took for granted that there are 'synthetic *a priori* judgements'. For Kant, the question is how this is possible, not *whether* it is possible. And the answer is that 'synthetic *a priori* judgements' are possible because there are certain forms, in all knowing subjects, that are conditions for ordered experience.

What does Kant mean by 'synthetic *a priori*'? He defines the term as follows:

a priori: independent of experience – e.g. 'A bachelor is an unmarried man.'

a posteriori: dependent on experience – e.g. 'This house is green.'

analytic: 1 statements in which the logical predicate is 'a part of' the logical subject; e.g. 'A bachelor is an unmarried man.'
2 statements in which the negation leads to a logical contradiction; e.g. 'A bachelor is not an unmarried man.'

synthetic: 1 statements in which the logical predicate is *not* 'a part of' the logical subject; e.g. 'This house is green.'
2 statements in which the negation *does not* lead to a logical contradiction, e.g. 'This house is not green.'

We then have:

	synthetic	*analytic*
a priori	'Every event has some cause.'	'A bachelor is an unmarried man.'
a posteriori	'This house is green.'	

In other words, analytic *a priori* statements correspond to insight into the relationship between concepts, according to the rationalists and empiricists, and synthetic *a posteriori* statements correspond to experience, according to the rationalists and empiricists. The critical point is *the synthetic a priori judgements*. These are statements that are independent of experience (*a priori*), and in which the logical predicate is not given in the logical subject (synthetic). Kant was convinced that statements (*Urteile*) like these exist, and that the statement 'Every event has some cause' is an example. This is in opposition to the empiricist view that would have interpreted this statement either as analytic (*a priori*) – we can define 'every event' in such a way that 'has some cause', by definition, belongs to the concept 'everything that happens' – or as synthetic (*a posteriori*) – the statement is a generalization from particular experiences; consequently, we do not know whether the statement will apply in the future. Kant claimed that it is *not* analytically given, with the concept *every event*, that every event *has its cause*, and that we do not need to look to experience in order to know that every event has some cause, since the cognition of causality is built in with our forms of thought.

The statement 'Every event has some cause' thus belongs with the basic principles of natural science (such as Newton's mechanics) that Kant considered universally valid and necessary. Correspondingly, for example, Kant thought that the statement 'the shortest distance between two points is a straight line' is a synthetic *a priori* statement within mathematics. Thus, mathematics and natural science are firmly anchored sciences, according to Kant. The anchoring is based in the ordered forms found in all subjects.

Kant thus rejected what he saw as empiricist scepticism: there is, according to Kant, a reflexive insight into the conditions of knowledge, an insight showing that the two previously mentioned sciences rest on a secure foundation. Kant also rejected what he saw as rationalistic dogmatism: speculative rationalism (metaphysics) does not have a firm foundation and, consequently, is not a science. The rational intuition that the rationalists claimed, as in regard to God, is only quasi-insight. Here, Kant's critique of speculative reason began: traditional rationalism is a pseudo-science. We *can* reflect on the conditions of experience, as Kant did in his philosophy. But the rationalists tried to move beyond experience, to the transcendent, to what lies beyond the limits of sense experience. But we cannot know anything about what transcends the conditions (and limitations) of knowledge. Kant advanced two arguments to support this view: on the one hand, we *cannot* have sense experience of the transcendent, because that lies *beyond* such experience. On the other hand, when the rationalists theoretically dispute God's existence, for example, the arguments for and against are *equally weighty*. This theoretical dead end (*aporia*) also shows that it is impossible to *know* anything about the transcendent.

But does not Kant's epistemology presuppose that we receive impressions that ultimately originate from the thing-in-itself, that is, from a transcendent object that lies beyond experience? How can Kant know that this is the case? This is one of the objections raised by Hegel, among others.

Kant criticized metaphysics. But, unlike the radical empiricists, he did not think that the era of metaphysics was over. On the contrary, Kant thought that the metaphysical questions are unavoidable. Asking these questions is a part of human nature, although we can never arrive at a scientific answer.

Personally, Kant was a pietistic Protestant, and his transcendental philosophy, which both rejects rationalism and conceives of the metaphysical questions as being unavoidable, harmonizes well with central Protestant concepts: we can neither prove nor disprove the fundamental religious questions. And since we are not able to break free from these questions, the answers must be based on *faith*. We thus end up with a distinction between *knowledge* and *faith* that is typical of Protestantism. Room is made for religion. We can neither prove nor disprove the existence of God, but we can believe in the one or the other. At the same time that Kant 'preserved reason' in the natural sciences and mathematics against Hume's empiricism, he left room for a simple faith in religion.

We have seen that Kant's transcendental philosophy, which includes a reflection upon the epistemological limits of knowledge, involved an attempt to form a synthesis of rationalism and empiricism. Kant touched on something essential: in addition to our statements about states of affairs — statements that in varying degrees are true or false to the extent that the statements correspond with the objects of experience — we may reflect upon the *conditions* that make such true or false statements *possible*.

In this sense, we may take the principle of contradiction — 'a thing cannot, at the same time, be ascribed the property A and the property *not-A*, in the same sense' — as such a condition for empirically true or false statements. According to normal linguistic use, the statement 'this pencil is simultaneously red and blue all over' is a breach of the principle of contradiction. This statement is neither empirically true nor false since it breaks a condition of the statement's being empirically true or false.

Correspondingly, we may interpret the principle of causality – 'all events have causes' – as a condition for meaningful statements, as for example, within the natural sciences. Suppose a medical researcher says: 'It is not just the case that the causes of certain forms of cancer are unknown. Several forms of cancer do not have any cause.' This researcher has done something different from, and something worse than, making an *empirical* mistake; that is, to have attributed certain forms of cancer to the wrong cause. This researcher has broken a *condition* of meaningful cancer research. In other words, the principle of causality may be said to function as a necessary principle within the natural sciences. If scientists transgress this principle, they are not making a factual mistake, they are overstepping the bounds of scientific research.

One major criticism of Kant is directed against his attempt to find all of the basic principles of knowledge, *once and for all*, and to locate all of these principles in the cognizant *subject*. Some critics have claimed that there are many different principles that partially apply to certain areas, but not to other areas. Thus, we may say that the principle of contradiction applies to a larger field (for example, to both physics and text interpretation) than does the principle of causality (which applies to physics, but not to text interpretation). Other critics have claimed that certain of these principles are inherent in language, as more or less indispensable principles of linguistic meaning or convention, in the *intersubjective life world* (cf. Chs 26 and 27).

However these principles may be interpreted, the decisive point is that, in an epistemological sense, they are *prior* to common empirical knowledge. These conditions are presuppositions for empirical knowledge (empirically true statements), approximately in the same sense that the rules of chess are presupposed in the moves in a chess game: the rules in chess are like a frame which makes the variously good and bad moves possible. These rules make the moves possible, they 'constitute' the moves.

The point of transcendental philosophy is precisely that there are such enabling conditions which, epistemologically, have a more fundamental status than empirically true and false statements, that is, than empirical statements. Transcendental philosophy tries to clarify the conditions (rules, presuppositions, principles, and frames) which constitute (make possible and form) experientially true and false statements. We will later see how Hegel modified Kant's transcendental condition in the direction of social conditions, that is, in the direction of ideologies.

TRANSCENDENTAL PHILOSOPHY – MORAL THEORY

As we have mentioned, Kant attacked Hume's scepticism both in natural science and ethics. Kant's answer to Hume's *ethical* scepticism was, in many ways, parallel with Kant's epistemological answer: Kant took it as *a given* that there is a 'you shall'. He asked: *how* is this possible?

Since this 'you shall', according to Kant, is an absolute obligation, it cannot stem from experience – because the experiential does not embrace (according to Kant) what is normative; moreover, the experiential is never completely certain. This 'you shall' must then be inherent *in us*.

Furthermore, this unconditional moral imperative ('you shall') cannot apply to the *consequences* of our actions, because we do not have complete knowledge or control over the consequences. This moral imperative must therefore apply to our *moral will*, according to Kant.

Kant's moral theory was an ethics of moral will, not a consequentialist ethics: the decisive factor is that the will is good, not that the consequences of the actions are good. Here Kant distinguished himself from the utilitarians, who advocated a consequentialist ethic: morally good actions are those that lead to the greatest utility (happiness, pleasure) for the greatest number of people.

Moreover, Kant's ethics of moral will was an ethics of *duty*. He held that we are first able to *test* our moral will when we do something reluctantly, motivated by our sense of *moral obligation*. This does not mean that Kant advocated displeasure and pain, but it shows how far removed he was from all forms of morality based on pleasure (hedonism). This unconditional moral imperative, 'you shall', is thus inherent in us, just like the transcendental forms of space, time, causality, etc. This means that *all* human beings are subject to this moral obligation. Morality thus has an *absolute* anchoring, according to Kant. In other words, Kant based an absolute morality on the subject, while Plato based an absolute morality on 'objective' ideas.

In this connection it is helpful to see how Kant's epistemology made a fundamental distinction between the empirical and the transcendental, between *what we experience* and man as *thing-in-itself*. What we experience represents the *realm of necessity*, since everything there is comprehended in terms of causal connections. This also applies to man. To the degree that we experience our own empirical ego, we understand it as being causally determined. But the consciousness that conceives is not itself the consciousness that is conceived. The consciousness that conceives cannot be said to be causally determined, since causal determination is something that follows from the circumstance that phenomena are shaped by our transcendental forms. And the consciousness that conceives is not anything that we experience in this way.[6] Hence, for Kant, there was a distinction between man as a creature of reason and man as a creature of nature. As a rational being, man is subject to absolute moral obligations in the form of laws that an autonomous person follows on the basis of reason. As a natural being, man is subject to causality; it exists in the realm of necessity.

In his view of man, Kant envisaged a series of oppositions reminiscent of Plato's distinction between the world of ideas and the perceptible world. Man is said to belong to the realm of necessity, but he can also be said to belong to the realm of freedom. The sharp distinction between the transcendental and the empirical, between man as a rational being and as a natural being, renders ethics independent of empirical factors. Ethics is grounded in man as a rational being. This may be said to safeguard morality against criticism based on empirical factors. But at the same time, there must be some kind of connection between these spheres, between the transcendental and the empirical. How does this occur? Kant thought that the will mediates between the two spheres, in that the will is influenced by our natural inclinations, although the will is ruled by the law that we acknowledge with our free reason.

This absolute moral obligation has the status of a *categorical imperative*, which, according to Kant, takes the following form: *act only on that maxim that you can at the same time will that it should become a universal law*. The maxim for our actions is the universal rule that an action follows. If you lie to obtain an advantage, the maxim for your action would be: 'If we can obtain an advantage, we shall lie'. Hence, both moral and immoral actions are based on maxims. But Kant's point is that even though immoral actions do follow maxims, these maxims cannot be made into universal laws.

From Kant's formulation it is clear that he understood the moral obligation to be *universally valid*: the test of a moral action is that the action would be right *for everyone* who is in the same situation. Thus, it is not right to lie since we cannot make lying a universal norm: 'I cannot will that everyone should lie when it is advantageous to do so.' Kant gave an example: a kind of self-contradiction arises if we attempt to universalize a maxim that a man may escape financial difficulties by making a promise that he does not intend to keep. To put it another way, not all maxims can be universalized. For example, it is not possible to universalize a maxim advocating the breaking of promises. If we make such a maxim into a universal law, a contradiction arises on the practical level: we cannot consistently will such a maxim.

The demand to act on the basis of maxims that can be made *universal* is connected with the principle of acting towards others on the basis that they are an end in themselves. We are all ethically obligated not to treat other people only as a means for our own ends: we are all ends in ourselves. Although we must often view people as means, we should not view them as no more than that.

Kant's categorical imperative is a so-called meta-norm, that is to say, a norm about norms, namely, an ideal standard for deciding whether norms about actions are valid or invalid. But norms for right actions are not only to be legitimized from such a meta-norm. The norms for right actions must also be applied correctly. For Kant, there was also a tension between justification (the categorical imperative) and the application of this meta-norm in concrete situations. Such applications require an understanding of how the situation may best be understood. This raises the question of how we, as agents, may be certain that we possess adequate concepts for interpreting the situations in which we find ourselves.

The moral law, in the form of the categorical imperative, is connected to us by virtue of our being rational beings. The categorical imperative is *a priori*, since it is not grounded in experience. But it is not analytic; thus, it is *synthetic*. The categorical imperative is synthetic *a priori*. To put it in other words, the duty of all rational beings to act on the basis of universal laws is valid, independently of what people actually do, or of what they actually seek. The categorical imperative that expresses this duty is thus independent of, and prior to, empirical factors; it is *a priori*. Furthermore, this duty cannot be derived by conceptual analysis from the concept of a rational being or from a rational will. The categorical imperative that expresses this duty of all rational beings is thus not analytic, but synthetic. The categorical imperative is a practical, synthetic *a priori* proposition.

In addition to the unconditional categorical imperative, Kant assumed various *hypothetical* imperatives: if we want to achieve this or that end, we have to act in this or that way. These imperatives are not absolute, since it is not given that the end is good in and of itself. These imperatives are teleological in the way that they connect means to ends. 'If you want better grades, you will have to work harder on your assignments.' 'If we want to defeat our enemy, we will have to build more cannons.' The hypothetical imperatives represent a means-to-an-end rationality. The goal is taken for granted, as a hypothesis – we do not attempt to legitimize it rationally – and rationality is used to find the best means of reaching this goal; that is, rationality becomes instrumental: on the basis of confirmed experimental knowledge, we set up a calculation and a strategy for action. The action is successful when this strategy leads us easily to the goal. The hypothetical imperative has the form: 'if we want to reach goal *A*, we should follow strategy *S*'. Thus, to formulate hypothetical imperatives, according to Kant, is to postulate a causal relationship. The means are understood as the cause that leads to the goal. Kant therefore held that the promotion of hypothetical imperatives is actually a function of the theoretical use of reason, and not the genuine practical use of reason.

If the goal is of the kind that cannot be shared with others without loss – such as scarce material goods, a loaf of bread, a country, or a sum of money – and if everyone is seeking such a goal on an egotistic basis, the result is a situation where everyone is fighting against everyone else (Hobbes). By requiring that we should also view our fellow human beings as ends in themselves, Kant distanced himself from such an asocial state: my fellow human beings should not be viewed only as a means in my own calculations and actions, and they should be viewed not only as counter-agents, acting against my goals, but also as agents who have legitimate ends in and for themselves. And by requiring a universalization of maxims for action, Kant distanced himself from a manipulative strategy: when we manipulate and indoctrinate others, it is presumed that our own deliberations must not be made known to the others. By universalizing our maxims, we counteract manipulative techniques of domination.

The requirement of viewing our fellow human beings as ends in themselves, and the requirement of universalization – both of which are found in Kant's categorical imperative – thus represent a guarantee for the civil community: the technical or instrumental strategy in favour of egotistic goals must never become absolute. The respect for the moral law may thus be seen as an expression of the mutual recognition that enables a norm-regulated, non-strategic form of life. Thus, the moral law and respect for the moral law make a civil community possible.

Kant's argument concerns ahistorical individuals. Hence, his point is somewhat abstract. For example, in practice, we find questions of this kind: should we also view those who do *not* act towards others as ends in themselves, as ends in themselves? In what sense should we, in practice, view those who oppress others, as ends in themselves? It is clear that the categorical imperative is *formal*. It is to be absolutely binding for all people at all times. But in concrete situations, empirical factors necessarily enter the picture, factors which imply that what is morally right for one person is not always right for another. For example, at the scene of an automobile accident, a police officer and a doctor should act differently, by the requirement of universality. The police officer should not begin to treat the victims, and the doctor should not direct traffic. The universal requirements applying here are 'being a doctor at the scene of an automobile accident' and 'being a police officer at the scene of an automobile accident'.

Kant thought that this categorical imperative refuted what he viewed as Hume's ethical scepticism. But Hume also thought that we arrive at a correct moral judgment by being neutral and impartial. There is thus a certain parallel between Hume and Kant, since they both claimed that the practical criterion for right morals is universality; that is, that the norms for actions may be made universal. But, for

Hume, universality was grounded in similar feelings for all impartial observers, while Kant meant to build on firmer ground than feelings: the categorical imperative is necessarily inherent in us, just like the transcendental forms of knowledge. Here we must make a reservation. It is true that even the moral principles are found in us 'just like' the transcendental forms of knowledge. But we *can violate* the moral principles, something that we *cannot* do with natural laws (as in physics). Therefore, to say that the categorical imperative is inherent in us does not mean that we are all actually moral, but only that we all possess a moral will.

According to Kant's theory of knowledge, we cannot have knowledge of anything other than formed experience and the forms of experience. But, on the basis of the principle of duty, 'you shall', Kant held that we can accept certain implications that we cannot know anything about, but that still present themselves to our conscience. Kant called these implications 'practical postulates':

1   If we all possess the absolute principle of duty 'you shall', it must be the case that we *can* do our duty ('*ought* implies *can*'). Otherwise, the requirement would be meaningless. Thus, we must possess *free will*.
2   The absolute principle of duty demands that we seek *perfection*. But in this life this is impossible. Thus, we must be *immortal* in order for the requirement of perfection to have meaning.
3   All of this shows that there is a moral world order that creates a harmony of duty and consequence, so that what we do on the basis of good will also has good consequences. Therefore, a moral world Orderer must exist; that is, *God must exist*.

These are not arguments for God's existence, nor proofs of a life after death, or of free will. They are conditions for action that we cannot *know* anything about, but that still present themselves as unavoidable to the conscience. These conditions belong to the *practical*, moral reason, not to the *theoretical* reason. In Kant's philosophy, the postulate that we have free will is made possible by the distinction between the transcendental and the empirical: our empirical ego is necessarily conceived as causally determined, but, according to Kant's epistemology, free will *can* be ascribed to the transcendental ego. Hence, the first practical postulate can legitimately say that we as actors *must* have free will, in order to make sense of the categorical imperative.

POLITICAL THEORY

For historical reasons, Kant, like the liberalists and the utilitarians, did not have a sociological approach to man and society. He primarily took the individual as his theoretical starting point. But by opposing duty to pleasure, and moral will to consequence, Kant distinguished himself from the utilitarian theoreticians. A basic idea in Kant's political theory is the notion of the individual's self-worth. This self-worth is transcendentally based on the individual's freedom, that is, in the individual's own ability to make moral laws and to follow these laws. This means that everyone is, in principle, equal. The legal rights and the political institutions should aim to protect this freedom and equality. Kant was thus a defender of the individual's rights. This defence is based neither on an objective natural rights philosophy, as in Thomas Aquinas, nor on a subject-centred natural rights philosophy, as in John Locke. For Kant, the individual's rights are based on what Kant saw as an inalienable feature of human beings.

While the utilitarians, like Helvétius and Bentham, tried to base law and morality on the principle of the best possible consequences for the greatest number of people, Kant tried to establish law and morality as transcendentally necessary properties of man: the individual rights include what is necessary for a person to live in moral liberty. Whatever goes *against* these rights is evil, whether or not it leads to general utility or pleasure. In other words, while utilitarians debated the question of whether we should sacrifice a few for the benefit of the majority, Kant held that it is always wrong to violate the basic rights of an individual.

For people to live in moral liberty, the requirements include constitutional government, the abolition of slavery and other forms of inequality, and the abolition of war. These requirements reflect our right to be our own master, to live in liberty and peace – since it is only *then* that we can be ourselves.

We will unite this line of thought with what we have previously mentioned about transcendental philosophy and ethics. Kant started with the notion that human beings are moral creatures; he took this as given. The question becomes, what are the conditions for moral being? The answer is that we all have the ability to make a moral law for ourselves. Thus, we are all our own moral lawmaker; we are all *morally autonomous*. This presupposes that human beings are, in principle, free to make such laws, and reasonable enough to do so. Free and reasonable individuals will further understand that they cannot make whatever laws they want for themselves. They will understand that other individuals are as they themselves are, and therefore that we must not treat ourselves or others only as means, or things, but always as free, rational creatures who are, in themselves, an end. Thus, individuals will also understand that good actions are those that do not harm our moral freedom or that of others. This consideration provides us with both the categorical imperative, 'I ought never to act except in such a way that I can also will that my maxim should become a universal law', and the foundation of moral and legal rights and duties, 'Do not harm the moral freedom of yourself or of others!'

With his transcendental philosophy, Kant wanted to revolutionize philosophy and give it a new and certain foundation. Although it is not always easy to follow Kant's thinking, several branches of philosophy and other disciplines were fundamentally changed by his 'Copernican revolution'. These include epistemology and moral philosophy, but also jurisprudence and political science. In many ways, Kant's political thinking expressed that of the Enlightenment. He quoted the slogan of the Enlightenment: *Sapere aude!* ('have the courage to use your own reason'). During the most turbulent phase of the French Revolution, Kant noted that a people will mature to *reason* only through their *own efforts*. With a polemical thrust at the contemporary reactionary and conservative circles, Kant insisted that a people cannot mature to *freedom* unless they are first *set free*. The key concepts of Kant's philosophy, reason and freedom are also central to an understanding of the French Revolution. His political philosophy may therefore be understood as a legitimization of the transition from absolutism to constitutional and democratic forms of government.

Kant's philosophy of law begins with a basic transcendental question: what is the condition for *coexistence* among people who freely seek to realize their own ends? Kant was thus seeking a universally valid criterion for human coexistence. This criterion will, at the next stage, make it possible to evaluate the legitimacy of existing legal systems and forms of government; that is to say, to determine whether they satisfy the requirements of political justice. On the surface, Kant asked the basic question of the philosophy of law in a very abstract manner, but it is easy to see that this question is, at the same time, the great challenge of political liberalism: how can the freedom of citizens be reconciled with a state and a legal system that necessarily place limits on this freedom? Where are the limits for legitimate state intervention in the freedom of citizens? The proponents of anarchism and modern libertarianism ask the question in a more radical way: why cannot free citizens manage without government (Greek: *anarchy*)?[7] Is it ever legitimate to regulate a human being's natural freedom and inalienable rights? Kant's philosophy of law is, in many ways, an answer to such questions. Like the liberals, he presupposed that the citizens have a legitimate right to realize their own ends in the way they deem best. Neither the state nor other forms of authority may determine happiness for its citizens. They have to find it on their own. However, our goals and projects are not necessarily rational and thus universalizable. Human beings who share a finite space – and the Earth has a finite surface! – may therefore come into conflict with one another. One person's freedom to act may threaten another person's freedom to act. Thus, this basic human situation has certain features in common with Hobbes' state of nature: potential conflicts are always imminent.

For Kant, therefore, the problem was how the greatest possible freedom for human beings may be reconciled with a guarantee that one person's freedom will not infringe upon another's freedom. It is against this background that he formulated the universal legal principle to secure both freedom and coexistence: 'Justice is therefore the aggregate of those conditions under which the will of one person can be conjoined with the will of another in accordance with a universal law of freedom.'[8] To put it in other words, Kant's fundamental natural, or rational-legal, principle states the conditions under which the free choice of one person may be reconciled with the free choice of another in accordance with a general law of freedom.

Kant's point is thus that the individual's unlimited freedom of action must be restricted in such a way that it is compatible with the freedom of everyone else, according to a general law. An effective law based on this principle would limit everyone's freedom of action in the same way. This is the condition for peaceful coexistence among people having different and even contradictory goals. At the same time, it is a restriction on freedom that aims at securing the greatest possible freedom of action within the framework of general law. Therefore, Kant's philosophy of law primarily contains principles of *regulating conflicts* fairly.

Kant linked the criteria for the universal validity of laws or of constitutional principles to the citizens' autonomy or self-legislation: constitutional principles and effective law must, in principle, have the full support of all the involved parties (universal consensus). In practice, a legislator must strive to pass such laws that the citizens, in principle, *could* have given their support to them. This is the testing ground for the legitimacy of the laws. Only laws that satisfy this requirement are suitable to regulate the mutual relationship of individuals.

Kant's rational conception of law has a family resemblance to the categorical imperative. In both cases we are challenged to carry out a thought experiment. It is either a question of universalizing maxims (moral philosophy) or universalizing principles of law (philosophy of law). Kant's thinking also required a practice that corresponds to our rational thought experiments (cf. a corresponding procedure in John Rawls' thinking, Ch. 26). Kant showed that these experiments can have a critical-normative function: he thought that freedom of the press and freedom of speech ('freedom of the pen') are in accordance with consensus-based principles of law. The privileges of the nobility, serfdom, despotic regimes, and torture are clearly not things to which *all* involved parties would give their support. Consequently, such institutions and practices are not based on universal principles of law. In such arguments, Kant became an ardent spokesman for democratic reforms in the spirit of liberalism.

Kant was thus one of the first political thinkers to discuss the question of *human rights* as a general principle. In accordance with the basic attitude of the Enlightenment, he held that each person has innate and inviolable rights. These rights are in accordance with the rational conception of law, but are now formulated as subjective rights, that is, rights belonging to the individual subject: each person has the right to the greatest degree of freedom of action that is, at the same time, compatible with every other person's freedom of action according to a general law. If human rights are to provide a genuine guarantee, it may occasionally be necessary to intervene against persons or institutions that suppress legitimate freedom. Therefore, the state has a legitimate right to intervene in cases where human rights are violated. We may note that Kant does not limit this violation to atrocities such as genocide or torture. The most common breaches of human rights are 'normal' crimes and everyday criminality. In this way, Kant believed that he has justified the state's legitimate use of force and criminal prosecution.

As a liberal, Kant opposed all attempts to moralize law. The duties that are connected with personal morality, that is to say, duties we have towards ourselves and duties that we have towards others, are not necessarily *legal* requirements. For example, Kant viewed suicide as morally despicable, but he criticized legislation to punish suicide attempts. Self-preservation is a personal duty, not a legal requirement. It is our duty to show gratitude and compassion, but these are not legal requirements. We cannot be punished for lacking a humane disposition, but we can be punished for inhumane actions. Even though an act is immoral, it should not necessarily be made the subject of criminal prosecution. That something is immoral does not mean that it should be illegal in a juridical sense. Laws forbid everything that makes human coexistence *a priori* impossible, such as theft, murder, and breach of contract (lies). Here legal requirements and moral duties are identical, but Kant does not require that law-abiding persons should have moral incentives for acting in accordance with law and right. The state legal code does not require that we should act on the basis of respect for the moral law. Consequently, Kant distinguished between morality and law. He neither legalized morality nor moralized law. This is an attitude that characterizes all modern liberal societies.

According to Kant, the international scene is marked by 'everyone's fight against everyone else'. There is a lawless state of nature among sovereign states. The 'right of the strongest' is the dominant principle in international politics. Kant found this

an unworthy and irrational situation – in this area, too, we must 'have the courage
to use our own reason'. Thus, in his short essay *Perpetual Peace* (1795), he defended
the notion of a global 'league of nations' to regulate relationships among sovereign
states. The basic idea is largely the same as that found in his philosophy of law: a
league of nations must be based on universal principles to regulate conflicts and
peaceful coexistence; that is, principles which all involved parties should be able to
support. In practice, this is, of course, easier said than done: some states are small
and weak, while others are large and strong. States may also, as we know, have
greatly differing interests. They have different economic systems and are often
based on different political ideologies. On what kind of principles can such states
agree? According to Kant, only 'limited' principles of justice are appropriate for
regulating conflicts; for example, 'No independently existing state, whether it be
large or small, may be acquired by another state by inheritance, exchange, purchase or gift.'[9] It is characteristic of Kant's principles that he seeks systematically to filter out substantial questions of religion and ideology. States do not need
to agree on all kinds of controversies. It is sufficient that they agree on a *modus
vivendi*. Kant emphasized that the goal is to create a peaceful community, but not
necessarily a friendly community, among all peoples. Kant's philosophy of peace
had its first genuine fulfilment with the founding of the United Nations after
World War II.

Not surprisingly, many aspects of Kant's political philosophy relate to issues of
his own day. In practical politics he did not always manage to sustain a principle-
based and universal position. Although Kant insisted that laws must express the will
of the people, he did not support general voting rights for all citizens; consequently,
the citizens at large are not given any part in legislation. Women are excluded without any further justification, as are all others who are not economically and socially
'independent' (temporary workers, servants, etc.). For such persons, it is no longer
a question of maturing to reason through their *own attempts*. At times he also
defended extreme and abstractly rationalistic viewpoints. Like Locke, Kant held a
liberal and contractual view of marriage. The old bachelor began a discussion of
marital law as follows: 'The domestic relations are founded on marriage, and marriage is founded upon the natural reciprocity or intercommunity (*commercium*) of
the sexes. . . . Marriage . . . is the union of two persons of different sex for life-
long reciprocal possession of their sexual faculties.'[10] He also laid down strict
requirements for a natural sex life – without having much experience in the area.
He continued: 'This . . . is either natural, by which human beings may reproduce
their own kind, or unnatural, which, again, refers either to a person of the same sex
or to an animal of another species than man. These transgressions of all law . . .
are even "not to be named"; and, as wrongs against all humanity in the person, they
cannot be saved, by any limitation or exception whatever, from entire reprobation.'[11]
Apparently, Kant had no respect for the rights of homosexuals.

Kant was a son of the Enlightenment. He defended enlightenment and autonomy. For Kant, enlightenment is using our reason publicly: we become enlightened by reasoning in community with others. And this public use of reason must
be exercised in freedom (cf. John Stuart Mill's view of public opinion). The future
thus offered a hope that continuing free discussion between rational individuals in
public would gradually make the truth more apparent.[12]

JUDGEMENT – TELEOLOGY AND AESTHETICS

Kant's philosophy is thought by many to be complex, difficult to grasp, and difficult to maintain. But those who make such criticisms should, at the same time, keep in mind what Kant achieved. Firstly, he reinforced modern empirical science, with physics as its paradigm. Kant cleared the ground for causal explication in all areas accessible to our experience. Secondly, he fully supported the view that man is a free and morally responsible creature. He established a basis for morality. Thus, he had it both ways, accepting determinism and causal explanation on the one hand, and justifying indeterminism and morality on the other. Hence, Kant gave an answer to one of the fundamental dilemmas of modern philosophy, the relationship between science and morality. Moreover, Kant explained how religion, which is based on faith and revelation, is possible in a scientized society. Here, too, the answer lies in the Copernican revolution. The question of God's existence lies beyond our cognitive abilities; therefore, our attempts to answer such questions may be neither proved nor disproved. Kant thus laid a philosophical foundation for Protestant theology.

But on one decisive point, Kant's philosophy, as we have presented it here, is difficult to accept. We refer to the tension between the world of experience, where our explanations are based on causality, and the world of morality, where we are free and responsible – in short, the tension between necessity and freedom, between man as a cognizant and an acting being. On this point, Kant introduced his theory of 'judgement', as a mediating power: after the *Critique of Pure Reason* and the *Critique of Practical Reason*, came the *Critique of Judgment*. This is how Kant believed that he could mediate between the two worlds: judgement is the mediator between theoretical reason and practical reason.

This mediation is not something of which we can be *cognizant* (that is, of which we may have theoretical insight), because it would then have belonged to the realm of theoretical reason. But Kant thought that we have the ability to create a synthesis between theoretical and practical reason, and that we can reflect on this synthesizing ability. This is what Kant attempted to do in his critique of judgement.[13]

Kant held that judgement appears in two ways, as *teleology* and as *aesthetics*. We immediately think *teleologically* of forms of life, although we know that all explanations are actually causal; nevertheless, we reason as if life has an end and a meaning. In this way, the world becomes more meaningful to us. This spontaneous way of thinking, on the basis of end and meaning, helps ease the tension created by living in two worlds (necessity and freedom). Aesthetics reconciles the two worlds in a different way. Aesthetics is based on two basic experiences, according to Kant, the experience of something that is overwhelming or sublime – as in great art or nature – and the experience of something that is beautiful.

These are 'judgements of taste', not of cognition. But this does not mean that there is no accounting for taste, that taste is something that is purely subjective and arbitrary. Kant thought that we will also be able to arrive at a common opinion in this area. But this judgement is not formed as in experiential and theoretical cognition. The aesthetic judgement is, in a way, subjective, but still universally valid. It may be explained by that fact that we all experience the same aesthetic pleasure when we dispassionately view a work of art. When we are dispassionate, we may all be able to experience the same feelings towards a work of art, and, thus, our judgements of taste about this work of art coincide. Here, there is a parallel with Hume's theory of how various moral judgements coincide: we maintain a dispassionate attitude. Therefore, normal people will have the same feelings. These common feelings are the basis for correct judgements, which are thus universal. For Kant, the aesthetic experience is not subject to concepts. But the aesthetic feelings still follow certain rules, and we may, by the use of examples, show how these aesthetic experiences appear in different cases. Here we cannot claim that we have exclusive access to the truth about these matters, but we can appeal to others' experiences. (This is a kind of tacit knowledge; cf. Wittgenstein, Ch. 26.)

For Plato and Aristotle, art was an imitation of what is and what should be. For Plato, what is and should be are the ideas; for Aristotle, the substances and their forms. Seen in this way, aesthetics had an objective basis for Plato and Aristotle. The beautiful is connected with the true and the good. For Kant, there was a distinction between truth and morality (the latter as conceived by the categorical imperative). The beautiful, like the sublime (and the teleological way of thinking), is therefore to mediate between the two (between truth and morality); but, at the same time, aesthetics differs from both science and ethics. For Kant, the aesthetic judgement is simultaneously subjective, linked to our emotional life, and yet (potentially) universal.

After Kant's day, Romanticism developed an aesthetic that emphasized the subjective aspects of art even more strongly, especially in the creative process, but also in the experience of art. The genius, the great creative personality, moved to centre stage. Here, uniqueness was praised at the expense of the universal. Moreover, here, the creative and the renewing forces were strongly emphasized, in contrast to the classical emphasis on art as imitation. But for all their praise of uniqueness, the Romantic artist and critic still held that art can reach something that is common and universal for man. By means of uniqueness, the artist and the audience may reach a deeper insight into human life and its potential. (Cf. parallels in the post-Kantian philosophy of history, as in the thought of Herder, Ch. 16.)

QUESTIONS

Explain 'the Copernican Revolution' in Kant, and its role in his theory of knowledge.

How could Kant claim that he had simultaneously preserved a universal morality (based on human freedom) and a universal principle of causality (which implies that everything we acknowledge appears to be causally determined)?

Kant claimed that his transcendental philosophy had rejected both empiricist scepticism (as in Hume) and rationalist dogmatism (as in Descartes). Explain how he could make this claim.

Describe Hume's and Kant's views of the concept of causality and discuss in what sense Hume and Kant held opposite views in this respect.

'Since Hume bases morality on feelings while Kant bases morality on a universal law of reason, their moral philosophies lead in diametrically opposite directions'. Discuss this statement.

Both Kant and the utilitarians claimed to have found the true and universal criterion of right action. Kant's categorical imperative has a built-in protection against violation of a person's autonomy. Utilitarianism seeks the greatest happiness for the greatest number. Discuss these two criteria by using different examples (abortion and biomedical practice, for example).

SUGGESTIONS FOR FURTHER READING

PRIMARY LITERATURE

Gesammelte Schriften [collected works of Kant], 23 vols, edited under the supervision of the Berlin Academy of Sciences, Berlin, 1902–55.
Kant's Political Writings, edited by Hans Reiss, Cambridge, 1970.
The Metaphysical Elements of Justice, New York, 1965.
Critique of Pure Reason, translated by Norman Kemp Smith, London, 1929.
Fundamental Principles of the Metaphysic of Morals, London, 1873.
The Moral Law: Kant's Groundwork of the Metaphysics of Morals, translated by H. J. Paton, London, 1958.
Critique of Judgment, translated by Werner J. Pluhar, Indianapolis, IN, 1987.

SECONDARY LITERATURE

Allison, H., *Idealism and Freedom: Essays on Kant's Theoretical and Practical Philosophy*, Cambridge, 1995.
Bird, G., *Kant's Theory of Knowledge*, London, 1962.
Höffe, O., *Political Justice*, Cambridge, 1995.

NOTES

1 However, whether the natural sciences need an absolutely certain foundation, as Kant thought, is controversial.
2 The psychologist Jean Piaget (1896–1980) may be said to discuss the question of how children, through the process of socialization, gradually acquire 'transcendental forms'.
3 Kant's answer is subtle, and the subtlety of his answer should be seen in relation to the hard problems he tried to solve, that is, a justification of causality and of moral freedom, at the same time.
4 Kant first tried to show how the impressions are necessarily formed by space and time (in *Kritik der reinen Vernunft, Die transzendentale Ästhetik*). He then tried to show how the concepts are connected with these impressions (which are formed by space and time; ibid., *Die transzendentale Logik, Die transzendentale Analytik*): consciousness enters the picture as a principle superior to the statements (judgements) about the content of experience; and the categories, or concepts of reason, are incorporated in the statements. The concepts do not provide knowledge about reality without passing through the synthesis with the content of experience.

   Kant used the following twelve types of statements (the mind's forms of judgement) (ibid., A70/B95, standard pagination):

For the judgements:
- Quantity: universal, particular, singular
- Quality: affirmative, negative, infinite
- Relation: categorical, hypothetical, disjunctive
- Modality: problematic, assertoric, apodictic (possible, genuine, necessary)
And for the categories (ibid., A80/B106, standard pagination):
- Quantity: unity, plurality, totality
- Quality: reality, negation, limitation
- Relation: inherence and subsistence, causality and dependence, community
- Modality: possibility–impossibility, existence–non-existence, necessity–contingency
(Aristotle used the following categories: substance, quantity, quality, relation, location, time, position, condition, activity, passivity.)

5 This opposition should not be exaggerated: Hume also said that we have 'forms' within us that lead us to 'see causes', to the extent that we have expectations of what will happen. In this sense, there is something 'transcendental' about these expectations: they are forms that mark our experiences. But Hume interpreted these expectations as the result of actual (psychological) events; he did not view them as something that is given prior to experience (in the sense that Kant did).

6 It is true that we may turn towards a previous act of consciousness, but only because we now, in the present act of reflection, are ourselves a consciousness that conceives, not an experienced or conceived consciousness. This consciousness that experiences and understands, *the transcendental ego*, thus represents a thing-in-itself. Hence, the transcendental ego is embedded in the *realm of freedom*, in opposition to *the empirical ego* that takes part in the realm of necessity. The arguments so far have been based only on the notion that consciousness, as a thing-in-itself, *cannot* be said to be causally determined in the sense that this conceiving consciousness is not itself experienced. The arguments for the freedom of the transcendental ego are made in connection with the so-called practical postulates.

7 Concerning libertarianism see Robert Nozick, *Anarchy, State, and Utopia*, New York, 1974.

8 Kant, *The Metaphysical Elements of Justice*, New York, 1965, p. 34 (Introduction §C).

9 *Kant's Political Writings*, edited by Hans Reiss, Cambridge, 1970, p. 94.

10 Kant, *The Science of Right*, §24. Hegel, who was married and is said to have fathered an illegitimate son while writing *The Phenomenology of Spirit*, reacted by calling Kant's view disgraceful; see the quotation in Ch. 17.

11 Ibid.

12 Hence, Kant was part of a tradition originating with Plato and Aristotle, although Kant may be distinguished from them in that he conceives the realization of the enlightened society as a touchstone, an ideal task in history.

13 This is a controversial point in Kantian research. For example, it is argued that there is no synthesis, made by a third factor, between theoretical and practical reason, but that practical reason is ultimately the governing and determining power for theoretical reason.

16 The rise of the humanities

BACKGROUND

The second half of the 1700s saw the emergence of three relatively independent value systems within European culture: science, morality/ethics, and art. This intellectual differentiation was connected with three different claims to validity. Science took its stand on the *question of truth* (whether a claim is correct, in the sense of being true); morality/ethics dealt with *normative questions* (whether a command is valid, in the sense of being right); and the study of art raised specific *aesthetic questions* (whether a work of art is beautiful or tasteful). Thus, for example, it was regarded as a mistake to believe that normative and aesthetic questions can be answered by the sciences, and vice versa. Questions about *truth* (science), *right* (morality/ethics), and *beauty* (art) also had to be distinguished from religious questions. The sciences, morality, and the arts gained their independence (autonomy) from religion – the modern age had begun.

The first explicit thematization of these cultural spheres may be found in Kant's three critiques: the *Critique of Pure Reason* (1781) clarified the presuppositions of modern natural science; the *Critique of Practical Reason* (1788) gave morality independent status in relation to the natural sciences, and the *Critique of Judgment* (1790) established the boundary for aesthetics in relation to science and morality. In a sense, Kant was the culmination of a cultural development that began with the Renaissance.

An important turning point in this process was the rejection, by the natural sciences, of the teleological *understanding* of nature. Paradoxically, Galileo still thought of nature as a text or a book written in a mathematical language (cf. Ch. 7). The natural sciences of the Renaissance still held that nature contains a message from God. The goal of science was to understand this message. Thus, science had a hermeneutic or interpretative dimension. The natural sciences could therefore be legitimized as one of several paths to knowledge about God.

As a consequence of the increasing demystification and disenchantment of the world (cf. Max Weber) by modern science, the understanding of nature as a work of creation and revelation ('the Book of Nature') became restricted to mystics and romantic natural philosophers. It was only as mysticism that a hermeneutic natural philosophy could exist in the nineteenth century (Novalis, Schelling, and others). Modern science, on the other hand, offered power and control over nature and was legitimized by its beneficial effects. Natural science was no longer an inter-pretative or hermeneutic discipline that expounded the 'meaning' of the world. It sought to *explain* phenomena. To explain something, according to Kant, is to be able to trace the objects of experience back to known natural laws. From this per-spective, Newton's mechanics is the paradigm of a *scientific explanation*. From this point of view, it is difficult to find room for the *humanities*, or the *human sciences*, such as philology and historiography. In what sense do these disciplines contain *explanations* of the kind that we find in the natural sciences? Do they satisfy the requirements of 'good science'? Two strategies seem to be possible for the emer-ging human sciences at the beginning of the 1800s.

1   We may seek to give them the status of natural sciences: in the same way as the natural sciences, the humanities explain phenomena on the basis of uni-versal laws. Within the later positivistic context, this became the thesis of the 'unity of science'.

2   We may, for example like Vico, claim that the humanities and the natural sciences have qualitatively different objects of research and thus, different methods. Consequently, the humanities must be legitimized in a different way than the natural sciences.

These two strategies still figure in the contemporary discussion of the epistemo-logical uniqueness of the humanities. In this chapter, we will investigate the rise of the humanities and the problems facing the founders of this discipline.

HERDER AND HISTORICISM

The 1770s marked a decisive turning point in German intellectual life. More precisely, we can talk about a transition from a rationalistic Enlightenment to an antirationalistic pre-Romanticism – the so-called *Sturm und Drang* period.

Johann Gottfried Herder (1744–1803) was one of the central figures in this trans-ition period. He was the foremost representative of a new historical consciousness that entailed a new sense of *individuality* and historical *change*. This is the core of what was later to be called historicism. The roots of Herder's historicism go back to thinkers who, in different ways, found themselves on the periphery of the Enlightenment. From Hume, he inherited a sceptical view of the capacity of reason. He rejected the notion of universally valid human reason and timeless, universal standards. In Rousseau's cultural criticism and idealization of the happy 'natural man', Herder found the inspiration for a biting criticism of the Enlightenment's self-understanding and optimism about progress. This criticism was also strongly influenced by J. G. Hamann's (1730–1788) pietistic irrationalism.[1]

We have said that Herder may be seen as the founder of historicism. In the first place, historicism was a particular attitude and approach to history. Historicism awakened what we might call the 'historical sense'. History became the context and basic precondition for philosophy and human thought. Moreover, *histori-ography* became the dominant discipline, setting its mark on the other humanistic disciplines. The humanistic disciplines were 'historicized'; that is, they became historically oriented disciplines (as in the history of literature, the history of art, the history of religion, the history of language, etc.). Thus, we may say that historicism was both a view of reality and a research programme for the humanities.[2]

Historicism may firstly be characterized by its understanding of historical phenomena as *exceptional*, *unique*, and *particular*. Individuality is not limited to individuals or particular phenomena. Individuality may also be sought in the collective and 'superindividual': an epoch, a culture, or a people are something unique and specific. This is historicism's principle of individuation. Methodically, historical understanding should be based on the epoch's own premises, and all evaluations should proceed from *internal* rather than external criteria. Historicism aims for an immanent understanding, not one based on a later epoch's criteria of judgement. In this research programme, insight into historical context and historical connections becomes extremely important. A phenomenon gains meaning in the light of its original context. In a new context (such as our own), the phenomenon has a different meaning. Historical understanding is thus contextual understanding (cf. 'language game' and 'paradigm' in the philosophy of science in our day).

Secondly, historicism greatly emphasizes historical *change* and *evolution*. A static view of reality is replaced with a dynamic view of reality. Everything is subject to the stream of history. This emphasis on change has been interpreted as a decisive 'revolution' in Western thought.[3] As a consequence of the historicist revolution, the humanities in the 1800s developed a historical-genetic perspective of human life at the expense of a structural and systematic approach. Historicism's notion of individuation and its emphasis on historical change conflicted in various ways with several of the basic presuppositions of the Enlightenment; for example, the emphasis on universality and reason, the idea of an unchangeable human nature, and the notion of universally valid human rights. This gave historicism a certain relativistic tendency ('historical relativism') that became increasingly noticeable and problematic in the nineteenth and twentieth centuries.[4]

Herder's first contribution to the philosophy of history, *Another Philosophy of History* (1774), is often considered historicism's manifesto. From Montesquieu, Herder took the idea that naturally given conditions contribute to the determination of a people's individuality. Climate, geographical conditions, and other environmental factors determine the character of various historical expressions.[5] For Herder, these are physical-material conditions for cultural growth and development. This is the framework that forms the basis of all individuality.

According to Herder, each historical epoch has its own distinctive stamp. Any epoch is unique, and the spirit or mentality of the epoch makes its mark on all the particular phenomena and gives them a certain unity. In the 400s BC, the spirit of the Greek age permeated not only philosophy, but also art, poetry, and general intellectual life in a way that is typical of that period. The same applies to the national spirit. Each people, each national culture, is formed by its national spirit. For Herder, a country's language and folk tales exemplify its people's individuality and uniqueness. While two nations may be marked by the same spirit of the times, the national spirit comprises the principle of individuation within a given culture.

The ideals of various peoples, their norms of what is good and evil, ugly and beautiful, are marked by their national spirit. All criteria are thus related to the particular spirit of the people. There is no supranational or suprahistorical criterion for evaluating happiness and beauty. 'Each nation,' says Herder, 'has the *centre of* its happiness *within itself*, just as a ball has its centre of gravity within itself.'[6] Thus, all criteria are conditioned by historical and geographical circumstances. When the distance between two nations is great, they mutually regard each other's ideals as prejudices. But such prejudices are not necessarily negative, according to Herder: 'Prejudice is *good*, in its time, because it makes us happy.'[7]

But how can we gain a genuine historical understanding of the uniqueness of foreign nations and cultures? For Herder, no understanding or evaluation can be based on general or universal standards. Herder also refuted the notion that an epoch or nation may serve as a norm or ideal for others. Historical knowledge can occur only through empathy with historical phenomena. This type of understanding is not derived from universal principles of reason or universal laws. The historian's task is to imagine what it would be like to live in a distant past: 'Immerse yourself into the epoch, into the heavens, the entire history, feel yourself in everything.'[8] The historical approach, in other words, must be 'hermeneutically empathetic'. The historian must adapt to the uniqueness of the phenomena.

Herder's programme avoided a blindly ethnocentric attitude and allowed cultural tolerance. For Herder, nationalism has nothing to do with chauvinism. All nations are unique and equal. We can find a similar tolerance in his view of various historical epochs. For instance, in light of his notion of individuality, Herder wanted to re-evaluate the Enlightenment's negative attitude towards the Middle Ages: if each epoch has its own worth, has its 'centre' within itself, so must the Middle Ages (cf. Romanticism's positive view of the Middle Ages). In principle, the Middle Ages may be placed neither higher nor lower than any other epoch. Like all other historical epochs, it was an end in itself.

It is easy to see that the principle of individuation may come into conflict with the idea of historical progress and development. If history has a deeper meaning or is moving towards a particular goal, it is difficult to maintain that any epoch has its own absolute worth. If all epochs develop towards a common goal (*telos*), an *external* criterion of evaluation is introduced. The epoch then becomes meaningful in the light of the goal. This problem arises in various ways in Herder's philosophy of history. In *Another Philosophy of History*, he attacked the Enlightenment's superficial thesis of progress, while supporting Rousseau's idea of a historical decline from a golden age; he considered the Enlightenment to be 'decadent'.

For Herder, like Vico, nations and cultures go through 'life cycles'.[9] Although Herder used words like *development* and *progress*, he did not entertain the idea of unceasing progress or the idea that all cultures are moving towards the same goal. A culture develops analogously to the development of the individual, as if it followed a particular life cycle. Cultures and nations are born and die in the same way as all organic life. Thus, Herder used normative concepts like 'period of flourishing' and 'period of decline' (cf. his view of the Enlightenment as 'decadent' and 'senile'). All in all, he could not avoid a conflict between internal and external criteria of evaluation in his philosophy of history. In Herder's later works, such as *Ideas for the Philosophy of the History of Mankind* (1784–91) and *Letters for the Advancement of Humanity* (1793–7), the historical process found its unambiguous goal, namely, *humanity*. For Herder, the collection of folk poetry and the development of the new human sciences came to be connected with nation-building. In this way, he legitimized the relevance and the goal of the human sciences, but we can hardly doubt that this educational programme is contrary to a radical version of the idea of individuality.

In summary, we can say that Herder's contribution lay in his principle of individuation. All historical phenomena are conditioned by the spirit of the age and of the people, and by external physical-material conditions. Likewise, the overall mentality of an epoch and of a people determines the agent's self-understanding and understanding of the world. This is an idea that we will encounter again in Hegel. At the same time, historical phenomena have their own intrinsic worth and must be evaluated on the basis of their own premises. Obviously, this creates a certain tension between normative ideals and historical relativism. Perhaps Herder would say that we must distinguish between *understanding* a phenomenon (such as the blood feud or widow immolation [suttee]) and *accepting* it (on the basis of our moral criteria). His idea of humanity as the goal of history is, in a sense, an anti-relativistic stance, but it seems to be incompatible with a radical version of the principle of individuation. In many ways, this was an unresolvable dilemma for the historicism of the nineteenth century.

SCHLEIERMACHER AND HERMENEUTICS

Text interpretation was a discipline that lay outside Kant's field of interest. Although the art of interpretation, or hermeneutics, has always held a central position in the study of the humanities, modern hermeneutics began at the turn of the nineteenth century. A pioneer in this field was the German philosopher of religion Friedrich Schleiermacher (1768–1834). He is often deemed to have been the first to posit the *hermeneutic circle* as a basic principle of interpretation: the spirit that permeates the whole (such as a text) sets its mark on the individual parts. The parts are to be understood on the basis of the whole, and the whole is to be understood as an internal harmony of the parts. Schleiermacher's view of hermeneutics was influenced by Romanticism. A central aspect of hermeneutics was that of identifying with the individual, unique content of the soul ('individuality') *behind* the text.

For Schleiermacher, hermeneutics is not directed primarily towards the text, but towards the creative spirit behind the text. The basic problem of understanding is connected with our distance in time and space from the object being studied. Hermeneutics should contribute to the overcoming of historical distance. Like Herder, Schleiermacher emphasized the necessity of identifying with the text, the author's way of thinking, and the historical context. An important aspect of philology is therefore to place ourselves within the intellectual *horizon* of the author and the text. On the other hand, a better understanding of the text gives us better insight into the fundamental problems of the epoch. Here, hermeneutic interpretation may also be understood as a circular movement between the whole and the parts.

After Schleiermacher, hermeneutics became central to the new human sciences. In hermeneutics, there is common ground between not only theology, literary studies, jurisprudence, and historiography, but all of the human sciences. In a certain sense, this common ground contributes to the uniqueness of the humanities in relation to the natural sciences. From a hermeneutic perspective, the goal of the humanities is *understanding*, as opposed to the goal of the natural sciences, which is *explaining*.

THE HISTORICAL SCHOOL – VON SAVIGNY AND VON RANKE

Herder pioneered the 'historicization' of the human sciences. With the so-called *historical school* in historiography, a thoroughgoing historicization emerged within a number of central human sciences. In addition, the historical school promoted the scientization of the human sciences. The historical-critical method, with its emphasis on source criticism and its orientation towards facts, was a corrective of Herder's empathy and Romanticism's strong emphasis on the spirit of the age and the national spirit. 'The matter itself' now became of primary importance.

Like Herder and Romanticism, Friedrich Carl von Savigny (1779–1861) and Leopold von Ranke (1795–1886) emphasized that history is characterized by organic development. Radical interference with the development of history hinders its natural growth. In the 1800s, this idea became an argument for political stability and conservative resistance to reform. This is especially clear in the historical school of jurisprudence. After the Napoleonic Wars, the national impulse turned against French rationalism, natural rights theory, and the French civil legal code (*Code Napoléon*). The democratic and egalitarian elements in modern natural law theory were replaced by an antirationalistic, national historicism with roots in a specifically German juridical, historical tradition.

Von Savigny compared the organic development of law with linguistic changes. This perspective sets clear limits for legislation. Law, language, customs, and conventions are expressions of the soul of the German people. Consequently, the law must accord with the people's character, in the same way as language. A scientific approach to law must be historical-genetic, emphasizing both empathy and source criticism. Von Savigny thus viewed law and all other cultural phenomena as expressions of the national spirit.[10] The national spirit permeates all forms of life and creates a national individuality. There is an organic connection between law and the people's character. Thus, all valid laws are customary laws. The true legislator personifies and views himself as a representative of the national spirit. Von Savigny considered legal codes and constitutions based on the idea of human rights, such as 'the general customary law of Prussia', as un-German and unhistorical. Therefore, custom and tradition are given primacy over reason. This is precisely what became a central focus in Marx's criticism of the historical school of jurisprudence: according to Marx, von Savigny legitimized the irrationality and injustice of the present by means of the irrationality and injustice of the past. Hegel similarly criticized the historical school of jurisprudence because of its false view of the relationship between reason and reality. The legal reality (positive law) is not always rational and just.

This conservative, Restoration historicism was not an exclusively German phenomenon. We can find similar tendencies in the conservatism of Edmund Burke and in the French-Catholic Restoration philosophy (Bonald and de Maistre).

For Leopold von Ranke, the goal of historiography was objective reconstruction of the past 'as it actually was'. Von Ranke was primarily interested in political history. He had little interest in the role that economic and social conditions play in history. The primary purpose of historical research is not to understand the origin and background of our own age, but to understand the past on the basis of its own presuppositions. The historian must also avoid subjective and biased interpretations. A good aid is thus the historical-critical method and refined forms of source criticism. But von Ranke realized that historians can never be passive recorders of objective facts; they never start working without presuppositions. Without philosophy – by which von Ranke was probably referring to formative hypotheses or ideas – history is a chaos of facts. Although von Ranke rejected Hegel's philosophy of history as being both speculative and apriorist, he saw something universal in each particular phenomenon. Within each state of affairs and within each historical phenomenon, the historian finds something eternal that comes from God (*aus Gott kommendes*).[11]

Like Herder and Romanticism, von Ranke stressed the importance of *individuality* in his polemics against rationalism and the optimistic view of progress. If the thesis of progress is anchored in causal or teleological determinism, human freedom is annulled. However, historical development entails 'stages of freedom'. Historians must be able to trace historical phenomena back to *actions*. It is the concept of action alone which enables us to understand events as historical events. For von Ranke, furthermore, the thesis of progress was incompatible with the principle that all epochs and nations have equal worth ('are equally close to God', as von Ranke says). The very diversity is an expression of God's generosity. From the eternal perspective (God's perspective), all generations and epochs are of equal worth. We can say that von Ranke liberated the writing of history from philosophical speculation (Hegel). The institutionalization of historiography as a strictly empirical discipline may primarily be traced back to von Ranke and his school.

DROYSEN AND DILTHEY – THE UNIQUENESS OF THE HUMANITIES

Like von Ranke, Johann Gustav Droysen (1808–1884), the founder of the so-called Prussian school of historiography, saw God's hand in history, but, unlike von Ranke, he emphasized that the historian can never be totally objective: our understanding of the past is always determined by our perspective and interests. Therefore, each new generation will write history in a new way. This programme was formulated by Heinrich von Sybel (1817–1895) in the following way: 'Every historian who has had any significance in our literature, had his colours. There have been believers and atheists, Protestants and Catholics, liberals and conservatives, historians of all parties, but no longer any objective, impartial historians devoid of blood and nerves.'[12] Therefore, as the scholars of the humanities discover their own presuppositions and see that they always have a relationship with their own day, these scholars face an explicit problem of objectivity. The idea that historiography seeks to reconstruct the past as it 'actually was', becomes, in this programme, a naive illusion. On the other hand, it is difficult to reject the idea that the historian should still tell us what has been, and not only about his or her own position and perspective and about the 'toolbox' of the research community. The relationship between our unavoidable 'prejudices' and conceptual presuppositions, and our objects of research, has become increasingly problematic in the twentieth century. If it is no longer possible to obtain data that are independent of interpretation – that is, data that are independent of our theories and our understanding – we can hardly assess the validity of an interpretation. The traditional concept of truth ('the correspondence theory of truth') has been weakened.

The important distinction between the method of *understanding* (*Verstehen*) of the humanities and the method of *explaining* (*Erklären*) of the natural sciences also stems from Droysen's point that historiography is concerned not with inorganic objects (mechanics of the atoms), but with acts of the will. Since history is enacted on the stage of freedom, the historian cannot be satisfied with explanations that deduce phenomena from universal laws and historical presuppositions. In the humanities we seek to *understand*; in the natural sciences we seek to *explain*. This methodological dualism is one of the most important and problematic issues in the philosophy of the social sciences.

Every historical expression, according to Droysen, is a result of an *internal process*. The particular expression is understood by tracing it back to an inner, mental state of affairs of the historical agent (intentions, reasons, etc.). This programme for a human science that is based on understanding holds a central position in the thought of Wilhelm Dilthey and Max Weber (cf. Ch. 24).

While the historical school had demonstrated what the human sciences could be in practice, Wilhelm Dilthey (1833–1911) introduced a fundamental epistemological reflection upon what the humanities are and could be; he reflected on their status as a science and on what distinguishes them from the natural sciences.[13]

In Dilthey's work, the human sciences undergo a 'sobering' process. Dilthey was both a historian and a philosopher of science; he developed a theoretically and methodologically reflective historicism. For Herder, von Savigny, and von Ranke, there is a metaphysical-religious 'safeguard' against historical relativism. Dilthey rejected such a safeguard: a consistent historicism knows no ahistorical values, no absolutely valid norms, and no divine plans. Historicism recognizes the 'relativity' of all historical phenomena, without restriction.[14]

Dilthey is often mentioned as a *life philosopher*, meaning that *life* comprised the fundamental category in his thought. Obscure and inexplicable, life is the basis of our experience, and therefore cannot itself be explicitly and fully conceived: 'Knowledge cannot go beyond life.'[15] Life is thus a quasi-transcendental condition for the existence of the human sciences.

For Dilthey, the human sciences represent a hermeneutic *revolution*. Because they are hermeneutic disciplines, they have their centre of gravity in the interpretation of linguistic expressions, which must be traced back to the original experiences. Life itself has been objectified in texts and works of art. In other words, the object of investigation in the human sciences is the forms of objectification of the spirit within culture and society: morality, law, state, religion, art, science, and philosophy. Thus, the human sciences, in Dilthey's sense of the term, include the academic disciplines that today embrace a part of the humanities and the social sciences.

Understanding within the human sciences must therefore be based on the researcher's ability to revive, to re-experience, an original experience. But how can we be certain that *our* re-experience has anything to do with, for example, a Renaissance artist's original experience? Here, Dilthey introduced an important principle in his hermeneutics; he assumed that there are certain similarities between the subject that was the source of the expression and the subject that attempts to understand that expression. These similarities are ultimately based on a common human nature that is constant at all times and in all places. Life always shows the same sides, according to Dilthey.[16] He can therefore claim that there is an inner connection between life, life experience, and the human sciences. Within the process of understanding, it is life that understands life. We can understand what has been created by human beings. This was also Vico's fundamental idea. Like Vico, Dilthey thought that the first condition for the possibility of the human sciences lies in the fact that the person who investigates history is, in a certain sense, the same as the person who creates history.[17] Dilthey thus formulated the difference between human science and natural science as follows: 'Mind can only understand what it has created. Nature, the subject-matter of the physical sciences, embraces the reality which has arisen independently of the activity of mind. Everything on which man has actively impressed his stamp forms the subject-matter of the human studies.'[18]

As we know, there are great differences between individuals and between people living in different epochs and cultures. What must we presuppose if a *common* understanding is to be possible between individuals and between epochs and civilizations? According to Dilthey, this understanding implies that individuals recognize themselves in other individuals. Initially, this is something that we all are aware of and is thus uncontroversial: I understand what you mean when you say 'I am sad' because I know what I would feel myself if I said it. Understanding thus presupposes a similarity between people. If we were all 'the same', understanding would never be a problem. Understanding other people would be impossible if they were totally foreign to us, and understanding others would be unnecessary if there were nothing human that is foreign to us.

Like Droysen, Dilthey emphasized the creative element in understanding an expression. The expression is an objectification of a creative act, and understanding itself is a new creative act that may be objectified as an expression (such as a dissertation about a work of art). But what do we really mean when we talk about 'expressions'? According to Dilthey, there is an 'internal' life that can be expressed. Just as Kant's category of causality stipulated that we must always seek a cause, Dilthey required that we must begin with the inner side of external manifestations. This is what makes hermeneutics the key discipline and methodology of the human sciences. The next step is a consequence of Dilthey's understanding of expression: much of the hermeneutic interpretation by sociologists and social anthropologists is more similar to the systematic interpretation of literary texts than to the experiments that are performed by physicists and chemists. This does not mean that Dilthey considered hermeneutics to be the sole answer, to the exclusion of all other methods within the humanities and the social sciences. Several methods may be necessary, because human beings are not pure spirit. The method to be used in the human sciences will depend upon the nature of the object under investigation.

What, then, characterizes the research object in the human sciences, according to Dilthey? We may outline three characteristics.

1   The human sciences investigate what is individual and unique (cf. Herder and historicism). A physicist, too, is interested in particular phenomena (for example, how iron filings on a paper respond to a magnet), but he attempts to arrive at something that is universal or to test universal theories. When this goal is

reached, the particular iron filings are no longer interesting. This is not so in the humanities, or human sciences. The human sciences are not especially concerned with a search for general laws or statistical generalizations.[19]

2   The relationship between part and whole is also important for these sciences. An individual is a part of a larger whole (family, neighbourhood/city, society). A word is a part of a sentence, the sentence is a part of a paragraph, and so on. An action is usually a part of a larger, teleological, chain of action. Such chains of action may be parts of a larger whole (for example, a factory). One part may fit into various contexts and 'wholes' simultaneously. A speech, for example, may be a very personal psychological expression and a fateful contribution to a political debate, so that the politician's life and national politics coincide in the speech. Thus, within the human sciences, it is important to 'situate' parts into contexts and to view the parts on the basis of contexts (wholes). Here we meet the hermeneutic circle again. Dilthey rejected the idea that there is an absolute starting point in the human sciences. Every search for knowledge, he says, implies a circle. We must understand the words in order to understand the sentence, but we must, in turn, understand the sentence in order to understand correctly the meaning of the words. The categorical structure 'part – whole' is thus a necessary presupposition for all understanding.

3   Dilthey emphasized that the human sciences must conceive of man as both subject and object. As an object, a human being is a product that must be explained with reference to social conditions, background, etc. As a subject, a human being must be understood as an agent who creates his or her own surroundings. As an object, human behaviour may be explained in causal terms, but at the same time, we must recognize that human beings are creative subjects who make new things possible in history.

For Dilthey, the relativistic consequences of historicism became apparent. The human sciences show us that everything is conditioned by time and space: 'The historical consciousness points with increasing clarity to the relativity of each metaphysical or religious doctrine.' Comparative studies 'show the relativism of all historical convictions'.[20] According to Dilthey, values and norms can no longer claim to be absolutely valid when the historical-contextual analysis of norms and values has replaced the religious or metaphysical justification of those values and norms. Indeed, these types of justification are themselves the object of historical-contextual analysis in the history of science or the history of philosophy. For Dilthey, there is an insoluble, 'tragic' contradiction between a theory's claim of universal validity and the way that the historical consciousness makes all such claims relative; between what we *want* to justify and what we *can* justify.

When it comes to 'the ultimate values', modern man, in spite of great scientific progress, is still no wiser than the Ionic Greeks of 500 BC. In this age, says Dilthey, we despair more than at any previous time: we have become conscious of the anarchy of all deeper convictions. Everything has become fluid and all standards have been abolished. Like Nietzsche, Dilthey emphasized modern man's uncertainty and doubt about life's values and goals.[21]

But this is only one aspect of the problem of relativism. For Dilthey, the historical human sciences lead to a deeper form of self-understanding and have, in many ways, a humanizing and tolerance-creating effect. The human sciences also create a new feeling of freedom. They free us from the binding, limiting facets of a dogmatic position. In this connection, Dilthey said that man is in the process of becoming sovereign. But this is also the sovereignty of the nihilistic human being, beyond good and evil. It is hardly coincidental that the antihistorical movements of the twentieth century have insisted that it is necessary to return to the questions about what is true and false, just and unjust. The problem of validity again moves to centre stage in philosophy and science.

THE DISSOLUTION OF THE HISTORICAL SCHOOL

During the transition from the nineteenth to the twentieth centuries, we begin to see the contours of a series of new antihistorical research programmes. With Ferdinand de Saussure (1857–1913), linguistics gained a systematic and synchronic understanding of language that differed from a historical or diachronic approach. Thus, Saussure distanced himself from the notion that understanding something is necessarily synonymous with understanding a genesis or a development. For Saussure, linguistics is part of a general science of signs (*semiology*) (Greek: *semeion*, 'sign'). Since the 1930s, several interesting attempts have been made to transfer Saussure's structuralism to the social sciences (for example, the work of Claude Lévi-Strauss [1908–]).

Within the field of comparative literature, too, historicism and the psychological investigation of the author's 'inner experience' have been replaced by formalistic and structuralistic approaches (for example, Russian formalism and the Prager school from the end of the 1920s, with Roman Jakobson as one of the inspiring scholars). A similar tendency can be seen in the French Annales school of historiography, with Marc Bloch (1886–1944), Lucien Febvre (1878–1956), and others. At the same time, the human sciences have been challenged by functionalism and systems theory within the social sciences (Émile Durkheim, Talcott Parsons, and others). We can no longer talk about one specific method or approach within the humanities. Modern human sciences are, in various ways, marked by a new methodological pluralism and by shifting boundaries between various academic fields.

In our day there has also been a marked institutional differentiation. New disciplines and departments are an expression of an increasing specialization. Disciplines that were previously gathered into one faculty have gradually become independent faculties. At most universities today, the humanities have become institutionally separated from the social sciences, psychology, and jurisprudence. This has given rise to new disputes about the uniqueness and status of the humanities *vis-à-vis* other disciplines.

QUESTIONS

Explain what we mean by the principle of individuality in the human sciences. How can this principle lead to relativism?

What do we mean by historicism? What are its most important characteristics?

What is the hermeneutic circle? Use examples to illustrate your answer.

SUGGESTIONS FOR FURTHER READING

PRIMARY LITERATURE

Dilthey, W., *Introduction to the Human Sciences*, London, 1989.

Droysen, J. G., *Historik. Vorlesung über die Enzyklopädie und Methodologie der Geschichte* (1857), 6th edition, München, 1971.

J. G. Herder on Social and Political Culture, translated by F. M. Bernard, London, 1969.

Schleiermacher, F. D. E., *The Hermeneutical Tradition*, edited by G. L. Ormiston and A. D. Schrift, NY, 1990.

SECONDARY LITERATURE

Apel, K.-O., *Understanding and Explanation: A Transcendental-Pragmatic Perspective*, Cambridge, MA, 1984.

Iggers, G. G., *The German Conception of History: The National Tradition of Historical Thought From Herder to the Present*, Middletown, CT, 1983.

Meinecke, F., *Historicism: The Rise of a New Historical Outlook*, London, 1972.

NOTES

1 A specialist on this period, L. W. Beck, views both Herder and Hamann as philosophers of the 'Counter-Enlightenment' (*Early German Philosophy*, Cambridge, 1969, pp. 361 ff.).
2 The German historian Friedrich Meinecke emphasizes that historicism is primarily a *life principle*, a new way of looking at life (*Die Entstehung des Historismus* [1936], München, 1965).
3 See F. Meinecke, *Die Entstehung des Historismus*, p. 1.
4 The first exponents of historicism believed profoundly in a metaphysical reality beyond the historical world. They saw the various cultures and historical phenomena as expressions of this transhistorical reality (God). From such a perspective, history may be presented as a meaningful and reasonable process (cf. Hegel). When this belief was no longer credible, historicism entailed relativistic consequences. This change, at the beginning of the twentieth century, is often considered to be historicism's 'crisis', and questions of validity returned once more to centre stage.
5 J. G. Herder, *Auch eine Philosophie der Geschichte zur Bildung der Menschheit* (1774), Frankfurt am Main, 1967, p. 40.
6 Ibid., pp. 44 ff.
7 Ibid., pp. 46 ff.
8 Ibid., p. 37.
9 Ibid., p. 48.
10 Friedrich Carl von Savigny, *Der Beruf unserer Zeit für die Gesetzgebung* (1814). It should be emphasized that von Savigny stood within a conservative tradition that viewed rationalism and natural law as a major cause of the French Revolution. This is also the background for his criticism of Kant's philosophy of law.
11 Georg G. Iggers, *The German Conception of History. The National Tradition of Historical Thought from Herder to the Present*, Middletown, CT, 1968, p. 105.
12 Ibid., p. 117.
13 The term 'human sciences' (German: *Geisteswissenschaften*) can be traced to Dilthey's *Introduction to the Human Sciences* [1883], Princeton, NJ, 1989. The German term originated as a translation of John Stuart Mill's term 'moral sciences'. See K.-O. Apel, *Understanding and Explanation: A Transcendental-Pragmatic Perspective*, Cambridge, MA, 1984.
14 W. Dilthey, *The Construction of the Historical World in Human Studies*, in Dilthey's *Selected Writings*, edited, translated, and introduced by H. P. Rickman, Cambridge, 1976, pp. 183 ff.
15 W. Dilthey, 'Zur Weltanschauungslehre', in *Gesammelte Schriften*, vol. VIII, Stuttgart, 1960, p. 180.
16 W. Dilthey, 'The Types of World-View and their Development in the Metaphysical Systems', in *Selected Writings*, op. cit., pp. 133 ff.

17 W. Dilthey, *The Construction of the Historical World in Human Studies*.
18 Ibid., p. 192.
19 The cognitive interests of the human sciences cannot be reduced to that of explaining phenomena on the basis of universal laws (cf. the discussion, in the philosophy of science, of the Hempel model of scientific explanation).
20 W. Dilthey, 'Zur Weltanschauungslehre', in *Gesammelte Schriften*, vol. VIII, p. 194.
21 Ibid., pp. 193 ff.

17 Hegel – history and dialectics

Life. *Georg Wilhelm Friedrich Hegel (1770–1831), the son of a civil servant, initially studied theology at the Protestant seminary in Tübingen, Germany. As a philosopher, Hegel strove to develop a universal system. Although his works are abstruse, they have had a great impact on later thinkers, including Karl Marx. Privately, Hegel led a middle-class life, first as a family tutor, then as a headmaster, and finally as a professor in Berlin from 1818. His most important works include.* The Phenomenology of Mind *(1807),* The Science of Logic *(1812–16), and* Outlines of the Philosophy of Right *(1821).*

REFLECTION, DIALECTICS, EXPERIENCE

Hegel's background is the Enlightenment, as well as the Romantic reaction, and in his philosophy he attempted to grasp conceptually both recent history and the whole heritage of Athens, Jerusalem, and Rome. In his immediate past was the French Revolution and the reaction that followed. Reflection on history as the formative process for mankind was his main project. A basic question in the interpretation of Hegel's philosophy is the following: was Hegel progressive or reactionary? Was he in the vanguard of new thinking, or aligned with the old? We will here interpret Hegel as a progressive thinker who tried to grasp conceptually the new world. To simplify, we can then say that liberalist philosophers in the eighteenth century had placed reason above tradition, and the individual above society. The conservative reaction had reversed this, and placed tradition above reason, and society (the state) above the individual. Hegel claimed that he had found a dialectical synthesis of liberalism and conservatism, a true synthesis in which liberalism and conservatism are preserved as partial truths.

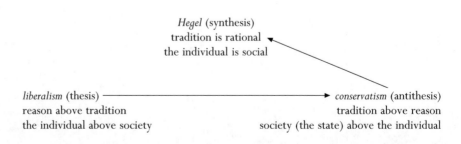

Hegel (synthesis)
tradition is rational
the individual is social

liberalism (thesis) ──────────────────────────────→ *conservatism* (antithesis)
reason above tradition   tradition above reason
the individual above society   society (the state) above the individual

We shall analyse what Hegel may have meant by this, and in so doing we shall adopt a 'left-wing Hegelian' interpretation of his philosophy.

TRANSCENDENTAL PRECONDITIONS – HISTORICALLY CREATED AND CULTURALLY RELATIVE

Kant thought that he had found *unchangeable* transcendental presuppositions. The two forms of perception, space and time, and the categories, including causality, are embedded in all subjects at all times. Hegel claimed that there is a wider spectrum of transcendental presuppositions, and that the transcendental presuppositions, to a great degree, are changeable. Transcendental presuppositions in one culture at one stage in history are not always valid in other cultures at other stages in history. Hegel claimed that the transcendental presuppositions are *historically created* and are therefore *culturally relative*. Briefly, some transcendental presuppositions are not universal to all human beings, but only to people in certain cultures.

We may define a transcendental presupposition as that from which we speak ('we' may be individuals, classes, or epochs). Kant was interested in the transcendental presuppositions that we can never abandon, but only talk about; Hegel was interested in transcendental presuppositions that we can both abandon and talk about.

While Kant sought what is certain and unchangeable, Hegel sought the historical formation process of different, changeable world-views. For Hegel, that which constitutes is something that is *itself* constituted, and the constitution of that which constitutes is *history*. For Kant, the constituting subject is the unshakable bedrock, unchangeable and ahistorical. For Hegel, that which constitutes is constituted by history, which thus becomes something different from and something more than a series of past events. History becomes a fundamental *epistemological* concept; history is understood as a collective process of self-development of different basic forms of understanding.[1]

For Kant, the relationship between that which constitutes and that which is constituted, between the transcendental and the empirical, was characterized as being absolutely distinct. For Hegel, the relationship became more fluid. This is connected with a basic difference in their ways of thinking: Kant often thought in terms of dualistic oppositions, while Hegel tried to reconcile the oppositions by placing the oppositions into a dialectical context. Thus, Hegel tried to overcome Kant's dualism between the phenomena of experience and the thing-in-itself (*Ding an sich*) by rejecting the idea of a thing-in-itself. Instead, he relied on the mutual relationship between a human being and the world. This relationship points to an ongoing conflict between that which *seems* to be (appearance) and that which *is* (being). This dynamic tension between appearance and being, within the relationship between a human being and the world, is fundamental in Hegel's dialectical thinking.

We have previously stated that a radical epistemological empiricism, in a certain sense, is self-defeating.[2] This empiricism claims that only empirical knowledge and analytical insight exist, although this empiricism itself is neither empirical nor analytical. In other words, this empiricism represents a philosophical position that we, for logical reasons, must reject after we have reflected upon it. Reflection upon this position leads us beyond this position. Reflection upon a transcendental presupposition that we can abandon may thus show that the presupposition is untenable, and therefore lead us away from this presupposition. Reflection may thereby create change, leading us in the direction of positions that are more tenable.

According to Hegel, *history* can be seen as such a chain of reflections in which various transcendental presuppositions are thoroughly tested and criticized, so that the human spirit advances towards positions that are increasingly true. (This, however, must not be understood to mean that Hegel considered history to be only reflection, and not action and fate.) Transcendental philosophy, for Hegel, was thus a philosophy of reflection and a philosophy of history: history is the internal dialogue which, throughout time, has led us towards more and more adequate philosophical opinions.

This means that Hegel held a specific notion of experience: in the empiricist tradition, experience was primarily understood as sense experience. But the word 'experience' may be used in different ways. In everyday language, for example, we talk about 'religious experience', 'sexual experience', 'work experience', etc. These usages of the concept of experience cannot be reduced to the passively receiving photography model, as in Locke. Hegel's conception of experience is in a sense closer to the everyday conception of experience in which experience is linked to our own activity. For Hegel, there is neither a passive subject nor a passive object, since human beings and reality mutually constitute each other, and in this process, experience plays a central role.

EXPERIENCE AS THE DRAMA OF SELF-FORMATION

Hegel's treatise *The Phenomenology of Spirit* is constructed around such a dynamic model. The path is the 'path of suffering'. It stretches out on two levels: partly, as a formation of the individual's consciousness from the simplest form of sense experience to philosophical knowledge; partly, as a formation of human history from the ancient Greeks to Hegel's own time. *The Phenomenology of Spirit* may be characterized as a philosophical travelogue: it provides us with a description of the journey of consciousness through history towards self-cognition. The various phases in this experiential process are discussed as the stages of the spirit's development.

Hegel held that each individual must *live through* the spirit's process of development, but in a shorter and more concentrated form. 'Autobiographically', we can recall our own development. We often say that we *mature* through religious, political, or existential crises: we then see the naive and deficient aspects of an earlier state of consciousness and are forced to move forward. Thus, the individual's development may be understood as a process of formation. For this reason, *The Phenomenology of Spirit* is often compared with the so-called *Bildungsroman* (such as Goethe's *Wilhelm Meisters Lehrjahre*). We may also think of Ibsen's *Peer Gynt*: here, too, the story is that of an individual's path towards his true self, an individual's attempt to find himself. This attempt to find oneself is, for Hegel, something that happens primarily through critical-historical reflection. Phenomenology, said Hegel, is the 'soul's path' through different stages whereby the soul little by little perceives the deficiencies of its various states of consciousness, the shortcomings of the various historical-relative transcendental preconditions from which we think and act.

The progress through the various forms of knowledge is a critical project. For Hegel, it is essential to show, by an inner critique, how a form of knowledge breaks down and points beyond itself. During each age, each of us may, at particular moments, find that 'the foundations shake', that there is an inner tension within consciousness between what we think we are and what we really are. The state of innocence is dispelled and 'the force of negativity' has done its work. The force of negativity is the dialectical tension which refuses to be at peace with a standpoint as long as it uncovers deficiencies. It is critical, but at the same time it allows a new and more adequate understanding of the situation. It is like Mephistopheles in Goethe's *Faust*:

> Part of that Power which would
> The Evil ever do, and ever does the Good.

DIALECTICS AND TOTALITY

This interpretation of Hegel, which emphasizes reflection as a political means of advancing development, shares some common traits with the Enlightenment philosophy of the 1700s: when we arrive at the truth, the world will move forward. But the philosophers of the Enlightenment largely viewed truth as scientific knowledge. According to Hegel, philosophical truth is grounded in our reflections upon the given, but insufficient, transcendental presuppositions. As we will later see, left-wing Hegelians (such as Habermas) placed great emphasis on this point. When they talk about emancipation, liberation, they do not mean (like the liberalists) an individual liberation from tradition and society as supra-individual dimensions, but a liberation from social irrationality as a step towards a more rational society, through a critical reflection (critique of ideology) that rejects insufficient transcendental presuppositions (ideologies) in favour of more adequate frameworks.

In the Hegelian view of liberating reflection, *history* is not a collection of isolated events. History is the process of reflection through which humanity fumbles its way towards the most adequate framework. Just as Aristotle held that human beings are first able to show what they 'are made of' through a realization of their abilities in the family, the village, and the city-state, Hegel held that humanity was first able to achieve self-realization and self-knowledge by living through and testing the different basic ways of existence. Human beings first understood their nature when they had 'lived out' the different frameworks and could look back at this process. In other words, history is the process by which human beings become themselves and, retrospectively, understand themselves, in that all transcendental presuppositions (ways of being) are lived out and tested. History thus leads towards self-insight that is more and more adequate.

History is not something external that we can observe from the outside. We always observe from some perspective, and these perspectives are formed *in* history. The perspective within which we think and experience is a result of the historical process of self-development. Hegel thus distanced himself from the ahistorical attitude that often appears along with radical empiricism. But how can we know whether *our* way of seeing the world is the correct and final perspective? Interpretations of Hegel have claimed both that he held that there actually is a set of perspectives that represents the correct and ultimate view (*absolute knowledge* = Hegel's philosophy), and that he held only that we are always on the path towards some perspective that should be more correct, but that absolute knowledge is an unachievable goal. The first interpretation is based on the idea of an ultimate completion of the historical process of self-development. However, in both instances, Hegel would say that our present position represents a higher synthesis than in earlier positions, and that we therefore are able to evaluate these earlier positions.

According to Hegel, this reflection which drives the historical process of formation forward follows certain laws, the so-called *dialectics*. Textbooks often say that Hegel's dialectic is a theory about how a thesis is transformed into an antithesis and this antithesis is again transformed into a synthesis, which is a thesis of a higher order; this synthesis, in turn, brings about a new antithesis, and so on.

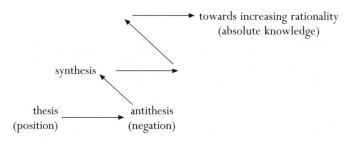

It is further pointed out that the word *dialectic* derives from Greek philosophy. *Dialego* means 'to discuss'. Dialectic was conceived as the philosophical dialogue whereby we arrive at truer standpoints through public discourse. But, for Hegel, dialectics is said to apply *both* to theoretical conversations and to the concrete historical process. In theory, dialectics emerges when concepts and positions point beyond themselves towards more adequate concepts and positions; in practice, dialectics emerges when the different transcendental horizons of understanding evolve towards their culmination in the state.

All of this is basically correct, but in order to grasp what Hegel meant by dialectics, we may find it helpful to *delimit* the dialectical insight in relation to empirical knowledge and pure analytic insight (even though such a delimitation is a simplification): insight into dialectical transitions is neither empirical knowledge nor deductive insight. Insight into dialectical transitions emerges from the insight that fundamental presuppositions (such as basic concepts in political theory) may be deficient, inadequate. Through dialectics we do not confirm and disconfirm by referring to experience or by arguing deductively, but by pointing out that presumably competent people agree that a certain position is 'deficient' in such a way that the position points beyond itself towards a less deficient position.

In this sense, dialectics is not a method that we can first learn and then apply to a particular case. Dialectical thought is *case-oriented* thought. The deficiencies in the case itself drive us towards a truer position. We are guided by 'the case', not by deductive rules of inference or by hypothetico-deductive methods. Thus, we cannot learn to think dialectically by means of a formal method. Dialectical thought can be learned only by thinking dialectically about particular cases. We must jump into the water if we want to learn to swim, as Hegel said. Therefore, the only satisfactory introduction to dialectics is a concrete dialectical analysis: our previous discussion of the internal transitions between various generations in pre-Socratic philosophy is an example of a dialectical interpretation. Therefore, instead of talking in formal terms about thesis, antithesis, and synthesis, we point to this example of dialectical thinking.

We can try to clarify this point with another example: if we think of the notion *to see*, we recognize that seeing is connected with seeing *something*, whether this something exists materially or not. And *what* we see appears against a *background*. And when we see something against a background, we see *from a particular place*. In other words, *the concept 'to see'* inevitably points beyond itself towards other concepts with which it necessarily connects. It is when we become aware of all of these mutually related concepts that we first understand the phenomenon – seeing – as it actually is. What drives cognition forward is not observations or experiments. Nor is this a deductive logic that begins with definitions and axioms. It is 'the case' itself that drives cognition forward. Here, the particular case was *the concept 'to see'*. This concept led us to think about the other concepts that are presupposed by this concept. We may thus talk about a 'content-directed' logic: we do not approach the case with ready-made methods and definitions; it is the case, the content, that determines the development of thought and that leads in the direction of more adequate concepts.

This development of thought thus moves in the direction of more and more comprehensive concepts: our understanding becomes truer the more comprehensive it is. Truth is totality. Truth is not found in parts, but in the interconnected totality (cf. similar views in Plato and Spinoza). We could have made a similar point by starting with the notion of action: it points to an agent, an intention, something that we act with, etc. The driving force in this reflective process is a striving to overcome the deficiencies of the various basic positions that prevail at various times. Reflection is a driving force because it *negates*: it tracks down deficiencies and creates an urge to overcome the deficiencies.

The word *overcome* ('*aufheben*') has several meanings in Hegel's dialectics. It is partly a question of *abolishing* the deficient aspects in a position, and partly a question of *preserving* those aspects that are not deficient. Finally, it is a question of *raising* the position to a higher level. A dialectical overcoming of a deficient position is therefore not a negative abolition of that position, but its critical preservation, within another and higher position. This is, in Hegel's terminology, what it means to think 'negatively': seeking the deficiencies of the present position so that we are driven towards greater insight. Thinking 'positively' is to think of the present situation as a complete and self-sufficient system. Thinking negatively is to think critically and progressively.

In this way, critical reflection upon changeable transcendental presuppositions forms a part of a dialectical overcoming which leads us forward towards truer transcendental presuppositions; that is to say, forward in the historical process of formation in which human beings realize themselves. And the goal of this process is complete insight into every possible transcendental presupposition. If human beings achieved this goal, they would possess perfect rational insight into themselves and the world, because they would, in principle, comprehend the totality of all basic positions. However, in practice, the goal is that of obtaining more extensive and complete positions than the earlier ones. The essential point is that of overcoming what is relatively more defective and incomplete, on the way towards better and more comprehensive totalities.

MASTER AND SLAVE – THE STRUGGLE FOR RECOGNITION AND SOCIAL IDENTITY

The historical process of formation is not purely theoretical for Hegel, something that only takes place 'in our head'. Hegel's theory of *master* and *slave* shows how concretely he imagined this historical process of self-development: when two people stand face to face a tension arises between them because each wants to be *recognized* by the other as the master of the situation, that is to say, as the one who defines himself or herself *and* the other. Hegel explained the historical process by this model: in this struggle for recognition, one will submit to the other. We end up with one who is superior, the master, and one who is inferior, the slave. The master forces the slave to work for him; thus, a mutual development arises whereby a human being (the slave) cultivates nature and the cultivated nature, in turn, changes the human being. When the slave ploughs the field, a material surplus is created that provides the basis for better work methods and better tools, something that again leads to a better cultivation of nature, and so on.

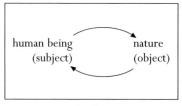

mutual cultivation

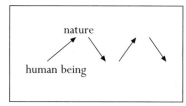

mutual formation process

We end up with a dialectical process of formative interchange between a human being (the subject) and nature (the object), and the slave is the one that stands closer to reality, and, hence, that learns more. It is the slave who becomes the scientist, according to Hegel, while the master functions as a necessary catalyst. With this, Hegel thought that he had overcome Kant's static distinction between subject and object, in which the subject never reaches out to the object (*Ding an sich*).

The master-slave interaction is a dialectical relation in the sense that there is a mutual, dynamic relationship between the two subjects. The master is master only because the slave (as well as the master) accepts the master as such, and the slave is a slave only because the master (as well as the slave) accepts the slave as such. This provided a sociological model for political power, which was later adopted by the existentialist Sartre[3] and by Frantz Fanon (1925–1961), one of the ideologists of the independence movements in Africa:[4] When a white person describes a black person's nature as inferior, the white person may be interpreted as 'master' in such a master-slave game. Whites *define* themselves as superior and the blacks as inferior, and the whites force the blacks to accept this definition both of the whites and of themselves. And the whites hide the fact that this is a social 'power move' by saying that this status is natural – and by making the blacks believe it to be natural that 'the black person's nature is inferior'.

Liberation must follow the same two steps. The blacks must personally realize that this is a *social* definition, not nature, and must learn to *redefine* their view of themselves and of the whites – and they must make the whites accept this redefinition of blacks and whites. The blacks cannot regain self-respect unless the whites also share this respect. With a little imagination we can see how this master-slave game functions on various levels in today's society (including the relation between men and women).

The theory of master and slave shows how the theoretical philosopher Hegel approached concrete political problems. This theory demonstrates, moreover, how Hegel refused to view the individual as being self-sufficient: we *are* what we *and the others* define us to be. What a person *is*, is to a great degree determined by other people and other groups.

Hegel viewed the French Revolution as an extremely important event. The theory of the master and the slave may be used to bring out the Hegelian points in this connection. Before the Revolution, the master was the self-indulgent, parasitic landowning class. The slave was the working, but politically impotent citizenry. During the Revolution, the game was redefined by the slave, that is, the hard-working bourgeoisie. After the Revolution, the mutual, but unequal recognition was overcome in favour of a mutual recognition based on equality: a society of free and rational equals – freedom, equality, and brotherhood. The equality of the civil society realized the Enlightenment's ideal of autonomy.

TRADITION AS REASON – THE TENSION BETWEEN THE UNIVERSAL AND THE PARTICULAR

History, for Hegel, is a process filled with tension that leads to increasingly richer and more adequate horizons of understanding. These different horizons of understanding are valid for complete epochs, and not primarily for particular individuals. The changing horizons of understanding are common, intersubjective, for each culture and era. There are two implications which are both important for political theory:

1   *The individual is an organic part of the community*. This means that the individual is a part of the community that exists during the historical period in question. This follows from the historical-sociological view of the transcendental horizons of understanding: the transcendental horizons of understanding are intersubjective, not private, and they are historically changing and historically created. To understand Hegel's point, we may consider *language*, understood as the common horizon of understanding within which we communicate (not language as sound waves or printer's ink). Language is not private, individual; it is common. We do not create language, but 'grow into' a common language and thereby learn to understand ourselves and the world from within this language. And language is historically changing and historically created. Our basic concepts of political theory today are not the same as they were in ancient Athens, but, at the same time, our basic political concepts have been created by historical-political development.

2   *Tradition is rational*. This follows if we accept the view that the criteria for rationality are determined by the transcendental horizons of understanding that history, or tradition, has brought about during each era: the common, historically created horizon of understanding that exists during a particular epoch

holds our criteria of what is meaningful or meaningless, rational or irrational. Again, we may think of language: in a certain sense, we *are* language, that is to say, the language (the basic concepts) that prevails in our day. We cannot simply leap back to the basic concepts of the ancient Greeks or into a future way of thinking that does not yet exist. Of course, we may change some of the basic concepts that form the basis of our understanding today. This is what happens in creative writing and science (cf. scientific breakthroughs by Newton and Einstein). But those who actively change and expand the horizon of understanding must also start within the horizon of understanding which has been inherited through tradition.

Such a view of history is both relativist and absolutist. It is relativist, because the claim is made that the criteria for reason and nonreason change throughout time. What was reasonable in Athens in 400 BC is not necessarily reasonable for us today. It is absolutist, because this view of history is not said to be relative itself, but, on the contrary, is said to be the ultimate horizon of understanding which embraces all previous and relative horizons of understanding. Hegel thought that his own philosophy was not relative, but absolute in the sense of being 'objectively true'.

In Hegel's thought, history was a crucial concern. The Greeks had largely been thinking ahistorically, and from the time of the Renaissance, philosophers had primarily been interested in the new natural sciences. But after the Enlightenment, human beings began, in a new way, to be problematic to themselves. History moved to the centre, in terms of both political history and cultural history (cf. Ch. 16). By the mid-1800s (with thinkers like Comte and Marx), interest in history increasingly included the problems of the day. The result was a social research that was historically oriented, in opposition to the social research inspired by natural science.

Hegel distanced himself both from individualism and from collectivism.[5] Both views are *abstractions*. Both views involve isolated fictions: individualism, with an atomistic, ahistorical, and self-sufficient individual; collectivism, with a state that emerges as something independent, divorced from living human beings. On the contrary, according to Hegel, human beings and the state are connected internally. Human beings first achieve self-realization in an 'ethical' (*sittlich*) community, which, for Hegel means the state. But we must live in smaller groups, like families and other social groups, before we become an organic part of the state. And the state, in turn, is not *made* by any contract, but rather grows out of history. The state, in Hegel's sense, thus forges the real bonds interlinking human beings. It is by virtue of these bonds that the state is an ethical community and that human beings can realize themselves as human beings. These ties, according to Hegel, are far more fundamental than any agreement based on individual pleasure-profit calculations. Hegel rejected the view that the state is a man-made convention or contract, without worth of its own and without an internal meaning for the individual person.

Consequently, *liberty* is essentially *positive liberty* for Hegel. Liberty is understanding the historical community and thus realizing our role in this community. Negative liberty, in which freedom is the absence of state coercion, is almost unthinkable for Hegel, because the state is nothing else than the human being, not *something* external that is capable of *coercing* a human being. The state is the ethical community of which human beings are organic parts. The will of the 'state' is therefore the will of the human being. Coercion is out of the question, unless there is something wrong with the individual human being or with the state.

In addition, it is worth noting that Hegel defends private property on the basis of the notion that human beings must *have something* by which they can *express themselves*. Human beings cannot only live 'within themselves'. They must have something in which they can express themselves, and in which they can recognize themselves. Therefore, everyone should own something. But according to Hegel, it does not matter that some own much and others little – as long as the economic inequality does not lead to discontent and political instability.

FAMILY, CIVIL SOCIETY, AND THE STATE

Hegel starts with the local environment, the family, in which the individual becomes socialized and individualized, that is to say, led into society and into tradition. Reconciling individual freedom with social solidarity was, for Hegel, the basic problem of modernity. His philosophy of the family should be understood in this light: the nuclear family of mother, children, and father who base their subsistence on familial wealth is, for Hegel, a necessary counterweight to the individualism of bourgeois society, because love and solidarity are basic values for the family.

The modern family is grounded on mutual love between man and woman. Through love the two mutually recognize each other. Each person's identity is co-determined by the identity of the other person. Each of them is defined by virtue of the other. Thus, their identity is not an isolated individual attribute, but is grounded on the interrelationship between the two persons. Marriage is thus something different from and something more than an external formality, just as love is something different from and something more than falling in love. Mutual recognition between a man and a woman within the socially recognized institution of marriage reconciles freedom in the form of love and romance with mutual identity and social recognition.

Hegel thought that the woman gains her complete recognition within the family, as wife and mother. The man also participates in work outside the confines of the family; he thus gains a part of his social identity outside the family and marriage. Hegel ascribed to the man a double role as father of the family and as an agent in the productive sphere. The woman, on the other hand, is connected to the family sphere in all of her tasks. This point reveals how Hegel's view of the family was based on the bourgeois family of his day. He regarded women and men as being different, and as having different functions. He did not champion gender equality.

Hegel's view of the family thus moved beyond the rather juridical view of the family as an external contract between two self-sufficient individuals.[6] In reference to Kant's discussion of marriage as a contract for the sharing of sexual organs and urges,[7] Hegel commented: 'To subsume marriage under the concept of contract is thus quite impossible; this subsumption – though shameful is the only word for it – is propounded in Kant's *Philosophy of Law*.'[8] It is also worth pointing out that while both Aristotle and Hegel (in opposition to Plato) viewed the family as fundamental to the socialization process, Hegel was somewhat less biologically oriented than

Aristotle, but more social-psychologically oriented with respect to formation of mutual identity.

From the family as the primary local community, Hegel moved to what he called the civil society, the foundation of which is 'the system of needs'; this was basically the market-economic system as Hegel knew it from the British political economists, and from his own age in general. Hegel emphasized the internal dynamic logic of this system. Actions mutually condition one another; and while the individuals act on the basis of partial insight, the system functions as a whole on the basis of its own logic, which is of a higher order. The system has a logic, a direction of evolvement, that the agents do not need to recognize. This is what Hegel called 'the cunning of reason'. This points to genuine sociological insight: when many individuals interact, results (and social patterns) may arise which no particular agent intended.

Hegel placed civil society in the interface between family and state. He is one of the first theoreticians to thematize the fact that manifold private and voluntary organizations have emerged in the modern world, with functions that cannot be adequately performed by the family or by the state. Professional life and the market economy are included in the broad version of this notion of a civil society. But under this term, Hegel also focused on questions that today are treated in opposition both to the state and to the market.

Moreover, it is striking that Hegel finally hinted at a crisis theory of *laissez-faire* capitalism: left to itself, this system (through expansion, the concentration of capital, impoverishment, and polarization between classes) leads to tensions and instability. At this point, intermediary organizations intervene, and along with them order and cohesion, and institutions and community, that is, the state in Hegelian terminology. In other words, Hegel distinguished himself from both the *laissez-faire* liberalists and from the Marxists, and he outlined a third path: capitalism is a self-destructive system that will not survive if left to itself, in contrast to what the liberalists thought. But Hegel did not think that capitalism would be overthrown by a revolution, as the Marxists claimed. If we may apply today's political terms anachronistically, we could in this connection think of Hegel as an early social democrat – but certainly with his own theoretical approach.

Hegel's thought is, in many ways, a philosophy about change, through tensions. From the French Revolution, among other events, Hegel had learned to view history as a surging process of formation; in any historical situation, we can always try to understand these historical changes by reflecting afterwards on what happened. For Hegel, wisdom belongs to the late hour of twilight.

OBJECTIONS TO HEGEL

Several objections have been made to Hegel's philosophy. We shall briefly mention some of these objections and show how sympathetic interpretations of Hegel may respond to these criticisms.

THE INDIVIDUAL HAS NO PLACE IN HEGEL'S SYSTEM

Kierkegaard, among others, made this objection when he supported the individual against what Kierkegaard viewed as a philosophical system in which what is unique, the individual, is subsumed by the universal, that is, by the state and by history.

It is basically correct that the individual, like morality and religion, is subordinated to the system in Hegel's thought. For example, he did not think that the individual can intervene in history: history is not formed by so-called great statesmen; but those whom we would call great men or women are used by history – often without these agents being aware of what they are *actually* doing. Napoleon thought that he was going to unite Europe, but history used Napoleon to promote a new nationalism ('the cunning of reason'). History achieves its objectively reasonable progress whether or not the people of that day understand what they are doing. History has its own logic that may be misinterpreted by the agents themselves.

At first glance, Kierkegaard's objection seems to be correct. There is something in each of us that is deeply personal, such as fear of death and self-consciousness. *How* this is formed may be determined historically and socially, but not *that* my death is mine and that my consciousness is mine. Morality and religion are in this sense not really preserved in Hegel's system. Thus, it is plausible to say that Hegel did not allow the individual, or the individual's moral and religious problems, to have their proper place.

On the other hand, Hegel would probably answer that the individual, the 'unique being' (*hin enkelte*) in Kierkegaard's thought, is an *abstraction*. The concrete human being always participates in a historical and social connection. We are therefore correct in emphasizing the historical and social connections. Only when we are able to grasp all of the connections within which people find themselves will we be able concretely to understand this person. The totality of connections is concrete and true. A part or an aspect gives us only an abstract and partially true picture. Moreover, the totality, the whole, is a process. The transcendental horizons of understanding evolve historically. Truth cannot be found through static concepts. We recognize truth – the totality of concrete connections – only by looking back on the entire historical process, with its dialectical tensions and leaps. In addition to such philosophical arguments against individualism, Hegel also had a political argument: unifying Germany was necessary in order to modernize the country, and in the Germany of his day, individualism was synonymous with regional division. Hegel was therefore *against* individualism because he was *for* German unification.

HEGEL'S PHILOSOPHY IS TOTALITARIAN

Hegel's support of German unification in order to strengthen the German state is easy to condemn in light of the next 150 years of German history. But to make such a judgement is anachronistic. At that time it was reasonable for a politically aware German citizen to want to strengthen the state. And although Hegel himself sometimes seemed to believe that he was almost omniscient, it is hardly correct for us to expect that he should know of, and also be held partly responsible for, the German political disasters of the twentieth century. It is also reasonable to believe that what Hegel wrote in *The Philosophy of Right*, under pressure from the censors, does not fully coincide with his own viewpoints: privately, Hegel expressed more liberal views.

On the question of Hegel's supposed totalitarianism, we may say that the official Hegel that we, for example, meet in *The Philosophy of Right* lent his support to the

Prussian state of his day (c. 1820). The ideal that Hegel publicly expressed is thus in many ways authoritarian but it is neither totalitarian nor fascist.[9] He supported a *constitutionally* strong government and he repudiated the notion that a dictator should govern by his own whims. Hegel wanted a state that is governed according to law and right, and he despised irrationality – while the fascists praised irrationality and unconstitutional rule.

HEGEL IS 'CONSERVATIVE'

The objection of Hegel's conservatism is frequently raised by left-wing intellectuals. But the word *conservative* has several meanings[10] – as well as both positive and negative connotations, all according to our perspective. If by 'conservative' we mean 'wanting to preserve the *status quo*', Hegel was not conservative. According to Hegel, we cannot always 'preserve' existing forms of government since everything that exists is subject to historical change. Hegel was thus directly opposed to a *static* conservatism. Historical change occurs in qualitative leaps. Therefore, seen from one perspective, Hegel was almost a 'defeatist radical': changes are unavoidable and occur through far-reaching transitions. But, at the same time, Hegel claimed that what is essential is always preserved in the form of higher syntheses. The unavoidable qualitative leaps always lead to syntheses which embrace both theses and antitheses, on a higher level. Thus, existing forms are preserved; but we should note that what previously existed is placed in a new and larger connection. Whether we interpret Hegel's thought in a radical or a conservative direction will thus depend on whether we emphasize that the overcoming to achieve the new synthesis is a rejection or a preservation.[11]

HEGEL'S VIEW OF HISTORY IS OVEROPTIMISTIC

Hegel's theory of the dialectical overcoming guarantees historical optimism: history gathers up all of the best aspects of earlier experiences. But is this certain? Can we be certain that our age is a synthesis of all of the good from the past? Is it not possible that essential aspects have been lost? Is it possible that not all change is a comprehensive overcoming to a higher level, but that most changes result from conflicts between various groups and various cultures in which some lose and some win? And cannot Hegel's philosophy represent a legitimization of the historical winners, a legitimization that might be politically 'dulling'?

We may reply that we are not going to experience *today* the great comprehensive synthesis that ensures that nothing is lost, but only when history is *consummated*. But this responsibility transforms the whole theory of dialectical overcoming into something distant and speculative, like a pious hope that 'everything will work out in the end'.

In addition, we may reply that it is *history*, and not we who are living today, that decides what is worth preserving. What a particular group may experience as a loss, is really – in a historical light – either neutral or a gain. But this answer approaches pure opportunism regarding the propositional content of good and evil: whatever happens, is good! Moreover, it becomes difficult to know what is 'really' good, since it is often difficult to know *where* history is going.

Some modern Hegelians think that history has reached its end: the final synthesis appears to be a weakly state-regulated and strongly market-oriented capitalism, with democratic government and recognition of human rights. There is no acceptable negation, no acceptable overcoming of these institutions. Historical progress will from now on mean only an improved capitalism and more democracy and human rights.[12]

Does this mean that the 'force of negation' is no longer operative in the modern world? If so, the right-wing Hegelians are correct as opposed to the left-wing Hegelians. In the right-wing Hegelian interpretation, Hegel emerges as a historical realist. But even if it were true that there is no possibility of qualitatively higher forms of societal institutions, and that history in that sense has come to an end, we could still experience breakdowns and regression. Life on Earth will hardly endure for ever, and there is always a danger of great crises, either by external causes (from nature) or by internal causes (from our social systems and culture).

HEGEL'S PHILOSOPHY LEAVES NO ROOM FOR ETHICS

Hegel claimed that the criteria for right are to be found in the horizons of understanding that history affords us at all times. An objective natural law does not exist. Those who emerge victorious are right. There is no room for ethics in Hegel's philosophy. Against this objection we can point out that, according to Hegel, the goal of history is a rational and free society. The goal is an objective and ahistorical good. But perhaps this counter-argument does not help very much, since this goal will be a part of the future, and we all must view the world from the perspective that we have been given.

Ethics, in a certain sense of the word, holds an important place in Hegel's thought. In fact, Hegel distinguished between abstract right, and morality, and 'the ethical' (*die Sittlichkeit*). The first distinction corresponds to Kant's treatment of the juridical as opposed to the moral sphere. But here, and elsewhere, Hegel criticized dualistic thinking: abstract law and abstract morality are connected in the ethical. The ethical comprises the concrete bonds, of the home, the community, and the state, that connect abstract right and morality. The central position that the ethical holds in Hegel's thought shows that it may be misleading to say that Hegel leaves no room for ethics.

HEGEL'S DIALECTICS IS NONSENSE

What Hegel calls dialectics is only a confused mixture of empirical science (such as psychology) and quasi-logic. This objection seems to spring from an extreme empiricism: there are no legitimate methods other than those of empirical science and deductive logic. But this empiricism is itself problematic. We have previously tried to show how dialectics may be understood as a 'softening' of transcendental philosophy. However, this is not meant to imply that Hegel's dialectical thinking is not problematic and questionable.

The simplest, but not the least important, criticism of Hegel is that he wrote in a way that is often unclear and hard to understand. It is thus an open question as to what Hegel might have learnt from Locke's sense of conceptual clarification or from Kant's will to explain and justify his claims.

QUESTIONS

Explain Hegel's view of history by using the following terms: 'dialectic', 'overcoming', 'synthesis', 'learning', and 'formation'.

'In Hegel's philosophy Kant's transcendental presuppositions are replaced by historically created presuppositions.' Discuss and take a position on this assertion.

'For Hegel the state is everything and the individual is nothing.' Discuss this assertion with regard to Hegel's view of dialectics and his view of the relation between the family, the market, and the state. Discuss Hegel's attempt to overcome liberalism and conservatism.

SUGGESTIONS FOR FURTHER READING

PRIMARY LITERATURE

The Hegel Reader, edited by Stephen Houlgate, Oxford, 1998.
The Phenomenology of Spirit, translated by A. V. Miller, Oxford, 1977.
Hegel's Philosophy of Right, translated by T. Y. Knox, London, 1952.

SECONDARY LITERATURE

Kojève, A., *Introduction to the Reading of Hegel*, New York, 1980.
Marcuse, H., *Hegel and the Rise of Social Theory* (1941), London, 1986.
Popper, K. R., *The Poverty of Historicism*, London, 1969.
Taylor, C., *Hegel*, Cambridge, 1975.

NOTES

1 When we here, in this history of philosophy, have tried to show how different political notions have changed – for example, how the Greek view of man as a social being changed into the Hellenistic view of man as an individual – we have worked in accordance with this Hegelian conception.
2 Ch. 9, Descartes – methodical doubt . . .
3 Cf. Sartre's theory about 'seeing'/the 'look', *le regard*.
4 Frantz Fanon, *The Wretched of the Earth* (1968), New York, 1991.
5 Cf. Ch. 13, Economic liberalism. It is not uncommon to interpret Hegel as a 'collectivist'. Especially in liberalist circles it is common to overlook the distinction between collectivism ('the state above the individual') and Hegel's dialectical view ('a human being is an organic part of the moral community which is the state').
6 Cf. this contractual view in Locke's *Two Treatises of Government*, VII, 78, 81.
7 Cf. Kant, *Grundlegung zur Metaphysik der Sitten, Rechtslehre*, 24, AB 107–8 (standard pagination).
8 Hegel, *The Philosophy of Law*, §75.
9 Herbert Marcuse, in *Reason and Revolution*, argues that Hegel was far removed from fascism because he supported the notion of a constitutional state governed by laws.
10 Cf. Ch. 13, Edmund Burke.
11 Cf. this chapter, Reflection, dialectics, experience.
12 Francis Fukuyama, *The End of History and the Last Man*, London, 1992.

18 Marx – productive forces and class struggle

Life. *Karl Marx (1818–1883) was the son of an affluent German lawyer of Jewish descent. A student of classical Greek materialism, he wrote his doctoral thesis on Democritus and Epicurus, but he was greatly influenced by the left-wing Hegelianism of his day. He became a journalist for the liberal* Rheinische Zeitung. *In 1843, after the newspaper was suppressed by the Prussian government, Marx went to Paris, where he came into contact with the French socialists. In France, he met Friedrich Engels (1820–1895), with whom he developed a lifelong friendship and a close collaboration. Through Engels, Marx gained insight into British economic theory and into the economic and social conditions in Britain. (At the time, Engels was the manager of a factory in Manchester.) When Marx was deported from France because of his political activity, he moved to Brussels. Marx and Engels developed a programme of action and published* The Communist Manifesto *in 1848, in connection with the founding of the Communist League. During the revolution of 1848, Marx went back to the Rhineland, but when the revolution was suppressed, Marx fled to London, where he spent the rest of his life.* The International Working Men's Association *(also known as the First International) was formed in 1864, and Marx was one of its driving forces. This organization was to represent the proletariat in all countries. After the defeat of the Paris Commune in 1871, the First International was dissolved. From then on, Marx concentrated on his economic analysis and was no longer actively involved in politics. Among his best-known works are* Economic and Philosophic Manuscripts *(1844–5),* The German Ideology *(1845–6),* A Contribution to the Critique of Political Economy *(1859), and* Capital *(1867).*

DIALECTICS AND ALIENATION

Marx was not satisfied with merely *interpreting* the world; he wanted to *change* it. In other words, Marx understood political theory as part of political activity: political theory is not contemplation of truth but is itself a manoeuvre in a political struggle for or against social changes.

Marx's scientific endeavour was not purely philosophy but also embraced history, sociology, economy, and philosophy. The transitions between philosophical analysis, empirical endeavours, and current political contributions were fleeting. As a Hegelian, Marx was unwilling to *separate* a uniquely philosophical theory: in reality, economy, sociology, history, and philosophy are connected.

Marx is often presented as one who propagated Hegel's philosophy: for Hegel, the world was a historical process in which the development of the *thoughts and ideas* was fundamental. Marx retained Hegel's view of the world as a dialectical historical process, but claimed that the development of *material life* was fundamental. At best, this presentation of Hegel as an 'idealist' and of Marx as a 'materialist' is a simplification. We have already seen that Hegel was concerned with social and material factors.[1] And we will see that Marx was not a materialist in a mechanistic sense.

If Hegel stood history 'on its head' (idealism) and Marx allowed history to 'stand on its feet' (materialism), it could be said that history should, of course, *walk* on its feet, but *think* with its head. In other words, it is not either/or, but both/and, in the sense that both material-economic and cultural-intellectual factors play their part. And as dialecticians, Hegel and Marx agreed on this. But at the same time, Hegel placed a *greater* emphasis on the cultural-intellectual aspect (*Geist*) than Marx, and Marx placed a *greater* emphasis on the material-economic aspect than Hegel. With this reservation, we may talk about a 'dialectical idealism' in Hegel and a 'dialectical materialism' in Marx.[2] In this chapter, we will not say much about dialectics, which we have already discussed with regard to Hegel.[3] Since dialectics is always determined by *the subject matter*, an exposition of Marx's dialectics would, at the same time, be an exposition of Marx's materialism. We will remind the reader of the general points surrounding dialectics as we mentioned them in connection with Hegel:

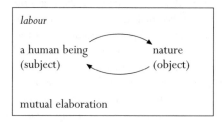

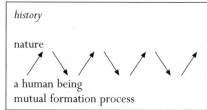

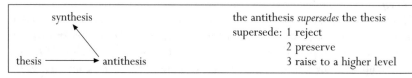

In order to make dialectics more concrete, we will sketch Marx's theory of *alienation* ('*Entfremdung*'). This is a theory that we find in his early works written when he was still strongly influenced by Hegel. Marx took his cue from the left-wing Hegelian Ludwig Feuerbach (1804–1872), who employed the following dialectical line of thinking in his critique of *religion*:

1   First, human beings lived in innocence, in harmony with themselves.
2   Eventually, human beings created an image of God, but they did not realize that this God was man-made. They understood this God as something *different* from themselves, as an external power that threatens and chastises. But, in reality, according to Feuerbach, this God was an external manifestation of human attributes: God had not created human beings, but human beings had created God. Human beings were now divided between what they recognized

as themselves and what they recognized as an external power, but which, in reality, was an external manifestation of themselves. This dichotomy was alienation: human beings in this condition are alien to parts of themselves. In this alienated condition, they experience God as an independent power, and themselves as powerless. Human beings became slaves in relation to an image of God which they themselves had created. They were oppressed by a product of their own making.

3   In order to overcome this miserable alienation, human beings must *recognize* the connection: that this God, which they conceive of as an external power, is really a human product, that is, a part of human beings themselves.

Feuerbach thought, in other words, that a *critique of religion* is sufficient to overcome this alienation. If people *recognize* the connection they will stop believing in God. They will no longer live with a painful dichotomy. They will become reconciled with themselves, with a product of their own making. We can illustrate Feuerbach's points in this scheme:

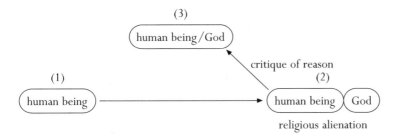

Here, our purpose is not to evaluate the validity of Feuerbach's atheism. As a disproof of God's existence, it is hardly free of objections. The decisive point for us is the dialectical scheme in which alienation represents the negation of an original state of innocence and in which the critique of religion represents an overcoming of this alienation. The result is a new harmony, but on a higher level, because through these processes, human beings recognized something about themselves that they did not know while they were in the original state of harmony. Marx employed this dialectical scheme. But he did not think, as did the left-wing Hegelian Feuerbach, that theoretical criticism is enough. As long as people need the comfort of religion, because they live under insufferable material conditions, no theoretical arguments will be able to overcome religious alienation.[4] Abolition of religious alienation presupposes an abolition of economic alienation.

Here we meet a version of Marx's 'materialism': religious alienation derives from political and social alienation, which again is based on economic alienation. In this sense, the economic ('material') factor takes precedence over the spiritual factor.

Marx | the religious level
the political and social levels
the economic level

Marx accepted the idea that human beings are religiously alienated. But this kind of alienation was not the most important for Marx. This religious alienation is only one aspect of a general alienation in capitalist society.

Labour creates alienation in the capitalist society. Because people (as opposed to animals) must work and produce in order to live, and because work creates a surplus product, the relationship between man and nature becomes a dialectical relationship in which each side mutually transforms the other. History is precisely this dialectical process of development in which nature becomes more and more transformed by human labour, and human beings are more and more shaped by the products they create. Nature, in the capitalist society, has been greatly transformed: people are surrounded by factories and cities. But at the same time, a drastic dichotomy has arisen between the capitalist and the proletariat, and between human beings and the product of their labour. Human beings are no longer the masters of their own product, which emerges as an independent power that forces human beings to work for it. The capitalist must invest and compete while the worker barely survives at the subsistence level. The machine and its development determine what happens to human beings, and not the reverse.

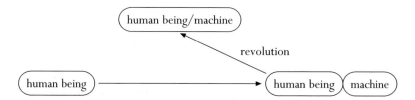

Here we have reached a salient point in Marx's thought: his indignation at human degradation in the capitalist society of his day (the mid-1800s). And it is important to see that Marx thought that this degradation affected both the capitalist and the labourer. Both are enslaved by the economic system. This degradation involves not only the economic impoverishment of the labourer, but human degradation in general: human beings are subject to external forces — reification and work pressures — which keep them from realizing themselves as free and creative beings, and they must function as automata, controlled by forces they themselves have created, but of which they are no longer master. Human beings — both capitalists and workers — are affected by this reified world. They feel *powerless* before 'transformed' nature as it functions in the capitalist society, and they view themselves and their fellow human beings as 'things'; as labour-power, as employees, as competitors. The alienation is thus twofold:

1   the economic impoverishment of the labourers
2   the human degradation of the capitalist and the labourer.

We can return to the dialectical 'triad': under capitalism, alienation is thus the *antithesis*. On the basis of a worsening of the situation — a crisis in capitalism — the workers make a revolution: they regain their human worth by *exerting mastery* over their own products, over the machines and the factories. When they have done this, they recognize themselves in this product and are reconciled with it, just as

Feuerbach thought that human beings become reconciled with their own divine attributes. Alienation is abolished through the revolution: human beings become conscious, free, and creative. Powerlessness and reification are superseded. Human beings gain control over the economy and are thus in a position to realize themselves.

Thus, Marx did not think that history moves smoothly and evenly forward. History is driven forward by qualitative leaps, by revolutions. The situation often gets worse before the transformation occurs. But the transformation results in a synthesis of a higher order. Thus, a proletarian revolution will come because of crises in capitalism, while the revolution will 'raise' the capitalist production ability to a qualitatively higher level, because the production apparatus will be under human control. Under capitalism, each person acts rationally on the basis of an ego-istic perspective, but the system as a whole functions anarchically and ultimately self-destructively. The sum of the individual actions leads to an unintended result. The system thus incorporates a logic that no individual person intends. But after the revolution, both the individual and the social structure will be rationally enlightened and rationally governed, according to Marx.

If Marx was a 'materialist' in the sense that he held that the economy is decisive for religious and spiritual life, he was *not* a materialist in the sense of taking the so-called *material values*, money and possessions, as an *ideal*. On the contrary, Marx viewed this 'have' attitude as a degradation.[5] Here, Marx shared the classical Aristotelian ideal: basically, a human being is a conscious, free, and creative being. Powerlessness and reification pervert these fundamental human attributes. Nor was Marx a 'materialist' in the sense that he held that human beings are at all times primarily *motivated* by material gain. On the contrary, he said that this, above all, is characteristic of the phase of history which is represented by the capitalist society.

HISTORICAL MATERIALISM

We said that Marx was not a 'materialist' in the sense of 'material gain is an ideal' (ethical materialism). Nor was he a 'materialist' in the sense of 'everything that exists is composed of material particles and follows mechanistic laws' (mechan-istic, atomistic materialism). Mechanistic materialism conflicts with two of Marx's basic notions:

1   For Marx, all change is not mechanistic. Historical-social change is dialectical.
2   For Marx, the world is not just a multitude of atoms. The historical-social real-ity is characterized by connections.

When Marx is called a materialist, it is, above all, in the following sense: 'economic-material factors are the driving force in the historical process' (historical materialism).

Marx shared the Aristotelian view of man as man-in-community, whereby human beings are first able to realize themselves in the context of various social groups. But labour, for Marx, is formative. This is a more positive definition of labour than what we find in Aristotle. Through labour, according to Marx, the social institutions are changed, so that other human properties can be realized in the new historical stages. People who live under capitalism can realize other abil-ities than those living in the city-state. History is the formative process whereby humanity realizes itself. (For historical reasons, this viewpoint is beyond Aristotle's philosophical horizon.) By becoming acquainted with history, we become acquainted with humanity and with ourselves. Marx thought that economic factors were decisive in the historical process of formation. History is the history of economics, the history of labour. The qualitative changes in economic life turn history into an irreversible process always moving forward.

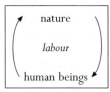 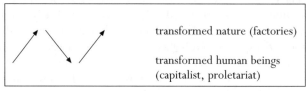

history = the history of economics, the history of labour

In this process of formation we have gone through these economic stages:

primitive society ⟶ slave society ⟶ feudal society ⟶ capitalism (communism)

The transition from one economic stage to the next represents a qualitative leap that necessarily occurs when the economy has developed to a certain saturation point. These qualitative leaps occur dialectically when one stage is 'negated' and 'superseded' by a higher stage:

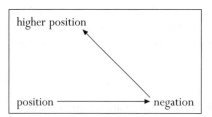

We may talk about a *higher* position, and about *progress*, because negation does not replace one economic system with another – just as we might depose one king and place another on the throne – instead, negation is a supersession in which essential aspects are realigned in a more rational connection. History, therefore, does not 'lose' anything. Thus, communism is said to develop the classless society from the primitive stage, the close ties of the feudal society, and the formal rights and great productive capacity of the bourgeois-capitalist society – and to integrate these factors into a system in which there is a rational and democratic control over the economy. Marx, like Hegel, thought that this process is inevitable because labour, the economy, will ultimately force these changes to occur regardless of what the individual persons think or imagine. Individual persons cannot influence this process to any degree according to whims. The process has been occurring even though people have not understood what they have participated in.

For Marx, the economy, not the spirit, is fundamental. Our thoughts are reflections of the economic-material conditions. The economic-material factors are therefore called the *basis*, and cultural phenomena, such as religion, philosophy, morality, and literature, are called the *superstructure*. In an extreme form, historical materialism means

1   that the basis is the driving force in history, not the superstructure,
2   that the basis determines the superstructure; the superstructure does not deter-
    mine the basis.

Thus:

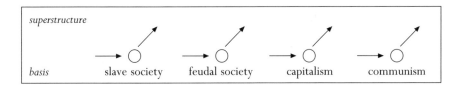

Interpreted in this extreme form, historical materialism becomes economic *determinism*. Both the historical process and human thought are determined by economic-
material circumstances. That is to say, human beings cannot think freely and thoughts
cannot influence events. But in such an extreme form, this economic determinism
becomes unsustainable:

1   It implies a rejection of all free rationality: our thoughts are always determined
    by economic *causes*, not by rational *reasons*. We think what we *must* think and
    not what we have reason to believe is true. But such a theory undercuts itself
    because it means that this theory, too, is only a result of certain economic
    causes. Therefore, there is no reason to accept it as valid. Moreover, the
    material conditions that are determinative today will be different from those
    that were determinative for Marx's thoughts.
2   This economic determinism is undialectical because it distinguishes between
    two different phenomena, the economy and thought, and it then says that the
    one phenomenon determines the other. Such a sharp dualism of two independ-
    ent phenomena is contrary to dialectics. One of the basic points of dialectical
    thinking is that a phenomenon such as the economy *cannot* be conceived of as
    a relatively isolated sphere. The economy is a part of society. Since economic
    determinism presupposes an undialectic dichotomy between economy and
    thought, and since Marx specifically emphasized that the factors are connected,
    it is unreasonable to ascribe such an economic determinism to Marx.
3   Texts in his works support the claim that Marx was not an economic deter-
    minist, even though he occasionally expressed himself ambiguously.

Hence, it is reasonable to interpret Marx's historical materialism as follows: economy and thought mutually influence each other, but economy has the decisive word:

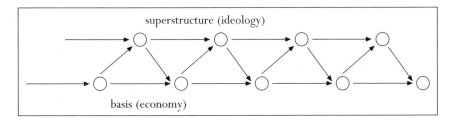

Moreover, we can complete the picture by including *the political-social factors*, in addition to the economic and conceptual factors:

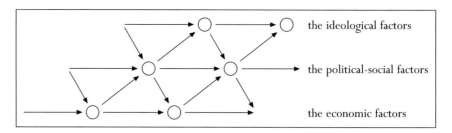

the ideological factors

the political-social factors

the economic factors

This is a simple and reasonable interpretation of Marx's materialistic conception of history. But this interpretation is ambiguous. What does it really mean to say that all of these factors play a part, but that the economy is 'decisive' or that it takes 'precedence'? We may interpret it as a *methodological rule*: 'look for economic explanations!', or 'place a special emphasis on the economic conditions within the socio-historical totality!' This is relatively unproblematic, but Marx was trying to say more than this. We may venture the following interpretation: 'The superstructure influences the basis in the sense that the superstructure is necessary for the basis, but the superstructure cannot direct the basis into new directions.' Here, the super-structure – the state, ideology, thought – is conceived of as a necessary part of the whole, but the changes, the new directions of development, are said to stem from the basis. On Marx's view of how the economy and thought are connected, we can add that the economy, for Marx, is based on *labour*. And labour is not a blind nat-ural process, but is social, human labour. Labour is the specifically human activity that puts us in touch with reality. Through labour, we learn about things and indirectly about ourselves. And because labour creates new products, and new social formations, we learn more and more about ourselves and about the world by means of this historical process. Labour is thus a fundamental *epistemological* con-cept in Marx's thought. It is through action that we become cognizant. This conflicts with the static and individual-centred model of cognition that was proposed by the classical empiricists, in which man is basically like a camera that receives optical impulses. If this interpretation of the epistemological connection between labour and cognition is correct, it is another reason to reject the sharp division between basis and superstructure, and the economic determinism based on such a dichotomy: labour and cognition are part of a dialectical process, and it is there-fore not correct to say that labour causally determines cognition.

Now the political consequences clearly differ between a Marxist defence of a strict economic determinism and an ascription to the superstructure of a certain influence. The first position sanctions political passivity: 'We must wait until the time is ripe.' The second position sanctions political activity. Furthermore, if we think that the superstructure is essentially determined by the basis, by economic conditions, it would be useless to debate with our opponents. The opponents' standpoint would simply be determined by their material position. Arguments can-not change such a standpoint; only a change in the material position can lead to a change of standpoint. This means, for instance, that a parliament has to be seen accordingly: power is 'extra-parliamentary', because power is found in the economic forces, *not* in the parliament. The parliament is only a political reflection of the prevailing economic power conditions.

Hence, discussions, subjective opinions, and the parliamentary system are all without import. All of these factors are basically passive reflections of the basis. In contrast, John Stuart Mill in *On Liberty* held that we can reach better informed opinion by the free exchange of ideas in discussion.

PRODUCTIVE FORCES AND THE RELATIONS OF PRODUCTION

Marx distinguished between three aspects of the basis: *productive forces*, *the relations of production*, and *natural conditions*. Productive forces are, in short, the labour force, with technological knowledge and tools, that is to say, the very source of the mutual development between human beings and nature. The relations of production are organizational forms; above all, the ownership conditions in regard to the means of production. The natural conditions are the given natural resources.

We said that Marx viewed the basis, the economy, as the decisive driving force in history. However, according to Marx, the genuine driving force is the productive forces. But the mutual development between human beings and nature that is embraced by the productive forces occurs within some organizational form (ownership form). Up to a certain point, the productive forces will be able to develop well, or at least without resistance, within the prevailing relations of production. But at a certain point, the prevailing forms of production begin to have a restraining effect on the growth of the productive forces. A tension then arises between the productive forces and the relations of production: the prevailing ownership conditions are harmful to a further exploitation of nature. A change will then occur as the productive forces forge *new* and more appropriate relations of production. Revolution comes. When the new relations of production are established, the productive forces may once again develop until these newly created relations of production begin to be restrictive, and a new revolution occurs. In other words, the productive forces evolve. Conflicts arise between the productive forces and the prevailing relations of production. The tension is resolved when a new and better relation of production is created.

Marx's concept of class is linked to the concept of the relations of production. Class is determined by relationship to the means of production (raw materials and production tools). Those who *own* the means of production are placed in a class opposition to those who do not own them.

This is an important point, since there are many who think that they can refute the Marxist concept of class by showing the great consumption of those who do not own the means of production. But Marx's concept of class does not primarily apply to consumption, subjective experience, or individual rights, but to the ownership of the means of production. As long as some own the means of production and others do not, according to Marx, there will be class oppositions and class conflicts. In the capitalist phase, the two classes are the capitalists, who own the means of production, and the proletariat, who do not own them. There are, of course, many kinds of oppositions that arc not based on conflicts over the means of production. There are, so to speak, benign oppositions. Class oppositions, on the other hand, are insurmountable oppositions, in the sense that they can only be overcome through revolution, through a change in the ownership conditions.

Since those who own the means of production will, as a rule, be against such a change, the revolutions will most often be violent. But violence is not a necessary feature of revolutions.

According to Marx, capitalism always suffers from internal crises. The proletariat will be impoverished. The lower middle class will become part of the proletariat because of the concentration of capital in the hands of the few. And the large businesses will create overproduction. This will become worse and worse until the proletariat rises and seizes control of the production apparatus in such a way that the international economy is brought under political control and production is geared to satisfy genuine needs. The working class has the historical mission to carry out the revolution and thus create a classless society.

SURPLUS VALUE AND EXPLOITATION

One of Marx's basic arguments against the classical liberalist economists (such as Adam Smith and David Ricardo) was that they thought abstractly, atomistically: they basically held the notions of the ahistorical individual and ahistorical laws. They did not correctly comprehend how the economy functions in society and history.

To put it roughly, we can determine price on the basis of supply and demand, where the demand is in turn determined by the need; but need then means purchasing power. However, we may very well need an item, such as food, without being able to pay for it. In that case, our need will not be registered as demand – on the other hand, a seven-year-old's power to purchase *brassieres* will be registered as demand even though she does not really need such an item. Needs and especially purchasing power are not ahistorical; we may ask how they are formed, and by whom. To overlook such points would be naive economic thinking.

Marx never hid the fact that he had learned much from Adam Smith and David Ricardo. We usually consider classical British political economy to be one of the three roots of Marxism:

1   German idealistic philosophy (Hegel), which contributed concepts such as dialectics, negation, and totality
2   French socialism (Saint-Simon and Fourier among others), which contributed concepts such as bourgeoisie, working class, and revolution
3   British political economy (Smith, Ricardo), which contributed concepts such as exchange value, use value, capital, production, and distribution.

What was Marx's contribution to classical political economy? Marx himself thought that the distinction between labour and labour-power was one of his most important contributions: labour-power is a commodity that has value, namely, the value of the commodities that are required in order to produce the labour-power. The use of the labour-power is labour, which creates value. We will see how these ideas introduce social and political conditions, at the same time that they represent a criticism of capitalism. A commodity may be defined partly by the need that the commodity satisfies, the use value, and partly by the exchange value. It is the exchange value that counts on the market. Under capitalism, everything is, in principle, a commodity, including the labour-power: within this comprehensive commodity market, we not only exchange things for things, but we also exchange labour-power for wages. Workers sell their labour-power to one who wishes to purchase it, that is, an employer, one who owns the means of production. The price is the wages. When things are traded for things, for example, a block of salt for two goatskins, the value does not increase; either both traders get just as much as they gave in return, or one gets more at the expense of the other, but, on the whole, the value has not increased. How, then, do we explain an increase in value? Marx's basic point is that the creation of value occurs through labour. In other words, the commodity of labour-power has a unique position in the market economy. Buying, selling, and finally using this commodity leads to a growth in value for the system as a whole. What becomes of the values that are created by the workers? When production costs are covered, and the workers have received their wages, what remains, the surplus value, is an expression of the portion of the labour for which the worker is not paid. This surplus value goes to the capitalist in the form of profit. According to Marx, since the surplus value, as unpaid labour, goes to one who has not personally created this value, the workers are always exploited under capitalism, regardless of their standard of living. The system is built on the acquisition of surplus value.

But the capitalists are themselves on the market, in competition with one another. The danger of bankruptcy drives them to avoid excessive consumption and to reinvest in factors such as better technology in order to strengthen their position in the competition with the other capitalists. In this way, surplus value is used for reinvestment and thus provides the basis for expansion within capitalism.

We now see how *surplus value* becomes a central concept in Marx's theory of the capitalistic society. This surplus value accrues to the capitalist in the form of profit. The profit represents exploitation of the workers. Part of the profit must be invested because of the competition. The process is continuous: new purchases of labour-power, increased surplus value, increased profits, new investments, etc. Money grows. That is to say, it is *capital*. An expansive economic system arises that has a profit rationale at the company level, but is without political direction at the national level. This system, capitalism, is self-destructive: it results in crises that cannot be solved within the system; therefore, it will be superseded by a different system.

OBJECTIONS TO MARX

As a political theoretician, Marx has undoubtedly had a great influence, both on politics and on the theoretical debate. Evaluations of Marx's thought must also deal with various Marxist factions. Few political theoreticians have been as abused and misrepresented as Marx. And few have been as adulated and misrepresented, as he. We can safely say that Marx was a pioneer in the sense that he, on the one hand, acknowledged the human alienation under capitalism and, on the other hand, sought to find a way to solve the problem by analysing the basic structure of capitalism. Another question is that of whether Marx's analyses are tenable. Therefore, we will briefly review some of the most common objections to Marx's theory.

MARX'S THEORY UNDERMINES ITSELF

Marx stated that all theories represent ideology (false consciousness), but since what Marx is asserting is also a theory, his statements undercut this theory. This objection that Marx's theory is self-referentially inconsistent has various formulations that all seem to go back to economic determinism. But we have already mentioned that it is unreasonable to attribute an extreme form of economic determinism to Marx.

MARX'S THEORY IS NOT EMPIRICAL

Marx's theory is both empirical and philosophical. We may then object that the empirical 'part' is not empirical enough. This is not, apparently, a serious objection – unless we must insist that *everything* Marx said is true. Occasionally, the objections are raised by empiricist circles.[6] Dialectics is, in principle, nonsense; we cannot predict the future (cf. Hume's and Popper's arguments that knowledge of the future is impossible). What we have said about the internal problems of empiricism and about the arguments supporting transcendental philosophy and dialectics makes this objection problematic. Without opposing all dialectics, however, we may object that Marx and Marxists do not generally distinguish between philosophical and empirical statements. This is an important point. If Marx claimed that a statement – for example, 'The crises in capitalism will become worse and worse' – is always true, regardless of what actually happens, it is clear that this statement cannot be empirical, since empirical statements are characterized by the fact that they can be confirmed or disconfirmed on the basis of what actually happens. And if the statement is philosophical, we should be able to argue philosophically for and against it, at least to some extent. In any case, Marx's theory does not represent an infallible truth for the initiated.

SOME OF MARX'S PREDICTIONS HAVE BEEN WRONG

Marx predicted that capitalism would lead to increasing class opposition. There would be a minority of capitalists and an increasing majority of the proletariat living at the subsistence level. In fact, most workers in the United States and Western Europe have a private consumption that corresponds poorly with Marx's theory of impoverishment. On the other hand, many people today are undernourished. Broadening the perspective to include an opposition between the imperialist nations and the colonized peoples was emphasized greatly by Lenin.

Moreover, Marx's concept of class is not linked to consumption, but to ownership of the means of production. Therefore, even though Marx may be *partially* refuted on his theory of impoverishment, it does not follow that we do not have a 'proletarization' in this sense, even in countries that have a high rate of private consumption: small businesses often fail as a result of the action of large international corporations and we have an increasing number of employees, that is to say, people who do not own the means of production.[7] But to what extent the working class, in *this* Marxist sense, will seek (and have the strength) to carry out an international revolution that could lead to a classless, rational, and humane society is at best an open question (to put it mildly). It is also claimed that Marx's theory was wrong because the revolution occurred in undeveloped Russia, and not in the countries where capitalism was most advanced. Lenin responded that we must evaluate capitalism as an international system: internationally, capitalism was fully developed, although not in Russia. But revolution occurs where capitalism is at the *weakest*, as in Russia.

MARX'S CONCEPTS OF CLASS AND CLASS STRUGGLE ARE INADEQUATE

Marx's concept of class and thus the concept of class struggle are problematic. If the concept of class is defined as the ownership of the means of production, certain problems arise in light of modern capitalism. Those who manage businesses today may not own the businesses or even have direct ownership interests in the business. They may be employed because of their qualifications and education, and not because they have inherited the ownership of the business. They may receive a high salary, but it may not necessarily be linked to the level of profits. It is therefore problematic to say that the capitalists, those who formally own the means of production, also decide how to use the means of production. It is at least necessary to recognize a certain distinction between the formal ownership of the means of production and the actual use of the means of production. We might add that even though these functions are, today, often split between two groups, both groups are still acting on the premises of capitalism. But the modern capitalistic system is not always a pure market system. We have monopolies and government intervention; in some cases, it may even be unclear to what extent businesses are subject to the bankruptcy principle. When a business enterprise is threatened by bankruptcy, the management often appeals to politicians, pointing out that jobs are in danger. Achieving economic support in the form of various governmental programmes, such as tax breaks, subsidies, etc., thus becomes part of the strategy to keep the business viable. This means that the managers, who do not need to own the means of production, and whose wages are not determined by the fluctuating profits, are not always forced to follow the theoretical rules of the capitalistic system. It is therefore problematic to say that owners and business leaders comprise the capitalist class because they both must act according to capitalistic principles. The statement must be amplified and made more concrete before it makes sense, that is, before we can decide to what extent it may be true or false.

Marx claimed that the workers produce the surplus value and the capitalist receives the profit. But what about workers who receive their wages in the public sector, those who do not work for a capitalist, and who consequently do not produce profit directly? This sector of so-called unproductive labour-power has increased greatly due to the rise of 'state-organized' society: public servants of all kinds; personnel in the armed forces; and staff employed in education, research, administration, health care, etc. To which class do they belong? The differences are quite large in wages, education, and attitude. The common factor of this group is that its members in some way or another contribute to keeping the system going. They may be said to contribute to better productivity for those workers who create profit.

MARX NEGLECTS THE IMPORTANCE OF 'THE NATURAL CONDITIONS'

The relationship between productive forces and the relations of production was of great importance to Marx. He seemed to think that 'the natural conditions' are relatively unproblematic. Raw materials, climate, air, water – all of these things *are there*. They are, of course, necessary to the economy. But Marx largely seemed to view these factors as being constant, and unchangeable, and therefore something about which not much can be done. In Marx's day such a view was reasonable enough. Moreover, there was nothing in his predictions that indicated that there would be important changes in this area. Marx predicted, as we know, that capitalism would 'explode' because of overproduction, among other things: capitalism would end in a crisis that resulted in a revolution because capitalists were too irrational to prevent overproduction. Here Marx was wrong. Capitalism has, so far, managed to avoid such a crisis by creating a consumer society throughout the world.

At the same time, it turned out that the earlier socialist countries in Eastern Europe were not in a position to manage their ecological problems in a rational and progressive way. The problem of pollution in Russia, Poland, and the former Czechoslovakia is a sad example. The ecological crisis is thus not an internal problem of capitalism. The Soviet system shows how 'the natural conditions' became a problem for Marxist economies too.

MARXIST SOCIALISM IS DEAD

Not only have nearly all Marxist regimes dissolved since the fall of the Berlin Wall, but also Marxist socialism has revealed its theoretical problems, not least with respect to normative questions concerning democracy and human rights. Nevertheless, Marxism remains an important analytic tool in modern societies, helping us to understand both capitalism as a system and human alienation. As a political theoretician, Marx is not dead, any more than Newton as a scientist, Darwin as an evolutionist, or Freud as a psychologist.[8]

FRIEDRICH ENGELS – THE FAMILY FROM A MARXIST PERSPECTIVE

Friedrich Engels (1820–1895) met Marx early in the 1840s. They were both German, and both later lived in England, where Engels worked closely with Marx on several important works, such as *The German Ideology* and *The Communist Manifesto*. After Marx's death (1883), Engels published the second and third volumes of *Capital*. Therefore, he is included in the classical Marxist literature. But Engels also wrote several important works on his own, treatises on natural philosophy and the family.

In his natural philosophy, Engels tried to show that nature (and not only society and history, as in Marx's thought) is dialectical. His theory of the dialectic of nature is controversial and is often considered speculative and unscientific. It is objected that his theory of the dialectics of nature blurs the distinction between society and nature (between subject and object), and that this theory does not accord very well with modern, experimental natural science. From the point of view of Hegelian idealism (where this sharp distinction between subject and object is 'superseded'), this theory may still be meaningful, in a philosophical sense.

In *The Origin of the Family, Private Property and the State* (1884), Engels, using the ethnographic literature of his day (especially the work of Lewis H. Morgan), tried to show that the family, and especially the woman's position, reflects historical development as determined by the development of the modes of production, and especially the forms of ownership. The view is Marxist in the sense that Engels described the development of the family in light of economic development, from the primitive community to the society of his day. Along with increasing trade and monetary transactions, a great social change occurred as part of the transition from a society based on blood lineage and an extensive barter economy to an industrial class society. This changed not only the class character of the state and the economic exploitation, but also the family relations and the relations between generations. Engels' special aim was to show that this development also led to 'the patriarchal family' and to 'the world-historical defeat for the female sex', in the sense that the oppression and exploitation of women was intensified. By referring to the middle-class nuclear family of his day, where the husband earned the money and the wife did housework, Engels emphasized that women, in this way, had become economically dependent on men, and hence, subordinate to them. As a contrast from the past, he presented the picture of an ancient society that was based on 'maternal rights'.[9] As a contrast from the future, he presented the picture of a communistic society in which women are not economically dependent on men in marriage: the state, not the family, will have the economic responsibility of raising children. The distinction between children who are born in and out of wedlock will disappear. Thus, women will be free, and hence the relationship between men and women will be marked by genuine love, according to Engels.

Engels thus contributed to the debate about the economic basis of gender roles and female oppression, and about how governmental welfare programmes may eventually replace (and largely abolish) traditional marriage supported by the husband's income. In summary, we could say that, while legally oriented theoreticians, like John Stuart Mill and Harriet Taylor, mainly focused on juridical equality (such as general voting rights), and while existentialist theoreticians, like Simone de Beauvoir, mainly focused on the mutual struggle for recognition (for equal social identity of men and women), Marxist theoreticians focus especially on the class conditions of exploitation and discrimination.

The Marxist perspective, in which the root of evil lies in the historical development of the modes of production, leads to the idea that the goal of political action is not mainly concerned with laws and rules, nor with social roles or 'the struggle for recognition' (in Hegel's sense), but primarily with the economic and social conditions that must change if we want to change the position of women.

QUESTIONS

Explain the main points in Marx's conception of history. Discuss his views of the driving forces and of the historical periods, and of class struggle and societal change.

Explain the main concepts in Marx's economics, such as productive force and the relations of production, class exploitation, and capitalism as a self-destructive system. Discuss these concepts; for instance, in relation to Adam Smith and liberalism.

Discuss Marx's view of alienation.

SUGGESTIONS FOR FURTHER READING

PRIMARY LITERATURE

Marx, Karl and Engels, Friedrich, *Collected Works*, London, 1975–.

SECONDARY LITERATURE

Elster, J., *Making Sense of Marx*, Cambridge, 1985.
Fromm, E. *Marx's Concept of Man*, New York, 1962.
Lukács, G., *History and Class Consciousness*, Cambridge, MA, 1971.

NOTES

1 See, for example, Ch. 17, Master and slave.
2 The expression *dialectical materialism* was not coined by Marx. In the Eastern European countries, Marxism was often officially called 'dialectical and historical materialism'. This was mainly a Soviet version of Marx, Engels, and Lenin.
3 E.g. Ch. 17, Reflection, dialectics, experience.
4 Cf. psychoanalysis: sometimes the psychiatrist's words do not help. A change of environment or medication must be prescribed to overcome the problem.
5 Cf. the existentialist antithesis between *being* and *having*, as in Gabriel Marcel, *Being and Having*, London, 1965.
6 Karl Popper, *The Open Society and Its Enemies*, London, 1962.
7 If we can thus 'save' Marx's concept of class by confining it to the ownership of the means of production, the next question is whether this class concept is especially interesting: a car maker in Detroit and a maid in Kerala (India) are, according to this definition, both 'proletariat'. But do we not then overlook essential differences between the two? – differences that are rooted in concrete, material basis, such as differences in resources and consumption.
8 Cf. the use of Marxist ideas, for instance, by Hannah Arendt and Jürgen Habermas (Ch. 27).
9 Here Engels borrowed from the ethnographic literature of his day, as in Morgan; the expression 'maternal rights' is taken from Johann Bachofen (1815–1861), who, in 1861, published a book on the history of the family.

19 Kierkegaard – existence and irony

Life. Søren Kierkegaard (1813–1855) was born in Copenhagen during the depression that followed the Napoleonic Wars. His father's family was from the poverty-stricken region of West Jutland, although his father had established himself as a businessman in the capital and managed quite well during the economic crises. Søren never suffered from financial hardship; he lived off his inheritance during his short life. His childhood home, however, was marked by spiritual crises. His father was melancholic. Deaths and accidents befell the family. At a young age, Søren learned what spiritual suffering means. Externally, his life was simple: he studied theology and philosophy, obtaining a degree for a thesis On the Concept of Irony. *He was a diligent writer, partly ironically withdrawn, partly polemically challenging. He made two trips to Berlin, where Hegel's speculative spirit permeated the atmosphere. He himself was responsible for the dramatic events in his life. This was true of his relationship with Regine Olsen, to whom he became engaged. He soon discovered that he could not live with her – a scandal in the Copenhagen of his day. This was also true of his polemical writings, especially the attack on Bishop Mynster in 1854. Mynster had been a close friend of Kierkegaard's family, but Kierkegaard felt that he had to react to what he saw as a counterfeiting of Christianity. Søren Kierkegaard died during this conflict.*

Kierkegaard was an industrious author who often used pseudonyms, and who composed his works in a literary form, often marked by irony and polemic. Among his best-known works are Either/Or, Fear and Trembling, The Concept of Dread, Philosophical Fragments, *and* Concluding Unscientific Postscript *– all published in 1843–6 – as well as* The Sickness unto Death *(1849) and* Point of View for my Activity as an Author *(1855). His diaries were published after his death.*

DIRECT AND EXISTENTIAL COMMUNICATION

As a person and as a writer, Kierkegaard was marked by tensions, that is tension between a brooding and introspective attitude, centred on guilt and anguish, and a self-conscious and masterful attitude, marked by a need for individual freedom and autonomy. Both attitudes derived from Kierkegaard's upbringing and environment: Protestant pietism, on the one hand, and the will and inclination to self-assertion among the emerging bourgeoisie, on the other.

These tensions are also evident in Kierkegaard's relationship to Hegel and to Romanticism. There are romantic features to Kierkegaard's thought, as in his presentation of the bohemian aesthete. But there are also anti-romantic features, as in his emphasis on the positive aspect of everyday, practical affairs. At times he used words and expressions that are reminiscent of a Hegelian idealist – antithetical words such as *subjective* and *objective*, and *particular* and *universal* – while ironically attacking Hegel and speculative philosophy. From out of these interrelated tensions between pietism and autonomy, and idealism and romanticism, Kierkegaard made his original contribution: the existential perspective.[1] Kierkegaard became a passionate spokesman for a sincere illumination and analysis of our human existence. In modern philosophy he is viewed as a pioneer of existentialism (cf. Ch. 26).

But what is human existence, and what about it did Kierkegaard deem important? The answer is anything but simple. The first problem is that Kierkegaard often used pseudonyms, such as 'Johannes Climacus' and 'Vigilius Hafniensis' (Copenhagen's night watchman). Does this mean that he himself did not seriously hold the opinions expressed by his various personae? Secondly, he wrote in an ironic, literary style. He seldom wrote traditional philosophical exposition in which propositions are discussed. It is therefore difficult to know what position Kierkegaard was actually taking, even when he signed a work as its rightful author, and not merely as the 'editor' of pseudonymous works. Thirdly, it is unclear whether Kierkegaard held the same opinions throughout his entire life, or whether his views changed. Was he more positive towards the practical tasks of life in his early writings than in his later writings when he polemically attacked Bishop Mynster and the Danish clergy? These are open questions in Kierkegaard research.[2]

It is therefore not surprising that there are different interpretations of Kierkegaard's philosophy – even doubt whether he can be said to have claimed that his endeavours were philosophical, in the usual sense of the word. But all of this was intentional on the part of Kierkegaard; he stated his intentions, for instance, as follows: 'In the pseudonymous books there is thus not a single word that represents myself; I have no opinion about them except as a third person, no knowledge of their meaning except as a reader, not the slightest relationship to them, which is impossible to have to a double-reflective communication.'[3]

Kierkegaard's use of pseudonyms and of literary forms is connected with the genuine difficulties of communicating insight into human existence. He was not trying to communicate propositional claims that may be read and conned by others. He was trying to mediate existential insight into what it means to be a human being. This requires an active acquisition, an act of internalization. Thus, on the one hand, readers must be provoked and seduced, and, on the other hand, must be freed to engage themselves and to develop in such a way that they are capable of seeing, and of being, in a more 'internalized' and sincere way.

In everyday prose, or in scientific exposition, we can be content with 'direct communication' – as when we say, 'The time is 12.30', or, 'The hurricane is moving in from the southeast'. But this kind of direct communication is not adequate to express what Kierkegaard had in mind. Here, other forms of expression are needed, forms of a more poetic nature. We are not mediating propositions *about* something; on the contrary, we are trying to mediate the entire attitude and 'mood' *from which* the state of affairs is to be understood – because, when it comes to human existence, the genuine theme is precisely this *relationship to* the various states of affairs. To mediate this relationship in such a way that it can be understood for what it is, and not as an objective state of affairs in the world, requires unique forms of expression. If we wish to mediate this kind of insight, we must be literary artists who have a reflective relationship to ourselves and to others. Hence, Kierkegaard spoke of a 'double-reflective communication'.

Correspondingly, we must personally make a special effort to acquire what is communicated in this way. If we are to understand it, and acquire it in such a way that it changes our own way of relating to the world, we must enter into a comprehensive process of formation – as part of a life-long formative task of living as a human being. It is also essential that the readers be free in regard to the text. Such a text must not coerce the readers as a scientific argument may. The salient point is that the readers may freely and responsibly choose their relationship to the text. This requires, at the same time, that a passionate involvement and a reflective distance exist simultaneously in a painful tension. Kierkegaard was certainly not a vulgar existentialist who proclaimed the unreflective and immediate experience, here and now. Nor was he an adherent of a theoretical reflection that is distant from life. The ironic passion and the distant presence – these concepts are probably more appropriate for what he was trying to do. But when we put it like this, we are already starting to betray Kierkegaard. We are already presenting his thought by means of simple and direct propositions. Here, we have already started to teach and explain Kierkegaard's work and forms of expression in propositional form: a mediation on, and refinement of, existential self-insight is the goal, and the means is the use of rhetoric and irony. We should now adopt an ironic attitude to what we have said. But we could also place Kierkegaard in the philosophical tradition of those who are concerned with 'tacit knowledge', and who try to 'show' what cannot be argued with propositions – like Socrates and Wittgenstein. In short, we should try to assume some of Kierkegaard's 'double reflection' and ironic distance. Perhaps we should have only presented quotations from Kierkegaard, so that he could have explained his ideas in his own way, without our interpretive intervention.

THE THREE STAGES ON LIFE'S WAY

Instead of trying to avoid the problems of interpretation by quoting Kierkegaard without comment, we will sketch three different interpretations of Kierkegaard's three so-called stages, namely, the aesthetic, the ethical, and the religious. In this way we will try to *show* some of the difficulties that arise in reading Kierkegaard.

THE EDIFYING INTERPRETATION

Kierkegaard not only turned against the speculative philosophers of his day, whom he accused of forgetting their own existence, but he also turned against a certain way of life by emphasizing the importance of taking existential responsibility for our own life. This became Kierkegaard's edifying message: be the 'unique being' (*hin enkelte*) that you basically already are, by choosing consciously. This is not a choice between things in the world, or between external actions. It is the choice of an existential attitude. We should acquire a more existential consciousness, both in the sense that we maintain a reflexive attitude towards ourselves and in the sense that this is done with a passionate inwardness. The three stages are thus not three developmental steps through which we all automatically progress, like a socio-psychological maturation process. The three stages represent different basic attitudes, or ways of being. These three different attitudes shape us completely, like comprehensive perspectives which mark everything in our lives: our attitude towards life is *either* aesthetic, ethical, or religious. Thus, we cannot choose between them, as we may choose between three kinds of cheeses in the shop, because there is no neutral position beyond these three attitudes. Nor can this dilemma be stated directly, and for this very reason! Therefore, Kierkegaard used an indirect form of expression, by maintaining ironic distance and by presenting examples of various attitudes towards life, as expressed by the persona of 'Johannes Climacus' and others. Nevertheless, the aesthetic stage may be characterized by a life experienced from a distanced and self-indulgent perspective. In this stage, we do not involve ourselves ethically and seriously in life, but remain passive observers, the same attitude that we tend to have towards art. We observe the tragedies and comedies of life but do not really participate. This is the reflective and uninvolved bohemian who seeks the beautiful and the sublime, but without being drawn into the duties and responsibilities that characterize bourgeois life, as well as the ethical stage. The aesthete is thus both privileged and despondent; privileged to stand outside the turmoil and the duties, but despondent because this form of life is empty and filled with despair.

Ethicists have chosen to say 'yes' to life as something for which they have personally chosen to accept responsibility, even though many factors lie beyond their control. We are all born into particular circumstances, and there are only some factors that we can change, or perhaps improve. When ethicists choose to accept responsibility, it is not under the illusion that they can change everything by their own efforts – as if they were in God's position. They choose in the sense that they accept life with passion and existential involvement; our actions are our own and our death is our own. It is thus an ethics based on a kind of moral will. But, unlike Kant's ethics based on a moral will, here, it is a matter of our own attitude – not the categorical imperative or other universal moral principles. Here, what matters is 'inwardness'. And as we could expect from an ethics based on a moral will, as opposed to a consequentialist ethics (such as utilitarianism), the consequences of our actions do not play a decisive role. This is what distinguishes the ethicist from the good citizen. Externally, they may appear to be the same, but, on the inside, they are different. Their attitudes towards life and their existential passion differ.

Aesthetes fly from flower to flower, like bees. They hover between different alternatives and different roles, one day choosing one, the next day, another. They are endlessly searching for something new, in the form of new experiences. Ethicists give meaning to life by following the road that has been chosen. Their life derives its meaning from this passionate involvement in their life project. Responsibility and duty characterize the ethicist's life, not as external requirements, but as integral elements of the ethical attitude towards life.

Here we have two fundamentally different perspectives towards life. The transition from the one to the other will therefore not occur by means of argumentation. It is, so to speak, a matter of two incommensurable paradigms, to borrow a term from the philosophy of science. There is no transition by virtue of arguments, nor by natural maturation. The transition occurs by means of an existential *leap*, according to Kierkegaard. The religious stage is characterized by the existential involvement not only of the individual alone, but also of faith in the living God. This faith is not a question of objective knowledge. Nor is it a question of intellectual insight. It is a question of a unique quality in our relationship to life, to ourselves, and to everything else. Externally, the religious person cannot be distinguished from the ethicist or from the good citizen. But again, this is only on the outside. Inwardly, they are radically different. This is also the case when these three all say that they believe in the same God. It is their relationship to God that is different – their passion in relation to the historical God and, thus, to their own existence.

We have so far been discussing the so-called edifying interpretation of the three stages.

THE SYNTHESIZING INTERPRETATION

The edifying interpretation points out the discontinuous aspect of the relationship between the three stages. There are qualitative leaps between them. Therefore, the existential choice is important. And hence, strictly speaking, it is not possible to talk about them and to compare them, as we have done here; therefore, a poetic form of expression suggests itself. Through indirect communication and personal effort, each person can personally choose one of the three. Those who have grasped this have been brought out of the state of innocence and must personally choose to take responsibility for their own lives in an *existential* sense.

But Kierkegaard can also be read as if he thought that there are qualitatively different levels. The religious stage is higher, both in insight and in the quality of life, than the ethical stage; and the ethical stage is higher than the aesthetic stage. It is not just a question of making a choice between three different attitudes towards life, all of which are on the same level. We may still talk about a positive development and a maturation in the transition from the aesthetic stage to the ethical stage and on to the religious stage. This does not mean that we deny the fact that there are leaps. And it is not a simple transition mediated by argumentation. Nor is this transition a Hegelian synthesis, where the lower levels are preserved, without vestiges, in the higher levels. But still, when we have moved from the aesthetic stage to the ethical stage and on to the religious stage, we recognize, through hindsight, that we have arrived at a higher level. What else could it mean to talk about a higher level? For example, we could perhaps say that this is similar to a successful treatment in psychoanalysis: when we have reached a new stage, we see that we were previously living under an illusion. But this is not something that we could see at an earlier stage. At that time, we would only feel a kind of vague discomfort.

In this sense, we could interpret the three stages as a step-by-step process of formation. We could claim that this is what is behind Kierkegaard's thinking. But by this interpretation we move in the direction of a Hegelian view of identity formation. Perhaps, here, we are moving closer to Hegel than Kierkegaard would have liked.

THE IRONIC-REFLECTIVE INTERPRETATION

The good citizen may both believe in God and go to church, be responsible and devoted to duty, and, furthermore, know how to enjoy beauty and pleasure.

Externally, the difference does not have to be very great between the well-adjusted citizen and the aesthete, or the ethicist, or the religious person. The difference, as we have said, lies within, or in their respective attitudes towards life.

The aesthetes thus distinguish themselves from the well-adjusted citizens, not because the aesthetes love beauty and the citizens do not, but because the aesthetes have an ironic-reflective relationship towards life. While the citizens spontaneously go about their daily tasks, worrying about the consequences of what they do, the aesthetes maintain a detached attitude towards all of these things. The aesthetes view all such worldly choices as being basically of no importance. It does not really matter to them what the consequences are. In this sense, the aesthete is the incarnation of European nihilism in the Nietzschean sense (cf. Ch. 21): no values are more valuable than any others. They are equally valid, and basically of no consequence.

Are we talking here about a choice, namely, a choice that means that all values are said to be equally valuable? Or are we talking about an insight, namely, an insight into the truth that all values are equally valid? Regardless of which answer we emphasize, the aesthete, in this interpretation, will not emerge as one who primarily enjoys life, and who loves beauty and pleasure, but as one who maintains an inner distance from life, a person who finds that life is ethically empty because everything is, basically, equally valid (*gleich-gültig*). Far from being a person with an immediate enjoyment of what life has to offer, the aesthete is closer to being a reflective cynic who heroically holds on despite the certainty that life is actually without objective meaning. This is the aesthete's inner despair, and this is what radically distinguishes the aesthete from the busy and compassionate citizen.

The leap to the ethical stage is not a question of choosing good values rather than bad ones. The leap is characterized by people choosing themselves as an end. It is not a question of choosing practical goals, such as particular trades or ways of life. We are talking about an inner or existential choice by which our attitude towards life is changed, thus allowing us to become someone else by claiming our own life as our own. Here we must speak merely in suggestive terms since personal experience of such choices is necessary to understand what is involved. But perhaps it is still the case that most people who have lived their lives have some idea of what is here being discussed. The catchwords may be *self-consciousness* and *the will to conduct our own life*, or *passion and sincere inwardness*, as Kierkegaard often says. Thus, the ethicist challenges life in a more engaged manner than does the aesthete. In this sense, the ethicist may overcome the gnawing existential despair of the aesthete. But again, the outward difference from the good citizen is rather small. The difference continually lies on the inner plane.

The ethicist is thus the 'unique being' (*hin enkelte*), who lives life passionately and reflectively, continually making new efforts. Externally, the ethicist is a member of the social community, as are other good people. He, or she, is not eccentric, externally. But while the narrow-minded bourgeois, in this sense, has a slumbering inner life, the ethicist is existentially conscious.

The leap to the religious stage is a leap into the unknown, without guarantees of objective knowledge, without convincing arguments, and without fully knowing what we are leaping to. Perhaps we may suggest that the ethicist feels the corrosive despair just under the skin. Everything depends on ourselves, and everything may fall to pieces. Through faith in the historical God, we may find an anchor in the universal, the temporal may be anchored in the eternal.

The historical God is Christ, who is not a doctrine, but life. To believe in him is not to know anything about something because Christ the Lord is not a something, but someone; that is to say, he is both a subject and a relationship. The human relationship will, in faith, relate to the divine relationship with an infinite passion. This is, for Kierkegaard, what it means 'to be in the truth'; that is to say, to have an inward and intense relationship of faith with the historical God. As a Christian, this is Kierkegaard's actual purpose. The philosophical and literary aspects gain their meaning only in this religious perspective.

Kierkegaard's sharp distinction between faith and reason, between faith and external works, falls within the Protestant tradition, where his Danish pietism belongs. But Kierkegaard did not defend a moralizing Protestantism. For Kierkegaard, neither good works (good consequences) nor good principles (the categorical imperative or the Ten Commandments) are morally decisive, but only the self-conscious choice of our own life. This is pietism, not Puritanism; that is to say, sincere inwardness, not good behaviour in the market place and in marriage.

Thus, Kierkegaard was not an ascetic nor did he reject society. For him, both ethically and religiously, it is the individual's attitude towards life and relationship with God that are the decisive factors. As a form of Protestantism, this is neither a happy and emancipated Christianity nor an ascetic and moralizing Christianity. This is a Christianity of existential pain, in a struggle with guilt and angst, in which we have a passionate and ironic-reflective relationship to ourselves and the historical God.[4]

SUBJECTIVITY IS TRUTH

Kierkegaard held two conceptions of truth. One was that of 'objective' truth. This conception of truth holds that propositions are true when they correspond with the actual state of affairs. This is often called the correspondence theory of truth: statements are true when they are in accordance with (correspond with) the actual state of affairs. If I say that the blackboard is green, this statement is true if the blackboard actually is green. Then there is a correspondence between the proposition and the state of affairs.

The other conception of truth applies to the quality of our relationship to the world. This is 'subjective' truth. When we are genuine and inward in our relationship, we express truth. Here, there is no question of propositional correspondence with external states of affairs, but of the intensity of our own relationship, of our own being. In this sense, we may, for example, talk about 'true love'. The point is not to obtain correct propositions about something, but to obtain a certain quality of the human relationship itself.

In ethical and religious questions, the point is just the quality of our existential relation to life and to the living God. Therefore, it is particularly relevant to focus on the 'subjective truth'. It is worth noting that in these cases the expression 'subjective truth' does not mean untruth or falsehood, that is, 'objective untruth'. The expression 'subjective truth' is only meant to preserve the notion that the human relationship, subjectivity, is decisive in such cases. The human relationship, subjectivity, is decisive both because in such cases there are no objective states of affairs or arguments that can be used to resolve the question, and because it is precisely the passionate and inward attitude towards life that is in focus. In scientific connections, Kierkegaard viewed 'objective truth' as a question of an endless approximation: in these connections, there are far more comprehensive and complex states of affairs than, for instance, that of the green colour on the blackboard. There are complicated theories that we can never fully confirm, but that we can test only through continuing research, so that we, in this sense, can approach the truth; and since we can never arrive at ultimate and absolutely certain knowledge through such scientific research, there will be a distinction between a research-based knowledge and personal faith in a personal God. Scientific arguments will never be decisive on this religious level, according to Kierkegaard. But he still did not think that Christian faith is only a question of 'subjective truth', that is, of an inward and passionate relationship of faith. Kierkegaard believed that Christ lived and died, as an 'objective truth'. This is no theory, but a historical event that is grasped by faith.

Kierkegaard thus offers alternatives. We may have a subjectively true attitude toward the objective truth (a genuinely believing Christian's attitude toward the Christian God). We may have a subjectively true attitude toward an objective untruth (a genuinely believing heathen's attitude towards his idol). We may have a subjectively untrue attitude towards the objective untruth (an existentially false prayer addressed by a heathen to his idol). We may have a subjectively untrue attitude towards the objective truth (an existentially false prayer addressed by a Christian to the Christian God). Kierkegaard's main purpose is not primarily to say something about 'objective truth', either in science or in religion, but to show how important 'subjective truth' is.

But it is even more complicated: Kierkegaard viewed human life as being surrounded by paradoxes and contradictions. Not the least of these is the Christian faith, which remains a paradox. Ultimately, faith becomes a puzzle – for our intellect. It is therefore important to maintain that life is characterized by leaps that no arguments and no maturation process can overcome. A passionate faith in the historical God is the greatest and most important of all paradoxes and leaps (cf. the similar ideas of the Roman Catholic theologian Pascal, Ch. 9).

DEMOCRACY AS DEMAGOGY

We often assume that all enlightened intellectuals in recent times have been adherents of democracy. When democracy first emerged, everyone realized that it was right, at least everyone who was thoughtful and disinterested. But this assumption is not correct. In a certain sense, Kierkegaard was anti-democratic. He admired the enlightened absolute monarchy that existed in Denmark.

It should be emphasized that Danish absolutism in the first part of the nineteenth century was an enlightened and benign rule. Moreover, for Kierkegaard, it was incomprehensible that everyone should participate in politics: those who ruled did generally a good job, and it was hardly the case that everyone wanted to participate in the everyday affairs of politics. And above all, it is essential for everyone to be active in ennobling the inner life. Political turmoil may detract from essential things. Finally, Kierkegaard feared that democracy would, in practice, become demagogy, that is, a society where the pressure to hold 'correct' opinions and conform could threaten the personal integrity of the individual. This would lead to increased alienation, or existential despair. The busy and restless bourgeois, as well as the busy and even more empty-headed amateur politician, would dominate society and displace the genuinely existential attitudes towards life. Kierkegaard's criticism of the emergence of democratic rule is thus a part of his general critique of alienation and existential impoverishment. Man might lose himself in what is nonessential and shallow, not only in the market place and in the workplace, but also in politics and in social life. The deeper relationships in life would be displaced. Life would become existentially impoverished.

For historical reasons, Kierkegaard could not draw on an empirical sociology, either for support or for correction. Democrats of our day would perhaps see in Kierkegaard's protest against democracy a reactionary, spiritual individualism. But as enlightened democrats we should become acquainted with Kierkegaard's objections. It is only then that we will know that he is wrong, if he is wrong. At any rate, the critique of modern society is a continuing process, with various contributors – and Kierkegaard is one of them[5] (cf. Chs 24 and 26).

QUESTIONS

'Kierkegaard is the exact opposite of Hegel.' Discuss this statement. Consider what Kierkegaard says about the 'unique being' and the three stages.

Explain what Kierkegaard means by saying that 'subjectivity is truth'. How should we communicate 'subjective truth'?

SUGGESTIONS FOR FURTHER READING

PRIMARY LITERATURE

The Concept of Dread, translated by W. Lowrie, London, 1944.
Fear and Trembling, translated by R. Payne, London, 1939.
Stages on Life's Way, translated by W. Lowrie, Princeton, NJ, 1941.

SECONDARY LITERATURE

Hannay, A., and Marino, Gordon D. (eds), *The Cambridge Companion to Kierkegaard*, Cambridge, 1998.

NOTES

1 Johannes Sløk, *Kierkegaards univers. En ny guide til geniet*, Copenhagen, 1983. Our discussion is indebted to this book.
2 J. Sløk, in *Kierkegaards Univers*, pp. 121–2, says that he is puzzled about whether or not Kierkegaard changed his basic presuppositions.
3 Quoted from *Kierkegaard*, ed. A. Næss, Oslo, 1966, Introduction, p. 11.
4 It is tempting to draw these parallels: the edifying interpretation, with its incommensurable life projects, has similarities with Kuhn's theory of (partly) incommensurable paradigms (Ch. 26); the synthesizing

interpretation, with its dialectical formation, has similarities with Hegel's view of personal growth and development (Ch. 17); and the ironic-reflective interpretation, with its meaning-constitutive life projects in a universe void of meaning, has similarities with Nietzsche's philosophy (Ch. 21).

5 At an early stage, Henrik Ibsen (1828–1906) was deeply influenced by Kierkegaard and the idea of existential authenticity (cf. *Peer Gynt* and *Brand*).

20 Darwin – the debate about our conception of man

Life. *Charles Darwin (1809–1882) was descended from a well-known British family that made major contributions in the fields of medicine and natural science. Darwin himself studied first medicine, then theology, and finally natural science. The great transformation of his ideas occurred when, as a young scientist (in 1831), he sailed with the research ship the* Beagle *on a voyage of almost five years. Before the voyage he thought that the biological species were immutable. But as a result of the material that he collected during this voyage to South America and to certain Pacific islands, he changed his view. For example, as a result of his studies of the variation among the birds on the various islands of the Galápagos, and of the mammalian fossils in South America, he found that the best hypothesis to explain the relationship between the various species and their environment was the view that species are not permanent and unchangeable, but that they have evolved by adjusting to the environment. The theory based on this hypothesis is still called 'Darwinism'. Darwin was young when he collected his material and arrived at this hypothesis, and it took a long time for him to systematize it all. During this endeavour he became acquainted with Malthus' theory that population growth follows a geometric progression, while food production can only increase in an arithmetic progression. According to this theory, more people will always be born than the given resources can sustain. Therefore, the lower classes will always live in poverty. For Darwin, this suggested an explanation of the evolution of species: the species that survive the struggle for limited resources are the ones best able to adapt to these conditions. In 1859 Darwin completed his work* On the Origin of Species by Means of Natural Selection, or the Preservation of Favoured Races in the Struggle for Life. *This work sparked a lively debate. Darwin himself chose to stay in the background. His health was poor, and until the end, he devoted himself to further studies of plants and animals. In 1881 he published a book about the importance of the earthworm for the soil. His other writings include* The Descent of Man and Selection in Relation to Sex *(1871) and* The Expression of the Emotions in Man and Animals *(1872).*

NATURAL SELECTION AND THE ORIGIN OF MAN

The biological species were traditionally seen as unchangeable. Each species (like horse, cow, and goat) had its permanent and specific forms and functions. This view was found both in Aristotle and among those who believed that the species were created directly by God, each with its permanent nature. Man is one of the species, and man, as a species, was thus understood to be both unchangeable and unique in relation to the other species. Darwinism argued differently. Organic life undergoes development: the different species are created and formed through an interplay with the environment. All species are thus created through dynamic chains of development, and hence there is a familial relationship between the species. From this perspective, no species, not even man, has a unique status, even though there are important differences between the species.

This assumes that each individual possesses characteristics that are genetically conditioned and that to some extent differ from the corresponding characteristics of other individuals of the same species. Furthermore, it is assumed that all organisms have a tendency to reproduce more offspring than the environment can support. Thus, some of the offspring do not survive. (If all fish eggs were to develop, the oceans would overflow with fish.) As a result there is a struggle for survival, and the outcome of this struggle is not fortuitous. Over time, the individuals with traits best suited to the given environment will survive. Those best suited by their inherited characteristics will be the biological winners, and they will transmit these characteristics to their offspring. In this sense, there is a natural selection. Due to the struggle for survival, there is in the long term a relatively stronger genetic transmission of those hereditary traits that allow an individual to adapt better to the environment than of less useful traits in other individuals of the same species.

Darwin, however, did not know the laws of genetic heredity. He did not know how traits are passed on. Therefore, he could not explain how a desirable characteristic (with respect to a given variation of that characteristic in a population) is transmitted genetically – finally contributing to the evolution of new species.[1] It was only with the theory of heredity of Johann Gregor Mendel (1822–1884) that the mechanism of genetics could be explained. Hence, Darwinism found a new foundation and a new shape.

However, there were two problems in Darwin's theory of natural selection: the problem of how traits were genetically transmitted and that of how new hereditary traits arise. The former was explained by Mendel's laws of inheritance, the latter by the concept of mutation, that is, sudden and relatively permanent changes in genetic material.

This brings us to an important theoretical point. Neither the emergence of variations in inherited characteristics through mutation nor natural selection are conceived of as occurring by will or by purpose. A mutation is an arbitrary occurrence; it is not intended. Mutations are conceived of as natural phenomena that, in principle, may be explained scientifically, that is, causally (in some sense), even if we cannot predict when a particular mutation will occur. Nor does natural selection occur by will or on purpose. Thereby, not only the *theo*logical explanations, based on a literal interpretation of the Bible, but also the *teleo*logical explanations of living nature were excluded. In the Aristotelian tradition, such teleological explanations, based on end and purpose, played an essential role.

Classical Darwinism thus reflects the conflict that arose between the Aristotelian and the Galilean-Newtonian concepts of scientific explanation.

However, the question of the nature of determinism in biology is a complex one, due to the interplay between genes, organisms, and environment.[2] In this connection it is also worth noting that in research on animal behaviour, biologists may use functionalistic explanations that are foreign to physics: 'The grouse has protective colouring *because* this colouring gives the bird a better chance of escaping its predators.' This hereditary trait (the protective colouring) is here explained by its functional effects. In the usual causal explanation, effects are explained by their causes. Here, the favourable effects, that is, the better chance of survival, explain why the trait (the protective colouring) exists. But this, of course, does not mean that protective colouring is something that is intended by the grouse.[3]

The major cultural challenge of Darwinism was its conception of man as a species among other species, created by natural selection.[4] Of course, human beings do have all of the characteristics that we recognize as human and that distinguish man from other species. However, Darwinism offers a perspective whereby all of these characteristics are viewed as the result of a process of adaptation of which the underlying mechanisms are basically the same for all organisms. What, then, becomes of man's unique place in the universe? Just as the heliocentric system seemingly reduced the position of Man in the cosmos from the centre to the periphery, Darwinism seemed to deny man a unique position among living creatures and consign humanity to a familial relationship with the other species.

There was a popular and polemical debate. Are we descended from the apes? However, Darwin did not propose such a direct descent. He argued that apes and man have common forebears, and that man evolved by natural selection over a long period of time, basically in the same way as all other species.

Does this scientific theory threaten our cultural conception of man? From the perspective of traditional Christian theology, Darwinism is problematic if we insist on a literal interpretation of the Bible. If, on the other hand, we hold that the Bible should be interpreted critically and freely, we may be open to a reconciliatory view that God created man through evolution. However, apart from the theological question of whether man was created by God, directly or indirectly, we have the ethical question of how Darwinism influences our view of ourselves as human beings. Does it really matter whether we have descended from primeval ape-like creatures? Is it important, or irrelevant? If we ignore the theological perspective, what remains is the view that humanity, in some way or another, emerged in the distant past, and will some day perish, but we do not know when or how. What does it mean, positively or negatively, if we, in addition, should be distant relatives of other species?

We may argue that human beings are what they are regardless of their descent. We build houses, bake bread, write letters, attend concerts, wage war, love and despair, live and die. All this we do – all these things that characterize us as human beings – fairly independently of the question of whether we are distant relatives of the apes. Human beings are what they are, and to find out what they are, we must study man, not apes: when something evolves from *x* to *y*, *y* is just *y*, and no longer *x*. (Some would say that if we want to know how human beings became human beings, it is more profitable to read Hegel than Darwin.)

However, we might also argue as follows. Human being are not what they are independently of how they *see* themselves. Hence, our conception of man is not irrelevant in this respect. For example, we often assert that human beings are altruistic, or at least that they can be altruistic. However, some people find it reasonable to interpret this apparent altruism to mean that all organisms shaped by natural selection are controlled by 'selfish' genes.[5] 'Altruistic' genes are 'loser genes'! People living today are therefore filled with selfish genes.

We shall not enter this debate surrounding altruism and selfishness in light of the theory of evolution.[6] We would merely draw attention to the view that we, as human beings, not only *are* what we are, independently of our self-understanding, but also, to some extent, are what we think we are. Our identity as human beings is open to interpretation. And one such interpretation is that 'basically', that is, genetically, we are selfish. (Compare a similar reinterpretation by Freud: 'basic-ally', action *x* and attitude *y* are different from what we thought; that is, they should be understood as expressions of underlying and suppressed sexual motives.) Such interpretations of what we 'really' are may affect our self-understanding. And if we are persuaded by one of these accounts of what we really are, we may, to some extent, begin to resemble it.

However, the question is not just what we *are*, but also what we *ought to be*. If we believe that man has come into being through a selfish struggle for existence, and hence that the relationships between human beings *ought* to be based on ego-istic principles, we have illegitimately moved from 'is' to 'ought' – the very log-ical leap that Hume, along with many others, warned us against. If we succumb to this fallacy, claiming to deduce an *ought* from an *is* (the so-called 'naturalistic fal-lacy'), we have moved beyond Darwinism as a scientific theory. That is what we may find in those political interpretations of Darwinism in which the rights of the fittest are promoted by developmental arguments, as a *norm* for how to organize society.

DARWINISM AND SOCIOBIOLOGY

The debate about our conception of man is connected with the debate about the epistemological status of Darwinism. These are debates on various levels, academic as well as popular. In the more popular debates we may encounter positions of this kind: if Darwinism has not been proven to be scientifically true beyond doubt, it is merely one hypothesis among others, and the so-called creationists, who believe in the biblical view of creation, in a more or less literal sense, do have a theory that can compete with Darwinism.[7]

In response to this position, we could refer to the argument that no scientific theories are beyond doubt; they may, for instance, be revised on the basis of new data acquired through new technology and new conceptual development. Hence, we should not argue that the fact that Darwin's theory of evolution has not been finally confirmed is in itself a decisive weakening of Darwinism and an indirect support of creationism. By this line of reasoning, we should not argue that since Darwinism is not beyond all doubt, any poorly supported opinions are equally valid: 'Darwinism is not finally proven, and creationism is not finally proven; therefore, both are on the same epistemic level.' It is certainly not that simple. Although scientific theories are fallible, some are better founded than others. For instance, modern Darwinism is part of a comprehensive scientific field, ranging from evolu-tionary research to modern genetic research based on the DNA molecule. Here, various theories and various methods participate in a fruitful interplay and mutual support. Such support gives us the right to view the theory of evolution as being fairly well founded scientifically, even though it is fallible and open to interpreta-tion. Creationism has no such system of coherent support.

To say that the species were created by God does not promote fruitful scientific research. It is an answer of another kind. To put it bluntly, we could say that the natural sciences are based on natural, not supernatural, causes, even though the nature of causal determinism in evolutionary theory remains to be explicated. Those who look to God as a cause are not scientific researchers, but perhaps natural philosophers. However, if, instead, we claim that God's acts are not supernatural, but are actual events, as recorded in the Bible, it remains to be shown that the Bible is true (and reasonably unambiguous), and that God exists, as the Bible states. If the latter claim were well founded, we could perhaps say that the origin of the species could ultimately be explained by these events, namely, by God's actions. This would be to trace explanations of a natural-scientific kind back to explanations from social science. However, whether we choose the supernatural or the 'social-scientific' approach, it is clear that we have defined our way out of the natural sciences.

To conclude, it is probably fair to say that in relation to the differentiation of the various epistemic spheres that characterize modern science, creationism seems to represent an intellectual confusion: today, in spite of difficult borderline cases, there are interesting distinctions between religion, science, morality, and the arts. Religious theories, for instance, do not answer scientific questions, any more than ethical or aesthetic theories do.

It is fair to say that when it comes to the question of 'what human beings really are', the answer cannot be found in one science alone, whether it is physics, evolutionary theory, genetics, psychoanalysis, neurophysiological psychology, behavioural psychology, social anthropology, economics, sociology, or . . . All of these disciplines have their own answers to propose, answers that are determined by their conceptual and methodological presuppositions. This multiplicity of perspectives is the unavoidable 'Tower of Babel' of modern society, a pluralism that we can seek to master only by reflexively recognizing the presuppositions and the limits of the various perspectives. Truth is not to be found in one thesis, or synthesis, but we may hope to achieve a well-founded insight if we maintain our critical reflection on the various relevant perspectives and positions.

For some, this pluralist argument may be seen as inspiring and liberating: the world is infinitely diverse and calls for all kinds of investigations! For others, it may be seen as depressing and confusing: the task of coping with the world becomes far too complex, without simple, clear answers! Perhaps modernity is 'out of its league', and the drive to return to our lost innocence – to the time before we ate of the tree of knowledge – has become overwhelming. This is when the siren songs of the new irrationalism may seem alluring, not only in Tehrān, but also in Los Angeles and London.

An interesting borderland between established academic disciplines is represented by the attempt to extend evolutionary theory to the study of human behaviour. This has occurred in sociobiology.[8] For quite some time, we have been studying animal behaviour on the basis of evolutionary theory. By building on the presupposition that human beings are the product of evolution, sociobiologists have tried to explain human behaviour on the same basis.

To start with, we should recall that different disciplines are entitled to explore the same phenomena. For example, sociology, social anthropology, social psychology,

and history, as well as sociobiology, can all legitimately investigate human behaviour. But then we must clarify our conceptual and methodological presuppositions, as well as how they may influence the result. When stating our results, we
should not say, 'Human beings are actually . . .', but rather, 'On the basis of the
following presuppositions within this specific research project, we have found convincing evidence that . . .' Within such interdisciplinary fields, 'muddy terminology' may easily arise if we, unreflectively, use concepts from one scientific tradition within another scientific tradition.[9] In such interdisciplinary fields, and especially when the field is relatively new and not well established, it is therefore
important that we carefully define the concepts that we use, especially distinguishing between the different concepts denoted by the same terms. For example, we
may recall that sociobiological debate has focused on the relationship between men
and women: are the differences in behaviour between women and men predomi-
nantly an expression of socially determined gender roles, or of evolutionarily conditioned oppositions? This is one variation of the extensive discussion of the intricate
interplay of genetics and environment. The problem, for example, is often framed
as follows: are men, on the whole, more aggressive and dominating than women?
If so, is this mainly a result of socialization or of evolutionary biological factors?

The debate that has followed in the wake of Darwinism is by no means finished,
either on the epistemological level or in the public debate about morality and our
conception of human nature.[10]

QUESTION

Discuss the conception of human nature in a Darwinian perspective.

SUGGESTIONS FOR FURTHER READING

PRIMARY LITERATURE

The Origin of Species, Harmondsworth, 1985.

SECONDARY LITERATURE

Dawkins, R., *The Selfish Gene*, Oxford, 1976.
Kitcher, P., *Abusing Science*, London, 1982.
Rose, S., *Lifelines. Biology, Freedom, Determinism*, Harmondsworth, 1997.
Ruse, M., *Taking Darwin Seriously*, Oxford, 1986.
Wilson, E. O., *On Human Nature*, Cambridge, 1978.

NOTES

1 For instance, there were reasons for claiming that atypical traits would be gradually neutralized
  through intermarriage within a given population.
2 Cf. the 'gene determinist' view in Richard Dawkins, *The Selfish Gene*, Oxford, 1976, and the criticism of
  this view in Steven Rose, *Lifelines. Biology, Freedom, Determinism*, Harmondsworth, 1997.
3 Jon Elster, *Ulysses and the Sirens*, Cambridge, 1979, pp. 1–35. To the extent that animal behaviour
  requires functional explanations not found in physics, this is an argument against 'reducing' biology
  to physics.

4 Michael Ruse, *Taking Darwin Seriously*, Oxford, 1986.

5 Altruism means love for others; its opposite is egoism, or self-love. On the argument for 'selfishness', see Richard Dawkins, *The Selfish Gene*, Oxford, 1976.

6 Cf. the criticism of Dawkins in Steven Rose, *Lifelines. Biology, Freedom, Determinism*, Harmondsworth, 1997.

7 See Philip Kitcher, *Abusing Science*, London, 1982.

8 See E. O. Wilson, *Sociobiology: The New Synthesis*, Cambridge, 1975.

9 Thus, for example, the term 'loser' in the biological context means an individual without offspring (that can carry on the parent's genetic code), while the same term in the context of the social sciences means a person who does not meet accepted social standards – a 'social winner' may very well be a 'genetic loser', and *vice versa*.

10 Michael Ruse, *The Darwinian Paradigm*, London, 1989; see also Richard Dawkins and Steven Rose (in secondary literature above).

21 Nietzsche and pragmatism

Life. *Friedrich Nietzsche (1844–1900), the son of a* Lutheran minister, *was raised in a Puritan environment. At an early age he developed an interest in philosophy, music, and literature. As a young student, Nietzsche studied classical philology, and at the age of 24 became a professor at the University of Basel. In 1879, he had to resign his position because of illness. He composed his philosophical works under difficult financial and personal conditions, at a hectic pace from 1878 to 1888. In Turin, in January 1889, he suffered an irreversible mental breakdown. During the course of his studies, Nietzsche had become acquainted with the pessimistic philosophy of Arthur Schopenhauer and with the music of Richard Wagner (1813–1883). From Schopenhauer, he took the notion of the* will *as the fundamental feature of life. In Wagner, he found the fruition of the Greek artistic ideal. In 1888, Georg Brandes lectured on Nietzsche's philosophy at the University of Copenhagen, and in the 1890s, the interest in his philosophy increased dramatically. European authors such as Thomas Mann, Albert Camus, Jean-Paul Sartre, August Strindberg, and Martin Heidegger are, in various ways, indebted to Nietzsche. Nietzsche left several unpublished manuscripts and notes at his death. His sister, Elisabeth Förster-Nietzsche, who was an anti-Semite and later a Nazi, edited and published these manuscripts after her brother's death, largely creating the myth of Nietzsche's anti-Semitism and proto-Nazism through her forgeries of his work. Nietzsche, like Kierkegaard, despised both the 'masses' and the complacent cultivated bourgeoisie. Both philosophers were convinced that they lived in a period of decline and opposed the dominant influences of their time. In Kierkegaard and Nietzsche, political thinking resulted in an 'aristocratic radicalism' (Georg Brandes), and both are central figures in modern existential philosophy.*

Nietzsche's most important works are The Birth of Tragedy from the Spirit of Music *(1872),* Human, All-Too-Human *(1878),* The Dawn: Reflections on Moral Prejudices *(1881),* The Gay Science *(1882),* Thus Spoke Zarathustra *(1886),* Beyond Good and Evil *(1886), and* Toward a Genealogy of Morals *(1887).* Ecce Homo *and* The Will to Power *were published after Nietzsche's death.*

'GOD IS DEAD' – EUROPEAN NIHILISM

The 1880s was the decade of optimism, progress, and development. It is against this background that Nietzsche announced his shocking discovery: 'The greatest event of recent times – that "God is dead", that belief in the Christian God has become unworthy of belief – already begins to cast its first shadows over Europe.'[1]

Nietzsche thought that this troublesome message would still need several centuries to become part of the European experience, but by then all traditional values would have lost their binding force; European nihilism would have become a fact.

For Nietzsche, nihilism was a necessary consequence of the bankruptcy of values and ideals. The devaluation of values, the revelation of their fictitious nature, pushed us into a void that we had never experienced before. For Nietzsche, the turning point of history had arrived: man will either sink into animal barbarism or overcome nihilism. But nihilism can only be overcome if it is lived to its extreme conclusion and then transformed into its opposite. Nietzsche's thought is meant to clear the way for something unknown that is to come. Thus, his thought is difficult to classify. He ranks with thinkers like Pascal, Kierkegaard, Marx, and Dostoyevsky. They are all radically different, but they are all 'sacrificial lambs of their epochs' who mark an epochal change in the conditions of humanity.[2]

Until Nietzsche, philosophers had viewed the world and history as being meaningful, rational, and just. Existence had a purpose, a meaning. It was not blind and accidental. There was a world order founded by God. The world was not chaos, but an ordered cosmos in which human beings held a meaningful place. It is this conception of man and existence that collapses with Nietzsche. For him, this conception does not represent a true picture of reality: the philosophical and religious world-views are only expressions of man's need to avoid chaos. Human beings cannot live without a continual 'forgery' of the world.

This view of the world as chaos reflects a basic mood in Nietzschean philosophy. The world is without a plan; it is a game played by fate. To put it another way, our thinking always requires a strictly logical form and structure. But reality is without form; it is chaotic. The threat of chaos forces us to create meaning, and thus to become 'metaphysical artists'. We give form to our existence and add 'meaning' and 'purpose' in order to survive. Philosophical systems and world-views are only fictions, serving to secure our existence. But man has a special ability to forget: the structure that *we* add to the world gradually comes to be understood as the world's *own* structure, as an order *created by God*. This is a presupposition for peace and security.

As God loses value and authority, we seek other guiding stars that can replace him: the categorical imperative, Hegel's reason, the goal of history, etc. Nihilism is a way of thinking and a psychological condition that arises as a direct consequence of the suspicion that there really is no external or internal moral authority. The feeling of valuelessness strikes when we realize that existence cannot be interpreted by concepts like 'purpose', 'unity', 'end', and 'truth'. These value-laden categories are those that *we ourselves have added to the world* — and when we abandon them, the world appears to be *valueless*.

It may be appropriate to interpret this as a form of 'philosophical alienation', in line with Feuerbach and Marx. Metaphysical systems are expressions of man's philosophical alienation. Therefore, Nietzsche wanted to return to human beings what had been 'alienated': 'All the beauty and sublimity we have bestowed upon real and imaginary things I will reclaim as the property and product of man.'[3]

The claim that the world is valueless does not mean that it has 'little value' or almost 'no value'. Strictly speaking, it is just as meaningless to claim that the world has value as it is to claim that numbers have colour or weight. Nietzsche seemed to think that the notion of *value* has a relational character: our claim that *x* has value is either an expression of our own evaluation or a descriptive statement of the following kind: 'John adds value to *x*.' To claim that *x* has value *in itself* is, for Nietzsche, a meaningless proposition.[4]

By nihilism, Nietzsche thus meant a completely disillusioned view of the world. The idea of 'God's death' awakens, in Nietzsche, a new understanding of the world without beginning and without purpose. Within the Christian tradition, morality and truth are anchored in God. Thus, if God is dead, the *foundation* of morality and truth is gone. Nothing is 'true'; 'everything is permitted!' However, nihilism was not Nietzsche's final word: his persona, Zarathustra, is to overcome God, nihilism, and the existential void. The condition is that we put our 'useful' lives behind us.

CRITIQUE OF METAPHYSICS AND CHRISTIANITY

Christianity, in Nietzsche's eyes, is 'Platonism for the people', the vulgarization of Western metaphysics. The life-denying Western understanding appears in Christianity and in metaphysics: that which is sensual, earthly, is understood in light of ideas or God, in light of the 'heavenly', 'genuine', and 'true' world. The earthly is devalued as 'unreal', 'pseudo', or 'the vale of tears'. All of Nietzsche's thought was directed towards turning this view of existence upside down. Consequently, he viewed his own thinking as reversed Platonism – or as a *revaluation of all values*.

By referring to *God*, Nietzsche was not thinking primarily of a religious power, but of the objectivity of values, independent of man: all values and moral criteria are given by God. Morality thus has a religious foundation. For Nietzsche, 'God's death' means an abolition of all forms of value transcendence and a rediscovery of values as human creations. Religion, morality, and philosophy are symptoms of human alienation. The destruction of these forms of understanding allows us to view man as the creator of what has been worshipped and bowed down to for almost two thousand years. The criticism of Christianity is followed by a criticism of metaphysics. According to Nietzsche, metaphysics rejects our earthly reality as non-existent (Parmenides) or as unreal (Plato). What the philosophical tradition understood as the actual being, 'substance', *is not*. Only the becoming and change of the visible world *is*. There is no substance or actual reality beyond space and time, no intelligible world, and no eternal ideas. There is only a sensual world that reveals itself in space and time. That is the real world. Thus Zarathustra exhorts: 'I implore you, my brothers, *remain true to the earth* and do not believe those who talk to you of celestial hopes! They are poisoners, whether they know it or not. They are contemptuous of life, dying off and poisoned by themselves. . . . let them go their way!'[5]

Our earthly world does not know anything eternal or underlying: all is movement, time, becoming, and 'nothing more'. Thus, Nietzsche basically said that Heraclitus was right. Unchangeable being is an empty fiction; everything is in flux: the so-called 'true' world is a lie. Hence, Nietzsche turned the basic metaphysical presuppositions of the Western world upside down. Metaphysics is, from the start, dualistic. Its essence is a dichotomy into a changeable sensory world and a static, transcendent world (where it may be said that what truly is, does not become, and what becomes, is not). Nietzsche aimed to overcome this contradiction between becoming and true being. Metaphysics, as he understood it, had devalued the world that reveals itself to us, and replaced it with an imaginary world, a fiction, that purports to be the real world. Philosophy distrusts the senses (cf. Plato) because they show us what is transient; it sees the main enemy of thought in the senses and in the sensual. Since what is eternal and imperishable cannot be found in the sensory world, philosophy appeals to a transcendent world that is furnished with the highest properties. The metaphysical construction is thus the following: metaphysics divides existence, into dichotomies such as 'appearance' and 'being', 'essence' and 'form of manifestation', 'thing in itself' and 'thing for me', 'genuine' and 'fake', and 'soul' and 'body'. In this way, metaphysics constructs a series of binary oppositions in which one link is seen as positive and the other as negative. The soul, for instance, has a positive value and the body a negative value. Each entity receives its *rank in terms of being*. Hence, metaphysics establishes hierarchic relations among various phenomena, and all ranking (as in Plato or Aquinas) is determined by the distance from the highest being, what we usually call 'the idea of the good', 'the absolute', or 'God'. The various phenomena are thus understood to be determined by an absolute standard. But the recognition that 'God is dead' makes it possible to overcome this understanding of existence, as in the Platonic and Christian dualistic theories.

What Nietzsche is rejecting with 'God' and Christianity is a moralizing ontology and an ontologizing morality: namely, the view that the imperishable is at the same time good, that man's moral task is to be raised above the sensual ('the needs of life') and turn towards the divine ideas. Dualism is, for Nietzsche, the greatest danger to man because it leads to a *turning away* from life. Nietzsche's struggle against 'God', that is to say, dualism, resulted in a view of life that is characterized by naivety, playfulness, and innocence. This is what he saw as a 'revaluation of all values' and as a correction of humanity's greatest mistake.

But when Nietzsche turned metaphysics upside down in this way, did he not then make use of what he was rejecting? Was he not himself using the very distinction that he fought against? Did he think that what is *earthly* is what is *genuine* and that what is metaphysical is only *imaginary*? Or was he inaugurating a new way of thinking that broke radically with philosophical tradition?

MORAL PHILOSOPHY

Nietzsche's moral philosophy is primarily a grand attempt to explain moral phenomena psychologically. He says little about what should replace the destroyed morality and how the new morality can possibly be grounded. Nietzsche insisted that no phenomena are moral or immoral in themselves. On this point, his position is reminiscent of Hume: there are only moral interpretations of phenomena. Nietzsche boasted of being the first to realize that there are no 'moral facts'. Nor do our moral codes serve to describe the world. Morality is a straitjacket: a useful means of preserving society and avoiding destructive forces. Morality uses *fear* and *hope* – among the strongest inventions are heaven and hell. Eventually, the mechanisms of coercion become internalized as the *conscience*.

In *Beyond Good and Evil*, Nietzsche announced his discovery of two fundamental types of morality: the 'master morality' and the 'slave morality'. It is true that they are mixed in all higher forms of civilization, and that elements of both may be found in the same person. In a radical form, the distinction may be made as follows: in master morality, 'good' is equivalent to 'noble', 'prominent', and 'magnanimous', and 'bad' to 'contemptible'. In slave morality, the question of good and bad is related to what serves the weak, 'the poor in spirit'. Attributes like sympathy, humility, and compassion are elevated to virtues, and the strong and independent individual is considered to be dangerous and 'evil'. By the standard of the slave morality, the good according to the master morality will be viewed as evil and immoral, since the master morality is based on strength and self-assertion. Slave morality, on the other hand, is based on weakness and submission. But although the masters are strong, the slaves are far more clever. The slaves do not dare to meet the masters in the open field, but they try to tame them by setting up their own moral evaluations as absolute: 'The beginning of the slaves' revolt in morality occurs when *ressentiment* itself turns creative and gives birth to values.'[6]

The aggression among the underprivileged is thus not expressed openly, but indirectly. In Christianity, Nietzsche saw the most effective destroyer of the master morality. Christians praise the attributes of the weak, humble, and meek – not because Christians love them, but because of a hidden hatred of strength, of the pride of life, and of self-assertion. Because of 'spiritual terror', the slave morality, which originally was only one perspective, becomes accepted by everyone as a *universal* standard: the masters assume the slaves' standard in regard to themselves. This 'revaluation of values' leads to an intense self-hatred among the natural aristocrats. They begin to hate their strongest desires and passions.

The weak shed only crocodile tears when others are made to suffer. The joy of suffering is human, according to Nietzsche, and humanity has never found barbarism to be despicable: 'To see somebody suffer is nice, to make somebody suffer even nicer – that is a hard proposition, but an ancient, powerful, human-all-too-human. . . . No cruelty, no feast: that is what the oldest and longest period in human history teaches us – and punishment, too, has such very strong *festive* aspects!'[7]

This does not mean that Nietzsche advocated heartlessness and bestiality. He wanted to show how complicated many of our desires can be, how much hidden joy is found in promising our opponents eternal torment!

We said that, according to Nietzsche, the weak made the strong accept their moral code. This produced a remarkable psychological phenomenon: when the strong could no longer turn their aggression outwards, it was channelled inwards, and it became gratifying in new, unexpected ways: 'All instincts which are not discharged outwardly turn inwards – this is what I call the internalization of man.'[8] And along with this, follows what we call *soul*:

> The whole inner world, originally stretched thinly as though between two layers of skin, was expanded and extended itself and gained depth, breadth and height in proportion to the degree that the external discharge of man's instincts are *obstructed*. Those terrible bulwarks with which state organizations protected themselves against the old instincts of freedom.[9]

Does Nietzsche mean that we should allow our passions and impulses to run wild, beyond good and evil? In morality, are we to adopt a *laissez-faire* attitude? For Nietzsche, all morality, including what is beyond good and evil, implies a certain tyranny over 'nature'. And this is necessary. Without morality, nothing emerges that makes life worth living. Neither art nor poetry (not to speak of great philosophy!) is possible without a certain amount of coercion, without an ascetic attitude towards life. The point is to discipline the passions and the desires; not to dry them up, but to cultivate them. *Sublimation* is the key. According to Nietzsche, a man with strong and terrible impulses is 'unhuman' because he has not learned the art of sublimating his impulses, as in the service of the sciences and the arts. But such a man is still much preferable to a 'Christian eunuch' who has nothing to sublimate, and, consequently, nothing to *create*. Through self-control, strong human beings will be able to realize themselves in a positive way. Nietzsche did not want to 'go back to nature', to a primitive expression of passions. All of this prepares the way for Nietzsche's ideal of humanity: 'the superman' (*Übermensch*).

ÜBERMENSCH, WILL TO POWER, AND ETERNAL RECURRENCE

Nietzsche did not give many indications of how we should understand his theory of the superman. Both Caesar and Napoleon (not to speak of Hitler and the 'Aryan race') have been taken as examples of what is meant by the superman. But such examples are not very appropriate. The 'Roman Caesar' became the first superman when 'Christ's soul' was bestowed upon him.[10] Nor does Napoleon do as an ideal. For Nietzsche, Napoleon was just a 'synthesis of *monster* [*Unmensch*] and *Übermensch*'[11] Nor did Nietzsche express any special affection for the 'Aryan race', whether anti-Semites or Germans.[12]

It was Goethe who seemed to come closest to Nietzsche's ideal of the superman. Goethe was driven by the strongest passions, but he overcame himself. 'What he wanted was totality; he fought against the division of reason, sensuality, feeling, will (– as it was taught in the most terrifying scholastic through *Kant* – Goethe's antipode); he disciplined himself to wholeness, he *created* himself.'[13] According to Nietzsche, Goethe was *tolerant*, not out of weakness, but out of strength. He was not a German, but a *European*. Goethe was a person who said *yes* to life. Such a free spirit does not deny, but accepts life. 'But such a faith is the greatest possible. I have baptized it with the name of *Dionysos*.'[14]

Nietzsche's *magnum opus*, *Thus Spoke Zarathustra*, was meant to articulate the unique vision that he had of the superman and the future. The historical Zarathustra (Zoroaster) believed that the world was the battleground of good and evil. Since Zarathustra was the first to make that mistake, says Nietzsche, he must also be the first to recognize it.[15] As a result, Zarathustra becomes the advocate of a new conception of values:

> Many things that one people called good, another called ridiculous and shameful: that is how I found things. Many things I found which in one place were called evil but which in another place were adorned with purple honors. . . . Truly – men gave themselves all their good and evil. . . . Things had no value until man put them there for his self-preservation; he created an aim and meaning! . . . There have been a thousand aims up to now, for there were a thousand peoples. Only the yoke for the thousand necks was still lacking – the one aim was still lacking. Humanity has no aim as yet.[16]

Zarathustra (Nietzsche) sets himself the task of positing and developing this *one goal*, and this is where the notion of the superman (*Übermensch*) finds its place: 'The Superman is the aim of the earth.'[17] Man is something that must be overcome. It is stretched between beast and superman. What can be loved in man is that he *transcends* and *descends*. Human worth lies not in what we *are*, but in what we can *become*. But in order to evolve towards the superman, we must get rid of all that is human, all too human.

Perhaps we have an idea of what we need to get rid of. What is lacking is a positive characteristic, if we do not wish to use Goethe as a standard, and a clarification of our potentiality. It may be that Nietzsche himself felt this deficiency: 'Never yet has there been a superman. I saw them naked, both the greatest and the smallest human being – All too similar are they still. In truth, I found even the greatest of them – all too human!'[18]

Zarathustra also proclaimed the idea of *the eternal recurrence of all things*. The idea is, roughly, that everything repeats itself in an infinite cycle. We also find this idea in the pre-Socratics, the Stoics, and ancient Indian philosophy: there will again be a Socrates and a Plato, each person will appear again having the same friends and enemies, performing the same actions, and suffering the same fate.

The idea may seem astounding, but Nietzsche accepted it as a hypothesis, a 'thought experiment'. It is based on the notion that everything happens in accordance with inviolable natural laws. As a scientific hypothesis, the idea of the eternal recurrence of all things relies on a series of problematic presuppositions: we must assume that there is a finite number of factors that determine all of the processes in nature. Given this, it follows that there are a limited number of possible combinations, and when this number is complete, previous combinations must be repeated. The presupposition is that the universe is finite.[19]

It is possible that Nietzsche was most interested in the *practical* meaning of the doctrine. It is, for example, incompatible with the notion that history has a final *goal*. It further implies a break with a linear-teleological view of history (Christian or Marxist). Perhaps the doctrine also favours the Stoic world-view, transcending resentment and thoughts of revenge – perhaps it implies that we should reconcile ourselves with the insight that our worldly task is Sisyphean (endless).

> My formula for greatness in a human being is *amor fati*: that one wants nothing to be other than it is, not in the future, not in the past, not in all eternity. Not merely to endure that which happens of necessity, still less to dissemble it – all idealism is untruthfulness in the face of necessity – but to *love* it.[20]

At the very least, the doctrine of the eternal recurrence of all things liberates us from traditional metaphysical and religious conceptions that promise future happiness and bliss. It also seems to imply that the eternal and the infinite are found only in this life: *This* life is your eternal life! What is more problematic is that this theory seems to collide with the theory of the superman. Is it at all meaningful to want to overcome 'the final human being' and create the superman if they are only figures that repeat themselves in an eternal cycle?

Much of Nietzsche's thought centred on the concept of *the will to power*, but this rarely received the same in-depth analysis as the concepts that Nietzsche attacked. Nietzsche seemed to think that human beings do not primarily desire 'pleasure' or

what is 'useful'. Nor do they desire freedom from something, but rather the freedom to realize themselves, to choose a 'lifestyle'. This occurs in the form of the
will to power. But power, here, does not mean power over others, but rather
power over oneself. The will to power is also expressed as a will to knowledge, an
instinct that leads us to organize chaos, to master and transform our surroundings.

Sometimes the concept takes on an ontological nature. The will to power thus
becomes the shaping force of existence. To the degree that the will to power is a
will to *something* in regard to the future, this mental image seems to conflict with
the doctrine of the eternal recurrence of the same. How these images are to be reconciled is a controversial question in Nietzsche research.

EPISTEMOLOGY

Before we close this chapter, we will review Nietzsche's ideas and examine his conception of truth. According to Nietzsche, all metaphysical systems are expressions
of the will to power. The same applies to the sciences. At the same time, they are
'fictions', that is to say, conceptual constructions that we impose on reality, a
Procrustean bed on which we distort it to serve our needs. These systems are 'physiological aids for the self-preservation of a particular species of life'.[21] Everything
is only a perspective and fiction. The perspectives are based on evaluations. Moral
evaluations are interpretations, a symptom of a particular physiological state.

Nietzsche held that there was a connection between *cognition* and *interest*,[22] but
at the same time the problems are reduced in a naturalistic-biological sense. Another
question also emerges: what about Nietzsche's own theories? Are they also fictions?
Or is it possible for Nietzsche's theories to avoid perspectivism and to give us
the truth about the world in an absolute sense? Nietzsche seemed to deny the latter
vehemently – he went so far as to question truth. Is not the belief in truth a
metaphysical belief?

> Our confidence in science continually rests on a metaphysical faith. And we who have
> knowledge, we who are godless and anti-metaphysical, we also take our fire from the
> same torch that was lit through a thousand-year old faith, this Christian faith that also
> belonged to Plato, that God was truth, that truth was divine. But what if this very belief
> becomes increasingly unbelievable? . . . If God now turns out to be our Oldest lie?[23]

The moment we deny the belief in the divine, said Nietzsche, a new problem
arises: the question of the value of truth: 'the value of true is tentatively to be *called
into question*'.[24] But what is to be our standard if it is not truth itself?

Thus, it seems that Nietzsche held two concepts of truth. Traditionally, we
understand truth as a *correspondence* between a statement and a state of affairs (what
this correspondence actually entails has been a controversial question since the time
of Plato). This is often called the correspondence concept of truth. Clearly,
Nietzsche had to reject this conception of truth. And the reason given is not without import: there are no neutral facts with which our theories may correspond. All
so-called facts are always already 'theory-loaded'. All *pure facts* or 'neutral description' is only a concealed interpretation, one perspective alongside a series of other
interpretations. In this sense, the theories of the will to power and the eternal

recurrence must also be fictions. For what distinguishes them from other fictions? In what sense did Nietzsche think that these theories are true (if there is no possibility of correspondence)? The answer is that some interpretations 'serve life'; they are useful for life and life-affirming. Nietzsche saw his own theories as being true in this sense. They are true, not in the sense that they express the truth about the world (for Nietzsche, there was no such truth), but in the sense that they *serve life*. This is what we may call a *pragmatic concept of truth*, and this is how we should understand Nietzsche's famous definition of truth as 'the kind of error without which a certain species of life could not live. The value for *life* is ultimately decisive.'[25]

But this pragmatic concept of truth still does not solve the problem. How does Nietzsche know this about truth? What kind of insight are we talking about? Moreover, Nietzsche claimed that the world in itself is chaos, but was he not then using the correspondence concept of truth that he is criticizing? If he claims that he *knows* it, then he at least cannot, at the same time, reject all objective theories of truth: the claim 'the world in itself is chaos and without order and purpose' would be *true* only if the world actually were chaotic and without purpose. For then the claim would correspond with the actual conditions. To be consistent, Nietzsche must view his philosophy as one perspective, among other possible perspectives. We have seen that Nietzsche defended this perspective because of its usefulness for life. But *what* is useful for life, and for *whom*? What may be useful to Nietzsche is clearly not useful to Plato. But what then is the criterion for saying that something is either 'life-affirming' or 'life-denying'? Would Nietzsche not have to say that an objective criterion is only a 'fiction' or a concealed perspective?

Perhaps we are pushing this too far. Nietzsche viewed himself and his philosophy as an *experiment*. He called himself a 'Don Juan in epistemology'. He placed our most deep-rooted convictions under analysis. He questioned the values that we often, dogmatically and unquestioningly, take for granted. He undermined what we take as self-evident. Nietzsche performed an experiment with truth. If we ultimately find out that this experiment in some sense or another presupposes what we have questioned, namely, the idea of absolute truth, this does not diminish the value of the experiment. On the contrary, Nietzsche's experiment has taught us something!

In many ways, Nietzsche recalls Socrates: a gadfly that is at his best when he stings us into defending ourselves.

TRUTH IS WHAT WORKS – AMERICAN PRAGMATISM

Pragmatism as a philosophical school was especially strong in the United States at the beginning of the twentieth century (as represented by William James [1842–1910], Charles Sanders Peirce [1839–1914], and John Dewey [1859–1952]). Both in its more refined and its unrefined versions, it has successors in contemporary philosophy.[26] Pragmatism has not only been important in philosophy (including political philosophy) but also in other fields such as pedagogy (cf. Dewey's work in this field).

The concept of truth is central in pragmatism. Roughly, pragmatism states that opinions are true when they *work*, when they are *useful*. We say 'roughly' because this may, for example, mean that what is called true is what is useful *for our own personal interests*. In that case we link the concept of truth to different kinds of political and practical interests. But the less 'rough' versions will appear if we take 'useful' as being what 'shows itself to work' when tested in everyday life and in scientific investigation and discussion.

To the more crude interpretation of the pragmatist conception of truth, it was objected by Bertrand Russell and others that it is often difficult to *know* whether one statement is more useful than another statement about the same state of affairs. For instance, how do we know that it is more useful to state that Columbus crossed the Atlantic Ocean in 1492 than to state that he did so in 1491? For whom, or for what, could the one statement be more useful than the other? And it is also objected that in order to know that something is useful, we must think that it is *true* that this something is useful, but if this again is to mean that it is useful to think that something is useful, we end up with the same question all over again, in an infinite regression.

In opposition to this more unrefined version of the pragmatic view of truth (which we also meet in some political ideologies), Peirce, among others, asserted that the *concept* of truth is to be understood on the basis of the way we *find* the truth (that is, validation), and that this validation must be understood as the consensus that all competent people would reach if they were allowed to work in open and free research without any time constraints. It is not the empirical fact of an agreement that harbours the truth, but the agreement that is achieved among competent researchers in a timeless research community. This is both a complex and important view (cf. Habermas' conception of truth, Ch. 27). In this connection it is sufficient to note that this view connects pragmatism with central problems in the philosophy of science and in the modern debate about human rights and their justification (cf. Chapter 26, John Rawls).

QUESTIONS

Explain Nietzsche's criticism of morality.

In what sense may Nietzsche's criticism of Platonism and Christianity be said to be appropriate?

SUGGESTIONS FOR FURTHER READING

PRIMARY LITERATURE

Beyond Good and Evil, translated by R. J. Hollingdale, London, 1990.
The Will to Power, translated by Walter Kaufmann and R. J. Hollingdale, New York, 1968.
Basic Writings of Nietzsche, translated by Walter Kaufmann, New York, 1992.

SECONDARY LITERATURE

Allison, David B. (ed.), *The New Nietzsche*, Cambridge, MA, 1986.
Danto, A. C., *Nietzsche as Philosopher*, New York, 1965.
Kaufmann, W., *Nietzsche: Philosopher, Psychologist, Antichrist*, Princeton, NJ, 1968.

NOTES

1 F. Nietzsche, *Die fröhliche Wissenschaft*, Werke II (Schlechta), p. 205, trans. from the German by R. W. and G. S.
2 K. Jaspers, *Nietzsche and Christianity*, trans. by E. B. Ashton, Chicago, 1961.
3 F. Nietzsche, *Nachlass (Der Wille zur Macht)*, Werke III (Schlechta), p. 680, trans. from the German by R. W. and G. S.
4 Cf. Arthur C. Danto's study: *Nietzsche as Philosopher*, New York, 1965.
5 F. Nietzsche, *Thus Spoke Zarathustra*, trans. by Marianne Cowan, Los Angeles, 1957, p. 5.
6 F. Nietzsche, *On the Genealogy of Morality*, trans. by Carol Diethe, ed. by Keith Ansell-Pearson, Cambridge, 1995, p. 21.
7 Ibid., p. 46.
8 Ibid., p. 61.
9 Ibid., p. 61.
10 *The Will to Power*, p. 513.
11 *Genealogy of Morals*, p. 36.
12 Nietzsche wrote of Wagner's friends in Bayreuth: 'Not an abortion was missing, not even the anti-Semite. Poor Wagner! To what a pass he had come! – Better for him to have gone among swine! But among Germans!' (*Ecce Homo*, translated with notes by R. J. Hollingdale, London, 1992, p. 60). W. Kauffmann gives a good account of the 'Nietzsche myth' (that is, of Nietzsche as a proto-Nazi) and his view of race in *Nietzsche: Philosopher, Psychologist, Antichrist*, Princeton, NJ, 1968, pp. 3–21, 284–307.
13 F. Nietzsche, *Götzen-Dämmerung*, Werke II (Schlechta), p. 1024, trans. from the German by R. W. and G. S.
14 Ibid., p. 1025.
15 *Ecce Homo*, p. 98.
16 *Thus Spoke Zarathustra*, pp. 62–5.
17 Ibid., p. 5.
18 Ibid., p. 106.
19 This is a problematic reconstruction. Perhaps Nietzsche did not think that the same individuals would recur, but rather the same type of individual. It is also possible that Nietzsche considered the doctrine of the 'eternal recurrence' to be a form of nihilism: 'This is the most extreme form of nihilism: the nothing (the 'meaningless'), eternally!' *The Will to Power*, p. 36.
20 *Ecce Homo*, pp. 37–8.
21 F. Nietzsche, *Jenseits von Gut und Böse*, Werke II (Schlechta), p. 569, trans. from the German by R. W. and G. S.
22 Compare the view that the basic needs of life are connected to 'cognitive interests' (see Ch. 27, Habermas).
23 *Die fröhliche Wissenschaft*, p. 208, trans. from the German by R. W. and G. S.
24 *Genealogy of Morals*, p. 120.
25 *The Will to Power*, p. 272.
26 Compare Habermas' theory of truth and the theory that 'truth is what serves our class/interests'. For Habermas' theory of truth, see Gunnar Skirbekk, 'Pragmatism and Pragmatics', in *Rationality and Modernity*, Oslo, 1993.

22 Socialism and fascism

COMMUNISM – LENIN: PARTY AND STATE

Lenin, or Vladimir Ilyich Ulyanov (1870–1924), was the leader of the communist revolution in Russia. His theoretical contribution was marked by the circumstances in which he found himself. Not only did Lenin lead the revolution, but he also had to expound the Marxist doctrine that applied to the transition from capitalism to the classless communist society. Marx had been rather careful in what he said about this transition.

Lenin had to explain why the revolution occurred in the industrially backward Russia, and not in the more developed capitalist nations in the West. He pointed out that capitalism is an international phenomenon. The industrialized capitalist countries and the colonies that produced the raw materials are two sides of the same coin in international capitalism. Internationally, capitalism had developed as far as it could, according to Lenin. The revolution had started where capitalism was weakest, not in the strongly capitalist countries like Germany and Britain, but in Russia. This theory of *imperialism* represents a certain revision of the theory of the historical periods according to which the revolution will occur in the most developed capitalist countries.

Communist doctrine held that the revolution would start in the countries where capitalism was most advanced, because a communist society would only be possible when the communists took over the production apparatus of a fully mature capitalism. First, a bourgeois revolution would occur, allowing capitalism to mature, and setting the stage for the communist revolution, which would introduce more rational economic conditions. Hence, there would be *two* revolutions separated by a certain amount of time. But, in Russia, the bourgeois revolution occurred in February 1917 and the communist revolution in October of the same year. The time between the two was too short. Russian capitalism had not expanded to its full potential within the framework offered by the bourgeois society.

Lenin explained what happened with his theory of two revolutions in one. Seen from an international perspective, capitalism was mature. This is why, in Russia, the bourgeois revolution could be followed immediately by the communist revolution. But this presupposed that the revolution in Russia would be followed by an international revolution that would allow the Russian communists to learn about industrialization from comrades in countries where the capitalist production apparatus was more developed. This also presupposed that the political will of the Russian communists would be a driving force in the industrialization of Russia. The last presupposition entailed a rejection of economic determinism. Here the 'superstructure', the political leadership, was supposed to *create* the 'basis', Russian industry. As time passed and no international revolution occurred, the Russians had to teach themselves almost everything, and this theory of leadership as a driving force became even more important. Therefore, Lenin's most important contribution was the development of a strong party organization. This is exactly the point where Lenin and the Bolsheviks came into conflict with the social democrats (such as Eduard Bernstein [1850–1932]), who wanted to organize a parliamentary socialist party, as well as with the liberal Marxists (such as Rosa Luxemburg [1870–1919]), who were opposed to Lenin's strict party discipline. Lenin was convinced that a strong, elite party of well-disciplined revolutionaries was necessary to lead the working classes to a communist society. Without such a party, the workers would not move any further than trade-union policies, in the style of the social democrats. Lenin had neither ends nor means in common with the social democrats. *They* wanted an egalitarian welfare society, and to achieve it would use legal political means to implement gradual reforms within capitalist society. Lenin wanted public ownership of all means of production, and to achieve that goal, he had to be revolutionary, aided by an elite party. Lenin had this basic goal in common with the liberal Marxists. But the liberal Marxists, such as Rosa Luxemburg, were more convinced that it was possible and necessary to maintain the usual democratic procedures in the party and in society in general. Iron discipline in the party and in society was not necessary; moreover, it was dangerous because it could later interfere with the restoration of a decentralized democracy.

To the extent that Lenin did manage to direct the revolution, we might in a sense say that history proved him right. But it also turned out that the Soviet communists were unable to allow sufficient latitude for democratic rights and procedures once they gained power. In this sense, Rosa Luxemburg was right.

Why was there a conflict between democracy and communism? Is there something in Marxism or Leninism, *qua* theory that makes democratization difficult? Or is it a purely sociological mechanism that people who have power are reluctant to give it up? Or is it connected with the fact that Russia had never experienced the liberal, bourgeois virtues: not only had the capitalist production apparatus never been fully developed in Russia, but Russia had never experienced the political ideals inherent in bourgeois society, such as parliamentary democracy and individual rights (such as freedom of speech and freedom of religion).

Classical Marxism claimed that the state would wither away once communism was introduced, that is to say, once the class society and oppression had been abolished. The state was seen as a form of oppression exercised by the ruling class against the lower classes. Once class oppression no longer existed, the state would be unnecessary. Lenin fully accepted the view that the state was a form of oppression in the hands of the ruling class. The police, the army, the legal system – all were aspects of the class state. But once Lenin gained power, it became necessary to answer the question of when and how the state would 'wither away'. The core of Lenin's answer was that in a transition period, of indefinite length, it would be necessary for the proletariat to put down all attempts at a counter-revolution. The capitalist class state, in this period, would have to be replaced by a *dictatorship of the proletariat*. But this would not be a new violent state, as in capitalism. It represented a step forward. Under capitalism – the bourgeois dictatorship – the majority, the proletariat, is oppressed by the minority, the capitalists. Under the dictatorship of the proletariat, the counter-revolutionary minority is oppressed by the revolutionary majority.

As a political thinker, Lenin emphasized the primacy of political action, not an impartial search for truth: his epistemological basis is the class point of view and loyalty to party positions. He rejected the idea of an independent, critical search for truth. This is the epistemological counterpart of a political theory that empha-sizes party discipline and rejects open discussion and criticism.

The following objection immediately suggests itself. If a leader thinks that the majority of the people are not able to recognize truth, because he holds – as Lenin did during the Russian Revolution – that the capitalists, as a result of their class situation, are unable to perceive reality without ideological distortion, and that the working class is not yet able to understand its own position correctly, that leader must assume that he himself has the right insight into all these matters. But, if so, he ought to believe that he should have been able to demonstrate all this to people who are on the same level as himself. In other words, party members should be able to discuss these issues rationally, and they should, in principle, be able to con-vince the masses of the truth of the decisions and basic position of the party. In short, irrespective of how convinced a leader might be of the irrationality and lack of judgement of the masses, he has to assume that he himself has correctly under-stood the situation on the basis of reasons that, in principle, also could have been recognized by others. In this sense, it is difficult to avoid the idea of truth as binding, despite all irrationality and power struggles.

So much for the theoretical level. However, today we know that Lenin, as a political leader, ordered drastic measures against large groups of people and the execution of innocent persons. He contributed actively to the establishment of the regime of terror and genocide for which Stalin was primarily responsible.

Since there had been no international revolution, and since the Soviet Union was surrounded by hostile capitalist nations, Joseph Stalin (1879–1953) pursued the establishment of an independent communist state, which, outwardly, closed itself off from the rest of the world, and which, inwardly, required great sacrifices in order to achieve industrialization without external capital and expertise. As a result, Stalin had to revise Lenin's theory on two points. He launched the doctrine of socialism in one country. Eventually, the result was a strongly nationalist Russian communism. In addition, he solved the problem that Lenin had in explaining why the state apparatus in the Soviet Union had not 'withered away'. The solution was simple: as long as communism in the Soviet Union was threatened by the capital-ist states, the Soviet state had to remain strong. This response might have been con-vincing had Stalin not, at the same time, announced that the opposition factions within the Soviet Union had been liquidated. For, why, then, were secret police, deportations, and purges necessary? Capitalist countries, which were not without inner opposition, had managed to maintain a front against external enemies with-out resort to such drastic internal measures (as in Britain during World War II). Finally, the Stalinist period was characterized by bureaucracy and a powerful cult of personality, and the latter is contrary to most versions of historical materialism, which holds that it is objective economic forces that determine history, not particular individuals. But even Lenin opposed radical economic determinism and advocated party discipline as the driving force in the industrialization process. And there was a fine line between worship of the party and a cult of personality.

With the fall of the Berlin Wall in 1989, Marxism and Leninism, as a significant political doctrine, became defunct. Politically, a world had disappeared, at least in Europe.

ANARCHISM AND SYNDICALISM

The Greek expression *anarchos* means '*without a leader*'. Anarchism was a political movement to abolish all forms of authority, and reorganize society on the basis of the social and economic needs that spontaneously arise among free individuals and groups. Among its most prominent theoreticians were Max Stirner (1806–1856) and Mikhail Bakunin (1814–1876). More specifically, anarchists held that this reorganization would be achieved through a network of communes: intimate communities, small enough to allow each individual to have a clear overview of the state of affairs in the community, as well as ensure daily communication with others, something that makes democracy possible. These units were to be self-governing and were not to be subject to an external power. In anarchist terminology, this was to be a society without a state. The necessary cooperation between the units was not to be directed by the laws of the market, nor by a central bureaucratic institution, but was to arise out of the specific needs of each group; this cooperation was to be developed on the basis of independence and mutual assistance. *Anarchy*, in other words, was not conceived of as a society without organization, but as a society in which the organization was spontaneous, that is to say, it was to emerge 'organically' from common interests and from a recognition of these interests. In the anarchist view, not only does such an organizational form secure the greatest possible freedom for each individual in a pluralistic social environment that can accommodate a multitude of desires, needs, and visions, but it also secures the greatest possible efficiency because there is no conflict between the rulers and those who are ruled, as in hierarchic organizations. Here we may recognize an affinity between this anarchist Utopia and the dream of a classless society in traditional Marxism.

But in Marxism, this goal is put off until after the revolution. According to traditional Marxists, we must first conquer the power of the state, and to do this, we need a centralized, elite party that can lead the masses and can establish the dictatorship of the proletariat. This line of argument was rejected by the anarchists, who held that the class system is kept in place by such methods; if the revolutionary movement uses these methods, it has been defeated before the battle has even started.

The anarchist concept of class differs from that of traditional Marxism. More basic than the distinction between those who own the means of production and those who own only their ability to work, according to the anarchists, is the distinction between the rulers and the ruled, between master and slave. *This* is the distinction that the anarchists primarily struggled against. Thus, the anarchists did not think that a 'transitional period' consisting of a dictatorial party state would lead to anything more than a new class society. If a genuine change in societal conditions is to be achieved, it must be based on the self-organization and action of the masses.

The nineteenth century was the main period of anarchism. Since the 1890s, anarchism as a political movement has played an important role only in Spain until the civil war in the 1930s, and in France. Today, some 'anarchist' ideas are incorporated in the 'alternative society' movement.

Syndicat is the French word for 'trade union'. Syndicalism arose in France at the beginning of the twentieth century. At that time, there was much dissatisfaction with the established labour organizations among certain workers, who turned to new forms of action. The critique was especially directed towards the socialist parties. From the point of view of the syndicalists, these parties did not distinguish themselves at all from the traditional conservative and liberal parties, but merely competed with them for the workers' support; but this did not remove the feeling of impotence that the masses felt in the political arena. The masses had become merely spectators, not political participants. The syndicalists also claimed that these socialist parties sought the support of the workers on the basis of ideas that often had little or no connection with the everyday conditions of the workers, and this caused more division than unity among the working class.

Against such a political backdrop, the syndicalists favoured direct economic action based on solidarity with the workers in their daily life. Syndicalism is a *theory of class struggle*. The syndicalist movement thus saw itself as emerging from the daily struggle of the industrial workers, firmly based on the factory floor, and challenging all authorities that denied the workers the right to govern themselves. The syndicalists supported extremely militant forms of action. These methods were an expression of the rejection, in principle, of government by the bourgeoisie. In their political practice, the syndicalists intend to break with the 'rule of the bourgeoisie', that is, with all legal political action.

The local factory trade union was considered to be the basic organizational unit in the struggle. The goal of the trade union, at factory level, should not be to enter into agreements with the management. Negotiations, agreements, and contracts were all viewed as bargaining and compromise within the framework established by capitalism. If the class struggle was to smash this framework, the workers had to develop their own, revolutionary form. *Externally*, this meant an uncompromising class struggle against the established power structures; *internally*, it meant organizing on the basis of a local self-rule that took its initiative from the grass roots. By organizing ourselves as we do, said the syndicalists, we are building the structure of a new society within the shell of the old.

The decline of syndicalism – today we can hardly talk about a syndicalist movement at all – seems to have been mainly caused by the difficulty of reconciling a revolutionary attitude with the struggle for the interests of the labour force within capitalist society.

SOCIAL DEMOCRACY – SOCIAL WELFARE AND PARLIAMENTARISM

Social democracy comprises a core of political opinions and attitudes drawn from different ideological backgrounds. Hence, it is not an unambiguous ideology, but represents a political programme that makes a priority of social equality and security, that is based on representative democracy, and that views public governance as a central political means.

This political movement has drawn on the same indignation that Marx and others felt at the systematic exploitation of workers under private capitalism. However, the social democrats distinguish themselves from the Marxists in both their means and the ends they wish to achieve. The social democrats support reform, not revolution. And they accept the parliamentary system and the liberal rule of law. By means of political and economic reforms, and by gaining power in parliament, they aim to achieve the welfare state. This will not create a completely classless society, but a good society, where no one is in need and where the economy is guided by governmental control. Not all economic activities need to be nationalized. How much to nationalize is a practical question. The social democrats support a mixed economy in which the state determines the limits of the market, and the state may own certain key businesses, although a major portion of the business activity remains privately owned.

In brief, the social democrats are characterized by political pragmatism. They want to do something here and now in order to improve the situation. They are sceptical of Marx's scientific socialism. This scepticism with regard to theory is, in many ways, theoretically based: reality is too complex and fluctuating to be grasped adequately by means of theoretical constructs. Problems of governance, bureaucracy and administration, education, and technology cannot be overcome by reference to a rigid ideology.

As a pragmatic movement, without an unambiguous ideology, social democracy has taken on slightly different forms at different times, in different countries. In Britain, social democracy emerged out of social liberalism, through the Fabian Society, founded in 1884: the British Labour Party, like the British labour movement, has shown little interest in Marx's materialistic conception of history. Pragmatism has held sway.

In Germany, social democracy arose more as a conscious opposition to Marxism. There, social democrats rejected both Marx's theory of unavoidable class conflict and revolution, and Lenin's theory of the party and the state. For example, Eduard Bernstein rejected Marx's theory of impoverishment and supported gradual reforms, enacted by parliament, in order to achieve concrete results within the existing system. He assumed that *real progress* would be made through the democratic parliamentarian system rather than by supporting class struggle and revolution.

The social democrats were, of course, clearly opposed to private capitalism. But after World War II, this changed. Capitalism became more favourable to governmental intervention (such as schools that train efficient and inexpensive labour forces, hospitals, social welfare, etc.) in order to 'pave the way' for business enterprise. Furthermore, modern capitalism favoured the increasing material welfare of large groups of the population. As a result, close cooperation between social democracy and modern capitalism often developed. The class struggle was apparently over. Both the trade unions and the capitalists had a common interest in increasing production. The only sore point seemed to be the specific distribution of the consumption and the extent and nature of governmental intervention.

We could say that as long as the social democrats were opposing private capitalism, the problems were relatively easy to see. The pragmatism embodied by the social democrats was an area of strength. But the problems connected with the new capitalism were not always as simple. Analysis was often needed in order to understand the problems. In this sense, this pragmatism might be a hindrance. On the other hand, it is claimed that the complexities of modern society are beyond the ability of traditional political theories to grasp, and, thus, pragmatism is the simplest and most realistic approach. The problem, of course, is the question of what theory offers the most adequate analysis of social and political reality. The questions of what this reality is, and what we want to achieve, and how we are to achieve it must be continually tested in a mutual interplay of theoretical activity and practical experience. (Note the connection between the social democrats' pragmatically testing approach and Popper's critique of totalitarianism and his theory of 'piecemeal social engineering', Ch. 26.)

FASCISM – NATIONALISM AND ORDER

The term *fascism* is used either in a narrow sense to refer to Italian fascism under Benito Mussolini (1883–1945) (as opposed to German Nazism), or in a broad sense, to refer generally to Italian fascism, German Nazism, and other related forms of government and ideologies.[1] Italian fascism and German Nazism were dominant movements in the interwar years and during World War II. Many reasons have been given for the emergence of fascism during this time;[2] for example, the harsh peace terms after World War I and the economic crises between the two World Wars.

Today, as we look back at the Hitler regime, it may be difficult to understand how so many people could have followed the fascists. But in the period between the two World Wars, fascism seemed to show a different face to many people. The economic and political systems were in chaos. In Germany and Italy, the democratic governments were weak. People were demanding order, and calling for strong-willed and powerful rulers to put an end to the turmoil. In the same way, a vigorous and viable idealism was needed to sweep away the unhealthy decadence that had tightened its grip. The workers needed work and better living conditions. In Germany and Italy there was a demand for compensation because of the losses suffered in World War I; and these countries were also demanding territorial expansion, *Lebensraum*. Britain and France were 'saturated' with colonies; now it was the underprivileged countries' turn. A strong nationalism, and an efficient and authoritarian government seemed, to many, to be the best way out of the impasse. The fascists, therefore, opposed both what they saw as the decadent liberals and impotent democrats, and international communism and socialism. And, initially, the fascists provided a certain sense of national self-confidence, as well as social welfare. 'Order' was achieved, although the methods were harsh and often violent.

This is roughly how fascism, including Nazism, appeared to many people between the two World Wars, especially in Germany and Italy, where the national wounds were the most painful and where the democratic tradition was weak. Fascism, however, may be understood in many ways: from the perspective of liberalism, fascism might represent a moral reversion to barbarism and absolutism. From the perspective of Marxism, fascism might represent a crisis in capitalism

– the capitalists had attempted to stabilize their tottering institutions through terror and violence. From the perspective of conservatism, fascism might be seen as the drastic expression of a culture that is out of balance – the people were following false prophets because the genuine community and the true authority (both represented by religion) had been lost.

It is difficult to draw up a list of defining features of the fascist movements. But the following characteristics are probably central to what is commonly called fascism:

1   Government-controlled corporatism, with repression of both unbridled liberalism and the trade unions.
2   A focus on common interests, not personal interests and class struggle, which were viewed as disintegrating tendencies in society.
3   Political mobilization of the masses and a rejection of parliamentarism.
4   Ambivalent attitudes both to capitalism and the very rich bourgeoisie, and to socialism and communism: on the one hand, the fascists did not reform the capitalist ownership conditions, but, on the other hand, they largely supported a planned economy under governmental direction; on the one hand, the fascists opposed class struggle, but, on the other hand, they supported political mobilization of the masses and a certain degree of social distribution.
5   A national crisis movement, in response to economic and political problems in the national state and in the local community, and often having social anchorings in the urban middle class and hard-hit rural communities.
6   Nostalgia for the pre-capitalist (pre-industrial) society, which took the form of romanticization both of the distant past (Teutonic Middle Ages, the Roman Empire) and of agricultural society.

However, in discussion of fascism (or Nazism) as an ideology, it is necessary to distinguish between theories expressed in the writings of prominent fascists, such as *Mein Kampf* by Hitler, and the opinions that emerge when we examine what the fascists actually did. Thus, we must distinguish between what the leading fascists *said* and what they *did*. Furthermore, it may be helpful to distinguish between strategic and theoretic elements in fascist ideology. And, finally, it may be important to distinguish between the ideology of the leading fascists and that of the 'common fascists'. These distinctions are important in all treatments of ideology, not only fascist ideology. Hence, the sources are different for the various types of ideology: for the official or prominent ideology, we can read fascist literature; for the ideology implicit in actions and that expressed by the 'common fascists', we can make use of a more empirically oriented investigation. The presentation of ideologies will vary depending on whether we assume one or another meaning of the term *ideology*. In the following discussion, when we refer to ideology as 'written theory', it is in many ways appropriate to talk about the irrationalism connected with fascism. But in the sense of 'written strategy', or 'opinion based on what they did', it may, on the contrary, be correct to emphasize a certain degree of rationalism: for instance, the fascists were skilled in making use of mass psychology. Furthermore, the beliefs of the common members and sympathizers certainly did not have to be identical with the theories of the leading fascists.

CRISIS AND ACTION

Intellectually, fascist and Nazi ideology (*qua* 'written theories as expressed by leading fascists') is not very satisfying. Both ideologies are in many ways irrationalist. Mussolini praised myths and action, and despised theory: fascism was to be built on an idealistic myth of Italy as the heir of ancient Rome, and fascism was to strengthen and unite the people through emotional ties, such as the willingness to make sacrifices and submit to discipline, so that the fascist rulers could create order and expand the Italian empire with a firm hand. Hitler also praised myth and action and disdained theory: the Nazis thought 'with their blood'. The 'Aryan' race was the supreme race, and this German myth, embodied in Nazism and the *Führer*, Adolf Hitler, offered the German people an opportunity to unite under his strong and cogent leadership. If the people were willing to make sacrifices and submit to discipline, he could restore to Germany the dominant place in history that belonged to the Aryan race.

Italian fascism and German Nazism may thus be said to be irrationalist in a double sense. Not only did the fascists claim that the world is governed by irrational forces (one kind of irrationalism), but they also maintained an irrational attitude towards the world (another form of irrationalism). Many might agree that much that happens in the world is irrational in some way. But the fascists were also irrationalist in the sense that they deliberately sought a solution to problems through myths rather than reason.

The Frenchman Georges Sorel (1847–1922) – a syndicalist advocate of the general strike – emphasized the importance of the emotional *myth* as a driving force for resolute political action: direct action and myth, this is the core of Sorel's message. Mussolini, among others, studied this message carefully.

As a possible socio-psychological explanation of certain features of fascism, we could perhaps say that when we lose control of a situation that seems overly complex, it may be tempting to react with a combination of black magic and aggressive action. This simple model is one that we may perhaps, with a certain justification, apply to fascism: fascism, in this sense, may be viewed as a kind of political spasm. We lose control and the reaction is panic.

What we have said here is *not* meant to be an historical explanation of Nazism (fascism), but only to serve as a model of links among some of the ideas and attitudes that comprised fascism (both in Germany and in Italy). But if we pursue this model of fascism as panic in a complex crisis, we may understand how fascism became action-oriented and myth-cultivating, and, at the same time, anti-intellectual. But this point of the irrationalism in fascism must be analysed further. In the *short* term, Hitler and Mussolini managed to accomplish much. They were able to unite their nations and reduce unemployment and social chaos. Therefore, the recourse to myth and action may even seem rational. We can almost see fascism as a kind of short-term pragmatism in a crisis.

In a fascist (Nazi) nation, the economy and society in general are in a virtual 'state of war' even during peacetime. Discipline and order are imposed. Thinking that may sow the seeds of doubt is eliminated. Self-interest is subordinated to the common interest. (But who determines what the common interest is?) To a great degree, problems are solved through commands and power. Business is brought under state control with price freezing, wage freezing, and abolition of strikes; at the same time, employment levels are high and the ownership of the means of production remains in private hands.

POLITICS AND ECONOMY

We have used a simple socio-psychological model to detect a kind of consistency in fascism as ideology. However, some analysts have looked for a connection between capitalism and fascism: the fascists were supported by the lower-middle class,[3] who feared the proletariat, and eventually received support from the world of high finance, which feared communism, and which tended to support right-wing parties, such as the fascists, when they came to power. But the earlier supporters of fascism were often anti-capitalist – something that does not conflict with the view that fascism resulted from a crisis within capitalism *as a system*; but it weakens the view that the fascists were capitalists, ideologically or professionally.

Furthermore, it is not correct to *identify* fascism with capitalism – as when it is claimed that fascism began at the same time as capitalism, and that it survives today, as in the United States and Europe. This is just as problematic as deploring fascism as an outbreak of certain eternal and ahistorical forms of human evil. Both are inadequate theories if we maintain that fascism is a government-led reaction to an acute crisis in private capitalism. Defined in this way, fascism is limited to the period between World Wars I and II, or to a society that finds itself in the same economic situation as the European countries between the World Wars: capitalism in chaos, as opposed to an organized capitalism; and capitalism that was largely national, as opposed to today's international capitalism.

If we disregard these features of fascism that were defined by history, we are thinking ahistorically, and we end up with a definition of fascism that is so broad that it might easily be useless – not the least because, by defining it in this way, we are probably no longer talking about what is usually meant by fascism.

Here, we are touching on the problem of what social phenomena really *are*, about what form of existence they have. Is a social phenomenon, such as fascism, a unique event that can be understood only in light of complex socio-historical conditions, or is a social phenomenon something that is relatively well-defined and unchangeable (as in psychological properties such as aggression and contempt for the weak), that recurs in different contexts? According to the former view, it is basically meaningless to ask whether or not Plato was a fascist, or whether or not the former Soviet Union and communist Albania were fascist states. According to the latter view, we may ask such questions, and find the answer by empirical research. Different views of what social phenomena really *are*, are thus connected with different views of what social research can and should be.

A leading ideologist of Italian fascism was the well-known philosopher Giovanni Gentile (1875–1944), who became a government minister under Mussolini. Gentile emphasized the state as a superior principle. Among the philosophical fathers of Italian fascism we also find the French-Italian Vilfredo Pareto (1848–1923), who held that *elite groups* rule in all societies. We may exchange one elite group for another, but we will always find that the rulers are an elite. Whether the government is a democracy or a dictatorship, an elite always rules the masses. Thus, all forms of government are equally viable as far as the masses are concerned. Pareto's theory may be applied to both the parliamentarian form of government, with elections and representation, and the Leninist party rule, with democratic centralism. His theory formed a part of the fascist mindset: if an elite invariably rules, let it be a nationalist or a socially unifying group; society should be ordered hierarchically with a leader or a council of superior people at the top.

Just as it is unreasonable to identify fascism with capitalism, it is also untenable to equate fascism with communism. However, both fascism and communism are based on a one-party system and reject the parliamentarian form of government, and both maintain a comprehensive control over the individual and suppress individual rights, such as freedom of religion, freedom of speech, freedom of opinion, etc. This limited comparison is largely correct; both systems are totalitarian in this sense. (See Hannah Arendt, Ch. 27.) But that does not mean that they are identical.

THE STATE AND RACISM

When we consider fascism from an ethical viewpoint, it is important to distinguish between Italian fascism and German Nazism. The latter was racist in a way that Italian fascism was not. In Nazism, the *race*, the people, was primary. For the Italian fascists, it was the *state*. There are Hegelian features in Italian fascism: the state, as an idea, stood above all else. But the fascist cultivation of the state was collectivistic and suppressed the individual. The Nazis placed the people ahead of the state. In a way, the Nazis were vulgar Darwinians, but not Hegelians.[4]

This distinction between Italian state fascism and German racial fascism is important. If our opponent is so because of race, there can be no rehabilitation, or reconciliation. The opponent and his family must be liquidated. The systematic extermination of the Jews was a 'logical' consequence. This was an implication of German racial fascism, but not of Italian state fascism. Since Hegel is sometimes blamed for the Nazi perversions, we should remember that it was in Italy, not in Germany, that a certain vulgar Hegelianism formed a part of fascist theory. Moreover, we note that the fascist cultivation of irrationalism contrasted with Hegel's demand for reason. Correspondingly, the fascist cultivation of the great leader, the *Führer* who decides what is true or right, stands in opposition to Hegel, who claimed that truth and right are found within the historical process, and are not defined arbitrarily by one individual. According to Hegel, the state was to rule constitutionally, not according to *one* person's whims. Hegel thus stood in opposition, in several ways, to both Italian and German fascism.[5]

The contradictions *within* fascism were many. The Nazis had a racist-communal view: the community, or the race, stands above the individual. Therefore, the individual must be sacrificed when it serves the community. But, *at the same time*, the Nazis cultivated the heroes, the great leaders. The Nazis praised the community, the race, above the individual with his or her subjective and confusing wishes. But they also exalted the *Führer*, who was called to rule the thoughtless masses with an iron hand. They praised the people above the individual, and the *Führer* above the masses.

QUESTIONS

Discuss different interpretations of the word 'ideology'. Take communism and fascism as a point of departure.

Discuss the different roles of the state in, for instance, Aristotle, Augustine, and Lenin.

SUGGESTIONS FOR FURTHER READING

PRIMARY LITERATURE

Engels, F., *Dialectics of Nature*, New York, 1940.
Engels, F., *Selected Writings*, Harmondsworth, 1967.
Hitler, A., *Mein Kampf*, translated by Ralph Mannheim, Boston, 1971.
Lenin, V. I., *Selected Works*, London, 1969.
Mussolini, B., *Fascism: Doctrine and Institutions*, New York, 1965.

SECONDARY LITERATURE

Marcuse, H., *Soviet Marxism. A Critical Analysis.*, New York, 1961.
Nolte, Ernst, *Three Faces of Fascism*, London, 1971.

NOTES

1 The word *fascism* derives from the Latin *fasces*, 'bundle of rods tied around an axe' – an ancient Roman symbol of authority.

2 Cf. Hannah Arendt, *The Origins of Totalitarianism*, New York, 1979, and E. Nolte, *Three Faces of Fascism*, London, 1975.

3 Lipset, for instance, claimed that it was primarily the liberal middle class who voted for Hitler – the conservatives, the Roman Catholic centre, the socialists, and the communists maintained better order. S. M. Lipset, *Political Man*, London, 1963 (part 1, chap. 5).

4 Cf. Herbert Marcuse, *Reason and Revolution*, New York, 1941, on the relationship between Fascism and Hegel.

5 Within fascism there persisted a conflict between the adherents of the *Führer* principle and the adherents of the 'principle of responsibility'. There was thus no agreement among the fascists in regard to the sovereignty of the *Führer*.

23 Freud and psychoanalysis

Life. *Sigmund Freud (1856–1939) was born in Freiberg, now in the Czech Republic, but then in the Austro-Hungarian Empire. He studied medicine in Vienna, where he lived and worked until the Nazis annexed Austria in 1938. Freud, who was a Jew, then took refuge in London, where he died in 1939 after a long struggle against cancer. Freud's most famous works include:* The Interpretation of Dreams *(1912),* Introductory Lectures on Psychoanalysis *(1915–17),* Beyond the Pleasure Principle *(1920),* The Future of an Illusion *(1927),* Civilization and Its Discontents *(1929), and* Moses and Monotheism *(1939).*

PSYCHOANALYSIS: A NEW VIEW OF MAN

Today, Freud is remembered as the founder of *psychoanalysis*. For this, he is often ranked with Darwin, Marx, and Einstein.

In many ways, Freud turned our notion of man upside down. According to Descartes, Locke, and Kant, nature endowed us with *free will*. This ability to make free choices is ultimately the core of our personality and is connected with a conscious 'self'. Freud considered this view of our psyche to be an illusion. The conscious 'self' is only the outward aspect of a powerful, unconscious mental life.

In this way, Freud caused a revolution in our view of the subject. He wanted to show that our conscious mental life is only a small part of our total mental life. Our conscious processes are strictly determined by unconscious factors. The analogy of the iceberg has often been used to illustrate this relationship: everything that is conscious and can be recalled is like the tip of an iceberg rising above the sea, while large masses of ice (the unconscious) lie unseen under the water. The invisible masses determine the centre of gravity as well as the movement and course of the iceberg. The unconscious is thus the core of our personality.

In two important works from the beginning of the twentieth century, Freud emphasized the existence of unconscious mental processes in all human beings, and showed that psychoanalysis can reveal the unconscious causes of the phenomena of daily life. In *The Interpretation of Dreams* (1912), Freud emphasized that dreams have *meaning* and that they express unconscious desires that erupt into our consciousness in a distorted and perverted form. Through a complicated process of interpretation, it is possible to determine the content of the unconscious that is hidden in dreams. In *The Psychopathology of Everyday Life* (1901), Freud analysed the trivial 'faulty acts' of everyday life, such as slips of the tongue and lapses of memory. According to Freud, such phenomena are neither accidental nor meaningless, but are, in fact, expressions of unconscious motives and intentions. For example, we lose or forget something given to us by a person whom we no longer like.[1]

Already, here, we may note that psychoanalysis allows a new understanding of the human mind. It claims that behind our dreams, trivial mistakes, and jokes, as well as our neurotic symptoms, lie unconscious (often sexual) motives. In other words, Freud suspected that things which are meaningful in light of the subject's conscious intentions and motives may gain a new meaning through psychoanalytical exploration of the unconscious. Symptoms that are apparently incomprehensible or meaningless gain *meaning* when we view them as expressions of unconscious motives and intentions. We may therefore say that Freud introduced a 'hermeneutics of suspicion'.

Through his work with neurotic patients, Freud found that patients were themselves unaware of the unconscious matter. The unconscious is the individual's 'foreign country'. But it is only the patient who can lead the analyst to the unconscious causes of the neurotic symptoms. The point is again that symptoms have meaning, but neither the patient nor the doctor has an immediate knowledge of this meaning. Interpretation is necessary.

Freud's thesis was that sexual desires (of a troubling or forbidden character) can be transformed into other, and essentially different, phenomena such as apparently meaningless symptoms and dreams. But why are such desires repressed in the unconscious? Freud assumed that there were repressive mechanisms that consigned emotionally charged material to an area of our mind that is not directly accessible to the memory. The symptomatic material is a *trauma* (the Greek word meaning 'wound'). The original trauma may ultimately be traced back to early childhood. Through a unique method of discussion ('free association'), the patient and the analyst work together to reconstruct the trauma. The therapeutic goal of psychoanalysis is to recapture unconscious and repressed material and make it accessible to the ego.

THE DREAM AS A GATEWAY TO THE UNCONSCIOUS

The unconscious may be investigated in various ways. It may be studied by free association, but also by a deeper hermeneutic interpretation of dreams and errors. For Freud, the interpretation of dreams quickly took a central place: 'Interpretation of dreams is in fact the *via regia* to the interpretation of the unconscious, the surest ground of psychoanalysis and a field in which every worker must win his convictions and gain his education. If I were asked how one could become a psychoanalyst, I should answer, through the study of his own dreams.'[2] In *The Interpretation of Dreams*, Freud emphasized that the dream possesses an outer likeness to, and an inner relationship with, the psyche. On the other hand, it is completely compatible with health and normality. The dream may, in principle, be treated as a 'symptom'; but what is it a symptom of? Freud pointed out that small children always dream about the desires and pleasures awakened in them during the previous day ('the dream day'), but which were not satisfied. The dream thus represents a fulfilment of their desires. The dreams of adults also contain vestiges of the dream day, but are much more complicated. The dreams are often incomprehensible and apparently far removed from wish fulfilment (fearful dreams and nightmares). According to Freud, such dreams have undergone repression. When the dream is associated with anxiety, it has been formed with the purpose of fulfilling repressed and forbidden desires that the *ego* does not accept.

To understand dreams, we must distinguish between *manifest dream-content* and *latent dream-thoughts*. Manifest dream-content is what we can remember when we wake up. Latent dream-thoughts are found on the unconscious level or on 'another stage', according to Freud. The manifest dream-content is the replacement through repression of unconscious dream thoughts. Repression is the result of mental defence mechanisms. When we are awake, these mechanisms prevent the unconscious and repressed desires from forcing their way into our consciousness. While we are asleep, such desires manage to slip through in a disguised state. Consequently, the dreamer is just as incapable of understanding the meaning of the dream as neurotic patients are of understanding the meaning of their own symptoms.

The dream as we remember it ('manifest content') is thus a *disguised* fulfilment of *repressed* wishes. Freud calls the process that distorts the unconscious dream thoughts the 'dream-work'. In many ways, this activity is identical with the process of repression that transforms the unconscious urges into neurotic symptoms when the repression has not succeeded. The dream-work makes use of condensation, displacement, dramatization, and symbolism. In addition, there is the secondary dream-work. The unconscious thus makes use of 'artistic' means. We are all artists in our dreams.

Condensation, for example, causes an occurrence in the dream (as recalled) to represent several different wishes. Displacement is a process by which a person or an event that is important to us is expressed in the dream as an unimportant memory or as a person or an event that we do not know. Something similar may occur when a dream of completely trivial content is associated with anxiety or strong emotions. Here, condensation and displacement have done their work, and we must use free association to reach the unconscious content. In the same way, symbolism is a variation of distortion. For example, the male genitalia may be replaced by objects having a similar shape, like canes, umbrellas, knives, and revolvers. The female genitalia are symbolically represented by objects that surround a hollow space and that can hold other objects (such as caves, boxes, rooms, houses, etc.). Secondary dream-work is derived from our attempt to describe the dream in a way that satisfies the demand for logical consistency. According to Freud, the (manifest) dream contains many different (and contradictory) elements. It can thus be said to be overdetermined. In the same way, various causal chains and factors overdetermine psychological symptoms.

Freud claimed later that the latent dream-thought is *censored*. To simplify, we can say that repressed and forbidden wishes must find their way past 'the censor' to become conscious. The dream-work transforms the latent dream-thoughts into a manifest dream-content in order to avoid censorship. The dream, as we remember it, contains a secret message that has been encoded. We can look at the manifest dream-content as a rebus to be deciphered. It is only when the analyst breaks the code that the dream reveals a new meaning. And what is this secret meaning? According to Freud, the dreams of adults are often sexually oriented; they express erotic desires. (This conclusion became problematic when Freud later discovered a unique aggressive or death instinct.)

We can summarize Freud's conclusions in *The Interpretation of Dreams* in five points:

1   The distinction between latent dream-thoughts and manifest dream-content is the key to understanding the meaning of the dream.
2   The manifest dream-content is a distortion of the latent dream-thought, that is to say, the product of the dream-work.
3   Free association may be used to analyse dreams as well as neurotic symptoms.
4   Dream interpretation suggests a general psychological model that may give us a richer picture of the human mental state.
5   The attempt to decipher dreams leads to an understanding of how the unconscious functions in accordance with certain 'grammatical' rules; that is, the unconscious is structured like a 'language' (cf. the dream as a rebus).

FREUD'S THEORY OF SEXUALITY

We have already emphasized the central role of sexuality in the psychoanalytical conception of man. Freud elaborated this theme in *Three Contributions to the Theory of Sex* (1905). This work leads us into the background of the process of distortion and to the source of the emotional energy that, according to Freud, forms the basis of our instincts and behaviour. This energy was later called the *libido*. This treatise also offered the first outline of a theory of infantile sexuality and sexual deviation. Freud's most important theses are the following:

1   Sexuality does not start with puberty, but is expressed fairly soon after birth.
2   It is necessary to make a sharp distinction between the concepts 'sexual' and 'genital'. The former is broader and comprises many activities which have nothing to do with the sexual organs.

Freud's theory of infantile sexuality met with great resistance, but it helped to revolutionize his generation's view of sexuality. It did not lessen his notoriety when Freud claimed to show a connection between child sexuality and adult 'perversions'.

According to Freud, the mouth is the first organ to be associated with pleasurable emotion. The infant begins to seek a satisfaction that is independent of its need of nutrition. Thus, this activity may be called *sexual*. The oral stage is then followed by the anal stage and the phallic stage. The *Oedipus complex* becomes especially important in the phallic phase (in Greek myth, King Oedipus unknowingly killed his father and married his own mother). Freud observed that a boy at this age (about three to five years old) starts to develop sexual desires for his mother and view his father as a threatening rival ('castration anxiety'). The Oedipus conflict is often resolved as the boy gradually identifies himself with his father and begins to assume his father's values and points of view (the formation of the 'superego'). Girls were supposed to be affected by a corresponding *Electra complex*.

For various reasons, the individual may become *fixated* on one of the infantile stages. In some cases, emotional and psychosexual development beyond this stage may be blocked (cf. 'anal' personality traits). Adults may also return to an earlier stage of development. Freud called this *regression*. Sexual deviation, according to Freud, may be understood as a fixation on sexual objects of a different kind than what is 'normal' for an adult. Because the perversions have their prototypes in the child's various sexual objects, Freud characterized child sexuality as 'polymorphous perversion' (characterized by multiple deviations). Consequently, adult 'perversions' are related to the diverse sexual activities of childhood.

THE MENTAL APPARATUS

Freud's theory of the mental apparatus is often difficult to understand for several reasons. First, during the different phases of the development of psychoanalysis, Freud changed and expanded his views of the human psyche. Although he tried to integrate the different perspectives, there remain many loose ends in his work. Secondly, Freud's physiological and vividly anthropomorphic terminology is ambiguous. When he says that 'the poor *ego*' must serve 'three tyrannical masters' (the *external world*, the *id*, and the *superego*), we may easily see that he objectified or personified mental functions.

Freud's first 'topographical model' (map of the psyche) distinguished between three areas of mental life. To simplify, we can say that the mental apparatus is spatial and is divided into three provinces: the unconscious, the preconscious, and the conscious. Consciousness may be characterized as everything that we are immediately aware of. Preconsciousness is the area for everything that we can reproduce or remember. Freud reserved the designation 'unconscious' for the mental processes that do not reach the consciousness easily.

In *Introductory Lectures on Psychoanalysis* (1915–17), Freud drew an analogy that may perhaps be more enlightening: a guest is in a large hallway (the unconscious) and wishes to enter the salon (the preconscious). But in the doorway between those two rooms there is a doorkeeper (the censor) who monitors the guests. If the doorkeeper does not like the guest, the guest is turned away, or *repressed*. Even if the guest manages to get into the salon, it is not certain that the host (the consciousness) will notice the guest right away. This corresponds to the notion that the ideas in the preconsciousness are not conscious, but that they may become conscious. In order for the ideas in the unconsciousness to become conscious, they must first gain admittance to the salon, or the preconsciousness. If a guest is turned away, the guest may later appear in a new disguise (cf. 'dream-work'). Then the guest may gain admittance to the party as a 'symptom', and the host may not recognize the guest's true identity. In this analogy, the doorkeeper corresponds to the individual's *resistance* to making that which is unconscious, conscious. When the doorkeeper becomes tired (or the individual sleeps), it becomes easier to enter in disguise (the manifest dream). We also see that the entire process of repression may occur without the host's being aware of it.

After 1920, Freud changed the topographical model and introduced the terms *id*, *superego*, and *ego*, which have met with great resistance from both other psychoanalysts (such as Jacques Lacan) and philosophers of science. Karl R. Popper scoffed that Freud's three-leaf clover has as little scientific status as Homer's myths of Mount Olympus.

We choose to interpret Freud's understanding of the mental apparatus as a *metapsychological* viewpoint. This tells us something about the perspective from which he studied man, and is an attempt to find a conceptual framework for the phenomena that he discovered in his clinical practice. In epistemological terms, we may say that the metapsychological framework is central to the research programme of psychoanalysis. It is in light of his theories of the mental apparatus, mental energy, and instinct that Freud tried to explain why rational arguments are impotent against irrational fear and obsessive actions. Thus, to elucidate the conflicts that exist between our instincts, our relationship to the external world, and our conscience ('inner voice'), he constructed a model of our mental life (id, ego, and superego). It is obvious that Freud here is stretching the border between fictions, concepts, and entities. Here is how he presents his view of our mental life: 'The hypothesis we have adopted of a psychical apparatus extended in space, expediently put together, developed by the exigencies of life, which gives rise to the phenomena of consciousness only at one particular point and under certain conditions – this hypothesis has put us in a position to establish psychology on foundations similar to those of any other science, such as physics.'[3] Apparently, Freud viewed psycho-analysis as being analogous to physics. This is connected with some of his basic meta-psychological presuppositions. He understood the mental life as being determined by mental forces and mental energy. Therefore, he can claim that psychoanalysis is a natural science.

Mental forces and mental energy can be found in the id, which is the oldest of the mental spheres. It contains the mental aspects of our instincts. Therefore, Freud compared the id to 'a kettle full of boiling excitement'. Our instincts are seeking to satisfy our needs. They obey the so-called *pleasure principle*. There are also other functions connected to the id that drive us. These stem from previous experiences that have been repressed. Freud spoke of 'memories' of ideas, actions, and feelings that are excluded from the consciousness, but which still drive us. These functions operate without logical organization; they are alogical. Yet, they still manage to force their way into our consciousness: they drive us to action, they make us depressed, or they result in dreams and fantasies without our understanding why and how. The unconscious is thus the supreme mental quality of the id.

The most important insight of psychoanalysis is that the processes of the uncon-scious or id follow other 'laws' than those that govern our conscious life. Freud called these laws *primary processes*. In our discussion of the dream-work, we pointed out a series of remarkable and intricate features in the processes found in the uncon-scious. Opposites are, for example, treated as being identical. The unconscious seems to be structured as a 'language', although it has different rules than our every-day language.

The id has a unique development due to the influence of the external world. A certain mental territory develops as a link between the id and the external world. This area of the mental life is what Freud called the ego. The ego's most import-ant task is that of self-preservation. In addition, it ensures that the satisfaction of needs occurs in a safe way. The ego makes decisions in regard to the postponement or suppression of the demands of the instincts. The ego obeys the *principle of reality*. Consequently, it must mediate between the demands of the id and of the external world. As long as the ego is weak and underdeveloped, it does not always manage to master the tasks that it will later need to perform without difficulty. The demands of our instincts and the demands of the external world may then result in *trauma*. The helpless ego defends itself by means of repression, which may later prove to be inexpedient. The ego is aided by the superego in this repression.

Freud was often struck by the fact that patients may view themselves as objects and may thus assume a critical and judgemental attitude towards themselves. He surmised that this reflective ability was developed at a later stage than the other abilities of the ego. This occurs gradually in children through the effects of socialization. The superego is a result of the unconscious *internalization* of the parents' norms and ideals. In a slightly broader sense, society and tradition exercise their moral authority through what we call 'conscience'. The superego can be said to observe the ego, make its recommendations, and threaten punishment. The superego requires that the ego give an account not only of its actions, but also of its thoughts and wishes. Consequently, the superego is the third force that the ego must reckon with. Freud's theory of conscience rejects the possibility of an innate or absolute notion of right and wrong. As an extension of his theory of conscience, Freud drew the conclusion that the idea of God is a projection of the child's relationship to the father.

In several places, Freud characterized dreams as a psychosis with illusions and unreasonable features. During sleep, the ego is weakened and other forces take over. A similar condition forms the basis of a series of illnesses. A disturbance in the functions of the mental apparatus finds its expression in neuroses and psychoses. The ego's relationship to reality is disturbed and partially abolished. This insight forms the background for the therapeutic goal of psychoanalysis: 'The analytic physician and the patient's weakened ego, basing themselves on the real external world, have to band themselves together into a party against the enemies, the instinctual demands of the id and the conscientious demands of the super-ego.'[4] Perhaps in this connection we may note a certain similarity between the therapeutic goal of psychoanalysis and Nietzsche's theory of the *Übermensch*: for both Freud and Nietzsche, it is a matter of overcoming the conflict between conventional hypermorality and the demands of the instincts; Nietzsche's *Übermensch* has overcome the self in the same way as the neurotic person after successful psychoanalytical therapy.

In later works, Freud distinguished between a life instinct (Eros) and a death instinct (Thanatos), pointing out that the idea of two basic instincts was already known in Greek philosophy (cf. Empedocles). Freud's idea of a unique death instinct met with great resistance in psychoanalytical circles and is still quite controversial. By introducing the death instinct, Freud hoped to clarify such phenomena as aggression and war, but he also emphasized that an excessive element of sexual aggression can turn the lover into a murderer. The aggression may also be internalized and become self-destructive.

REPRESSIVE CULTURE AND FEELINGS OF GUILT

In the period between World Wars I and II, Freud became increasingly interested in the critique of culture and civilization going on at the time. On both the Left and the Right, the decline and fall of Western culture was proclaimed. Freud's interest was concentrated on the psychological causes of these highly critical attitudes towards modern culture. He was especially concerned with 'the social sources of suffering'; that is, with culture as a possible cause of suffering and misery: 'It seems to be certain that our present-day civilization does not inspire in us a feeling of well-being'.[5] This thesis may seem surprising. It is a fact that scientific and technical achievements have given us power over natural forces; medical research has prolonged our lives and made life easier. Still, Freud emphasized that such progress is not the only condition of human happiness. The price we pay for progress is suppression of our instincts and an increase in individual feelings of guilt. This is the background of our discontent with civilization, according to Freud.

Freud was, of course, aware that culture protects us against nature and that it regulates relationships among unruly individuals. To understand his thesis, we must understand how he imagined the origin of civilization. According to Freud, the individual's freedom was greatest before civilization existed, even though this 'wild freedom' was almost worthless because the individual could not defend it (cf. the state of nature in Thomas Hobbes' thought [Ch. 8]). The first limitations of freedom came along with civilization. Thus, an opposition arose between individual freedom and civilized restraints.

This conflict is important for our understanding of the changes in human instincts. To some degree, all society must be based on a renunciation of our instincts. This is confirmed already in the first taboos. Among other things, there was a prohibition of incest (in a broad sense) as a source of sexual gratification. Custom set new limits on what is permitted. Most nongenital forms of satisfaction were forbidden as perverse. Freud characterized this process as 'the most maiming wound ever inflicted throughout the ages on the erotic life of man'.[6] Consequently, he concluded that the sexual life of the 'cultured' human being has suffered, and its importance as a source of happiness has been greatly reduced. At the same time, civilization derives its energy from suppressed sexuality. Sexual needs become desexualized and are fulfilled in other ways. Freud called this process *sublimation*. The supreme products within art and science are a result of the sublimation of instincts (cf. the Platonic Eros). In a certain sense, Eros was thus sacrificed on the altar of culture.

But Eros is not the only force in human life. According to Freud, human aggression holds a central place in the driving force of instincts. When restraints are removed, human beings reveal themselves to be wild animals. Culture is thus forced to make a vigorous effort and mobilize all of its resources in order to limit human destructiveness. The results in this area have been rather modest. It is apparently not easy for human beings to restrain their aggressiveness. Culture tries to channel the aggression towards external and internal enemies, but this often creates horrible suffering in modern civilization.

Against the background of these limitations of our sexual life and aggressiveness, Freud thought that he had clarified some of the causes of discontent in civilization. Thus, we have come to his critique of culture:

> In rightly finding fault, as we thus do, with our present state of civilization for so inadequately providing us with what we require to make us happy in life, and for the amount of suffering of a probably avoidable nature it lays us open to – in doing our utmost to lay bare the roots of its deficiencies by our unsparing criticisms, we are

undoubtedly exercising our just rights and not showing ourselves enemies of culture. We may expect that in the course of time changes will be carried out in our civilization so that it becomes more satisfying to our needs and no longer open to the reproaches we have made against it. But perhaps we shall also accustom ourselves to the idea that there are certain difficulties inherent in the very nature of culture which will not yield to any efforts at reform.[7]

As we have seen, Freud discovered a death instinct (Thanatos) in addition to Eros. The death instinct strives to disintegrate the living organism and lead it back to its original, inorganic state. It is not always easy to understand how this instinct works. Freud held that a part of this instinct turns against the external world and appears as aggressive and destructive actions. The restraint of the extroverted aggression increases the self-destructive activity that is always present. Thanatos may also be 'mixed' with Eros. An example of this is sadism, while masochism may illustrate the connection between introverted, destructive instincts and sexuality.

Freud thus held that man has an innate need for 'evil', for aggression and brutality. Aggression is an original and independent instinct in all human beings. Human aggression resists the attempt by culture to create peace and harmony among human beings: 'The natural instinct of aggressiveness in man, the hostility of each one against all and of all against each one, opposes this program of civilization.'[8] We may ask what other methods culture uses to inhibit aggression. We may best understand this by looking at the developmental history of the individual. What happens to an individual when the normal aggression instinct is curbed? As we have mentioned, the aggression is then turned inward, that is, against the ego. Aggression is put to use by the superego. As a kind of 'conscience', the superego threatens the ego with aggression. The struggle takes place *within* the individual. Freud calls the tension between the superego and the submissive ego, *the feeling of guilt*. It expresses itself as a need for punishment. Culture thus conquers the individual's aggressive instinct by setting up a mental apparatus that watches over the dangerous aggressive instinct.

In line with this, Freud rejected the idea of an original ability to distinguish between good and evil. Evil may sometimes even be desirable and pleasurable. It is the superego that decides what is good and what is evil. The fear of the superego is what creates the feeling of guilt. Furthermore, we develop a need for punishment because we cannot hide our forbidden wishes from the superego. Culture's attempt to prevent the satisfaction of our instincts results in an increasing feeling of guilt with which the individual can hardly cope. Consequently, it is not without reason that Freud held that the feeling of guilt is the greatest problem in the development of culture.

This analysis permitted a new view of morality. The purpose of morality is to inhibit man's instinctual need for aggression. ('Thou shalt love thy neighbour as thyself.') The morality of society may thus be understood as culture's superego. Freud's thesis was now the following: just as those undergoing analytical therapy must often struggle against their superego and make it reduce its demands, we must critically evaluate the ethical demands that culture makes. Freud suggested that many societies become 'neurotic' under the pressure of culture and should undergo therapy (cf. his critical evaluation of the sexual morality of his day in *'Civilized' Sexual Morality and Modern Nervous Illness* [1908]).

For Freud, the decisive problem in regard to humanity's fate was linked to the question of how culture can control the human aggressive and destructive instincts: 'Men have brought their powers of subduing the forces of nature to such a pitch that by using them they could now very easily exterminate one another to the last man. They know this – hence arises a great part of their current unrest, their dejection, their mood of apprehension. And now it may be expected that the other of the two *heavenly forces*, eternal Eros, will put forth his strength so as to maintain himself alongside of his equally immortal adversary.'[9]

Freud's reconstruction of the cultural history of humanity has several features in common with the models we have found in the thought of Hobbes, Locke, and Rousseau. Similarly, his negative anthropology (pessimistic view of man) has many features in common with Luther, and not least with Hobbes' idea of 'everyone's fight against everyone else' and the thesis that 'a human being is like a wolf in regard to other human beings' (*homo homini lupus*). In several areas, Freud's psychoanalysis shed new light also on the problems of sociology, such as internalization and the psychological mechanisms of socialization.

Freud's philosophical position is problematic in several ways. In the diagnosis of his own times, he advocated a higher degree of sexual satisfaction in order to reduce neurotic suffering. On the other hand, he thought that the suppression of instinct was necessary for a civilized life. He seemed, in other words, to lack adequate criteria to determine the border between the satisfaction and the repression of instinct. This was the more difficult because Freud did not sufficiently distinguish between happiness and pleasure (hedonism). Nor does it seem that he was able to justify the ethics necessary to develop a *rational* cultural superego, that is to say, an ethics that can restrain an arbitrary and 'wild' freedom. In general, it is unclear what status ethical questions and ethical arguments had for Freud. His view of an original subjective freedom may seem to be an illusion from a sociological perspective (cf. Hegel's and Émile Durkheim's theories of the historical genesis of freedom). It may also well be that Freud exaggerated the repressive character of modern culture. Much of his criticism of the sexual morality of modern culture seems to be quite out of date. Freud also neglected the cultural criticism that stems from sociologists like Durkheim. Durkheim attempted to show that the crisis in modern culture is based on an increasing dissolution of standards for moral orientation. In other words, Freud had little understanding of the inner connection linking anomie (the breakdown of social norms), conflicts of conscience, and feelings of guilt.

PSYCHOANALYSIS AND THE PHILOSOPHY OF SCIENCE

The epistemological debate about psychoanalysis has concentrated on its scientific status and on the content and importance of basic concepts such as mental determinism, explanation, the unconscious, the id, the superego, etc.

There is great disagreement about whether psychoanalysis may be said to be a science. To some degree, the conflict may be traced back to the fact that there is no unambiguous concept of science.[10] At the same time, the demands that we make of a scientific or scholarly theory vary greatly within the different sciences and scholarly activities, such as physics, sociology, and comparative literature. In other words, it is meaningless to deny the scientific status of psychoanalysis because it does not fulfil the unique requirements of physics. Although some of its theses may show a certain similarity with Homeric myths, this is hardly a sufficient reason for rejecting psychoanalysis in its entirety.

We may say that Freud understood psychoanalysis as a group of statements, some of which describe observed facts, others of which formulate general hypotheses, and still others of which interpret the observed facts in light of the hypotheses. As we have seen, he presents psychoanalysis as a natural science with terms such as 'force' and 'energy'. In more recent epistemological debates, many have viewed this as a misunderstanding. The claim has been made that psychoanalysis is actually an interpretative, 'deeply hermeneutic' discipline.

Psychoanalysis rests on the basic premise that there is an unconscious mental life. How the borders should be drawn between the unconscious, the preconscious, and the conscious are, however, questions that Freud answered differently in different periods. One of the theory's cornerstones is the thesis that sexual instincts are present from the time of early childhood. We can say that certain theses are basic because they comprise the presuppositions for other theses. Freud's theses thus form a kind of hierarchy. The hypothesis of repression must therefore be situated at a more basic level in the theory than that of the Oedipus complex, because the notion of repression is used to explain the origin of the various complexes.

Freud apparently held that some hypotheses are based on observed facts (or are inductively derived from facts), others should be understood as 'guesses' or 'constructions' confirmed by observation, and still others function as useful working hypotheses. Freud himself called metapsychology a 'speculative superstructure'. From this perspective, we may formulate the basic epistemological question as follows: to what degree does psychoanalysis fulfil the general requirements of an empirical theory? Two such requirements may be stated as follows.

1   An empirical theory must be testable (verifiable or falsifiable).
2   An empirical theory must be fruitful.

The requirement that an empirical theory be verifiable was formulated by the logical positivists between the two World Wars. There is little reason to believe that Freud's theory satisfies this verification criterion. Nevertheless, several prominent logical positivists respected psychoanalysis as a science and did not consider its propositions meaningless metaphysics. Freud himself respected 'positivism'.[11] As late as the 1950s, psychoanalytical theories were apparently approved by logical positivism.[12]

Karl Popper was far more critical. The fact that the theories of Freud, Adler, and Jung were apparently *confirmed* by experience and had tremendous explanatory force was viewed, by Popper, not as the strength of psychoanalysis, but rather as its weakness.[13] Popper's argument may be formulated as follows: while scientific theories are incompatible with certain possible observational results ('facts') and consequently may be *falsified*, psychoanalysis is compatible with all facts about human behaviour. Thus, psychoanalysis cannot be falsified and is, therefore, unscientific. The possibility of falsification is thus the general criterion for whether an empirical theory is to be considered scientific. If psychoanalysis is considered to be a scientific theory, it must, in principle, be able to tell us what facts would falsify it. The apparent success of psychoanalysis is thus due to the fact that it lacks content. Therefore, many philosophers of science have claimed that its presuppositions and hypotheses are not falsifiable.[14] This reduces psychoanalysis to a pseudo-science.

To understand this line of reasoning, we can consider some examples. Let us assume that the psychoanalyst's hypothesis is that the patient suffers from an unresolved Oedipus complex; he unconsciously hates his father. If he is aggressive towards his father, such behaviour, of course, will confirm the diagnosis. But if he shows respect and love for his father, this may mean that an unconscious fear disguises his feelings of animosity. Whatever the patient does, the analyst's hypothesis is confirmed. Let us take another example along the same lines. The psychoanalyst proposes an interpretation of a dream. If the patient accepts the interpretation, this may be viewed as grounds for the correctness of the interpretation; if the patient decisively rejects it, this may be viewed as evidence of the patient's *resistance* to the correct interpretation! Therefore, how can we disprove any interpretation?

Psychoanalysts object that such arguments miss the point. The interpretation of the patients' reactions is not based on isolated observations, but is compared with their way of reacting in different connections. The intensity of the rejection is also important: a furious and agitated rejection may be a sign that an interpretation is largely correct. Several of Freud's hypotheses do not fulfil the requirement of falsifiability. Certain facts which obviously conflict with one of Freud's basic hypotheses often led him to introduce additional hypotheses to vindicate the original hypothesis. Popper especially questioned the status of such additional or ad hoc hypotheses. Freud's additional hypotheses often cannot be falsified by experience. This creates problems for an empirical theory. For example, towards the end of his life, Freud concluded that certain dream-contents could be traced back neither to dreamers' adult life nor to their forgotten childhood. If Freud's conclusion were correct (but how could he *know* it?), it would falsify the hypothesis that the dream-content stems from the unconscious. But Freud did not draw this conclusion. Instead he proposed a new, ancillary hypothesis to 'sustain' the basic hypothesis: we must understand such a dream-content as a part of the unconscious, *archaic* inheritance that children, under the influence of ancestors, bring with them into the world.[15] This hypothesis of innate ideas is an ad hoc construction. Its only function is to support another hypothesis, and it can hardly be considered empirical. The thesis that dreams derive their content from the unconscious becomes impossible to falsify if the additional hypothesis is accepted. Similar constructions were to play an important theoretical role for the Swiss psychologist Carl Gustav Jung (1875–1961).

Such strategies to secure immunity to refutation conflict with the requirement of possible falsification. For this reason, Popper did not consider psychoanalysis to be a scientific theory. An empirical theory is always incompatible with certain events: if such events occur, then the theory is false. Popper claimed that Freud constructed theories in such a way that they are not falsifiable. But this does not render them either uninteresting or 'meaningless'. Psychoanalysis includes interesting hypotheses, but not in a form that is testable. Therefore, it is nonscientific (according to Popper). Only when psychoanalysis can indicate what would constitute its disconfirmation, that is, only when the theory becomes testable, will psychoanalysis cease to be a pseudo-science.

There is another point of Popper's criticism that should be mentioned: Freud, along with many other psychoanalysts, claimed that psychoanalysis is based on clinical observations. This is a naive view, according to Popper: all observations are actually connected to interpretations in light of theories or hypotheses. There are no 'theory-free' observations.

Many psychoanalysts have claimed that the patient improvement under psycho-analytic therapy confirms the theory: therapeutic success is a sign of its truth. But this is a dubious conclusion. At best, therapeutic success provides some validation of the theory when certain prognoses turn out to be accurate. Even though psycho-analytic treatment achieves good results, the theory on which it is built may still be false, partially or completely. Conversely, an unsuccessful outcome may be compatible with the fact that the theory on which the treatment is based is valid: the theory may be true but the analyst incompetent! It should also be emphasized that the criteria for success in analytic therapy are by no means clear.

Popper's conclusions are not universally accepted in the debate about the sci-entific status of psychoanalysis. Some theoreticians have viewed the falsification requirement as far too strict a criterion. It has also been objected that this require-ment 'kills' every new theory before it has a chance to develop. Since psycho-analysis, in certain areas, has succeeded in explaining facts that other theories could not explain, it may be said to satisfy the requirement of fruitfulness. A theory may also be said to be fruitful if it gives rise to new research programmes within vari-ous disciplines. Many have claimed that this is true of psychoanalysis. Some liter-ary critics have attempted to use psychoanalytic insights, especially in comparative literature, but it is still a controversial question whether, and in what sense, psy-chology can elucidate aesthetic phenomena. From the perspective of Thomas Kuhn and the so-called paradigm theory, we could perhaps say that Freud's metapsy-chology contains concepts that direct research, but that are themselves not subject to testing. From such a perspective we must look for an 'adequacy' criterion: are Freud's concepts *adequate*? How can they be criticized? This debate is not yet concluded.

A new approach to psychoanalysis may be traced in several schools in modern philosophy. The German social philosopher Jürgen Habermas has attempted to reconstruct psychoanalysis as a theory about systematically distorted communica-tion.[16] According to Habermas, Freud's epistemological self-understanding is based on a *scientistic* misunderstanding of the uniqueness of psychoanalysis. Psychoanalysis is not a natural science, but rather a kind of deep hermeneutics that attempts to grasp the meaning of distorted 'texts' (neurotic symptoms), dreams, etc. Psycho-analysis, consequently, must unite hermeneutic interpretation with psychological investigations of quasi-causal connections, that is to say, unconscious motives that function as causes unknown to the individual. We may therefore say that Freud developed a unique, demystifying 'deep hermeneutics', or interpretation technique for understanding and correcting systematically distorted communication. This raises difficult questions of the criteria of a *valid* interpretation. According to Habermas, psychoanalytical therapy may best be compared to an expanded 'self-understanding'. Individuals must no longer be governed by the 'causality of fate'; they must once again become free subjects. In line with this programme, psycho-analysis is 'critical theory', and not a natural science.[17]

Freud would probably have protested that he was not a philosopher. In a letter to a friend in the 1890s, Wilhelm Fliess, Freud said that he actually was neither a scientist nor a researcher, but a *conquistador*. Through psychoanalysis Freud became what he wanted to be: he conquered the realm of the unconscious.

QUESTIONS

Explain the main points in Freud's theory of the human mind, using concepts such as the conscious, the preconscious, and the unconscious, and the id, ego, and superego.

Describe the human condition from a Freudian perspective.

SUGGESTIONS FOR FURTHER READING

PRIMARY LITERATURE

The Standard Edition of the Complete Psychological Works of Sigmund Freud, ed. by James Strachey in collaboration with Anna Freud, 24 vols, London, 1953–64.

SECONDARY LITERATURE

Grünbaum, A., *The Foundations of Psychoanalysis. A Philosophical Critique*, London, 1984.

Ricoeur, P., *Freud and Philosophy: An Essay on Interpretation*, New Haven/London, 1977.

NOTES

1 Marie Jahoda claims that *The Psychopathology of Everyday Life* clearly reveals 'Freud's relentless belief in the total absence of chance in human actions' (*Freud and the Dilemmas of Psychology*, London, 1977, p. 53). We will return later to Freud's unique view of determinism.

2 S. Freud, *The Origin and Development of Psycho-Analysis*, trans. by Harry W. Chase, printed in *Great Books of the Western World*, vol. 54, Chicago, 1990, p. 11.

3 S. Freud, *An Outline of Psychoanalysis*, Penguin Freud Library, volume 15, translated by James Strachey, ed. by Albert Dickson, London, 1993, p. 431.

4 S. Freud, *An Outline of Psychoanalysis*, p. 406.

5 S. Freud, *Civilization and Its Discontents*, trans. by Joan Riviere, p. 777.

6 Ibid., p. 784.

7 Ibid., p. 789.

8 Ibid., p. 791.

9 Ibid., p. 802.

10 Cf. the broad sense of the word *Wissenschaft*.

11 H. F. Ellenberger, *The Discovery of the Unconscious*, New York, 1970, p. 809: 'A group of scholars [in 1912] founded a *Gesellschaft für positivistische Philosophie* (Society for Positivist Philosophy), with headquarters in Berlin, with the aim of arriving at a unified, scientific conception of the universe, and thus solve mankind's problems. Among the members of the society were Ernst Mach, Josef Popper, Albert Einstein, August Forel, and Sigmund Freud.'

12 P. Frank, 'Psychoanalysis and Logical Positivism', in *Psychoanalysis, Scientific Method and Philosophy* (ed. Sidney Hook), New York, 1959, p. 313. It should be emphasized that not everyone agreed with this assessment.

13 Karl R. Popper, *Conjectures and Refutations*, London, 1972, pp. 33 ff.

14 See, for example, Ernest Nagel, 'Psychoanalysis and Scientific Method', in *Psychoanalysis, Scientific Method and Philosophy* (ed. Sidney Hook), New York, 1959, pp. 38–57.

15 S. Freud, *An Outline of Psychoanalysis*, p. 399.

16 J. Habermas, *Knowledge and Human Interests*, Boston, 1971.

17 A harsh critique of Habermas' interpretation of Freud (and of psychoanalysis in general) is made by Adold Grünbaum, *The Foundation of Psychoanalysis. A Philosophical Critique*, Berkeley/Los Angeles, 1984.

24 The rise of the social sciences

BACKGROUND

Several sciences, some of which are as old as philosophy, fall under the umbrella of social research. Parallel with the history of philosophy we have previously discussed political theory (beginning with the Sophists). We have also mentioned historiography (from Herodotus and Thucydides to Vico and Dilthey), jurisprudence (Cicero and Bentham), and pedagogics (from Socrates to Dewey). Furthermore, we have discussed economics (Smith, Ricardo, and Marx) and the tendency to shape the social sciences through the use of utilitarian categories, and at the same time we have hinted at another more historically oriented type of social research (based on Hegel's thought). In this chapter we will survey the rise of sociology, with figures such as Comte, Tocqueville, Tönnies, Simmel, Durkheim, Weber, and Parsons. We will concentrate especially on their analysis of modern society and the status of sociology.

AUGUSTE COMTE – THE 'HIGH PRIEST' OF SOCIOLOGY

Auguste Comte (1798–1856) was a pioneer of the new science of society, sociology. The term 'sociology' is introduced in Comte's *Cours de philosophie positive* (1830–42) to replace *physique sociale* ('social physics'), which he had previously used.

Comte viewed the rise of sociology from a historical perspective: man's intellectual development, according to Comte, has passed through three stages, the theological, the metaphysical, and the positive. Mathematics, physics, and biology were already established on the positive stage. They were sciences that had liberated themselves from theological and metaphysical thinking. But the disciplines having man as their research object were still marked by theological and metaphysical speculations. Comte wanted to advance these disciplines to the positive, scientific stage. From this perspective, he became the advocate of sociology as a positive social science.

The words *positive* and *positivism* have a polemical edge. Comte's polemic was directed against theological and philosophical speculations. A positive discipline is empirical, objective, and anti-speculative. It concentrates on perceptible phenomena and on the ordered relationships that can be established through empirical research. Classical mechanics is the model of a positive science, and sociology ought to be modelled on physics as much as possible. Sociology should become the *natural science* of society. This approach is also 'positive' in the sense of being constructive and edifying. Like the Restoration thinkers (especially Bonald and de Maistre), who reacted to the French Revolution of 1789, Comte thought that the ideas of the Enlightenment had been negative and destructive. Its criticism of tradition and authority had led not only to the undermining of an antiquated political system, but also to a revolution that resulted in terror and chaos. He called Rousseau and Voltaire 'philosophers of the guillotine'. Like the Restoration thinkers, Comte was concerned with the moral crisis of the post-revolutionary period. He saw the origin of this crisis in the emerging *individualism* ('the sickness of the Western world') that had been introduced by the Reformation, and that had reached its climax during the Enlightenment. An important symptom of this 'sickness' was ideas such as popular sovereignty, equality, and individual liberty, as well as the accompanying negative views of the family, religion, the Church, and the community. This individualism had also been expressed as 'methodological individualism' in the tradition from Hobbes to Kant. For these thinkers, the *individual* is the starting point for social philosophy (cf. the social contract). But, according to Comte, society can no more be broken down into separate individuals than a line can be broken down into dots. Society can be broken down only into groups and communities. The most fundamental of these groups is the family.

Comte distinguished himself from the conservative Restoration thinkers on two points. First, he rejected the idea of Roman Catholicism as a socially integrating force. The conservative social philosophers in France wanted to return to the feudal-Catholic principles of the *ancien régime*. For Comte, such principles belonged to an earlier period in the development of man and must be replaced by the principle of positivism. Positivism is the only principle that can assume the role in society that was previously held by Roman Catholicism. Positivism is therefore the binding force (religion) in modern societies. Secondly, Comte was far more attuned to natural science and modern technology than were the Restoration thinkers. As a natural science of society, sociology might form the basis of a new and efficient social technology. It was to become an instrument for directing society so that society could once again function in an orderly and well-integrated manner.

For Comte, however, sociology was not a science among other sciences, but the apex of the scientific hierarchy. At the same time, it was the quasi-religious principle of integration in the new society, analogous to Catholicism in the Middle Ages. These views became more marked in Comte's later writings, where his earlier cool and anti-metaphysical attitude gave way to a fiery enthusiasm for the positivistic 'religion'. Comte's positivism, in this phase, reads as if Restoration Catholicism had been formulated in a new and secular language. For Comte, society itself, as understood by positive sociology, had become 'The Greatest Being' (*Le Grand Être*). In the latter part of his life, Comte virtually founded a 'religion of humanity', which gained much support, 'churches' being established in France, Britain, and the United States. Adherents of the early version of Comte's programme of scientific sociology, such as John Stuart Mill and Herbert Spencer, often chose to ignore the neoreligious ideas expressed in his *System of Positive Polity* ('*Système de politique positive*' [1851–4]).

Comte's basic view of sociology as the natural science of society gained many adherents in the second half of the nineteenth century (and far into the twentieth).

The influence of this 'high priest' of sociology may be seen, for example, in Émile Durkheim's reformulation of the basic features of sociological method (*Les règles de la méthode sociologique* [1895]). Durkheim had little use for the later Comte, but was greatly influenced by *Courses in Positive Philosophy*.

Comte's importance in the history of sociology can briefly be summarized under three headings:

1   He developed a programme for a positive 'natural science of society' which still has many adherents.
2   He maintained that 'social phenomena' can be studied objectively just like events in nature.
3   He maintained that sociological insight into the regular relationships in society allows the development of a new social technology to facilitate the solution of socio-political problems.

ALEXIS DE TOCQUEVILLE – AMERICAN DEMOCRACY

The French aristocrat Alexis de Tocqueville (1805–1859) is especially remembered for his study, *Democracy in America* ('*De la Démocratie en Amerique*' [1835–40]). Tocqueville thought that there was an irresistible development towards greater equality, both in behaviour and attitudes, and in politics and institutions. The country that had gone furthest in developing such a democratic equality was the United States, but Europe was to follow.

As a nobleman, Tocqueville was ambivalent towards this movement to political democracy. But as an intellectual kinsman of Montesquieu, he was realistic and open-minded. On the one hand, he viewed this democracy as being more just than the old regime. On the other hand, Tocqueville saw the dangers of a flattening out of society: if everyone becomes virtually equal, there will be a development of mediocrity. According to Tocqueville, what held Americans together was primarily a common interest in money and efficiency. Here, he foreshadowed modern cultural criticism of the so-called mass society.

But it was not only the aristocratic and elite intellectual values that Tocqueville felt were threatened. He thought that it would be difficult to reconcile individualism and liberty with democratic equality: when the democratic majority holds the power in all areas, the divergent minority and nonconformist individuals are in danger of being suppressed. And this suppression is the more dangerous since it is not a matter of open physical violence. Public opinion suppresses unpopular viewpoints in a quiet and painless manner. The slogan of the French Revolution was liberty, equality, and brotherhood. But Tocqueville thought that liberty and equality were hard to combine, and that equality tends to triumph at the expense of liberty. Furthermore, Tocqueville thought that democracy based on equality would lead to a strong state power, and that the state would regulate the material conditions of the people.

Tocqueville saw tendencies not only towards greater equality, but also towards new class divisions. The tendencies towards inequality were rooted in industrialization. On the one hand, Tocqueville thought that democratic equality promotes industrialization, both because its emphasis on material welfare for everyone creates a growing market for industrial goods, and because greater equality makes it easier to recruit talented people for work in trade and industry. On the other hand, Tocqueville saw tendencies towards the growth of inequality. Independent artisans were being turned into factory workers to perform monotonous labour, and the employers ran their large companies without contact with the employees other than the exchange of labour and wages. The reciprocal sense of responsibility that existed between the nobleman and his tenantry had been lost. Tocqueville saw a tendency towards a new inequality in the relationship between the new employers and their employees.[1] He thus predicted the development of both political equality and economic inequality. Tocqueville was one of the first thinkers to doubt the faith in progress, and he strove for a balanced view of the advantages and the disadvantages of the social development of the first half of the 1800s.

FERDINAND TÖNNIES – *GEMEINSCHAFT* AND *GESELLSCHAFT*

We will now take a closer look at what we may call basic conceptual pairs in sociology. Such conceptual pairs may be understood as perspectives or frames of reference for classical sociological argument. Perhaps the most important conceptual pair stems from the German sociologist Ferdinand Tönnies (1855–1936). It was introduced by the very title of his main work, *Gemeinschaft und Gesellschaft* (1887).

In this work, Tönnies tried to develop a comprehensive conceptual system with *Gemeinschaft* and *Gesellschaft* as the key terms. The usual English translation of *Gemeinschaft* is 'community' and *Gesellschaft* may be translated as 'society'. We will give some examples of this conceptual pair to help clarify Tönnies' point.

The concept of community is as central to classical sociology as the concepts of state of nature and social contract are to political philosophy from Hobbes to Kant. The tradition that developed from Hobbes used the idea of the contract to legitimize or justify social relations and political conditions. The contract provided a model for correctitude and justice in social life. All social relations that originated in contracts, that is, voluntary agreements, were legitimate. In the emerging sociology of the nineteenth century, the concept of contract was largely replaced by that of community as a basic category. At the same time, the community was the model of a good society. According to Tönnies, *Gemeinschaft* denotes all forms of social relations that are characterized by a great degree of personal intimacy, emotional depth, moral obligation, social cohesion, and continuity over time. The typical example of such a community is the *family*. Ties and relations exist between family members that are fundamentally different from the relations between, for example, the prostitute and her customers, or those between a corporation employer and an employee. In a *Gemeinschaft* relation, there are emotional ties (for better or worse, as in a love relation), and not the impersonal and anonymous relations characteristic of society (*Gesellschaft*).

In Tönnies' sociology, *Gesellschaft* (society) refers to a typologically modern relationship between human beings, relations that are characterized by a large degree of individualism and impersonal formality. These relations emerge from personal decisions and self-interest, and are distinct from the traditions and emotional relationships that form the basis of *Gemeinschaft*. In short, Tönnies viewed *Gemeinschaft* as a lasting and genuine community, and *Gesellschaft* as a passing, accidental, and mechanical form of life.

We have said that the prototype of *Gemeinschaft* is the family. The individual is born into a family. Blood ties and family relationships are thus basic pillars in *Gemeinschaft*. But individuals are also united by various forms of friendship and by their local environment. Among the many manifestations of *Gemeinschaft* are guilds, various occupational and intellectual communities, and religious congregations and sects. Typical *Gemeinschaft* relations include the traditional relationship between master and apprentice or between the master of the house and the members of the household (including the servants).

Tönnies emphasized that the moral aspect often holds an important position in the popular characterization of *Gemeinschaft*. A society marked by *Gemeinschaft* relations often strikes us as being 'warm', 'close', and characterized by 'personal relations'. However, these premodern features may accompany widespread corruption, nepotism, and essential deficiencies in the legal code.

According to Tönnies, gender issues are also reflected in these terms: women are traditionally more oriented towards the 'gentle values' than are men. Women's liberation demands that women enter the 'men's world', that is, into *Gesellschaft* relations. Through this process, women become 'hard', 'enlightened', 'aware', and 'calculating', just like men. It is the *Gemeinschaft* element in women and children, Tönnies claimed, that explains why women and children could so easily be exploited in early industrial society.

The conceptual pair *Gemeinschaft* and *Gesellschaft* hold a central position in Tönnies' understanding of the great social changes which have occurred in Europe in recent times. Tönnies emphasized that European society has moved from *Gemeinschaft* relationships to *Gesellschaft* relationships based on agreements and contracts. This process created new bonds between people, destroying traditional authority and replacing it with new forms of authority. Competition and egoism became increasingly predominant, for the core of *Gesellschaft* is rationality and economic calculation:

> The theory of the *Gesellschaft* deals with the artificial construction of an aggregate of human beings which superficially resembles the *Gemeinschaft* in so far as the individuals live and dwell together peacefully. However, in the *Gemeinschaft* they remain essentially united in spite of all separating factors, whereas in the *Gesellschaft* they are essentially separated in spite of all uniting factors. . . . Here everybody is by himself and isolated, and there exists a condition of tension against all others. Their spheres of activity and power are sharply separated, so that everybody refuses to everybody else contact with and admittance to his sphere; i.e., intrusions are regarded as hostile acts. Such a negative attitude toward one another becomes the normal and always underlying relation of these power-endowed individuals, and it characterizes the *Gesellschaft* in the condition of rest; nobody wants to grant and produce anything for another individual, nor will he be inclined to give ungrudgingly to another individual, if it be not in exchange for a gift or labour equivalent that he considers at least equal to what he has given.[2]

Some would perhaps interpret this as a negative characterization of modern society. Did not Tönnies see anything positive in *Gesellschaft*? He was by no means a reactionary, and he emphasized that without *Gesellschaft* we would not be able to imagine the rise of modern liberality and culture. The city and the urban life are likewise connected with *Gesellschaft*. Associated with the city are science, trade, industry, and everything that we understand by modern Western civilization. *Gemeinschaft und Gesellschaft* may be a nostalgic work, but this is a nostalgia that is built into the basic concepts of classical sociology. This nostalgia expresses a problem that still marks our society.

According to Tönnies, the culmination of the *Gesellschaft* period is long past. The need for *Gemeinschaft* relationships has become increasingly more noticeable as we move into modernity. Already in the 1880s, attempts were made to include community relations and safety mechanisms in *Gesellschaft* (social politics, welfare state, etc.). Our current interest in neighbourhoods, private spheres, social networks, lenient values, and decentralization may all illustrate that the problems defined by Tönnies are still relevant.

We have attempted to show how the conceptual pair *Gemeinschaft* and *Gesellschaft* characterize different types of social relationships, and how they can be connected to two different phases of European history. We can also regard *Gemeinschaft* and *Gesellschaft* as two extreme types which have never existed in a pure form in the empirical world. In this sense, our modern society is closer to *Gesellschaft* than *Gemeinschaft*.

Tönnies' conceptual pair came to play an important role in sociology. They turned up again in the works of the American sociologist Charles H. Cooley (1864–1929), who distinguished between *primary groups* and *secondary groups*. Primary groups are characterized by close contact and 'face-to-face' relations. A group is primary when it shapes our social nature and ideals. The most important primary groups are the family, the neighbourhood, and adolescent groups. They comprise, in various ways, a 'we'. Organizations and political parties are examples of secondary groups. While the frequency of contact and the relationships in the primary group are, respectively, continual and intimate, in the secondary groups relationships are arbitrary, formal, and impersonal. The means of communication in the primary group are speech, mimicry, and gestures; in the secondary group, they are usually letters, newsletters, and telephone conversations.

We will later look at how Max Weber and Talcott Parsons developed the basic concepts introduced by Tönnies.

GEORG SIMMEL – THE SOCIAL TISSUE

Georg Simmel (1858–1918), a German Jew, was the great essayist among the classical sociologists. His most important works are *On Social Differences* (1890), *The Philosophy of Money* (1900), and *Sociology* (1908). In addition, he wrote studies of philosophy, art, and other cultural issues, such as *The Cities and Intellectual Life*, *The Tragedy of Culture*, and *Oneness and Twoness*.

For Simmel, sociology was a science concerned with the interplay, or social interaction, between individuals. As such, sociology is relational thinking. Social interaction is 'life as a process'. This implies that social reality is an open process and not a virtually closed system. Sociology should therefore start with the simplest elements in this process and discover their interrelations.

For Simmel, sociology was, in many ways, social microscopy. In a series of interesting essays he described loneliness and 'twosomeness'. He also discussed the social situation of the 'stranger' in the interaction context. In the essay *Conflict* (1908), he examined how conflict between groups can bring the members of a group even closer together against an enemy, but the interaction between the conflicting groups may also bring them closer together. For Simmel, society was a 'tissue' of innumerable interactions. To understand this interaction, we must carry out sociological investigations at the microlevel. Such an investigation should start with the simplest forms of interaction and the invisible threads linking individuals. Only in this way may we be able to follow the threads in the social labyrinth.

In his essay *The Cities and Intellectual Life* (1902), Simmel showed how the modern city creates new forms of interaction and new people: in the large city we are bombarded with impressions. Each individual's 'nerve life' becomes intensified, according to Simmel. Modern people become hypersensitive. To avoid this intense pressure, they create a *distance* between themselves and the physical and social surroundings. To guard themselves from an increasing number of impressions – sounds, lights, pictures – they try to shut out reality. In this way, a characteristic *blasé* state of mind emerges among modern city-dwellers. They become reserved and have to develop a certain distance from their surroundings in order to survive. Ultimately, the hypersensitivity of modern Man places him in a vacuum. People of our time, according to Simmel, suffer because they are both too close to reality and too far removed from it.

Simmel started not with macrosociological concepts, but with microsociological analyses of details. He thought that our concepts have to be adapted to what they have to grasp. For Simmel, the modern world was fissured and fragmented. It was no longer possible to grasp the 'totality'. Only in the details of life and in kaleidoscopic fragments was it possible to glimpse a larger interconnection. The methodological gateway is thus composed of 'snapshots', fragments, and particular impressions. And a simple element can reveal social connections. For example, a *coin* (or a key) is a symbol of important social relations. In modern society, money mediates between people. Simmel inspired the incipient sociology of the twentieth century. Many other authors, including Max Weber, borrowed ideas from him. In his long monograph *The Philosophy of Money* (1900), Simmel explained how the calculation of means–ends chains has become more prevalent in modern life: in others words, instrumental (purposive) rationality submits to other forms of rationality. Because of the money economy, the relations between people are transformed into relations between things. In these analyses, Simmel developed a unique theory of alienation and reification in social relations. The things we have created become increasingly our masters. Similarly, social interaction may 'harden' to objective and supraindividual structures. In modern life, we have little understanding of the technology that surrounds us. The same is true for culture; we no longer understand the spirit that is immanent in cultural forms. Thus, the results of the spirit become alien to us.

It is often said that Simmel is an 'impressionistic' social researcher who, like Impressionist painters such as Monet, Renoir, and Seurat, wanted to grasp the spontaneous experience. As a sociological Impressionist, he was a master of capturing the immediate first impressions of social phenomena. His picture of reality is thus composed of such transitory impressions. In many ways, Simmel was sociology's 'pathfinder', seeking to map the fragmentary terrain of modern life. His 'fluid' picture of social life also affected his form of presentation. As a result, his arguments are often hypothetical and tentative. There is hardly another sociologist and philosopher who uses 'perhaps' as often as Simmel. Consequently, it was not without reason that he was called a 'perhaps-thinker'. In this sense, the essay as a literary genre suited well his attempt to grasp some aspects of a fragmentary world. Nor did he lay claim to anything more. But in addition he had aesthetic aspirations. He was a master of language. Hence his style is difficult to imitate. His thoughts lose something essential when they are translated into ordinary prose. Simmel evinced a fluid transition between poetic expression and sociology. Both in style and theme, he anticipated the postmodern experience.

ÉMILE DURKHEIM – SOCIETY AND SOCIAL SOLIDARITY

Life. Émile Durkheim (1858–1917) came from the German-French border area of Lorraine. His father was a rabbi, but Durkheim adopted an agnostic view on religious questions. He studied philosophy and political theory in Paris, taught pedagogy and social science at the University of Bordeaux, and later became a professor at the Sorbonne, first of pedagogy and later of sociology. He conceived it as his task to launch the new science of society, sociology. He championed political causes, for example, Alfred Dreyfus (1859–1935), *in the famous miscarriage of justice, and the struggle against German militarism during World War I. His most important works are* The Division of Labour in Society *(1893)*, The Rules of Sociological Method *(1895)*, Suicide *(1897), and* The Elementary Forms of the Religious Life *(1912).*

Durkheim's basic idea was that society is based on the forces that hold people together. When social solidarity is weakened, society falls ill. We must then find the correct therapy to restore this socially vital solidarity. Sociology, for Durkheim, was the science of this solidarity: its foundation, how it is weakened, and how it can be strengthened. Durkheim thought that the France of his day was a society in which solidarity had been weakened; that is, it was a sick society.

Durkheim rejected the view that sociology should use the same social concepts that the members of society use to understand their social interactions (cf. Winch, Ch. 26). According to Durkheim, sociology has to find better concepts. He illustrated this point by the concept of suicide. Starting with everyday language and everyday life, Durkheim sought for a conception of suicide that can be treated statistically in regard to various social conditions, that is, in regard to variations that are not of a psychological nature. By ignoring the various emotional and individual aspects of suicide – what each victim felt and thought – Durkheim, as a sociologist, distanced himself from psychology. He looked for variations in the frequency of suicide in regard to gender, age, marital status, religious affiliation, nationality, social class, etc. Such statistics form the basis of Durkheim's theoretical work as a sociologist. (That is, he did not stop with statistics.) On the basis of these statistics, he tried to formulate a theory of society, that is to say, of social solidarity, whereby the high frequency of suicide is a sign of a weakened sense of solidarity.

Durkheim's method is sometimes called *positivist*. This word is so ambiguous that it is always necessary to explain what we mean by it. Durkheim was not a positivist in the sense of logical positivism, but in the sense that he was interested in *what is given* (the given is 'the positive'). He wanted to observe how society functions. He was not trying to make radical changes or 'negate'. Durkheim wanted to understand the things that are, as they are, in order to find a remedy or therapy for unhealthy social disintegration (he viewed the social changes of his day mainly as a weakening of society).

When he said that a sociologist should view social phenomena *as things*, he had in mind the use of statistical material and practical concepts to develop theory. This approach represented a break with the social research that is purely based on understanding. But a naturalistic reduction — whereby social phenomena are said to have the same ontological status as objects of nature — is not a necessary part of such a statistical-theoretical approach. On the basis of his work with the statistical material on suicide, Durkheim thought that he could explain social solidarity, and determine the causes of the weakening of social solidarity. He called this weakened social solidarity *anomie* (Greek: *anomia*, 'no law/norm'), that is, lawlessness, normlessness. Briefly, a state of anomie represents a weakening of the bonds between people. When anomie develops, individuals become less resistant to pressure and hardship, and the frequency of suicide increases.

Thus, Durkheim assumed that he had statistical evidence that there is less anomie (stronger social solidarity, less suicide) among married than among unmarried men, among married couples who have children than among married couples without children, among Roman Catholics than among Protestants, etc. Marriage, family, and religion (*qua* a social form of life), especially Catholicism, are thus binding factors in society.

Durkheim did not think it necessary to abolish the division of labour in order to have a humane society; on the contrary, a thoroughgoing division of labour could allow society to become once again harmonious: when the division of labour is not developed, there is equality among people, but little individuality. A 'mechanical solidarity' then prevails, as Durkheim put it. But along with an increasing division of labour, individuals become more dependent on one another. The result is what Durkheim called 'organic solidarity': everyone is dependent on everyone else, like the parts of an organism. Such an increasing division of labour leads to specialization and individualization.

But, according to Durkheim, a society based on the division of labour can be both healthy and sick. The question is whether the economy functions according to the correct norms. When that does not happen, we have anomie (as in a heightened class struggle). Durkheim did not look back towards a society without a division of labour, but rather forwards to a harmonious society based on a division of labour.

The strengthening of the norms of socio-economic life that, according to Durkheim, are necessary to overcome anomie will not occur by simple moralizing, or by mere state power. There must be institutions within the state that can regulate the economy in a harmonious way. Here, the corporations enter the picture. Durkheim wanted a corporate state, that is to say, a state in which corporate organizations regulate the economy efficiently and reliably.

Durkheim, like Hegel, provided a kind of 'social democratic' answer: he opposed both the uncontrolled expansionism of pure liberalism and the Marxist theory of drastic changes. Durkheim's argument was largely directed against what liberalism, socialism, and Marxism have in common, that is to say, against their common political inheritance from the Enlightenment: the ideas of development, liberation, and progress. These ideas, which other theoreticians strongly emphasized, were viewed by Durkheim as dangerous tendencies towards dissolution. Society ought to be stable, though not static, or unchangeable. Durkheim questioned concepts such as development and progress: when such terms are applied to all kinds of change, they may actually be describing exactly the destructive anomie in a harmless manner. We should not 'liberate' ourselves from everything, but should try to achieve the social solidarity that is a prerequisite for our social stability and happiness, according to Durkheim.

It is common to distinguish between two kinds of social theories; those assuming a basic *conflict* and those assuming a basic *harmony*. In this regard, Durkheim was definitely a theoretician of harmony, while Marx was a theoretician of conflict (that is, for history *prior* to the communist classless society). Historically, Durkheim's ideas hark back to pre-Renaissance political theory; for example, to the political theories of Plato and Aristotle, who emphasized integration and stability. Today, his theory is also of interest in the ecological context, as a contribution to a sociology of ecological equilibrium.

With regard to the relationship between individual and community, Durkheim emphasized community and solidarity. Individuals have to adapt themselves to the norms and rules necessary for a well-functioning society. The alternative is, in principle, anarchy (anomie), something which does not serve the individual. The question still remains as to whether individuality and liberality could be secured within a functioning community by means of a dialectical mediation between what is unique and what is universal – to use Hegelian terms. The problems surrounding such a mediation between the individual and the community are hard to solve, both theoretically and practically. But some critics still hold that Durkheim did not deal sufficiently with this problem.

MAX WEBER – RATIONALITY AND 'HEROIC PESSIMISM'

THE PHILOSOPHY OF SCIENCE AND IDEAL TYPES

Max Weber (1864–1920) is probably the classical sociologist who has had the greatest impact on the development of this discipline. We will first look at his philosophy of science and his view of 'ideal types'.

According to Weber, there is a fundamental difference between facts and values, between what *is* and what *ought* to be. As scientists, we can comment only about facts, not about values. Of course, we may investigate the values that people actually accept. That is an empirical question. Of course, we may also become politically and morally involved. But this involvement stems from our position as citizens, not as scientists. Hence, we must not mix these two spheres, as for example, by promoting political propaganda under the guise of science. Science may, of course, tell us something about the means appropriate for achieving a certain goal.

It can also tell us something about the 'cost' involved in reaching that goal. But once such facts are presented, the agent must personally make a *choice*. This is Weber's thesis of the *value freedom* of science, that is to say, that science, *qua* science, can only say something about what is, not about what ought to be. In science, we seek truth which is *valid* for everyone: 'It has been and remains true that a systematically correct scientific proof in the social sciences, if it is to achieve its purpose, must be acknowledged as correct even by a Chinese.'[3]

Weber's conception of value freedom does not mean that values do not play an important role in science. There are always some basic viewpoints and perspectives that determine which themes become the object of scientific research. According to Weber, all knowledge of culture and society is conditioned by value conceptions. Like the neo-Kantian philosopher Heinrich Rickert (1863–1936), Weber held that the cultural sciences characteristically give the subjects of historical research form and position in relation to 'cultural values'. But on one decisive point Weber did not share Rickert's view that there are objective cultural values. Weber's view was similar to that of Nietzsche; namely, that there is a diversity of subjective values, attracting the researcher's interest to certain themes rather than others. The second premise in Weber's philosophy of science is thus the idea of a general *pluralism of value*.

Weber asserted that the world and life, to start with, appear as an infinite diversity, a virtual chaos of events and actions. If we wish to describe the world 'without value presuppositions', we discover an infinite number of observations and opinions, and a chaos of relevant and irrelevant facts. Weber's position on this point has much in common with Karl Popper's criticism of naive collections of facts. We structure this chaos in such a way that only a portion of reality becomes significant to us. A particular issue such as the French Revolution means something to us because it represents ideas of cultural value. It is in light of such cultural values that we distinguish the essential from the non-essential, as *we* see it. This is what makes phenomena relevant and what gives them meaning. Value conceptions are thus quasi-transcendental presuppositions for the cultural and social sciences.

Weber realized that the value conceptions, which in effect cause the relevant problems that a researcher and a research community study, may change over time. Changes in the social sciences may therefore be the result of profound changes in self-perception and in the view of the value conceptions of a given epoch. Weber described such changes in words reminiscent of Thomas S. Kuhn's exposition of scientific revolutions (cf. Ch. 26), but Weber placed a great emphasis on cultural changes *outside* the social sciences that influence the choice of problems within these sciences. A central element in this connection is changes in the value conceptions of an epoch or a researcher:

> But there comes a moment when the atmosphere changes. The significance of the unreflectively utilized viewpoints becomes uncertain and the road is lost in the twilight. The light of the great cultural problems moves on. Then science too prepares to change its standpoint and its analytical apparatus and to view the streams of events from the heights of thought. It follows those stars which alone are able to give meaning and direction to its labors.[4]

In accordance with Wilhelm Dilthey and the German intellectual tradition (cf. Ch. 16), Weber maintained that the social sciences must use a 'method of understanding' (*Verstehen*). It is not accidental that his sociological *magnum opus*, *Economy and Society*, has the subtitle *The Foundation of a Sociology of Understanding*. Sociology should not merely be confined to finding general rules that govern social action, but it should also seek to *understand* the agent's subjective intentions and motives. Such subjective motives may, at the next stage, be viewed as causes of social action and may be developed into a causal sociological explanation. This corresponds with Weber's definition of sociology. 'Sociology (in the sense in which this highly ambiguous word is used here) is a science which attempts the interpretive understanding of social action in order thereby to arrive at a causal explanation of its course and effects.'[5]

We may notice two things concerning this definition: the starting point is what is often called methodological individualism. This means that Weber was sceptical of collective concepts in sociology. If concepts such as spirit of the times and character of the people cannot be traced back to social action, they are 'biting off more than they can chew'. But if sociology limits itself to the agent's own understanding, its 'bite is too small'. There is also a distinction, implicit in Weber's definition, between *action* and *event*. Sociology is concerned with motivated actions; natural science is concerned with unmotivated events (for example, planetary motion). The meaningful character of human action does not have a counterpart in nature. But this does not exclude the possibility of making predictions in sociology. An action has a specific property that makes it more calculable than a natural process: the action has an understandable motive. Hence, an action is less 'irrational' than an event.

Weber thus held that understanding (*Verstehen*) does not exclude explanation (*Erklären*). An understanding (hermeneutic) method is complementary to a causal-explanatory method. An intuitive 'empathy' with other people is not sufficient. An understanding interpretation of motive and purpose must be supplemented or controlled by a causal explanation. Statistical statements which describe human courses of action (such as the frequency of suicide) may, according to Weber, first be said to be sufficiently explained once the *meaning* of the actions has been clarified. Therefore, social science must progress *via* the agent's subjective intentions and perspective.

We have said that research themes are constituted by value conceptions and that science should be *value-free*. For Weber, there was no contradiction in this. It is by means of values that something becomes a relevant research theme, but what we as scientists say about this theme must be said *without* making value judgements.

In this connection, 'ideal types' play a central role, as they do in Weber's philosophy of science. Ideal types may be understood as basic concepts used in science. They form a 'model' of reality. For Weber, who was basically a nominalist, ideal-typical concepts (such as 'economic man') do not represent the characteristics of reality. In accordance with Rickert and neo-Kantianism, Weber held that an ideal type is only a formal instrument that is used to help us order the diversity of reality. It cultivates particular aspects of subject matter and has no normative importance. (Ideal types do not have anything to do with 'ideals' in a normative sense.) The ideal type 'charismatic kingdom', for example, describes a type of kingdom that is never found in a pure form in any society. The same applies to ideal-type constructions such as 'Renaissance', 'Protestant ethics', 'spirit of capitalism', 'goal-rational action', etc.

Weber's view of ideal types may be understood in light of Kant's categories. Just as Kant's categories are conditions for a possible cognition of reality, Weber's sociological ideal types are nets which are meant to capture some of the infinite diversity of reality. Unlike Kant's categories, ideal types are not eternal and unchangeable. They are constructed by the researcher, but they must still be logically consistent and 'adequate' in relation to the given state of affairs.[6]

TYPES OF ACTION AND FORMS OF LEGITIMIZATION

Weber based his sociology on four 'pure' types of actions (ideal types).

1   An action may be rationally oriented with regard to a given goal (*goal-rational action*).
2   An action may be rationally oriented with regard to an absolute value (*value-rational action*).
3   An action may be determined by states of emotion in the agent (*affective or emotional action*).
4   An action may be determined by traditions and deep-rooted habits (*tradition-oriented action*).

In the two first types of actions, the actions are *rational*. The term 'rational' indicates certain criteria that distinguish the first two types of action from the latter two. The first type of action is rational because it is oriented towards a consciously and unambiguously formulated goal and adopts the means, on the basis of available knowledge, that will lead to the realization of this goal. Goal-rationality may thus be characterized as *means-to-an-end rationality*. The work of Wernher von Braun to develop a rocket that could reach London and other large cities during World War II is an example of a goal-rational action. A successful medical strategy is another example.

The second type of action is rational because it is determined by the agent's ethical or religious belief that a form of action has an absolute value independent of the result. The captain that goes down with his ship because of the dictates of honour or duty is acting according to value-rationality. Actions that are based on an 'ethics of moral obligation' will, in most cases, be actions that are value-rational. The examples show that what for one agent may be 'rational' may be 'irrational' for another. We may also note that 'rationality' is defined on the basis of the *agent's* goal, value, and knowledge, not on the basis of what the social scientist thinks are relevant goals, values, and knowledge.

Weber did not characterize the third type of action as rational. It is a direct consequence of the agent's emotional state. A neurotic action or an uncontrolled reaction to an unusual stimulus may be said to be a passionate action. Such an action is on the border between meaningful action and meaningless behaviour.

The fourth type of action embraces everything that we almost 'unconsciously' do by virtue of custom and habit (or norms) of which we are not aware. This type of action, too, describes behaviour that often exceeds what is considered mean-ingful action. Traditional actions approach value-oriented action if the link to what is 'deep-rooted' is consciously appropriated. When we are consciously traditional, our actions are value-rational.

For Weber, meaning was closely related to rationality. Meaningful actions are linked to goal-rationality and value-rationality. Traditional and passionate actions are borderline cases. As an 'understanding sociology', Weber's project is based on the notion of rational action.

These four types of action make it possible to define more closely what *rational-ization* and *modernization* mean in the development of European culture. For Weber, the Western rationalization process may be described as a development in which an increasing number of fields of action are permeated by goal-rational action. Actions within spheres such as economy, law, and administration are close to the ideal-type 'goal-rational action'. If we regard goal-rationality as a basic cultural value, we may consequently talk about 'progress' within each of these spheres; that is, rational-ization and modernization in the direction of a growing *goal-rationality*. If, on the other hand, we regard religious 'brotherhood ethics' as a basic cultural value, we must, perhaps reluctantly, realize that as the world becomes secularized, this ethics of brotherhood gradually disintegrates in an increasing number of spheres of action. These are the kinds of problems that are central in Weber's diagnosis of modernity.

Weber's theory of action also clarifies a phenomenon such as *bureaucratization*: modern social life carries with it a growing bureaucratization. This is connected with the fact that business and society in general require increasingly better plan-ning and organization. Science becomes a part of administration, and thus enters into society as a whole. This process makes actions more goal-rational because we then have a greater security and fewer losses from accidental and unforeseen factors. Hence, we have, at the same time, bureaucratization, scientization, and increased rationalization.

For Weber, this development represented both alienation *and* increased goal-rationality. He did not believe in a qualitative change in this area. Increased democratization is at the same time increased bureaucratization. Here we see a clear distinction between Weber and Marx: Weber could not imagine a decisive change in the structure of society. Nor did socialism appear to be a qualitative improve-ment; Weber held that the abolition of the market economy would, in fact, strengthen bureaucratization.

Weber developed three ideal types for the legitimization of state authority: the *traditional* authority, the *charismatic* authority, and the *legal* authority. Along with bureaucratization, the legitimization of the state has also changed – or vice versa, the changes in the forms of legitimization have led to bureaucratization: in relat-ively static and traditional societies, the state's authority is never really called into question. State authority rests on tradition. But with a weakening of tradition (scientization, rationalization), this type of authority will also become weaker. An alternative legitimization is what Weber called charisma: the charismatic authority is legitimized by virtue of the subjects' emotional ties to the ruler as a person (cf. passionate action). Charismatic leaders are obeyed because of their personal attributes, not because of law or tradition: 'Ye have heard . . . [what] was said by them of old time . . . but *I* say unto you' (Matthew 5:21–22). In modern society, on the other hand, it is the bureaucratic rationalization that legitimizes state authority: what happens is rational and in accordance with law and justice. The actions of the state are rational and transparent. A verdict, for example, is not handed down on the basis of whims, but on the basis of fixed, universal laws. Weber thus spoke of *legal authority*.

The question of the legitimization of state power is important also because Weber regarded the state as the institution that may legitimately employ violence. In other words, this conception of the state says something about the means which the modern state has, *de facto*, not about the tasks or functions that the state ought or ought not to have.

The four types of action and the three forms of legitimization are Weber's *generalized* ideal types. They may, in principle, be used in the analysis of all social forms, regardless of time and place. Generalized ideal types may therefore be said to build a bridge between nomothetic and idiographic sciences; that is, sciences that work with universal laws and sciences that describe particular instances. Other ideal types may be adapted to specifically historical phenomena, for example, 'the Protestant ethic', 'the Renaissance', etc. To simplify this concept, we may distinguish between generalizing sociological ideal types and individualizing historical ideal types (see below).

PROTESTANTISM AND CAPITALISM

Rationality and rationalization are the common threads in Weber's historical-sociological research. In his extensive empirical work, Weber tried to explain the development of the specific rationality of the West. The central question is formulated as follows: 'A child of the modern European cultural world will unavoidably, and correctly, treat universal historical problems from the following perspective: which chain of events has led to the result that in the West, and only here, there arose cultural phenomena which still – as we would at least like to imagine – pointed in a direction of *universal* significance and validity.'[7]

Weber thus sought the characteristic social and cultural features of the West as distinguished from those of other civilizations. According to him, only in the West was *science* developed, the science that today is regarded as being valid for everyone. Empirical knowledge, and philosophical and theological wisdom are found also in other cultures, such as those of India, China, and Persia. But in those cultures, the acquired knowledge lacks a mathematical foundation and rational proofs; nor is it based on scientific experiments.

In art, we see something similar: musicality is present in all peoples, but only the West has developed a rational harmonic music (counterpoint and chordal harmonics), orchestras, and musical notation. During the Renaissance, a rationalization took place within the fine arts with the introduction of linear and spatial perspectives. And it is only in the West that 'the state' has been recognized as a political institution, having a rational and formal constitution and rational and formal laws. Scientifically specialized experts and high-ranking technocrats are found only in Western culture, according to Weber.[8]

The same applies to what Weber called 'the most fateful force in our modern life', namely, *capitalism*. The search for economic benefit is known in all epochs and in all nations of the world. But it was only in the West that a rational capitalist organization emerged that was based on a (formally) free labour force. Modern

Western capitalism is dependent on the fact that all economic factors can be calculated. Ultimately, this is made possible by rational science. Modern capitalism also requires a legal system and a government bureaucracy to create a predictable field of action. It was only the West that could offer this to business.

Why were not such rationalization processes developed outside the West? And why was modern capitalism first developed in Europe?

According to Weber, 'the citizen' personifies a unique type of action, goal-rational action. The decisive question is then: why is this type of action especially prevalent in the West?

We have seen that Weber pointed to several external conditions behind the triumph of capitalism in the West (science, jurisprudence, etc.). But he was also interested in what we could call internal causes. This has to do with causes that are connected with man's disposition for certain forms of 'practical-rational *ways of life*'. Weber emphasized, not unlike Freud, that when such a way of life is restricted by inhibitions of a religious and ideological nature, the development of a rationally capitalist business life will also meet with great internal opposition.[9] Such problems are well-known in the industrialization process in all countries. In *The Protestant Ethic and the Spirit of Capitalism* (1904), Weber attempted to identify the specific factors, during and after the *Reformation*, that broke down these inhibitions and made the rise of modern society possible.

According to Weber, the Reformation led to a radical change in the traditional ethical notions of duty and prepared the way for an ethic which legitimized a new rational way of life. Hence, the Protestant ethic justified a previously unknown work ethic and a new rational attitude towards life. This work ethic was even seen as enjoined by religion. Indeed, productive work gained a religious significance for Protestants; it became a 'vocation'. Business success was interpreted as a sign of belonging to the 'elect'. Therefore, profit could, in itself, not be immoral. And the negative attitude towards the 'flesh' and the pleasures of the 'senses' limited consumption and facilitated the accumulation of capital. In this way, Protestantism created what Weber called a 'worldly asceticism'. Such a worldly asceticism restructured personality. There appeared an *inner* rationalization of personality in the direction of work and methodical self-control. The internal rationalization supported, at the next stage, an *external* rationalization of economic life.

Weber did not claim that Luther and Calvin had intended to establish the intellectual conditions for the rise of capitalism. Nor were the ethics of capitalism developed with this as a goal. Weber held that the rise of capitalism in the West was an unintended effect of ethical-religious attitudes developed in Protestant sects. The bourgeois way of life and the capitalist spirit emerged from behind the scenes.

Weber's theory has been intensively discussed throughout the twentieth century, and it is often seen as an alternative to the Marxist conception of the relationship between basis (economy) and superstructure (ideology and religion). In this connection, it is important to be aware of what Weber was *not* saying. He did not claim that the Protestant ethic was a necessary and sufficient condition for the rise of capitalism. Weber rejected monocausal models of explanation (explanations based on *one* cause). He emphasized that there were many causes of the rise of capitalism in the West. The Protestant ethic was thus a necessary, but not sufficient condition for the rise of capitalism.

WEBER'S DIAGNOSIS OF THE MALADY OF HIS DAY: 'HEROIC PESSIMISM'

Like Nietzsche, Weber broke in many ways with the Enlightenment belief in progress. His view of his own day and of the future was influenced by Nietzsche's diagnosis of nihilism. The rationalization of business life had created an amazing economic growth, but it had also created what Weber called the 'iron cage' of capitalism and the mechanistic force that determines our lives with 'overwhelming coercion'.[10] The rise of modern science provided new insight into natural processes, but this insight also brought with it a definitive 'demystification of the world' (*Entzauberung der Welt*). While science had emptied the world of religious-metaphysical content, our *existential* need for meaning had increased. This need, Weber emphasized, cannot be satisfied by science.

> The fate of an epoch which has eaten of the tree of knowledge is that it must know that we cannot learn the *meaning* of the world from the results of its analysis, be it ever so perfect; it must rather be in a position to create this meaning itself. It must recognize that general views of life and the universe can never be the products of increasing empirical knowledge.[11]

Scientific rationalization had led to what Weber called the loss of meaning, and our subsequent inner need. In his diagnosis of the malady of his own day, he thus faced the problem of the 'meaninglessness' of modernity. In the absence of a convincing ethics, it was the struggle of everyone against everyone else. The outcome of this struggle could not be decided by rational arguments and criteria. Like many existentialist philosophers, Weber held that in this struggle we must make a *choice* that could not be rationally based. This is Weber's so-called 'decisionism', also called 'the battle of the gods'; i.e., the struggle between basic values that cannot be rationally reconciled.

By Weber's own presuppositions, an irrational decisionism in ethical-political questions is not very satisfying. As we have seen, he pointed out that certain fundamental values are inherent in scientific activity in general. *Truth* and *validity* are basic for all research. But will not something similar occur in a discussion of ethical-political questions? When we uphold certain values against other values, are we not presupposing that what we are saying is *right* and *valid*? We will see later that these are objections that the German philosophers K.-O. Apel and J. Habermas raised against 'decisionism' and 'ethical relativism/subjectivism'.

We pointed out that Weber regarded the growing rationality and bureaucratization as a threat to our freedom. The only political alternative that he found to this development was a charismatic 'leader-democracy' (*Führerdemokratie*); that is government by a charismatic leader who can give society a *new direction*. After World War I, pessimism permeated his view of the future. It is only by having a heroic attitude towards life that modern man, according to Weber, can learn to measure 'up to the world as it really is in its everyday routine'.[12] For Weber, any optimism was an illusion: 'Not summer's bloom lies ahead of us, but rather a polar night of icy darkness and hardness, no matter which group may triumph externally now. Where there is nothing, not only the Kaiser but also the proletarian has lost his rights.'[13] Weber showed a certain similarity in moral temperament with his contemporary, Sigmund Freud: the centre of their sombre moral vision is not a new society, but a new individual, an individual who neither harbours nostalgia for a lost Golden Age nor prepares for a future millennial kingdom, but who has a painfully acquired and scrupulous view of the world, and who is able to face life stoically.

TALCOTT PARSONS – ACTION AND FUNCTION

The American Talcott Parsons (1902–1979) was the last great sociologist in the classical tradition. At the end of the 1930s, Parsons tried to develop a general theory to describe varying social conditions. In many ways, Parsons' complicated and many-sided thinking is a grand synthesis of classical sociology, Freud, and modern system theory. In later works, Parsons tried to rehabilitate a theory of universal features for social evolution. Here the concepts of rationalization and differentiation play a central role.

Already in the important work *The Structure of Social Action* (1937), Parsons maintained that classical sociological thinkers, such as Durkheim, Weber, and Vilfredo Pareto, *converge* on a common theoretical position. Parsons tried to formulate this common goal in terms of a theory of action: action presupposes, among other things, that agents must orient themselves according to means and ends, but the action has direction only by virtue of supraindividual norms and values. Strictly speaking, it is this community of values that makes interaction and society possible. The cultural sphere thus becomes very important in Parsons' sociology.

Parsons' theory of action may be said to represent a criticism of utilitarianism. In opposition to utilitarianism, which does not rely on normative limitations on what various individuals conceive of as ends or on which means they use to achieve them, Parsons held that common values and norms set limits to and coordinate individuals' actions. This early action theory was later incorporated into a structure-functionalist frame. Parsons' theory of action implies that we always choose between different alternatives. These choices are presented as a series of dichotomies. A pattern variable is thus a dichotomy in which the agent must choose one of the alternatives so that the meaning of a situation will be determined. Parsons introduced five such dichotomies.

EMOTIONS – EMOTIONAL NEUTRALITY

For example, teachers in their professional role must choose the normative pattern that prescribes emotional neutrality. They must not become too emotionally involved with their students. The same applies to various professional roles such as judge, psychologist, etc. On the other hand, a father's or a mother's role implies emotional involvement. An interesting question is whether modernization – rationalization and differentiation – creates a normative pattern in which an increasing number of relationships are marked by emotional neutrality (cf. Tönnies' distinction between *Gemeinschaft* and *Gesellschaft*). While work and the professional life of most people is, or ought to be, characterized by emotional neutrality (cf. the debate about sexual harassment in the workplace), the private sphere becomes the place for emotional actions (tears, caresses, etc.). The family normally had this *catharsis* function. However, in our day, we have seen an emotional draining of the family. This is perhaps why modernity is characterized by institutions specializing in provision of outlets for suppressed emotions.

UNIVERSALISM – PARTICULARISM

Should phenomena of practical action be judged on the basis of more universal rules (such as Kant's categorical imperative) or on the basis of more particular rules? For example, in modern society we emphasize professional competence and examination results in the search for a job, not familial relationships, gender, ethnic background, etc. This, according to Parsons, is to make evaluations on the basis of general rules. Here, too, it is a question of whether modernization implies that an increasing number of phenomena are evaluated on the basis of universal, and not particular, rules (cf. 'equality under the law').

EGO-ORIENTATION – COLLECTIVE ORIENTATION

Here the choice is between taking care of ourselves or taking care of others. Does the normative pattern allow agents to use the situation to their own advantage or should they primarily think collectively? Speculators on the stock market, for example, should, by virtue of their role, act on behalf of their own interests or their company's interests, while the doctor and psychologist should primarily be concerned with the patient's interests. In accordance with Durkheim's sociology, we could perhaps say that ego-orientation is first possible in a modern society on the basis of organic solidarity. Collective orientation, or altruism, becomes, from such a perspective, characteristic of a society based on mechanistic solidarity. Again, the question is whether modernization entails a normative pattern which gives ego-orientation priority over collective orientation.

ASCRIPTION – PERFORMANCE

This conceptual pair is based on a distinction between ascribed and achieved qualifications as the basis for determining social status. Should we, for example, give priority to qualifications such as gender, age, and group affiliation or should we give priority to achievement? We often think that the modernization process means (or 'ought' to mean) that achieved qualifications are decisive ('we should be open to talent'). For example, certain professions are no longer reserved exclusively for the nobility or for a particular caste ('the warrior caste', 'the merchant caste', etc.).

SPECIFICITY – MANY-SIDEDNESS

This dichotomy distinguishes between a specific/narrow and a many-sided/diffuse relationship to a phenomenon. The normative pattern here prescribes either limitation of the relation to a specific aspect (cf. the bureaucrat's casework) or expansion of the relation to comprehend more aspects. The modern process of differentiation seems to imply increasingly more specific relations. But there is also another trend that is expressed in the requirement that the bureaucrat should take 'human factors' into account, or that the teacher should be a social worker and a psychologist. Of course, many-sidedness is characteristic of the *Gemeinschaft* sphere in modern society; for example, the relationship between parents and children.

These conceptual pairs represent Parsons' attempt to combine some of the basic concepts in classical sociology; for example, Tönnies' concepts of *Gemeinschaft* and *Gesellschaft*, Weber's *types of action*, and Durkheim's distinction between *mechanistic* and *organic solidarity*. These basic concepts tell us that certain social roles 'predispose' to the choice of a specific side of a dichotomy. One professional role requires that we choose ego-orientation; another requires the choice of collective orientation. For example, a father, in relation to his children, must choose emotion, many-sidedness, particularism, ascription, and collective orientation. If he is his children's teacher, he must correspondingly choose the other side of the dichotomies.

With the help of these conceptual pairs, we can also describe the priorities of a society's norm or value structure. Thus, Parsons sketches several social structures: for example, the universalist performance-oriented pattern characterizes modern industrial societies. We find other patterns in premodern societies. Thus, conceptual pairs form a part of a theory of rationalization and differentiation.

In various ways, Parsons attempted to show that social systems encounter so-called system problems. Here, the basic concepts are connected with biology. In a social system there are mechanisms to ensure that a system is kept in balance when changes occur in the environment. Here we find the *functionalist* model of explanation. Certain mechanisms function to create a balance in a social system; for example, role differentiation must be understood as an attempt to solve 'system problems' on the microlevel. On the macrolevel, there is a corresponding functional differentiation (culture, politics, and economics considered as subsystems). Society is thus equipped with subsystems to deal with adaptation problems in relation to nature, social and normative integration problems, etc. If society exclusively concentrates on instrumental questions, the value community will suffer. Here, culture is important to Parsons, in the form of schools, universities, art schools, etc.

In more recent works, Parsons attempted to revive the theory of universal features of social evolution ('evolutionary universals'), as in various forms of social stratification, written language, law, science, money, bureaucracy, and democracy. The development in a society of such institutions (for example, science and democracy) will decisively influence this society and its future. According to Parsons, it is the increasing functional differentiation – as a society develops new specialist institutions – that brings about these universal developmental features. From this perspective he proposed a theory of development in which the modern Western societies are seen as the end product of this historical process. The collapse of the Soviet Union has strengthened this theory: all societal development seems to move in the direction of the modern Western society and its universal institutions – everything else is a dead end. Here history has reached its conclusion (for the time being). Although Parsons rejected the idea of a teleological explanation of historical development, he may in a sense be seen as a 'modernized' and 'sociologized' Hegelian. Like Hegel and the Enlightenment philosophers, Parsons thought that he had found the mechanisms that create a modern society.

QUESTIONS

Discuss Weber's view of the relation between Protestantism and the rise of capitalism.

Discuss how classical sociology regarded 'the discontents of modernity'. In what sense can this diagnosis be said to be appropriate?

In what sense was classical sociology 'positivistic'? How is this positivism to be distinguished from the positivism of the logical positivists?

SUGGESTIONS FOR FURTHER READING

PRIMARY LITERATURE

Durkheim, E., *Suicide*, Glencoe, IL, 1951.
Parsons, T., *Social Systems and the Evolution of Action Theory*, New York, 1977.
Tocqueville, Alexis de, *Democracy in America*, London, 1994.
Weber, Max, *The Theory of Social and Economic Organization*, New York, 1966.

SECONDARY LITERATURE

Giddens, A., *Capitalism and Modern Social Theory – an Analysis of the Writings of Marx, Durkheim and Max Weber*, London, 1971.

NOTES

1 But Tocqueville also noted that the majority in a democracy are often guaranteed a reasonable portion of the production so that they do not think they have anything to gain by revolution. The minority that would clearly benefit from a revolution may thus be restrained by the majority.

2 Ferdinand Tönnies, *Community and Society*, trans. and ed. by Charles P. Loomis, New York, 1957, pp. 64–5.

3 Max Weber, *The Methodology of the Social Sciences*, trans. and ed. by Edward A. Shils and Henry A. Finch, New York, 1949, p. 58.

4 Ibid., p. 112.

5 M. Weber, *The Theory of Social and Economic Organization,* trans. by A. M. Henderson and Talcott Parsons, New York, 1947, p. 88.

6 Here, Weber is confronted with a serious epistemological problem. As we have previously seen, empirical reality, for Weber, had an almost amorphous character (here he followed Nietzsche and, to some extent, neo-Kantianism). It is therefore difficult to see how we can determine whether ideal-type concepts are adequate or not in relation to an empirical state of affairs. For Weber, there did not seem to be any form of mediation between the nominalistic sphere of the ideal types (that is, Weber had a nominalistic theory of concepts) and the meaningless infinity of the empirical world. Weber, it seems, did not realize that social reality is 'always already' interpreted and given meaning by social agents *before* the researcher starts to work.

7 M. Weber, *Gesammelte Aufsätze zur Religionssoziologie*, vol. 1, Tübingen, 1963, p. 1. This 'preface' is in many ways the key to Weber's sociology.

8 Cf. M. Weber, *The Religion of China: Confucianism and Taoism*, New York/London, 1964, and *The Religion of India: the Sociology of Hinduism and Buddhism*, New Delhi, 1992.

9 M. Weber, *The Protestant Ethic and the Spirit of Capitalism*, London, 1956, pp. 17 ff.

10 Ibid., pp. 181–2.

11 M. Weber, *The Methodology of the Social Sciences*, p. 57.

12 Max Weber, 'Politics as a Vocation', in *From Max Weber: Essays in Sociology*, ed. with an introduction by H. H. Gerth and C. Wright Mills, London, 1970, p. 128.

13 Ibid.

25 New advances in the natural sciences

EINSTEIN AND MODERN PHYSICS

In recent times there has been an explosive growth in the research community. This applies both to the number of active researchers and to the number of topics and approaches. This expansion applies to all branches of research, but especially to the natural sciences and their offshoots in the development of technology. The civilian and military industries are both closely involved in many of these activities. We may point out three scientific-technological revolutions of our time: those of physics, informatics, and biology. We will glance at the development of modern physics, emphasizing the relation between scientific development and technology. But our concluding remarks on the need for interdisciplinary and public discussion also apply to the problems of information technology and biology.

FROM 'SEEING NATURE AS TECHNOLOGY' TO 'SEEING NATURE WITH TECHNOLOGY'

Galilean-Newtonian physics inspired the mechanistic world-view with its basic concepts of material particles and mechanistic causes. In Renaissance science, 'the book of nature' was assumed to be written in mathematical language: geometry allowed access to the inner structure of nature, beyond the knowledge of natural phenomena attainable by immediate perception. The laws of physics and astronomy were thus formulated in mathematical terms. Geometry became an integral part of architecture and art as well as technology. And there was a close connection between geometry and technology: if comprehensible in the language of geometry, nature could at the same time be handled technologically, since in the new perspective nature was seen not only as mechanical movements of material particles, but also as material objects formed according to geometric design – in terms of straight lines and angles, plane surfaces, and circles and spheres, and of balance wheels and pendulums, with linear and circular movements. Nature was thus seen as a gigantic machine. Hobbes, a proponent of the mechanistic-materialistic world-view, compared society with a watch, and Harvey saw the heart as a pump. Epistemology accordingly distinguished between the perceiving subject and the perceived object, man as perceiving subject seeking to perceive nature as a technological system.

The transition from classical Galilean-Newtonian physics to modern physics entailed various changes. There was a redefinition of basic concepts, such as the notions of mass and energy, space and time, and causality. The focus was on Einstein and the theory of relativity. At the same time, there was a redefinition of the conception of nature and of epistemology – in short, as nature had earlier been regarded as technology, technology now became necessary to study nature. Experimentation and exact measurement of phenomena in experiments little by little became totally dependent on an advanced and comprehensive technology.[1] We came to 'see' by means of technology. Technology thus became an extension of the recognizing subject, and thereby the traditional epistemological model of subject–object became problematic. We now discuss causality and uncertainty, and the ontological status of elementary particles: how far has observation become dependent on the concepts and the technology by means of which we observe?

With the transition from classical physics to modern physics, we thus find an epistemological transformation. To put it roughly, while we previously thought that the researcher was cognizant of natural processes as they exist (with their mathematical properties), and that nature therefore could be understood by the principles that we find in engineering – with balance wheels, falling balls, etc. – we now find that natural events have become products of our experimental and observational equipment, determined by the technology of our day and by the art of engineering. We use mathematical models to express what our observational conditions allow us to grasp, but without the requirement that what we are observing exists independently of the concepts and apparatus that we use to measure and observe. 'Realistic' epistemological presuppositions are thereby brought into question.

The unavoidable effect that 'subjective' factors have on the 'object' extends even to our definition of concepts. For instance, in Euclidean geometry, only one straight line is possible between any two points; but when the concept of a straight line is defined operationally, with the aid of measurement by light, the concept of a straight line depends, by definition, on light as it figures in our set of operations. Since light 'bends', we have more than one 'straight line' between the two points. This means that we as researchers, with our equipment and our operational definitions, affect the form of what we investigate.

A GLANCE AT PHYSICS

Research on the atom was crucial for modern physics. In 1911, Ernest Rutherford (1871–1937) proved that the atom is composed of a nucleus orbited by electrons. One of Rutherford's students, the Danish physicist Niels Bohr (1885–1963), further developed this model. The different electrons revolve in particular paths, or orbitals, and if they jump from outer to inner orbitals nearer the nucleus, energy is emitted from the atom, and by the transition in the other direction, energy is absorbed. Thus, we observe surges of discrete quanta of radiation energy. Through further theoretical and experimental research, it was discovered that electrons simultaneously have the character of both particles and waves. Some physicists attributed this paradox to the effect on the research object of our concepts and methods. The electrons appear as waves under certain research conditions and as particles under other conditions. Bohr therefore concluded that the property of being a particle and that of being a wave are complementary.

Werner Heisenberg (1901–1976), who worked at Bohr's institute in the 1920s, emphasized a similar epistemological point: on the microlevel, there will always be an effect by the research conditions on the research objects, so that we cannot measure simultaneously a particle's momentum and spatial position (energy and temporal position) with precision. When we are able to measure exactly where a particle is, we cannot, at the same time, determine its momentum; and when we exactly measure its momentum, we cannot, at the same time, determine where the particle is. This so-called uncertainty principle, along with the discontinuous quantum leaps, led to a statistical view of causality, which is sometimes called indeterminism: cause is not sought for each particular event, but only for a certain number on a statistical basis.

Just as classical physics led to a comprehensive philosophical discussion, from the empiricists and rationalists to Kant, modern physics has also given rise to philosophical discussions: on ontological questions (of elementary particles, matter and energy, and space and time) and epistemological and methodological questions (of how this can recognized). Logical positivism, which was the dominant school in the philosophy of science between World War I and World War II, was heavily influenced by modern physics. Furthermore, many of the leading physicists, such as Heisenberg, Bohr, and Einstein, were personally interested in philosophy. Modern physics has been developed by a large research community in many countries. But it may still be interesting to focus on one person, and Einstein is the obvious choice.

Albert Einstein (1879–1955) was born into a Jewish family in Germany. After a stay in Switzerland, he became, in 1914, professor and director of the Kaiser Wilhelm Institute of Physics in Berlin, where he worked until 1932, when he left Germany because of the rise of Nazism. He settled in the United States at Princeton University. In 1921 he received the Nobel Prize in physics (but not for his theories of relativity). He published his special theory of relativity in 1905, and his general theory of relativity in 1916. Einstein was a pacifist who abominated the German methods of warfare during World War I. He was an advocate of individual liberty and peaceful international cooperation (the League of Nations). He saw Nazism as a major menace that had to be fought, even if it meant using nuclear weapons. Early in World War II, as he became aware that it was theoretically possible to construct atomic weapons, he appealed to President Roosevelt (1882–1945) to produce such weapons. Einstein himself took no part in this work. After the war he opposed further development of nuclear weapons, and he urged other atomic physicists to work for nuclear disarmament. In the mid-1950s, Einstein and the British philosopher Bertrand Russell established an international organization, known as the Pugwash movement, to bring together scientists from the East and the West in order to promote peaceful solutions to international conflicts. Einstein also helped to plan the Hebrew University in Jerusalem, but he refused the invitation to settle there, just as, in 1952, he refused to accept the presidency of Israel. Einstein, with his Jewish background, was a religious person, but he did not believe in a personal God. For Einstein, divinity was to be found in the laws of physics (a parallel with Spinoza?).

Einstein's theories of relativity represent a new interpretation of the concepts of space and time. The special theory of relativity deals with constant motion in a straight line and explains why observers who move in this way in relation to one another arrive at the same invariant formulations of the physical laws. The general theory of relativity deals with accelerating motion and describes gravitation as a property of the four-dimensional space–time continuum.

The results of our measurement are dependent on our measuring equipment. If we measure with a rubber band, the result will be dependent on how far we stretch it. But even an iron rod varies in length depending on the temperature. Einstein worked with concepts such as 'length contraction' and 'time expansion': the length of a rod appears to be shorter when it is measured by a person who is moving past the rod than when it is measured by a person who follows it (and thus is standing still in relation to the rod). The time between two events seems to be shorter when people observe the events in the same location in relation to themselves than when they find that the events occur in two different locations because they are moving in relation to the events. In other words, in motion, length becomes shorter and time longer! This was experimentally confirmed by showing that unstable element-ary particles have a longer lifespan when they are in motion (near the speed of light) than when they are not in motion. This would not be noticeable at a slower velo-city, but it is noticeable when the velocity approaches the speed of light. Moreover, we cannot add velocities in the same way as we do in classical physics.[2]

The velocity of light cannot be surpassed. A twentieth-century German philo-sopher (Hans Blumenberg) saw in this principle a fundamental limit to human cogni-tion: we will never be able to test our hypotheses about the universe because its dimensions are so vast that it would take billions of light years before 'we' would get a result – and by then it would no longer be a problem for 'us'! Therefore, we will always be in the dark regarding questions about the cosmos as a whole.[3]

Modern physics requires coordination of theoretical and experimental research. Important aspects of experimental research today require massive equipment and an extended organization, such as the CERN facility. Many thousands of scientists, engineers, technicians, and workers have participated in building and maintaining such equipment. Its building and service are astronomically expensive. Technology, economy, and administration thus become integrated factors in research. Inter-disciplinary cooperation and research-political management have become neces-sary, but they are not always problem free. To recapitulate, while we earlier used to see nature *as* technology, we now see nature *with* technology. This increased use of technology in the process of research requires extensive organizational and eco-nomic efforts. Modern physics plays an important role in modern society, which, to a great degree, is permeated by scientific conceptions and by scientific products and solutions. To a great extent, we think in terms of scientific concepts, and by using scientific and technological innovations we can change the conditions of life on Earth. Never before have we known and mastered as much as today. At the same time, we live in the shadow of innumerable threats, from those of war and ecological crises to those of material injustice and the decay of social institutions. How should we, theoretically and practically, improve our conceptions and mas-tery of what we have brought about?

SCIENTIFIC DIVERSITY AND TECHNOLOGICAL DEVELOPMENT – THE APPLICATION OF SCIENCE AND INTERDISCIPLINARY APPROACHES

USEFULNESS AND LIMITS OF INSTRUMENTAL REASON ILLUSTRATED BY NORMATIVE DECISION THEORY

In modern times, man's relationship to nature has become one of increasing domination, scientifically and technologically. In this process, nature has been conceived of as an unproblematic source of resources for the realization of human goals. We did not hold ourselves responsible for our actions in regard to nature. We were all free to exploit nature, at least to the degree that our neighbours' property rights were not harmed.

This attitude rests on the presupposition that nature is infinitely renewable. But this presupposition has gradually proved to be untenable, and, in our day, technological domination has caused permanent and complicated crises. These crises become especially noticeable in their various and often unforeseen harmful consequences in nature as well as in society. The key themes here are energy crises and pollution, social and regional conflicts, and endangered animal and plant species. It has become more and more clear that the ecological conditions of life are vulnerable. Finally, we have come to realize that a more careful interaction with nature is necessary for our survival. This experience of crisis has shown not only the limits of nature but also the inherent limits of a purely instrumental rationality and practice.

We will examine certain interdisciplinary and practical problems connected with such an instrumental scientization. We will first look at the usefulness of cost-benefit analyses in connection with modern technology, and we will do so by focusing on normative decision theory, while also considering some of the limitations of such an approach. We will emphasize the philosophical aspects of these problems, not the empirical ones, in that we will discuss the question of what is rational and moral, without considering the political and economic conflicts of interest and other empirical questions.

Normative decision theory proceeds from a given situation for decision-making in which we can choose between alternatives, each having different, and more or less probable consequences. Decision-makers are rational, according to this theory, when they choose the alternative that has the highest mathematical score for the probability and value of its estimated consequences. This is a procedure reminiscent of utilitarianism (cf. Bentham's proposal of a utility calculation). Hence, we find this kind of reasoning in economic calculations. In normative decision theory, the utility calculation is thus embedded in a mathematical model: we try to find the mathematical expression for the probability and for the desirability of the various consequences, and on this basis we decide, by calculation, which alternative to choose.

We will briefly illustrate how normative decision theory covers an interplay of utility morality, scientifically established conceptions of probability, and mathematical calculations. We will at the same time discuss the role that instrumental rationality plays in this connection and the need for interdisciplinary procedures and public discussion. We may, for instance, have the following problem: 'How are we to obtain enough inexpensive energy in the next five years?' We then have to investigate the various alternatives and their consequences, and, on this basis, arrive at a rational choice. If we were to use normative decision theory in such a problem, we would take the following steps:

1   formulating the goal
2   investigating the alternatives
3   analysing their consequences
4   making an evaluation
5   making our choice.

1   Formulating a goal is a *normative* task. Evaluating whether the goal is desirable and just is a question that lies outside all sciences. But there are many practical problems surrounding the goal which are open to scientific investigation. Formulating the goal is often conceived as a part of the way decision-makers describe the situation. In the standard case, we assume that both the situation and the goal are clearly and correctly acknowledged by the decision-makers. In real life, this is certainly not always the case.

2   Different alternatives may be chosen. It could, for instance, be a question of the relation between different ways of generating energy – power from water, oil, gas, nuclear, wind, etc. – and different ways of using this energy – including different forms of energy saving. It is part of the decision-maker's role to be cognizant of these alternatives; but further elaboration of this knowledge requires, in principle, scientific support. It is *science* which helps us to see more clearly what alternatives we have, and which means (technological solutions) are possible. And it is science that helps to make the new instrumental approaches possible.

3   In the same way, knowledge of the different consequences of each alternative can be further developed through *scientific* effort: it is through scientific research of various kinds that we can arrive at reasonably good answers to the question of the possible consequences of each alternative, and how probable these different consequences are.

4   In decision theory, the degree of probability of the different consequences is quantified with *numerical values*. Correspondingly, we attempt to quantify with positive and negative numerical values *what* the consequences *mean* for the involved parties. (Cf. the problems connected with such a quantification in the utilitarian calculus.)

5   The greater the value, positive or negative, that a consequence is assumed to have, the more weight we give this consequence in weighing the different alternatives with their respective consequences. At the same time we give more weight to the consequences that are more probable than to those less probable. In order to account for both of these concerns, in normative decision theory we work with the mathematical products of the numerical values of the probability and of the desirability of each consequence. Each alternative is then evaluated by the sum of these products. *Rational choice*, according to normative decision theory, is the choice of the alternative having the *highest sum of the products* (or the lowest sum, if the sums are negative).

The following diagram, with given numerical values illustrates these points:

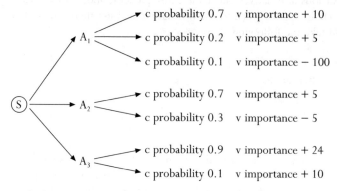

Explanation:
S: choice situation; A: alternative; c: probability; v: importance (value, desirability)

In order to quantify probability (c) we have chosen here to use a scale from zero to one.[4] If we want to 'play safe', we may (pessimistically) assign the unwanted consequences the higher numerical value for probability and the desired consequences the lower numerical value. In order to quantify the importance (v), we have chosen to use the complete scale from zero to (nearly) infinity, both in a positive and a negative direction. In this way it is possible to use 'absolute values'. The extermination of the human race may thus be characterized as 'infinitely negative'.

In our example, we get the following sums of the products:

A_1: $0.7 \cdot 10 + 0.2 \cdot 5 + 0.1 \cdot (-100) = 7 + 1 - 10 = -2$
A_2: $0.7 \cdot 5 + 0.3 \cdot (-5) = 3.5 - 1.5 = +2$
A_3: $0.9 \cdot 24 + 0.1 \cdot (-10) = 21.6 - 1 = +20.6$

In this case, it is therefore rational to choose the last alternative (A_3), and to prefer the second (A_2) to the first (A_1).

Such an abstract case of normative decision theory may seem remote from what we actually do. It may also invite objections to the attempt to assign numerical scores to the different kinds of values. Such objections should be taken seriously. At the same time, it is important to see that normative decision theory is not supposed to be able to explain *actual* behaviour, but to help us determine what a rational choice *ought to be*. And most people will probably agree that such a scheme accounts for many of the intuitions that we have of reasonable choice, as for example, when we plan to build a power plant or a bridge. It is probably quite accurate in assessing the underlying rationality of modern technological projects, from the choice of medical treatment to energy and defence policies. We shall outline certain positive aspects of such a procedure.

1   This way of developing the different alternatives may strengthen our sense of reality because it forces us to look at the various alternatives and their respective consequences in a systematic and scientific way. At the same time, it may help us to develop our imagination because it requires that we make an effort to find alternative solutions.

2   This approach indicates that we ought to concentrate our research on the con-
    sequences that have the greatest importance, positively or negatively, and, cor-
    respondingly, direct less effort into the consequences that are unimportant.
    This provides direction for our work, distinguishing what is important from
    what is unimportant.

3   This way of distinguishing between different kinds of questions may help us to
    become aware of their epistemological status. Is the question normative, or
    does it pertain to some scientific discipline, and, if so, which one? This helps
    us to see more clearly what we know and what we do not know, what we may
    find out scientifically and what requires ethical discussion.

THE NEED FOR INTERDISCIPLINARY ANALYSIS

The value of interdisciplinary analysis may need further explanation. The decision-
theoretical scheme makes it clear why we often need an interdisciplinary approach.
For example, when we are planning a nuclear power plant, questions about the different alternatives and their respective consequences are, of course, not questions
that can be clarified by means of different forms of physical-technical expertise
alone. Here we also need economic, ecological, and social-science expertise. Cost
and risk are involved at all of these levels. If we are to make a rational decision,
we must obtain the most realistic picture of all of these aspects of the project, and
this task requires the use of all relevant disciplines. Many projects have foundered
unnecessarily because of blindness on the part of overspecialized expert advisers to
certain implications of the undertaking.[5] In such cases, an interdisciplinary approach
is required. The scientific development of different alternatives and their possible
consequences requires more than technical expertise. For example, a well-drilling
project in an underdeveloped country also needs insight into economy, health care,
education, and social and cultural conditions. The more comprehensive the consequences of a project, the more important it is to develop the best possible
consultative approach. Such examples illustrate the point that a given group of
experts may prove to be too one-sided. In such cases, a reasonable requirement
is to expand the number of disciplines represented in the project. We must do this
to attain an adequate understanding of the project.

Ideally, we ought to include all relevant disciplines and carry out thorough investigations on all levels. But, in practice, this requirement must be moderated in light
of the cost, both in time and money. Research may continue forever, while practical resolutions are subject to time limits. In the example of the well-drilling project, the need to supplement the original technical expertise with expertise in health
care, education, and social conditions may seem fairly obvious. But in other cases
it may be difficult to say exactly what is 'enough', in the sense of 'optimal', given
the objective need for more insight of varying kinds, and given the cost of obtaining this insight in relation to its actual usefulness.

At some point, the different groups of experts must *cooperate*, at least in such
a way that the various disciplines are presented 'in one intelligible package' to the
'employer'. In that sense, the representatives of the various disciplines, such as
economists and ecologists, should be able to communicate with one another on an
academic level. This requires that they be able to discuss their own methodological
and conceptual presuppositions. This is often difficult.

Hence, there is often an objective need to expand the range of scientific expertise; for example, from one natural-scientific discipline to several such disciplines, or to a group of disciplines including the social sciences. When human factors are involved, we need the expertise of the social sciences. However, there are specific problems in predicting the possible consequences of human behaviour. Predictions may be difficult enough in many natural sciences, such as meteorology and somatic medicine. But in many social and psychological settings, prediction seems to be very problematic.[6] In part, this is also a problem of logic: what we do is in some degree determined by what we know. Research gives us new insight. Thus, in the future there will be forms of insight that we do not possess today, and that will influence what we do then. Those aspects of our future actions cannot possibly be predicted today.[7] Therefore, it is difficult, in principle, to use numerical values for probability when human factors are involved.

If we decide to play safe, we must be even more cautious in making decisions involving high risk. It is worth emphasizing that this strategy is not 'less rational' than gambling. We may rather argue that it is more rational to be careful than to be daring, especially when the well-being of others is at stake. Furthermore, it is clear that those who generally want to include only a small portion of the natural sciences in the decision-making process are thereby not especially rational. On the contrary, it is a rational demand that, for example, ecological and sociological disciplines in many cases *ought* to be included – and this also applies to the risk factors of nuclear power plants, where the human factor enters the picture, both as intended actions (such as terrorism) and as unintended actions (such as poor safety routines).

During such an investigation of the different alternatives and their probable consequences, the persons who are to make a decision may find that the entire situation appears in a new light. For example, it could turn out that the project has possible negative consequences that had not previously been thought of or realized clearly enough – possible negative consequences that put the original goal in a new and critical light: should the whole project now be revised or rejected in light of the new insight and in view of more important goals in our society? The project may prove to be something different than what we originally thought, and this requires its complete revision. This is a decisive point.

That a rational demand for an expansion of the spectrum of expertise may lead to a revision and, eventually, a change in the entire project shows that we have gone beyond the limits of strict decision theory to a self-critical and reflexive discussion. This does not mean that the analysis based on decision theory is rejected; it has been placed within a broader frame of 'freely-arguing' analysis where we, in the community, try to combine the different perspectives and to evaluate the project in question in relation to other goals and values.

In more comprehensive industrial and military projects, the possible negative consequences are often of a deep-rooted, global, and long-lasting nature. The consequences last longer than the election term of politicians and longer than the time frame for business calculations. In many cases (such as radioactive contamination), it is a question of future generations. And quite often, the consequences extend beyond a nation's borders (as in the case of pollution). In such situations, and in light of the interdisciplinary expertise that is often required, there is an objective need for an open and enlightened public debate in which all of the perspectives and all of the involved parties may, in principle, participate. Ideally, a continual and intensive interdisciplinary exchange is needed on alternatives and consequences, and a critical discussion covering the possible revision and rejection of the project.

So far we have not commented on the purely *normative* questions, either in connection with the goal of the project or in connection with the importance of the various consequences. We shall briefly comment on some aspects of these normative questions. First, it is worth noting that critical reflection on the project as a whole may represent a learning process in which we simultaneously try out and reshape our concepts and preferences. It is not only empirical questions that are under discussion, but also the question of how adequate the concepts are that we use in the various disciplines. Since *normative* questions are always formed within a conceptual framework, the attempt to improve the conceptual 'grasp' is already relevant to the normative discussion. This point needs a few comments: the sharp distinction between facts and values is somewhat unfortunate because *concepts* play a formative role, both for facts and values (or norms). Thus, normative debates are often discussions about what the matter actually *is*; that is, about which concepts should be used in describing and explaining it.

The decision-theoretical scheme is tailor-made for many economic decisions; for example, whether or not to invest in a new factory. Here the question of value is, in principle, simple enough. It is a question of money, of cost and profit based on market prices. But when this scheme is used on comprehensive projects, such as nuclear power plants and defence installations, we encounter not only all of the intricate interdisciplinary problems that we have mentioned but also more acute questions of value, such as the relationship between money and health, or between our costs and those of other agents, etc.

The scientization of modern society is characterized by the fact that such comprehensive problems have become normal. The result is not only epistemological and normative problems, but also problems of political governance. The problems of governance are manifold, and they also include the need already mentioned for sufficient overview and insight. Here, the solution seems to lie in a Sisyphean task of internal, interdisciplinary cooperation and open public discussion.[8]

That the sciences have become more varied and complex can also be illustrated by modern physics. While a scientist in Galileo's day could observe swinging pendulums and falling balls, scientists today have a wall of technology between themselves and their research objects. The CERN nuclear research centre in Switzerland has a particle accelerator with a circumference of 27 km in order to 'observe' nature. Today we relate to nature by virtue of complex technology and complex theoretical presuppositions that require lengthy training to use and understand. But also in everyday life, our relationship to nature and to one another has become increasingly characterized by such a mediation via technology and science: most people no longer write with pen and paper, but with word processors that represent a barrier of theoretical and technical sophistication between the writer and what is written – a sophistication that few understand fully. This also applies to everyday life in general, where, for example, television and radio increasingly mediate life experience and codes for interpreting it. The process of scientization thus creates a technical and theoretical medium for our relationship to things, to our fellow human beings, and to social phenomena. It is therefore vital, both for what we do and for what we are, that one-sidedness and banality do not characterize our grasp of science and technology.

In light of the ecological crisis, this need for better scientific analysis and more rational long-term preferences and attitudes has become urgent. Here there is also a need for a rational formation of public opinion, in the sense that we must be open to the possibility of changing our orientation and projects. We may thus say that scientific development has given us a disciplinary diversity and an instrumental type of decision-making that brings us face to face with entirely new problems. Is it possible to break out of this cycle of development, or is the only responsible answer to go further in our rationalization, along the lines that we have suggested in this section? We will take a look at both of these viewpoints, as represented, respectively, by Heidegger and by Habermas (Ch. 27).

QUESTIONS

'Earlier we saw nature as technology; now we see nature with technology.' Comment on this statement, and discuss the epistemological differences between classical Galilean-Newtonian physics and modern physics (Einstein).

Discuss the kinds of expertise that should be included in the planning of a complex facility such as a power plant.

SUGGESTIONS FOR FURTHER READING

PRIMARY LITERATURE

Einstein, A., *Relativity, the Special and the General Theory: A Popular Exposition*, London, 1954.

SECONDARY LITERATURE

Churchland, P. and Hooker, C. A. (eds), *Images of Science*, London, 1985.
Jonas, H., *The Imperative of Responsibility: In Search of an Ethics for the Technological Age*, Chicago, 1984.

NOTES

1 For example, the particle accelerator at CERN (European Laboratory for Particle Physics).
2 According to classical physics, if a passenger runs forward at 10 km/h (v) while riding in a railway carriage that is rolling at 90 km/h (u), the passenger should be moving forward in relation to the ground at a velocity of 100 km/h, i.e. $(10 + 90)$, or $(v + u)$. However, in Einsteinian physics, the passenger's velocity in relation to the ground becomes:

$$\frac{v + u}{1 + \dfrac{v + u}{c^2}} \quad \text{or} \quad \frac{10 + 90}{1 + \dfrac{10 + 90}{c^2}}$$

where c is the speed of light ($= 300,000$ km/h). This contradicts classical physics, in which velocity is said to be an additive physical quantity.

Even unlimited increasing force will not cause a body to exceed the velocity of light, which is the maximal velocity in nature; that is, it is a physical constant. Mass increases when its velocity changes by the formula:

$$m = m_0 \gamma$$

where m_0 is the mass at rest and gamma (γ) is equal to:

$$\frac{1}{\sqrt{1 - \dfrac{v^2}{c^2}}}$$

When the velocity approaches c (the speed of light), the mass therefore increases towards infinity. This means that the speed of light can never be exceeded. When v approaches c,

$$\frac{v^2}{c^2} \text{ approaches 1, and } 1 - \frac{v^2}{c^2}$$

approaches zero; the result is the square root of a fraction whose denominator decreases towards zero, and whose numerator is always 1. Gamma (γ) and thus the mass (m) therefore approach infinity when v approaches c.

3 Einstein showed the equivalence of mass and energy with the formula:

$$E = mc^2$$

As follows from this formula, light possesses mass and momentum. Because of its mass, light is attracted by bodies of mass and its trajectory is bent. If we define a straight line as a light ray's trajectory of motion, it is possible in a space with centres of gravity to connect any two points by more than one straight line. This 'curved' space is described by means of non-Euclidean geometry.

Thus, the general theory of relativity says that the velocity of a point mass that is influenced by gravitational forces may be conceived of as a geometric property of the space–time continuum. We cannot distinguish between a body undergoing uniform acceleration and a body subject to a gravitational field. In his theory of general relativity, Einstein predicted several observable phenomena and their magnitude. One of his famous predictions was confirmed by measuring the light deflection from a star during a solar eclipse (1919). Other predictions were experimentally confirmed in the 1960s.

4 We are ignoring the margins of the numerical values, such as 0.7 ± 0.02. By using such margins above and below the chosen numerical value, we can make calculations with upper and lower limits (such as 0.72 and 0.68).

5 The so-called Green Revolution in grain production is one example. Western style well-drilling projects is another. See Mette Jørstad's report to NORAD (Norwegian Agency for Development Cooperation) (15 December 1982), 'A social scientist's view of strategies in order that water development programmes in Central and East Africa may attain their explicit and implicit goals'. The report shows that the managers of the project concentrated on one-sided technological expertise with the result that the social conditions necessary for the project to function were overlooked.

6 An extreme case: who can say what the British government will do with its radioactive waste in 30 years?

7 Cf. Popper's argument questioning the idea of total predictability of human behaviour (Ch. 26).

8 An open interdisciplinary debate between researchers is necessary, but not sufficient. Objective, detailed, and complete journalistic information is also necessary, but not sufficient. We need free communication between the research community and journalists.

26 A glance at contemporary philosophy

In this chapter we will briefly survey contemporary philosophy, focusing especially on logical positivism and analytical philosophy, phenomenology and existentialism, and feminism. It is important to remember that all great philosophy lives in contemporary philosophy. Platonism, Aristotelianism, Thomism, Spinozism, Kantianism, etc., all form a part of contemporary philosophy; therefore, we can understand today's debates only by becoming familiar with the history of philosophy.

LOGICAL POSITIVISM – LOGIC AND EMPIRICISM

In the period between World Wars I and II, several new initiatives in philosophy emerged. For instance, modern physics exerted a new influence that was mediated through extensive epistemological discussions within logical positivism, and the new existential situation in a complex and science-based society was discussed not only by the emerging social sciences, but also by philosophical schools such as phenomenology and existentialism.

Logical positivism, or logical empiricism, as it is also called, may be seen as a descendant of British empiricism (Locke, Berkeley, Hume) and of Enlightenment philosophy. At the same time, it may be seen as a philosophical response to the new achievements of modern physics (Einstein) and of the new logic. Finally, it may also be seen as a reaction to the rise of totalitarian and irrationalist ideologies in the 1920s and 1930s, especially Nazism in Germany.

Today, few would espouse logical positivism as a position in its orthodox form. But this school has played an important role by emphasizing the basic importance of sober and argumentative procedures in philosophy and in intellectual work in general, and by its criticism of conceptual opaqueness and seducing rhetoric. In this way, logical positivism has had an important civilizing effect, despite the criticism that gradually was directed against some of its basic philosophical claims – a criticism which was formulated not least by the proponents themselves. After World War II, logical positivism evolved into various forms of the philosophy of science, with an emphasis either on logic and formal language or on conceptual analysis (cf. Wittgenstein and analytical philosophy).

Classical British empiricism, from Locke to Hume, started primarily with the senses. This empiricism was thus based on psychology. Unlike British empiricism, logical positivism was based on linguistics. It was primarily concerned with methodological questions of how knowledge could be confirmed, of how our state-ments about reality should be formulated, and of how claims are strengthened or weakened when tested by experience. We may, in this sense, speak of a synthesis of classical empiricism and modern methodology and logic, resulting in a logical empiricism. Hence, this philosophy appeals to the logical structure of language (syn-tax) and to methodological verification. Its name, 'logical empiricism', indicates this shift away from psychology towards language and methodology.

NEW LOGIC

From Aristotle to the nineteenth century, logic had not changed radically. But with the pioneering work of thinkers like Gottlob Frege[1] (1848–1925) and later Bertrand Russell (1872–1970) (and Alfred N. Whitehead [1861–1947], who worked with Russell[2]), logic underwent a radical development. Their goal was to show that mathematics could be regarded as a branch of logic – they claimed, in effect, that mathematical concepts could be defined precisely in terms of concepts from logic. This project also led to a 'mathematization' of the discipline of logic itself, as math-ematical symbols and forms were used to express logical relations. In mathemati-cal language we can say that 'a' is greater than 'b' by the formula 'a $>$ b'. Now, the sign '$>$' marks a specific relation; if we wish to represent the more general case of 'a' being related in some way to 'b', we can write 'aRb', where 'R' stands for an arbitrary relation. Modern logic is divided into several subdisciplines. Its most basic divisions are propositional logic, which deals with the logical relations between propositions, and quantification theory, which deals with the logical force of quantifiers – words such as 'some' and 'all'. Set theory, or the theory of classes, plays an important role; it was conceived of by Frege and Russell as a point of transition between logic and mathematics, and it is still used as a formal instrument for setting up (explaining) the various other disciplines of logic. Another special discipline of importance is modal logic, which treats of the logical properties of the notions of possibility and necessity. Furthermore, we have the theories of argu-mentation and of interpretation.

We may here mention certain features of propositional logic. Consider the two sentences, 'My dog is green' and 'My dog is big'. These are simple sentences in the sense that they are not built out of other, simpler sentences, as in the com-pound sentence, 'My dog is green and my dog is big'. It can easily be seen that the truth value of the compound sentence (proposition) – i.e., the question of whether it is true or false – depends on the truth value of the simple sentences. If 'My dog is green' is true and also 'My dog is big', the compound sentence formed by link-ing the two sentences with 'and' must also be true. If one (or both) of the con-stituent sentences is false, the compound sentence must be false. Therefore, we can construct a calculus of sentences (propositions) that can be used to calculate the truth value of compound sentences on the basis of possible combinations of truth values for the simple sentences occurring in them. For the case 'My dog is big and green', we have these possibilities:

p = 'My dog is big'
q = 'My dog is green'

p·q (p and q) = 'My dog is big and green' (t = true, f = false)

p	q	p·q
t	t	t
t	f	f
f	t	f
f	f	f

For the case 'My dog is big or green' (p v q), we have the following table of possible truth values:

p	q	p v q
t	t	t
t	f	t
f	t	t
f	f	f

    The truth values of the simple sentences (propositions) must be decided empirically: we have to determine (see, in this case) whether the proposition expressed by the sentence, 'My dog is green', is true or not (it will be true if the dog actually is green). This may give rise to a general picture of how thoughts (propositions) relate to reality: only if can we show an arbitrary sentence to be a determinate compound of simple sentences, each of which can be verified empirically, does the sentence have a clear meaning. Such an approach shaped the kind of philosophy that came to be known as logical empiricism or logical positivism: the role of philosophy became analytical, showing whether and how particular sentences (propositions) could be related to reality in the required way.

LOGICAL POSITIVISM AND LOGICAL ATOMISM

Originally, the term 'logical positivism' was applied to a group of scientifically oriented philosophers in Vienna during the 1920s and 1930s – the Vienna Circle – which included Moritz Schlick (1882–1936), Otto Neurath (1882–1945), and Rudolf Carnap (1891–1970). Other German-speaking philosophers, such as Hans Reichenbach (1891–1953) and Carl Hempel (1905–), were also a part of the same school. The early work of Ludwig Wittgenstein (1889–1951) was a source of inspiration for the logical empiricists (cf. his *Tractatus Logico-Philosophicus* [1921]). The logical positivists had in common the distancing of themselves from speculative philosophy. For them, metaphysics was obsolete! The basis of philosophy should be logic (including mathematics) and the empirical sciences, with physics as a model. Beyond this, the only philosophy that they respected was the analytical philosophy of science that they themselves practised.

    We find a corresponding attack on traditional philosophy in the British philosophy of the time. In part, this was a conceptual criticism based on everyday language, as in the analytical philosophy of George Edward Moore (1873–1958); in part, a

more formal criticism, as in the logical atomism of Bertrand Russell. A prominent defender of logical positivism in British philosophy was Alfred Jules Ayer
(1910–1989).[3]

Russell held that there is a one-to-one relation between language and reality:
language consists, in part, of 'atomic' verbal expressions that refer to atomic facts,
and, in part, of the logical relationship between these verbal expressions – and these
logical relationships correspond to formal logic. For example, the words 'cat' and
'mat' are used as atomic verbal expressions to refer to atomic facts, that is, to the
cat and to the mat. The sentence, 'The cat is lying on the mat', stands in a one-
to-one relation to the fact that the cat is lying on the mat, since simple linguistic
expressions refer to simple states of affairs. At the same time, the syntactical
form of the sentence correctly expresses the relationship between the cat and
the mat. Thus, we have the thesis that reality consists of simple, delimited facts,
and that a cognitively meaningful language consists, in the same way, of simple,
delimited expressions that refer to these facts, while the correct logical relationship between these linguistic expressions corresponds to the relationship that
exists between the given facts. The interesting verbal expressions are sentences that
claim that something is the case. Such statements can stand in a one-to-one relation
with reality, and may thus be cognitively meaningful. Other forms of verbal expression such as exclamations, single words, commands, questions, value judgements, and lyrical formulations cannot have such a function, and thus they fall
outside the field of interest. This thesis represents *atomism* in the sense that reality
is said to be composed of simple, delimited facts, that language is composed of
simple delimited expressions, and that the two have an external relationship with
each other.

Logical atomism is thus opposed to dialectical reasoning in which different concepts and states of affairs are said to go beyond one another and point towards other
concepts and states of affairs. Dialectics tends to point towards totalities based on
internal relationships between concepts. We have an *internal relationship* when a
concept cannot be defined without this relationship to other concepts; the complete definition of the concept is dependent on other concepts (cf. the view that
the concept of action has to be defined in relation to concepts such as those of intention, agent, and objects). In logical atomism, we have an *external relationship* when
a concept is what it is, independently of its relationship to other concepts – as when
the cat is understood to be what it is regardless of whether it is related to the mat
or not.

In logical positivism, two conditions must be fulfilled before a statement can
express knowledge:

1 The statement must be well-formulated; that is, it must be grammatically (logically) correct.
2 The statement must be empirically testable, that is, verifiable.

Statements that do not fulfil these conditions do not express knowledge. They
are cognitively (epistemically) meaningless. Ethical, religious, and metaphysical
statements – 'thou shalt not kill', 'God is love', 'substance is one' – are thus cognitively meaningless according to these positivist criteria for cognitive meaning.

These statements do not express knowledge. That such statements may be emotionally meaningful is, of course, not denied. Value statements, for example, often have great meaning, for the individual as well as for society. The point, according to this thesis, is that these statements do not represent knowledge.

We can briefly summarize logical positivism as follows: there are only two kinds of cognitively meaningful statements, namely, analytical statements and well-formulated, synthetic *a posteriori* statements. In other words, the only epistemically meaningful statements are those of the formal sciences (logic, mathematics) and verifiable empirical statements. In simple terms, this was the core of logical positivism in the period between World Wars I and II among the Vienna Circle.

The distinction between cognitively meaningful statements and cognitively meaningless statements, between genuine knowledge and pseudo-knowledge, is here defined by the distinction between statements that are verifiable and statements that are not verifiable, and this distinction is identified with the distinction between science and pseudo-science. Like other forms of empiricism, logical positivism was a reaction against rationalism, that is to say, against statements that purport to give true insight but do not fulfil the testing requirements of observation and hypothetico-deductive research. Theology and classical metaphysics (such as ontology) are thus rejected as being cognitively meaningless. As we have previously mentioned, this rejection is problematic since we have to ask whether this empiricist thesis itself falls into the category that it declares to be cognitively meaningless: can this thesis itself be tested empirically? This objection has been mentioned earlier in connection with Hume among others.

Value judgements – ethical and aesthetic statements – are cognitively meaningless, according to this positivist position. But in this case the rejection has a different character than it does in regard to theological and metaphysical statements. We may say that ethical and aesthetic statements are *cognitively* meaningless, but that such statements, as opposed to theological and metaphysical statements, are not supposed to be cognitively meaningful: they are meant to express and mediate attitudes and evaluations that cannot be based cognitively, but that still play an important role in our lives.

The Vienna Circle was anything but indifferent on political questions. They firmly opposed fascism in the period between the two World Wars: the empiricist thesis necessarily rejected aspects of fascism as cognitively meaningless. The logical positivists could thus allow themselves to take a political and ethical stand. But the salient point is that they did not think that they could base their choice of a normative position on rational argument. Ultimately, on ethical-political questions, we must rely on non-rational decisions: we make a decision which, in principle, cannot be rationally legitimized. Regardless of whether logical positivism could expose the nonsense of fascism, according to the empiricists' definition of nonsense ('scientifically unverifiable'), it still could not reject the basic norms of fascism. In other words, the logical positivists could reject what was empirically unverified and the unverifiable in the fascists' statements (such as anti-Semitism, and the millennial visions of the Third Reich). But the logical positivists explicitly denied the possibility of argument on basic norms and principles: argument in this area cannot lead to compelling conclusions.

KARL POPPER AND 'CRITICAL RATIONALISM'

We have previously mentioned that an inductively established general statement can never be verified (cf. Ch. 7, The dispute over method). We can never verify that 'all swans are white', since all new observations of white swans will only add to the, in principle, *finite* number of confirming observations, while this general statement refers to an *infinite* number of cases ('*all* swans . . .'). On the other hand, one black swan will falsify the statement.

This kind of reflection led to a shift of the criteria for scientifically meaningful statements, from the requirement that the statement must be verifiable *to* the requirement that it must be *falsifiable*: in order for a statement to be scientific, it must, in principle, be falsifiable. This point was central in the thought of Karl Popper (1902–1994).[4]

We are talking about statements which are falsifiable *in principle*: the question of what we, at any given time, can actually falsify, is dependent on the technological situation. A certain technology is required to falsify a statement about the temperature on the dark side of the moon, or in the core of the moon. Today, we can falsify statements about the temperature on the dark side of the moon; but we still cannot falsify statements about the temperature of the core of the moon, although, in principle, we could be able to do so in the future with better technology. Therefore, the statement, 'the temperature of the core of the moon is 70°C' is scientifically meaningful, because it is, *in principle*, falsifiable.

But what about the statement, 'the average temperature on the surface of the earth when the human race is extinct, will be 70°C'? This statement is, in principle, not falsifiable since no one will be alive to falsify it (assuming that no other intelligent creatures replace human beings). But is this statement, then, cognitively meaningless, and not scientific? Scientists would probably be reluctant to draw this conclusion: they would hardly think that such statements are scientifically meaningless.

This shows that it is problematic to identify the distinction between statements that are falsifiable-in-principle and statements that are not falsifiable-in-principle with the distinction between science and non-science, and even that between cognitively meaningful and cognitively meaningless statements.

Popper's *The Logic of Scientific Discovery* ('*Logik der Forschung*') (1934; English translation, 1959) is a seminal text in the philosophy of science. It stands in a close, but critical, relationship to logical empiricism, and it derives from the empirical tradition going back to Locke. This empirical attitude requires clear formulation and rigorous testing of claims in order to promote the growth of knowledge. Popper himself used the term *critical rationalism* in reference to his theory. He disputed the view that there is an inductive method of legitimate inference from specific to general statements. Regardless of how many white swans we have seen, we cannot conclude that all swans are white (cf. Hume on induction). Furthermore, we cannot extrapolate from observations of particular events to *hypotheses* of *theoretical notions* (such as $F = ma$; that is, force equals mass multiplied by acceleration [cf. Ch. 7]).

How can we, then, justify general statements in the form of hypotheses or laws? According to Popper, we can do so by a *deductive* method of testing. This implies that hypotheses are first tested empirically after they have been proposed. The question of how we arrive at a hypothesis should thus be distinguished from how we justify, or test, this hypothesis. The question of how we arrive at a hypothesis is a psychological question – a question that can be clarified through empirical research. How to justify a hypothesis is a logical or methodological problem that cannot be solved by empirical research, since empirical research presupposes that the method of empirical research is legitimate. We thus arrive at a fundamental distinction between questions of fact, which pertain to the empirical sciences, and questions of justification or validity, which are to be clarified by the logic of research.

How, then, do we test the proposed hypothesis? Empirical testing is carried out by deducing specific statements from the hypothesis and these statements are then verified or falsified according to whether they fit the observational statements. The deduced statements say what will happen under given conditions. The statement is true if what it says will occur does occur. If this does not occur, the statement is false. When the result is positive, the hypothesis has passed the test – this time. But this was just one of an infinite number of possible deductions and tests. Consequently, we cannot know whether the hypothesis is universally true. But if the result is negative, the hypothesis has been proved to be wrong.

Thus, there is an asymmetrical relationship between what follows from an empirically confirmed implication of a hypothesis, and what follows from an empirically disconfirmed implication of the same hypothesis. If one of the deductions of a hypothesis is true, we still do not know whether the hypothesis is true. But if one of the deductions is false, we know that the hypothesis is false. Consequently, the genuine test is found in falsification, not in verification, which is, in principle, unachievable. This means that the best way to check a hypothesis is not by performing many 'easy' tests, but by performing the most difficult. If a hypothesis holds up under such testing, we may begin to view it as confirmed – but this result is always open to later falsification. Furthermore, it is important to express and present our results clearly and accessibly, so that others can readily detect any weakness.

The logical positivists were very concerned to distinguish clearly between science and metaphysics. They defined this as a distinction between what is verifiable and what is not verifiable, and this again was a distinction between what is cognitively meaningful and what is cognitively meaningless. A central point for Popper was his denial that scientific hypotheses and theories are verifiable. According to Popper, *falsifiability*, not verifiability, is the criterion of *science*. Popper, too, was interested in the distinction between science and metaphysics, and this is defined by the distinction between what is empirically falsifiable and what is not: to the degree that a theory is not falsifiable, it is not scientific, according to Popper. But he did not claim that this distinction is, at the same time, a distinction between what is cognitively meaningful and what is cognitively meaningless. Here, Popper did not share the logical positivistic view.

But what is the logical status of this criterion of demarcation? How do we know that this is true? Popper replied that his criterion is ultimately a conventional proposal, something that we decide to accept, and that is beyond rational argument. Popper thus maintained a form of *decisionism*: on this level, a binding rational discussion is not possible; here, we must decide in favour of one or the other.[5] But at the same time, Popper added that he 'believes that a reasonable discussion is always possible between parties interested in the truth, and ready to pay attention to each other'.[6]

Popper used the term 'critical rationalism' to refer to his own position, in connection with the emphasis that he placed on rational discussion, on reason, both in scientific and in practical connections. For Popper, it was a question of maintaining an open trial in which we challenge falsification by possible opponents who can dispute our claims, an attitude that means that we do not argue in order to 'win', but in order to learn. We remain open to the possibility that the opponent may be right and our own position wrong. We have confidence in the common use of reason as an aid for both parties. For Popper, this was rationalism, the reliance on the exercise of reason in open debate. The *critical* aspect is that we attempt to falsify theories, and the method is at fault if we can show that it is counterproductive to the promotion of knowledge. We may thus be able to criticize a philosophical position without being able to falsify it.

If falsifiability is to serve as a defining criterion of science, there must be specific statements that can serve as premises for the falsifying inferences. Deduced specific statements are not tested directly on reality. They are compared with observation statements claiming that the case is such and such. But how do we know that these observation statements are true? When we have an immediate sense experience and express it by a specific statement – 'This house is now green' – there does not seem to be any other way of testing this statement than by another specific statement of the same kind. Statements about states of affairs are controlled with new observations that are also formulated as statements about states of affairs. How, then, can we be sure that these new statements are not wrong?

Popper took a pragmatic approach: when many people experience the same thing, and when the same thing is experienced repeatedly, we have the objective foundation that we need. The guarantee that our sensory experiences are valid lies in the intersubjective test. This means that only what is reproducible and intersubjectively accessible – what repeats itself and is common – can be a content of science in the form of observation statements. Nor is this an absolute guarantee. There is an infinite regression in connection with the testing of observation statements, and no test can, in practice, continue infinitely. However, Popper's point is not that all scientific statements must be tested, but that they all *can* be tested.

It is not just Popper's methodology and epistemology that are intertwined. These are again connected with his political theory: in order to discover mistakes, we must participate in free discussion; to participate in free discussion, we must have institutions and traditions which make this possible, that is to say, we must have a society formed according to the scientific *ethos*, and, for Popper, this is the open, liberal society. With his view of knowledge and of how this society is formed, Popper joined the political debate, as for example, in his two-volume work *The Open Society and Its Enemies* (1945). This work attacks Plato, Hegel, and Marx for their lack of concern for an open and gradual promotion of knowledge and for the liberality that this presupposes. For Popper, these philosophers based their doctrines on a weak foundation, and on the basis of this ill-founded dogmatism constructed a theory of society that is harmful to rational discussion and progressive development of knowledge. In this way, Popper championed tolerance and liberality.

Popper's book *The Poverty of Historicism* (1957) is dedicated to the 'memory of the countless men and women of all creeds or nations or races who fell victims to the fascist and communist belief in Inexorable Laws of Historical Destiny'. This book attacks the thesis that we can make predictions about society as a whole, the thesis which he calls historicism. Popper outlined his basic argument in the preface:

1   The course of human history is strongly influenced by the growth of human knowledge. (The truth of this premise must be admitted even by those who see in our ideas, including our scientific ideas, merely the by-products of *material* developments of some kind or other.)

2   We cannot predict, by rational or scientific methods, the future growth of our scientific knowledge. (This assertion can be logically proved, by considerations which are sketched below.)

3   We cannot, therefore, predict the future course of human history.

4   This means that we must reject the possibility of a *theoretical history*; that is to say, of a historical social science that would correspond to *theoretical physics*. There can be no scientific theory of historical prediction.

5   The fundamental aim of historicist methods . . . is therefore misconceived; and historicism collapses.

The argument does not refute the possibility of every kind of social prediction; on the contrary, it is perfectly compatible with the possibility of testing social theories – for example, economic theories – by way of predicting that certain developments will take place under certain conditions. It refutes only the possibility of predicting historical developments to the extent to which they may be influenced by the growth of our knowledge.

Thus, Popper did not deny that we can make predictions about partial processes. On the contrary, he held that we ought to form hypotheses about the future, test them and learn from the result, adjust the hypotheses and again learn from the result, and so on. In other words, he applied central features of his philosophy of science to his political philosophy. The result is a tentative, piecemeal politics, a scientific reformism.

The approach is basically neutral on the question of whether it is to be used for the best of a particular group in society; that is a question of political choice. What is essential for Popper is that politics become scientific by means of 'piecemeal social engineering'. It is the desire to plan society *as a whole*, a totality, that Popper rejected. That is impossible. We cannot transform everything at the same time. Those who think that we can, not only become utopian, but also tend to become authoritarian since they want everything to proceed according to their plans. We should proceed in an orderly, step-by-step fashion, scientifically and openly, in the sense that we investigate whether the result was as we had assumed, and that we are willing to adjust our plans as we go along.

Popper maintained that social phenomena are different from natural phenomena; social phenomena, even less than natural phenomena, can be observed without pre-conceptions of what we are looking for. For Popper, the objects of social science are, to a great degree, theoretical constructions. In this connection, he mentioned war and the military, which he viewed as abstract concepts, while the many that are killed, the soldiers, etc., are all concrete. Along with this, Popper introduced the principle of *methodological individualism*: 'The task of social theory is to construct and to analyse our sociological models carefully in descriptive or nominalist terms, that is to say, *in terms of individuals*, of their attitudes, expectations, relations, etc.'[7]

Popper's view of the testing of hypotheses has been sharply criticized. Some of his criticics claim that Popper's model is naive and simplistic. The core of this criticism – some of it voiced by Popper's own pupils – may briefly be formulated as follows:

'H' stands for hypothesis. 'I' stands for the implication of the hypothesis, that is to say, one of the statements about special states that logically follow from the hypothesis. This statement (a prediction deduced from the hypothesis) may then be tested by observation. If this statement is confirmed, we get:

$$\frac{H \supset I \\ I}{H}$$

In other words, 'H implies I, and I, therefore H'. But this is not a valid deduction. Thus, H is not verified. If the statement about the observed case proves to be inaccurate, we get:

$$\frac{H \supset I \\ -I}{-H}$$

In other words, 'H implies I, and not-I, therefore not-H'. This is a valid deduction. It is therefore possible to falsify H. Universal statements are therefore falsifiable, but not verifiable.

One of the objections to this viewpoint may be formulated as follows: statements about special cases are deductions from the hypothesis *plus additional conditions* (A); for example, conditions of the experiment (such as the equipment). The formula is therefore:

$$\frac{(H + A) \supset I \\ -I}{-(H + A), \text{ i.e. } -H \text{ or } -A}$$

In other words, 'H and A imply I, and not-I, therefore not-H *or* not-A'. This means that an implication (I) that is not accurate does not require us to reject (revise) the hypothesis, but it indicates that the hypothesis *or* other premises are rejected (revised). If we have a hypothesis that in other cases has proved to be fruitful – and, for now, we do not have any alternative hypotheses with which to replace our original hypothesis – it is hardly reasonable that we will reject (revise) the hypothesis. It is more reasonable that we will try to change one or more of the other premises (A). This was also a main point in Kuhn's criticism of Popper's falsification thesis.

THOMAS KUHN – PARADIGM SHIFT IN THE SCIENCES

Thomas S. Kuhn (1927–1996) proposed a basic criticism of Popper's falsification thesis by developing a perspective on scientific activity from the *history of science*.

He tried to show that his theory most accurately describes what scientists actually do. This was his theory of *paradigms* and the relationship between *normal science* and *scientific revolutions*. The hypothesis that is being tested forms a part of a comprehensive set of presuppositions which, to a great degree, are implicit (tacit). Included in these implicit presuppositions is the research competence that scientists acquire during their studies of the discipline. Being taught a subject is not just a matter of learning facts, but also of being socialized into a community of perception and thought – of acquiring concepts and norms of research. To show that explicit and implicit hypotheses and conjectures form a part of a larger set of presuppositions, Kuhn introduced the term 'paradigm' for this more comprehensive set of presuppositions.

During the research process, we may, in various degrees, feel the need to reflect upon, and perhaps change, some aspect of this comprehensive collection of presuppositions. When this kind of reflection and testing begins, we enter into a revolutionary phase, according to Kuhn – as opposed to normal scientific research, where we work with particular hypotheses (problems) on the basis of presuppositions that are unquestioned. Since this comprehensive set of presuppositions also includes the criteria for important and correct research, a rationally unresolvable problem arises, according to Kuhn, when two or more paradigms come into conflict.[8] For the same reason, there is no neutral position from which we can evaluate such a conflict, and eventually characterize the result as progress. Other philosophers of science claim that there are certain universal forms of competence and norms for scientific research and argument that cannot be denied or rejected (unless we thereby presuppose them), and which therefore, in one way or another, form a part of all paradigms (cf. Habermas, Ch. 27).

Because Kuhn assumed that there were leaps between different paradigms in science, we may no longer talk about scientific progress as an uninterruptedly linear development. We may talk about a growth in knowledge within a paradigm, but not so easily of a transition from one paradigm to another.

It is also difficult to create a mutual understanding between the representatives of the two different paradigms. The representatives view the discussion from the perspective of their respective presuppositions, that is to say, their paradigm. Communication is possible within a paradigm, but not so easily between different paradigms. A radical interpretation of this view is that there is no neutral observational language; all data are stamped by the paradigm in question. Nor are there any methods which are neutral in relation to the particular paradigm. All criteria of relevance, objectivity, and truth are thus dependent on particular paradigms; no criteria exist beyond the different paradigms, and none are common to all paradigms.

If this means that the question of what is true and valid is relative in regard to the different paradigms, the result is a problem of relativism and scepticism: truth is relative. But this is a problematic standpoint. We then have a problem of self-reference: if this sceptical claim is meant to apply universally, it must also apply to the claim itself – and then the claim supersedes itself. And if the claim is not meant to apply to the claim itself, there must be universal and paradigm-independent insight, namely, what the claim itself states (cf. corresponding problems of self-reference in radical interpretations of positivism, at the beginning of this chapter.)

Kuhn himself was not willing to go so far,[9] but other philosophers of science with the same inclinations, such as Paul Feyerabend (1924–1994), clearly moved in a relativistic direction. Feyerabend rejected the idea of universal rules of method for science ('anything goes'). The distinction between science and non-science then becomes fluid.

The paradigm concept is decisive in Kuhn's philosophy of science. But different interpretations of this have been given. It is, however, worth emphasizing that it includes both basic understandings about *what there is* (some kind of ontology) and *norms for good research* (some kind of methodology), in addition to the fact that it includes an *education*, with the aid of examples, in scientific practice. In accordance with this last point, the paradigm also includes a scientist's socialization into a research community where it is also a question of acquiring the competence to be able to use the basic concepts (the ontology) and the methods (the methodology) in question. As we shall see, the notion of 'tacit' knowledge based on practice plays a fundamental role also in the later work of Wittgenstein.

LUDWIG WITTGENSTEIN – ANALYTICAL PHILOSOPHY AS PRACTICE

To the degree that the distinction between statements that are falsifiable-in-principle and statements that are not falsifiable-in-principle proves not to function as an adequate criterion for the distinction between cognitive meaningfulness and cognitive meaninglessness, the question arises of how we should distinguish between what is meaningful and what is meaningless. An answer to this question was suggested by a school of Anglo-American philosophy that was inspired by the later writings of Ludwig Wittgenstein (1889–1951). This school, *analytical philosophy*, started with an analysis of everyday language as it functions in its diverse uses – that is, analytical philosophy went beyond merely analysing statements with a descriptive content: linguistic expressions are meaningful when they are in common use; meaninglessness is to be understood as a break with common linguistic use.

Briefly, we could say that analytical philosophy rejects the thesis of a one-to-one-relation between language and reality, and hence that there is one particular language that is basically correct: the language of the natural sciences. Analytical philosophy asserts that words and sentences have a variety of different functions. The words 'five red apples', for example, have a different meaning according to the context. For instance, spoken in a greengrocery, the words function as a purchasing order; spoken by a student in a mathematics class, the words may express the correct answer to a calculation. Similarly, we could say that the same piece of wood can be two different pieces depending on whether it is used in chess (as a pawn) or in draughts (as a draughtsman). The question of what kind of piece it is can only be answered by referring to the game in which it is used. Hence, the same word has different meanings in different contexts, and the question of which meaning a word has can only be answered by pointing to a concrete way in which it is used. Seen in isolation, words and sentences only have *latent* meanings. It is not until they are put into a particular context that they have actual meaning. Thus, we can say that the *use* defines the *meaning*. And since a word or a sentence can be put into many contexts, the word or sentence has many meanings. Hence, there is not a one-to-one-relation between language and reality. There is no single correct language, 'the scientific language', that reflects the world as it actually is.[10]

The sharp distinction between meaningfulness and meaninglessness must yield to the question, what kind of meaning, in what kind of use? And in many contexts, language does not function descriptively. In poetry and morality, language is not primarily used to claim something about actual states of affairs. We should, therefore, not reject, as cognitively meaningless, all language that does not correspond to the language of empirical science. Our task is to find the unique linguistic use that governs each context – such as poetry, ethical interaction, or practical life.

In everyday life, linguistic use is generally meaningful, in some sense or another. Hence, it is important to clarify the kind of use we have in each case. We should therefore analyse everyday language as it functions, when it functions. Analytical philosophy is thus an 'ordinary language philosophy'.

What is meaninglessness, according to the Wittgensteinian tradition? It is misuse of meaningful everyday language: classic philosophical problems often arise from such misuse. We use words that have a meaningful function in *one* context, in a different context where they do not belong.[11] This is like mixing chess and draughts. To take another example: if a man waiting for the bus is asked whether he knows when the bus is due and he answers, 'I do not know anything for certain', he is misusing language. What he says does not make good sense in *this* connection. In the question, the word 'knows' is used meaningfully; it fits the context of waiting for the bus. But his use of the word presupposes a completely different context; that is, a context of epistemological discussion. 'An ordinary language philosopher', such as Wittgenstein, would thus claim that many philosophical debates, such as those about epistemology and scepticism, are largely illustrations of the misuse of everyday words in theoretical contexts where these words do not belong. Hence, complex philosophical problems arise, problems that actually are pseudo-problems stemming from a misuse of language. A standard point in this context has been the claim that classical ontological definitions actually are a projection of linguistic distinctions onto things – for instance, the categories that Aristotle found in things are ultimately distinctions *in language* that are naively thought to be properties of the things. The distinction between substance and property, for example, is a projection onto things; of the linguistic distinction between the grammatical subject and predicate.

Described in this way, ordinary language philosophy becomes a kind of nominalism. But it is not quite so simple. As we will soon see, the central idea in the Wittgensteinian *language game*, according to which that language is basically expressed in speech acts, is that utterances, tasks, and objects constitute a whole, thus overcoming the distinction between language and reality. It does not make good sense to insist that we have language with its distinctions, on the one hand, and things on the other hand, as though they were epistemologically independent.

Analytical philosophy strives not only to 'diagnose', but also to 'cure': it seeks to provide 'therapy' for the linguistic disorder caused by our misuse of ordinary language. For analytical philosophers such as Wittgenstein, this therapy is especially meant for classical metaphysical problems. This view of philosophy as therapy thus contains an anti-metaphysical tendency. So far, analytical philosophers and logical empiricists agree. But when analytical philosophers, such as Wittgenstein, view philosophy as therapeutic practice, they also hold that philosophy does not provide answers in the form of theses and standpoints; philosophy as therapy means that philosophy is to be understood as a practice, an activity that untangles linguistic (conceptual) knots, without making any claims itself. Here there is a certain affinity with the Socratic method.

The therapeutic method aims to show what can and cannot be said in different linguistic contexts. Generally, the method presupposes that those living in a linguistic community possess an implicit knowledge of the rules of meaningful linguistic practice in that community – without such knowledge, a linguistic community is impossible. In some sense, philosophical linguistic analysis tries to make what is implicit, explicit, revealing, through analysis and arguments, the unspoken rules of linguistic use. Thus, we may say that the basic rules in ordinary language function as a court of appeal: linguistic expressions are meaningful when they accord with the existing basic rules. But how do we decide who is right in disagreements about the basic rules? We can only find out by *pointing* again to usage: to say, 'The number seven is green', is meaningless in ordinary language because it breaks the basic rule that numbers cannot be predicated with colour – the meaninglessness that we experience in connection with this utterance points to this basic rule.

In *Philosophical Investigations* (1953), Wittgenstein analysed language as something that is internally connected with our various activities: language is embedded in language games, that is to say, concrete practical contexts where language and use form a unity. In a language game – such as buying five red apples in a grocery, or asking for beams and blocks at a construction site – there is no external relationship between things and language; phenomena, as they exist in this language game, can only be satisfactorily described by means of the concepts in the game, and the concepts gain their meaning through the phenomena as they appear in this game.

The various language games generally overlap. The rules of the language games may be more or less unique for one language game, or common to several language games. Hence, a linguistic expression may have a common meaning across different language games. In such cases we may talk about a *family resemblance*: there is not one clearly defined common identity across the different language games, but we are still able to recognize certain common features (as among family members).

Wittgenstein thought that he could show that language is embedded in such manifold activities, without himself claiming to use a higher-order language game having all of the other language games as its object. He rejected the idea of a higher-order language game that could represent a common frame of understanding for all of the language games in everyday life, including the language games of the sciences.

On the other hand, one of Wittgenstein's followers, Peter Winch, developed a philosophy of social science by using the theory of language games as a starting point.[12] Understanding a society is like understanding a set of language games. To understand a language game is to understand the game on the basis of its own concepts and rules. We cannot use other concepts and rules, such as a causal explanation of speech acts. Winch is thus an exponent of a social science based on *understanding*, not causal explanation And he proposed a theory of language games that has the status of a higher-order standpoint, a metatheory, in relation to the various language games.

In what sense are the basic rules of the language games such that we can do without them, and in what sense are they such that we cannot do without them? If we hold that there are certain basic rules which necessarily form a part of *all* language games – so that we cannot avoid or do without these rules, but we can analyse and discuss them while using them – we are left with a kind of transcendental linguistic philosophy. There are certain common, unavoidable rules or principles in language – rules that are necessary for linguistic meaning in general – constituting a final standard for all linguistic meaning. If so, we have certain common, basic conditions for linguistic meaning in general.

Other analytical philosophers, such as Gilbert Ryle (1900–1976), used linguistic analysis in a somewhat more constructive manner.[13] By clarifying how our concepts are interconnected in various meaningful ways, we may see more clearly what language and phenomena actually are. The method is to determine, through analytical thought experiments, what concepts are internally connected with one another, and what concepts cannot be combined (the result being meaninglessness when such concepts are combined). Thus, the concept of action is necessarily connected with the concepts of agent and intention, while conceptions of number cannot be combined with predicates of colour.

In some analytical philosophers, such as Ryle, the anti-metaphysical tendency is less pronounced, and analysis becomes a means of gaining insight into classical problems, such as the question of what an action is, or what an agent or a person is.[14]

If the conditions for meaning are tied to language in use, what, then, is the relationship between language and the user? Is not language necessarily connected with a language user, a subject? Moreover, does not language imply something intersubjective and socio-historical? Is not language something that the user inherits, something that the user becomes acquainted with from and through others? These problems of the internal relationship of language to the speaking and cognizant subject, and also to the historical and social community, go beyond the semantic approach and lead us in the direction of speech-act analysis and of phenomenology and existentialism.

ORDINARY LANGUAGE PHILOSOPHY AND SPEECH ACT THEORY – AUSTIN AND SEARLE

The school known as *ordinary language philosophy* arose in Britain in the 1930s as a counter-movement to logical positivism. While the logical positivists were inspired by formal logic and by the mathematical language of modern physics, the proponents of ordinary language philosophy emphasized the analysis of the multitude of expressions found in everyday language.[15] We may distinguish between different groups within ordinary language philosophy:

1   *common-sense* philosophy, represented above all by George Edward Moore
2   the *Cambridge* school, including Wittgenstein (in his later phase), John Wisdom, and Norman Malcolm
3   the *Oxford* school, including Gilbert Ryle, Stuart Hampshire, Peter F. Strawson, Stephen Toulmin, and John L. Austin.

These groups had in common the analysis of everyday language as the starting point for criticism of the idealized language used in the mathematically formulated empirical sciences and of the idealized language used by the philosophers who were inspired by formal logic. The *ordinary language* philosophers defended everyday language and *common sense* (note the parallel with phenomenology).

By a careful analysis of common language usage, John L. Austin (1911–1960) criticized philosophers making what he saw as pretentious and opaque claims (cf. John Locke's linguistic clarification). By pointing to the insight found in everyday language, Austin thus articulated a sceptical critique of metaphysics and logical positivism, while at the same time trying to refute philosophical (theoretical) scepticism. Austin distinguished between *descriptive* statements ('constative') and what we could call *executive* statements ('performative'). The statement 'I am walking' is a *descriptive* statement. It *states* something. The statement 'I promise . . .' is a statement that is, at the same time, an *action*. The statement *performs* an action.[16] If the mayor, in an official ceremony, says, 'I name this street State Drive', he or she is not describing, but is *performing an action*, namely, giving the street a name (this obtains as long as everything is carried out as it should; that is, that the protocol is correct for such a ceremony). In this way, Austin focused on the relationship between the language users and the linguistic expression and on the social context within which the language users express themselves. The relationship between the language user and the linguistic expression may be investigated psychologically. But, for Austin, it was a question of philosophical analysis. Research into the relationship between language user and linguistic expression is often called 'pragmatic', while research into the structure of language is called 'syntax' and research into the content of meaning in language is called 'semantics'. On the basis of such terminology, Austin was concerned with pragmatics in a philosophical sense.

Austin was thus a key figure in the shift towards linguistic philosophy, including speech-act philosophy, the so-called *linguistic turn* (or *pragmatic turn*). For better analysis and comprehension of different kinds of speech acts, Austin also introduced a tripartite conceptual scheme: locutionary, illocutionary, and perlocutionary. The *perlocutionary force* of a speech act is connected with causal relationships. If I say, 'The hand grenade behind you may explode at any second', this utterance may cause others to run away; by saying this, I am 'causing' an action on their part. The speech act thus has perlocutionary force. But even if they do not start running, I have still warned them by uttering this sentence. In accordance with the conventions of warning others (and for thus being able to say that I am innocent in the event that another person is hurt), my speech act has been successful even though they ignored my message. The *illocutionary force* of a speech act is connected with the fulfilment of conventions, not by causal effects. (Note the parallel: when the mayor names a street, it is in accordance with conventions, not as a causal effect.) The *locutionary* aspect is based on what we call the content of the claim (what we are expressing). One and the same speech act can, in different ways, be characterized by all of these three aspects.[17]

Speech act theory has been further developed by the American philosopher John R. Searle (1932–).[18] Starting with the idea that speech acts have illocutionary force, Searle tried to uncover the rules of successful speech acts, that is to say, rules that are 'constitutive' (and not only 'regulative') in successful speech acts. In short, the rules for chess are *constitutive* for chess moves because the individual actions in the game, the individual moves, are what they are only in view of these rules. But the prohibition, 'Do not smoke in your office', regulates only behaviour that already exists, to smoke or not to smoke, without itself being a condition for the existence of these types of behaviour. The rules for speech acts that Searle attempted to uncover are those that, for example, are based on the fact that we usually assume that people are truthful, that we normally assume that what they are talking about exists, and that roles and institutions are normally such that their speech acts are meaningful. When we hear that the mayor says, 'I name this street State Drive', we usually assume that the mayor means what he or she says, that there is a street to be named, and that the mayor is really performing an official act. When speech acts are meaningful and successful in the interaction between human beings, it is precisely because of such rules, which we often do not think about, but generally take for granted, both in speaking and listening. Such implicit rules for speech acts are thus constitutive conditions for mutual understanding in linguistic interaction. In practice, there are, of course, all kinds of factors that prevent us from understanding one another. Of course, one or more of these rules are often broken, intentionally or not. But just as speaking truthfully precedes *lying* (because, in order to be able to lie, the liar must assume that the listener believes the liar to be speaking the truth), these rules also precede their violation. That they are often broken is neither doubtful nor deniable. In this connection, Searle also introduced the term 'institutional facts' to denote social conditions (facts) that would not have existed had they not been placed within certain institutional frameworks, including the rules for speech acts which 'constitute' these conditions (facts).[19]

PHENOMENOLOGY AND EXISTENTIALISM – HUSSERL AND SARTRE

Phenomenology is not a homogeneous school. Its founder, Edmund Husserl (1859–1938), developed his theory during the course of his career. Among those who are often said to belong to the phenomenological school, such as Martin Heidegger (1889–1976), Jean-Paul Sartre (1905–1980), and Maurice Merleau-Ponty (1907–1961), the contrasts are great. Sartre, for example, may also be called an existentialist. We will here briefly discuss some of the main points of phenomenology.

Phenomenology (literally, the theory of phenomena) is a philosophical school that attempts to *describe* events and actions as they appear. It criticizes the tendency only to accept as real what is described by the natural sciences. Phenomenology aims to describe the everyday items that we use, as they appear to us: the pencil with which I am now writing is described as it is in this context. Phenomenology attacks the view that the pencil is only a collection of atoms. In this sense, we can say that this school aims to reconstruct the universe in all of its diversity and fullness, with all of its qualities, as opposed to a one-dimensional standardization based on scientistic philosophy. Thus this school opposes the view that only the concepts of natural science grasp things as they actually are.

Here we see a parallel with the concept of the language game that we found in the ordinary language philosophers; there, the view that the language of natural science is the only correct language was rejected in favour of a presentation of the diversity of different linguistic contexts – linguistic meaning was defined by the context. In phenomenological descriptions, phenomena, not primarily language, take centre stage. But here, too, we have criticism of the absolutist view that only the concepts of the natural sciences are valid. At the same time, it should be emphasized that neither analytical philosophy nor phenomenology oppose natural science! What is being criticized is the philosophical theory that only the concepts of natural science grasp reality.

Phenomenology often describes simple everyday activities: grinding grain, forging a horseshoe, writing a letter. We often use the Husserlian term *life world* (*Lebenswelt*): the world in which we live, with its everyday articles and its ideas (phenomena, agents, and linguistic expressions) as they appear to the users. Hence, language-in-use forms a part of the *Lebenswelt*, as do the language users (cf. the parallel with language games, which are not merely linguistic in a semantic or syntactic sense, but in a pragmatic sense).

Phenomenology does not present its notion of the life world as an alternative to scientific notions. The life world has an epistemological precedence. It is not simply that the sciences arise historically out of the life world; the life world is the epistemological precondition that makes scientific activity possible. Husserl thus regarded phenomenology as an extension of the scientific development in European history. Philosophy, as well as science, is committed to rationality as an end ('*telos*'), and phenomenology has the task of enlightening and clarifying the basic problems of science. Husserl thus spoke of his own phenomenology as a 'rigorous science' and as a 'transcendental phenomenology' that should provide support in 'the crisis in the European Sciences'. The redemptive efforts of phenomenology in regard to the scientific aspects of the sciences reside in its ability to present the life world as the meaning-constitutive ground of the sciences in order that they should not overlook the question of knowing whence they come and where they are going.

The task of phenomenology is therefore not only to describe phenomena (tools, intentions, fellow human beings, etc.) as they appear in various contexts. The deeper goal is to discover the conditions within the life world that make human action (scientific activity included) possible. The goal is that of discovering the *meaning-constitutive* conditions of human action and rationality. This goal is thus sought in the basic conditions that make the life world what it is. (Take again our chess example: the rules of chess are meaning-constitutive for the various good and bad moves in the game; without these rules it would not make sense to talk about moves in chess.) In this sense, there is here, as in the speech-act philosophers, a certain transcendental philosophical argument, but this is a transcendental philosophy that seeks the more or less varying preconditions of the linguistic-practical community, not a transcendental philosophy in a strictly Kantian sense with unchangeable preconditions embedded in each person.

Thus, the clarification of the structures in the life world has an *epistemological* aim. It is important that the life world is practical, with purposive tasks and norm-regulated actions. Epistemological problems are discussed in terms of *action* (tasks, labour, interaction), not in terms of passive sense experience, as in Berkeley. The insight that we have about what we do is understood as being fundamental. This insight cannot be reduced to simple sense impressions. For example, when I chop wood, I know, instinctively, what I am doing; and what I know, for example, about the movements of my arm is not something that I know by *looking* at my arm, as if it were an object of observation. Of course I look at my arm when I am chopping wood, but my vision of the arm is part of a context of action in which the observation that my arm is moving is different from the observation when I am merely looking at my arm as a foreign object.

The fact that phenomenology starts epistemologically with our everyday tasks, and not with passive sense impressions or with pure thought, means that the problems connected with the relationship between subject and object, with the concepts of things and of personal identity, have a unique twist in phenomenology. As acting persons, we have immediate access to these activities; there is no absolute dichotomy between subject and object. Phenomena reveal themselves as they are in a given situation, as the things that they are; and the agent's consciousness, in the time span of the action, guarantees a continuity and an identity for the agent. Phenomenological descriptions that start with action are interesting for the social sciences and their basic debates: in phenomenological analyses of life contexts, based on the concept of action and related concepts such as those of intention, agent, co-agent, and objects of action, we aim to present the field of action in terms of the categories that the agent is using. Thus, phenomenology is closely related to the *understanding* approach to social research, as opposed to the explanative approach. This is in line with Winch's analysis of society in accordance with the language-game model.

But, as we have mentioned, phenomenology mainly aims to find the elements that constitute meaning, not merely a description of the situation. It is therefore important to be aware of which logical level we are on, at any time. For example, when Sartre discusses freedom in *Being and Nothingness* ('*L'Être et le néant*' [1943]), he conceives of freedom as having a constitutive meaning. Freedom has the logical status of being a necessary *condition for* action: to act is to act intentionally, consciously, in some sense or another. Action *presupposes* that we see that the situation could have been different than it actually is, that there is an alternative to what is given, a possible alternative that we, through a particular series of actions, may hope to realize. In other words, action surpasses the given – action 'negates' the given – in light of another state of affairs. In this sense, what is possible is given precedence over what is actual; what is possible is what is not yet actual but which may be actualized through action. If we did not see that the situation around us could be different in some way or another, as a result of our efforts, we would not be able to act. This possible intentional negation of 'the given' indicates freedom as a condition of action. Freedom thus *constitutes* action. It is by virtue of freedom, in this sense, that action is possible.

However, at the same time, Sartre held that human beings can lose their freedom. How can this be possible if freedom is a basic, constitutive element in us? The answer is that basic freedom, which we always possess latently, may be lost in specific situations if we do not recognize the situation as one that can and ought to be changed, and ourselves as the agent who can and should effect the change. We then view ourselves as a kind of *thing*, without the ability to act. Hence, freedom is not actualized. This is how freedom can be lost. But as an essential property of human beings freedom is latently present even in these instances.

We have so far primarily discussed phenomenology in connection with epistemology and action theory. However, phenomenology has been just as fruitful within art and literature, since it restored qualities to our world: once again, we could legitimately discuss phenomena in their qualitative fullness – whether it be one of Nerval's poems or one of van Gogh's paintings. In literary research, phenomenology, like hermeneutics, has functioned as an interpretative science.

In his later work, *Critique of Dialectical Reason* (1960) (cf. Kant's titles), Sartre discussed the relationship between his earlier existentialist phenomenology and Marxism: starting with individual activities, he attempted, by dialectical transgression, to arrive at a theory of the socio-historical totality. His theory of how manufactured structures – streets, houses, stairs, markets, etc. – define our fields of action, is important in this connection. These structures are material mediations between human beings, and between human beings and the community. Otherwise, group formation represents such a 'mediating' factor; the *group* expresses a spontaneous common action to achieve common goals, while in what Sartre calls the *series*, the particular individuals form part of an aggregation without communication and community (as in a bus queue). To escape from our alienated situation, we must activate ourselves in the 'group', and move beyond the situations where the sum of our individual actions leads to unintended results – as when each farmer's sensible action of felling trees leads to an imprudent deforestation and natural disaster. We should try to avoid having the sum of our particular actions backfire; Sartre here spoke of counter-finality.

Sartre, who, in *Being and Nothingness*, advocated an individualistic standpoint, later tried to develop a kind of Marxist philosophy to mediate reasonably between the individual and the community. He said that Hegel, with his concept of the totality, was right in comparison with Kierkegaard, and that Kierkegaard, with his concept of 'the unique one', was right in comparison with Hegel – both conceptions being mediated through Sartre's version of Marx. Here, Sartre emphasized the family – the medium of the child's primary socialization and individuation – as the mediator between the universal and the particular.

Sartre is often said to be an existentialist. But existentialism is not a philosophical school in a strict sense. The term is applied to contrasting thinkers, such as the Roman Catholic Gabriel Marcel, the atheist Jean-Paul Sartre, the feminist Simone de Beauvoir, the deist Karl Jaspers, and the philosopher of Being Martin Heidegger. But, to use Wittgenstein's phrase, there is a certain family resemblance. And the roots of this way of thinking go back to Kierkegaard, Pascal, Augustine, and Socrates. The family resemblance can been seen in the way that these thinkers interiorize man's Being, as a finite and mortal individual, often tragic and filled with paradox, in an unfinished life where self-consciousness is fundamental and unshakable. A basic feature of existential philosophy is therefore the view that we must all meditate on our own life. In such existential thought – where we are also personally cognizant of our own death – we are roused, virtually reborn with a consciousness that plumbs greater depths. If we cannot find an answer to what Dostoyevsky called the 'damned questions' – from where do we come? what are we? where are we going? – we still retain this consciousness of the uniqueness of human existence, the pure flame of life. As the Norwegian author Arne Garborg put it: life is 'completely unmotivated, perfectly contrary to reason, a bare postulate

– but an energetic postulate, that we cannot avoid; a postulate so superior that it refuses legitimation, so sovereign that even when we deny it, we are subjected to its laws or whims in every fiber of our being'.[20]

Here we will say a few things about Sartre's specifically existential viewpoints, especially as they are expressed in *Existentialism and Humanism*. Sartre held that, for human beings, 'existence precedes essence'. By this, he meant that there are no norms, no 'divine ideas' implanted by a Creator that tell us what we ought to do with our lives. We are therefore free in the sense that there are no objective norms or prescriptions. (Compare the difference between this conception of freedom, based on a lack of norms, and the conception of freedom as a condition for action in *Being and Nothingness*.) We may use the following illustration to clarify Sartre's view: we are like actors who suddenly find themselves on stage in the middle of a performance, but without having a script, without knowing the name of the play or what role they are playing, without knowing what to do or say – yes, without even knowing whether the play has an author at all – whether it is serious or a farce. We must *personally* make a decision, to *be* something or other – a villain or a hero, ridiculous or tragic. Or we can simply exit, immediately. But that is also choosing a role – and that choice, too, is made without our ever knowing what the performance was about.

This is how we are plunged into existence. We exist, we find ourselves here – free, because there are no prescriptions – and we must decide for ourselves, define ourselves as the kind of person we are going to be. The essence (the definition) thus follows existence (that we are already living).

In Sartre's version of existentialism, *choice* is important. This is not choosing things by means of a standard, but 'choosing' the standard, choosing ourselves *as a person*. But such a choice of a basic position cannot be rationally defended, according to Sartre. On the contrary, all attempts to defend a position must start with something, but, here, the choice is the very starting point. There is then something arbitrary about this choice. This fundamental choice is something that we do alone – even if we ask for advice, we have chosen to ask for advice, and we choose how to interpret the advice, and to follow or not to follow that advice. In this sense, the choice represents a decision, something arbitrary. We may choose altruism or egoism, communism or fascism. The choice itself cannot be rationally based (note the parallel with Popper). But at the same time, according to Sartre – interestingly enough – we, as individuals, still choose on behalf of *everyone*. Here we see a Kantian idea: a universalization of the norm for action.

Still, we may well ask, are we really so sovereign that we can define our identity in this way? Are we not vitally linked to the community – through socialization, through mutual recognition later in life, through the objective, necessary world of labour, and through language? There seems to be something problematic in the relationship between individual and community as conceived in Sartre's existentialism.

In existentialism, the question of *identity* is central: basically, who am I? Sartre thought that we are, in principle, free to define our identity. There is no script for our roles! There is no 'essence' that tells us who we are and what we ought to be. We are all free, and we all bear the responsibility to find the answer – make up the answer – to this existential riddle.

Sartre inherited the problem of identity and recognition from Hegel, who viewed the question of identity as a question of the relationship between human subjects: when two subjects meet, a struggle for *recognition* arises, a struggle to determine how they are mutually to view themselves as well as each other. This is a 'spiritual' struggle in the sense that it is not primarily a struggle for material things, but for mutual recognition. Still, for Hegel, it was a struggle of life and death; the question of who we are in relation to others is vital for us. Moreover, from Hegel's perspective, it was a question of being recognized either as superior or as inferior. It was a struggle to determine who is to be 'master' and who is to be 'slave' – and Hegel also related these positions to material conditions: the slave must work for the master on pain of death.

Hence, Hegel conceived of human identity – our self-understanding and our understanding of the other(s) – as a vulnerable product of an ongoing socio-psychological process. Identity is not something that we *have*, like hair colour or genetic makeup. It is something that we gain through a tension-filled intersubjective process, and it is something that can be endlessly rechallenged. We are vulnerable not only as physical beings, in regard to sickness and death, but also as social beings, in regard to others' definition and redefinition of our identity.

But by pretending that our identity is merely a product of nature, we can give the impression, to ourselves and to others, that this socially defined identity is as unchangeable as other natural phenomena. The slave is a slave by nature, and the master is master by nature, or by the grace of God, but not as the result of a social power game, which, in principle, can always be redefined in a new, and different, way. Thus, the nobleman may view himself as master by nature, and view the servant as slave, also by nature – as something eternally fixed. Hence, both the nobleman and the servant subvert the thesis that social status is really a socially defined mutual understanding that can be changed. This is how we may interpret Hegel's point, and these were the kinds of interpretations that Sartre inherited from Hegel. For Sartre, such a rationalization would be an example of 'bad faith', that is to say, self-deceit: a failure to take the existential responsibility for our own life, for answering the question of who we are. But this is actually part of a struggle, for Sartre as well as for Hegel: there was always, for Sartre, the perception of a power struggle when two people face each other: who will gain control, who will define their relation?

Even in the unequal forms of mutual understanding and identity, both parties are involved, both parties accept the inequality. It is a question of a mutual relationship. We cannot have the identity that we want without the acceptance of others. Therefore, it is precisely because we are dependent on what others think of us that the struggle is inevitable. These ideas of social identity represent a transition between theory and practice, in the sense that these ideas indicate how we may understand inequality in social relationships, and thus how we may try to redefine these relations. Theory, then, influences and legitimizes political action.

These ideas were adopted by groups which felt that they were oppressed, such as indigenous peoples in the anti-colonial struggle after World War II (like Frantz Fanon). These ideas also inspired the emerging women's liberation movement after World War II, with Simone de Beauvoir as one of its foremost representatives.

IDENTITY AND RECOGNITION – SIMONE DE BEAUVOIR AND FEMINIST PHILOSOPHY

Simone de Beauvoir (1908–1986) grew up in a traditional bourgeois milieu in France, where women did not gain general voting rights until after World War I, when she was nearly 40 years old. She also became an early member of the radical existentialist circle along with Sartre. During this time of upheaval, de Beauvoir became concerned with the unequal social role imposed upon women, as a group, in this society: women were defined as *the other* in relation to men. It was the male viewpoint that defined both men and women, and that defined women as 'the second sex'. The male self-perception and perception of 'the other' prevailed. Women were thus defined as second class, and were taught to accept this view of themselves and this view of men. As a result, women had an inauthentic identity.

This social definition was understood, and thus legitimized, as something inherent in nature. For an existentialist like de Beauvoir, this was an especially rankling offence, since human beings, for existentialists, are primarily defined by freedom, freedom to decide personally who they will be. Women, as a group, had even less freedom to shape their own lives, freedom being viewed as a basic feature and basic value of human existence. Women were defined as 'the second sex', and this role was thought to be permanently assigned by nature.

To redefine this role model, we must establish that it is a question of social definitions, and not of nature, and then we must – with theoretical and practical efforts – get both parties, men as well as women, to understand themselves and the other in a new and more equitable way. De Beauvoir's life's work was to deal with this issue in terms of both theory and practice, and in terms of both philosophy and literature. Her life was devoted to books, philosophical essays for clarification, and literary works to give substance to the issue. As an intellectual, she also became politically active, especially in the cultural sphere where the feminist struggle for recognition and identity took place. But she also supported more practical causes, such as a woman's right to be free of an unwanted pregnancy and to remain childless if she so chooses. Here, her support for a woman's right to abortion was central. The biological coercion to which a human life is subject bears a tension-filled relationship to the existentialist emphasis on our basic freedom. Like Sartre, de Beauvoir personally chose to minimize this 'coercion of nature' by not having children.

In many ways, de Beauvoir's goal was equality. Men and women should mutually recognize each other as equals. This does not mean that everyone is the same, that there will not be varying individual careers. But the general oppression of women must be opposed. There is, however, another way to reinterpret women's roles and identities. We may claim that it is neither possible nor desirable to strive for equality in mutual understanding. We may claim that men and women *are* different, that they understand themselves and others in different ways, and that it is therefore an illusion to believe that they will at any point recognize each other as being the same. They may only recognize each other as equal, but as fundamentally different. Both men and women are 'the other' in relation to the other. That is how it is, and how it ought to be. This tension-filled recognition without complete mutual understanding may degenerate into rejection and oppression. This is what has traditionally happened in regard to women. This must be corrected.

But the goal cannot and must not be complete mutual understanding and equality: legally, socially, and materially, there must be equality. But for equality in identity, the mutual understanding and recognition of both sexes, it is important to realize that this cannot be achieved completely, and ought not be tried. This is the position developed by the feminist phenomenologist Luce Irigaray (1932–). On the basis of the philosophy of language and of psychoanalysis, she has argued that men and women are necessarily different, and that the best we can achieve – and ought to strive to achieve – is a *recognition* of the basic *difference*, of this 'otherness'. Irigaray has little use for equality in the sense of viewing human beings as *one* kind of being. There is not one kind of human being, but *two* – woman and man. This is something that we must acknowledge. This is her critique of much of the philosophical discussion of gender, including that of de Beauvoir. While de Beauvoir is an *equality-feminist*, Irigaray is a *difference-feminist*. The conflict is about how differences in body and sexuality ought to be interpreted. How essential or non-essential are these differences for human identity, for our conceptions of value, and for our view of reason and justice? This summarizes the conflicts that exist between these two types of feminism.

Recognizing the other as equal, but as being fundamentally different, has gradually become a central theme in modern (postmodern) discussions. We have reached a socio-critical defence of difference, in regard to gender, but also to ethnicity and culture in general. We now have a 'politics of recognition' in which different groups demand this form of recognition because they do not want to become like the dominant group(s).[21] There has been a flowering of discussions of minority cultures in North America, of homosexuality, and of 'difference-feminism' in some feminist groups. Seen from this perspective, de Beauvoir may look like an old-fashioned conformist. The monoculture of modernism is under pressure, and postmodern cultural plurality is pushing its way to the fore!

In 'late-modern' society, there are many opinions on most issues, including the question, 'what is a human being?' The biological and genetic perspectives of human life have to be seriously considered, while there are various social, psychological, and human sciences that, each in its own way, have something to say. If I, as philosopher, wish to make a significant contribution to the debate on human nature, I certainly will not maintain my position without meeting formidable criticism. But even if I cannot unambiguously establish my position, I may still present interesting perspectives, and perhaps also better arguments than my opponents.

Identity – individual or collective – has become a central theme in our society. It is not only nature that can no longer restore itself. Social and existential meaning has also become a scarcity. Even in so-called *realpolitik* contexts, we no longer speak only in terms of power or money, but also of identity. We have a new religiosity and a new nationalism. The question of identity is complex: who are we? Who am I? Perhaps I am a working-class Jewish mother, 60 years old, who is a native of France. Socially, who am I, *really*? French? Middle-aged? Proletarian? Jewish? Mother? Or woman? All of these, and more, in varying degrees. Under normal conditions, it is to some extent up to me what I want to emphasize – or up to my various roles and institutions. But sometimes it is not a personal choice. During the years of the Vichy regime, the Jewish identity would have been decisive since it could have taken me to Auschwitz.

In view of the cultural plurality of modern society (in regard to identity), some philosophers have thought it necessary to find something that is *universally valid*, in the form of norms that can regulate conflicts between different cultures and values. These are ideas that we find in the thought of John Rawls and Jürgen Habermas. But this attempt to find a 'thin' universality (of general norms, not of concrete cultural values) has brought new objections: an ideal universality of general norms must also be related to concrete situations. Universal justification of general norms requires, in turn, a discernment that makes us capable of applying these norms correctly in concrete situations.

One of the philosophers who has contributed to this discussion is Seyla Benhabib (1950–), a professor, a Turkish Jew married to a German, a mother, and a resident of the United States. She is very much of our age and our world. The title of her book published in 1992 is significant: *Situating the Self. Gender, Community and Postmodernism in Contemporary Ethics*. She has attempted to mediate between the *universalistic* positions that we find in Habermas and the *contextualist* positions of Gilligan and other feminists.[22]

Benhabib agrees with Habermas that, in a modern pluralistic society, we need the concept of a *formal universality* – if not, we will end up with an eternal battle between perspectives and values,[23] without any basis for impartial criticism; all impartial rationality, theoretical and normative, will then be impossible. But a certain amount of minimal rationality is needed if we are to develop critical comments, and if we are to be able to claim that something is better than something else, that something is fair or just in relation to something else.

According to Benhabib, we can argue for such a minimal rationality, in line with Habermas. On the other hand, Benhabib emphasizes that we are always *situated*. We are formed by a specific background, we live in a specific context, and we relate to specific people. Consequently, we should bring our situated identity with us into philosophy. Not only 'the generalized other', whom we recognize as a human being and as a potential discussion partner, but also 'the concrete other' must be considered. Not only general norms for justice, but also concrete ties and feelings, in connection with the 'close' other, must be reflected in our philosophy. If de Beauvoir can be called an equality-feminist and Irigaray a difference-feminist, Benhabib can perhaps be called a universalist situating-feminist! The philosophical possibility of normative critiques of established formations is a central theme in Benhabib's philosophical discussions, just as it is presupposed in the thought of both de Beauvoir and Irigaray.

JOHN RAWLS – JUSTICE AS 'FAIRNESS'

In the first part of the twentieth century, logical positivism aimed to rule out all forms of normative philosophy. But in recent decades, we have witnessed a new and increasing effort in moral philosophy and the philosophy of law. This applies to the basic problems in practical philosophy as well as to applied ethics such as biomedical ethics, eco-ethics, business ethics, etc.

One of the leading representatives of this new trend within practical philosophy is the American John Rawls (1921–). His book on the notion of justice and the principles of a just society, *A Theory of Justice* (1971), is today regarded as a seminal work. We shall here look at some of the main concepts in Rawls' theory of justice as fairness.

Let us look at the basis of his theory. We live in a time when we can no longer expect philosophical or religious consensus on the aim and meaning of life and on what is the good life. This is the lesson of the wars of religion in the seventeenth century: we must distinguish between politics on the one hand, and religion and metaphysics on the other. If we want a society in which people with different 'comprehensive doctrines' and basic convictions can live peacefully together, we must establish neutral principles for the organization of society. We must have a society based on principles that all its citizens can recognize as just. Rawls' notion of justice thus relates to the basic institutions of a just society. Justice is here understood as 'fairness': principles that can guarantee the freedom of the individual as long as it does not harm the freedom of others, and that lead to an impartial distribution of opportunities in society.

Rawls' moral intuition maintains that the welfare calculations of utilitarianism do not appropriately grasp all aspects of what we understand by justice. Such calculations do not give an adequate conception of the idea of a basic respect for the person, and they may arrive at resource distributions that are to the disadvantage of the underprivileged. He therefore proposed a procedure that compels us to be impartial and thus just. This procedure is based on the idea of the 'original position': we imagine that we do not know who we are with regard to gender, age, race, social status, innate abilities, etc., but that we do know how different political institutions will function for people with different backgrounds and different resources. Behind this 'veil of ignorance' we then choose the principles of the organization of society. In such a thought experiment, we should all choose the institutional order that we think is best for ourselves. But there is a built-in coercion to impartial role-taking: we do not know who we are as persons, but we know the various ways in which society can be organized, and we are therefore interested in choosing a political order that will serve us best regardless of who we might be, whether a black unmarried mother or a Kennedy born with a silver spoon in his mouth. We act out of enlightened self-interest, but without knowing who we are, so that we are forced to choose an impartial solution. This is exactly the point of the 'original position': it guarantees justice in the form of impartial and reasonable equality within the basic institutions of society: justice as fairness. In such a situation, according to Rawls, we will choose the following principles for the basic institutions. First, we will respect personal integrity and freedom. Each of us should enjoy the freedom that does not harm the freedom of others. We will therefore support political institutions allowing all citizens the same access to social advancement. We will not choose a society based on the principle that certain persons have a privileged access to higher positions. We will also choose a social order in which the well-to-do cannot increase their wealth at the expense of the worst off.

These are the principles of the just society that Rawls aimed to generate from the original position. If we put ourselves in this position and evaluate the political institutions from behind the veil of ignorance, we will, in this moral 'situation of coercion', out of enlightened self-interest, have to choose as follows:

1   The principle of personal autonomy or freedom. Regardless of whom we should turn out to be, we have overwhelmingly strong reasons for this choice.

2a The principle of equal opportunity to rise in society. Again, the reasons are overwhelming to choose this principle.

2b A political order in which the well-to-do cannot make themselves even more wealthy at the expense of those who are worst off. This is an insurance against radical exclusion from the resources of society and marginalization.

The point of this thought experiment is to compel us to imagine what it is like to be in various positions in a given society, by a kind of hypothetical role-play. This thought experiment puts into operation an intuition that is close to the Kantian categorical imperative: a just political order is one that is based on the principle of universal impartiality.

As a thought experiment, the original position functions as a procedure to generate the principles of justice of the basic institutions of society. In that sense, it is a metanorm, or a norm for norms.

These are some of the main points of Rawls' theory of justice as fairness as expressed in his book published in 1971. This book, *A Theory of Justice*, also presents comprehensive analyses of problems in juridical, political, and economic theory. This work had a considerable impact not only in philosophy, but also in related fields such as economy, political science, and law.

It is interesting that Rawls, in his main theory, combined liberal and Kantian points with welfare considerations. This he did without burdening his theory with controversial metaphysical or religious positions on the good life. We may therefore say that Rawls' theory of justice is largely neutral: this theory does include procedures to estimate principles of justice for political institutions. It is not a theory of value questions that will turn out to be controversial because of conflict with basic views and convictions.

There has been extensive discussion of Rawls' theory since 1971. Some thinkers have criticized the idea of an 'original position' since they find it unrealistic to imagine that people could be able to disregard totally what and who they are. Similarly, it has been objected that the presuppositions are far too idealized: it is unlikely that subjects could disregard who they are and in that sense be ignorant, while at the same time having an excellent grasp of how society functions.

Others have objected to this thought experiment as too monologic: everything happens in a 'single room', as it were – and thereby we disregard the value of real discussion and real confrontation between persons. In such concrete discussions and attempts at so-called role taking, we can actually learn to see ourselves and the others in new ways. They represent innovating learning processes that the thought experiment of the original position cannot bring about.

Regardless of how we judge these objections, it remains true that Rawls' ideas have contributed to a fruitful normative debate in many forums. We should add that Rawls himself has gradually reached the conclusion that the idea of the original position assumes a particular view of man as a rational agent, and that it might be better to prefer a political theory based on the idea of overlapping consensus between different comprehensive doctrines. If we want to achieve a peaceful society of citizens holding diverse views on basic issues, all reasonable ('free and equal'), we must recognize that we cannot intrude our own personal beliefs into politics; instead, we must base society on an overlapping consensus between free and equal citizens. This is a philosophy of a just society in which the philosophical contribution is reduced compared with the theory of justice based on the idea of the original position. Rawls calls this new version of this theory of justice 'political liberalism' (which is the title of his book published in 1993).

We shall later see that some of Rawls' basic ideas of a minimum conception of justice for modern societies are also central to the philosophy of Jürgen Habermas. But much more than Rawls, Habermas has emphasized both the Kantian concept of justification and the Hegelian concept of history and the development of modern institutions.

QUESTIONS

Describe the relation between classical empiricism (Locke, Hume) and logical positivism, and discuss the development of logical positivism into analytical philosophy (ordinary language philosophy and the later work of Wittgenstein).

Discuss the relation between Popper and Kuhn with respect to falsification and scientific progress. What are Kuhn's arguments against Popper's thesis of falsification? Does Kuhn finally adopt a kind of relativism?

Explain the relation between the later work of Wittgenstein, the philosophy of ordinary language, and phenomenology.

Discuss Sartre's views of the epistemological status of norms (and values).

Discuss the various views of the gender question held by Simone de Beauvoir, Luce Irigaray, and Seyla Benhabib.

What are the main ideas of Rawls' theory of justice as fairness?

SUGGESTIONS FOR FURTHER READING

PRIMARY LITERATURE

Ayer, A. J., *Language, Truth and Logic*, London, 1936.
Beauvoir, S. de, *The Second Sex*, Harmondsworth, 1972.
Benhabib, S., *Situating the Self*, Oxford, 1992.
Irigaray, L., *An Essay on Sexual Difference*, London, 1993.
Kuhn, T., *The Structure of Scientific Revolutions*, 1970.
Lakatos, P. and Musgrave, A. (eds), *Criticism and the Growth of Knowledge*, Cambridge, 1974.
Popper, Karl R., *The Logic of Scientific Discovery*, London, 1959.
Rawls, J., *A Theory of Justice*, Cambridge, MA, 1971.
Rawls, J., *Political Liberalism*, New York, 1993.
Russell, B., *The Problems of Philosophy*, London, 1962.

Ryle, G., *The Concept of Mind*, London, 1963.

Sartre, J.-P., *Existentialism and Humanism*, London, 1948.

Searle, J. R., *Speech Acts*, Cambridge, 1972.

Wittgenstein, L., *Philosophical Investigations*, Oxford, 1963.

SECONDARY LITERATURE

Hospers, J., *An Introduction to Philosophical Analysis*, London, 1963.

Moi, T., *Simone de Beauvoir*, Oxford, 1994.

Urmson, J. O., *Philosophical Analysis, Its Development between the Two World Wars*, Oxford, 1960.

NOTES

1 Central to the foundation of modern mathematical logic was the German mathematician and philosopher Gottlob Frege. His well-known works on the philosophy of language include *On Sense and Reference* ('*Über Sinn und Bedeutung*') (1892). One of the most influential modern philosophers to be inspired by modern logic is the American Willard van Orman Quine (b. 1908), author of 'Two Dogmas of Empiricism,' in *Philosophical Review* 60 (1951), later collected in *From a Logical Point of View*, Cambridge, MA, 1953, and *Word and Object*, Cambridge, MA, 1960. On modern logic, see, for example, Benson Mates, *Elementary Logic*, Oxford, 1962 (2nd ed., 1972), and W. V. Quine, *Methods of Logic*, New York, 1950 (4th ed., 1972).

2 They were the co-authors of *Principia Mathematica* (1910).

3 See his *Language, Truth and Logic*, London, 1936.

4 'One can sum up all this by saying that the criterion of the scientific status of a theory is its falsifiability, or refutability, or testability.' Karl Popper, 'Science: Conjectures and Refutations', in *Conjectures and Refutations*, London, 1972, p. 37.

5 The philosopher Karl-Otto Apel objected that it does not make sense to say that we can choose to be rational (in the sense of being interested in truth), since the act of choosing between rationality and irrationality presupposes that we already are rational.

6 Popper, *The Logic of Scientific Discovery*, Ch. 14, note 5.

7 *The Poverty of Historicism*, Ch. 29, p. 136.

8 Cf. Paul Hoyningen-Huene, *Reconstructing Scientific Revolutions. Thomas S. Kuhn's Philosophy of Science*, Chicago, 1993.

9 Ibid.

10 This means that Wittgenstein rejected his earlier position in *Tractatus Logico-Philosophicus*.

11 Cf. the analysis of the dilemma of Achilles and the tortoise, in *Dilemmas* by G. Ryle, London, 1964.

12 P. Winch, *The Idea of a Social Science*, London, 1958.

13 Cf. G. Ryle, *The Concept of Mind* (1949), London, 1990.

14 Cf. Stuart Hampshire, *Thought and Action* (1959), London, 1960, and Peter E. Strawson, *Individuals* (1959), New York, 1963.

15 In this sense, the mathematically formulated language can be said to be 'idealized'.

16 J. L. Austin, *How to Do Things with Words*, Oxford, 1962.

17 Jürgen Habermas developed a distinction between the illocutionary and the perlocutionary aspects in the direction of a comprehensive speech act theory in which the distinction between *communicative* and *strategic* action is basic (cf. Ch. 27).

18 J. R. Searle, *Speech Acts*, Cambridge, 1969.

19 The concept of *brute facts*, as a counterpart to the concept of institutional facts, was developed by Elizabeth Anscombe. 'On Brute Facts', *Analysis*, vol. 18, January 1958.

20 Arne Garborg in *Tankar og utsyn* (translated by R. W.).

21 Cf. Amy Gutmann, ed., *Multiculturalism and 'The Politics of Recognition'*, by Charles Taylor, with commentaries by Amy Gutmann, Steven C. Rockefeller, Michael Walzer, and Susan Wolf, Princeton, NJ, 1992, p. 661.

22 Carol Gilligan, *In a Different Voice*, Cambridge, 1982. See also Lawrence Kohlberg, *Essays in Moral Development*, San Francisco, CA, 1984; Seyla Benhabib and Drucilla Cornell (eds), *Feminism as Critique*, Minneapolis, MN, 1987; Nancy Fraser, *Unruly Practices*, Cambridge, 1989.

23 'The Battle of the Gods' (that is, the battle between different fundamental values), as Max Weber put it.

27 Modernity and crisis

CRITIQUE OF MODERNITY

In this book we have followed Western thought from antiquity through the Middle Ages and down to our own time. What, then, is 'modernity' in such a perspective, and what is the critique of modernity? The problems of modernity have been implicit throughout our discussion, and in several cases they have been mentioned explicitly – for instance, in connection with the Renaissance and the philosophy of the Enlightenment, and also with Kant and Hegel – and critical views of modernity have been discussed in various cases, from Rousseau and Burke, through Marx, Freud, and Nietzsche, to Durkheim and Weber. We will now outline one view of modernity, as the background to a discussion of Heidegger, Arendt, and Habermas; Gadamer and Derrida; and Foucault and Rorty.

After the Renaissance, the cognizant subject became the philosophical starting point. This is true of the empiricists as well as the rationalists and Kant. In political theory (from Locke and Mill), the individual is the bearer of rationality, whether it is in the marketplace or in politics or law. The enlightened subject stands against ignorance and prejudice. Progress is growth in science and enlightenment, in technological control over nature, and in material welfare. The notions of an independently acting and cognizant subject, of science and enlightenment, and of progress and reason – these are characteristic concepts of modernity.

Burke and Tocqueville, Rousseau and Herder – these and others expressed criticism: they emphasized the power of tradition, the ambiguity of progress, and the destructive tendencies that result from the autonomy of the individual. These were the major themes of conservative criticism of the 'modern project'.

In our own day, scientization and technological development have increased. At the same time, social integration and political governance have become more complex and problematic. Our mobility and role repertoire have increased, as has control over nature and society. These are 'modern times', in work and leisure, with much freedom of choice and much centralized power, and with short-term perspectives and long-term anarchy.

Marx, Freud, and Nietzsche poured out a stream of *criticism* of the optimistic faith in reason and liberty – a critique of ideology in Marx, a critique of reason and autonomy in Freud, and a critique of morality in Nietzsche: what we believe to be rational explanations of free and moral behaviour and attitudes are exposed as rationalizations, as unconscious distortions of reality, and as illusions. The image of the free and rational individual has been shattered. We are left with a murky sea of hidden needs and desires. Enlightenment and knowledge are merely an external varnish, and belief in them may be a dangerous illusion. This gloomy Freudian view of the discontent of modernity matches Nietzsche's critique: when we talk about truth, the will to life lies below the surface! All statements filter out something and leave something else lying in the shade. They reveal something by simultaneously covering up other aspects of the phenomena. Hence, truth and untruth walk hand in hand, and beneath it all lie the life forces and the will to power. The *rationality* that is praised in scientific activity and in political life is actually *hidden power*. *Values*, both theological and humanistic, are thus exposed as *illusions*. There is no longer anything to believe in. All false hope is gone. European nihilism is finished. Only through art and sublime actions can we break free from the iron cage of rationality. Poetic speech is the only thing that remains of philosophy – for those who have ears to hear. Beyond this, we have another form of criticism, 'deconstruction', to expose the hidden power behind words and actions.

This is the absolute criticism of modernity. The pure ideals of progress in enlightenment, government, and the exploitation of nature are rejected as decay and stupidity, as a suppression of the life forces and as a foolish undermining of natural conditions. In the period between the two World Wars, this total criticism was also expressed by the political Left, such as the Marxist-inspired Frankfurt school, including Theodor W. Adorno (1903–1969), Max Horkheimer (1895–1973), and later Herbert Marcuse (1898–1979). They no longer believed in 'the revolutionary subject' (the proletariat) who will lead us into the good society. They no longer believed, without reservation, in the ethos of enlightenment, for it seemed ambiguous, but they still believed in the enduring value of criticism and in the liberating potential of aesthetics. This radical self-criticism within modern society has later been carried on by the postmodernists, such as Foucault and Derrida. Starting with the experience of crisis in the intellectual milieu between World Wars I and II, we will trace the attitude to modernity in Martin Heidegger (1889–1976), Hannah Arendt (1906–1975), and Jürgen Habermas (1929–): Heidegger hesitated at a distance from modernity, Arendt revitalized the Aristotelian conception of politics, and Habermas has sought a universal 'minimum reason' in a world in crisis. We will also glance at Gadamer, as well as Derrida, Foucault, and Rorty.

MARTIN HEIDEGGER – THROUGH THE POETIC

For Heidegger, Western history is no triumphant march towards light and happiness. On the contrary, this history is permeated by a *basic decline*, from the pre-Socratics to our time. The more intensively man has tried to grasp the various essences with his theoretical concepts and technical achievements, the more he has *forgotten* what is *essential*. History is thus a fateful decline from what is essential towards an impotent search for non-essentials – whether it is theoretical insight, technical force, or ways of life.

Plato marked an early step in this direction. He placed all beings of this world under the yoke of the ideas. Later philosophy and theoretical science further developed this tendency, with an increasing strength and expansion, until there was hardly any phenomenon exempt from the yoke of the ideas. Similarly, technological development represented a practical parallel with the theoretical development. Everything was to be placed under rational control – nature, society, even man. But who was controlling whom? Thought or thoughtlessness? Were these wise actions, or an unstoppable and short-sighted drive for what is new (but which was still in essence the old)?

On one hand, Heidegger was an existentialist (cf. Ch. 26). He was concerned with authentic and inauthentic existence, with our unique consciousness, our choices, and death, which is 'always mine'. He may be said to be a phenomenologist, with his description, in his book *Being and Time* (1927), of the basic features of human existence: we understand the world on the basis of our 'projects'. We have no access to the world without such formative projects, and the phenomena always appear as they do in light of each particular project. The insight included in such a project may either be expressed by statements or remain implicit as 'tacit knowledge', as in our familiar grasp of a hammer and a saw.

Our understanding can be developed and deepened. This always happens against the background of something that we think we already know. We see new things in light of what we already know. We are therefore never without presuppositions. But we can moderate and reshape the presuppositions that we have had until the present. Hence, our insight can change. Thereby we also are changing ourselves, in a sense – we form ourselves – because we follow not only explicit hypotheses (so to speak), but also basic, implicit presuppositions that 'we are' and that we often are not aware of. In this way, the *hermeneutic* process moves on a personally deeper level than does hypothetico-deductive research in which expressed hypotheses are put to the test. But, for Heidegger, hermeneutics was not primarily a method among other methods. Hermeneutics is the basic pattern of human cognition. We sway between the known and the unknown, between part and whole, so that in our search we see new sides, and probably see better and truer – but always as fallible creatures.

From a cultural-political perspective (which is not his), Heidegger seems like a critic of reification and the loss of historical awareness – in line with the existentialist criticism of mass society (Kierkegaard, Jaspers, Marcel). But behind it all lies Heidegger's complete critique: no compromises, with their illusory attempts at 'brightening up' this gloomy development! We live under technology as destiny, and will only fall back into its web if we adopt shallow solutions. The crisis embraces the entire history of Europe, with scientific rationality and technology as its major examples. Therefore, a transformation must be sought on the deepest level, where the forgotten and essential is concealed.

What, then, is the essential? It is not an 'essence'; it is neither a god nor a principle. The essential is what is close to us, yet to which we have become strangers. Nevertheless, we can attempt to rediscover it through the philosophers from the time before Platonic ideas took precedence. It is 'the Being of being', according to Heidegger – and he adds that it is still enigmatic for modern man. We must learn to listen to the language, so that the essential can speak to us. Language is an opening, especially poetic language, which is especially sensitive to what is difficult to convey. Genuine art is important for the same reason. Language is speech. We convey ourselves in speech. By expressing ourselves, we communicate what we are. Thus, we not only talk *about* something, but, through speech, we communicate *ourselves*. Through speech we express our current state. Our situation is communicated. We convey our mood, as a revealing relation to the world and to ourselves. This is how it always is. But this communication of who and how we are, of our mood, varies from scientific language to poetry. In poetry, what we say is relatively unimportant. What is essential is the communication of a particular mood, as an unveiling of a way of being toward that which is. Poetry is thus active in establishing meaning, in opening a world. By reading a people's poetry, we may gain insight into their mode and mood of being. In this way, we may also more easily find ourselves. Heidegger held poetry, the word, in high esteem. Language is the house of man. And poetry is our creative re-creation and actualization. The impoverishment of language – through empty talk, clichés and chatter – is impoverishment of the essence of man. For Heidegger, the poets, not the scientists or the politicians are the vanguard! The poets and the poetic philosophers are the vanguard of man's concealed essence. Rational discussion, whether it takes place in the city-state, the lecture room or the laboratory, does not hold a prominent position in Heidegger's thought. Such discussion, despite its triumphs, is not genuinely essential.

Heidegger, the poet philosopher, was not an ordinary philosopher of history. Reflecting on history, he envisaged the emergence of the Word in the beginning. And as an apolitical critic of modernity and its roots, he was a consistent 'oikologist': for Heidegger, the forms of life represented by village life, the daily life of the farmer and craftsman, were less degenerate and more authentic than urban life, with its alienation and rootlessness. He was a rustic thinker who viewed rural life with more pleasure than urban life. In his remarkable 'double-reflective' way, Heidegger was a kind of 'homestead thinker': poetically, human beings live on the earth, where they care for their households ('*oikos*') with deliberate thought ('*logos*'). He sees something that is still genuine – and, at the same time, universal – in what is local and characteristic. He did not argue for this view, in any usual sense. For that, language is (still?) insufficient. But he tried, poetically, to communicate what is essential. His criticism of modernity and its origin is brought to bear *through the poetic*.

HANNAH ARENDT – *VITA ACTIVA*

Hannah Arendt was of the same generation of Jewish intellectuals as Herbert Marcuse, Theodor W. Adorno, and Walter Benjamin (1892–1940). She was born in Hanover, Germany, in 1906 and grew up in Königsberg (Kaliningrad) in what was then East Prussia. Arendt studied philosophy under Martin Heidegger, Edmund Husserl, and Karl Jaspers in the 1920s. As an 18-year-old student, she developed a close relationship with Heidegger, who was then finishing his *magnum opus*, *Being and Time*. Five years later, Arendt completed her doctorate in philosophy with a dissertation on Augustine's concept of love. After Hitler came to power in 1933, she was arrested for anti-Nazi activity. Arendt later fled to Paris and then emigrated to the United States in 1940, where she remained until her death in 1975.

Arendt is one of the most important political thinkers in the twentieth century. However, it is difficult to place her within the political landscape. Labels like 'left-wing', 'right-wing', 'radical', or 'conservative' do not fit her philosophy. Above all, Arendt wanted to be an independent thinker and not a representative of some 'ism' in philosophy.

For Arendt, politics should not be reduced to power and violence, or to empty rhetoric or 'horse-trading'. Nor is politics, in a genuine sense, a matter of striving for political power or of gaining influence in the corridors of power. The essence of politics is to be found in debate and discussion — what the Greeks called *praxis*. Arendt's goal was to reclaim a conception of politics that has often been suppressed and forgotten, but which still shows up regularly in the historical process, namely: politics as participation in the public arena, on the model of the Greek city-state (*polis*). Arendt found traces of authentic political life in the American Revolution (1776), in the Paris Commune of 1871, in the socialist council movement after World War I, in the Hungarian rebellion of 1956, in the American civil rights movement of the 1960s, and in the student riots of 1968 in Paris. The common factor in these examples is that agents who were politically paralysed found an expression for their individuality and spontaneously organized themselves by creating new forums for political liberty. According to Arendt, this is the highest form of *vita activa* – the active life. Consequently, Arendt had little interest in party politics. Special interest politics, parliamentary democracy, and political compromise held no interest for her.

To clarify Arendt's objectives, we will take a closer look at her analysis of three basic forms of activity in her *magnum opus*, The Human Condition (1958). In this book, Arendt distinguished between *labour*, *production*, and *action*. Through labour, a human being becomes *animal laborans*, a labouring animal. The labouring human being obtains food and what else is needed for survival. This elementary activity of sustaining life does not leave any products. It secures only survival. For the Greeks, labour belonged to *oikos*, the sphere of the household. *Oikos* was, in the Greek world, the private sphere which shunned publicity. Through *oikos*, the family patriarch ruled despotically; the Greek word *despotēs* simply means the master of the house. Necessity, coercion, and lack of freedom prevailed here (cf. the slave's role in the household). Through production, a human being becomes *homo faber*, a creative being which transforms itself and its surroundings. For Arendt, production corresponded with what the Greeks understood by *poiesis*, namely, producing an 'artificial' or man-made world of objects. What primarily characterizes human beings, however, is their ability to act spontaneously and unpredictably, to bring something new into the world. Action, in this sense, requires a sphere of action, a public arena that makes participation and discussion possible. Action may then be said to be more than just labour and production. Arendt's model is here the *praxis* that unfolds in the *polis* between equal citizens.

Why was the distinction between labour, production, and action so important for Arendt? Arendt's point is that political movements in the nineteenth and twentieth centuries have tried to reduce action to labour and production. They have treated politics as if it were a form of political technique or 'social engineering'. Thus, the field of action dissolves. Labour and production 'colonize' political life. Political questions are reduced to 'social problems'. Arendt's criticism struck at the heart of many contemporary political movements, especially Nazism and Stalinism. The problematic relationship between labour, production, and action therefore play an important role in her first major work, *The Origins of Totalitarianism* (1951). Arendt was one of the first to apply the term 'totalitarianism' to both Nazism and Stalinism. According to Arendt, what was new in Stalin's Soviet Union and Hitler's Germany was the attempt to *produce* a new human being and a completely new political order. Unlike previous dictatorships, these regimes based themselves on a total ideology, a large-scale mobilization of the masses, systematic manipulation and indoctrination, and a consistently technocratic view of politics. The charismatic *Führer* wanted to create a new human being and a new society, just as the craftsman shapes an object from formless raw material: human beings and society were like putty in the *Führer*'s hands! In these totalitarian regimes, action was reduced to production; *praxis* to *poiesis*. The same technocratic attitude is seen in the struggle against presumed enemies: the Nazi extermination of the Jews (*Endlösung*) was not like the traditional pogroms, but was a well-planned, bureaucratic mass execution. Adolf Eichmann ensured that the goal, a Germany cleansed of 'foreigners', was achieved in the most efficient way. In the Stalinist view of reality, the 'class enemy' (which also included the old Bolshevik elite) had to be exterminated in order to achieve a classless society. A pathological concept of the ends justifying the means applied in both cases.

Arendt's major concern was to reveal how this could have happened. We cannot go into her historical analysis of the origin of totalitarianism, but must be content with an outline of two fundamental points: the fact that political leaders could treat human beings as pliable material (and as a means to an end) reveals a basic truth about the human condition in the twentieth century. Under totalitarian conditions, human beings are robbed of their ability to act. Totalitarian regimes view action as a threat and strive for predictable behaviour in their citizens' lives so that they can be controlled more easily. These regimes do everything to shut down all 'public arenas' in order to isolate and atomize the people. One of the preconditions for totalitarianism, according to Arendt, is the emergence of the isolated and atomized individual – a negative aspect of the liberal society – without the ability or chance to act authentically. Hence, modern 'mass man' is a correlate of the new dictatorship. What is fascinating – and deeply unsettling – about Arendt's analysis is that the differentiation and rationalization of modernity brings with it individuals with no roots or identity, people who feel superfluous and are therefore attracted to leaders who can provide them with a new goal and a new identity.

Some of the intellectual preconditions for totalitarianism can be found in antiquity. In her analysis, Arendt tried to connect the idea of progress and of modernity with the idea of the totalitarian temptation. Modernity, by definition, exceeds all limitations. Modern man always wants to go further, and never accepts the limitations of his existence. He never becomes 'weary of the journey' and seeks immortality. He wants to surpass his earthly attachment and has already begun to plan a future in outer space. For Arendt, this idea of progress is a form of *hubris*. It suggests that modernity is rebelling against humanity's fixed limits. Arendt thought that she could trace the historical origin of this *hubris* back to the idea of power and control over nature that has been gaining momentum since the Renaissance. In the twentieth century, this idea has gained acceptance in all fields – nature, society, and human beings have all become the object of control and manipulation. From this perspective, totalitarianism is merely an extreme version of the mentality that also characterizes democratic and liberal societies. Modern technology has assumed supernatural dimensions and has become an all-encompassing system that measures everything by the same standard.

Arendt's criticism was directed not only against political ideologies. She also developed an accurate and apt analysis of modern philosophy. Like Jürgen Habermas, she criticized Marx for reducing *praxis* to labour. Although Marx anticipated many of Arendt's concerns, his focus was not on politics, but on economics. For Marx, human alienation from labour was the most important obstacle to freedom and self-realization (cf. Ch. 18, Dialectics and alienation). The primary goal of the socialist revolution was to change the conditions of labour and production so that human beings could realize themselves through their labour. In the future communist society the state would 'wither away' and politics would be replaced by 'an administration of things'. Marx was thus remarkably silent about *praxis*, about the conditions for the acting human being. Not only, therefore, does Marxism lack an adequate political theory, but also the entire ethical-political dimension is reduced to labour and production. As we know, the socialist 'experiments' had catastrophic results.

A similar criticism may be made of Heidegger. In *Being and Time* Heidegger provided instructive descriptions of man's various tasks, but, like Marx, he reduced *vita activa* to labour and production. It is the farmer's and the craftsman's lives that take centre stage. But Heidegger's hand hammers; it does not caress. In the workshop and in the farmer's work, there is no place for the ethical-political discussion.[1] Heidegger thus developed a philosophy of *praxis* – a 'praxeology' – without *praxis*. He became an *oikologist* and was, at heart, an apolitical thinker. It is true that in his later work Heidegger recognized many of Arendt's problems. He was keenly aware of the dangers of technological development, but his thesis that poetry ('the poetic') is the only possible answer to this challenge shows once again that he lacked adequate political concepts.

We have emphasized that Arendt's concept of politics assumes a discussion between free and equal agents. The goal of the discussion is to clarify and test our views and opinions. For Arendt, it became important to distinguish between truth and opinion. She referred to the struggle between truth (*aletheia*) and opinion (*doxa*) as, for example, in Plato's struggle with the Sophists. In this conflict, Arendt defended political *doxa* against philosophical *truth*, but without taking a sophistic position. She emphasized that we do not 'have' opinions. We form well-informed opinions when private viewpoints and ideas are tested in a genuine meeting between those with different opinions. Only in this way can we learn to view a case from different sides and thus form reasonable opinions. Through such discussions we may revise our conceptions in the light of better arguments. Arendt also emphasized, like Aristotle, that politics requires a unique form of wisdom (*phronesis*); that is, the practical discernment that is always exercised in our evaluation of a specific situation or case. Theoretical insight, therefore, can never replace political wisdom. Even though Habermas has not made the same distinction between theoretical and practical discourse as Arendt, both agree that political discussion should be open to rational arguments and not degenerate to sophistic rhetoric.

Not all of Arendt's political philosophy is as well-thought out and to the point. Arendt may be said to have advocated an elitist participatory democracy in which only a few are politically active. She had a somewhat romantic view of politics: politics is the communicative battleground on which citizens seek honour and recognition; it becomes an arena for each person's self-realization. This conception may best be characterized as a *self-realization democracy*; politics is to some extent reduced to expressive action. Thus, for Arendt, authentic politics has similarities to great drama. In this perspective, not only does the idea of everyday politics disappear, but also the fact that politicians face deadlines, that they are forced into compromise and strategic decisions, etc. Nor is it always clear what Arendt considered to be political themes or cases. In various contexts, she distinguished sharply between 'social matters' and 'political matters', and insisted that social questions do not belong in politics: 'Nothing . . . could be more obsolete than to attempt to liberate mankind from poverty by political means; nothing could be more futile and more dangerous.'[2] To this, we could object that liberation from poverty is a presupposition for political participation, in Arendt's sense, and that it is therefore also a political question. But for Arendt, neither poverty nor other social problems can be solved by political means. These are not matters that belong to the *polis*. They must either be solved in the sphere of the household or left to the experts to solve. This is, however, a questionable position: if all social questions are excluded from politics, as Arendt proposes, the consequence will be that political life is emptied of substantial content. What are the discussions to be *about*? Arendt did not see that the participants themselves must decide – with political arguments – what is and what is not politics. Political philosophers cannot set the political agenda. It should be emphasized that Arendt's strength lay in her *diagnostic* vision, not in her development of a political programme.

GADAMER – THE HERMENEUTIC TRADITION

We may distinguish two main traditions after Heidegger. The first, which we can call the *hermeneutic tradition*, is centred on Hans-Georg Gadamer (1900–). The second, which we may call the *deconstructionist tradition*, has several heirs; here we have chosen to discuss Jacques Derrida, Michel Foucault, and Richard Rorty. The first tradition has elaborated ideas from the early work of Heidegger and developed a philosophy of understanding and interpretation. This tradition has roots that go back to Schleiermacher and Dilthey (cf. Ch. 16).

While the early work of Heidegger focused on human action as he developed his philosophy of understanding and interpretation, Gadamer turned primarily to historical *texts*. For Gadamer, as for the older hermeneuticians such as Schleiermacher and Dilthey, the paradigm for hermeneutics can be found in the *understanding of texts*. But while the earlier hermeneuticians had studied texts primarily in order to obtain historical insight, Gadamer viewed literary texts, along with religious and juridical texts, as a basis for developing a hermeneutic philosophy. In this connection, the problem of human nature was central for Gadamer, who, like Heidegger, was primarily interested in understanding man; the interest in questions of method was secondary to the anthropological question of what a man is as cognizant creature.

The second tradition, the deconstructionist one, began with Heidegger's philosophical critique of tradition, that is to say, with Heidegger's attempt to answer the profoundest questions about those forces that have been presupposed but not 'seen', and that have shaped history. We seek the tensions in the philosophical texts that have been handed down, in order to 'come behind the text' and reveal the contradictions that the author may have overlooked, but which critical interpretation can bring to light. The texts are thus 'deconstructed'. Deconstruction is, in this sense, a critical activity that tries to show that the traditional texts are not really what they claim to be, but something else. Hence, the deconstructionist tradition offers a programme that is radical and critical of tradition. As we will see, this undermining of tradition has been understood differently by the various deconstructionists. But they still have some common features that, among other things, puts them in opposition to the tradition represented by Gadamer, in which respect for tradition is basic. If Gadamer's predecessors were the hermeneuticians such as Schleiermacher and Dilthey, Nietzsche and Freud are the pioneers of the deconstructionist tradition.

In spite of this clear opposition between a 'radical' and a 'conservative' hermeneutic programme, the fact remains that both traditions are critical of modernity. While Gadamer, in keeping with the humanistic concept of *Bildung* (*formation*), was especially critical of the cultural decay of modern society, the deconstructionists are primarily critical of the type of rationalism that they find in, and behind, modern society, a rationalism that they often interpret as a covert and oppressive force imposing discipline homogenization.

We shall take a closer look at Gadamer's philosophy before our discussion of deconstructivism.

During his twenties, Gadamer came into contact with Heidegger's thought and became especially inspired by Heidegger's interpretation of philosophical texts. Here, systematic thinking was carried out in the explication of earlier philosophers. Heidegger's ideas were developed through a creative interpretation of these historic texts. This was to be Gadamer's own method. The main presentation of his hermeneutic philosophy is found in his book *Truth and Method* (1960).

As a hermeneutician, Gadamer was also inspired by Schleiermacher and Dilthey. Schleiermacher emphasized that hermeneutic interpretation must go behind the text to the authors and their life's work. Thus, we should try to understand the specific part of the text not only in light of the author's entire body of work, but in light of the author's personal life, intellectual life, and career. The so-called hermeneutic circle is thus not merely a question of the relationship between the part and the whole in a text. Textual understanding is not only an alternation between interpretation of *parts* of the text on the basis of the text as a *whole* and interpretation of the *whole* on the basis of the *parts*, but also a hermeneutic circle which draws in the author's life, preferably the work of the author as a reconstructed whole. But this means that text interpretation becomes largely a psychological (or historical) project. On this point, Gadamer expressed his reservations.

Gadamer did not deny, of course, that there are many kinds of psychological and historical facts that form the basis of a text. But he emphasized that a text still claims or states something – directly or indirectly – and that we have to take these text-immanent propositions seriously if we want to understand the text as a text. Understanding a text is therefore a question of understanding what it is stating. Understanding a text's meaning is thus linked to understanding the truth claims of the text. Of course, it is possible that what the text says is meant as a joke. It is therefore important to find out what kind of claims the text is making. It may also be that the text has no meaning at all – the author, for example, may have gone mad – and in such cases it is necessary to change our method of approach and instead look for psychological causes. But this is still not the standard example of text interpretation, according to Gadamer. Normally, we try to understand what the text is saying, what it is claiming.

Immersing ourselves in a text is therefore not a question of immersing ourselves in the intellectual life of another person, but of immersing ourselves in the meaning of the text. And the meaning of the text is found in the 'truth claims' that the text makes. To understand a text, we must actively try to determine whether its truth claim is reasonable or not. This does not mean, of course, that we need to agree with what the text says, but complete neutrality is not possible.[3]

Once we undertake to understand a text, we must, moreover, adopt the basic view that the text is meaningful and that it is without contradiction in regard to the truth claims that it makes. Here, Gadamer held that with our pre-understanding of the text we assume that it is 'perfect' (*Vorgriff der Vollkommenheit*).[4] The following two important linguistic-philosophical points are involved:

1   Language is not only determinative for texts, for also for human understanding in general, and thus for the life-world in which we live. Here, language is not understood 'objectively', as either sounds or letters. Nor is it understood as a specific national language. Language is understood as the inherited 'horizon' of meaning in which we are socialized and through which we understand ourselves and the world. Language in this sense is what connects us together as human beings and what mediates between us and the world.

2   The meaning of a text does not lie in the text as an object to be found. The text's meaning is only what it is in light of the *horizon of meaning* in which the text is placed. We will always see the text from our own horizon of meaning. Therefore, to understand the meaning of a text we try to find the questions to which the text may be the answer; that is to say, we are really looking for the meaning horizon which makes a certain type of question possible. When we find the kinds of questions that seem to open up the text for us, it means that we, with our horizon of meaning, have managed to approach the horizon of meaning from which the text is shaped.[5]

When a text and an interpreter belong to the same world (horizon of meaning), the work of interpretation is, in principle, manageable. This work becomes very difficult when the text belongs to a culture different from that of the interpreter, whether it is a different culture in our own day or that of a past age. It is precisely in such cases that the work of interpretation becomes an intellectual challenge.

In such cases the text also speaks to us personally. To understand the meaning of a text, I have to take the text seriously. As an interpreter of the text, I have to try to understand the questions the text is answering. The text is written from its own horizon of meaning, not mine. The text is written on the basis of its own 'pre-judices' from which it speaks. I have my own 'pre-judices' from which I speak and interpret. The degree to which I manage to understand a foreign text thus depends on whether the two horizons of meaning can communicate with each other, can merge together. This is what Gadamer called 'fusion of horizons'. But this does not mean that the two horizons have simply become one and the same. The 'one' horizon is different from the 'other'. What has happened is a transformation of my horizon of meaning. In this sense, I have undergone a deep formation, 'deep' because it is not a question of acquiring new knowledge from a given background, but of a transformation of my own 'frame of reference'. This formation (*Bildung*) is a learning process in the sense that I, in this way, expand my horizon and understand more, and in a different way, than I previously did. At the same time, this shows the close relationship between hermeneutics and education for Gadamer. This formation process towards a fusion of horizons is something that happens to us. We cannot plan it or survey it in advance, as if we were assuming a position outside history. We are always in the process; we never stand outside and survey the process. As a result, we can improve our insight, and thus learn – grow in age and wisdom – but we cannot pretend to have the 'final' truth, from a timeless position outside history. In this sense, we are always on the path. Our understanding is always historically determined and the process of interpretation never ends.

This brings us to the core of Gadamer's philosophy. What he was driving at was an improved understanding of human beings as 'historically understanding' beings. He was not primarily trying to give advice in regard to the question of method in the human sciences. He was trying to clarify the conditions that make human understanding possible. Put in this way, his project becomes an epistemological project or, more precisely, a transcendental philosophical project. But Gadamer distinguished himself from the epistemologists, including Kant, by starting with language as a horizon of meaning and by understanding any interpretation as a formation process that seeks a fusion of horizons. He saw language and interpretation as essentially historical phenomena. Thus, there are clearly Hegelian features in Gadamer's philosophy; but Gadamer interpreted texts while Hegel built systems.

Two critical traditions have their roots in Gadamer's thought. The first asks whether or not our historical contextualization is so basic that it is problematic to talk about 'truth' as something universal. This is the criticism made by the deconstructionists. The second asks whether or not 'truth claims' ought to be interpreted on the basis of a general theory of speech acts and a theory of cultural modernization. This is the criticism made by Habermas.

DERRIDA, FOUCAULT, AND RORTY – DECONSTRUCTION AND CRITIQUE

Jacques Derrida (1930–) has continued Heidegger's effort to bring metaphysics to its logical conclusion. In this critical project, he is also the heir of Nietzsche and Freud. As in these pioneers, Derrida's criticism of metaphysics is, at the same time, a criticism of Western thought in general, including the scientization, in theory and practice, that has emerged from Western history and that characterizes modern civilization. Derrida criticizes from the inside, through deconstruction; that is to say, by a method of reading texts that seeks the built-in contradictions in the text, and that thus induces the elements of meaning in the text to fall apart.[6]

Derrida has broadened the concept of text, or of writing, so that language is understood as 'writing', and everything ultimately is 'writing'. This he does by interpreting writing as an activity which establishes differences; that is, defines and distinguishes. The basic mistake of metaphysics is that it has always sought a foundation and has sought this foundation in what is. But, like Heidegger, Derrida seeks to show that it is futile to seek such a foundation. The world, in this sense, is without foundation. It is futile to seek a foundation in 'what is' in the form of 'being'. What characterizes 'writing' is 'distinguishing' (*la différance*). Writing appears to be a continual contest between new differences, a contest between what is present and what is absent. In this open contest, 'the other', what is different, will always resist definition, in spite of all attempts to grasp it with our concepts. Born in Algeria, Derrida is a French philosopher with a Jewish background. As such, he has always been, in his own words, 'the other' in relation to the dominant culture. The problem for Derrida is the well-known question of self-reference. We could put it bluntly as follows. If deconstruction means that all of the classic concepts in philosophy are 'dissolved', including the concept of truth, it is imperative for Derrida to explain whether he still thinks that what he says about this is true. If he answers in the affirmative, he is self-referentially inconsistent. If he answers in the negative, it is difficult to see that he is saying anything that we need to take seriously. Or is there a third answer?

Michel Foucault (1926–1984) became especially known with the book *Words and Things* ('*Les Mots et les choses*' [1966]), in which he advocated a structuralist position: man is a social construction. Reality is basically structures. Like the other French structuralists, Foucault criticized theories supporting the concept of man as an autonomous individual, instead of giving precedence to concepts of structural conditions. Foucault was searching for what he called the 'archaeology' of the humanities, that is to say, the underlying structural connections of a given epoch. Foucault called the determining structure, which also determines the thoughts and actions in a given epoch, the *epistémé*. Foucault's work is just as much intellectual history as philosophy. His book on the history of madness (*Histoire de la folie* [1961]) is an example of this. It is characteristic of Foucault's 'archaeological' analyses that his aim was practical (political), in spite of the scientific form that his work takes. His aim was to expose power structures, to show how something that seems to be rational is really functioning as covert suppression, often in the form of discipline and indoctrination. Foucault's heart was with those who are marginalized in society, such as the 'insane', homosexuals, or prison inmates. With his critique of traditional Western rationalism, Foucault was aligned with the deconstructionists. Like Derrida, he defended those who are defined as 'the other', but Foucault's political commitment was so strong and his antagonism to philosophical justification so consistent that there was an obvious tension between his philosophical scepticism and his practical commitment. How can a sceptic know that there are good causes worth fighting for? In brief, a consistent answer could be that this is a matter of making a decision, a decision that could just as easily have been in favour of the powerful as of the weak; for Stalinism or for Hitlerism. But this was certainly not Foucault's view.

Richard Rorty (1931–) was trained in analytical philosophy.[7] In his book *Philosophy and the Mirror of Nature* (1979), Rorty articulated a radical criticism of the traditional subject–object dichotomy in epistemology (from Locke to Kant) and also of the idea of truth as a *one-to-one relation* between thought and thing, or between proposition and state of affair. He criticized the notion of truth as *correspondence*. Rorty emphasized usefulness in preference to the idea of the truth as correspondence; therefore, he has moved in the direction of pragmatism.[8] At the same time, he has emphasized that thought is always 'situated' in particular contexts. Rorty is thus a contextualist. His pragmatism and contextualism mean that, for him, the political tradition takes precedence to philosophy. Rorty is thus a supporter of the liberal and democratic tradition of his native United States. This is his 'context' (contextualism). This context decides what is useful, and hence valuable, without the support of philosophical arguments. Rorty believes such philosophical argumentation to be impossible. This is the crucial point of a contextualism that holds that arguments have meaning only within a particular context. The transition from classical analytical philosophy to a form of contextualism is not unusual (it is also found in the later work of Wittgenstein).[9] What is characteristic of Rorty's contextualism is his emphasis on the importance of the political culture of his country.[10] It is also characteristic of Rorty that he, as a former analytical philosopher, supports the deconstructionists not only in their basic views, but also in their method. Rorty tries to carry on a 'conversation' with the great thinkers, but always by deconstructing their philosophical propositions and ideas (such as the idea of truth). Hence, philosophical texts, for Rorty, are no different than literary texts. It may be interesting and edifying to read them, and they offer us views and visions, but not as anything that can claim to be true or valid. Finally, it is characteristic of Rorty that he assumes a sharp distinction between the private and the public spheres. A private person may be edified and enriched by reading the great classics, but without taking what they say as dogmas on truth or how we ought to organize society. The question of how society ought to be organized is a question for the public sphere, as divorced from the private sphere, and on this level, Rorty supports the liberal society.

As a private person, Rorty reads Nietzsche and Heidegger but maintains ironic distance from their claims. As a political thinker, he considers philosophers such as Nietzsche and Heidegger utterly unacceptable and even dangerous, and he supports an open and enlightened, liberal society, free from philosophical dictation.[11] He has thus criticized the French deconstructionists (such as Derrida and especially Foucault) for confusing a philosophy of life with politics. In politics, according to him, we must be liberal and not support radical criticism based on philosophical projects. For Rorty, everything is contextual and contingent; no propositions or norms are strictly universal or necessary. Rorty's deconstructive approach is marked by that fact that he has been an analytical philosopher and knows this school intimately, a knowledge which allows him to argue with great precision. He is not content with showing how ideas and arguments pertain to particular contexts, but also tries to show how we can manage without philosophical distinctions (such as the one between truth and falsity). He does this by showing that these distinctions break down when we take them to extremes; for instance, in the sense that the idea of absolute truth becomes problematic. Rorty has taken the criticism of philosophy seriously. He has personally renounced philosophy as a profession and transferred to a university department of literature. Rorty is well aware of the problems of self-reference that arise with a sceptical position. Hence, he always proceeds carefully. He makes few claims, but 'suggests' and 'hints' at alternative ways of discourse. Rorty has had a great influence on many aspects of textual studies. But those who follow him in these fields often lack his philosophical education, and their argumentation is often far less subtle and far more vulnerable to counter-arguments, as in self-referential inconsistency. But it remains to be seen whether Rorty manages to extricate himself from all such problems of self-referential inconsistency.[12] Furthermore, it is striking that Rorty often tries to dissolve conceptual distinctions by focusing on and criticizing their extreme versions. But a rejection of extreme versions does not justify a rejection of the more moderate versions, such as the concept of truth.[13] Finally, it is difficult to see how Rorty can consistently maintain such a sharp distinction between the private sphere and the public sphere – and this point is especially ironic because he has specialized in dissolving such sharp conceptual distinctions.[14]

JÜRGEN HABERMAS – THROUGH THE ARGUMENTATIVE

The hermeneutic tradition and critical deconstruction both start with language as text. They therefore have a close relationship with comparative literary studies, historical research, theology, and jurisprudence. Jürgen Habermas (1929–) has always been interested in the social sciences, and initially conceived of language as speech act. For Habermas, the concept of action (and of institutions) takes precedence over the concept of text.

Habermas was trained in the Frankfurt school. But he broke with the full-scale criticism and pessimism that characterized the early generation of this school (Adorno and Horkheimer). This break was related to Habermas' distinction between different so-called *cognitive interests*: we must be able to dominate nature in order to satisfy our vital needs. In connection with the extension of instrumental forms of work, we have the development of applied science and nature-controlling technology. This is the *technical cognitive interest*. At the same time, we are dependent on common action and social interaction. Interaction is internally connected with language, and interactive understanding is developed further in hermeneutic sciences, ranging from social anthropology to history. This is the *practical cognitive interest*. Finally, we need to liberate ourselves from ideological ties through critical reflection, as in psychoanalysis and the critique of ideology. This is the *emancipatory cognitive interest*.

In regard to nature, our rationality is controlling. And that is how it has to be since the technical cognitive interest is indispensable. Habermas does not see anything blameworthy in this. This is how it should be; this is where this type of power belongs. But, according to Habermas, there is also a form of knowledge and rationality that does not control. It is based on the practical cognitive interest. It is here decisive that Habermas does not conceive of rationality only as oppressive and controlling. In interpersonal relationships, we can use *either* the technical cognitive interest *or* the practical cognitive interest. Instead of a kind of fatalism in regard to one kind of controlling rationality, we have the important task of seeking a reasonable balance between the technical and the practical rationality, between control and understanding.

Emancipatory cognitive interest also belongs on this social level, and is important in the struggle against reification and inner oppression.

In other words, in regard to nature, only *one* cognitive interest is current. It is the explanatory and controlling cognitive interest. In regard to society, all three cognitive interests are current. Therefore, we must struggle to find the right balance between the three, especially between the technical on the one hand and the practical and the emancipatory on the other.

Methodologically, this means that Habermas holds that we, in regard to nature, can only carry out hypothetico-deductive research which results in causal explanations. In regard to social phenomena, we can carry out *both* hypothetico-deductive research *and* hermeneutic research ('understanding sociology'). In the larger, historical-critical perspective, this means that Habermas aims to show that there is one type of rationality whose essence is not controlling, but which implies mutual understanding. We have communicative rationality and communicative action.

We will not go into the philosophical problems connected with this division into different cognitive interests and forms of research, but only point out what is reasonable according to Habermas' basic intuition. If a person exhibits asocial behaviour, we may try to find causes for this, of either a physiological or psychological nature, and on the basis of our knowledge of causal relationships, we may try to cure the person. The person in question has then become *objectified* for us. By virtue of such insight, we may control this objectified person. *Or* we may consider the person to be sane and reasonable, and thus responsible, since we are trying to find out the reasons for this behaviour – perhaps there are good reasons that we have not recognized, or perhaps the person in question simply is reprehensible and should be urged to reform.

Occasionally, we may use *both* approaches, as with neuroses and alcoholism. But in some cases it is reasonably clear that a person's behaviour is causally determined, as in drug addiction, and in other cases it is reasonably clear that the person is sane and responsible, as during academic examinations. In the latter case, the teachers are not interested in the causes that lead the examinees to write answers but rather in the reasons that justify those answers.

This is the difference between *reasons* and *causes* in the determination of a person's response. Reasons can be understood, expanded, and disputed. To understand Einstein's theory of relativity and test it, we ask whether there are good reasons to accept the validity of this theory. But of course there were also causes determining the fact that Einstein proposed this theory. We may, for example, be interested in the psychological factors that caused him to become a physicist. Such causes are interesting in many contexts, but not in regard to the question of whether the theory is valid or not. Even if Einstein proposed his theory because of unconscious Freudian compulsions, his theory may still be valid! The answer to the question of its validity is determined through further research, not by investigating Einstein's childhood and private life.

Thus, it is correct that we maintain two kinds of attitudes towards one another (and towards ourselves). It is also correct that we may have a less free and more restrictive society if the tendency to find causal explanations becomes excessive (the therapeutic society). But it is also true that we might search for reasons where we should rather have sought for causes, and hence that we might be moralizing in cases where therapy would have been the appropriate course (as in an example of an overly moralistic society).

Habermas has tried to show that differentiation in the process of modernization has led to fundamental tensions between two spheres: what he calls *system* and *life-world*.[15] We can say that 'system' embraces the economic and political fields. Here we have progress in the form of an increasing scientific and technological domination. Hence, there is room for rationalization in the sense of an improvement in regard to rationality; namely, in the knowledge of which means lead to which ends (means-to-an-end rationality). However, Habermas' main point is that this is not the whole story: at the same time that we have institutions that develop in the economic and political fields, with accompanying learning processes, we also develop competence within the life-world, in the form of a better developed communicative rationality. In short, this differentiation between system and life-world means that we learn to master certain basic distinctions: we no longer whip the sea when we dislike its 'behaviour' (as did King Xerxes of Persia in the fifth century BC), because we have learned to distinguish between nature and society, between things that we can influence only by having insight into causal relations, and things that we can communicate with and rebuke. We have learned this distinction, and, hence, we are on a higher stage of development than those who have not yet learned it. We assume that those today who seriously 'whip the sea' are mentally disturbed.

Furthermore, we expect that sane adults have learned to master the distinction between truth and falsehood, between understanding that something is the case and that something else is not. Of course, we all occasionally make mistakes in regard to this distinction. And of course, we are not all equally good at talking *about* it. But we can all make *use* of this distinction in practice, once we have reached a certain age. We also consider psychopathological the failure to distinguish between reality and fantasy. In addition, we distinguish between what is right and wrong. The person who does not know (not even roughly and implicitly) what is appropriate in different situations is an outsider in the life-world. Finally, we can distinguish between a genuine expression of what we are feeling and thinking, and a simulation.

This kind of progress in reflexive and communicative competence leads towards an ability to thematize and discuss the questions of what is true and what is right, when uncertainty and disagreements arise about such questions. Instead of searching for answers in tradition and in canonical works, we learn to follow arguments. To reach the truth, we have to rely on different forms of research and discussion. In normative questions, according to Habermas, it is also a question of seeking a reasonable agreement between the parties involved. If we arrive at a free agreement on the basis of an open and informed discussion, the answer can be assumed to be the normatively correct answer. Habermas thus thinks that adults in our culture are, in principle, able to decide in regard to basic normative questions by argumentation among those who are affected. This is a version of the viewpoint that there are universally valid answers to normative questions, and that we, in principle, are capable of reaching such answers by the discursive use of reason.

For Habermas, this argument is directed against both ethical relativism and ethical dogmatism: deductive proofs are excluded because such proofs lead either to a logical circle, an infinite regression, or an arbitrarily chosen stopping point. Nor does he rely on self-evident or revealed normative truths; in this field we have long had *different* metaphysical and theological answers that contradict one another. Nor does he think that free and reasonable subjects can reason their way to such conclusions on their own. We need one another in order to understand that our perspective is one among many – and to become aware of our unconscious distortions, so that we may correct them. We need other people because we need a pluralistic reason, theoretical as well as normative, in order to discuss the given conceptual frameworks and in order to balance the various arguments against one another.

Here we meet an intersubjective and procedural rationality: *intersubjective*, because discussion is crucial; *procedural*, because it is not specific theses or standpoints that are the 'final ground', but the procedure itself. This procedure is that we proceed objectively and questioningly. The particular view that we, at various times, accept to be true or correct may later prove to be doubtful. This is the only approach that we, as fallible creatures, have at our disposal; that is, to acknowledge our mistakes and to move forwards. This procedural approach is therefore basic.

Habermas, like his colleague Karl-Otto Apel (1922–), has emphasized in this connection that there are certain unavoidable conditions that make it possible for us to argue. As participants in serious argumentation, we must be able to follow the argument, and be willing to submit to 'the force of the better argument'. Furthermore, we must mutually recognize one another both as reasonable and fallible – reasonable enough to be able to follow an argument, and fallible because we have something to learn. A know-it-all can give advice, but cannot argue; there is nothing for such a person to discuss. There is a normative element in this mutual recognition: equality. This means that there is a restriction on egoistic and ethnocentric answers. Moreover, there is a requirement of universalization, because valid arguments must be valid for everyone. An argument is not private property, like an IQ or a dental chart. Arguments are not valid for some and invalid for others. The concept of a valid argument means that the argument is universally valid, that is to say, valid in all cases of the same kind.[16] This conception of rationality is daring in the sense that it claims to embrace basic normative questions. But at the same time, it is careful to emphasize that this is a question of a fallible process in which we may continually seek to improve our opinions through research and discussion, but where we are never guaranteed to possess the final truth.

This conception of rationality is opposed to decisionism, as in the thinking of Popper, Weber, and Sartre. Enlightened and public discussion between reasonable persons is Habermas' answer. This fallible process is, according to him, all that we have. The alternative is an appeal either to basic metaphysical truths, which we no longer think of as credible, or to a rationally ungrounded decision. Habermas' answer is, in many ways, modest, but it is also problematic, both in regard to the practical actualization and in regard to further philosophical discussion. But its theoretical strength lies in the fact that it is difficult to avoid: if we disagree, we must argue against it – but then we are trapped by what we want to reject. If we do not argue against it, we have not made any criticism. If we do argue against it, we are standing within the argumentative situation, with its built-in requirement of enlightened discussion and mutual recognition between the parties involved. Those who disagree must show that they have better arguments than Habermas. This is the 'magic ring' of argumentative reason. Argumentative reason represents an unavoidable fate. Not that we should always discuss. But in many cases of uncertainty or disagreement, we should look on a procedural and reflexive rationality as the final court of appeal. According to Habermas, this is a basic feature of modernity. Modernity is characterized not only by differentiation and division, but also by unity around a discursive rationality, which is defined not according to content, but procedurally. Habermas is thus the heir of the Enlightenment, although he is free of its naive optimism.

QUESTIONS

Discuss Hannah Arendt's view of politics in modern societies. How is Arendt's view related to that of Heidegger (on the one hand) and that of Habermas (on the other)?

Discuss the strengths and weaknesses of deconstructive philosophy (Jacques Derrida, Michel Foucault, and Richard Rorty).

In what sense does Habermas think that validity claims for basic normative questions can be decided rationally?

SUGGESTIONS FOR FURTHER READING

PRIMARY LITERATURE

Apel, K.-O., *Towards a Transformation of Philosophy*, London, 1980.
Arendt, H., *The Human Condition*, New York, 1958.
Derrida, J., *Of Grammatology*, Baltimore, MD, 1976.
Foucault, M., *Madness and Civilization: A History of Insanity in the Age of Reason*, New York, 1965.
Gadamer, H.-G., *Truth and Method*, New York, 1975.
Habermas, J., *Theory of Communicative Action*, 2 vols, Boston, MA, 1984, 1987.
Habermas, J., *The Philosophical Discourse of Modernity*, Cambridge, MA, 1987.
Habermas, J., *Between Facts and Norms*, Cambridge, MA, 1996.
Heidegger, M., *Being and Time*, New York, 1962.
Rorty, R., *Contingency, Irony, and Solidarity*, Cambridge, MA, 1989.

SECONDARY LITERATURE

Bernstein, R. (ed.), *Habermas and Modernity*, Cambridge, 1985.
Bernstein, R., *The New Constellation*, Cambridge, 1991.
McCarthy, T., *Ideals and Illusions*, Cambridge, MA, 1991.
Skirbekk, G., *Rationality and Modernity*, Oslo/Oxford, 1993.

NOTES

1 See Anne Granberg's analysis of Heidegger in her dissertation, 'The Death of the Other. The Making of the Self and the Problem of the Ethical in Heidegger's "Being and Time" ', Oslo, 1995.

2 H. Arendt, *On Revolution*, London, 1990, p. 114.

3 Gadamer's thesis of truth claims being built into the texts may be compared with Habermas' thesis that all speech acts make validity claims. But it is worth noting that, for Habermas, this primarily applies to the speech acts as interactions *between persons*, and that it only indirectly applies to *texts*.

4 Against this, the deconstructionists, such as Derrida and Foucault, would claim that we, on the contrary, ought to use the 'hermeneutics of suspicion' and look for what is conflicting and contradictory in the text.

5 Here we have a 'transcendental-philosophical' view of language in which the horizons of meaning function as a transcendental framework. Hegel viewed the shifting 'time spirits' (and ideologies) as such horizons of meaning.

6 J. Derrida, *De la grammatologie* and *L'Écriture et la différence* (both published in 1967). This idea of text 'deconstruction' has gained acceptance in literary studies of various genres and periods. The term 'postmodernism' followed in the wake of 'post-structuralism', as in Jean-François Lyotard, *La condition postmoderne* (1979).

7 Cf. Ch. 26, Logical positivism and Ludwig Wittgenstein.

8 R. Rorty, *Consequences of Pragmatism*, Minneapolis, MN, 1982. In regard to pragmatism, see above, Ch. 21, Truth is what works.

9 See also, the discussion about this transition in *After Philosophy: End or Transformation?*, eds. K. Baynes, J. Bohmann, and T. McCarthy, Cambridge, MA, 1987.

10 R. Rorty, *Achieving Our Country*, Cambridge, MA, 1998.

11 R. Rorty, *Contingency, Irony, and Solidarity*, Cambridge, 1989.

12 See Richard Bernstein, *The New Constellation*, Cambridge, 1991, pp. 258–92.

13 See Thomas McCarthy on Rorty in *Ideals and Illusions*, Cambridge, MA, 1991, pp. 11–42 (on Foucault, pp. 43–82; on Derrida, pp. 83–123).

14 Here we may ask: does literature occasionally have a certain political importance, whether we like it or not?

15 J. Habermas, *Theory of Communicative Acts*, Boston, MA, 1984 and 1987.

16 See G. Skirbekk, *Rationality and Modernity*, Oslo/Oxford, 1993.

Index

and text 460–3; growth from Greek and Hebrew scholars 107; Heidegger's basic pattern of cognition 455; interpretive methodology 155; Schleiermacher and text's soul 297; scientific interpretation of Bible 162–3

Herodotus 7, 102

Hildegard of Bingen 145

Hippocrates 102–4, 144

Histoire de la folie (Foucault) 464

historicism: antihistorical structuralism and functionalism 303; Dilthey on relativism of human sciences 300–3; Herder's individual and historical change 294–7; Popper's attack on 'historical destiny' 431–2; von Rank and von Savigny 298–9

history and historiography: Christian linear view 249; circular view of Stoics 97; dialectic 309–10; discipline of 294; Droysen's and Sybel's Prussian school 299–300; the 'end' of 319; French Annales school 303; Hegel 307–10, 313–15, 318–19; Heidegger perceives decline 454–6; historiography 102; Marx's materialism 325–9; tradition 313–14; transcendental presuppositions 307–8; universal and particular 313–15; Vico's historiography and individuality 197–200

Hitler, Adolf: Arendt's analysis 457–8; features of fascism 371–4; *Mein Kampf* 372; racism 373

Hobbes, Thomas: clockwork society 181–4; *De cive* 181–4; enlightened self-interest 184, 186; and Freud 384, 386; life and works 180; monarchy 141; as a political and economic 'liberalist' 187–8; reductionism 215

holism 52–3; Plato's ideas 62–3

Homer 200

homosexuality 288

Horkheimer, Max 454

human beings: Aristotle's anthropology and sociology 78–80; Christian anthropocentrism 110, 114; Darwin's theory of natural selection 347–50; egoism 59; equality 95, 96; Hegel's historical process 313–14; Hobbes' enlightened self-interest 184, 186;

Plato's ideas 55; Protagoras on man as the measure 35–8; Spinoza's substance 208–9; *see also* individuals

The Human Condition (Arendt) 457

humanities: separation from religion and science 293–4

Hume, David 221; and Burke 259; causality 321–4; comparison to Buddhism 26; emotions and learned conventions 236–8; empiricism 155; ethical scepticism 283–4; 'ideas' and 'impressions' 229–31; 'is' and 'ought' of moral philosophy 234–6; Kant's criticism of 273–5; life and works 229; and Rousseau 252–3; science and philosophy 152

Hunayn ibn Ishaq 146

Husserl, Edmund: phenomenology 440, 441

Hypatia 107

Ibn al-Shâtir 147

Ibn-Rushd *see* Averroës

Ibn-Sinâ *see* Avicenna

Ibsen, Henrik: *Peer Gynt* 308

idealism: Berkeley's *esse* is *percepi* 225–9

Ideas, theory of 47–51; art as imitation of ideal 62; objections to 52; as a yoke 454–5

Ideas for the Philosophy of the History of Mankind (Herder) 295

identity: complexity of issues 446

ideology, defined 372

imagination 198

India: *Bhagavad-Gita* 26–7; Buddhism 24–6; Burke's defence of culture 260; historical background 21–2; Vedic beliefs 22–4

individuals 90; Burke's conservativism 257–61; Hegel places in community 313–14, 316–17; Kant's moral liberty 284–8; Leibniz's monads 210–11; liberalism 244–6; Vico 199–200; *see also* human beings

inductive reasoning 153–6; Hume's concept of causality 233

infinity 215–16

Innocent III, Pope 138

Innocent IV, Pope 138

The Interpretation of Dreams (Freud) 377, 378–80

Schopenhauer, Arthur 21, 25–6, 354

sciences: Aquinas' realism 131–2; Arab cultures 147–8; from classical to modern physics 412–15; Darwin's natural selection 347–50; demystification of the world 407; early university education 144; empiricism 217–18; experience and observation 156–7; Galileo's new view of cosmos and nature 163–6; Greek thought 9–10, 105–7; influence on Kant 274–5, 278–9; Kuhn's history of scientific paradigms 433–5; methodology 151–6, 163–6; need for interdisciplinary analysis 419–22; phenomenology describes world 440–1; question of truth 293; rationalism *versus* empiricism 238–9; relation to philosophy 2–3; Renaissance paradigm-shifts 169–73; unpredictable future knowledge 432; validity of psychoanalysis 386–9; Vico on methodology and humanities 197; vitalism *versus* mechanistic reductionism 169; Weber's 'value freedom' 400–2

Searle, John R. 439–40

self: Buddhist impermanence 26; Indian reincarnation 22–4

semiology 303

Seneca, Lucius Annaeus 93, 94, 105

sensory experience: Aquinas' realism 130–2; Democritus' atomism 18; Descartes' methodical doubt 191; Descartes' rationalism 193–4; divided from soul 55; Galileo' s subjectivism 165–6; Hume's 'ideas' and 'impressions' 229–31; Kant's epistemology 275–9; Parmenides 14–15; Platonic ideas 48–9, 52; relativity 226; Scepticism 98–9; subjectivity 216

Sextus Empiricus 98

sexuality and roles: Aristotle 80; Freud's theory of 380–1; Plato belief in equality 60–1

Sic et Non (Abelard) 144

Siddhartha Gautama 24

Simmel, Georg: *The Cities and Intellectual Life* 397; *Conflict* 397; *The Philosophy of Money* 397; sociology of interaction 396–8

sin 111

Situating the Self. Gender, Community and Postmodernism in Contemporary Ethics (Benhabib) 448

slavery 6, 79

Smith, Adam 188, 266, 330; liberal economics 249–51; *Wealth of Nations* 249

social democracy: Durkheim's solidarity 399; political pragmatism 369–71

social sciences: Dilthey's characterization of research 301–2; Habermas' cognitive interests and reasons 466–8; Hobbes' thought experiments 182–3; methodological pluralism 303; need for interdisciplinary analysis 419–22; Popper's methodological individualism 432–3; relation to philosophy 2, 3–4; sociobiology 351–2; use of Darwin's 'survival of the fittest' 270; Weber's value freedom 400–2; *see also* anthropology; psychology; sociology

socialism: J. S. Mill's social liberalism 266–9; merges with social liberalism 270; syndicalism 369

society: Althusius' social contract 179; anarchy 368–9; Burke's conservatism 257–61; Enlightenment harmony of self-interests 244; Freud's criticism of repressive culture 383–6; Green's liberalism within community 269–70; Hegel's theory of master and slave 312–13; Hellenistic-Roman community 90–1; Hobbes' clockwork analogy 181–4; Hobbes' enlightened self-interest 184, 186; Hume's learned conventions and reactions 236–8; Indian caste system 23; Locke's order over state of nature 218–23; philosophical knowledge 2; Plato's hierarchical structure 55–8; public opinion and debate 267–8; Pythagorean order 20–1; Rousseau's belief in returning to nature 253–6; social contract 184, 221–3; Tönnies' community and 394–6

sociology: Aristotle 78–9; Comte's positivism 391–3; Cooley's primary and secondary groups 396; Durkheim's social solidarity 398–400; functionalism 410; outlined and defined by Weber